graphic arts encyclopedia

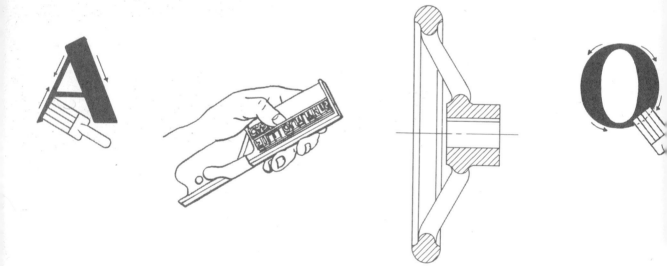

George A. Stevenson

graphic arts encyclopedia

second edition

new york **McGRAW-HILL BOOK COMPANY**
st. louis san francisco london paris
düsseldorf singapore new delhi
bogotá johannesburg montreal
toronto auckland são paulo
madrid sydney tokyo

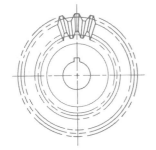

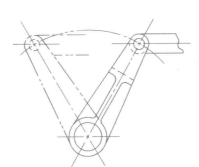

Library of Congress Cataloging in Publication Data

Stevenson, George A.
    Graphic arts encyclopedia.
    Bibliography: p.
    Includes indexes.
    1. Printing—Dictionaries.   2. Graphic arts—
Dictionaries.   I. Title.
Z118.S82 1979   686.2'03   78-7298
    ISBN 0-07-061288-9

    567890   VHVH   86543

*The editors for this book were W. Hodson Mogan, Virginia Fechtmann Blair,
and Susan Thomas, the designer was Naomi Auerbach, and the production
supervisor was Teresa F. Leaden. It was set in Electra
by York Graphic Services, Inc.*

Printed and bound by Von Hoffmann Press, Inc.

contents

127361

The *Graphic Arts Encyclopedia* is designed to provide basic understanding and practical guidance in the reproduction of words and pictures. As such, it deals with (1) the products and tools with which an image is formed, (2) the kind of image, and (3) the surface or material upon which the image is produced.

The aim has been to consolidate in one volume all the most useful techniques, processes, concepts, and methods required in the graphic arts professions. Clearly, restraint has had to be exercised to hold the book within reasonable bounds; the process has been more one of selection and elimination than of compilation.

Much is said in these pages that has never been said before. The author's intention has been to view the subject matter in the light of actual working experience rather than to parrot catalog descriptions that usually present only ideal or "typical" situations. Moreover, he has felt free to present not only the "what" but also the "why" and the "how." A purposeful book is an instructive book.

It was inevitable that the *Graphic Arts Encyclopedia* undergo a second edition, mainly because of its wide acceptance both on this continent and in foreign countries. Its value as a worthy and constructive publication, therefore, speaks for itself. Be that as it may, many significant changes in the graphic arts industry have taken place since publication of the original edition. The *Encyclopedia* is divided into two broad divisions that are intermixed in the subject matter. The first division includes treatment of graphic arts equipment with supplementary photographs. Virtually all photographs were replaced with those of modified or new equipment. The second division includes treatment of all descriptive terms and illustrations not included in the first division. A very large percentage of these terms remains unchanged. These terms have been with us for many years and represent the art and technology of our communicating with each other in these fields. However, hundreds of new terms have been added.

Of particular concern is the broad coverage of very impressive computerized photographic typesetting and support equipment, such as keyboarded composing machines and editing and correction video display terminals. Facsimile transceivers are shown for the first time. New and advanced electrostatic copying machines, very popular in almost all industries, are included and screen-process printing is abundantly dealt with. Considerable new copy has been included for printing inks, a major industry in itself, and the presentation of this new material is as thorough as possible within a book of this nature. While electrostatic stencil-screen printing is not new (it has been in the development stage since as far back as 1968), it is beginning to emerge as a viable method of printing with great possibilities. The process is covered adequately in this edition.

Because conceptual understanding has been the foundation of the working descriptions, the *Encyclopedia* should be especially useful to beginners, to students at the secondary and college levels, and to those working on the fringes of the graphic arts or attempting to use a method or a process for the first time.

The assistance of the many manufacturers who provided photographs and literature about their products strongly contributed to this volume. Without their cooperation and worthwhile contributions the work would have been severely handicapped. The author regrets that not all manufacturers could be represented in this edition. Omission of a product or a service is no reflection on its quality. Inclusion of all manufacturers of graphic arts products and materials was virtually impossible.

The author is extremely indebted to the staff of consultants who gave unstintingly of their time and knowledge to the end that the *Encyclopedia* would be a reliable reference work. To single out any one consultant as being exceptional would be an injustice to the others, because all are exceptional. Their objective advice and comments have added greatly to the exactness of the contents. These consultants are Cecil W. Birnbaum, Carl D. Buchanan, Arthur E. Gleason, Henri A. Lindeman, Jerry F. Mc-Cosky, and Arthur F. Meier.

It would be ungracious not to mention the illustrator, Clifford D. Lang, who is outstanding as a technical illustrator and artist. He deserves high praise for his work. The author is fortunate that Mr. Lang's experience, knowledge, and expertise have become a part of this work.

If the reader, student, or craftsman benefits from the *Encyclopedia* even in small measure, the author will be well rewarded for his work. Suggestions and constructive criticism are invited, with the hope that they will be fruitful in leading to the next edition.

George A. Stevenson

how to use the encyclopedia

The *Graphic Arts Encyclopedia* can be used for ready reference, as one normally uses a reference book, or for prolonged study of the many fields of interest in the graphic arts professions. It may therefore serve not only as a reference book but also as a textbook.

As a reference book. When the subject is known, refer to the main body of the text and find the topic heading, which appears in its alphabetical position.

When the topic heading is not known but a product or material can be assigned to a class or group, turn to the Product Index on page 425, find the classification or group to which the product or material belongs, and then find the product. The topic heading in the *See* column shows where the product or material may be found in the main body of the text. For example, if information concerning microfilm equipment is desired, a complete list of such equipment is found under the classification "Microfilm equipment" in the Product Index. By selecting the particular equipment in the *Product* column and by checking the *See* column, the topic heading for the product or material can be found in the main body of the text.

When the name of a product or material is not known but the manufacturer's name is known, turn to the Manufacturers' Index on page 432 and find the name of the manufacturer. The topic heading in the *See* column shows where the product or material may be found in the main body of the text. For example, assume that information concerning Itek's platemaking equipment is desired. Refer to the name "Itek Business Products" in the Manufacturers' Index, and in the *See* column note that information on this equipment may be found under the topic heading CAMERA, PROCESS: PAPER PLATES.

As a textbook. Prolonged study implies specializing in a selected vocation. The chosen subjects can be studied in the classroom under supervision, or the *Encyclopedia* can be used as a home study course. Because topic headings indicate the various fields of interest to which they pertain, it is a simple matter for the reader or the instructor to select headings in a specific field. Any attempt to study the *Encyclopedia* in its A-to-Z format, with a view to gaining an overall knowledge of its contents, is not practicable. The range of subjects is so extensive that a good grasp of them is unlikely if this method of study is pursued.

It is suggested, instead, that the instructor, student, or practicing technician commence at the beginning of the book and make a list of topic headings pertinent to the specific field of interest. Another alternative is to make a list of topic headings from the alphabetical index which starts on page 453. Once the list has been completed, it will serve as an outline for an excellent approach to a study. Or, the instructor making the list can arrange the topic headings in any desired sequence to conform with the curriculum. For example, if the field of interest is technical illustrating, the list would commence with these topic headings: ACETATE, ACETATE INK, ACETATE OVERLAY, AIRBRUSH, AIRBRUSHING, AMBERLITH, ANGLE OF VIEW, APRON, ART FILE NUMBER, ARTIST, ARTIST AID, ASSEMBLED VIEW, and so forth.

If the interest is in the field of process-camera work, the following topic headings would start the list: ACETATE, ACETATE FILM, ACETATE ORTHO LITHO FILM, ACETATE OVERLAY, ACTINIC LIGHT, ACTINIC TRANSMISSION, AMBERLITH, ARC LAMP, ASSEMBLED NEGATIVE, BACK UP, BACKGROUND, BASIC REPRODUCTION PAGE, BENDAY, and so forth.

A few other examples of fields of interest are platemaking, films, paper, editorial functions, overhead projection, color separation, cold-composition copy, bookbinding, typography, copying machines, engineering drafting, microfilming, duplicating machines, hot-metal and cold-composition work, and the methods of printing: letterpress, gravure, letterset, planographic, stencil, and screen-process printing.

graphic arts encyclopedia

AA *See* AUTHOR'S ALTERATIONS.

absorbency Property of a porous material, such as paper, which causes it to take up liquids and moisture with which it comes in contact.

absorption Penetration of one substance into the mass of another.

abstract Brief statement in outline or summary form, often prefacing a report or proposal and presenting the complete subject matter. An abstract tells what the report or proposal is about and what conclusions have been reached. It should be to the point and contain no more than 150 words.

AC Abbreviation for author's correction. A similar abbreviation is AA for author's alteration.

accordian fold Paper or stock having folds like the pleated bellows of an accordian.

acetate Transparent or translucent plastic material. It is available either clear or in colors and in smooth or matte finishes. Pyroxylin and cellulose acetate compose the base for some photographic films. It has been a practice in the graphic arts field to call any transparent or translucent material acetate. A thin transparent paper material, for example, may be called acetate. Acetate typewriter ribbons, however, are opaque.

acetate film Sensitized film having an acetic acid base. It is used in photomechanical platemaking.

acetate ink Ink with special adhering qualities intended for drawing or printing on such materials as films and acetates. It is employed specifically in making projecturals for overhead projection and in printing on foils. Available in black and in colors, acetate ink is used in making transparencies, slides, and color overlays, as well as with plastics, drafting films, and so forth.

Acetate Ortho Litho film Du Pont film that has an acetate base. It is designed especially for camera and contact applications which require intricate stripping, cracking, and scribing and in which dimensional stability is of secondary importance.

acetate overlay Thin sheet of transparent plastic mounted by flapping to artwork. Acetate overlays have many useful applications in artwork and process-camera photography. To protect a mounted photograph that is to be made into a halftone, a clear acetate overlay of sufficient dimensional stability is flapped over the photograph by means of tape fastened across the top. Instructions for reworking by airbrushing are indicated on the overlay with a wax pencil. This use of an overlay is common when another copy of the photograph is not available for marking. A register mark is drawn on the overlay, keying it to the photograph. Marking an acetate overlay does not affect the surface finish of the photograph, whereas pencil may pierce a tissue overlay and harm the photograph. Vellum paper should not be used as an overlay because of its oily nature.

An acetate overlay is mounted on a photograph or other artwork when nomenclature or callouts are required. The nomenclature, consisting of typeset preprints or paste-ups, is placed on the overlay in register with the photograph. Register marks similar to those shown in Figure A-1 should be used. The marks should be equidistant. If five marks are used, marks are positioned in the lower right- and left-hand corners and the bottom center mark is eliminated. Register marks must be placed outside the crop marks. The process photographer registers the work, photographing it through the acetate overlay. Screening nomenclature with the photograph does not degrade ordinary production work, for the nomenclature retains a good definition. If a second set of nomenclature is required for a photograph, a second overlay must be made with the new nomenclature and used with the photograph.

Acetate overlays can be employed for color separation of line and continuous-tone copy. As an example, the colors red, blue, and yellow are to be used in conjunction with the black plate. Register marks are applied to the black, or base, art as well as to all three color overlays. Four negatives are made, and from these the process photographer separately photographs the black art and the three color overlays, all in register. Four plates from which the black and colors will be printed are made, and the color separation is complete. Caution must be exercised in using acetate overlays when close registration is required, for acetate is susceptible to expansion and retraction with changes in humidity. The cost of color separation is lowered and accurate registration is obtained in photo-mechanical work when color-separation negatives are produced by photographing the multicolored orginal successively through three color-separation filters and by using the black printer to add density to

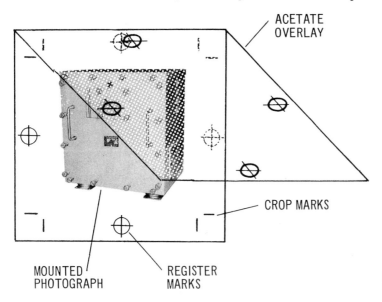

Fig. A-1 Registering an acetate overlay with art.

dark areas of the photograph or other artwork. (*See also* COLOR SEPARA-TION.)

Acetate overlays are also used for running heads or feet when headings, titles, or logotypes are repeated on each page of a publication or for pamphlets or booklets in which an image is repeated on each page. The overlays are hinged with masking tape and affixed to the copyboard. The copy is placed in register with the preprinted overlay, and the combination is photographed.

In addition, acetate overlays may be used to represent one or more configurations of like objects. The original represents one configuration, and an overlay represents another configuration on which undesirable images have been blocked out with white pressure-sensitive tape and new callouts added. A second overlay may be used to show an entirely different configuration.

acetate proof Thin acetate sheet, taken directly from the pressplate, on which is imposed a positive inked reproduction proof of the image. The proof is used for making contact negatives or for stripping up a positive flat.

acknowledgment Author's statement expressing thanks and appreciation by listing the names of individuals or organizations that have contributed to his or her work. The acknowledgment may appear in the front matter, either as a dedication on a separate page or in the preface or foreword. It may also appear as a footnote.

actinic light Light in the ultraviolet region of the spectrum that causes a chemical change in photosensitive materials, as in photography.

actinic opacity Imperviousness to actinic light of specified spectral character, usually in the near-ultraviolet region of the spectrum.

actinic transmission Transmission of actinic radiation by light-sensitive emulsions.

addendum Something that supplements the main content of a book or other printed matter.

advance Money paid by a publisher to an author and charged against future royalties.

aerate To introduce air between sheets of paper, either by riffling them manually or by employing a device in order to facilitate feeding in the printing press or to establish uniform thickness during bookbinding. Some printing and reproduction machines have small tubes from which streams of air are directed between the sheets to separate them. Aerating is also accomplished mechanically in some copying machines.

afterword Composition at the end of a written work (usually of fiction) that comments on the history of the author and other aspects of the work. It may be written and added at any time after initial publication. The lapse of time between the first printing and the appearance of the afterword may be any number of years.

against the grain   Folding or using paper at right angles with the grain. Grain in paper results from the alignment of fibers during vibration of the pulp along the traveling belt during the manufacturing process. *See also* PAPER MANUFACTURING.

agate   Type size of 5½ points (1.93 mm), used in stock exchange market reports, box scores, some classified advertising, and so forth.

agate line   Measurement of advertising space which is ¼ inch high and one column wide.

air   Excess space in line or photographic art or in text matter. Too much "air" is indicative of poor planning and layout. However, space can be used to advantage to improve the eye appeal of an advertisement.

airbrush   Atomizer that by compressed air discharges a spray of water-color pigment on artwork.

airbrushing   Act of using an airbrush to produce art or to improve the appearance of art. It is a graphic arts technique that stands by itself as a specialty. Airbrushing is used extensively in retouching photographs for fine reproduction. It is also used in the creation of art, particularly industrial art, where cutaway views are required for machinery, equipment, devices, etc. Line drawing is combined with airbrushing to produce the artwork. A small hand brush may be used to touch up details, but an airbrush is needed for larger areas, as in taking out or altering background, removing shadows, and coloring planes of an object with parallel or dissimilar tones. Highlights are added or deleted to produce varying effects. Glossy prints are recommended for best results.

Good photography eliminates the need for considerable retouching. Photographs should always be larger than the size intended for reproduction. The quality of artwork is normally improved when it is reduced, because small imperfections and fuzziness drop out, lines become firm, and tones stabilize. However, caution must be used to avoid loss of detail, because fine light tones merge with surrounding heavier tones if the reduction is too great.

Sheets of thin transparent material called frisket paper are available for blocking out areas on art to protect the image from particles of spray. The frisket paper is pressed on the image and cut along areas and outlines of the image. The paper has a slightly adhesive quality which makes it stick to but not harm the print. The frisket paper is removed after airbrushing has been completed. A careful choice of colors (tones) is most important, as watercolors have a tendency to reflect different tones when dry and when spread in a mass. Test samples should be taken on a glossy sheet and tones compared for color density after drying.

album paper Paper used in photograph albums. Manufactured from mechanical or chemical wood pulp, it has an antique finish and is available in solid colors only. Black album paper is the most popular. Basic weights range from 80 to 110 pounds (36.3 to 50 kg) for 500 sheets of the standard size of 24 by 35 inches (61 by 89 cm). The 80-pound (36.3-kg) weight is used extensively.

albumen plate Surface printing plate used in offset lithography that utilizes the albumen from eggs as the sensitized coating.

algebra symbols *See* TABLE 10, *page 446.*

alphabet length Length of the 26 lowercase letters of the alphabet as measured in points. The ideal measure for a line of printed text matter is considered to be 1½ alphabets, or 39 characters.

alphanumeric Consisting of alphabetical characters, numerals, symbols, and punctuation marks. Alphanumerics is the arrangement and placement of these elements on the universal typewriter keyboard. An alphanumeric system can be used in computer and phototypesetting work.

alterations Changes made in text copy after a job has been set in type and proofs have been pulled for checking.

alternate-position lines *See* PHANTOM LINES; *see also* LINE CONVENTIONS: ENGINEERING DRAWINGS.

Amberlith Amber-colored masking and stripping film coated on a polyester backing sheet. Amberlith is a registered trademark of the Ulano Company. *See* MASKING AND STRIPPING MATERIALS.

ammonia-light process Dry diazo or whiteprint process. *See* WHITEPRINT PROCESS.

ammonia print Whiteprint copy produced by the dry diazo process. *See* WHITEPRINT PROCESS.

ampersand Symbol &, used in lieu of the word "and." The symbol is called a "short and." It should not be used in text copy unless it is part of the official name of an organization, but it is sometimes used in tables and illustrations when space does not permit spelling out "and."

analog A physical variable which remains similar to another variable; for example, voltage as a representation of temperature.

anchoring Securing metal printing plates on wooden blocks by using screws and pouring solder through holes drilled in the blocks.

angle bar (turning bar) In a web-fed printing press, a metal bar arranged between printing units at an angle to the direction of the press to turn the web (paper) as it feeds from unit to unit. Angle bars are often filled with air and perforated to reduce the heat caused by friction as the web travels through the press.

angle of view   Angle from which an object is viewed either in real life or in an illustration. In technical illustrations, the most appropriate angle of view is that which not only most adequately portrays the object in its normal configuration but shows the greatest number of parts or those surfaces which readily distinguish the article. In the fine arts, the most desirable angle of view is that which enhances the aesthetic value of the art.

anhydrous ammonia system   System used in the developing section of some whiteprint machines. Ammonia gas, stored in a high-pressure tank, is fed through a low-pressure line into the developing chamber. There it is mixed with water from a separate source and vaporized. The vapor then rises between and through perforated rollers to develop the material. This system makes possible the use of remote and multiple ammonia-supply facilities. In a remote installation, the storage tank and high-pressure lines are stored together in a separate room or building or in a sheltered area or shed outside the building that houses the machine. Only the low-pressure line to the machine enters the reproduction room. In a multiple installation, any number of interchangeable tanks can be connected to a single supply line to provide an uninterrupted flow of ammonia gas to any number of machines. The multiple installation is recommended especially for large departments.

aniline   Oillike liquid originally obtained from indigo but now prepared by the reduction of nitrobenzene and used as the basis for various inks and dyes.

animal sizing   Gelatin used for coating certain grades of paper. The gelatin is appled on the surface of the paper rather than made an ingredient of the pulp mixture from which the paper is manufactured.

animation   Effect of drawing pictures, such as cartoons, in time sequence so that when the assembled pictures are viewed in rapid succession, the characters appear to be moving as in real life.

annex   Increment bound as part of a technical publication. It thus differs from an attachment, which is bound by itself. While an annex is related to the main body of the subject matter of which it is a part, its content is such that it can be more conveniently used by the reader as a separate entity within the publication.

annotate   To furnish explanatory notes which may or may not complement the subject matter of the text. Usually the notes are made in the margin.

anodized plate   Offset printing plate that has been specially treated to increase the hardness of the metal surface and make it strongly resistant to press wear. Kodak's LN-L plate is an example. It is coated on grained anodized aluminum and is contact speed. It is also negative working, has short exposure and process time, and is subtractive-processed. The sensitized coating is a special colored photopolymer which becomes insoluble when sufficiently exposed to light. The unexposed areas are softened and removed during development. Photopolymer is reputed to have outstanding ink-carrying and ink-release capabilities.

antihalation backing   Protective coating on the back of films and plates (that is, opposite the emulsion side) that absorbs the image light and prevents the light from reflecting back into the emulsion. It is washed off during the developing process. *See also* FILMS AND PLATES.

antique finish   Rather rough finish of paper having low-bulk characteristics. It is designed to imitate the finish of handmade paper. The finish is not recommended for letterpress halftones but may be used for sheet-fed gravure halftone printing. Caution should be exercised in selecting an antique finish when halftones are to be used.

antique paper   Printing paper classified as an exotic type with a rough finish. It is especially suitable for printing type and line engravings by letterpress. Halftones may be printed by offset presses as well as by gravure presses on certain antique papers. Antique papers are used chiefly in booklets, books, folders, and brochures.

antique wove paper   Paper of low-finish characteristics. Laid lines or chain marks are not visible.

aperture card   Die-cut card containing an aperture for mounting a microfilm of text or illustrated matter. The image may be duplicated in a microfilm duplicator or enlarged on a screen for viewing on a reader, or a printout may be produced either on a reader-printer or on a printer alone. Figure A-2 is an example of an EAM (electrical-accounting-machine)

Fig. A-2 Tabulating card with mounted microfilm.

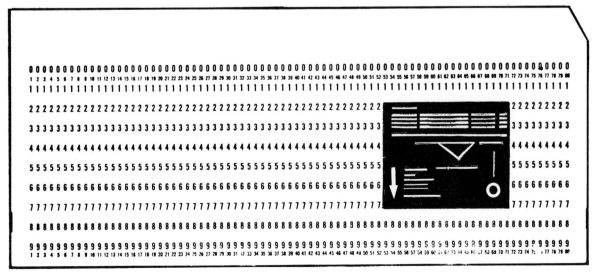

tabulating aperture card with a 35-millimeter microfilm mounted in the aperture. Index information is provided at the top of the card for manual storage and retrieval. The card can also be retrieved with a sorting machine by using information punched in the card. *See also* MICROFORM.

appendix Part following the final text page of a book, as distinguished from a supplement, which may be published separately. An appendix usually contains matter that is relevant but not essential to the body of the book and that would be awkward or distracting if it were presented in the main text.

application software In computer work, the level of software which encompasses not only primary software and functional subroutines but includes special user requirements such as data acquisition.

apron White space allocated at the margins of an engineering drawing for the protection of the drawing when rolled; also, additional white space allowed on a foldout page. When text matter or an illustration exceeds normal page dimensions, thus requiring a foldout, and the size is such that a convenient foldout cannot be made, an apron is left along the binding margin.

aqueous ammonia system System employing a mixture of ammonia and water that is used in the developing section of some whiteprint machines. The mixture is supplied from a storage bottle, carboy, or drum through rubber tubing to the developing section. Liquid flow is controlled by a solenoid pump synchronized with the machine speed. The mixture is vaporized in the developing section. The ammonia vapor then rises between and through perforated rollers to reach the sensitized material, thus bringing out the latent image. Complete development is effected at all machine speeds.

arabic numerals Figures 1, 2, 3, 4, 5, 6, 7, 8, 9, 0, as distinguished from roman numerals.

arc lamp Electric lamp in which light is produced by an arc made when current leaps the space between two electrodes. Figure A-3 is a simple drawing illustrating the principle of "burning" an image with an arc lamp through a photolithographic negative onto a sensitized plate. The negative, produced by a process camera, has a translucent image and a black background. The negative is stripped into position on masking paper known as "goldenrod," with only the image showing. The whole is then mounted in a vacuum frame with the negative in front of a thin, flexible printing plate that bears a sensitized emulsion. The arc lamp burns the image through the translucent portion of the negative onto the plate. The latent image is then developed with a chemical wash, dried, and mounted on the printing press.

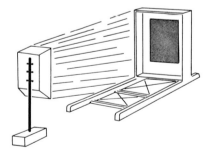

Fig. A-3 "Burning" an image with an arc lamp.

architectural floor plan Line drawing that shows the physical location of various elements and inside and outside perimeters of a house or other

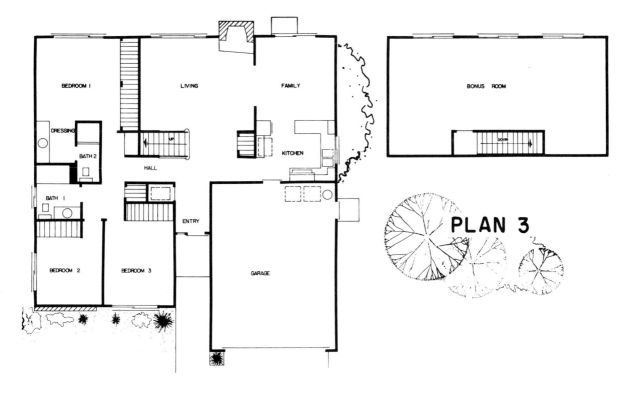

ELEVATION A

Fig. A-4 Architectural floor plan and elevation drawing.

building structure (*see* Figure A-4). Floor plans are used in conjunction with elevation drawings of the structure. *See also* ELEVATION DRAWING: ARCHITECTURE.

architectural rendering Perspective drawing of a house or other building structure as illustrated in the elevation drawing of Figure A-4. While renderings of this type are usually done in watercolors, other media such as oils, pencil, ink, charcoal or chalk, and airbrush are common. The renderings are used as sales drawings for real estate promotion. The oversize originals are displayed in the sales office, and the renderings are reduced for reproduction as illustrations in sales literature and newspaper or magazine advertising. Because tones vary through the range from white to black, the renderings are screened with a 133- to 150-line screen when they are reduced. Variations in exterior design are indicated by the designations "elevation A," "elevation B," etc., but floor plans remain the same.

arithmetic scale Scale of lines equally spaced vertically and horizontally, It is thus distinguished from a logarithmic scale. A chart using an arithmetic scale has equidistant lines which represent equal values. *See also* LOGARITHMIC SCALE.

arithmetic symbols *See* TABLE 10, *page 446.*

arrangement drawing Engineering drawing which shows any projection or perspective of objects, with or without controlling dimensions, to indicate their relationship.

arrowhead Indicator shaped like an arrowhead and used at the end of a lead line to direct attention to an object or a point of reference in conjunction with a callout number, letter, or other symbol. Caution should be exercised in using arrowheads. If an exploded view is congested with many callouts, only lead lines should be used. When practicable and when paste-ups or transfers are used, white lead lines and arrowheads are employed in dark areas. Black lead lines and arrowheads are used in white or highlighted areas. When a lead line crosses both white and black areas, a white-and-black lead line is used.

art In the graphic arts field, any line drawing, photograph, or continuous-tone of halftone illustration. Only two kinds of art are considered for reproduction purposes: line and halftone. The term "art" is commonly used to mean any copy other than text.

art brushes *See* BRUSHES, ART.

art file number Key file number placed within the image area of each piece of original art. When an organization puts out publications in which numerous illustrations are used, an art filing system should be established to provide ready access to negatives and illustrations for future use or for rework. Filing all negatives or illustrations by groups is preferable to segregating the negatives and illustrations used in a particular publication or to filing according to product or article. Negatives should be filed with key numbers indicating (1) the type of art, (2) the equipment classification, and (3) the basic negative number within the classification.

The following suggested system may be enlarged or altered to satisfy individual requirements. The first symbol is a letter indicating the type of art:

E—Exploded view
S—Schematic (electrical, hydraulic, pneumatic)
T—Tool drawing
A—Assembled view (frontispiece)
B—Block diagram
P—Pictorial drawing
I—Inspection drawing
W—Wiring diagram

The second symbol is a number preceded and followed by a dash; it denotes the type of equipment and is assigned arbitrarily to a particular item or to similar items. The third symbol is the sequential number assigned to the illustration. For example, in the file number W-3-47, W indicates a wiring diagram, the numeral 3 indicates a particular class or type of equipment, and the numeral 47 represents the forty-seventh wiring diagram of the class or type that has been logged in. Care should be taken to avoid filing art negatives in groups by specific publications because it would then be necessary to trust to memory to find them. A logbook should be maintained to serve as an index and reference. In addition, reverse blueline copies can be made from each art negative and a file maintained by equipment classification for research and reference purposes. Reproduced type size for art file numbers should be no larger than 6 point (2.11 mm). File numbers must be placed within the image area of the original art, adjacent to either the right or the left crop mark, in whichever location has the more open space. This system of filing negatives is advantageous in reworking art of the same family, since an enlarged print can be made from the art negative bearing the appropriate file number.

art knife *See* FRISKET.

art-lined envelope Envelope with an extra-fine paper lining. The lining paper may be plain or fancy.

art parchment *See* DIPLOMA PAPER.

artist Person engaged in fine, commercial, or industrial art. There are several types of artist: (1) the fine artist, whose work is motivated by values in which perception and taste govern the manual execution; (2) the commercial or industrial artist, who creates material used in advertising, magazine illustrations, labels, decorative packaging, displays, etc.; and (3) the technical illustrator, whose work is considered separately because this is the only work in which execution is based on technical knowledge of equipment or in which the objects depicted are of a technical nature.

Artist Aid Trademark of paste-ups and transfers. Artist Aid sheets include almost any character or symbol that can be printed (or drawn and then printed). Various letters, numbers, shadings, and symbols are printed on thin transparent or opaque acetate sheets having adhesive backs. These are termed "paste-ups." The desired design or character is cut out and burnished in position on the reproduction copy. With transfers, cutting is not required: the characters and symbols are affixed to the copy merely by burnishing.

artist's board *See* ILLUSTRATION BOARD.

artwork Illustrations, drawings, photographs, renderings, paintings, sketches, and copy of any kind—except text copy—that is being prepared or used for reproduction.

ascender Portion of a lowercase letter which rises above the body of the letter, such as the upper part of the letters h and d. A descender is just the opposite, being that portion of a lowercase letter which descends below the body of the letter, as in p. (See Figure A-5.)

ASCENDER

h p
DESCENDER

Fig. A-5 Ascending and descending characters.

ASCII or USASCII Abbreviations for United States of America Standard Code for Information Interchange; a coding system.

aspect ratio Ratio of width to height of an alphanumeric character; used in computer graphics.

assembled negative Photolithographic negative, consisting of line and halftone copy, from which a combination plate is made for printing. *See* COMBINATION PLATE.

assembled view Line drawing, halftone, or photograph of an object drawn or photographed to show the object assembled as one piece. The term is employed in technical publications. Assembled views may be used as frontispieces to give the reader a visual introduction to the equipment to be discussed, or they may appear in a box in an appropriate corner of an exploded view of the object in a parts list. While isometric projections are used more frequently in exploded views (because they are easier to execute than perspective drawings), assembled views should be drawn in perspective to eliminate distortion. Figure A-6 shows a line illustration of a modified van which serves as a frontispiece for visual introduction to the equipment. The symbols *A* through *D* indicate the physical location of various components and are keys to subsequent illustrations of the components. This method of showing a breakdown is used for equipment having several components, assemblies, or subassemblies.

Fig. A-6 Assembled view.

assembly In engineering and manufacturing, a multiple-piece item that can be disassembled into its component parts or units without destruction. An assembly does not independently perform or fulfill a specific or complete function but is essential for the completeness or proper operation of more complex equipment with which it is mechanically or electrically combined. When assemblies are part of a larger assembly, they may be referred to as "subassemblies."

asterisk Symbol *, used to key text or tabular matter to a footnote. It is the first of a series of reference marks. *See* REFERENCE MARKS.

asynchronous Operating with data entry at varying and irregular intervals, such as the data rate incoming to computer peripheral devices. Some printers/plotters, for example, have the ability to assimilate data at varying rates and intervals, and these are referred to as "asynchronous."

author's alterations Changes made to manuscript copy by the author after the copy has been typeset. In book publishing, extensive corrections may be charged to and paid by the author. Alterations include not only text copy but illustrations as well. The cost of typographical typesetting and corrections made by the publisher is borne by the publisher.

author's proof Proof taken from set type, arranged in galley form, and printed as a strip. The galley is the first printing of the copy as it comes from the typesetting machine and is not page-numbered according to final page format. The copy is proofread by the printer, and typesetting errors are corrected. The author then proofreads and checks the proofs, using standard proofreader's marks. After all corrections have been made, the copy is arranged in pages, which include both text and illustrations. The author is usually required to check the copy again from page proofs. Great care should be used in making changes and corrections. While the publisher will make allowances for a reasonable number of corrections, the author will be charged for excessive rewriting and changing to defray the additional typesetting costs. The alphabetical index, when required, is prepared by the author from the page proofs.

auto indent In photocomposition, a discretionary command entered into the system indicating that text copy is to be indented automatically by the phototypesetter until the command is canceled.

autogeneration Duplication of an image on the same material.

automated drafting *See* DRAFTING, AUTOMATED.

automated publication Publication of any kind that has been published and copy retained on a tape, disk, or other element for future printing. This method of storing copy is used with computerized cold composition typesetting. The system is used for revising the publication in part or whole. For example, a technical publication, such as those used by government agencies, can undergo revision of certain pages and be reprinted. Or a hardcover book having a singular style and format as to type size, type-face, type style, line measure, leading, and the like can be reprinted as a paperback edition with different style and format requirements.

automatic linecasting control *See* LINECASTING MACHINE.

automatic scanner *See* ENGRAVING, ELECTRONIC.

Autopositive materials *See* KODAK AUTOPOSITIVE MATERIALS.

Autoscreen Ortho film *See* KODALITH AUTOSCREEN ORTHO FILM.

autospacer Automatic quadder mechanism in an Intertype automatic linecasting machine. It consists of space matrices used in conjunction with spacebands. The quadder mechanism in a Linotype machine is called a "self-quadder."

auxiliary roll stand Additional roll stand for holding the web (paper roll) as it unwinds and feeds into the press. It may be mounted on top of another roll stand to permit one stand to be reloaded while the roll on the other stand is still unwinding. Unless such a dual roll stand is installed, only one web can be fed at a time.

auxiliary view Engineering drawing showing the true shape of objects which have inclined faces or other features that are not parallel to any of the three principal planes of projection. The auxiliary view should be arranged as though the auxiliary plane were hinged to the plane to which it is perpendicular and had been revolved into the plane of the paper. *See also* ORTHOGRAPHIC PROJECTION: ENGINEERING DRAWINGS.

Avery (colloquially called **sticky back**) White adhesive paper with a backing sheet, used in applying typed, printed, or drawn nomenclature. The nomenclature is cut out and pasted in position on line and halftone copy. The term is in common usage among illustrators and artists.

Avery is a product of the Avery Label Company. The company was founded by R. S. Avery, who, in 1935, perfected the first die-cutting machine that could cut through labels while leaving the backing paper intact. After being removed from their backing, the labels thus produced could be applied simply by touch, either by hand or with an automatic dispenser. This development, which made self-adhesive labels practical for manufacturing purposes, resulted in the founding of a new industry. Avery's self-adhesive labels and paper utilize chemical-release coatings which allow all types of adhesives to be removed from their protective backings. Avery industrial and consumer self-adhesive products include more than 100 combinations of materials and adhesives for self-adhesive labels. Among other products are labeling systems, dispensers, imprinters, and affixing equipment.

axis Imaginary line about which a body rotates; also a line around which structural parts are symmetrically arranged. An axis is any imaginary line which defines the position of planes of an object. An ellipse has two axes: a major and a minor axis. The major axis is that of an imaginary line extending through the center of the ellipse at its longest dimension; the minor axis is the imaginary line which extends through the ellipse at its shortest dimension. (*See* Figure A-7.)

axonometric projection Drawing that shows the inclined position of an object with respect to the planes of projection. There are three types of axonometric projection: isometric, dimetric, and trimetric.

1. Isometric projection is the projection of an object upon a plane equally inclined to the object's three principal axes. Parallel dimensions are shown in their true proportions. Isometric projection is the most common form of illustrating objects in an exploded-view format, because drawing is faster and easier than in perspective projection. However, an isometric view distorts the object. For example, assume that two sides of an object are in exact parallel. The parallelism is reflected in the drawing, and the plane, represented by lines indicating the two sides, is in true proportion. Thus when the drawn object is viewed, parallel lines do not merge in a vanishing point as in perspective projection.

2. Dimetric projection is a tetragonal representation in which the three principal axes are at right angles to one another, two equal lateral axes having a different length from that of the opposite axes.

3. Trimetric projection is the representation of an object which has three unequal axes intersecting at right angles.

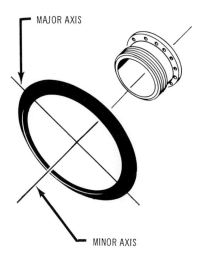

MAJOR AXIS

MINOR AXIS

Fig. A-7 Minor and major axes of an ellipse.

back cover Back outside surface of a case-bound or soft-cover book. The inside surface of the back cover is called the third cover for advertising purposes. (The inside surface of the front cover is called the second cover.) If a book has a self-cover, meaning that it is coverless, a blank page inserted at the end of the book is called a dust cover.

back jacket flap Back, folded-inside portion of a jacket on a case-bound book. It usually contains copy that is continued from the front jacket flap and may include a photograph of the author.

back matter Portion of a book or other publication that follows the main body of the text. Back matter includes such elements as exhibits, appendixes, a glossary of terms, the bibliography, and the index. It is generally folioed in sequence following the text.

back slant Inclination of a typeface, usually a display face, in which the characters slant backward, as opposed to italics or script, in which the characters slant forward.

back to back In printing, on both sides of a sheet.

back up To print or cause an impression to be made on the back of a sheet of orange or black carbon paper which is reversed in typing, thereby causing an impression to be made on the same sheet on which the material is typed. The resulting strong image offers resistance to light, and good reproduction is obtained when such copy is used for whiteprint reproduction. The term "back up" also means to print on the reverse side of a printed sheet. *See also* ORANGE BACKING.

backbone (shelfback; spine) Portion of a book normally seen when the book is placed upright on a shelf or desk.

background Portion of an image that is behind the principal object being illustrated or photographed.

background art Design, texture or pattern, or other form of artwork used to create a background effect for type and illustrations.

backing up Using solder to build up the thickness of metal for line and halftone etchings used in patent bases. Also, printing on both sides of a sheet.

backlining Paper cemented to the backbone of a book, binding the signatures and allowing space between the backbone and the cover.

baking oven Oven heated by incandescent lights to dry typed reproduction copy. It may have a series of mesh trays for holding separate pages and be lined in part with some heat-reflecting material, such as aluminum foil. The oven offers an advantage when ink rules are required, since a

B

b

resin fixative is unnecessary. The term "baking" is also applied to drying the toner in xerographic copying and electrostatic printing.

balance Arrangement of text illustrations in a manner pleasing to the eye. The copy should be balanced on a page or facing pages. Heavier elements should be placed at the bottom of the page and lighter elements at the top. A half-page illustration occupying the entire image width of the page should be placed at the bottom with text above it. The layout of two facing pages shows good judgment when the text and illustrations on both pages are in direct balance with each other. *See also* LAYOUT.

balloon Rough circle or envelope used in cartoon strips and sometimes in advertising illustrations to encircle dialogue spoken by the characters. The term "balloon" also refers to any circle which encloses copy, such as index numbers or letters placed beside the bill of material on an engineering drawing and keyed to material on the face of the drawing. In technical illustrating a similar circle is commonly called a "bubble." *See* BUBBLE.

banner heading Large caption placed across the top of a page.

bar chart Graphic representation comparing numerical values by means of rectangles of equal width. The bars extend horizontally on the chart and usually represent quantity, as in Figure B-1. Time, distance, or some other value is shown on the other dimension of the chart. Shaded patterns may be used to construct a chart with parallel double bars, divided bars, and symbols. A bar chart may also have a vertical base line that divides the bars. Distances to the left of the base line should show negative results,

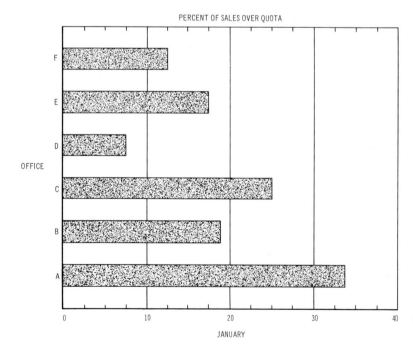

Fig. B-1 Bar chart.

while those to the right should show favorable results. *See also* COLUMN CHART; CURVE CHART; PIE CHART; SURFACE CHART.

base   Metal or wood structure on which printing plates are installed.

base art   *See* BLACK ART.

base line   Last line or space occupied by type on a page. In printed material, the base line on all pages of text copy should be on the same base line as measured from the bottom of the page or for a page line count.

base material   Material to which a coating or plating is applied.

base stock   Foundation stock from which various papers are made.

basic   Colloquial term for an original work, such as a technical manual, a planning document, or a commercial brochure, in which changes and revisions are made.

basic art   *See* BLACK ART.

basic reproduction page   Page containing camera-ready copy; also, reproducible copy that is photographed and made into a page. *See also* REPRODUCTION COPY.

basic size   Predetermined size assigned to a class of paper. For example, the basic size of bond and writing papers is 17 by 22 inches (43.1 by 55.8 cm). Although a basic size is a standard size, it should not be confused with the regular sizes into which paper is cut. While 17 by 22 inches (43.1 by 55.8 cm) is a basic size for bonds, bond paper may also be cut in sizes of 17 by 28, 19 by 24, 22 by 34 inches (43.1 by 71, 48.2 by 61, 55.8 by 86.3 cm), etc., and all are considered standard or regular sizes. *See also* TABLE 2, page 440.

basis weight   Designated fixed weight of 500 sheets (one ream) of paper of the basic sheet size, used as the basis for measuring the substance of paper by weight. Different classes of paper, such as writing, cover, and book, have fixed measuring sizes that determine the designated weights. For example, the basic size of Bible paper is 25 by 38 inches (63.5 by 96.5 cm) and the basis weight of 500 sheets is 20 pounds (9.08 kg); book paper (process-coated) is 25 by 38 inches (63.5 by 96.5 cm) and the basis weight for 500 sheets is 50 pounds (22.7 kg); writing paper is 17 by 22 inches (43.1 by 55.8 cm) and the basis weight for 500 sheets is 13 pounds (5.9 kg). Papers may be bigger or smaller than the basis weight size. Obviously, the weight of 500 sheets of a basis weight size will be proportionate to the size. The proportionate weight is called the "equivalent weight." The weight of 1,000 sheets of paper is called the "M" weight, found by doubling the 500-sheet weight. This M designation is convenient for printers because their work necessitates figuring in sheet numbers and the page-size sheets that must be cut out of a designated size.

bas-relief Form of low-relief sculpture in which the image is raised slightly above the background surface. The intent is to portray an illusion of a three-dimensional image on what amounts to a two-dimensional surface. The effect is obtained by emphasizing planes of the object in relation to their importance and magnitude. Foreground objects are given a deeper and more refined definition, whereas background objects are less clearly defined and are blended to suggest distance. The modern technique incorporates the use of a plastic powder and paint to make the relief. The image is first sketched or drawn with charcoal on a material such as masonite or plywood. Then the plastic powder is moistened to a working consistency and applied with a palette knife. When the relief is dry, the image is painted with oils and the bas-relief framed as desired.

bastard title *See* HALF TITLE.

battered type Type that has been damaged or broken or is otherwise defective.

beard Portion of metal type that extends from the face of the type to the shoulder. (*See* Fig. T-8.)

bearer In letterpress platemaking, a piece of wood or metal used to hold and protect the type mass of foundry-proof pages. In electrotype and molding work, a bearer is any excessive metal retained on surrounding areas to confine the molding material.

bearoff Filling of spaces between type characters, numbers, symbols, rules, or other type elements to improve composition and justify copy.

bed Surface of a flatbed printing press, either inclined or horizontal, on which the chase of composed type is secured for printing.

bellows Folding portion of a process camera that expands and retracts between the front and rear case.

benday Mechanical shading tint applied to a plate or artwork to give a variety of tones in line drawing. Originally the term was limited to the process named for its inventor, Benjamin Day.

bevel Edge around solid printing plates that provides a surface for clamping the printing plate.

Bible paper (india paper) Light, thin, strong, opaque paper used for Bibles, dictionaries, sales manuals, and other purposes. Basic weights are 12, 20, 24, 30, 35, and 40 pounds (5.44, 9.08, 10.9, 13.62, 15.9, and 18.16 kg) for 500 sheets of the basic size of 25 by 38 inches (63.5 by 96.5 cm).

bibliography List of books, articles, or papers placed at the end of a chapter or in the back matter of a publication. It includes works from which the author has made excerpts or which the author used as reference material to substantiate a fact or theory, as well as works recommended for study. The name of the author, the title of the publication, report or reference numbers, the publisher, the place and date of publication, and any other information which will aid the reader in securing the cited material should be given.

bicycling Utilizing the same engraving, film, or copy in two or more publications having close publishing dates. The material is used and shipped from one printer to the next.

billboard Outdoor advertising poster, preferably now called a poster.

billhead Blank form used for posting billing charges. The name and address of the seller are at the top of the form.

bimetal plate Printing plate composed of two metals. One metal rejects ink, while the other does not. Such plates are used in planographic printing (printing from a plane surface).

binder's board Heavy paperboard that is covered with cloth and used for covering books.

binding, mechanical Binding by means of metal clasps and prongs, rings, screw posts, or other metal fasteners, as distinguished from the standard methods discussed under BOOKBINDING. Mechanical binding also includes plastic methods of binding, sometimes called "comb binding." Plastic binding has gained in popularity, primarily because of low costs, attractive appearance, and the growing number of industrial brochures, booklets, and other publications bound on company premises. Companies have found it convenient and efficient to have the binding equipment available.

Plastic binding is available in a great variety of colors and is used for binding practically any sheets or pages into an assembly. All pages lie flat when the book is open, and binding margins are visible. Plastic binding is obtainable in diameters from $\frac{3}{16}$ to 2 inches (4.76 mm to 5.08 cm). Depending on size, the back may be imprinted with a title or other descriptive material. Two operations are required for plastic binding: (1) the sheets are hole-punched on a punching machine, and (2) they are bound together with a binding machine.

Mechanical binding machines that combine both the punching and the binding operations are available. The machine may be manually or electrically operated.

In addition to plastic and loose-leaf binding, common forms of mechanical binding include post binding for loose-leaf publications, saddle stitching, sidestitching, and spiral binding. In post binding, screw posts are placed in the margin of the book as illustrated in Figure B-2. This method of binding is used for publications which are subject to revision or for which it is desirable to add or remove sheets without difficulty. However, post-bound publications tend to close when used. If the reader is not required to hold the publication open, another form of binding should be selected. When post binding is used, ample space should be allowed at the binding margin. A minimum of 1 inch is recommended.

Saddle stitching (see Figure B-2) is a lasting method of binding short permanent publications. It should not be used for publications having more than 120 to 140 pages (60 to 70 sheets), for which this type of binding would not be durable. No less than ½ inch (1.27 cm) should be used at the binding margin.

SADDLE STITCHING . The term is derived from the method of sewing the cover and pages together. In this illustration, staples are used instead of binding thread.

POST BINDING.   This method of binding employs three screw posts inserted through holes punched in the cover and pages of a publication.

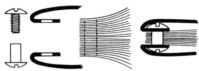

SIDESTITCHING.   This is a method of binding in which the cover is glued to the pages and the publication is then stapled through the side of its spine.

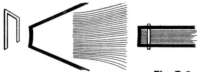

Fig. B-2   Types of mechanical binding.

Sidestitching should be used for publications consisting of more than 140 pages. Publications with sidestitched binding also have a tendency to close when not held open, and a minimum binding margin of ¾ inch (1.902 cm) should be used.

Spiral binding consists of helical metal wire inserted through punched holes in the binding margin. This type of binding is used for thin publications and for those from which pages will not be removed.

Figure B-3 is the Velo-Bind Model 123 desk-top binder, a new innovation in mechanical binding. The machine is designed for binding reports, proposals, presentations, marketing plans, photographs, research reports, computer printouts, and other documents up to 1 inch thick and as much as 14 inches (35.5 cm) wide. The binding process utilizes a "hot knife" system, common to all Velo-Bind binding machines. Both bind and punch cycles are performed by a single U-shaped control bar that can be operated by either left- or right-handed personnel. It has a punching capability for handling stock 14 inches (35.5 cm) wide by ⅛ inch (3.17 mm) thick. A range of covers, both hard and soft, is offered in an assortment of sizes and colors. The Velo-Bind Model 201 Mark IV binder (not shown) handles materials up

Fig. B-3   Velo-Bind Model 123 desk-top binder.

to 3 inches (7.62 cm) thick and 14⅞ inches (37.7 cm) wide and has the capability to punch, bind, and hard cover books in less than ninety seconds, and to softcover documents in less than sixty seconds. Punching capability is up to 14⅞ inches (37.78 cm) wide in stacks of ⅛ inch (0.317 cm) (20,000 sheets per hour). The machine is push-button and power-operated. As a safety measure, two binding buttons must be pressed simultaneously to activate the binding cycle. Figure B-4 illustrates the sequence of the binding operation and the elements that compose the binding function from the cover to the top binding strip. Over 50 sizes and color combinations of binding strips are available.

Figure B-5 is General Binding Corporation's Autobinder II, Model 346 BN. The machine plastic binds 500 to 1,000 booklets per hour. When in the automatic mode, it feeds, positions, opens, and closes plastic binding without operator handling. For long runs, cartridge packs of binding material are used and the machine is switched to the automatic mode. For shorter jobs, the binding material is placed in guide vanes by hand and the machine is switched to the manual-feed mode. The machine has a binding width capability (the binding margin) of from 6 to 23 rings, and a binding diameter of plastic material from ¼ to ⁹⁄₁₆ inch (0.635 to 1.43 cm) that includes both the automatic and manual-feed binding of wide-back material. The weight of this machine is 54 pounds.

Figure B-6 is General Binding Corporation's automatic punch. A feeding hopper is adjusted to accommodate the sheet size (5½ by 8½ to 9 by 12 inches) (13.9 by 21.6 to 22.8 by 30.4 cm) and paper is loaded to be punched. The operational sequence then starts: A blade separates a lift of 15 to 25 sheets from the bottom of the stack, the lift of paper is advanced under the punching dies, punching occurs when the paper touches the back guide, and the paper is automatically ejected into the stacker. Then a new cycle

Fig. B-4 Velo-Bind sequence of binding operation.

Fig. B-5 General Binding Corporation's Autobinder II Model 346 BN plastic binding machine.

Fig. B-6 General Binding Corporation's automatic punch.

begins. Speeds are adjustable to handle 30 to 70 lifts per minute, with an overall capability of punching 75,000 to 100,000 sheets per hour. The machine punches bond or ledger stock in weights from 16 to 28 pounds (7.26 to 12.7 kg), and punching dies can be selected to punch from 1 to 27 holes having $\frac{9}{16}$-inch (1.43-cm)-diameter centers.

binding edge Edge of a sheet or page that is nearest the saddle of the book. Right-hand pages are bound at the left side and left-hand pages at the right side. Ample space for binding should be allowed. If binding is such that the pages lie flat when the book is open, less binding edge is required. For small books, with a page size of 6 by 9 inches (15.2 by 22.8 cm) or less, an allowance of not less than $\frac{5}{8}$ inch (1.58 cm) should be made for pages that lie flat. The minimum binding edge for brochures, pamphlets, and booklets is 1 inch for a page size of 8½ by 11 inches (21.6 by 28 cm). In typing composition for printing, the edge of the left-hand page should have the same dimensions from edge to image as the right-hand page has from edge to image. Similarly, the binding margins of the two pages should have the same dimensions. If a page is printed horizontally, the margins should have the same width as on other pages. If possible, horizontal pages should be right-hand pages so that the copy may be read by turning the book clockwise.

bit Single character of a computer language having only two characters, such as either of the binary digits 0 and 1. Also, a unit of information equivalent to the choice of either of two equal likely states of an information-containing system, as well as a unit of information storage capacity as of a computer memory.

bit density Number of bits of information contained in a given area, such as the number of bits written along an inch of magnetic tape.

bite In photoengraving, the successive steps of etching by corrosion of the metal plate with acid. Each bite necessarily makes a deeper etch.

black and white *See* REPRODUCTION COPY; REPRODUCTION PROOF.

black art (also called **base art; basic art; key art**) Basic art used in making process plates for illustrations of two or more colors. As the name implies, it is art that will be printed black and used in combination with color work.

black patch (also called **blackout; window**) Black masking patch that is pasted or mortised into position in the exact size of a photograph on reproduction line copy. (A red patch serves the same purpose.) The photograph is screened and reduced if necessary, and the halftone negative is stripped into the window of the line negative, thus making a composite, or assembled, negative of line and halftone copy. If the photograph requires reduction—and it often does—the reduction must be in exact proportion to the window and the line negative left by the black patch.

black printer Printer's term for the film (and subsequently the plate) that prints black in the color-separation process. The plate is also known as the key plate.

blackline Black-lined copy, either text or artwork, produced by the whiteprint process. The only difference between blacklines and bluelines lies in the type of diazo-treated copy paper used.

blackout *See* BLACK PATCH.

blanc fixe White material used with china clay as a filler for coating and enameling book papers.

blank Heavy paper used for advertising display purposes such as posters and window displays. Blanks are designated by ply, the ply indicating thickness.

blanket Rubber sheet covering the cylinder of an offset press. The cylinder on which the blanket is mounted is called the blanket cylinder. The blanket receives the impression from the plate and transfers it to the paper. Since the image is right-reading on the master cylinder, the image of the blanket will be wrong-reading; thus a right-reading image is transferred to the paper.

blanket cylinder Cylinder or cylinders on offset printing presses which contain the blanket and which deposit the inked image on the substrate.

blanket-to-blanket press (unit perfecting press) Offset printing press in which the rolled web (paper) is fed between two blanket cylinders, each of which serves as an impression cylinder for the other. Figure B-7 illustrates the blanket-to-blanket relationship of cylinder plates and blankets.

bleed To extend to the edge or edges of a page, said of line or halftone work. The effect is produced by printing a fraction of an inch (usually ⅛ to ¼ inch) (3.175 to 6.350 mm) of the image beyond the desired dimension and then trimming the sheet to obtain the bleed. Printers consider bleeding an additional cost factor.

blind copy Typewritten carbon copy of a letter directed by the writer to an interested recipient without the recipient's name being listed on the original under the distribution notice. The recipient's name is listed only on the copy he or she receives and on the file copy.

blind embossing Embossing without printing.

blind folio Page number counted but not printed. It is sometimes necessary to identify a page as having an assigned number without printing the number. For example, to identify an inside title page with a printed page number is of no importance insofar as a point of reference is concerned. An

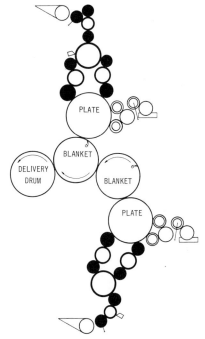

Fig. B-7 Blanket-to-blanket relationship of plates and blankets.

inside title page therefore does not warrant this reference, and the page is counted but not printed with a page number. Pages in the body of a magazine are often counted but not numbered because an overprint of the page number on a colored bleed could not be distinguished if it were printed. However, during the manufacturing process it is imperative that individual pages be identified by number even if the number is not printed.

blind punching   In automatic linecasting control, perforating tape without producing decoded copy to be checked and edited. The copy must be proofed from the tape.

blind stamping   Pressing a design on a surface merely by using a die. Ink or other materials, such as gold leaf, that would give a more distinct image are not used.

blinding   In photomechanical platemaking, a condition in which, despite a strong-looking image, a printing plate prints very weakly or not at all. Blinding may be caused by an excess of gum on the image, which therefore does not accept ink. The plate may be rubbed down with fountain solution to remove the excess gum. Some plates require going over with the developer. The manufacturer's directions should be followed in using the correct chemicals for final gumming. Blinding is also produced by glazed ink rollers or by a strong fountain solution that has worked into the ink, causing the ink to emulsify.

blister card   Printed display card to which merchandise is affixed and over which a transparent material has been shaped in the form of a "blister" covering the article. Such items as combs, toothbrushes, razors, razor blades, and the like are common examples of merchandise displayed in blister cards.

block   Metal or wooden base upon which a printing plate is mounted. "Blocking" is the process of mounting the plate on the block.

block diagram   Drawing in which blocks or rectangles are used to show the relationship between the components of an item or a piece of equipment. Lines and arrowheads indicate flow or sequence.

block in   To make the principal outline of an object during initial preparation by sketching blocks which are then usable as reference points.

block letter   Character inscribed in relief on a wooden block from which an ink or dye impression can be made. The typeface is square-cut, sans serif, and without hairlines.

block printing   Earliest-known form of printing, in which impressions were taken from wood. It followed the taking of rubbings. The material used in block printing was generally pearwood. The block was planed and squared to the desired page size, and the surface was rubbed with paste or sizing. The page was first written carefully on thin paper, which was made to adhere facedown on the block. The paper itself was then rubbed off, leaving the inked impression of the letters on the wood. The carver cut away the wood surrounding the characters, leaving them in relief. Actual printing was done by brushing ink on the block, laying a strip of paper on it, and then rubbing the paper with a dry brush. This method is still used in Asia today.

Origins

The Chinese consider block printing rather than the invention of movable type to be the real origin of printing. The exact date when true block printing began is not known, but scholars believe that the years 712 to 750 may be taken as approximate dates. While block printing undoubtedly originated in China, the earliest-known specimen of block printing, or of printing of any kind, is from Japan; it was produced between 764 and 770. It is of interest to note that the earliest-known work of printing and publishing was done during this period and is a most important event in the history of Japan and of the world. The empress Shōtoku, an ardent Buddhist, ordered the printing of 1 million charms, each to be enclosed in a little wooden pagoda and to be distributed among 10 Buddhist temples. The Japanese government has preserved a number of these pagodas and charms in the National Museum. According to the best information available, there are three of the original pagodas and charms in the British Museum, one in the Leipzig Museum, and at least two in the United States.

The first printed book known was produced by Chinese block printing. The book is the *Diamond Sūtra*. It was found in 1900 by a priest near the city of Tunhuang in northwestern China, where it had been preserved in a sealed cave, one of the Caves of the Thousand Buddhas. Now in the British Museum, the *Diamond Sūtra* is a landmark in cultural history. It is made up of six sheets of text, measuring about 1 foot high and 30 inches long, and a smaller sheet with an illustration. The seven sheets are pasted together to form a book roll. Toward the end of the text is a statement that it was printed on May 11, 868, by Wang Chieh, ". . . for free general distribution, in order in deep reverence to perpetuate the memory of his parents."

Linoleum-block Printing

Block printing from linoleum is an old craft which is gaining in popularity among both adults and children, no doubt because of a strong desire for individual expression of creative ideas. It is one of the few forms of graphic expression in which the individual has complete control of his subject from creating the design to printing it.

A plain "battleship" linoleum block without pattern is used in block printing. Linoleum blocks are available either unmounted or mounted on plywood to make the printing block type-high. This height, 0.918 inch (23.3 mm), is a standard dimension for the thickness of the printing block or form. Blocks with a white or gray surface are used for ease in transferring the design to the block. When the linoleum block is cold or old, it should be warmed to soften it for cutting. Figure B-8 shows some of the tools and techniques used in linoleum-block printing.

Other materials, including carbon paper for transferring the image, a triangle for squaring blocks, india ink, scotch tape, hard and soft pencils, paste, and art gum, are used from time to time. The printing paper should

MOUNTED AND UNMOUNTED LINOLEUM

CARVING THE LINOLEUM BLOCK

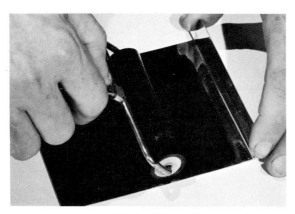

USING BRAYER AND INKING PLATE

ROLLING INK ON THE CARVED BLOCK

be soft and absorbent. Onionskin and newsprint are both excellent papers for proofing prints. Rice paper is ideal for finished work, although school sketching or drawing paper is suitable. Hard-surfaced, glossy, or enameled papers should not be used. For hand production of prints, small presses manufactured especially for block printing are available. Pressure is applied to the block on the paper with padding to ensure good printing. Industrial printing presses may be used for runs with relief printing plates, but the plates must have a reverse-reading image in order to produce a right-reading image. Inks for linoleum-block printing are made water-soluble for easy cleaning, as well as with an oil base. A full range of colors, including gold and silver, is available. Reducers and extenders for all conditions are also available.

Water-soluble ink is the most popular because the blocks can be cleaned easily with water. This kind of ink also blends well into light pastel colors and is excellent for school use. If a permanent color or black printing is desired, an oil-based ink is used. Oil solvents such as kerosine or benzine are employed for cleaning when oil-based inks are used. A roller called a

Fig. B-8 Instruments and techniques used in block printing. (*Courtesy of Hunt Manufacturing Co.*)

"brayer" is used to roll the ink from an inking plate onto the printing surface. Any nonporous material such as tin may be used as an inking plate.

blocking out Eliminating characters, portions of art, or any part of an image on reproduction copy or negatives by pasting them over, whiting them out with paint, or masking them. Blocking out can be used to great advantage in the whiteprint process.

blotting paper Paper made especially to absorb ink or other liquids. It has a low finish and readily absorbs writing inks. Blotting papers are available in a wide range of colors and finishes and in 100- and 120-pound (45.4- and 54.4-kg) weights. Sheet sizes are 19 by 24 and 24 by 38 inches (48.2 by 61 and 61 by 97 cm). *See also* TABLE 5.

blow up To enlarge by photography an advertisement or preprinted text for advertising and display purposes; also, to enlarge an illustration or a photograph for any purpose.

blowback Act or result of making an enlarged print or copy, particularly from a microfilm such as 16, 35, 70, or 105-millimeter film. The term is derived from "blow up" (to enlarge) and "back" and means reproduction back to a larger size.

blue-sensitive Sensitive to blue and ultraviolet light, said of a plate or film which has little or no sensitivity to light of other colors.

blue streak Streak of blue ink imposed along the margin and on the front page of some daily newspapers to indicate a specific edition when more than one daily edition is published. Ink is applied with a cylinder wheel mounted on the press. The device has its own ink supply.

blueline Copy having blue lines with a white background. Bluelines are made from vellum, film positives, or any translucent or transparent original on which an image has been made and reproduced by the whiteprint process. Photolithographic negatives may produce what are commonly called "reverse bluelines" by utilizing the whiteprint process. Since these negatives have a translucent image and a black background, they produce a white image on a medium or dark blue background. *See also* REVERSE BLUELINE.

blueline print Print in which the image is formed of blue lines. Such prints are durable and permanent, but the scale is only fair. They are made by contact with any negative on iron-sensitized paper or cloth by developing and washing. The paper has a rag content of 50 to 100 percent.

blueprint Print in which white lines are produced on a blue background by the direct contact of pen or pencil positive originals with vellum or other translucent materials. When pencil is used, the original must be firmly defined and solidly delineated for fine reproduction. All blueprints are of contact size, as no enlargement or reduction can be obtained without a lens. Blueprint copies may be made 54 inches (137.1 cm) wide and in any length and are economical for a run of 1 to 100 copies. A portion of the original drawing can be used merely by placing the desired portion over the sensitized copy paper or other material. Blueprints are popular for production, construction, and architectural drawings. Because of their ability to stand hard usage, they are common in shops and in the field, where they may be exposed to direct sunlight. It is difficult to keep blueprints to exact scale, however, for the paper is subject to warping and shrinking because of the wet process of developing and washing. If the vellum or cloth original has been drawn with pencil, an ordinary pencil eraser will suffice to make corrections, but if ink has been used, an eradicator must be employed. *See also* DARK-PRINT PROCESS; REPRODUCTION FLOW.

blueprint paper Direct-copy-process paper manufactured with a good rag content to produce a smooth finish, wet strength, and good absorbency. To make the copy, the original or translucent master is placed in direct contact with the blueprint paper.

blueprint process *See* DARK-PRINT PROCESS.

blurb Copy slanted toward a sales angle, particularly copy on a book jacket. A blurb is usually written in brief paragraphs.

board Any heavy board material, such as that used for mounting art or making displays. Also, heavier art stock may be called board, as in illustration board, canvas board, etc.

board art Any artwork, especially original art, mounted on heavy board stock. Figure B-9 illustrates what may be done with original board art in sequence. It shows practices common to handling art for photo-offset printing, as well as some side steps that may be taken. Once an image has been produced, many processes and variations can be involved. The choice depends on what is required of the end product, the types of reproduction and printing equipment available or desired, the quality of the final publication, time limitations, and other factors.

In Figure B-9, the original board art *A* may be twice up or once and a half up in size. The art should be protected with a tissue overlay and mounted and flapped with kraft paper on rigid board stock. It should be identified with the figure number and title, the desired reduction size, and any other information consistent with art department policies and specifications. The art is photographed with a process camera, which produces the 8 by 10-inch (20.3 by 25.4-cm) art negative *B*. The negative is known technically as a photolithographic negative; it has a translucent image and an opaque background. From the negative is made a photoprint *C*, which may have a matte (dull) or a glossy finish. The photoprint is enlarged or reduced to match the size of the reproducible copy. The required dimensions for enlargement or reduction may be indicated on the negative by

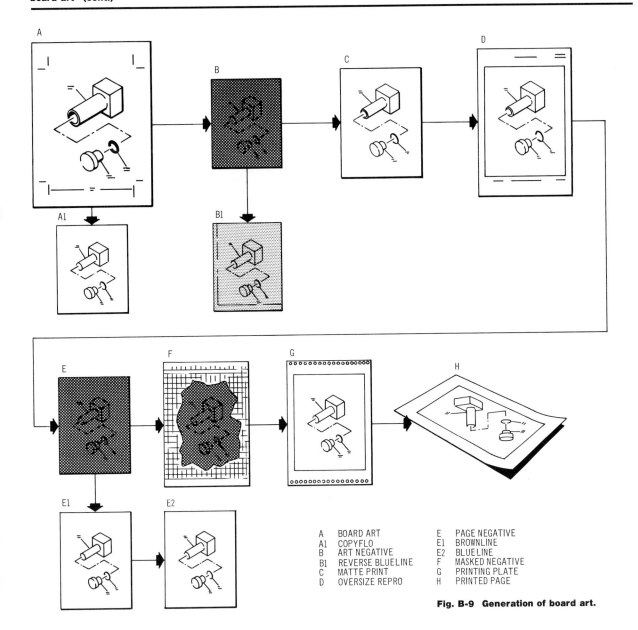

A	BOARD ART	E	PAGE NEGATIVE
A1	COPYFLO	E1	BROWNLINE
B	ART NEGATIVE	E2	BLUELINE
B1	REVERSE BLUELINE	F	MASKED NEGATIVE
C	MATTE PRINT	G	PRINTING PLATE
D	OVERSIZE REPRO	H	PRINTED PAGE

Fig. B-9 Generation of board art.

placing a strip of masking tape along the bottom (outside the crop marks) and writing the dimensions on the tape. A horizontal line, terminating at both ends in arrowheads to denote the dimension width, is drawn along the tape. The photoprint is then stripped in or pasted on the oversize basic reproduction page D and ruled or boxed in.

Before the art is stripped in, the basic reproduction page may be called a "skeleton," a "page frame," or a "page mask," usage varying with the organization. The figure number and such marginal information as the page content heading, running head, folio, or security classification are typed on the reproduction page. Whether it contains text or art, the page is known as "repro" or "camera-ready" copy.

The process camera is again employed, and a page negative E is produced from the basic reproduction page. The negative, which is reduced to page size, is a photolithographic negative having a translucent image and an opaque background. It may also be called a "base plate." The printer strips the page negative into orange masking paper containing grid lines to ensure exact positions, as in Figure B-9F.

The assembled masking paper and negative are now placed over a sensitive flexible printing plate, and the combination is positioned in a glass frame, where it is firmly held. A vacuum is employed to compress negative and plate within the frame. The negative and plate are subjected to strong arc lights which "burn" through the translucent image of the negative and activate the light-sensitive emulsion on the plate, leaving a latent image. The plate G is then developed by washing with a developer and water, and the page H is printed from the plate.

Many other steps may be taken with the materials produced, as indicated in Figure B-9. For example, if a piece of art similar to board art A is to be originated, the original art should not be reworked because it would then lose its identity. Instead, an enlarged matte or glossy print is reworked; when completed, it will have an identity of its own. For every piece of effective art, there should be an original piece of art with its own identity. When art must be submitted with manuscript copy for approval, the art negative B is used in making a reverse blueline $B1$ by means of a whiteprint machine. The negative is placed over the copy paper with the upper right-hand corners in register. The reverse blueline has a white image and a black or dark blue background. Since the negative measures 8 by 10 inches (20.3 by 25.4 cm), the blueline will have a white binding margin on the left and a 1-inch (2.54-cm) white space at the bottom for figure number and title when 8½ by 11-inch (22 by 28-cm) copy paper is used.

When an art negative is not available for the submittal of manuscript and art copy, Copyflo copies can be made and reduced to fit 8½ by 11-inch (22 by 28-cm) bond paper. Copyflo is made by the xerographic process of reproduction on 35-millimeter film. The black image is suitable for reference or review copies.

Figure B-9 also illustrates a brownline $E1$ produced from the page negative E. When a government procurement agency orders technical manuals, it usually requires brownlines in addition to the reproducible copy and page negatives. Brownlines are made from sepia brownline paper of 100 percent rag content by running the negative and copy paper through the whiteprint machine. They are long-lived intermediates which may be filed as permanent copies. Bluelines, made from the translucent brownline as indicated in Figure B-9E2, have blue images with white backgrounds. Blueline copies are used for reference or as review copies.

body Piece of type on which a character is cast. The term also denotes a block of text copy, as well as the main part of a book or other publication exclusive of front and back matter.

body type (reading type; text type) Type of a size used for printing text material. Popular sizes range from 8 to 12 points, 9 and 10 points being quite common. *See also* TYPE SPECIMENS.

boiler plate Centrally prepared material of a stereotyped nature, supplied especially to small newspapers. The term "boiler plate" may also refer to artwork in common use, as well as to text copy that may require only slight alteration in context.

boldface Typeface that is heavier and darker than the body typeface, used especially for center and side headings to distinguish them from related text. The term is opposed to "lightface."

bond paper Paper used for ruling, printing, typewriting, and pen writing. Since bond paper is employed extensively for correspondence, which must be handled and filed, strength and permanence are paramount requirements. The surface characteristics of bond paper are therefore important. Three methods are used to size bond paper: engine, surface, and tub sizing. Engine sizing is accomplished by adding resin to the pulp while the pulp is in the beater. In surface sizing, the paper is sprayed with sizing solution on both sides before the web (paper) is advanced to the dryer rolls on the paper machine. Tub sizing is accomplished by immersing the paper in a solution of gelatin or starch. Better grades of paper are made with surface and tub sizing techniques.

Bond papers require an even finish, which is obtained by machine speeds that permit a "close" formation of fibers. There are two kinds of bond papers; one has a cotton or rag content, and the other is made from chemical wood pulp. All rag-content and 100 percent rag papers are sized by tub and surface processes. Practically all rag-content bonds are watermarked by the dandy roll; laid marks are obtained as desired. Rag-content bonds come in four grades, of 25, 50, 75, and 100 percent rag content, respectively. High-quality bleached wood bond paper is produced from various combinations of sulfate, sulfite, and soda pulp; all sizing is accomplished by the engine process in the beater. Most wood bonds are dried on the machine rollers. Several grades are made by each manufacturer, the better grades being watermarked. Standard weights of bond paper are 9, 13, 16, 20, and 24 pounds (4.08, 5.9, 7.3, 9.08, and 11 kg) for 500 sheets of the basic size of 17 by 22 inches (43.1 by 58.8 cm).

bond typewriter paper Boxed paper, or paper that has already been cut to the regular size of 8½ by 11 inches (22 by 28 cm) or to legal sizes of 8½ by 13 and 8½ by 14 inches (22 by 33 and 22 by 36 cm). Usually manufactured in white only, bond typewriter paper may have either a cockle or a smooth vellum finish. Standard weights are 9, 11, 13, 16, 20, and 24 pounds (4.08, 4.9, 5.9, 6.8, 9.08, and 11 kg) for 500 sheets of the basic size of 17 by 22 inches (43.1 by 55.8 cm). *See also* BOXED PAPER.

book endpaper *See* ENDLEAF.

book face Any typeface suitable for the text of a book. Book face is also an old term, used especially in technical publication circles, for a special kind of typeface known as IBM's Bold Face No. 1.

book-form drawing In engineering drafting, an assemblage of drawings and related data pertaining to an item or a system under a single identifying drawing number and title. It is intended for special-purpose applications and employs combinations of printed or typewritten data and illustrations to show requirements. Book-form drawings should not be used to circumvent requirements for furnishing the individual drawings normally needed for items or for a system.

book lining *See* ENDLEAF.

book makeup Act of collating, arranging, and numbering pages of reproduction copy of a publication. It is the last function in preparing the publication for printing. A blank preprinted form showing individual pages may be used to assist makeup personnel and to direct the printer in the placement of each page. As many sheets of the form as are required are used to depict the pages of the complete publication. Page 1 of the body of the publication begins on a right-hand page. All matter preceding page 1 is front matter and can be laid out in reverse order from the last element to the cover page. Following are some elements which should receive consideration when organizing elements (not all the elements may be present in a given publication).

1. Front matter
   a. Half title page
   b. Title page
   c. Copyright notice
   d. Contents
   e. List of illustrations
   f. List of tables
   g. Foreword
   h. Preface
   i. Introduction
2. Body
   a. Parts
   b. Chapters
   c. Sections
3. Back matter
   a. Exhibits
   b. Appendixes
   c. Glossary of terms
   d. References
   e. Bibliography
   f. Alphabetical index
4. Pagination
   a. Front matter (lowercase roman numerals). Identify each element as to placement for a right- or a left-hand page.
   b. The first page of the first division of the body begins with a right-hand page and is assigned the arabic numeral 1. Succeeding pages are numbered in sequence.
   c. Consider that a part or a chapter in a particular publication may be designed to begin only on a right-hand page.
   d. Back matter is paginated either by continuing the numbering in sequence

from the body (this practice is most popular) or by defining the element at the bottom of the page and beginning the first page with the arabic number 1. For example, Appendix A appears at the bottom left margin, for a right-hand page, with the numeral 1 at the right margin (for a left-hand page, Appendix A is placed at the right margin and the numeral 1 at the left margin).

5. Illustrations
   a. Define a foldout illustration by using the symbol F/O.
   b. Define a halftone page by using the symbol H/T.
   c. List the figure number of the illustration or the art file number, or both, for all illustrations.
   d. If an illustration consists of more than one page, show the figure number followed by "page 1 of 5," "page 2 of 5," etc.
6. Tables
   a. List all table numbers.
   b. Note that a particular table is a foldout by using the symbol F/O.
   c. If a table consists of more than one page, show the table number followed by "page 1 of 10," "page 2 of 10," etc.

book paper   Classification of paper that includes various grades and many finishes. Among the grades are uncoated book paper, coated book paper, rotogravure paper, Bible paper, and offset paper. Book papers are used by printing establishments, publishers, manufacturers, educational institutions, and business, social, and other organizations. Most are manufactured from various combinations of sulfite, sulfate, and soda-bleached pulps. Some rag may be used. (*See also* separate articles on the various grades of paper.)

bookbinding   Bookbinding as it is known today consists of a number of methods of holding pages together to form a book, booklet, magazine, or other multipage piece of visual material. Premodern bookbinding was an art invented out of the need to protect valuable manuscripts written on papyrus or parchment scrolls and lavishly decorated with designs and bookplates. The invention of the printing press gave great impetus to bookbinding. In modern hardcover bookbinding, the binder receives two or four signatures consisting of 16 or 32 pages each, or quadruples of 16 pages each, which are bundled into convenient folded units. The signatures are arranged in page sequence. The books are then sewn by machines which pass threads through their spines. Air is driven between the pages to establish uniform thickness. After the book has been trimmed, the edges may be stained, marbled, or gilded. The back of the book is then treated with hot glue, and strong endleaf paper is affixed to hold the inside of the book and the cover together. Paste is applied to the outside of the endleaf, and the cover is encased. The book is pressed until the paste dries. It is then ready for marketing.

The growth of industrial soft- and self-cover booklets, brochures, pamphlets, and similar matter has led to mechanical binding. Loose-leaf metal-ring binding, metal-prong binding, post binding, stapling, etc., are common in offices. Wire-spiral binding and plastic-comb binding are convenient and inexpensive methods. Since pages lie flat when the book is open, handling and reading are easy.

Figure B-10 shows the Sheridan hinge-clamp binder, a heavy-duty, high-speed binder designed to operate at up to 250 cycles per minute. The

Fig. B-10 Sheridan high-speed, heavy duty hinge-clamp binder.

hinge-clamp feature incorporates improvements in adhesive binding from infeed to delivery. Gathered signatures are fed into the machine vertically, while jogger units ensure positive register of the gathered signatures. Connections are available for quick connection to any arm or rotary-type gathering machine. The backbone of the book is prepared by using carbide-tipped dustless saws and a precision cutter to cut off the back of the signatures to extremely close tolerances. Additional saw and rougher units are available for particular applications. A hot-melt unit features easily accessible adjustments and controls to allow quick setup of the binding glue. The unit is compact and insulated, and the heat is thermostatically controlled. The cover feeder consists of a long feed board and ratchet-controlled feed-up belts that ensure efficient loading and accurate register to suckers with automatic control. The cover feed rate is regulated by a detector system. An applier drum receives covers from the cover raceway and provides register control of cover to the book. The cover feeder system, as used with all Sheridan binders, includes "no book/no cover" missing-cover detectors. Bound books are delivered vertically from the binder through conveying equipment or other in-line equipment.

Signature sizes are 5 by 7 inches (12.7 by 17.8 cm) minimum to 11½ by 16½ inches (29.2 by 41.9 cm) or 8 by 18 inches (20.3 by 45.7 cm) maximum. The book thickness finished is ⅛ inch (3.175 mm) minimum up to 1½ inches (3.81 mm) maximum. Both 25- or 33-clamp machines are available.

The Sheridan XG standard rotary gatherer (Figure B-11), designed for medium- to short-run operations, utilizes the rotary principle of placing

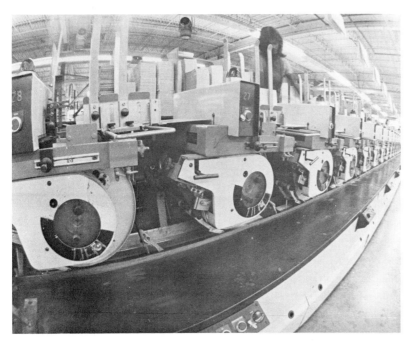

Fig. B-11 Sheridan XG standard rotary gatherer.

signatures on the raceway in the direction of raceway flow. The machine is powered to run at 10,000 cycles per hour (167 cycles per minute). It accepts signature sizes from 4 by 6 inches (10.16 by 15.24 cm) minimum to 12 by 20 inches (30.48 by 50.8 cm) maximum, and the signatures may be fed from either side of the machine. Machine setup is controlled from the operator side. Makeready of caliper and paper size adjustments on the pocket is completed in seconds. Caliper wheels, visible to the operator, allow faster timing of each pocket and detect variation. A cam-operated reciprocating needle supports the pile on each hopper, and a separator disk positions each signature for efficient gripper action. Drum-mounted grippers pull signatures from the hopper and place them in the gatherer raceway at pin speed. Push-button stations are mounted on each four-pocket section. The operator can control the machine remotely from any of eight stations with the portable jog button. Signature types handled are double parallel, open three sides, and close head. Thickness can be accommodated up to 72 pages per signature (⅛ inch; 3.175 mm). The minimum this machine can handle is a two-page signature of 22-pound (10-kg) stock; the maximum for loose-gather bulk is 2½ inches (6.35 cm).

The Sheridan straight-line trimmer (Figure B-12) has been designed for continuous heavy-duty and long-run book, publication, and trade production. Flexibility includes connections to side-wire, sewn, or adhesive-bound binding lines. The machine is available in three-knife or five-knife versions to trim piles up to a maximum of 6 inches (15.24 cm) high and a minimum of 4¾ inches (12.06 cm) high. Standard mechanical advantages include speeds up to 42 cycles per minute for a three-knife trimmer and up to 36

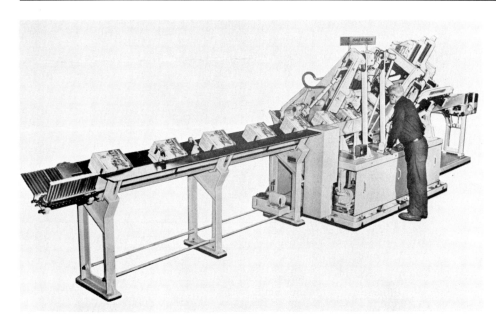

Fig. B-12 Sheridan straight-line trimmer.

cycles per minute for a five-knife trimmer. A notcher on the five-knife trimmer eliminates the cover break when cutting apart two on work, and a higher clamp pressure is fully adjustable for better pile control and trim quality. Other features include automatic sorting of two on work with the five-knife trimmer utilizing a belt conveyor delivery, and a new transport system resulting in station-to-station movement with high registration accuracy.

booklet Small book consisting of as much as, but not more than, 24 pages, yet having a sufficient number of pages not to be classified as a pamphlet. According to United States postal laws and regulations, for mailing purposes a book must have 24 pages or more (including the cover) in order to qualify for book mailing rates.

bookplate Label pasted on the inside of a book bearing the owner's name or other identification. For ornate bookplate designs, the term *ex libris* (Latin for "from the library of") may be placed before the owner's name. Very old books are often considered collector's items when they bear bookplates created by eminent designers or when the bookplates carry the name of a famous owner.

bottom out Term used in page layout to indicate that a page of text closes near the bottom limitations of the page. Text or copy should be conveniently aligned within the prescribed vertical dimension of the page. Text should not ordinarily be set in type or typewritten as reproducible copy with the first line of a paragraph standing at the bottom of a page. It is preferable to leave the page short and begin the paragraph on the next page, for typewritten matter, or to take up the space with additional quadding or by adding space, as is done with proportional-spacing machines. Two lines of a paragraph may appear at the bottom of a page if the carry-over lines on the next page number two or more. A single word (orphan) or part of a sentence (widow) should never stand alone at the top of a page or column. The last word of a column or page should not be hyphenated, and a page should not end with a reference to a following list; instead, one or more items of the list should be placed at the bottom of the page. Care should be used to have no more than three broken words, requiring hyphens, at the right-hand margin of justified copy.

bounce Effect of "bouncing" characters, produced by type, usually display type, set with a photographic typesetter.

bourgeois Old type size. The nearest equivalent in the point system is 9 point (3.16 mm).

box tilts *See* WEB ALIGNERS.

boxed paper (typewriter paper) Paper that has been cut and boxed (or wrapped), such as bond, onionskin, manifold, mimeograph, and duplicating paper. Cutting sizes are the letterhead size of 8½ by 11 inches (22 by 28 cm) and the legal sizes of 8½ by 13 and 8½ by 14 inches (22 by 33 and 22 by 36 cm). These are the utility sizes for offices, homes, libraries, schools, and almost any other place where a typewriter or an office duplicator machine is used. The government size for boxed paper is 8 by 10½ inches (20.3 by 27 cm).

boxhead Columnar headings in a table that appear between the head rule and the first cutoff rule, under which pertinent matter appears for each heading. Parts of a boxhead are the head rule, stubhead, columnar heads, spanner head, subspanner heads, date and figure heads, reading column heads, and the cutoff rule. (*See* Figure B-13.)

boxing Enclosing an illustration or other material in a drawn or printed frame. When lines are drawn with ink, the proper weight must be used if the art is to be reduced.

B/P Symbol for blueprint.

BPI Abbreviation for bits per inch; a data density usually found with magnetic tape.

brace Symbol or sign used to enclose, connect, and show relationships of text or illustrative matter. In technical illustrating, a brace encloses and identifies subassembly details of the main illustration of an exploded view. The brace indicates origin with respect to the main illustration. The word "bracket" is often used erroneously when "brace" is correct. (*See* Figure B-14.)

SPECIAL TOOLS, FIXTURES, AND EQUIPMENT

A

PART NUMBER	MANUFACTURER'S DESIGNATION	APPLICATION
34321	Inner Section Tube Flattener	To flatten inner tubes of core assembly.
78909	Tube Tool Holder	To hold tube puller and bumping tips.
35678	Tube Puller	To remove broken or damaged tubes.
78645	Tube Tool Handle	Used with tube puller and tool holder to remove broken and damaged tubes.

B

Part Number	Manufacturer's Designation	Application
34321	Inner Section Tube Flattener	To flatten inner tubes of core assembly.
78909	Tube Tool Holder	To hold tube puller and bumping tips.
35678	Tube Puller	To remove broken or damaged tubes.
78645	Tube Tool Handle	Used with tube puller and tool holder to remove broken and damaged tubes

Table 1. Special Tools, Fixtures, and Equipment

Fig. B-13 Application of boxheads in technical publications.

brass Alloy essentially composed of zinc and copper used largely in manufacturing printing types, rules, and characters where hardness and durability are required. Uses for brass type include stamping book titles on book covers, stamping gold leaf where heat is required, and embossing work.

brayer Hand roller used to distribute ink over a printing plate. *See* BLOCK PRINTING.

break line Discrete line used on an orthographic engineering drawing. Long break lines are designated as "thin" lines; short breaks are indicated by solid freehand lines and are designated as "thick" lines. For long breaks, full ruled lines with freehand zigzags are used. Shafts, rods, tubes, etc., which have a portion of their length broken out are drawn as illustrated in LINE CONVENTIONS: ENGINEERING DRAWINGS.

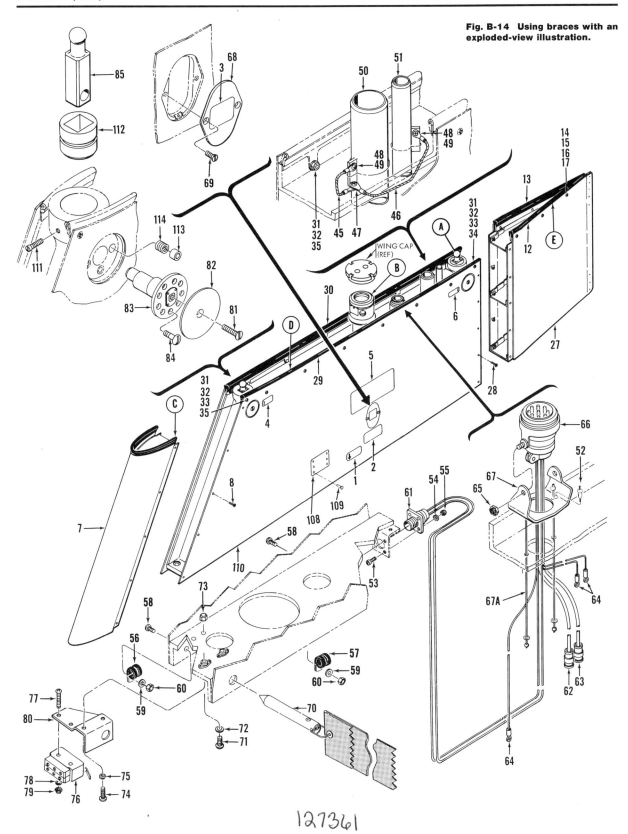

Fig. B-14 Using braces with an exploded-view illustration.

127361

breakline In composition linecasting, the end of the last sentence of a paragraph where quads are inserted to complete the line with a blank space for the line of type. Quads, or quadrats, do not print.

brevier Old type size. The nearest equivalent in the point system is 8 point.

briefing chart (flip chart) Visual aid that graphically presents a story to an audience. The speaker or briefer uses the chart to monitor, illustrate, and emphasize pertinent points of the subject. Briefing charts are prepared with black or colored lettering and lines, as well as with pastels, and generally on a white stock sufficiently stable and rigid for mounting or standing. Sizes vary from the desk size of 10¼ by 13 inches (26.03 by 33 cm) for an audience not exceeding 10 persons to 30 by 40 inches (76.2 by 101.6 cm) for audiences from 10 to 40 persons and 42 by 52 inches (107 by 132 cm) for audiences from 40 to 70 persons. Copy on briefing charts should be confined to short descriptive phrases. Briefing-chart books may be prepared from the charts when a wider dissemination or a permanent record of the material is desired. The text on each chart should cover one major topic and not be congested.

brilliant Old type size of 3½ points (1.23 mm). It is seldom used.

broad fold Having the grain running along the short dimension, said of paper. It is the opposite of "long fold."

broadside Advertising sheet, usually a self-mailer. The word is probably derived from the old practice of printing on only one side of a sheet and then folding as desired. Today a broadside may be printed on both sides or on portions of a single fold.

broadside page (horizontal page; landscape page) Page that must be turned 90° clockwise for right reading.

brochure Pamphlet said to be of deluxe design and high quality.

broken images Unfavorable condition found in photomechanical plate-making in which the image is absent in certain areas and fingerprints have developed on the plate. There are several causes for broken images. Tape or opaquing solution may be covering a portion of the image on the stripped flat, or tape or opaquing solution may have come off on the underside of the vacuum-frame glass. The plate may be underexposed, the image disappearing after a few revolutions of the press. Broken images may also be due to moisture on the plate prior to exposure. Plates should be handled by the edges only and fingerprinting avoided. They should be stored in lighttight containers away from moisture.

bromide print (silver print) Print made from copy or photographic paper that has been treated with silver halides. The bromine halogen is compounded with silver halides to form the light-sensitive emulsion.

bronzing Printing with a sizing ink and applying bronze powder that adheres to the paper and gives the effect of printing with a bronze metallic ink. The sizing in the bronzing ink has adhesive characteristics.

brownline print Brownline image on a white background, sometimes called a silver print. It can be used as an intermediate or as a finished print. If printed on thin paper or transparentized film or paper, it can be used as both a reproducible and a finished print. If printed on thick paper, it is used for reference or display only. The process is wet, but a darkroom is not required. The print can be 54 inches (137 cm) wide by any length. Exposure is made by contact with any translucent original. *See also* BROWNPRINT.

brownprint Whiteline image produced on a brown background. The brownprint process is a reversal process in which a negative is produced from a positive original. Prints so produced are usually intermediates. Brownlines and brownprints are made by the same process. Quite often, brownprints are made wrong-reading. This technique produces a sharper image than a right-reading image because of the emulsion-to-emulsion contact when printed. A brownprint is recommended for use as an intermediate in making positive blueline, brownline, wash-off, or photographic prints. The process is wet, but a darkroom is not required. The print can be 54 inches (137 cm) wide by any length. Exposure is made by contact with any translucent original. Brownprints and brownlines are made on the same material. The brownprint is a negative made from a positive; the brownline, a positive made from a negative.

brush pens *See* PENS, TECHNICAL.

brushes, art Brushes used for fine artwork as well as for such applications as show cards are divided by source into two categories: those manufactured from the red sable and the less costly grades whose hair is taken from squirrels, goats, fitches, other fur-bearing animals, and camels. The finest hair used commercially for brushes is taken from the thick center section of a sable's abdomen. The hair must be firmly rooted in the ferrule of the brush to a sizable depth for security and must have the maximum amount of snap to spring it back to normal shape. Moreover, the hair must have fine pointing qualities. Quality brushes are also distinguished by their seamless nickel or copper ferrules. Stroke brushes (brushes with square ends used for lettering or filling in solid areas) are of high quality when the hairs cling together and have a sharp, clear-cut definition at the brush edge. Sable or other brush hair that is set too shallowly in the ferrule has a tendency to pull out. Inferior brushes, such as those containing a mixture of dyed foreign soft hair with pure red sable, may be detected by an awkward thickness at the base of the brush at the ferrule, little or no ability to spring back to the original shape, and a tendency to bulk at the working end.

In the manufacturing process, art brushes must be cemented, oven-baked, crimped, and pressed. Not all fine brushes are made of red sable. Application and use may require other brushes. For example, white and black boar hairs, selected from spine bristles having tone and fiber, make excellent oil brushes. Each bristle has a natural curve and, in the manufacturing process, is "toed in," or interlocked, to produce a brush with a stroke that can be controlled. Brush size must be left to the discretion of the user because the choice of a given size depends on skill, the type of painting or lettering undertaken, the viscosity of the paint used, and, sometimes, the surface of the material to which the paint is applied. (*See* Figures B-15 and B-16.)

Fig. B-15 Red-sable watercolor and graphic arts brushes. (*Courtesy of M. Grumbacher, Inc.*)

Fig. B-16 Camel's-hair lettering quill brushes. (*Courtesy of M. Grumbacher, Inc.*)

bubble In technical illustrating, a circle enclosing a detailed drawing on a piece of art or on a second sheet. The drawing is drawn separately from the main illustration from which it originates (*see* Figure B-17.) The term "bubble" also refers to the formation of air beneath loosely mounted copy. This defect may be corrected by pricking the bubble with a pin.

buckram Coarse cloth of linen, hemp, or particularly, cotton, used in bookbinding as the exterior surface of a hard-cover book.

bug Colloquialism for a letter scriber such as the Leroy or Wrico scribers. The term is also used colloquially to mean the union label of the printing industry, as well as a logotype of any kind.

bulk Thickness of paper; also, the thickness of the total number of pages in a publication.

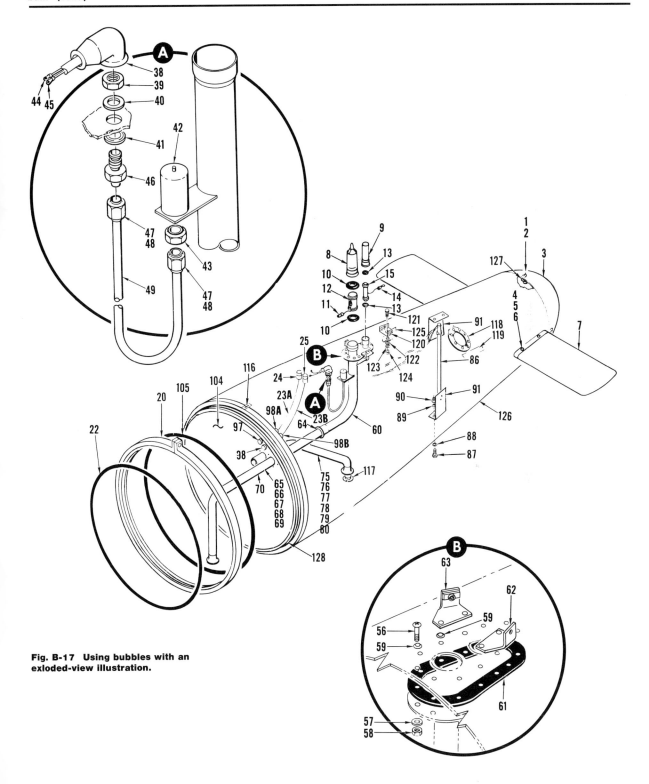

Fig. B-17 Using bubbles with an exloded-view illustration.

bulldog Printer's idiom for the first daily issue of a newspaper.

bullet Symbol •, used to preface listed items or a phrase, add emphasis, and generally embellish copy. It is sometimes called a "meatball." An example of the use of bullets follows:
- Quality control
- Reliability assurance
- Maintenance procedures

bumping See DRY-DOT ETCHING.

bundle Two reams of paper, or 1,000 sheets. Also, a fixed unit of 50 pounds (22.7 kg) used with paperboards. The number of sheets in a bundle will vary according to size, thickness, and weight of the paperboard.

bundling Tying signatures of a book together during the binding process.

burn through Sensitized condition of film caused when enough light penetrates a masking sheet to expose a film or plate beneath the sheet. Masking sheeting is supposed to prevent light from penetrating to the film, but accumulated exposures, as in step-and-repeat exposures, sometimes sensitize the film.

burnish To secure paste-up or mortised copy to the basic reproduction page or to material prepared for printing. A smooth burnishing bone, available in art and stationery stores, is most suitable. The copy is secured in place by heat from friction and pressure. A piece of clean paper or a tissue overlay should be placed over the copy while it is being burnished. However, if the table surface is clean, the copy may be turned over and burnished.

burnout In the whiteprint process or any other process in which light penetrates the original copy during exposure, the act or result of placing an opaque material, usually a sheet of paper, over the original copy to preserve space where new copy is to be added. After the first exposure, the opaque material is removed and the new copy is placed in position over the burned-out area, exposed, and developed.

burnout density Density remaining and read on a diazo material after exposure to sufficient actinic light to decompose the diazo salts and achievement of full development. The term is analogous to "fog" in photographic terminology.

burr Metal that protrudes above the printing surface when a routing machine has been used on a printing plate.

by-line Name of the author that appears above a magazine or newspaper article that he or she has written.

calculus symbols *See* TABLE 10, *page 446.*

calender rolls In paper manufacturing rollers through which paper is passed in order to finish it to the desired quality. *See also* PAPER MANUFAC- TURING.

calendered finish Degree of smoothness imparted to paper as a result of running it through the calenders of a papermaking machine. Smoothness varies with the number of times the paper is calendered.

California job case *See* CASE.

caliper In paper, a measurement of thickness expressed in thousandths of an inch; also, the instrument that measures the thickness.

call out In technical illustrating, to call attention to a part or item in an illustration by indexing it, i.e., by assigning it a number in the illustration (*see* Figure C-1). A lead line points, or "leads," to the part or item. The assigned number is found in an accompanying legend or parts list where other information concerning the particular part or item may be obtained. When an exploded view with callouts is keyed to a parts list, it is called an illustrated parts list, an illustrated parts breakdown, or a provisioning parts breakdown. To call out means also to refer to or discuss a thing in text.

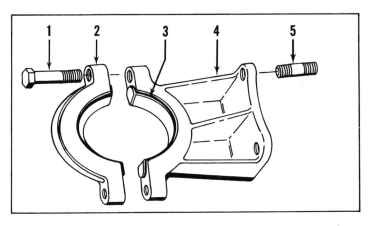

1. BOLT   3. CUSHION
2. CAP   4. BRACKET
     5. STUD

Fig. C-1 Using callouts on artwork.

camera, microfilm Camera designed to reproduce microfilm images of documents, newspapers, books, magazines, engineering drawings, re- ports, and any other information capable of being photographed. It is the microfilm camera that first photographs the document from which a microform is produced. "Microform" is a generic term for a reduced image made on film in sizes ranging from 16, 35, and 70 millimeters to 105 millimeters for roll microfilm or as a film unit cut and mounted for insertion in an aperture card. In addition, microfiches containing multiple images on a single microform are produced in microform sizes of 3 by 5, 4 by 6, and 5 by 8 inches (7.62 by 12.7, 10.16 by 15.24, and 12.7 by 20.32 cm). Related equipment for processing and handling microforms includes microfilm duplicators, readers, printers, reader-printers, processors, and retrieval systems.

Bruning's 750 microfiche camera processor (Figure C-2) is an automatic, self-contained system for producing microfiche forms from original documents. External plumbing or auxiliary reproduction equipment is not required. Originals are photographically copied at a specified reduction ratio (20, 24, 27, 30, 42 or 48:1) onto a microfiche. The film sheet is then automatically processed inside the machine. The finished microfiche is delivered to the operator in ninety seconds. Film is contained in individual sealed packets. A packet is inserted into the machine. When the wrapper is withdrawn, the film sheet remains inside, positioned for the first exposure. The operator then places a document to be photographed faceup on the exposure table and presses the print button. The reduced image is recorded on film. The 750 camera processor is 48 inches (122 cm) wide, 52 inches (132.08 cm) high, and 35½ inches (90.17 cm) deep, and it weighs less than 500 pounds (227 kg).

Fig. C-2 Bruning's 750 microfiche camera processor. (*Addressograph-Multigraph Corp.*)

camera, process Photolithographic camera especially designed for process work, that is, for copying, making halftones, color separation, and the like. While some cameras are comparatively large, ruggedly constructed, and mounted to minimize vibration, other models are designed to supplement small printing departments by extending the application and utility of small offset duplicators. Large process cameras are mounted with their rear cases in darkrooms.

Photolithographic negatives are produced from which printing plates are made by offset printing. The image is "burned" through the translucent image area of the negative into the printing plate. The latent image on the plate is then developed and the plate mounted on the press for printing. A single page may be mounted in the copyboard, or, with cameras capable of handling large copyboards, pages may be photographed simultaneously in "groups" of 4, 8, 16, 32, and 64. The number of pages depends on the copyboard size and the capability of the printing press. Multiple-page photography is referred to as "gang shooting," and the original copy placed on or in the copyboard is called a "flat."

Figure C-3 is the LogE Robertson 500 graphic arts process overhead camera. Low-bed models of the 500 series are also available. The copyboard springs open at thumb's touch of the release lever, closes with double-hatch security, and eases into shooting position with one pull on the release knob. Lights can be moved behind the copyboard for backlighting through a 20 by 30-inch (50.8 by 76.2-cm) transparency opening. The vacuum-back door moves down or sideways with springboard counterbalance. The vacuum for this mechanism is actuated by a thumb switch. The camera holds a variety of film sizes. The following are some features of the Robertson 500: an 11-foot 16-inch (3.35-m 40.6-cm) track; a glass-covered, 30 by 40-inch (76.2 by 101.6-cm) copyboard of rotating type with

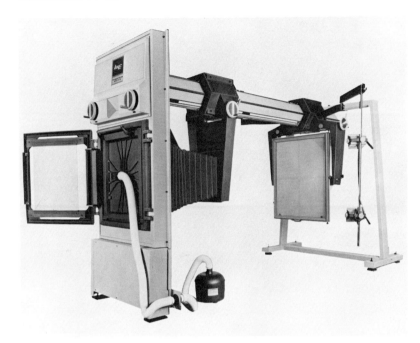

Fig. C-3 LogE Robertson 500 process camera. (*Courtesy of LogEtronics, Inc.*)

automatic positioning to shooting position; a 20 by 24-inch (50.8 by 61-cm) film size; a 21 by 24-inch (53.3 by 61-cm) contact screen size; a 20 by 24-inch (50.8 by 61-cm) ground glass with inch markings, mounted in a side-swinging cast-metal door; a tapered bellows with a 60-inch (152.4-cm) maximum extension; and a 19-inch (48.26-cm) apochromatic lens, flat field type, including a quick-change lens board and manual iris diaphragm control for 2X enlargement to 4X reduction.

Figure C-4 is LogEtronics' 432 Mark II vertical process camera. The hinged glass copy cover locks in open position, freeing both hands to position copy. Film is held securely by a high-volume vacuum pump. The vacuum back has a machined surface to ensure that the film remains in the focal plane. The operator sets enlargement and reduction percentages on direct-reading scales, and an automatic reset dual-range exposure timer combines two timers for control over long and short exposure times. Holder capacity for maximum film or contract screen is 20 by 24 inches (50.8 by 61 cm). The standard lens focal length is 10½ inches (27 cm), and the auxiliary lens focal length is 6⅜ inches (16.2 cm). Enlargements and reductions are 2X for the standard lens and 5X for the auxiliary lens. The maximum acceptable image area at same size (100 percent) with the standard lens is 18 by 22 inches (46.7 by 55.8 cm). Ground glass size is 19 by 23 inches (48.2 by 58.4 cm). Maximum copy size for the copyboard with front lighting is 20 by 24 inches (50.8 by 61 cm); with the transparency opening backlighting, the maximum copy size is 17 by 22 inches (43.18 by 55.8 cm).

Model SST-1418 is the nuArc process camera with film capacity of 14 by 18 inches (36 by 46 cm). See Figure C-5. The copyboard has a spring latch and a copy platen of the pressure type with a plate-glass cover. The platen

Fig. C-4 LogEtronics' 432 Mark II vertical process camera.

**Fig. C-5 nuArc's Model SST-1418
process camera.**

accommodates copy material ranging from thin typewritten pages to paste-ups on thick board stock. To move the copyboard in a horizontal loading position, it is swung to a resting position on a stop plate. A locking pin then engages and locks the copyboard; and the glass frame rises and locks in position. The platen is rectangularly zoned for centering copy material on the copyboard. A quartz iodine cycle lighting system is used to illuminate the copyboard.

The operation of the lens shutter is solenoidal. A manual setting arm on the lens board is used to control the diaphragm opening by reference to a lens-diaphragm chart. Copy is scaled by direct percentage focusing. For example, if a line on the original measures 10 inches (25.4 cm) and is to be reduced to 5 inches (12.7 cm), the negative is reduced to 50 percent of the size of the original.

When the master switch on the control panel of the exposure console is turned to the ON position, power is provided for all accessories. Two cranks on the control panel are moved to obtain the correct percentage of reduction or enlargement of the copy material. One crank operates the lens board and the other the copyboard. Corresponding tape viewers display the desired percentages, which are automatically focused.

**Fig. C-6 nuArc's Model 2024V Rocket
vertical process camera.**

When a toggle switch on the control panel is turned to FOCUS, the copy lights turn on and the lens shutter opens. Film size is determined by viewing the scale on the ground glass. The film is loaded on the back film holder (with a screen for continuous-tone copy) and is held in position by a vacuum that draws the film and screen tight to the film back.

Exposure time is based on the speed of the film, the intensity and distance of the light, the distance from the copyboard to the lens, and the distance from the lens to the film. All these factors, with the exception of film speed, have been compensated for in nuArc cameras with the lens-diaphragm and percentage setting systems. The exposure timer is numbered in seconds and has two hands, one green and one red. A black dial is turned to set the timer to the desired exposure time. Turning the dial moves both green and red hands from an exposure to a new setting. The red hand moves toward zero when the exposure button is pressed, while the green hand remains stationary for another exposure at the same setting. After exposure, the red hand on the timer returns to its position under the green hand, the lens shutter closes, and the copy lights turn off at the instant the exposure is completed.

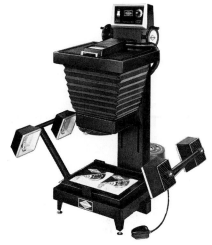

Figure C-6 shows the nuArc Model 2024V Rocket vertical process camera which holds odd-size film as well as standard-cut film image sizes up to 20 by 24 inches (50.8 by 61 cm), with a film size of 21 by 25 inches (53.3 by 64 cm). The metal back for loading is machined flat to keep the film in the correct focal plane. The camera loads at the front, then slides back to the expose position. Direct-reading percentages are calibrated on focusing tapes, one set for each lens, and are positioned at the front of the control console; enlargement and reduction percentages are dialed. A dual-lens system with two color-corrected lenses (6½ inches, 17 cm; and 10¾ inches, 27.3 cm) provides flipping from one lens to the other by means of a specially designed lens slide. Contact screen capacity and copyboard sizes are both 21 by 25 inches (53.4 by 64 cm). The reduction range is from 50 percent (2X) to 20 percent (5X), and enlargement range is up to 200 percent (2X). The opening for backlighting is 19 by 23 inches (48.2 by 58.4 cm).

Fig. C-7 nuArc's Model VV1418 vertical camera.

Figure C-7 is nuArc's Model VV1418 vertical camera for making stats, proofs, screened prints, special-effects screens, and film positives. A master switch (with built-in circuit breaker), an automatic reset timer, and a manual switch for special exposures are featured on the control panel. A digital scaling system shows the percentage of enlargement or reduction ratios translated into digits from a conversion chart mounted on the vacuum back. Film size for the VV1418 camera is 16 by 20 inches (41 by 51 cm). Image size is 14 by 18 inches (36 by 46 cm), and both copyboard and contact screen capacity are 16 by 20 inches (41 by 51 cm). The lens is color corrected for maximum sharpness and coverage.

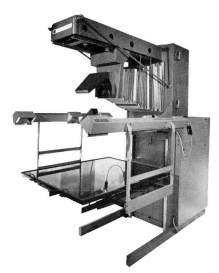

The Itek 480 camera processor is shown in Figure C-8. The 480 camera produces high-contrast line and halftone film or paper prints, sized as required and delivered dry. A darkroom is not required. Exposure, processing, and drying of film or paper prints is automated. Three-dimensional objects, difficult drawing patterns, and fabrics can be placed directly on the copyboard and reduced to size for use in layout work, illustrations, and the like. The 480 camera processor is used by newspaper and book

Fig. C-8 Itek's 480 camera processor.

publishers, engineering reprographics, commercial printing, and with phototypesetters and printed circuitry. Extended enlargement and reduction ranges are 33⅓ percent to 300 percent. Roll-fed material is in widths of 8½ to 18 inches (22 to 46 cm), and operator-selected lengths are available from 10 to 24 inches (25.4 to 61 cm).

camera, vertical Process or other camera placed in a position that permits photographing copy or objects in the vertical plane only. The copy must be mounted or lie flat on a horizontal surface.

camera-ready copy See REPRODUCTION COPY.

canvas board Board or canvas panel manufactured especially for oil painting. A 35-ply board has the desired surface characteristics and construction. This board is available in sizes from 8 by 10 inches (20.3 by 25.4 cm) to 25 by 30 inches (63.5 by 76.2 cm).

cape Complete set of engineering or other drawings for a piece of equipment or an installation.

caps Common abbreviation for capitals.

caption In general, any heading or title; more precisely, a descriptive title for an illustration or a table.

carbon paper Paper used mainly to make duplicate typewritten copies. The name is derived from the carbon deposited on the paper, which is transferred to copies by percussion. A recent development is fluid-ink paper, from which ink is transferred instead of carbon. Paper used as typewriter carbons must be of good quality to withstand blows from keys. Typewriter carbon papers may have cut corners and an extended edge at the top for pulling them free from the copies. Standard typewriter carbon and fluid-ink papers are 8½ by 11, 8½ by 13, and 8½ by 14 inches (21.6 by 27.9, 21.6 by 33, and 21.6 by 36 cm) in size; they are sold in boxes of 100 sheets with 25 sheets to each folder. Colors are black, purple, red, blue, brown, and green.

carbro Process of making color prints by using the negative of each of the printing colors, produced photographically, and developed with sensitized gelatin. The blue-filtered negative is printed on a paper backing with a light-sensitive emulsion that becomes a bromide print. The bromide print is then placed in contact with sensitized gelatin that has a tissue backing. A yellow pigment is contained in the gelatin, and a yellow image is produced after processing. The gelatin is transferred to a support and the tissue backing removed. The red and blue images, produced in the same way, are transferred in turn and the backing removed to register over the yellow image, thus completing the print.

card-to-card printout Producing a duplicate microfilm aperture card from an original microfilm aperture card by using a microfilm duplicator. An up-to-date master file of cards can be maintained by providing duplicate copies on request.

card-to-paper printout Producing paper copies of a microfilmed image from the aperture card on which the film is mounted. Depending on the copying machine, xerographic, diffusion-transfer-reversal, electrolytic, diazo, or stabilization processes of reproduction may be used. Copies can be made on plain bond paper, translucent stock for whiteprint reproduction, offset paper plates, or tracing paper suitable for reworking prints. Sizes vary with the machine.

cardboard Thick display material, not to be confused with the ordinary gray paperboard commonly known as cardboard. Cardboard is thick paper manufactured in a variety of colors and used for display, poster, and other advertising purposes. Finishes accept images applied by any medium, including printer's ink, crayon, watercolors, and pastels. The standard size is 28 by 24 inches (71.1 by 61 cm) in 8-ply and in 14-ply, the most popular thickness. A special board for illustrations may be obtained in either hot-pressed or cold-pressed form. The cold-pressed board is slightly toothier than the hot-pressed board. Novelty cardboards may be obtained in various colors.

caret Mark ($_\wedge$) used extensively in all stages of copy and proof preparation to indicate where an insertion or correction is to be made by the typist, compositor, or other individual.

caricature Representation of a person or thing that shows a deliberate exaggeration and distortion of features or mannerisms. Caricatures may be good-humored or bitterly satirical.

carrier Copyholder made of clear acetate backed with a paper of no more than 20-pound stock. It is used to protect the original while making copies by feeding the original into the machine manually. Using 8½ by 11-inch (22 by 28 cm) copy as an example, cut the acetate to this dimension but allow ¼ inch (0.635 cm) of acetate along the leading edge. Fold and crease the acetate along this length and affix the backing paper to the ¼-inch (0.635-cm) fold with clear tape. The original is then inserted between the acetate and paper backing with the image area exposed through the clear acetate for copy making.

carry-over line Second or any succeeding line of a sentence, paragraph, or nonsentence list item. The carry-over line may be either flush left or indented in what is called a "hanging indention."

case Container having two drawers that are separated into compartments for holding individual pieces of type. The various pieces are hand-selected and placed on a composing stick to form a line of type. Capital letters are stored in the upper drawer, or case, and lowercase letters in the lower drawer, or case. (The terms "uppercase" and "lowercase" are derived from this storing method.) The California job case, however, has only one storage drawer for all characters, sorts, rules, and the like. Printing students must know the location of compartments and the particular types each contains. The term "case" also refers to a hard or stiff cover into which a sewn book is bound.

case-bound book (hard-cover book) Stiff-covered book. The cover is manufactured separately, and the sewn book is inserted and affixed to the cover. *See also* BOOKBINDING.

casein Phosphoprotein derived from milk and used to sensitize the surface of lithographic plates. Casein also serves as an excellent base in manufacturing glue and as an ingredient of artist's paints.

casein plate Sensitized plate. Casein is an ingredient of the sensitizing material.

cassette reader Cartridge that holds magnetic tape on which information can be stored that corresponds in appearance and function to the common audio tape cassette. In photocomposition work, the information is "read" from the magnetic tape that drives the phototypesetter to produce the copy on paper, or on photographic film or paper.

cast-coated paper *See* COATED BOOK PAPER.

casting Molten electrotype metal that backs the shell to a desired thickness.

casting box Enclosed box made of metal that is used for casting stereotypes from molds called "mats" (abbreviation for matrices). Molding mats are made of papier-mâché.

catch line Temporary heading used to identify a proof.

cathode-ray tube (CRT) Vacuum tube in which a hot cathode emits electrons that are accelerated as a beam through a relatively high-voltage anode, further focused or deflected electrostatically or electromagnetically, and allowed to fall on a fluorescent screen. It is the same as an ordinary television tube screen. The CRT also is used in some phototypesetters as a character-exposure device. The term is sometimes used to indicate the display seen on a screen (as noted above) resulting from keyboarding during photocomposition typesetting. However, it is more popularly called a "video display terminal" (VDT).

CB print Print produced by a wash-off process that was pioneered and developed by the Charles Bruning Company, from which it gets its name. A CB print is made as follows:
1. Sensitized CB material is placed on close contact with a negative of the original.
2. This material and the negative are exposed to intense light. Light penetrates the translucent image area of the negative.

3. The unexposed sensitized coating on the material is washed off.

4. The material is then immersed in a developer, and the print is again washed to remove the developer.

A CB print is used to replace a poor original, to produce an inklike substitute original, or to make a tracing-cloth revision of an original. Composite CB prints can be produced by combining negative intermediates made from several drawings or parts of drawings. A replacement facsimile of a lost or destroyed original can be produced by using a negative intermediate made from a whiteprint, a blueprint, or some other type of copy of an original.

cell Typesetter's name for stock having no adhesive backing; also, a hand-cut or photographically prepared mask used to block out light in areas where light is not wanted (same as mask). The term "cell" is also used extensively in the production of animated cartoons. A cell consists of a sheet of clear acetate on which a cartoon image is drawn. The artist places one cell over the other and draws each cell to an advanced configuration. The series of cells is photographed, and when the completed film is projected rapidly on a screen, the result is one of animation.

cellophane Group of clear, transparent, flexible, cellulose films. Most cellophanes are coated to provide combinations of properties to guard against moisture, oxygen, grease, and other contaminants. They are also treated to have heat sealability and deep-freeze stability when such an application is required.

cellulose Fibrous residue remaining after the chemical treatment of base papermaking materials.

center fold *See* CENTER SPREAD.

center heading Caption or title that appears in the center of a page or column. Chapter titles are often center headings.

center line Line used in orthographic engineering and mechanical drawings to indicate the axis of a depicted object. Center lines are composed of alternating long and short dashes with a long dash at either end; they are designated as "thin" lines. Very short center lines, however, may be unbroken if they cannot be confused with other lines. Center lines are used to indicate the travel of a center. *See also* LINE CONVENTIONS: ENGINEERING DRAWINGS.

center spread Two center pages of a publication, used as a double spread (double truck) for advertising. In book work, the center spread is the center fold, where one printing plate may be used for both facing pages. The two pages are necessarily imposed in page-numbering sequence. There are as many center folds as there are signatures.

chain delivery Delivery of printed material as it emerges from the rollers on a conveyor that is driven by a link-chain and sprocket-wheel arrangement.

chain marks Vertical and horizontal lines produced by laid wires on the dandy roll of a papermaking machine. The finish on laid antique paper is an example.

change bar In a revised technical publication, a vertical rule placed adjacent to text matter. The bar denotes a change in text and is extended to include the number of lines affected by the change. Change bars should be inserted to the left of the text for left-hand pages and to the right of the text for right-hand pages; they may be lost to view if they are placed in the binding margins. Such bars are useful because the reader can determine at a glance what text has been changed. A 3- or 4-point (1.05 or 1.40-mm) rule set out no more than ¼ inch (6.35 mm) from the text is recommended for a change bar.

chapbook Small, inexpensive book or pamphlet of poems or ballads, sometimes of a religious nature. The name is derived from chapmen (peddlers, hawkers) who sold the books on the streets.

character Any letter, number, punctuation mark, or space in printing matter. The average number of characters that can be set in 1 pica (there are about 6 picas to 1 inch, or 2.54 cm) is known as "characters per pica."

character generator Hardware or software device which provides the means for formulating a character font and which also may provide a controlling function during printing; used in computer graphics.

characteristic curve Curve drawn on a graph to represent the response of photographic material to varying amounts of light.

charcoal drawing Drawing made with fine artist's charcoal. The paper used should have a rib finish. The technique of rendering charcoal drawings is difficult to master. The drawing should be fixed with a material such as gum arabic dissolved in alcohol. Charcoal sketches are often used by commercial illustrators to outline an object before completing the work in oils or other media or to obtain client approval of a layout before finishing it.

chart Graphical representation showing values and quantities by means of bars, curves, columns, and symbols. *See* BAR CHART; COLUMN CHART; CURVE CHART; PIE CHART; SURFACE CHART.

chart, organization *See* ORGANIZATION CHART.

charting media Papers used by chartists to compose graphs and scale drawings. *See* GRID.

chartist One who has become proficient in the production of graphical representations.

Chartpak® Trade name for preprinted, pressure-sensitive, adhesive-backed tapes and components made by Chartpak. These products are used as paste-ups for charts, graphs, map overlays, advertising layouts, newspaper borders, printed-circuitry configurations, and layouts of almost any design. Transparent tapes are available in colors or patterns for use on slides or transparent overhead projectors, for blueprint or whiteprint reproduction, and for occasions when the copy underneath must remain visible. Solid-color tapes with a glossy, matte, or fluorescent finish and pattern tapes or special printed tapes with an opaque white background are used for visual presentations, opaque overhead projectors, photographic reproduction, and in making contact prints. These tapes can be reproduced by the diazo process and with most office copying machines. In addition, Chartpak provides transfer lettering, graphic films, and symbols and accessories such as graphic arts knives, blades, scalpels, and burnishers. *See also* OVERHEAD TRANSPARENCY; TAPE, PRESSURE-SENSITIVE; TRANSFER SHEET; and FRISKET.

chase Rectangular metal frame in which composed type and printing plates are locked for printing. As a transitive verb, "chase" means to ornament metal by embossing or engraving.

check-out chart (also called **specification tree**) Chart form of presentation resembling a Christmas tree, a name by which it is sometimes known. It is used in technical publications as a kind of trouble-shooting chart to check the operating accuracy of a system in logically sequenced steps.

chill rolls (also called **cooling rolls**) Rolls located immediately after the drying oven which are used to reduce the temperature of the web and to set the ink.

china clay Filler used with blanc fixe for coating book papers during the paper-manufacturing process.

choke Contact process by which letters, solids, or other shapes are made thinner without altering their shape or relative positioning. Amount of choke is controlled by exposure.

chopper Device used in a web-fed printing press to make the chopper fold. The signature is conveyed from the first parallel fold in a horizontal plane, with the binding edge forward, until it passes under a reciprocating blade. The blade then forces it down between folding rollers to complete the fold.

chopper fold (cross-fold; right-angle fold) Fold made in a web-fed printing press after the first parallel fold and at right angles to it. Signatures are produced in 16-page multiples of the number of webs (rolled paper stock) in the press with one-fourth of the web width by one-half of the cutoff length.

Christmas tree *See* CHECK-OUT CHART.

chuck Device inserted in the core to support the paper roll on the roll stand in a web-fed printing press.

chute delivery Delivery of printed material from the press by forcing it between the cylinders into a chute.

circular Advertising piece in the form of a single sheet or a leaflet.

circular grid Grid used to form pie charts and plot data in polar coordinates. It is also employed in trigonometry, calculus, and analytic geometry. Circular grids are popular in light studies to plot flux determination in light beams and to show the relation of an illuminating source and points of illumination. In addition, they are well suited for plotting stadia survey notes. The center of the ordinates represents the station from which the stadic observations were taken. Horizontal angles, distances, and elevations are plotted, and the appropriate points are then connected by contour lines.

circular screen Photographic screen used with a process camera which is adjusted for each color to eliminate the undesirable wavelike or checkered effect called "moiré."

classified ad Advertisement composed of words only and sold by the line, as distinguished from a display advertisement, which is sold at a given rate per column inch. Word-line advertisements are set on linecasting machines and photographic typesetters.

Clearback Ortho Litho film Lithographic film produced by Du Pont on a Cronar polyester film base. Fast, even exposures can be secured through the back of the film, thereby permitting reversing or "flopping" to obtain emulsion-to-plate image contact. The film is suitable for all line and halftone work but is particularly good for deep-etch lithography and photoengraving applications.

Clearbase film Lithographic film produced by Du Pont on a Cronar polyester film base. The film has a special subcoating designed to hold opaques and blueline solutions without cracking or chipping. It is particularly suitable for stripping and lay-up.

closed loop System with a feedback control in which the output is used to control the input.

coated book paper Paper manufactured especially for printing fine-screen halftones. The base paper is the same as for English-finish book paper, but casein, starch, or glue and certain pigments are added. While coated book papers are usually glossy, some dull coated papers are manufactured. Coated papers are used when high printing quality is desired for color-separation work. They are divided into several classifications: coated-one-side, coated-two-sides, dull coated-two-sides, process- or machine-coated, and cast-coated.

Coated-one-side book paper is used for offset or letterpress printing of labels, posters, or any other type of application for which high-quality printing is required and for which one side may be adhesive-backed or pasted. Standard basic weights are 50, 60, 70, and 80 pounds (22.7, 27.2, 31.7, and 36.3 kg).

Dull coated-two-sides book paper is used for illustrated booklets and books and for other applications in which glare must be avoided. This paper is suitable for halftone work of 120-line screen. Standard basic weights are 50, 60, 70, 80, 90, 100, and 120 pounds (22.7, 27.2, 31.7, 36.3, 40.8, 45.4, and 54.4 kg) for 500 sheets of the basic size of 25 by 38 inches (63.5 by 96.5 cm).

Coated-two-sides book paper is suitable for 133- to 150-line screens, but 120-line screen is recommended for fine reproduction of the highest quality. This paper is used extensively by printing establishments for catalogs, direct-mail pieces, brochures, pamphlets, and other applications for which quality printing is essential. The medium-priced, coated-two-sides paper is the paper most commonly used by printers. Standard basic weights are 50, 60, 70, 80, 90, 100, and 120 pounds (22.7, 27.2, 31.7, 36.3, 40.3, 45.4, and 54.4 kg) for 500 sheets of the basic size of 25 by 38 inches (63.5 by 96.5 cm).

Process- or machine-coated papers are made by applying coating on the surface of the paper as it passes through the drying end of the papermaking machine. The paper is then supercalendered, and the result is a high-quality coated paper of lighter weight. This paper is used for magazines, direct-mail pieces, catalogs, brochures, booklets, and other applications for which light weight and high-quality printing are desired. The basic weights are 45, 50, 60, 70, and 100 pounds (20.4, 22.7, 27.2, 31.7, and 45.4 kg) for 500 sheets of the basic size of 25 by 38 inches (63.5 by 96.5 cm).

Cast-coated papers have a high gloss and an exceptionally smooth surface. Advertising pieces, direct-mail pieces, fine wrapping papers, and labels are some of the applications to which the good appearance of this paper is well suited.

coated-one-side paper Book paper coated on one side only. See COATED BOOK PAPER.

coated paper (smooth finish) Paper necessary when faithful reproduction of the image is desired. Sizing, which decreases porosity and absorbency, is added to the paper during manufacturing. The paper web is passed between metal rolls under pressure. During this process, called "calendering," a coating containing finely divided pigments and a water-base bind can be deposited on the paper. The coating may consist of styrene-butadiene or polyvinyl acetate latex, or starch, protein, or casein, or various combinations of each. These papers are called machine-finished, supercalendered, coated, and cast-coated papers. Magazines, books, booklets, trade journals, and catalogs use these papers for high-quality printing. Letterpress and lithographic inks for these papers are more viscous than inks of uncoated papers and are more dependent on oxidation than on absorption for complete drying. Inks are manufactured especially to accommodate printing presses for long and short runs of large circulation periodicals or for limited circulation of single-run jobs. Press speed, therefore, is an important factor in ink selection because of ink drying characteristics. Heat-set inks that dry by rapid evaporation with the application of heat are largely replacing inks that dry by oxidation.

coated-two-sides-paper Book paper coated on two sides. *See* COATED BOOK PAPER.

cocking roller (guide roller) Device used in a web-fed printing press to compensate for slight paper variations while the web (paper roll) is feeding. The "cocking" roller is located on the roll stand between the roll of paper and the "dancer" roll.

cockle finish Rough, wrinkled, irregular finish in paper.

cold composition Composition by machines such as typewriters and photocomposing machines or in any manner in which no molten metal is used to form the image. Apparently the term "cold composition" was derived as the opposite of "hot composition," which refers to casting slugs of type with molten metal on linecasting machines such as the Linotype and the Intertype. Movable type set by hand is referred to as "cold type" when it is contrasted with hot-metal type. Pressure-sensitive adhesives containing preprinted or photographically composed nomenclature, symbols, and the like are also called cold type.

The Varigraph is operated by moving a swivel handle which follows guide grooves in the selected matrix or template. (*See* Figure C-9.) A

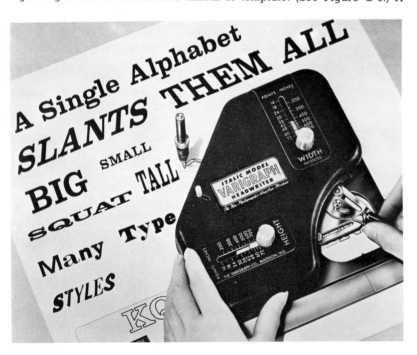

Fig. C-9 Varigraph headline composing machine.

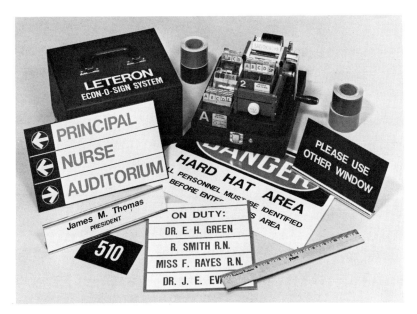

production pen of the desired line weight sets the image in response to the pattern followed on the matrix. Two controls are added features. One control establishes the width of individual characters and the other the height. These controls are calibrated in both points and inches in sizes from 14 to 72 points. The operator can select any desired intermediate size from one matrix. Different matrices are available for popular headline typefaces, any of which may be used as variations for intermediate sizes as well as providing condensed, open-faced, extended, shadow, dancing, reverse, and other effects. An italic model produces back-slanted and vertical or italic characters from any Varigraph matrix.

Figure C-10 shows the Leteron automatic lettering system that uses acrylic material Letertape and Letertype alphabets, numerals, and punctuation sets. The machine is operated by dropping a Letertype die in a slot and pressing an actuator for each character; the tape is then removed from the Leteron and the image separates with one carrier; the word strip is placed on any smooth, dry surface, and the second clear carrier is peeled off.

Figure C-11 shows the Xerox 800 electronic typing system (ETS). The machine is available in four configurations: single and dual magnetic tape cassettes and single and dual magnetic cards. A new interchangeable typing wheel (see Figure C-12) enables a typing speed of up to 350 words per minute. The wheel is available in 17 color-coded type faces. The machine enables three spacing alternatives: 10-pitch, 12-pitch, and proportional spacing. To operate the ETS, the typist selects a typing wheel with the desired type style and types a draft, which is automatically stored on magnetic tapes or cards. Corrections can be typed over errors and revisions inserted. The ETS can then type the document automatically, printing it out from left to right or in reverse from right to left. When revisions are made to early drafts, as many as 78 characters per line can

Fig. C-11 Xerox 800 electronic typing system (ETS).

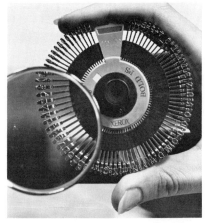

Fig. C-12 Xerox interchangeable typing wheel.

be inserted without retyping the entire document; and the carriage returns without operator attention while the operator is typing.

The Xerox 850 display typing system consists of a group of modular components that provide selectivity in word-processing functions. The system is designed for users with heavy typing and moderate to heavy revision requirements. The 850 can add, delete, change, or move characters, words, lines, paragraphs, or pages. The system is compatible with Xerox 800 typing systems, computers, and with some competitive word-processing systems. Components can be added as requirements change. The 850 system consists basically of the following:

1. *Controller* (Figure C-13*A*). The unit contains two flexible floppy disks that can store up to 280 pages of text. The controller contains a mini-

Fig. C-13 Xerox 850 electronic display typing system.

computer and associated electronics. It drives the 24-character display and the 66-lines per page display as required.

2. *Printer* (Figure C-13B). The printer has a printout speed of 35 characters per second. While the operator is typing or editing a new document, the printer can be playing out previously typed or edited documents. A printing mechanism uses a composite wheel and provides 10-pitch, 12-pitch, and proportional spacing.

3. *Display typewriter* (Figure C-13C). The display typewriter has a 24-character display screen, a keyboard, and a bidirectional printer combined as one unit. The printer is the same as in Figure C-13B, except the display screen and keyboard have been added.

4. *Page display typewriter* (Figure C-13D). The typewriter has a display capacity of 66 lines per page and 102 characters per line. The screen can show characters in black on white or the reverse. The cursor can be operated to move in any direction on the screen.

Four components are provided that are compatible with the Xerox 800 electronic typing system: card and tape units and IBM card and disk units. The smallest 850 typing system consists of the controller and the 24-character display typewriter. The smallest full-page display system consists of the controller, page display screen, the keyboard, and the printer.

Figure C-14 is a photograph of IBM's Magnetic Tape Selectric typewriter (MT/ST). The typewriter is capable of automatically producing error-free copy at a speed of 150 words per minute. The machine uses a magnetic tape which stores typed information in coded form. As the typist operates the keyboard, the words and numbers are recorded and stored on a ½-inch (1.27 cm) tape. The tape is 100 feet (30.5 m) long and can hold 24,000 characters, roughly the equivalent of one day's typing. When an error is made in spelling, grammar, or punctuation, the typist back spaces and

Fig. C-14 IBM's Magnetic Tape Selectric typewriter.

strikes the correction over the incorrect character or word. Back spacing automatically erases the magnetic tape, and only the new typing is recorded. When a word, sentence, or paragraph is to be deleted, the typist presses a button on the machine's console, and the MT/ST searches the tape at 900 characters a second until a precoded reference point is located. These reference points may be designated at any place on the tape, such as a page, chapter, paragraph, or the beginning of a letter. After this is done, the typist deletes the material. Similarly, the typist can stop the tape at any point to insert new text. When the typing has been completed and all corrections have been recorded on the tape, the typist presses a button on the MT/ST console, inserts a fresh piece of paper into the typewriter, and the machine reads the magnetic tape and types the recorded material. A two-tape model of the MT/ST is available, on which stored information from alternate tapes can be merged to produce a finished document. A special remote recording feature of the MT/ST enables one MT/ST to send typewritten information to another MT/ST over a telephone line. The MT/ST is designed to prepare technical reports and papers, manuals, legal briefs, insurance reports, reproduction masters, repetitive business forms, complex statistical work, and other documents that require periodic revision.

Figure C-15 shows IBM's Magnetic Tape Selectric composer (MT/SC), which produces composition at 14 characters per second automatically. The primary application of the composer is to prepare large volumes of body text composition automatically, including the following applications: instruction manuals, pamphlets, technical manuals, catalogs, newsletters, bids, proposals, legal briefs, magazines, journals, books, and newspapers. The machine is popular in the commercial graphics industry and in-plant

Fig. C-15 IBM's Magnetic Tape Selectric composer.

printing facilities. The machine features two distinct parts for automatic typesetting: (1) the recorder, which is the operator-input device for keyboarding original source material for automatic typesetting, and (2) the console, which has solid-state logic and comprises the reader, which has two stations, and modified IBM Selectric composer. The recorder has the following features: the ability to produce hard copy for proofreading, the Selectric typewriter touch, 10- or 12-pitch spacing, one magnetic tape station for recording only (no playback capability), load and unload magnetic encode reference code for searching, back space and strikeover for corrections on hard copy and magnetic media, line return for correcting magnetic tape and hard copy, and magnetic tape cartridges that are 120 feet (36.5 m) long with the capability of storing approximately 28,800 characters and spaces. The composer console consists of two freestanding units: (1) the two-station magnetic reader console, which reads magnetic tape at approximately 20 characters per second, searches magnetic tape at approximately 900 characters per second, merges magnetic tape for correction procedures, rereads characters for parity error checks, and loads and unloads magnetic tape on right and left stations; and (2) the composer control with a desk housing core memory and solid-state logic. The unit automatically performs the following composition functions: It prepares body text composition with correct justification, leading, centering, and flush left and flush right of copy; it prepares copy in line measures up to 9 inches (22.8 cm) with 11- and 12-point typeface sizes; the unit permits an operator to choose variables for good typography, such as choice of amount of minimum and maximum interword spacing, choice of maximum quad, and choice of line length or measure, from a minimum of a fraction of an inch to a maximum of approximately 9 inches (22.8 cm); and it allows the operator to select the amount of the paragraph indentation or line indentation, the amount of space between leadered dots, and whether or not to hyphenate. The MT/SC, which can be used in an automatic or manual composing mode, accommodates leading ranging from 5 to 20 point, and popular printer's type styles in various weights ranging in size from 3 to 12 point. The machine features an automatic velocity control, which provides the ability to do multilingual composition and adjusts impression of different-size characters for the English used in the United States, the English used in the United Kingdom, Norwegian, German, French, French-Latin, and Latin. A dead-key disconnect provides the ability to have dead-key disconnect selection of positions 41–43 or 38–43 for multilingual compatibility of all foreign keyboard arrangements.

The VariTyper (Figure C-16) is a cold-composition, direct-impression composing machine having a universal keyboard. The machine composes reproducible copy in various type styles, sizes, and formats. There is a choice of over a thousand type styles and sizes in many languages as well. Two type fonts can be used in the machine at one time, and changes from one to the other are made by turning a control knob so that matching italics, boldface type, and so on may be used in the same copy with text type. A wide choice of leaders and rules is available with three selections on a single type font. Once the machine is programmed for the desired column width, the operator produces a justified column of text. As each line

Fig. C-16 VariTyper cold-composition composing machine (*Addressograph-Multigraph Corp.*)

is typed, the justifying mechanism automatically adds the exact amount of extra space between words to produce even margins. Composing also may be done on paper plates for offset duplicators or stencil work.

collating Arranging proofs or sheets in order; hence, organizing, gathering, and assembling a book or other publication in page sequence. Hand collating for long runs is time-consuming and therefore quite expensive. Figure C-17 shows A. B. Dick Company's Model 7124(S) automatic collator. The collator has 24 bins, each with a capacity of 2½ inches (6.35 cm) or 450 sheets per bin. Sheet sizes are 5 by 8 inches (12.7 by 20.3 cm), adjustable to 13 by 18 inches (33 by 45.7 cm). Operating speed is 28,800 sheets per hour, and 1,200 sets can be collated in one hour. Operating speed is based on the cycles per hour of the unit. For example, this collator operates at 1,200 cycles per hour and therefore operates at a sets-per-hour speed of 1,200. To determine sheets-per-hour speed, multiply cycles or sets per hour by the number of bins. Paper ranges in weights from 13 to 110-pound (5.9 to 50-kg) stock. The unit has a preset/reset counter and a dual miss detection system. Programmers can be used to permit running different sets at the same time.

Figure C-18 is A. B. Dick Company's Model 720 copy sorter. Operating the buttons on the control panel enables the sorter to do the following: Run more than one job without unloading, thus enabling the use of any number of bins less than the maximum without going through the full bin cycle; skip unwanted bins; interrupt the feed system; route sheets to the proof tray; and supply a specific bin with any number of extra sheets. The 720 magazine consists of two banks of 50 bins each for a total of 100 bins. Bin capacity is 100-plus sheets or 20-pound (9.08-kg) stock or equivalent. Sheets sizes range from 5 by 8 inches (12.7 by 20.3 cm) to 11¾ by 18 inches (29.1 by 45.7 cm). Weights of stock are from 13 to 100 pound (5.9 to 45.4 kg), depending on size.

Figure C-19 is General Binding Corporation's 20-Station Rollomatic

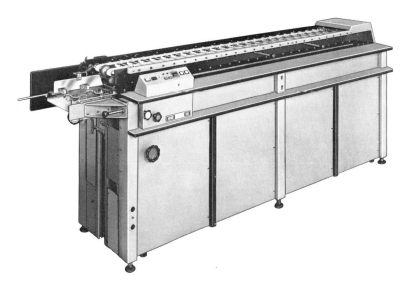

Fig. C-17 A. B. Dick Company's Model 7124(S) collator.

collator. The machine features electronic sensing for each bin to ensure accurate feed and count. Each bin has an individual indicator light and on-off switch. The indicator light shows a fail-to-feed condition for its particular bin. A vibrating jogger and offset stacker attachment is included for jogging paper, and the stacker separates sets by 90°; or the stacker can be operated to "marry" sets. Maximum paper sizes is 11 by 17 inches (27.9 by 43.1 cm) and minimum size is 5½ by 8½ inches (13.9 by 21.6 cm). Cycling speed is 1,000 sets of 20 (26,000) sheets per hour. Station pockets have a capacity of 200 to 250 sheets of paper.

Figure C-20 shows the Schriber 750A business forms collator designed to operate at speeds up to 750 feet per minute (228.6 m/min). It will collate from 2 to 12 parts and takes paper rolls 24 inches (61 cm) in diameter, and carbon rolls 18 inches (45.7 cm) in diameter for web widths from 5 to 18 inches (12.7 cm to 45.7 cm). The 750A has an adjustable-flow, automatic lubrication system providing lubrication to critical parts. Standard safety features include enclosed drive shafts and couplings, guarded main drive belts, warning labels, and sound-dampening devices, all removable for machine accessibility. The delivery table/descender combination enables rated speeds to be maintained, and the descender mechanism moves the folded forms, ready for boxing, from the delivery table to a vertical stack. A top and bottom perforating head is available for cross-perforating continuous forms. In order to furnish various lengths of forms, the collator can be equipped with a head to match each press circumference on which forms will be produced. The fine-line cold-glue system consists of one pump element for each glue line and nozzle orifice in order to provide positive adhesive flow at all times. A crimp lock is built into the main collator frame behind the cutoff head to enable the forms to be crimped before they are cross-perforated. The constant feed of paper and carbon necessary for registration of multiple forms is maintained by a redesigned air-operated brake acting against the roll arbor. Optional accessories consist of an across-the-web glue system, a crash numbering unit, a file punch unit, an adjustable feed chain, and a mechanism to produce unit-set forms by changing from perforation rule to cutoff rule and by changing from up-and-down heads to top-only heads.

Fig. C-18 A. B. Dick Company's Model 720 sorter.

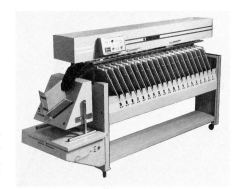

Fig. C-19 General Binding Corporation's 20-Station Rollomatic collator.

Fig. C-20 Schriber 750A business forms collator.

collimate To render parallel to a certain line or direction, as with light rays. Contacting lamps attempt to collimate the light source within the practical limits of a lamp housing.

collotype process *See* PHOTOGELATIN PROCESS.

colophon Brief technical description placed at the end of a book, giving information on the typeface and design, the paper used, production facts and printing techniques, or other physical aspects of the work. The term "colophon" refers also to an emblem or device identifying a printer or publisher; it may appear on the cover, title page, backbone, or jacket of a book.

color-blind emulsion Emulsion that is sensitive only to blue, violet, and ultraviolet light.

color break Line or edge along which different colors start or end, said of an image.

color burnout An objectionable change in the color of a printing ink which may occur either in bulk form or on the printed sheet. In the first case, it is associated primarily with tints and is caused by a chemical reaction between certain components in the ink formulation. In the latter case, it is generally caused by heat generated in a pile of printed material during the drying of an oxidizing type of ink.

color chart Chart used to evaluate matching of colors as indicated on proofs. Proofs should be on the same stock and printed with the average amount of ink to be used for the pressrun. Solids and screened images should be used for comparison with the chart.

color coder Instrument used to compare the intensity of colors on printed samples and so permit faithful reproduction.

color correction Change made in reproduction work to correct the rendition of a color.

color dimensions Properties that compose the various forms of color composition. There are three dimensions of color: hue, saturation, and lightness. *Hue* is a quality that distinguishes colors in the visible spectrum, such as red, yellow, green, blue, and the like. *Saturation* is the character-istic of colors that expresses the amount of a given hue in a color, that is, the intensity of the hue; for example, the difference between a dark-grayish purple and a vivid purple or the difference between a grayish red and a vivid red. *Lightness* is the quality of a color that expresses various shades of tones within the same color range, or the discrimination of all colors within the same color range from the intense to the soft, delicate hues; for example, the different values of lightness between white, the many shades of gray, and intense black, or from light pink to intense red. The Munsell and Ostwald color systems are popularly used in the industry to order and

distinguish colors. The scientific study of color is termed "chromatic
"chromatology." Color harmony and the use of colors is an extensive
of art in the printing industry and is not treated herein. However, ther
many books available covering the subject.

color filters   Colored screens consisting of thin sheets or disks of gel
glass, or plastic that are placed in front of the camera lens or in a sl
the lens mounting during photographic work. The various filters trar
light of certain colors while absorbing light of others, and there
selected colors of light from a multicolored object are filtered out
reduced. The photograph then records only the colors transmitted thro
the filter.

color identification   Designation of the color of each process plat
illustration copy having two or more colors. The identification is mar
outside the reproducible area on each overlay. When a color other than
primary or secondary colors is required, a swatch should be provided to
identify it.

Color-Key   *See* CONTACT IMAGING MATERIALS.

color proof   Sample impression of a printed color work combining all
colors. The proof is checked for proper color determination, size, registration, and the like.

color reproduction   Any of several methods in which photographic masks
are used to obtain better rendition of colors in the reproduction process.

color sensitivity   *See* FILMS AND PLATES.

color separation   Division of colors of a continuous-tone multicolored
original or of line copy into basic portions, each of which is to be reproduced by a separate printing plate carrying a color. Usually three separations are made for continuous-tone work and any combination for line
work. Basic methods of separating colors for printing are (1) using acetate
overlays from which three black-and-white negatives are made to represent each primary color; and (2) employing different filters in the process
camera, each of which allows some of the color in the multicolored original
to be imposed on the negative, thus separating colors for reproduction by
printing. Because acetate is subject to molecular change with changes in
humidity, fine color registration is best achieved by using filters.

Acetate-overlay color separation involves the initial preparation of the
black plate from which the black image is produced. A separate plate is
used for each color. Primary-color plates should be on a matte-finish
acetate film of sufficient body to withstand warping or shrinking. The color
area to be printed from a plate appears in permanent black on the plate
and is in perfect register with the other plates comprising the artwork.
When secondary colors are required, they are obtained by overprinting
the primary colors. Areas to be printed in secondary colors are also
defined in permanent black on the appropriate primary-color overlays.

color separation, direct

Each color plate should contain
marks, which appear outside
marks should be finely detai
of each overlay to ensure
perfect register of eac
each plate should b
When a color oth
should be incl
should app
printed i
in a
add

a minimum of four equidistant register
he reproducible portion of the plate. The
ed and placed on the corresponding position
accurate register of each plate, thus producing
n color from the plates. The name of the color for
scratched on the plate outside the reproducible area.
r than primary or secondary colors is required, a swatch
ded with the printing instructions. Paste-ups and preprints
ear on the overlay containing the portion of art that is to be
the same color. When paste-ups and preprints are to be printed
olor that is not provided for by the art separation overlays, an
itional overlay registered to the key, or black, art is used.

Color separation of multicolored originals by means of filters ensures accurate registration and produces colors of the highest quality, all other factors being equal. The work is accomplished by the person operating the process camera. A filter transmits light of certain colors while it absorbs light of others. The most common filters are thin sheets or disks of gelatin or glass placed in front of the lens of the process camera or in a slot in the lens mounting. By using the proper filters, selected colors of light from a multicolored object are filtered out or reduced. A negative will then record only the colors transmitted through the filter. A filter never changes the color of light: it can only allow a part of some colors to pass through and stop other colors. In color-separation work, the colored original is photo-graphed successively through three color-separation filters. The three black-and-white color-separation negatives thus produced are used in making the three printing plates which print the respective colors on paper. A fourth plate, called the "black printer," is usually made to add density to dark areas of the picture.

color separation, direct *See* DIRECT COLOR SEPARATION.

color separation, indirect *See* INDIRECT COLOR SEPARATION.

color-separation filters *See* FILMS AND PLATES.

colors, primary *See* PRIMARY COLORS.

colors, secondary *See* SECONDARY COLORS.

columbian Old type size. The nearest equivalent in the point system is 16 point.

column One of the sections of text or other matter, such as display advertisements, that make up a vertically divided page. It is measured horizontally and is usually justified. Each column of a page is established by a line measure for justified copy. The term "column" also refers to a vertical section of a table.

column chart (also called **vertical column chart**) Graphic representation having juxtaposed vertical columns that usually denote a quantity, with the horizontal dimension representing time or some other value (*see* Figure C-21). An additional value can be represented by using double or divided columns or symbols such as a pig, cow, and sheep, interpreted to indicate pork, beef, and mutton. *See also* BAR CHART; CURVE CHART; PIE CHART; SURFACE CHART.

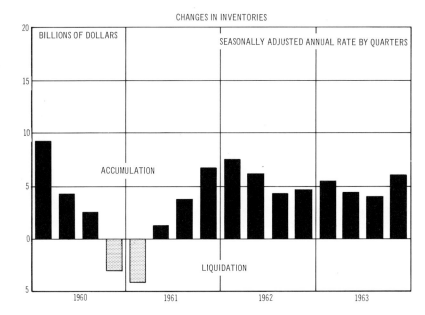

Fig. C-21 Column chart.

column inch Space one column wide and 1 inch high, used to establish rates for display advertising. If, for example, a magazine has an established rate of $40 per column inch, the cost of an advertisement one column wide and 1 inch high would be $40. If the advertisement is one column wide and 2 inches high, the advertisement would cost $80. If the advertisement is two columns wide and 2 inches high, the cost would be $160.

columnar arrangement Division of a page into two or more columns of display or text matter. Columns may be justified or run "ragged."

comb binding (plastic binding) Form of mechanical binding with a plastic center strip from which curving prongs extend. The prongs are inserted in holes punched in the paper. Apparently the name is derived from the resulting comb effect. Plastic binding affords a solid spine on which the title of the book or other information may be printed. *See also* BINDING, MECHANICAL.

combination plate (also called **composite**) Plate containing both halftone and line copy. A black or red patch in the exact proportions of the halftone is mortised or pasted into the camera-ready reproduction copy in the position that the halftone will occupy. The halftone negative is stripped into position in the line negative, and the combination plate, containing both line and halftone copy, is made. Two negatives are necessary because halftone copy requires screening and line copy does not.

commercial Relating to any product manufactured and sold for commercial use or to any service so sold. Although a proposal may ultimately embrace a product or service purchased by the military, it is considered commercial if it is company-funded and if the company's style and format are used in the publication that supports the product or service. If, on the other hand, the publication is funded by the military and government specifications are required to prepare it, the publication is classed as military. A military publication, such as a handbook or a technical manual, has a publication number that is assigned to it by the cognizant agency.

commercial art Artwork of any kind that is prepared for predetermined commercial purposes such as advertising and general promotion. It is distinguished from fine art. Commercial art may be used by government agencies or by private industry.

commercial reproduction copy Reproduction copy which is not intended for government agencies or services and to which a publication number is not assigned.

Commercial S film Film using Du Pont's Cronar polyester film base to make continuous-tone negatives and positives, positive and canceling masks for color-separation techniques, and black-and-white film copies when red and green sensitivity are not needed. It is also well suited to the reproduction of artwork that combines continuous-tone and line material.

comp Abbreviation for compositor or for comprehensive. "Comp" is also used in art departments to mean to apply ("compose") nomenclature on artwork.

compensator Adjustable roller used in a web-fed press to control the tension of the web (paper roll) and maintain paper smoothness.

complementary flat Flat which contains material that is exposed in successive "burns" onto the same plate. This procedure is often necessary when several negatives must be pieced too closely together to be handled in a single flat, as is the case with halftones with close-fitting captions, or when halftones require longer exposure than line work.

composing stick (job stick) Device for holding and arranging type while a line of type is being set by hand. It is made of metal and is adjustable so that a line can be set to the desired measure. The nicks (grooves) in the type are visible to aid in aligning it for right-reading printing. (See Figure C-22.)

Fig. C-22 Printer's composing stick.

composite *See* COMBINATION PLATE.

composition Material consisting of text in typewritten form for photo-offset reproduction or in typeset form for letterpress and other methods of printing. The material is better known as reproduction copy when it is composed on a cold-composition machine and as reproduction or etch proofs if it is in letterpress format. *See* REPRODUCTION COPY; REPRODUCTION PROOF.

compositor One who sets type by hand, with an automatic typecasting machine, or by using a keyboard in connection with a photographic typesetter system.

comprehensive Layout of art and type, either in black or in colors, that is used as a presentation for advertising or other purposes. The comprehensive is neither a rough sketch nor a completed product but should be of sufficient quality and clarity to carry a message. The meaning and purpose of the theme should be readily understood. While the comprehensive should represent the end product as faithfully as possible, it need not be an exact facsimile. Several comprehensives covering the same subject may be produced for comparison.

computer graphics Science of using computers to generate and interpret pictures.

computer language Code used to provide data and instructions to computers.

computer photocomposition work Computers have many different capabilities ranging from simple to complex to highly sophisticated designs. The mini-computer was invented by Digital Equipment Corporation in the late 1950s and was used primarily for problem-solving operations. However, it has had a large impact on the printing industry and has gained rapidly in popularity because of the development of fast, accurate, and versatile computer phototypesetting equipment. In photocomposition work, computers are programmed to perform many functions upon command of the keyboard operator as well as automatic functions under certain conditions. The computer stores formats, lines, and tabulated columns, and some perform all three automatic justification routines for processing unjustified tape, i.e., use of no hyphens, discretionary (operator decision) hyphenation, and logic (machine intelligence rules), with prefix and suffix dictionary capability. The computer also controls the following: typeface and size; the line measure in picas (length); leading (the space between lines of type); automatic quad right, left, or center; leader dots; vertical rules; indentions; runarounds; kerning; letterspacing; and variable character fitting and set-width.

concordance Alphabetical listing of all the important words in a book with page references to the passages in which they occur.

condensed type Type with a narrower face than that used in the same family of type.

construction drawing Engineering drawing that illustrates the design of structures and surrounding areas, individually or in groups, and includes pertinent services, equipment, and other features required to establish all the interrelated elements of the design. Construction drawings, in general, present design information by pictorial plans, elevations, sections, and details. Maps (except those used in construction), sketches, presentation drawings, perspectives, and renderings are not considered construction drawings.

construction paper Type of school paper manufactured from groundwood for use in the elementary grades for coloring, cutouts, pencil or charcoal drawings, etc. The basis weight is 80 pounds (36.3 kg) for 500 sheets of the standard size of 24 by 36 inches (61 by 91.4 cm). Construction paper is manufactured in red, black, orange, yellow, green, dark blue, scarlet, light blue, light red, dark green, brown, white, gray, and light green.

contact imaging materials Material used in the preparation of art comprehensives, packaging design, film cels and slides, and other visual aids. The material is a clear polyester film overlaid with an ink-pigmented coating that is sensitive to ultraviolet light. It can be imaged by any type of transparent, translucent, stencil, or cut-out original through which light can pass. It is available in three basic types:

1. Negative transparent, which acts to reverse the image of the original copy or film; for example, a film negative will produce a positive-reading image, and a positive stat will produce a negative-reading image. In either case, the image produced will be transparent.

2. Positive transparent, which acts to duplicate the image of the original copy or film; for example, a film positive will produce a positive-reading transparent image.

3. Negative opaque, which acts to reverse the image of the original as in the negative transparent above, except that the image made is opaque. Color-Key, 3M's trade name for contact imaging material, is packaged in six standard sizes with more than 50 colors, including 48 colors that are matched to the Pantone coordinated ink matching system. Some common originals are photographic film or paper negatives, photographic film positives, transfer letters on clear film or vellum, dense pencil or ink drawings on vellum or lightweight paper, negative stats and glossy photographs that have been transparentized to pass light, painted art on clear acetate, and orange Color-Key, which acts as a special no-darkroom negative or positive. Some uncommon originals are Japanese rice and tissue papers, tablecloths and other lightweight fabrics, leaves and flowers, pieces of burlap, linen cloths, lace, fishnet, and textured screens. All types of opaque art, type, photographs, and other designs can be converted to photographic negatives or positives. The following are the processing steps for Color-Key: (1) Make a sandwich of the original, a sheet of Color-Key, and a sheet of goldenrod or dull black paper; (2) expose these materials to an ultraviolet light source; and (3) develop out the image, rinse, and blot dry. For further information concerning Color-Key, refer to the *"How To" Guide For Design Graphics, 3M Color-Key Contact Imaging Material*, 3M Industrial Graphics Division.

contact print Print or copy made in the same size as the original negative or master copy without the benefit of a reduced or enlarged print. It is made on sensitized paper by direct contact with the master or original.

contact printing frame Glass-topped frame used to bring a film into contact with another film or plate for the purpose of making an emulsion-to-emulsion contact. The frame may or may not be vacuum-operated.

contact screen Halftone screen made on a film base with a graduated-dot pattern. The screen is placed in direct contact with the film or plate to obtain a halftone pattern from a continuous-tone original. Specifically designed for making halftone negatives and positives for photomechanical reproduction, they are composed of vignetted dots on a flexible base support and are used with high-contrast film or paper on which the halftone is to be made. The Estar-base support gives the contact screen maximum durability and extended life. The dots composing the contact screen may be the conventional square-dot shape or may be elliptical in shape. The elliptical-dot screen produces an elliptical dot in the middle tones. This feature of the screen eliminates the sudden jump in density that is usually encountered in vignetted areas of the reproduction and which results because all four corners of the dots join at the same place in the tonal scale. With the elliptical dot, only two diagonal corners join at any one place in the tonal scale. As a result, a smoother reproduction is obtained and graininess is minimized. This screen is used in the same way as a square-dot contact screen.

When a contact screen is used in a process camera, the screen must be in the closest possible contact with the sensitive material. This requires the use of a vacuum film holder for the screen and the sensitized material on the camera back. To illustrate, place a sheet of film, emulsion side up, in the center of the vacuum holder. The screen must be large enough to cover the film and extend far enough (at least 1½ inches [3.81 cm]) beyond it on all four sides to provide good contact. Wipe the contact screen lightly with a clean, dry photo chamois; place the screen emulsion (or dull) side down over the film; and turn on the vacuum pump. If the screen shows a tendency to wrinkle, use a rubber roller to work the unevenness to the edges. When good contact is established, close the camera back and make the exposure. The lens opening does not affect contrast or dot formation. Therefore, use an aperture of f/16 or f/22, because most process lenses give the sharpest results at these settings. For making enlargements or reductions, either the aperture or the exposure time must be changed. Of course, if the lens aperture is not changed, enlargement of the image size necessitates longer exposure; reduction of the image size, shorter exposure.

For many purposes, halftones can be made by contact from continuous-tone negatives or positives of the desired size. Since the closest possible contact with the sensitive material is again necessary, a vacuum holder or vacuum printing frame is needed. For example, to make a halftone positive from a continuous-tone negative, place a sheet of film so that its emulsion side faces the exposing light. Wipe the contact screen gently with a clean, dry chamois and place it, dull side down, over the film. Next, place the cleaned negative, dull (or image) side down, over the contact screen. Lower the glass of the frame over the assembly and turn on the vacuum. Then make the exposure with an exposing lamp, and be sure that the lamp is far enough from the frame so that illumination will be even across the entire image area.

When any positive or negative type of screen is used for its intended purpose, it will give good results without complicated exposure techniques. However, if a positive screen is used in a normal manner for making negatives, or a negative screen for making positives, the resulting reproduction will usually lack sufficient highlight contrast. Excellent halftone negatives can be made with a positive screen if a no-screen, or highlighting, exposure is added. However, there is no way to overcome the loss in highlight contrast if positives are made with a negative screen.

Eastman Kodak Company provides five basic types of contact screens. These screens are discussed as follows:

Kodak magenta contact screen (*negative*).   The screen is available in sizes from 9 by 11 inches (22.8 by 28 cm) for 8- by 10-inch (20.3 by 25.4-cm) film, to 31 by 31 inches (78.7 by 78.7 cm) for 29- by 29-inch (73.6 by 73.6-cm) film, and in rulings of 110, 120, 133, 150, and 175 lines per inch. All screens have elliptical dots. These screens have various highlight-contrast improvements built into them to meet the needs of the processes for which they are normally used. They can be used with white-flame arc or pulsed-xenon lamps on the camera, with only small differences on tone reproduction. Tungsten lamps give somewhat less contrast. The magenta dye in the screen permits tone-reproduction changes to be made with filters. The controlled-flash method is the simplest method of controlling halftone contrast. Two exposures are required: The main exposure, made through the screen, depends primarily on the highlight density of the original copy, on magnification, and on lens aperture. (It can be computed readily with a Kodak halftone negative computer or with the Kodak graphic arts exposure computer.) The second exposure is a flash exposure through the screen. The actual flash exposure to produce a satisfactory shadow dot depends on the density range of the original, but the density range of most originals is long enough to require a flash exposure. Figure C-23 shows an extension of tone scale by using the controlled flash. The five scales reproduced were all made with a magenta contact screen from an original gray scale represented, at somewhat reduced contrast, on the left. All five reproductions were given the same main exposure, but the flash exposure was varied as shown. Note how increasing the flash exposure lengthens the tonal range. The main exposure in each case was a single white-light camera exposure of one minute at $f/16$ with two 35-ampere arc lamps.

A satisfactory lamp for flashing can be set up in the camera darkroom as shown in Figure C-24. The lamp can be attached permanently above the camera if the camera back opens on the horizontal, as shown at the top of the illustration, or it can be mounted in any convenient position opposite the camera back if the back opens on a vertical hinge, as shown in the bottom diagram. Such a lamp can be made conveniently from a Kodak Adjustable Safelight Lamp with a 7½-watt, white-frosted lamp and a 5½-inch (13.9-cm) diameter Kodak Safelight Filter 00 (light yellow), and should be used at a distance of approximately 6 feet (1.83 m). A lamp for

Fig. C-23 Extension of
tone scale using a
controlled flash.

Original Scale	1 No Flash	2 10 Sec	3 17 Sec	4 21 Sec	5 24 Sec

flashing can be mounted as shown on top for cameras which have backs
that open to a horizontal position and, as shown on bottom of the illustration, for cameras which are hinged vertically.

When increased highlight contrast is needed for making halftone negatives, an additional highlighting image exposure can be made without the
screen. The no-screen exposure may be from 2 to 15 percent of the main

exposure, depending on the amount of highlighting required. With the film in place on the vacuum back of the camera, make the no-screen, or "bump," exposure first. Then place the screen over the film and give the screen main exposure, followed by the flash exposure through the screen.

Kodak magenta contact screen (positive).   This screen is available in the same sizes as the Kodak magenta contact screen (negative) and in rulings of 120, 133, 150, 175 (with elliptical-dot screen), 200, and 300 lines per inch. The tone characteristics of the "positive" screen are especially suitable for screen positives from continuous-tone separation negatives in color work. The preferred method of contrast control is to use Kodak color-compensating filters, generally known as "C" filters. (The controlled-flash method will usually result in poor highlight contrast.) These gelatin filters of high optical quality were originally designed for corrective color balance in color photography. They are supplied in six colors (blue, green, red, yellow, magenta, and cyan) and in a wide range of densities (0.025 to 0.50). They are available in 2-inch, 3-inch, and 4-inch (5.08, 7.62, and 10.1-cm) sizes. Only the yellow and magenta filters are used for contact-screen work.

A typical filter designation is "CC20Y." The "CC" stands for color compensating, "20" for a density of 0.20, and "Y" for yellow. The density designation applies only to the light of the color that this filter is designed to absorb, in this case blue light. Yellow CC filters, in combination with the magenta color in the magenta contact screen, reduce the contrast of a halftone; hence, yellow filters permit the use of negatives of higher contrast. Magenta filters increase contrast of a halftone; that is, they permit use of negatives of lower contrast.

Kodak magenta contact screen (for photogravure).   This screen is available in the same sizes as the magenta contact screen (negative) in a ruling of 133 lines per inch. A screen ruling of 150 lines per inch is available in film size of 24 by 24 inches (60.9 by 60.9 cm) and 29 by 29 inches (73.6 by 73.6 cm). It is designed for making intermediate halftone negatives for intaglio halftone (hard-dot) processes in both the publication and packaging fields. It is used mainly in color work for making intermediate halftone negatives from color-corrected, continuous-tone positives by contact printing. However, it can be used in the camera in place of the conventional crossline screen or for screening directly onto resist film.

Kodak gray contact screen (negative).   The screen is available in the same sizes as the Kodak magenta contact screen (negative). Screen rulings are 65, 85, 100, 110, 120, 133, 150, and 175 lines per inch in elliptical-dot screens. (The 100-lines-per-inch screen has been designed to lighten the middle-tone area of reproductions. This screen is especially well suited to web offset printing of newsprint.) The gray contact screen (negative) is used to make halftone negatives and direct halftone separations from color originals. This is the easiest screen to use and is recommended for processes that do not require magenta dye to control tone reproduction. The controlled-flash method is recommended for controlling halftone contrast. The flash exposure is made through the screen by using the same flash lamp and flashing procedure as that recommended for the Kodak magenta contact screen (negative). A white-light flash exposure rather than a

Fig. C-24   Example of lamp for flashing exposures.

yellow-light flash tends to minimize the effect of Newton's rings when the gray screen is used.

For most work, the gray screen (negative) will give adequate highlight contrast. For any situation that requires additional highlight contrast, a no-screen, or highlighting, exposure can be given. To do this, make an exposure without the screen before the screen is put in place for the main exposure. The highlighting exposure time may be from 2 to 15 percent of the main exposure. If the highlighting exposure time becomes too short for control, use a neutral density filter (Kodak Wratten Neutral Density Filter No. 92). With a filter having a neutral density of 1.00, the same exposure time used for the main exposure will yield a 10 percent highlight exposure.

Kodak PMT gray contact screen. This contact screen is available in film sizes of 11 by 14 inches (27.9 by 35.5 cm) and 24 by 24 inches (60.9 by 60.9 cm), with screen rulings of 65, 85, and 100 lines per inch. These are elliptical-dot screens designed for use with Kodak photomechanical transfer materials. The screens are used for making screened paper prints for use as camera line copy. The screen has an extra-long screen range to maintain the tone separation in the shadow areas of the print. Without this added range, screened prints may appear to lose shadow contrast and shadow detail.

The foregoing discussion was provided through the courtesy of Eastman Kodak Company and are extracts from their Pamphlet No. Q-21, *Kodak Contact Screens, Types and Applications.* For details concerning the preparation of direct-screen color separations, refer to Kodak Pamphlet No. Q-121, *Kodak Contact Direct-Screen Color-Separation Method.*

contact screen: angling Act of rotating contact screens away from the normal horizontal-vertical axes of a camera back whenever several screened impressions are printed on top of each other. Superimposed screened impressions are necessary for a number of printing applications: process-color (three- or four-color) reproduction, posterization, duotone printing, rescreening of preprinted copy, screening of continuous-tone copy that has screen-type patterns (plaid fabrics, window screens), printing multiple screen tints, and others. The angle away from the horizontal or vertical axis is critical; contact screens must be positioned and registered carefully to minimize moiré patterns. Even at the optimum angles, a subtle high-frequency moiré or rosette pattern is formed. Proper alignment of screen angles prevents moiré from becoming objectionable. A screen angle of 45° is generally used in single-color printing. In this way, the rows of dots will not run in either the horizontal or vertical directions, where they would be the most noticeable.

In angling and punching either a set of screens or a single circular screen for color reproduction, the same principle is followed. The strongest color, usually the black, is printed at the 45° angle. The yellow, the least noticeable color, is printed at a screen angle of 90°. The magenta and cyan are printed at angles of 75° and 105°, respectively. This arrangement may be varied as needed. For example, with a weak black printer, the black and cyan angles could be interchanged with the cyan as the strongest color. With elliptical-dot screens, there is a special requirement for a set of angled screens. The dot-chaining direction of the 75° printer must be set at a right angle (90°) to the stated angle of 75°. The other printers will have the dot-chaining direction along the angle axis. This requirement, illustrated in Figure C-25, is automatically established when a single elliptical-dot screen is prepared for color reproduction. The figure shows the direction of the dot chain in the contact screen in relation to the conventional angles. The illustration is viewed down for magenta screens and emulsion up for gray screens. Table C-1 shows the largest size screen of each angle that can be cut from each available size of a Kodak contact screen. Detailed directions for angling screens and an indicator for screen angles are available in Kodak publication No. Q-31. Kodak publication No. Q-82 covers their contact screen cutting template. *See also* CONTACT SCREEN and CONTACT SCREEN: PREANGLED.

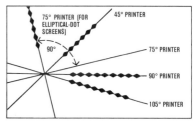

Fig. C-25 Dot-chain direction of elliptical-dot screens for color reproduction.

TABLE C-1

Size of uncut screen	45° angle	75°, 90°, and 105° angles
9 × 11 in. (22.8 × 25.4 cm)	9 × 11 in. (22.8 × 25.4 cm)	5½ × 7 in. (14 × 17.7 cm)
12 × 15 in. (30.4 × 38.1 cm)	12 × 15 in. (30.4 × 38.1 cm)	7 × 9 in. (17.7 × 22.8 cm)
15 × 18 in. (38.1 × 45.7 cm)	15 × 18 in. (38.1 × 45.7 cm)	9 × 12 in. (22.8 × 30.4 cm)
17 × 21 in. (43.1 × 53.3 cm)	17 × 21 in. (43.1 × 53.3 cm)	11 × 13 in. (25.4 × 33 cm)
25 × 25 in. (63.5 × 63.5 cm)	25 × 25 in. (63.5 × 63.5 cm)	15½ × 19½ in. (39.3 × 49.4 cm)
31 × 31 in. (78.4 × 78.4 cm)	31 × 31 in. (78.4 × 78.4 cm)	19 × 23 in. (48.2 × 58.4 cm)

contact screen: preangled Contact screens manufactured with their rulings accurately pre-positioned at specific screen angles. Kodak preangled magenta contact screen (positive) and preangled magenta contact screen (photogravure) are available for making halftone positives, and Kodak preangled gray contact screen (negative) is produced for making halftone negatives. The gray contact screens (negative) are elliptical-dot screens, available for film sizes of 11 by 14, 16 by 20, 24 by 24, and 29 by 29 inches (25.4 by 35.5, 40.6 by 50.8, 60.9 by 60.9, and 73.6 by 73.6 cm) in rulings of 85, 110, 133, 150, and 175 lines per inch. Screen angles are set at 45°, 75°, 90°, and 105°. The magenta contact screens (positive) are available for film sizes of 11 by 14, 16 by 20, 24 by 24, and 29 by 29 inches (25.4 by 35.5, 40.6 by 50.8, 60.9 by 60.9, and 73.6 by 73.6 cm) in rulings of 133 (square-dot), 150 (square- and elliptical-dot), and 175 (elliptical-dot) lines per inch. Screen angles are set at 45°, 75°, 90°, and 150°. The magenta contact screens (photogravure) are lateral-dot screens available for film size of 14 by 17 inches (35.5 by 43.1 cm) in a ruling of 150 lines per inch. Screen angles are set at 45°, 60°, 75°, and 105° for intaglio halftone (hard-dot) processes.

In order to obtain full advantage of the accuracy of the angling, certain precautions must be observed. Every screen is supplied with a clearly designated reference edge. This edge is shown by large lettering and an arrow at the edge. The ruling and the angle are also marked in the same way. This reference edge must be accurately positioned against a fixed edge on the camera back, printing frame, or wherever the screens are to be used. If a punch method is to be used, the reference edge must be held firmly against the punch guide edge as each screen is punched. Individual Kodak preangled screens purchased for replacement may be used with other Kodak preangled screens already in use. *Note:* The screens which have an elliptical-dot structure require that the dot-chaining direction of the 75° printer (magenta) be maintained at a right angle (90°) to the stated angle of 75°. All screens labeled 75° have been properly oriented. When a preangled contact screen is used in total darkness, a code-notch method is useful for identifying the screen angle. Notches can be made on the edge of the contact screen or on the edge of the screen holder. Round notches can be made with a single-hole paper punch, or V-notches can be cut slightly into the screen edge. The following is a code-notch method that is easy to remember: No notch in the screen indicates a 45° angle, one notch is the 75° angle, two notches indicate the 90° angle, and three notches the 105° angle. If the notches are made in the upper right edge of the screen when the reference edge is at the top and the emulsion side is away from the user, the notches will also identify the emulsion-down position of the screen. *See also* CONTACT SCREEN; CONTACT SCREEN: ANGLING.

contact size   Size of a print or an image reproduced or copied in the same size as the original, without enlargement or reduction.

contents   Portion of the front matter of a publication that lists the parts, chapters, sections, and sometimes the numbers and titles of paragraphs. A list of illustrations and a list of tables may also be included and follow in that order. The page on which each entry may be found is given opposite the entry. The single word "contents" is replacing the phrase "table of contents."

continuous form   Series of perforated sheets attached in roll form. The sheets are fed into a printing press or other device, such as a computer printout, and are separated into individual sheets by tearing them apart along the lines of the perforations.

continuous-form press   Printing press designed especially to print on continuous forms. The continuous-form press is used both for printing custom business forms and for imprinting. Custom forms are usually prepared and printed to individual specifications. Imprints are stock forms that are rerun by the printer to add a heading or a vertical rule or a combination of captions and vertical and horizontal rules. Among the custom forms the press will produce are payroll registers, payroll checks, invoices, purchase orders, statements, insurance-premium notices, tax notices, earnings and withholding-tax statements, and bills of lading. Imprints include ledgers, cash and general journals, columnar forms and pads, visible binder forms, machine-bookkeeping forms, and data processing forms.

Figure C-26 shows the Kluge web-flow continuous-form press. Accessories consist of an unwind unit and pneumatic roll loader, a line hole punch unit, fan folder, sheeter, and a line-slitting and/or line perforator. By use of a special bed casting, the press will accommodate an over type-high numbering machine with numbering type faces as high as 2 inches (5.08 cm). With this design, the press can be returned to standard for use with conventional numbers and printing. The Kluge web-flow press is manufactured in three sizes: 12 by 18 inches (30.48 by 45.72 cm), 14 by 22

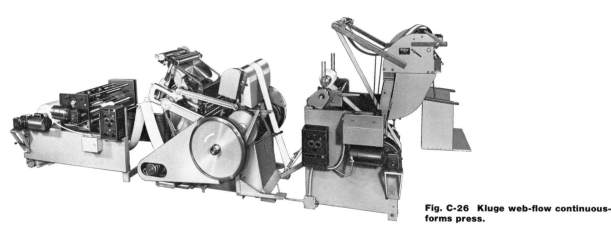

Fig. C-26 Kluge web-flow continuous-forms press.

inches (35.56 by 55.88 cm), and 17 by 19 inches (43.1 by 48.2 cm). Each model has stock advancements variable from 3 inches (7.62 cm) to 22 inches (55.8 cm). Web widths are 2½ inches (6.35 cm) through 19 inches (48.2 cm) for the 12 by 18-inch (30.4 by 45.7-cm) and 17 by 19-inch (43.1 by 48.2-cm) models, and 2½ inches (6.35 cm) by 22 inches (55.9 cm) for the 14 by 22-inch (35.5 by 55.8-cm) model.

The Kluge web-flow press produces pressure-sensitive labels as well as commercial. The pressure-sensitive roll material is line-hole punched and then moves on into the press. The press prints, die cuts, and foil stamps the labels on a multiple-press basis. Waste is stripped from the backing and the completed label or panel of labels are either fan-folded or rewound as desired in one continuous operation. The tandem web-flow heat-seal process produces labels on heat-seal material in one, two, three, or four colors. It utilizes the vertical punch unit for optical scanning of identification punches for automatic label-dispensing machinery. The press handles tag- and ticket-printing requirements including perforated labels, inventory or piece work, tags and labels, library cards, and index record control cards. Vertical punch units are available for stripping action or for punching of special configurations. The 12 by 18-inch (30.4 by 45.7-cm) press has a speed of 3,500 impressions per hour, the 14 by 22-inch (35.5 by 55.8-cm) press 3,000, and the 17 by 19-inch (43.1 by 48.2-cm) press 3,300 impressions per hour.

continuous-tone art Photograph, wash drawing, or oil painting without a halftone-dot screen. Any image with a tonal gradation is a halftone[1] when screened and, in the graphic arts, is contrasted with line copy. After continuous-tone art has been screened, it becomes a halftone. A halftone is identified by examining the paper surface with a magnifying glass and noting the presence or absence of dot formations. *See also* HALFTONE SCREENING.

[1]Because the meaning of words is based on general usage and acceptance, the definition of a halftone given here is used throughout the *Encyclopedia*. However, some authorities are of the opinion that screening continuous-tone copy does not cancel the full range of tones. Their preference is to call this copy full-tone instead of halftone. They contend that a halftone is actually continuous-tone copy altered to the extent that it is treated as line work when it is engraved for printing. *See also* LINE CONVERSION.

contour Form of an object drawn in outline. In mapmaking, contour lines are lines that connect points of equal elevation.

contrast In photography, the separation of tones; the range of differences from white through black; the density of certain areas of the image as compared with others. When tones are slightly defined, the image is said to be "low" in contrast, but when they are readily identified from white through black, it is said to be "high" in contrast.

contrast index Average slope or gradient of the characteristic curve of a film between two points representing the maximum and minimum densities normally used in making high-quality negatives. Contrast index is determined by measuring the slope of a straight line between these two points. This measurement can be more useful than "gamma," since it includes the toe portion of the characteristic curve which is used in practical negative making. *See also* GAMMA.

control guide, contact Guide for making high-quality contact reproductions of line and halftone negatives or positives. *See* Figure C-27. A clear area, about ½ inch by 3¾ inches (1.27 by 9.53 cm), is in the lower left section of the guide. In this area, mount Kodak Control Scale T-14. The complete guide contains the reference areas listed below:

Area 1. A continuous-tone density scale for exposure control and adjustment.

Area 2. A calibrated guide for checking the amount of spread (or choke) that is obtained in the contact print of a line image. The amount of size change is measured in points.

Area 3. A detailed halftone scale for checking dot rendition and dry-dot etching. Note that the two halves of the halftone scale are mounted to allow direct negative-positive comparisons.

Area 4. Two small line targets for checking line intersections; one is negative and the other positive. They are also useful for alignment and register.

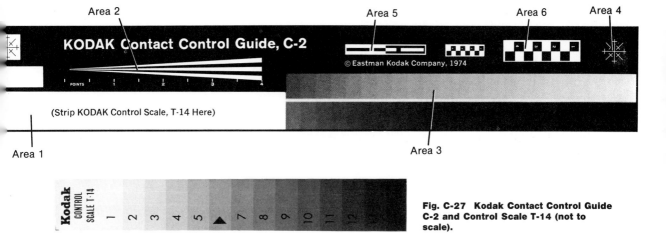

Fig. C-27 Kodak Contact Control Guide C-2 and Control Scale T-14 (not to scale).

Area 5. A negative and positive guide for checking either inside or outside corners of line images.

Area 6. Another type of line guide useful for checking corners, intersections, and spreading and choking effects.

To assemble the guide, carefully cut out the area of the guide provided for attaching Kodak Control Scale T-14. Attach the control scale with small pieces of transparent tape. Be sure that the emulsion side of the scale faces the same way as that of the guide. If desirable, a soft-dot halftone scale can be stripped along the edge of this guide. Make the soft-dot scale by exposing a reflection gray scale to a sheet of film with a contact screen. The Kodak Reflection Density Guide (24-step) works well for this purpose.

Using the Guide

The guide should be positioned adjacent to the image area of the negative or positive that is to be contact-printed. Be certain that the emulsion side of the guide is facing the same direction as the emulsion side of the material from which a contact print is to be made. ("Contact print" refers to the result of printing onto film, paper, plate, or any other photosensitive materials by contact.) It is important to have this same orientation for the original and the guide in order to get a reliable interpretation of exposure and development effects which relate to the original. At this point, under normal exposure and processing conditions, the guide can be used to make a reproduction of a familiar original. This will show how the various areas of the guide reproduce. If checking the result obtained under normal conditions is not desired, make a few test prints under varying exposure conditions. Do not vary processing conditions, however. By checking the reference areas in the prints of the guide with those in the prints of the original, the guide will soon be able to be interpreted to establish the best procedure. The reference areas of the guide can then be relied on to assist in controlling the many conditions which influence the making of contact reproductions.

Interpreting the Guide

Area 1. Kodak Control Scale T-14: The continuous-tone scale indicates the speed and, to a slight degree, the contrast at which the sensitized material was exposed and processed. After making trial negatives that represent the type of contact print needed, the best result is selected. Use the step (speed-point) indicated on the density scale as a standard for making contact reproductions to similar originals. It is desirable to use a densitometer to measure the density of the control step established on the density scale. This gives the best accuracy for controlling repeatability. However, if access to a densitometer is not possible, a careful visual comparison of the step-density of a new contact print with that of a standard print should be quite satisfactory. When examining trial prints, it may be found that contact prints made from a good original will be acceptable within a plus or minus tolerance of one or more steps. If the exposure must be adjusted to produce a different control step, or an exposure which produced the wrong control step must be changed, follow these instructions: For negative materials, to print two additional steps, double the exposure. To print two less steps, cut the exposure in half. For positive materials, to print two additional steps, cut the exposure in half. To print two less steps, double the test exposure. The continuous-tone density scale is sensitive to the contrast of the sensitized material on which it is being exposed. Therefore, the control step that is established for use with one type of material cannot necessarily be used with different types of sensitized materials. The control scale should always record similarly when printed in the same manner on the same sensitized material.

Area 2. Spread-and-choke guide: Three lines converge in a wedge shape over a scale of point sizes to monitor image size change when making spreads and chokes. Where the wedge is shortened by choke techniques or where the lines converge after "fattening" from spread techniques, look down at the point-size scale: one-half the value indicated by the scale is the actual amount of the size change (normal spread and choke is distributed equally from the center to each side of the given line; for example, if the indicator measures a two-point spread, then the image has swelled one point on each side). *See* Figure C-28. For other measuring methods, a point equals about $1/72$ inch, and there are 12 points to a pica. (There are other interpretations, but this is most common.) The conditions of exposure and processing that produce a certain value of spread or choke should again produce the same value of spread or choke for other line images of different sizes, when accurately repeated on the same film. *Note:* The amount of spread or choke indicated by the Control Guide C-2 applies to any size of line image, provided the guide is positioned during exposure at the center, or within a reasonable distance from the center, of the exposing plane or image area. Otherwise, some distortion could result which might affect the guide's accuracy.

Area 3. Intersect target: A contact print made from Control Guide C-2 will disclose any variations in line intersections that result from changes in exposure or processing conditions. The line-target print is also very sensitive to alignment changes in any direction. If desirable, its sharp character can be retained when overexposed to make spreads or chokes. Cover it with a neutral-density filter so that it receives a normal exposure.

Area 4. Negative-positive corner guide: A contact print made from the control guide will disclose any variations or distortions of inside or outside corners, in positive or negative form.

Area 5. Halftone scales: These are hard-dot scales. The ends of the scales are reversed to show a direct negative-to-positive or positive-to-negative dot area relationship. In other words, 99 percent is opposite 1 percent, 56 percent is opposite 44 percent, and so on. The results of dry-dot etching (that is, changing halftone-dot size by adjusting the exposure during contacting) by exposure on Kodalith Duplicating Film 2574 (Estar Base), Kodak High Speed Duplicating Film 2575 (Estar Base), or Kodalith MP High Speed Duplicating Film 2565 (Estar Base) can be checked by observing corresponding dot sizes in the scales. When the dots in the halftone scales of the control guide are reproduced accurately but the dots in the contact print from the original halftone are changed in size (sharpened), the size change in the dots is due to a low-density edge on the dots in the halftone. In this case, a soft-dot scale, previously discussed under instructions of assembling the guide, may be a good addition to clarify the relationship between the guide and the original halftone. However, if original halftones are continually made under the same conditions and on

WEDGE LOOKS LIKE THIS FOR A ONE-POINT CHOKE

WEDGE LOOKS LIKE THIS FOR A ONE-POINT SPREAD

Fig. C-28 Wedge indications for spread and choke.

the same sensitized material, the dots on the contact prints should always sharpen the same amount.

Area 6. Miscellaneous targets: The miscellaneous targets are borrowed from a lens-resolution chart. The numbers in the boxes have no bearing on the spaces and adjoining corners of the boxes, but are useful as reference numbers. As the numbers progress, the space or the thickness of the connector between sets of boxes increases. If the exposure sharpens the connector, then duplicates are being overexposed and contact reverses are being underexposed; consequently, the image is being undercut. If the exposure "spreads" the connector or connects the spaces, duplicates are being underexposed and contact reverses are being overexposed. Use the small or large boxes, depending on the critical nature of contacting needs. For more details on contacting work, see *Contacting Procedures for the Graphic Arts*, Kodak Publication No. Q-4. *See also* CONTACT SCREEN.

controlling dimension Dimension, either horizontal or vertical, that determines the enlargement or reduction of an image.

cooling rollers In a web-fed press, a roller installed immediately following the drying oven. It reduces the temperature of the web from oven temperature to the setting temperature of heat-set inks, which is approximately 80 to 90°F.

copy Any matter, including photographs, rules, designs, and text, that is used in reproduction for printing in any manner.

Copy Block Product of Craftint Manufacturing Company, consisting of preprinted blocks of copy in 10, 12, and 14 point to indicate the size of type and the area the copy will occupy. The material has an adhesive back and is pasted in place on a dummy layout to instruct the typesetter. Copy Block contains the normal leading (spacing between lines) applicable to text material.

copy card. Electrical-accounting-machine (EAM) tabulating card containing a frame of unexposed microfilm mounted in or over a rectangular aperture for subsequent exposure and development while still mounted in the card. Microfilm duplicators are used to make copies on copy cards from the original microfilm. *See also* APERTURE CARD.

copy casting *See* COPYFITTING.

copy-dot reproduction Photomechanical reproduction of halftone illustrations and associated line copy without rescreening of the illustrations. The halftone dots of the originals are copied as "line" material. Very careful photography is necessary to obtain good results.

copy paper *See* DUPLICATOR PAPER.

copy scaling *See* COPYFITTING.

copyboard Frame that holds original copy while the copy is being photographed. It is called a "vacuum frame" when vacuum suction is used in conjunction with the board. Without vacuum suction, the copy must be tacked or taped to the face of the board or inserted in a glass-faced frame in which it is secured by pressure. Vacuum copyboards are glass-covered and can be tilted and rotated for easy loading. Vacuum-blanket inserts may be used to keep thin copy, such as tracing, flat within a copyboard. The inserts are mounted in the board, and a vacuum pump and meter are supplied to create the vacuum. Open-faced copyboards (without glass) are available to hold large drawings or sensitized materials for the production of photo templates.

copyfitting (copy casting; copy scaling) In letterpress printing, arranging original copy by type and line measurements so that it will fit the available space. Each letter, space, and punctuation mark is counted as a character. Characters on an elite typewriter measure 12 to the inch and pica characters 10 to the inch. Leading is the space between lines of type. The most accurate system of typing copy to fit space is based on the character count. By multiplying the average number of characters per line by the number of lines of copy, the total number of characters can be found. For example, assume that the copy has an average of 40 characters to a line and that there are 50 lines; multiply 40 by 50; the total is 2,000 characters. To find out how much space the copy will occupy when set in type, determine the measure, which is the width of the line of type in picas, in the typeface and point size desired. This information may be taken from a sample catalog furnished by the compositor. The characters in the given typeface and size are counted in the amount equal to the measure, e.g., 30 characters per line, 40 characters per line, etc. Assume that the copy is to be set in 8 point to a measure of 20 picas and that the selected typeface is found to average 67 characters to the measure. Then, by dividing 67 into 2,000, it is seen that the copy will make 30 lines of type. For convenient assistance to the compositor, copy may be typed so that each line will approximate the measure in picas.

To establish the depth of copy required, the foregoing calculation is used to arrive at 30 lines of type set in 8 point. If the type is to be set 8 on 8, indicating no leading (extra spacing), 30 is multiplied by 8 and a total of 240 points is the depth. The total number of points is divided by 12 (the number of points in a pica), and the total depth is found to be 20 picas. If the 8-point type is to be set on a 9-point body (1 point of leading), expressed as 8 on 9, or on a 10-point body (2 points of leading), expressed as 8 on 10, the point or points of leading are multiplied to obtain the depth in points and divided by 12. To find the depth in inches, divide by 72, which is the number of points in 1 inch (2.54 cm).

It has been established that the ideal line of type should be about 39 characters in any type size set in lowercase letters. Lines of more than 50 or less than 30 characters should be avoided.

copyholder Person who holds and reads aloud the original copy during proofreading while the proofreader marks the proof (in the case of hot composition) or the reproducible camera-ready copy (in the case of cold composition). The term "copyholder" also denotes a frame or stand for holding copy.

copying machines Machines normally used to reproduce copy in offices, company-operated reproduction departments, and printing and duplicating establishments. Included are the larger whiteprint copying machines employed not only in manufacturing plants but in commercial blueprinting and printing shops. Several of the smaller types of copying machines are known as photocopying machines. These produce copies from opaque as well as transparent and translucent originals. The larger copying machines, with which diazo salts are used as a sensitized emulsion on the copy paper and which can make copies only from transparent and translucent originals, are more properly referred to as whiteprint machines.

The copy paper used in copying machines may or may not be sensitized. With some processes it is necessary to produce a master from the original and then make additional copies from the master. The xerographic process copies from an original or a copy onto nonsensitized stock without the use of masters or intermediates. For the whiteprint process, the original must be on a translucent or transparent material that can be penetrated by light during exposure, and the copy paper must be capable of being developed because of light-sensitive characteristics. While most copying machines will reproduce color from originals, it is, of course, impossible to reproduce and impress a color on the copy without the use of colored ink. Copies are black regardless of the color of the original.

Copying machines are not classed as duplicators, although the copies they produce may be correctly termed "duplicate copies." Duplicating machines are those that employ a metal plate, a paperplate master, or a stencil master as the form from which the image is transferred to stock. Offset duplicators, which use paper and flexible metal plates as the image source, are in fact small printing presses. Other types of duplicators are those that employ stencils in mimeographing, such as the mimeograph, and those that use masters to transfer dye images to stock in the spirit duplicating process.

Figure C-29 is the Bruning pressure diazo copying machine Model PD 80. This whiteprint process offers a dry, odorless operation without heaters or ammonia fumes required for development, and therefore venting or mixing of chemicals is not required. The development system is replenished with a cartridge of activator. In this process, the exposed copy material travels through the developer section where a thin film of activator is metered under pressure for development of the diazo material. Metering and pressure blades withdraw automatically from contact with the applicator rollers when the machine is turned off. When the machine is turned on for operation, the blades return to position for development. The Model PD 80 copying machine contains one instant-on, high-intensity fluorescent exposure lamp, a rated printing width of 42 inches (106.6 cm), a maximum printing speed of 15 feet (4.57 m) per minute, front delivery, and manual separation of originals. The machine is 13½ inches (34.3 cm) high,

Fig. C-29 Bruning's pressure diazo copying machine Model PD 80. (Addressograph-Multigraph Corp.)

64 inches (162.5 cm) wide, and 16 inches (40.6 cm) in depth, and weighs approximately 220 pounds (99.8 kg). An optional cabinet stand is available.

Figure C-30 shows the Multigraphics AM 5000 copier. This electrostatic copying machine produces copies at the rate of 50 per minute. There is no minimum size for originals; maximum width for originals is 8½ inches (21.6 cm) and maximum length is 14 inches (35.5 cm). Books of any thickness can be copied, as well as three-dimensional objects. Copies may vary from a maximum width of 8½ inches (21.6 cm) to a minimum width of 3½ inches (8.9 cm); minimum length is 8½ inches (21.6 cm) and maximum length is 14 inches (35.5 cm). An automatic counter provides dialing for up to 99 copies. The 5000 copier uses roll copy paper that is spindle-loaded. Copy sizes can be varied from 8½ to 14 inches (21.6 to 35.5 cm) long by turning a dial. Up to 1,300 8½ by 11-inch copies (21.6 by 27.9-cm) can be obtained from a single roll. Weight of the copier is approximately 440 pounds (199.7 kg).

Figure C-31 shows the Multigraphics 4875, called a both sides copy maker because the machine prints on both sides of a sheet of paper at one pass through the press. A document control unit makes sure that if the 4875 misfeeds or does not receive a master, the duplicating cycle will stop until the problem is corrected. The rate of speed is 17,000 8½ by 11-inch (21.6 by 27.9-cm) copies per hour. By reproducing standard-sized originals two-up on both sides of 11 by 17-inch (21.6 by 43.1-cm) stock, the rate is increased to over 30,000 copies per hour. Minimum paper size is 8 by 10½ inches, (20.3 by 26.6 cm), and maximum paper size is 11 by 17 inches (27.9 by 43.1 cm). Image area is 10½ by 16½ inches (20.3 by 42 cm). Stock used can be 16-pound (7.26-kg) bond to 70-pound (31.7-kg) offset.

Figure C-32 shows the Multigraphics Total Copy system. The system is an integrated combination of the copier and an automatic offset duplicator that produces copies at the rate of 154 per minute on bond paper. Copies are produced using originals ranging from 2½ by 6 inches (6.35 by 15.2 cm) up to 11 by 17 inches (27.9 by 43.1 cm). Paper sizes are 3 by 5-inch (7.62 by 12.7-cm) minimum and 11 by 17-inch (27.9 by 43.1-cm) maximum. Image

Fig. C-30 Multigraphics AM 5000 electrostatic copier. *(Addressograph-Multigraph Corp.)*

Fig. C-31 Multigraphics Both Sides copymaker. *(Addressograph-Multigraph Corp.)*

Fig. C-32
Multigraphics Total
Copy system.
(Addressograph-
Multigraph Corp.)

area is 10½ by 15½ inches (20.3 by 39.3 cm). Paper feeder capacity is 5,000 sheets of 20-pound (9.08-kg) bond. Computer printouts can be reduced to 8½ by 11-inch (21.6 by 27.9-cm) size, and fixed reduction ratios are 20, 25, 30, and 35 percent; special dual-mode capabilities are available, such as 4 percent and size-for-size, 4 percent and 25 percent, and 4 percent and 35 percent.

Figure C-33 shows the Xerox 4500 copier. The machine features two-sided copying, on-line collating, and the capability of remembering where each copy is located when there is a job interruption. A particular feature of the copier is that transparency material can be used for overhead projection presentations. Two paper trays are provided for different colors or sizes of paper. Each tray holds up to 500 sheets of 20-pound (9.08-kg) stock. Speed of the copier is 45 copies per minute, with the first copy in less than 7 seconds in the nonsort mode and 7.5 seconds in the sort mode. The sorter operates on-line and gathers one-sided or two-sided copies. Originals can be up to 8½ by 14 inches (21.6 by 35.5 cm) from bound volumes and three-dimensional objects, as well as from ordinary, unsensitized stock of various weights, sizes, and colors.

Figure C-34 is the Xerox 6500 color copier. The copier makes dry color copies on ordinary bond papers without need of intermediates, special chemicals, or critical exposure adjustments by the operator. Three basic colors—magenta, cyan, and yellow—generate the seven-color range. Four buttons offer color control. The full-color button is the full-color copying mode. The other three one-color buttons can be used singly or in combinations of two. A seven-color copy can be produced in eighteen seconds and a single color copy in six seconds. Best copies are made from originals of solid colors. When a color photograph or any color continuous-tone original is used, a representative color copy is produced. Copy paper weights of from 20 to 24-pound (9.08 to 10.9-kg) substance are accepted, and paper sizes accommodated are from 8 by 10 inches to 8½ by 14 inches (20.3 by 25.4 cm to 21.6 by 35.5 cm). Paper capacity is 500 sheets of 20-pound (9.08-kg) substance. Maximum image area is 8½ by 13¾ inches (21.6

Fig. C-33 Xerox 4500 copier.

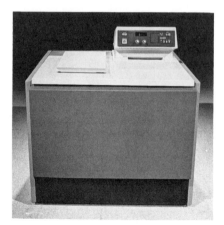

Fig. C-34 Xerox 6500 color copier.

by 34.9 cm). In the full-color mode, 3.2 color copies can be produced in one minute, in the three-color mode 4.8 copies in one minute, and in the single-color mode 9.6 copies can be produced in one minute. The 6500 accepts color copier transparency film and makes color transparencies for overhead projection. There is a multiple-print-selector dial that counts from 1 to 99.

Figure C-35 is a photograph of the Xerox 9200 duplication system. The reproduction system duplicates 7,200 impressions an hour directly from the original without interruption, feeds different weights of paper without adjustment, and automatically sorts and collates the output. By using the programmer, the operator controls quantities needed, both paper trays, and the automatic document container; activates the sorters/collators; and controls the built-in reduction camera. In addition, the quality of impressions is improved from light originals or originals with a color background. When there is a requirement to change weights of paper, the system adjusts automatically to handle paper weights from 16-pound (7.26-kg) bond to 110-pound (51-kg) index. The system is equipped with two paper

Fig. C-35 Xerox 9200 duplication system.

trays. The main tray holds 2,500 sheets of paper and a second tray holds 400 sheets. Originals are cycled automatically, with a capacity of up to 50 of 20-pound (9.08-kg) bond stock of size 8 by 10 to 8½ by 14 inches (20.3 by 25.4 to 21.6 by 35.5 cm). After each original is imaged, it is returned in proper sequence. Since each original is changed and positioned in ½ second, the duplicating process is continuous from one page to the next until the job is completed. The collator has 25 sheets per bin and can be present in the stacking mode. In the sets mode, 100 sheets per bin of 20-pound (9.08-kg) bond paper is accommodated. Paper sizes handled by the collator are 8 by 10 to 8½ by 14 inches (20.3 by 25.4 to 21.5 by 35.5 cm). Reduction ratios of the original size are 65, 74, and 98 percent.

Figure C-36 is A. B. Dick Company's Model 675 electrostatic copier. The machine copies single sheets or from bound materials. An electronic sensor automatically adds toner as required to ensure uniform copy density. A panel light signals when dispersant should be added. One setting on the countdown makes from 1 to 20 copies continuously. A counter in the control

Fig. C-36 A. B. Dick Company's Model 675 electrostatic copier.

panel registers up to 999 with a button for resetting to zero. Minimum copy size is 3 by 5½ inches (7.62 by 13.9 cm) and maximum size is 10 by 15 inches (25.4 by 38.1 cm), and copy paper may be cut to any length from 5½ to 15 inches (13.9 to 38.1 cm) long. Ten 8½ by 11-inch (21.6 by 27.9-cm) copies can be produced per minute. Offset printing masters can be imaged at the rate of 10 per minute. Copy paper capacity is a 460-foot (209-m) roll available in 3, 5½, 8, 8½, or 10-inch (7.62, 13.9, 20.3, 21.6, or 25.4-cm) rolls. Offset master copy paper capacity is 9 by 10-inch (22.8 by 25.4-cm) widths. A totalizer keeps a cumulative record of all copies made up to 99,999 copies and is not resettable.

Figure C-37 is IBM's Copier II. The machine accepts an original and automatically positions it on a stationary flatbed. Using an advanced document feed, the first copy is delivered in six seconds. Subsequent copies of the same or different originals are produced every 2.4 seconds, or 1,500 per hour. The copier reproduces items such as bound volumes, halftones, colors, low-contrast images, oversized originals, and three-dimensional objects. To facilitate copying of large rolled documents such as wiring diagrams, blueprints, engineering drawings, construction plans, maps, and architectural drawings, the Copier II is equipped with a rolled-document holder. The holder allows feeding of a rolled document onto a flatbed document glass measuring 8½ by 14 inches (21.6 by 35.5 cm). A copy selector allows from 1 to 20 copies at one setting. A continuous-setting calibration on the selector permits the copier to produce multiple copies until the operator resets the dial to "1," thereby completing the copying cycle. A separate counter is used to maintain an accurate count of copies produced on a continuous setting. The machine also features a copy darkness control for increased readability of those documents with a faint text or image. The Copier II copies both letter-size (8½ by 11 inches) (21.6 by 27.9 cm) and legal-size (8½ by 13 inches or 8½ by 14 inches) (21.6 by 33 cm or 21.6 by 35.5 cm) documents.

Fig. C-37 IBM's Copier II.

Figure C-38 is IBM's Copier that is a compact, flatbed console that operates from a separate 115-volt, 15-ampere power source. A specially developed photoconductor enables the machine to provide consistent quality on plain paper. The Copier has a transparent toner carriage that holds enough toner for a period of up to three months of copy production and enables the operator to observe the amount of toner in the carriage at any given moment. A mechanism built into the machine automatically stirs the toner. Copies are produced at the rate of 600 per hour. The plain bond paper used by the machine is roll-fed, and each roll has a capacity of approximately 625 letter-size copies. The roll feed enables the operator to select either letter- or legal-size copies by pressing a button. To operate the copier, the user selects the number of copies desired, places the original facedown on the flat document bed, closes the document cover, and depresses the start bar. No warm-up period is required, and the first copy is produced in fifteen seconds. Subsequent copies are produced every six seconds. The copy selector is calibrated from 1 to 10. If set for more than one copy, it automatically moves back to the "1" position in measured increments as each copy is produced. When the copy is completed, the document cover automatically opens both to facilitate paper handling and

Fig. C-38 IBM's Copier.

to remind the user to retrieve the original document. Simultaneously, the machine shuts off automatically.

The machine shown in Figure C-39 is Itek's A.D.S. automatic duplicating system. The A.D.S. can produce 1,000 impressions in less than ten minutes, or 20,000 impressions of medium-run-length jobs in one day's work. The machine produces from originals typed on regular bond paper, corrected with fluid, tape, or any other method. Industry, educational institutions, government, business services, and wholesale/retail outlets are examples of organizations where this duplicating system is used.

copywriting Writing advertising copy and literature.

core Paper or metal shaft around which the paper (web) is wound. It may be either returnable or disposable.

Fig. C-39 Itek's A.D.S. automatic duplicating system.

cornerer Device equipped with a semicircular die that is used to cut round corners on printing stock.

correction overlay Additional tissue overlay affixed to a board art for making corrections. Before the corrections can be made, the overlay must be registered to the art by drawing crop marks. A wax pencil should be used when marking an overlay attached to a photograph. Once corrections have been made, the overlay is replaced and returned with the art so that the corrections may be checked.

correction sheet Sheet of paper, coated on one side, which is deposited over a typewritten error for correction. *See* Figure C-40. These sheets are manufactured by Eaton Allen Corporation under the trade names of Ko-Rec-Type and Ko-Rec-Copy. Ko-Rec-Type is convenient for correcting letters and small words; the corrected original is suitable for high-level distribution, and machine-made copies do not show the error when made properly. Ko-Rec-Copy is used to correct carbon copies.

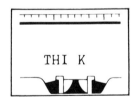

1. BACKSPACE TO TYPEWRITTEN ERROR.

2. PLACE CORRECTION MATERIAL DIRECTLY ON THE ORIGINAL WITH COATED SIDE FACE DOWN. RETYPE THE SAME LETTERS AS THE ERROR.

3. REMOVE CORRECTION MATERIAL. YOUR ERROR HAS DISAPPEARED. TYPE IN CORRECTION.

Fig. C-40 Using Ko-Rec-Type to make typing corrections.

correction tape (spirit process) Tape employed to make corrections on masters used with spirit-process duplicators. The tape is mounted on an adhesive backing with ⅙-inch (1.58-mm) widths for single-spaced copy and

⅓-inch (8.46-mm) widths for double-spaced copy. To make a correction, the tape is removed from its backing and cut to the exact length of the error. The tape is pressed over the error on the back of the master. A clean strip of dye-carbon paper is then placed over the error, and the correction is typed over the error on the face of the master.

correction tape (typewriters) Tape used for correcting errors on ordinary typewritten copy. The tape has an adhesive backing and is useful for quick correction of words or long lines of copy, from which copies may be made for local distribution. The original, however, with the tape affixed, is not of sufficient quality for high-level distribution. To make a correction, a strip of tape is removed from the backing and affixed directly over the typed error or over a typed lined the length of the paper. The correction is then typed on the tape. This tape is available in ⅙-inch and ⅓-inch widths. Rolls are 50 inches (127 cm) in length and are packed in dispensers.

cosmetics In computer graphics, a term designating the general characteristics of copy as to image sharpness, contrast, uniformity, and the presence of unwanted images areas.

count Number of sheets of paper in a given size, thickness, and weight required to make a bundle of 50 pounds (22.7 kg); used with paperboards.

courtesy copy In business correspondence, a tissue copy (manifold or onionskin) that accompanies a signed original. It may be routed to interested persons while the original is held by the recipient for reference or action.

courtesy line (credit line) Line of text placed at the bottom of an illustration or in a parenthetical phrase following the figure title, in which credit is given to the person or organization supplying the illustration. The courtesy line may read, for example, "Courtesy of John Doe Art Studios." The type should be no smaller than 6 point. Credit should be given at all times, but in lieu of a courtesy line a product may be identified in the figure title. Examples of such identification are "Robertson's Model E process camera" and "The Model E process camera manufactured by Robertson."

cover flap *See* MOUNTING AND FLAPPING.

cover paper Paper used as covering to protect the contents of advertising brochures, pamphlets, books, booklets, etc. It may be obtained with finishes such as ripple, smooth, linen, fabric, corduroy, and antique. Antique is the most popular finish, followed by smooth and ripple. Base stock ranges from mechanical wood pulp to sulfite, sulfate, soda-pulp, and rag papers. Various coated cover papers, including plain heavy, plastic-coated, cast-coated, metallic, and cloth-lined papers, can be obtained. These coats and finishes meet almost every requirement of good appearance and durability.

Basis weights range from 40 to 100 pounds (18.16 to 45.4 kg), 40, 50, 60, 65, and 85 pounds (18.16, 22.7, 27.2, 29.5, and 38.6 kg) being the most popular.

Some cover papers that are exceptionally heavily coated or are pasted in double thickness are sold in weights by points (10, 16, and 20 points). The basic size for all cover papers is 20 by 26 inches (50.8 by 66 cm), in 500 sheets, except for weights sold by points. *See also* TABLE 4 *on page 443.*

Craft-Color   Trade name for thin colored self-adhering acetate sheets manufactured by Craftint. The sheets are available in a glossy finish for display as well as in a matte finish for pencil and ink work. Thirty-five or more colors are available. The sheets are used for multicolor layouts, dummy packages, displays, color reproduction, charts, maps, graphs, etc. The vermilion color photographs black and may be used through its transparency for accurate layout register. The colors are available in specific degrees of transparency or opacity, designated as T for transparent, ST for semitransparent, and O for opaque.

Craf-Tech   Trade name for paste-ups by Craftint that include common pieces of hardware reproduced in various isometric views. These are especially useful in technical illustrating. *See Figure C-41.*

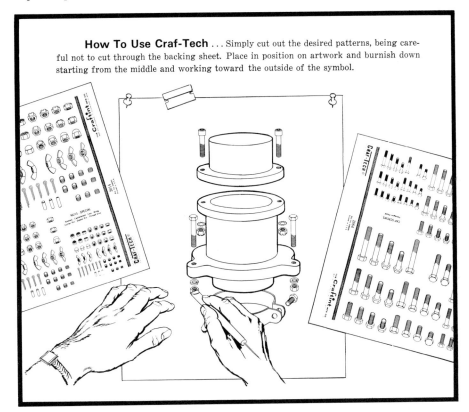

How To Use Craf-Tech ... Simply cut out the desired patterns, being careful not to cut through the backing sheet. Place in position on artwork and burnish down starting from the middle and working toward the outside of the symbol.

Fig. C-41 Application of Craf-Tech patterns.

Craftint   Trade name for paste-up and direct-transfer products of the Craftint Manufacturing Company. The products are used in newspaper

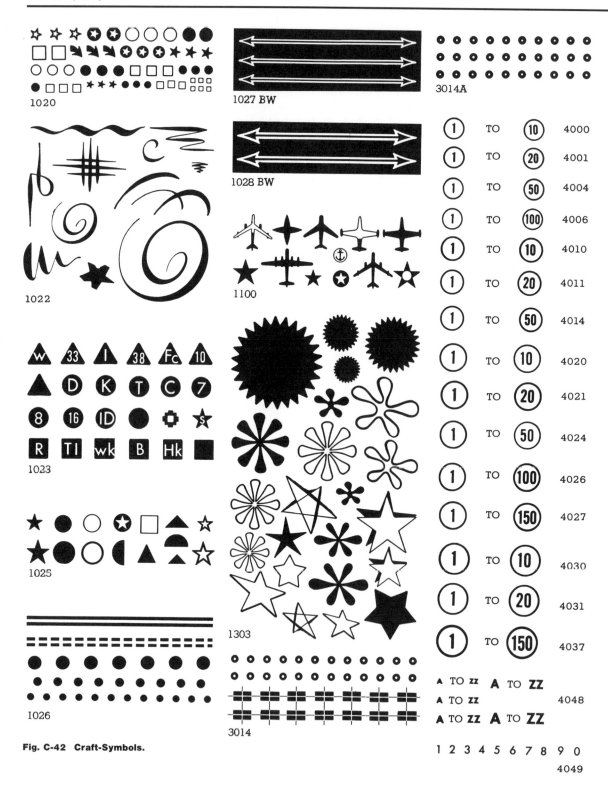

1020

1022

1023

1025

1026

1027 BW

1028 BW

1100

1303

3014

3014A

1	TO	10	4000
1	TO	20	4001
1	TO	50	4004
1	TO	100	4006
1	TO	10	4010
1	TO	20	4011
1	TO	50	4014
1	TO	10	4020
1	TO	20	4021
1	TO	50	4024
1	TO	100	4026
1	TO	150	4027
1	TO	10	4030
1	TO	20	4031
1	TO	150	4037

A TO zz   A TO ZZ
A TO zz   4048
A TO zz   A TO ZZ

1 2 3 4 5 6 7 8 9 0
                  4049

Fig. C-42   Craft-Symbols.

advertising, direct-mail pieces, catalogs, sales manuals, maps, graphs, cutaway drawings, architectural drawings, television and motion-picture titles, and other applications. Craftint categorizes its products as follows: Craf-Tech (line drawings of common hardware), Craf-Tone (shading mediums), Craf-Type (typefaces, symbols, sorts, etc.), and Letter-Set (dry-transfer sheets of alphabetical characters). For a discussion of these products, see CRAFT-TECH; CRAF-TYPE; SHADING MEDIUMS; TRANSFER SHEET.

Craft-Symbols Symbols manufactured by Craftint. They provide the artist with a library of symbols, from arrows to stars, to be used on layouts, finished art, and sign or presentation jobs. *See* Figure C-42.

Craf-Type Assembly of standard wax-backed acetate sheets of various typefaces and type sizes, symbols, characters, sorts, and designs by Craftint. A great variety of faces and sizes of type are obtainable (*see* Figure C-43). The range of sizes, which extends to a height of 1¼ inches (3.17 cm), permits pasting up for layouts of all kinds. The sheets are available in 35 colors for convenient use on direct chart presentations.

Pt.

18 Craf-Type. . .The Best and Fastest Method for Creative Letter 12345678
CE-25-3-18

24 Craf-Type. . .The Best and Fastest Method 12345
CE-25-3-24

NEW ANZIO 36 Craf-Type. . .The Best and 12345
CE-25-3-36

48 Craf-Type. . .The B 12345
CE-25-3-48

BARNUM 48 Craf-Type...The B 123
AU–2–3–48

84 craf-t 12
G-4-2-84

36 *Craf-Type. .The 12*
G-4-3-36I

18 Craf-Type . . .The Best and Fastest Metho 1234
G-45-3-18

BODONI 24 Craf-Type . . .The Best and Faste 123
G-45-3-24

36 Craf-Type...The Best a 123
G-45-3-36

48 Craf-Type..The B 12
G-45-3-48

Fig. C-43 Craf-Type (not actual size).

Thermo sheets, which have a specially prepared heat-resistant back, are obtainable for processes that involve heat during exposure, such as whiteprinting.

crash finish Linenlike paper finish. Its appearance is generally considered one of good taste.

creasing Making a partial fold in paper or board. Creasing by printing machines improves the endurance of sheets that must be folded, such as ledgers and heavy stock for cartons that are shipped "knocked down" and later assembled and formed for use.

credit line *See* COURTESY LINE.

creeping Movement of packing sheets on the blanket or plate cylinder of a printing press.

crimping Creasing paper, especially at a binding edge where pages fold, so that the pages will be exposed and the book will open easily. *See also* SCORING.

critical step Highest-numbered solid black step developed on an offset plate as indicated on a sensitivity guide. *See* SENSITIVITY GUIDE.

Cronar Registered trademark of Du Pont's polyester photographic film base. A fundamental study of polymer chemistry was made by Du Pont as long ago as 1928. In chemistry, polymerization is a reaction in which two or more molecules are combined to form larger molecules. In 1951, Du Pont produced experimental quantities of Cronar polyester photographic film base. This production demonstrated the feasibility of extruding a thick narrow web of polyester material and continually stretching and treating it to lock in the strength, durability, stability, and flexibility that are required in an ideal support for photographic emulsions. In January, 1957, the first polyester-based photographic product was made commercially available. The 0.004-inch (0.1016-mm) Cronar film base was designed for applications in which flexibility and tear strength are essential. Shortly thereafter Du Pont was able to supply a complete line of color-separation, color masking, and lithographic films on a common support, thereby eliminating the problem of trying to get different materials, such as glass and acetate, to register to each other. Polyester films are flexible, are only slightly affected by changes in relative humidity and temperature, and will not crack or break in normal use. They are extremely resistant to tearing, lie flat, have excellent optical characteristics for assuring maximum image sharpness, and will not become brittle or change size with age.

Du Pont manufactures 21 graphic arts products for offset lithography, letterpress, letterset (modernized dry offset), gravure, and silk-screen use. All but 3 are on a Cronar polyester photographic film base. *See also* ACETATE ORTHO LITHO FILM; CLEARBACK ORTHO LITHO FILM; CLEARBASE FILM; COMMERCIAL S FILM; HIGH CONTRAST PAN FILM; LITHO T PHOTOGRAPHIC PAPER; LOW CONTRAST PAN FILM; LOW GAMMA PAN FILM; MASKING (BLUE-SENSITIVE) FILM;

MEDIUM CONTRAST PAN FILM; ORTHO A FILM; ORTHO D FILM; ORTHO M FILM; ORTHO S FILM; PAN LITHO FILM; PAN MASKING FILM; SCREEN-PROCESS FILM.

crop mark Mark used to define the limit of the reproduction area of an illustration and to establish the portion of the image that is to appear in the reproduction (*see* Figure C-44). Crop marks determine the size the image will take. They should appear on all illustrations at each of the four corners, marking the vertical and horizontal dimensions of the image area. Crop marks should be definite, be drawn with black ink, and extend no closer than ¼ inch (0.635 cm) to the outside of the reproduction area. The area designated by the crop marks should be a true rectangle. Though crop marks do not appear on final reproduction copy, they may be retained on the negative as evidence of the dimensions of the art.

cropping Defining the reproduction-image area of line and continuous-tone art by drawing crop marks or of continuous-tone art by producing windows in negatives by means of dropout masks. Figure C-45 illustrates one method of cropping continuous-tone art. It includes the following steps:

1. Use a ruby- or amber-colored opaque stripping film slightly larger than the desired reproduction area of the photograph.

2. Secure the film with a strip of masking or other pressure-sensitive tape to the right of the mounted photograph along the vertical dimension. The tape serves as a hinge. Its left side must be straight and aligned to serve as the right edge of the masking window.

3. Place a piece of mounting stock beneath the mask to avoid cutting through to the photograph.

4. Use a frisket knife and cut the film in a true rectangle on the three remaining sides to form the reproducible area of the photograph.

5. Peel and strip away excess masking outside the rectangle.

6. Tape the whole to the camera copyboard.

7. Tape a sheet of white enameled paper between the photograph and the mask, making certain that the mask is correctly aligned.

8. Photograph a line negative of the mask and leave the negative in the camera.

9. Remove the enameled paper. Swing the mask on its taped hinge and tape it flush against the copyboard, exposing the photograph.

10. Make a normal screened-halftone exposure of the photograph.

The line shot photographs only the mask and entirely eliminates the image of the photograph. The negative is still light-sensitive where covered by the opaque mask and will accept the halftone image. Any instructions pertaining to the size, title, or classification of the photograph may be written on the mask with a black grease pencil. This technique can be varied by cutting the mask into the shape of a heart, letter, numeral, or any other configuration or symbol desired.

This use of a line shot and a screened shot should not be confused with cropping continuous-tone with line copy in a combination plate. In the latter technique, the line copy and continuous-tone copy are photographed by using two distinct negatives. The halftone is stripped into the line negative. *See also* COMBINATION PLATE.

Color blocks are fashioned by using various tints and shadings, as well as an opaque material (screened by the camera) that may be overprinted.

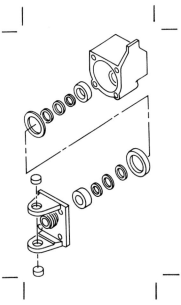

Fig. C-44 Application of crop marks.

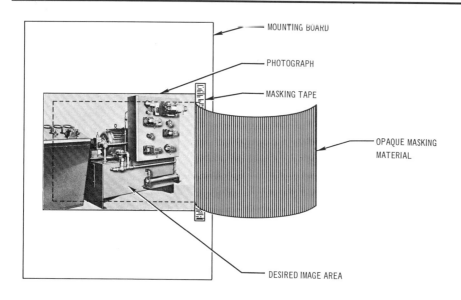

MOUNTING BOARD

PHOTOGRAPH

MASKING TAPE

OPAQUE MASKING
MATERIAL

DESIRED IMAGE AREA

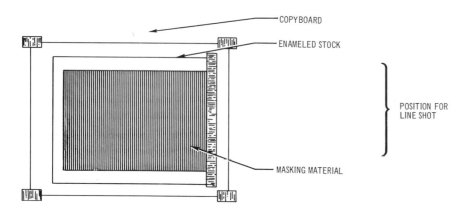

COPYBOARD

ENAMELED STOCK

POSITION FOR
LINE SHOT

MASKING MATERIAL

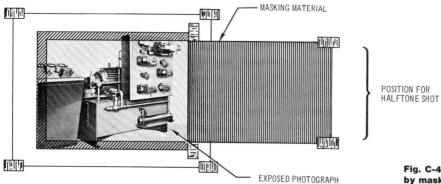

MASKING MATERIAL

POSITION FOR
HALFTONE SHOT

EXPOSED PHOTOGRAPH

**Fig. C-45   Cropping continuous-tone art
by masking.**

cross perforations In web-press work, perforations made across the web, at right angles to the direction of web travel, to prevent signatures from bursting during folding. The perforations emit air trapped between the sheets and relieve sheet tension.

cross-fold *See* CHOPPER FOLD.

cross-reference Direction to a reader to refer to related matter in another part of a publication.

cross-section grid *See* SQUARE GRID.

cross-section view Technical illustration of an object in which all or part of the object is cut away to show the shape and construction of the cutting plane and the relationship of adjacent parts. In Figure C-46, parts of an object are designated by numbers keyed to a legend (not shown) describing them. This type of view is used in technical manuals to illustrate maintenance instructions for the overhaul of equipment and repair of parts when the interior construction or hidden features of an object cannot be shown clearly by other views.

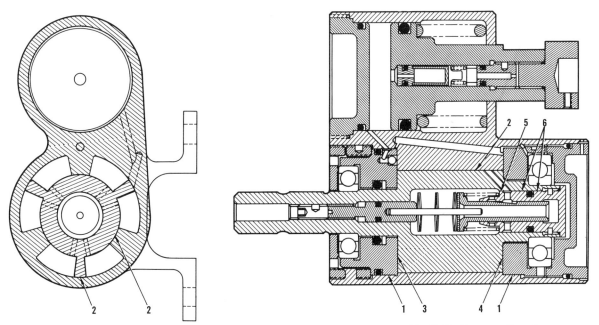

Fig. C-46 Cross-section view.

crow quill Very fine writing and drawing pen. The name is derived from the quill of the crow's wing, which was formerly cut to a fine point and used for writing with inks.

CRT Abbreviation for cathode-ray tube. *See* CATHODE-RAY TUBE.

cumulative supplement Supplement that includes all information contained in the preceding supplements of a publication and therefore supersedes them.

curl Measurement of the vertical distance above a surface to which the edges of a sheet of paper will curl. The measurement is used especially with papers that become damp or wet during a development process.

cursive Typeface that resembles handwriting; a designation for writing where the strokes of the letters are joined in each word.

cursor Seen on video display terminals, a visible position occupied anywhere on the screen within the appropriate unit of copy displayed. It serves as a reference point enabling the operator to position and arrange text copy on the screen.

curve chart Graphical representation that uses curves to reflect values such as time, distance, or any other condition desired (*see* Figure C-47). For example, the base of a chart may show a time value in years, months, weeks, or days, and the vertical dimension may reflect quantities. The curve chart is probably the most popular type of chart. *See also* BAR CHART; COLUMN CHART; PIE CHART; SURFACE CHART.

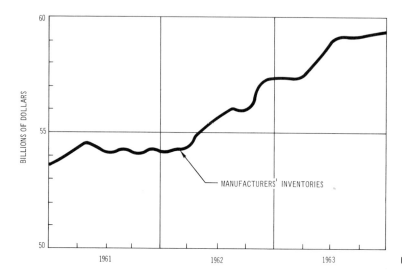

Fig. C-47 Curve chart.

curved plate Printing plate, commonly a stereotype or electrotype plate, that is curved to fit the plate cylinder of a rotary printing press.

cut Metal plate of an image from which the image is printed. The cut is prepared by photoengraving and has a relief (raised) surface. It is in reverse reading. When the image is imposed on stock, a right, or positive, reading results.

cut dummy Cut proofs of illustrations arranged in sequence to facilitate page makeup.

cut-in initial *See* INITIAL

cut list List of illustrations for a publication.

cutline Placing of a caption in an illustration. In addition, the meaning of the term has been broadened to include instruction to the printer to insert an illustration during makeup. An example is "CUTLINE: Fig. 1. Rate-control mechanism."

cutoff Paper dimension fixed by the size of the press cylinder, which limits the cutoff at right angles to the travel of the web. The opposing dimension is the width of the web; this can be varied. Common dimensions for a web-fed press are 36 inches (91.4 cm) in width by a 22¾-inch (57.8-cm) cutoff.

cutoff register control Auxiliary electronic device used to control register between the printed image and fold or web cutoff point. It involves photoelectric detection of the position of the image and automatic adjustment of web compensator rollers.

cutoff rule In a boxhead, the rule that separates divisions of a table and which extends for the full width of the table.

cutout Piece cut out of stock by a steel die. A rectangle may be cut out of the cover of a soft-cover booklet to expose the title or other pertinent information printed on an inside page.

cutting chart *See* TABLES 3, 4, *and* 5 *(pages 442–443)*.

cutting-plane line In engineering and mechanical drawings, a line indicating a plane in which a section is taken. It is designated as an "extra-thick" line. The line, together with arrows and letters, forms the cutting-line indication. The arrows, which are placed at the end of the cutting plane, indicate the direction from which the sections are viewed. The cutting plane may be a single continuous plane, or it may be bent or offset if details can thus be shown to better advantage. *See also* LINE CONVENTIONS: ENGINEERING DRAWINGS.

cylinder press, flatbed Printing press in which the printing form remains on a flatbed and the paper, which receives the impression, is held by grippers and revolves on a cylinder. The pressure applied between the cylinder and the form is controlled by packing the cylinder surface. A flatbed cylinder press is suitable for all kinds of work, from printing on heavy rough stock to producing delicate halftones and color reproductions. It may be used to print books, folders, broadsides, catalogs, printed forms, and brochures. With slight modifications, it may also be used as a cutting and creasing machine for heavy stock.

A two-color cylinder press has a single bed on which the plates for two colors are installed. Two fountains of different-colored inks are used, and each color has its own impression cylinder and ink-distributing system. When the first color has been printed from its impression cylinder, a transfer cylinder receives and transfers the paper to the second color-impression cylinder and prints the second color. Thus two colors are printed on one side of a sheet in one trip of the paper through the press.

cylindrical casting Stereotype cast into a curved mat for use on a rotary press. It is employed only in letterpress printing.

dagger The symbol †, used to key text or tabular matter to a footnote. It is the second of a series of reference marks. *See* REFERENCE MARKS.

daguerreotype Early type of photograph or photographic process in which the image is made on a light-sensitive silver-coated metallic plate or copper plate and developed by mercury vapor. The name is derived from the French inventor Louis J. M. Daguerre.

dampening Moistening the printing plate of an offset press. Lithography is based on the principle that grease and water do not mix. When ink rollers come in contact with the printing plate, its surface must be kept moist enough to prevent the ink from adhering to the part of the plate that has no image. The water solution is carried from the water pan to the plate by a roller partially immersed in the pan and then to dampening rollers, which moisten the plate. Considerable skill and experience are required to maintain the proper proportion of ink and water.

dampening solution *See* FOUNTAIN SOLUTION.

dancer roll Name given to the rider roller in a web press. *See* RIDER ROLLER.

dandy roll In paper manufacturing, the roller that contains the design, trademark, name, etc., and impresses these on the paper to form the watermark image.

dark-field illumination Method of viewing halftone dots on film. By viewing the halftone against a dark background with illumination coming from a side angle, one can observe the amount of fringe surrounding the solid core of the dot.

dark-print process Wet or dry process used to make the common blueprint. It was the first method of reproducing large drawings in quantity. In the dark-print process, copies are made from right-reading translucent originals. The image is white on a medium or dark blue background of contact size. Copies are made by exposure to light and development in an aqueous solution. The copies are then dried, either in the blueprint machine or by exposure to air.

The dark-print process is the opposite of the whiteprint process. In the dark-print process, what was black is made white and what was white is made black; in the whiteprint process, what is black stays black and what is white stays white.

The copy paper used in making blueprints is called blueprint paper. It is iron-sensitized (by impregnated ferric compounds), whereas in the whiteprint process material coated with diazo compounds is used for copy paper. Formerly, the translucent original drawing used in making a blueprint was placed in an ordinary glass frame on top of what was then called litmus paper. The exposure was made by holding the frame to the sunlight for a few seconds. Light penetrated the nonimage area, where it destroyed the dye in the litmus paper. The image protected the image area of the paper from the sunlight. The paper was then submerged in water and washed. The result was a blueprint, which was hung up to dry. The principle is the same today, but the method of production has changed from hand to machine. The blueprint machine operates by ultraviolet-light exposure, and the print is developed, washed, and dried in the machine. It is also possible to make blueprints in a whiteprint machine by using only the exposure unit and bypassing the development stage. Blueprint paper must be used. The prints are then washed and air-dried.

Blueprints can stand hard usage because the copy paper contains a good percentage of rag, and they hold up well in shop and field. As blueprints are made by a wet process, however, the linear scale is only fair.

data points Symbols used for plotting events or other information on graphs and charts. Data points (Figure D-1) are used with straight lines or with curves. A legend or key explains the meaning of each point. As an example, data points may be used to chart a sequence of events as the events take place or a sequence of proposed steps for a project. When open-faced data points are used, an event can be shown as having occurred by filling in the relevant point.

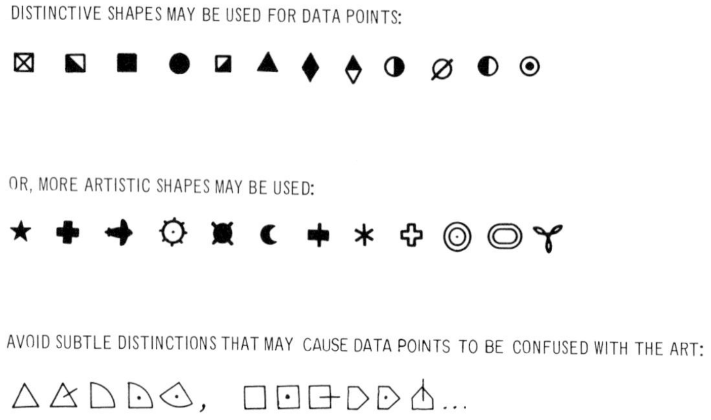

DISTINCTIVE SHAPES MAY BE USED FOR DATA POINTS:

OR, MORE ARTISTIC SHAPES MAY BE USED:

AVOID SUBTLE DISTINCTIONS THAT MAY CAUSE DATA POINTS TO BE CONFUSED WITH THE ART:

Fig. D-1   Data points.

datum line Line used in engineering and mechanical drawings to indicate the position of a datum plane. It is designated as a "thick" line and consists of one long and two short dashes evenly spaced. See also LINE CONVEN-TIONS: ENGINEERING DRAWINGS.

dead matter (killed matter) In hot-metal composition, lead type masses, plates, cuts, etc., that are no longer required and may be melted down, or "killed," for reuse of the lead.

dead metal Waste or unnecessary metal around or on a photoengraving. The metal is removed by cutting out, routing, or deburring.

dead time See DOWNTIME.

deadline Final time set for the completion of a task of any kind.

deaerate In printing and reproduction work, to remove the air between sheets of stock, particularly as applied to "jogging" by the use of joggers.

decalcomania (abbreviated **decal**) Art or process of transferring pictures and designs from specially prepared paper to china, glass, or other materials. Modern usage of decalcomania has been extended to include transferring images to almost any surface.

deckle edge (featheredge) Natural uncut feathery edge of paper. The effect may be produced either by hand or by machine, usually in antique papers because of the decorative value it adds to booklet covers, brochures, and direct-mail pieces.

dedication Brief inscription in which an author dedicates a book, usually in personal terms, to someone of his or her family, kin, or acquaintance. The dedication appears on a separate page in the front matter.

deep-etch plate Special offset plate printed from a film positive instead of a film negative. The unexposed image is given a surface etch to provide "tooth" for the enamel. The portion of the enamel or bichromated coating left on the plate after burning in or developing, which protects the covered areas from the acid etch, is removed later. The deep etch provides a rugged image because the enamel is laid directly on the etched surface rather than on the bichromate.

deglaze In lithography, to remove the dried layer of ink and gum from the press rollers and the offset blanket.

delayed dwell In a platen press, the time delay necessary in quality foil-stamping and embossing work, for which a combination of heat, impressional strength, and dwell-on impression is required. The heat is needed to soften the binders and coatings in paper, board, and other materials. Once the fibers in the stock have been softened, they can be realigned and reshaped to permit a sharp embossment. Heat is also required for foil stamping, and the increased dwell allows time for the heat to penetrate from the embossing or stamping die to the foil and thence to the stock. The delayed dwell is necessary to obtain proper adhesion of the foil to the stock. See also PLATEN PRESS.

dele Proofreader's mark indicating that a letter, word, phrase, sentence, or paragraph is to be deleted.

delineate In the graphic arts, to give depth to line art by making certain outlines heavier. The word also means "to describe in detail."

densitometer Photoelectric device that measures the density of photographic images and color printing.

density In general terms, the relative darkness of an image area as seen by the eye; in technical usage, a measure of light-stopping ability or blackening of a photographic image as read on a densitometer.

density, burnout *See* BURNOUT DENSITY.

density, maximum Highest density obtainable with a particular photographic or sensitized material after complete development. When one looks at a negative or a positive, the maximum density is the highest density noted.

density, minimum Lowest density noted on a photographic or sensitized material. The term is used in contrast to maximum density.

density range (density scale) Measured difference between the minimum and maximum densities of a particular negative or positive.

depth Thickness, measured downward from the surface of an object. The term "depth" is used only with objects having a third dimension, never to describe a plane surface.

descender *See* ASCENDER.

desensitize To render a photographic material less sensitive or insensitive by varying the application of light during exposure or developing. Increasing or decreasing exposure and developing will desensitize the material and cause over- and underdeveloping respectively.

detail assembly drawing In engineering drafting, an assembly drawing on which some items are shown in detail in lieu of preparing separate detail drawings.

detail drawing Engineering drawing that gives detailed information on an item. It includes the form, dimensions, material, finish, tolerances, and other requirements of the item. The term also denotes a drawing used to show parts of structures and the relationship of parts, their sizes, contour, and construction materials.

detail view In engineering drawing, a view which shows part of the principal view of an item, using the same plane and arrangement but in greater detail and on a larger scale. *See also* ORTHOGRAPHIC PROJECTION: ENGINEERING DRAWINGS.

developer In photography, a chemical used to render visible the image recorded on the photosensitive film, paper, or metal plate.

diagram drawing Engineering drawing that uses symbols to show the features and relationships of items and systems.

diamond Old type size. The nearest equivalent in the point system is 4½ point.

diazo compound   Mixture of diazo salts combined with an azo dyestuff component. The salts are sensitive to light, especially when ultraviolet light reflects on treated paper. The light destroys the salts, but the dye remains to reflect the image of the original. The whiteprint process of reproduction, as well as other methods of copying, uses paper, cloth, or film coated with diazo compounds. Diazo-treated film is employed extensively in microfilming.

diazo film   Film used as a flexible transparent base and coated with emulsions of diazo salts and couplers.

diazo-generated reproduction   Reproduction made from an image that has itself been reproduced by the whiteprint process or some other process in which a diazo compound is used as the emulsion-sensitive base.

diazo paper   Paper treated with a diazo compound and an azo dyestuff component. Reproduction of the image depends on the light sensitivity of the dye. Development is achieved by destroying the diazo compound, the dye remaining to reflect the image. By varying the azo dye, black, red, blue, or sepia colors are produced to form the image. Reproduction is accomplished by utilizing ultraviolet light for exposure; therefore, all originals or masters must be on transparent or translucent material such as vellum, tracing cloth, or film. *See also* WHITEPRINT PROCESS.

diazo print   Reproduction made by using the whiteprint process.

diazo process   *See* WHITEPRINT PROCESS.

Diazochrome projecturals   Diazo-sensitized films that produce colored-dye images on a transparent plastic base. Diazochrome is a trade name of Scott Graphics, Inc. The films are designed for use in overhead projectors and lend effectiveness to the 3¼ by 4-inch (8.3 by 10.1-cm) standard stereopticon. They are also used for displays, overlays, and novelties.

diazotype process   *See* WHITEPRINT PROCESS.

die cutting   Cutting cardboard, paper, card stock, or other material with regular or irregular designs formed into dies. Pressure is applied to the die press containing the die, and a lift of the material is cut. If the cut stock is to stay in the material, small pieces of cut material are left to hold the die-cut piece together until they can be punched out later, as is done during the assembly of a point-of-sale display box.

die stamping   Method of using steel, brass, or bronze dies to impress an image on a surface by using a relief counterpart or the reverse thereof. As a material such as paper, card stock, or foil is placed between these counterparts, impression rollers press and form the image. *See also* PLATEN PRESS.

dielectric-coated paper   Paper which is electrostatically charged in the desired image areas in a dot pattern and then passed through a liquid toner suspension of charged particles. The toner particles adhere to the paper wherever a charge exists, resulting in a permanent, high-content image. This paper is used in computer work and graphics.

differential letterspacing *See* PROPORTIONAL SPACING.

diffraction Apparent deflection of light into the geometrical shadow of an obstacle. Light appears to bend slightly around the edges of opaque material.

diffusion screen Screen used in photographic work to tone down or "soften" the image by eliminating glare and excessive highlights.

diffusion-transfer process Successful and popular method of producing an image from an original by the diffusion of chemicals, in which the image is transferred from a negative to a material such as paper or a flexible printing plate. The original may be opaque or translucent or may have copy on both sides of the sheet. The process is used largely by manufacturers of photocopying machines. Though grossly exaggerated for clarity, Figure D-2 portrays the negative-paper and copy-paper relationship. The center line divides the two papers. The original has already been exposed to the negative. The sensitive-emulsion side *B* of the negative paper is composed of gelatin and grains of silver salts. Transfer layer *C* of the copy paper is composed of gelatin also, in addition to silver sulfide or colloidal silver.

After exposure and during development, the negative paper is pressed against the copy paper as illustrated, with the emulsion side *B* of the negative paper and the transfer layer *C* of the copy paper in close contact. During development, the grains of silver salts in the emulsion side *B* of the negative paper which have been exposed to light (have not been protected by the image) are converted into black metallic silver; that portion of the negative appears black. Where the silver salts have not been exposed to light (have been protected by the image), they remain intact and the negative paper remains white. Thus a black-and-white negative image is formed on the negative paper. The undeveloped silver salt grains, which now represent the image, pass by diffusion into transfer layer *C* of the copy paper or other material, where, by chemical action, the salts are converted into black metallic silver and form the image on layer *C*. Thus black areas on layer *C*, which represent the image, are formed under the white areas of layer *B* of the negative, and a positive image of the original appears on the copy paper.

The Kodak PMT metal litho plate is a grained, anodized lithographic printing plate capable of providing run lengths up to 25,000 copies. The plate is coated on one side only with a non-light-sensitive layer that can be imaged from a special silver halide negative paper by the diffusion-transfer process. The plate is capable of copy-dot and normal line copy reproduction. The plate is available in most standard press sizes and with different end configurations to fit the plate cylinder requirements of most presses. The plate is for use on all types of offset presses and duplicators for in-plant printing work, general commercial work, newspapers, techni-

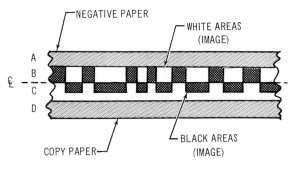

A. NEGATIVE – PAPER BASE
B. SENSITIVE – EMULSION SIDE OF
   NEGATIVE PAPER
C. TRANSFER LAYER OF COPY PAPER
D. COPY – PAPER BASE

Fig. D-2   Diffusion-transfer process.

cal bulletins, forms, and yearbooks. Exposure of the copy to Kodak PMT
litho negative paper creates an image that is conveyed chemically to the
lithographic plate by diffusion transfer in a special plate processor. After
transfer, application of a plate fixer to the plate makes the image area
receptive only to ink and the nonimage area receptive only to water. The
plate and the companion negative paper can be processed in a temperature range between 18.5 and 29.5°C (65 and 85°F). Although there is no
means provided for making additions to the plate, deletions are readily
accomplished. The plate will operate satisfactorily with a wide range of
fountain solutions and printing inks.

Deletions can be made either on the press or prior to mounting the plate
by following these steps:

1. Sheet the ink off the plate, if necessary.
2. Apply Kodak Litho plate gum wash to the area to be deleted.
3. Remove the unwanted image with a hone.
4. Treat the honed area with the gum wash and buff dry.

To process the plate, proceed as follows:

1. Position the exposed negative paper with its emulsion side in contact
with the coated side of the plate.
2. Align the plate/paper combination on the feed tray of the diffusion-
transfer processor according to instructions supplied with the processor.
3. Feed the paper and plate into the processor. When they exit, hold
them in contact for thirty to sixty seconds, remaining under safelight
conditions. Periods longer than sixty seconds may result in separation
problems.
4. Peel the negative paper away from the plate and discard the paper.
(Lights can now be turned on.)
5. Place the processed plate on a clean, dry surface such as a bench top
covered with newspapers.
6. Immediately after peeling, pour at least ¼ oz (7 or 8 ml) of Kodak PMT
metal plate fixer per square foot (929 square centimeters) of plate material
onto the plate. With minimal pressure, work the plate fixer evenly across
the entire plate surface with a fiber pad for a minimum of thirty seconds.
The plate surface should still be damp after thirty seconds of fixing.

Caution: The fixing step is very important; either decreasing the amount of fixer or reducing the length of time of fixing may cause blinding.

7. With the plate still damp with fixer, and using the same fiber pad used for fixing, apply the gum wash to the plate surface. Use at least ¼ oz (7 or 8 ml) of gum wash per square foot (929 cm^2) of plate and work into the entire plate. With a dry fiber pad, buff the plate to dryness. *Caution:* Do not use water on the plate during either the fixing or gumming operation.

The Kodak PMT paper litho plate is composed of a resin coating on a paper support. It is a lithographic printing plate capable of providing run lengths of at least 2,000 copies under normal operating conditions. The plate is coated on one side only with a non-light-sensitive layer that can be imaged from a special silver halide negative paper by the diffusion-transfer process. The plate is capable of copy-dot and normal line copy reproduction. The plate is available in most standard small press and duplicator sizes and with different end configurations to fit the plate cylinder requirements of most presses. The paper plate is for use on all types of small offset presses and duplicators. Web press work is not recommended. Exposure of the copy to Kodak PMT litho negative paper in a standard process camera creates an image. This image is conveyed chemically to the paper plate by diffusion transfer in a special plate processor that is recommended, although any processor capable of handling Kodak PMT negative and PMT receiver paper may be used if set up properly. After transfer, application of the paper plate fixer to the plate makes the image area receptive to ink and the nonimage area receptive to water. The paper plate and negative paper can be processed in temperatures ranging between 18.5 and 29.5°C (65 and 85°F). Additions and deletions are readily accomplished. The plate will operate satisfactorily with a wide range of fountain solutions and printing inks. The plate itself is unaffected by light, but negative paper, onto which the exposures are made, is an orthochromatic material that must be handled under red safelight illumination for both exposure and processing.

To process the plate, proceed as follows:

1. Position the exposed negative paper with its emulsion side in contact with the coated side of the paper plate.

2. Align the plate/paper combination on the feed tray of the diffusion-transfer plate processor according to the instructions supplied with the processor.

3. Feed the paper and plate into the processor. When they exit, hold them in contact for thirty to sixty seconds while under safelight conditions. Periods longer than sixty seconds may result in separation problems.

4. Peel the negative paper away from the plate. Discard the negative paper. (Lights can now be turned on.)

5. Fix the plate with Kodak PMT paper plate fixer. The actual process/fix/run sequence will vary slightly as shown in Table D-1, but the procedure for fixing does not change. The fixing procedure is as follows:

    a. Pour a liberal amount of paper plate fixer onto the plate surface (at least ¼ oz [7 or 8 ml] per square foot [929 square centimeters] of plate material).

    b. With minimal pressure, work the plate fixer evenly across the plate

TABLE D-1 Process, Fix, Run Sequence

If Plates **Can** Be Fixed at the Press (Preferred)	If Plates **Must** Be Fixed During Platemaking	If Plates Are Run **Immediately** After Platemaking
1. Process in a diffusion-transfer processor.	1. Process in a diffusion-transfer processor.	1. Process in a diffusion-transfer processor.
2. Peel away negative paper.	2. Peel away negative paper.	2. Peel away negative paper.
3. Wipe excess activator from both sides of plate.	3. Apply and work in fixer.	3. Apply and work in fixer. Remove excess fixer from the plate with a clean pad dampened with water.
4. Allow to dry. Stack plates only when completely dry.	4. Rinse both sides of the plate thoroughly in room-temperature running water for at least 15 seconds.	4. Plate can be run while still damp. Use normal start-up procedures.
5. Fix immediately prior to running on press. Remove excess fixer from the plate with a clean pad dampened with water or fountain solution. Use normal start-up procedures.	5. Air-dry completely.	
	6. Run when desired, using normal start-up procedures.	
Plates processed in this manner can be stored, unfixed, for 3 to 4 weeks.	*Plates processed in this manner can be stored for 3 to 4 weeks.*	*Plates processed in this manner should be started on press within 1 hour of fixing, and should not be stacked.*

surface with a clean fiber pad for a minimum of thirty seconds. At the end of thirty seconds, the plate should still be wet with plate fixer.

c. Remove excess fixer from the plate with a clean pad dampened with water or fountain solution. The plate is now ready for the press. Refer to Kodak Publication No. Q-207 for additional information.

Figure D-3 shows nuArc's Model P2500 diffusion-transfer processor. The machine has been designed to accommodate large copy such as full newspaper pages. Two feed rollers feed the material into a chemical tray at a constant speed for uniform end-to-end processing. An adjustable side guide ensures precision lineup for small or large sheets. The material is held in a carrier after it leaves the processor; a timing lever is pushed and an indicator light goes on for thirty seconds and then goes off; then a timer bell rings to signal that the material is ready to be pulled apart. The P2500 processor has a wide material capacity of 24 inches (61 cm) to any length. The processor and table has adjustable leg levelers. Chemical capacity of the processor is 3½ quarts (3.71 L).

Fig. D-3 nuArc's Model P2500 diffusion-transfer processor.

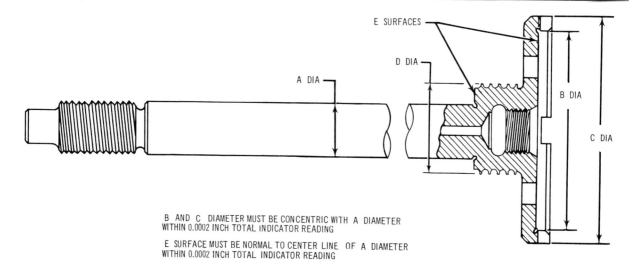

B AND C DIAMETER MUST BE CONCENTRIC WITH A DIAMETER WITHIN 0.0002 INCH TOTAL INDICATOR READING

E SURFACE MUST BE NORMAL TO CENTER LINE OF A DIAMETER WITHIN 0.0002 INCH TOTAL INDICATOR READING

A	B	C	D
0.3936 IN. MIN	1.4370 1.4372 IN.	1.62 1.64 IN.	0.6545 IN. MIN

Fig. D-4 Dimension or inspection drawing.

dimension drawing (inspection drawing) Cross-sectional illustration used in overhaul and maintenance technical manuals to instruct personnel how to inspect, repair, and replace parts of equipment so that the equipment may be kept within designed operating tolerances. In Figure D-4, supporting text instructs repair personnel on the disposition of parts that do not meet the requirements outlined in the illustration.

dimension line In orthographic engineering and mechanical drawings, a line used to indicate the dimension between two points. It is designated as a "thin" line. Dimension lines are unbroken except where space is required to insert the dimension. *See also* LINE CONVENTIONS: ENGINEERING DRAWINGS.

dimensional stability, photographic film *See* FILMS AND PLATES.

dimensioning *See* SCALING.

dimetric projection *See* AXONOMETRIC PROJECTION.

dinky In newspaper jargon, a half roll (web) of paper measured along the width, not along the diameter. For a 14-page newspaper, 12 pages would be produced from three full rolls and a dinky roll would be provided to print the remaining 2 pages. The four webs (three full webs and one dinky) would then be joined at the former section to produce the 14 pages.

diploma paper (art parchment) Fine printing paper manufactured especially for greeting cards, official documents, certificates, awards, diplomas, and the like. The paper may contain up to 100 percent rag; the basic size is 17 by 22 inches (43.1 by 55.8 cm) and the basis weight 50 pounds (22.7 kg).

direct color separation Color separation in which the various separation exposures are made through a halftone screen so that screened separation negatives may be obtained directly. *See also* COLOR SEPARATION.

direct-copy process *See* WHITEPRINT PROCESS.

direct entry In photographic typesetting, a term used to describe a keyboard that inputs directly to the phototypesetter, as opposed to a paper tape, wire service, or other remote method.

direct image Image applied directly to a paper or printing plate. *See* DIRECT PLATEMAKING.

direct mail Literature mailed by an advertiser directly to an addressee, usually to promote or sell a product or a service.

direct platemaking Any method of applying an image on the surface of a coated printing plate without intermediate steps (*see* Figure D-5). Direct platemaking is particularly suitable for producing an image on paper plates. Intermediate steps are used for indirect plate making with a process camera, xerographic photocopying machines, and other processes. Any typewriter can be used for typing text on paper plates, although lines are ruled with ink or drawn with a special reproducing pencil. Corrections are marked on the plate with a nonreproducing pencil. The nonreproducing-pencil marks dissolve when washed off the plate by an aqueous solution during the first few revolutions of the master cylinder.

An image may also be applied directly to the plate by preprinting or with an ink pen, graphite or grease pencil, ball-point pen, rubber stamp, brush, or crayon. Colors are produced by making separate color plates in register with the use of a light table.

The offset method of printing is based on the principle that grease and water do not mix. The master plate is placed on the master cylinder of the duplicator, and the aqueous solution is applied to the plate from a fountain. The solution is repelled by the grease-receptive image but is accepted by the nonimage area on the master. The ink adheres only to the grease-receptive image and is repelled from the wet nonimage area of the plate. As the master cylinder revolves, the various rollers continue to supply the solution and ink to the plate on the master cylinder. The image is transferred from the master plate to a cylinder containing a rubber blanket. An impression cylinder then brings paper in contact with the blanket cylinder, thus offsetting the image from blanket to paper.

display advertisement Advertising matter, with or without illustrations, composed of a size, design, and variety of typefaces to attract reader attention and promote or sell a product or service.

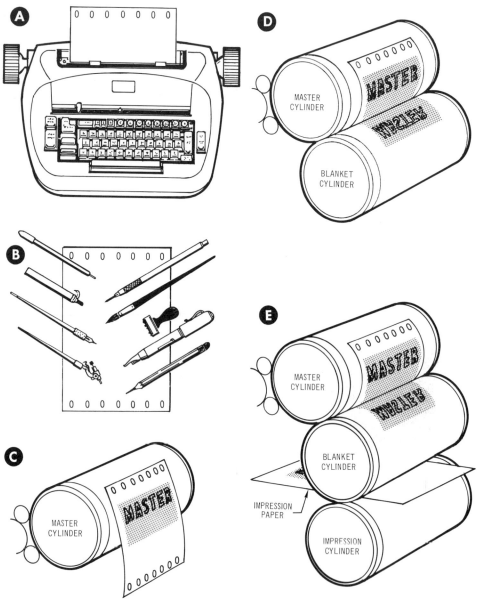

display blank Paper manufactured especially for show cards, posters, outdoor advertising, etc. Standard sizes are 22 by 28 by 44 inches (55.8 by 71.1 by 111.7 cm). Display blanks may range in thickness from 2-ply (0.012 inch; 0.304 mm) to 16-ply (0.056 inch; 1.422 mm). The most popular thicknesses are 6-ply (0.024 inch; 0.609 mm) and 8-ply (0.030 inch; 0.762 mm). Popular colors are velvet white, white, ivory buff, light tan, yellow, light green, light blue, pink, oyster gray, black, imperial blue, scarlet, orange, and shamrock green.

display board Heavy blank board used for display advertising. The standard size is 40 by 60 inches (101.6 to 152.4 cm). Some boards are coated and colored on both sides with the same color; coats are usually dull. The popular thicknesses are 14-ply, 28-ply, and 43-ply [0.048 inch (1.220 mm), 0.096 inch (2.440 mm), and 0.159 inch (4.038 mm-ply)]. Colors are ivory, canary, ultramarine, blue, shamrock green, black, cardinal, and snow white. The surfaces have a good tooth for crayon, charcoal, ink and paint.

display type Large type used for magazine and newspaper headings, posters, etc. The type is distinguished from body type, or text type, used for text material, and is always larger than 12 point in size. Display type is also used for display advertising. *See also* TYPE SPECIMENS.

display typesetters *See* TYPESETTERS, PHOTOGRAPHIC.

discretionary In phototypesetting, a term used to describe the method by which an operator may inhibit the automatic mode by overriding that which has already been introduced on the keyboard, as opposed to logic where machine intelligence rules.

disk (variant of *disc*) Flat photomatrix used in phototypesetting equipment that contains an assortment of typeface designs. The characters bear a transparent image, for light emission, with an opaque background. The number of typeface designs on the disk multiplied by the number of type sizes in the lens system is the mixing capability equivalent to the number of fonts at a one-time machine setup.

distemper *See* TEMPERA.

distribution rollers Printing press rollers that mesh and operate to deliver an equal distribution of ink to the form roller of the printing press. The ink is picked up from the ink fountain by the fountain roller.

divider *See* INDEX GUIDE.

doctor blade Blade that wipes clean the flooded ink on the surface of a printing press and leaves only the ink remaining in the recesses of the plate to form the image. The doctor blade is used only in intaglio (gravure) printing.

document, engineering *See* ENGINEERING DOCUMENT.

dodger Small handbill. *See* HANDBILL.

dodging Method used in printing photographs to create greater contrast between light and dark areas. The effect is obtained by moving a light screen between the light-exposure source and the photographic paper. Dodging is used in the aerospace industry to improve photographs photographed from outer space.

dogleg Colloquial term for a bent lead line. A lead line is drawn off in one direction and turned at an angle to point to or indicate an item or to call out an item or part on an illustration. The first part of the lead line is horizontal. The line then "doglegs" to point out the object and, in most cases, terminates in an arrowhead.

dot Smallest individual element of a halftone negative or halftone printing plate.

dot area Halftone pattern consisting of dots and the clear spaces between them. The percentage of the area that is occupied by the dots (which may consist of developed silver, printing ink, etc.) is known as the percentage of dot area. In a checkerboard pattern the percentage of dot area is 50 percent.

dot etching Changing tone values by chemically reducing the size of, or "etching," halftone dots. This method is used in lithography when tone values or color strength must be changed during the photographic steps rather than on the printing plate.

dot formation Arrangement of dots in halftone screens. Continuous-tone art, that is, art as it appears before being screened (such as in the common photographic snapshot), is composed of various tones or shades. The tones range from white through a variety of grays to dense black. The tones cannot be reproduced as they appear to the eye but must be reduced to many rows of dots that stand apart so that the dots will receive ink. To produce a halftone, the photographer or engraver places a fine transparent halftone screen containing many broken or dotted lines in front of the negative material in a process camera to break up the continuous-tone image into dots of black and white. There are two types of screens: ruled glass screens and contact screens. *See also* HALFTONE SCREENING.

dot gain Slight enlargement of a halftone dot during exposure or development or on the printing press.

dot leaders *See* LEADERS.

dot loss Disappearance of a halftone dot from the printing press plate.

double-burn To "burn" images in register on a sensitized plate from two or more different negatives.

double-coated paper Heavily coated paper. It is not necessarily coated on two sides but may be double-coated on one side only. Requirements for coated-two-sides, double-coated-one-side, or double-coated-two-sides paper should be stated specifically.

double-digest fold One of the four basic folds used in web offset printing to produce signatures. The other three basic folds are the newspaper fold, tabloid fold, and catalog or magazine fold.

double former folder Auxiliary device used in web offset printing that produces a double fold for further folding, or cutting and folding, or for finishing in the bindery. This device is available for handling various paper widths. *See* Figure D-6.

double image Two impressions of an entire image or of a portion of an image. A double image is, of course, undesirable. In printing, a double image may be caused by pages touching each other during the pressrun while the ink is still wet. In the process of making plates, negatives, or projection or contact prints, a double image may be caused by a movement of the copy, plate, or negative during exposure.

double-imprint unit In a web-fed press, a unit with two sets of cylinders that permits an imprint to be changed while the press is running at full speed.

double spread (double truck) *See* CENTER SPREAD.

double sticky back Tape composed of a backing upon which an adhesive is affixed. The tape is burnished in place with the adhesive side placed down. The backing is then removed, exposing the adhesive to which paper, film, acetate, plastic, or wood can be attached. The tape is supplied in rolls of various widths and thicknesses. It is useful in many applications.

double up To set lines of type in columns when a line set will be too wide. Lines are usually doubled up when a line measure is 30 picas (127 mm) or more in width.

Doubletone Sheet of high-grade board stock manufactured by the Craftint Manufacturing Company. It is processed with two invisible shading screens, one of a light tone and the other of a dark tone. The artist applies one of two different developers to bring out the tone desired on the drawing. *See also* SHADING MEDIUMS.

downtime (dead time) Lost time due to malfunction of equipment, such as a breakdown during a pressrun, or loss of time when the time is chargeable to a job. The term also denotes a period of time when personnel are not working and are charging time against an assignment or a work-order number.

draft To compose a drawing or an illustration, usually with the intention of adding refinements after examination; also, to sketch an object. As a noun, the term denotes a preliminary version, such as a rough draft or first draft of a manuscript. A final draft is the copy to be printed, duplicated, or reproduced.

drafting, automated Method of producing an image by means of a computer, the graphic information being transposed into digital form and the digital data converted into a graphic display. Originally, automated drafting was confined primarily to engineering design and drafting work.

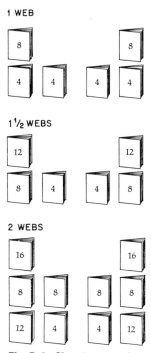

Fig. D-6 Signatures produced by the double-former folder. (*Courtesy of American Type Founders.*)

Now art pieces, such as electrical and mechanical schematics, flow diagrams, and charts as well as other line drawings, are made with the aid of computers. Isometric, perspective, trimetric, and dimetric illustrations are all possible. Automatic drafting equipment is complex and sophisticated, and a complete explanation of its operation cannot be presented here. The following discussion is intended to show technological advances and trends in automated drafting.

There are four general procedures for producing images with automated equipment:

1. The designer makes a layout of the object and designates reference points with dimension values, which the computer interprets as connecting lines.

2. The reference points are converted to numerical values, and these values are inserted in electrical-accounting-machine (EAM) cards as punched holes.

3. An individual called a "programmer" sorts the cards in a succession of desired drawing steps according to the value expressed by the punched holes.

4. A magnetic tape is produced by the computer from the deck of punched cards. The tape operates in conjunction with a device called a "plotter," which contains the inking pen that forms the image on paper.

Figure D-7 shows Gerber Scientific Instrument Company's laser-controlled photoplotting system Model 1434. It has the capability of producing large-scale artwork in sizes up to 16 by 22 inches (40.6 by 55.9 cm) at a maximum speed of 170 inches (431.8 cm) per minute on a high-resolution glass plate. The ultra-precise laser interferometer measurement system advances the precision of large area photoplotting from the "mil" to the "microinch." The system optically measures the distance from the exposing

Fig. D-7 Gerber's laser-controlled photoplotting system Model 1434.

light beam to the outer references of the plotting material and eliminates potential error sources including thermal growth, mechanical distortion of machine elements, roll, pitch, yaw of the X and Y carriages, guideway straightness, and orthogonality. The optical exposure head is capable of drawing lines from 0.00050 to 0.060 inch (0.0127 to 1.524 mm) and flash exposes precomposed images. Because a single objective lens is used to plot on photosensitive material, only one point must be located precisely over the photographic emulsion. The optical photohead enables lines as small as 0.001 inch to be drawn to width tolerances of 50 microinches. While a wide variety of standard apertures is offered, special apertures are available to meet unique user demands. The 1434 Photoplotter has a mini-computer controller designed for use with Gerber's Model 34 plotting table.

Software package functions include: linear interpolation of English or metric coordinate data, data buffering, "look ahead" for velocity optimization, smoothing on straight lines, and 10-microinch input resolution. While the 1434 is used as either an off-line or on-line terminal to Gerber's Interactive Design System (Figure D-8), the system can be interfaced to input devices such as cards or magnetic or paper tape, or directly on-line to another computer system. The computer is of solid-state integrated circuit construction, with a 12K word core and 16-bit word length. It has a 70-instruction repertoire. In the line drawing mode, image rotation is 360° in 0.1° increments.

Figure D-8 is Gerber's Interactive Design System (IDS) for use by circuit designers, mechanical designers, cartographers, architects, and engineers in general. It provides hardware and software tools needed to create, compose, digitize, draw, and edit mechanical drawings, artwork masters, photogrammetric plans, schematics, and manufacturing and architectural drawings. The system combines a full three-dimensional design and

Fig. D-9   Gerber's automatic artwork generator Model PC-740-E system.

drafting capability with a set of algorithms which utilize the drawing data to automatically generate the tool paths for numerically controlled (N/C) machining. The software system is constructed as three sets of applications functions, all working on the same data base. The geometric construction subsystem provides the mechanical designer with the ability to describe the geometry of a part utilizing interactive graphics instead of the conventional drafting tools. The designer may then call upon the drafting subsystem which aids in dimensioning, labeling, and adding notes to complete documentation of the design.

To complete the transition from design concept to manufacturing release, the N/C programmer utilizes the N/C portion of the system. Working with the geometric description created during the design process, the programmer then selects the sequence of machining operations to be performed. The system will automatically generate the necessary N/C tool paths to machine the part based on parameters entered by the programmer. Included in the system's repertoire are algorithms for drilling, pocket and profile cutting, and three- to five-axis surface contouring. During the N/C programming process, the programmer receives immediate visual verification of each tool path; this enables correction of any errors during the programming process and eliminates test cutting to prove out a tape. The system is built around a central process which includes a 24K minicomputer with floating-point hardware and a 2.4-million-word disk. Attached to the central processor is a selection of up to six terminals.

Figure D-9 is Gerber's automatic artwork generator Model PC-740-E system. It is a self-contained computer graphics center that provides control over printed circuit artwork generation. (*See* Figure D-10.) Specifically, aspects such as data preparation, input, processing, and output for artwork masters are controlled, and finished artwork masters are produced, starting with a rough gridded layout of the circuit board. Because all processing is accomplished within the mini-computer, no additional computer capability is required. The system consists of a Gerber GCD-PC digitizer connected to a customer-supplied card punch, a stored program Model 700 control unit, a high-speed photoelectric card reader, and a Model 40 precision plotting table. The table includes a

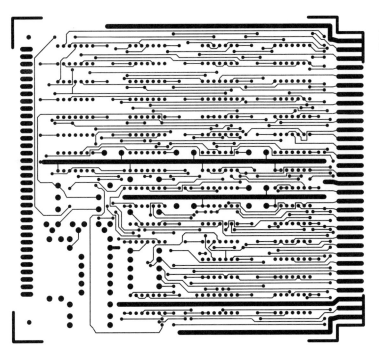

Fig. D-10 Example of printed circuit master.

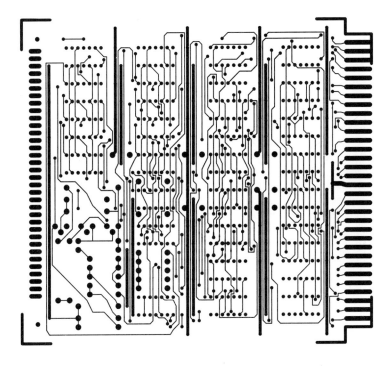

photo-optical exposure head whose light source is a tungsten halogen incandescent lamp. The Gerber turnkey feature ensures compatability between digitizer output, command language, processor input, and artwork generation. Correcting and editing is done instantly.

The PC-740-E system has an automatic artwork generator designed for the production of full size (1:1) printed circuit masters (*see* Figure D-9). The table provides a 16 by 20-inch (40.6 by 50.8-cm) drawing surface which moves under the photo-optical exposure head mounted to a fixed beam over the plotting table. The table has a positioning accuracy of 0.001 inch (0.0254 mm) and repeatability of 0.0005 inch (0.0127 mm) at a speed of 150 inches (3.810 m) per minute.

drafting machine Machine (*see* Figure D-11) that combines the functions of a T square or straightedge, a triangle, scales, and a protractor in one unit. Since it is controlled entirely by one hand, the other hand is left free for drawing. In operation, the scale assembly moves only in parallel. Thus, when the machine is set so that one scale is horizontal and the other vertical, the operator has a T square horizontally and a triangle vertically. When a triangle angle is required, the operator can shift and snap the scale assembly into place at any unit multiple of 15°. By releasing a lever, the scale assembly can be shifted without changing the zero setting of the protractor. This adjustment is used to align the scales to the base of a new drawing. Since the adjustment has a range of 180°, the scales can be set to operate from any oblique base with a zero setting of the protractor. Scales are available in a wide variety of graduations suitable for any type of work. They are adjustable and interchangeable.

drafting and tracing materials Paper, cloth, or film may be used for drafting and tracing. These materials are characterized by their stability, tear strength, erasability, translucency, permanency, and ability to accept pencil and ink. Drafting papers must be translucent for whiteprint reproduction, be sufficiently translucent for tracing, and have good erasing characteristics. Erasability is of major importance. The weight, transparency, and strength of tracing papers vary with their manufacture. The greater the rag content, the greater the strength; but transparency may thus be sacrificed. Natural tracing paper should be used for sketching only when permanency is desired. Prepared tracing papers, which are treated with synthetic resins for translucency and drawing finish, combine strength and transparency.

Drafting cloth combines the advantages of transparency, strength, surface finish, and permanency. It will withstand repeated erasures without major surface deterioration, and aging does not affect its drawing or reproduction capability. Although drafting cloth is erroneously referred to as linen, it consists of cotton fibers treated with starch in the manufacturing process so that they will accept ink or pencil. Unless the cloth is resistant to moisture, however, white spots will appear because starch is water-soluble. If the cloth is exposed to excessive moisture, it will shrink and lose stability and the surface finish will be destroyed.

drawdown Speed and effectiveness with which air is evacuated from a vacuum contact printing frame. Also, in inspecting printing inks, the act of

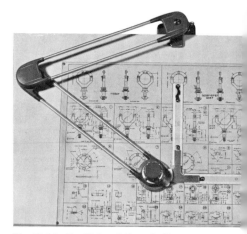

Fig. D-11 Keuffel and Esser's Paragon drafting machine.

depositing ink on paper by using a smooth-edge blade to evaluate under-tone and mass-tone of the ink.

driers Substances added to inks to hasten their drying. They consist mainly of metallic salts which exert a catalytic effect on the oxidation and polymerization of the oil vehicles employed.

drilling Using a rotating die or drill to make holes in sheets of stock or binding. It is preferable to employ the term "drilling" when this method is used and "punching" when ordinary paper punches are used.

drop folio Page number appearing at the foot of a page.

drop-out blue *See* FADE-OUT BLUE.

drop shadow Shadow of an image appearing behind the image, pro-duced in such a manner that it is subordinate to the image. Drop shadows are common in logotypes and display advertising.

dropout Halftone negative, print, or plate from which certain areas present in the original have been removed by masking or opaquing. A silhouette dropout is one in which the entire background has been removed to emphasize the central image. The term "dropout" is also widely used to describe the blocking or masking out of any undesirable or unwanted image area.

drum Drumlike photomatrix, containing an assortment of typeface de-signs, that is used in photocomposition equipment. The characters bear a transparent image for light emission with an opaque background. The number of typeface designs on the drum multiplied by the number of type sizes employed in the lens system is the mixing capability and is equivalent to the number of fonts used at a one-time machine setup. Because of interchangeability of photomatrices, the number of fonts will vary in proportion to the number of typeface designs on the photomatrix.

dry diazo process Whiteprint process that employs ammonia vapor in the developing stage to reproduce contact-size copies from transparent or translucent originals. The development of this process dates to World War I, when a substitute reproduction process was needed to relieve the shortage of critical photographic papers. In Germany, a Benedictine lay brother named Koegel knew that certain combinations of diazo chemicals were sensitive to light. Believing that these chemicals could be applied to paper and other materials, he got in touch with a dye manufacturer, who provided him with chemicals for experiment. The result of his success, combined with the many improvements that have been made in the process, is evident. Figure D-12 illustrates how colored image lines are formed by the chemical reaction of two substances in the coating, one a light-sensitive diazo compound and the other an azo dyestuff component, which produces the color when the component couples with the diazo compound. Coupling takes place when the coating is subjected to ammonia vapor.

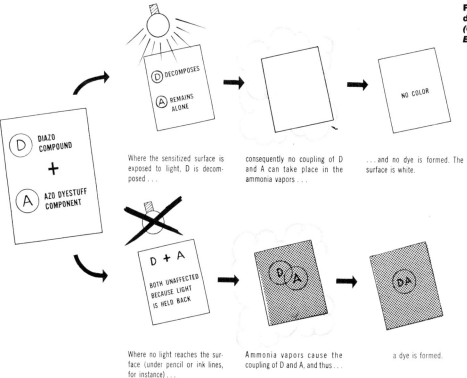

Fig. D-12 Principles of dry diazo process. (Courtesy of Keuffel and Esser Co.)

D DIAZO COMPOUND + A AZO DYESTUFF COMPONENT

D DECOMPOSES A REMAINS ALONE

NO COLOR

Where the sensitized surface is exposed to light, D is decomposed . . .

consequently no coupling of D and A can take place in the ammonia vapors . . .

. . . and no dye is formed. The surface is white.

D + A BOTH UNAFFECTED BECAUSE LIGHT IS HELD BACK

Where no light reaches the surface (under pencil or ink lines, for instance) . . .

Ammonia vapors cause the coupling of D and A, and thus . . .

a dye is formed.

dry-dot etching Manipulating contact exposures to increase or reduce dot sizes. Selective etching, or etching more in one place than another, is accomplished by using a mechanical or photomechanical mask in the contacting procedure.

dry finish High finish obtained in paper without the use of moisture while the paper is being processed through calender rolls during manufacture.

dry ink (also called **powder ink: toner**) Very fine powder used to form the image in some copying processes and in electrostatic screen printing. In the electrostatic process, dry ink, when automatically brushed onto the surface of the copy paper, adheres to a defined area to form the image by electrostatic attraction. The xerographic method employs a selenium-coated drum to which the image is attracted by electrostatic forces. The image is transferred to copy paper by rotating the drum. Electrostatic screen printing involves the deposit of dry ink on the receiving substratum. In all cases, the ink must be fused by heat or chemical means to fix the image.

dry mat paper *See* MATRIX PAPER.

dry mounting Method of mounting photographs without paste or rubber cement. A light thin paper called mounting tissue is used in conjunction with heat to mount photographs, prints, or other materials. The tissue acts as an adhesive between the copy or print and the mounting board. The procedure is as follows: (1) the mounting tissue is tacked to the back of the print with a hot iron, leaving the corners free; (2) the tissue is trimmed to the same size as the print; (3) the tissue and the print are positioned on the mounting board; (4) the face of the print is covered with clean paper and placed in a hot mounting press at a temperature ranging from 200 to 250°F, and pressure is applied for about ten seconds or longer. The duration of the pressure, which depends on the thickness of the print, allows the print to adhere to the mounting board as the result of heat. An ordinary electric hand iron may be used if a mounting press is not available. Care should be taken to have the iron hot enough to render the adhesive, but not hot enough to scorch the print. When color prints are being mounted, a somewhat lower temperature should be used. An electric hand iron should not be employed because its lowest setting may be too hot for color prints.

dry offset   *See* LETTERSET PRINTING.

dry-offset printing plate   Printing plate designed for use without the necessity of using a fountain solution.

dry stripping   Removal of the stripping layer from a film after the film has been processed and dried.

dry-to-dry processing   Method of operation of an automatic film processor. The processor is loaded with unexposed dry film; it processes the film automatically through the stages of feeding, developing, fixing, washing, and drying, and then deposits the dry processed negative in a receiving tray.

drybrush   Rendering technique used to give a shaded or hatched effect to art. The drawing medium—ink, watercolors, oils—is laid on in excess while it is wet. Then a stiff dry or damp brush is used to spread and brush the medium to other areas of the drawing.

dryer (or **drying oven**)   In web-press work, an oven located after the last printing unit through which the web passes. The dryer heats the web roll to a temperature as high as 350°F to dry heat-set inks. Gas, electricity, or steam may be used as the heating medium. Air blasts are employed to disperse volatile gases.

drypoint   Engraving made by using a sharply pointed instrument or needle directly on a copperplate. Drypoint engraving is an etcher's art. As the needle scores the plate, a ridge of copper is thrown up in relief to form the image. Drypoint is also used in retouching etched plates.

DTR   Abbreviation for diffusion-transfer-reversal, a method of reproduction used in office copying machines. *See* DIFFUSION-TRANSFER PROCESS.

dual roll stand   In web-press work, a roll stand that supports two units, one mounted above the other, in order to feed two rolls through the press at the same time. Production is higher than if only one web were used at a time.

ductor roller Ink or water roller that alternately contacts the fountain roller and the distribution roller.

dull coated paper Paper that has a dull finish, although it is coated. Paper may have a dull finish on one side and a highly polished coat on the other. Such paper may be used for fine color work or halftones on the glossy side and text on the opposite side, where the dull finish eliminates glare for reading solid copy.

dull coated-two-sides paper Book paper having a dull finish but coated on both sides.

dull finish Matte paper finish without gloss or luster.

dull seal Typesetter's term for stock having an adhesive back.

dummy Rough draft or proposal of a piece of printing material, pasted or bound together in the exact reproduction size and showing the areas that illustrations and text will occupy. Rough sketches and copy are usually included. The term "dummy" also denotes a sample book made up to show bulk, size, binding, paper, etc. For example, a dummy book consisting of blank pages and cover can be used to determine the size of the jacket.

duotone Two-color halftone print made from a screened photograph when one color or hue is desired. Two identical plates are made. The first plate is run in the desired color, and the second plate is run in black. During exposure, the second screen is turned at an angle of 15° to 30° to the first screen to prevent the screens from meshing. (Meshing causes an undesirable checkered pattern called "moiré.")

duplex paper Paper having a different color or finish on each side of the sheet.

duplicate Identical copy of an original. A duplicate must be identical in every respect to the original. It is not a duplicate unless it is an exact likeness, and the image must therefore be of the same size, although the paper may be of any size. An enlargement or a reduction is not a duplicate.

duplicating, offset See OFFSET DUPLICATOR; see also DIRECT PLATEMAKING.

duplicating, spirit See SPIRIT DUPLICATING.

duplicating, stencil-method See MIMEOGRAPH.

duplicator, microfilm See MICROFILM EQUIPMENT.

duplicator paper (copy paper)   Paper designed specifically for use as a master paper with spirit, gelatin, and other office duplicators (but not offset duplicators). Duplicator papers are available in basis weights of 16 to 24 pounds (7.26 to 10.9 kg) for 500 sheets of the basic size of 17 by 22 inches (43.1 to 55.8 cm). Most duplicator papers are boxed in cut sizes of 8½ by 11, 8½ by 13, and 8½ by 14 inches (21.6 by 27.9, 21.6 by 33, and 21.6 by 35.5 cm).

Duplimat masters   *See* MULTILITH DUPLIMAT MASTERS.

dust cover   Blank page inserted at the end of a coverless book for the protection of the last page that contains copy; also, the jacket of a hard-cover book.

dwell-on impression   *See* DELAYED DWELL.

dye transfer   Absorption process for making color prints with gelatin relief matrices. The matrix film produces a relief image in the gelatin when it is exposed through a color-separation negative. The three matrices are soaked in appropriate dye solutions. First the yellow printer is placed in contact with a gelatin-coated paper, which absorbs the dye. The matrix is then removed, and the red and blue printers are applied in turn and in register to complete the color separation.

EAM Abbreviation for electrical accounting machine.

EBCDIC Abbreviation for extended binary code decimal interchange code, a standard character code used in computer work.

edge marks *See* HANGER MARKS.

edge shadow Dark area along the edge of a halftone caused by halation.

edges, plate type *See* PLATE TYPE EDGES.

editing Preparation of a manuscript for publication. It may include revision, rewriting, and checking for accuracy, as well as what is usually termed "copy editing." Unless a copy editor is technically qualified, he or she should not make technical changes. Copy editing includes checking numerical sequence, marking for type, and making the style of the manuscript consistent. Spelling, punctuation, and grammar are corrected. Modified proofreader's marks are used in editing the manuscript. When possible, however, the corrections are written above the affected word or words rather than in the margin. Colored inks or colored pencils are generally used.

edition When a book is published for the first time, all copies are said to be the first, or original, edition. Reprintings of the first printing are called the second printing, third printing, etc. When an edition has been revised substantially, it is a second edition as well as the first revised edition; the first pressrun of this edition is the first printing of the second edition or of the first revised edition. These sequences keep recurring. A new edition requires a new copyright notice to protect rights to added material, but reprints from the original plates are protected under the provisions of the original copyright notice and date.

EF Abbreviation for English finish.

eggshell finish Finish similar to the texture of an eggshell, applied to book papers or boards.

electrical schematic Diagram of the operational functions of an electrical or electronic system. The system's parts and components are represented by lines and symbols. When the electrical energy source is shown, it should originate at the left of the schematic, flow to the right, and then flow up or down, depending on the system. Adjacency of parts and components need not be depicted, but the system must function graphically. The schematic must be so drawn that the circuitry can be traced from component to component in the sequence of their respective functions, although no attempt is made to indicate the actual physical size and location of parts and components.

electrolysis Chemical decomposition of a compound by the passage of an electric current through an electrolyte. *See* ELECTROTYPE PLATE.

electrolytic engraving Photoengraving process in which the nonimage area on a relief printing plate is charged positively and then etched away. It is the reverse of electroplating.

electrolytic reproduction Process of reproducing an image from film onto sensitized copy paper. The copy paper consists of a paper base, a thin layer of metal foil, and a coating of zinc oxide with resin as a binder. The coating is photoconductive and sensitive to light. In darkness, it is impervious to an electrical charge and has a high resistance. During exposure, light lowers the resistance of the translucent areas of the film that it penetrates, and a latent image is formed on the copy paper. Thus, a difference in resistance values is established between the image and nonimage areas. The image area has become an electrical conductor. After exposure, the copy paper is subjected to an electroplating solution, and direct current flows between the solution and the foil. The solution contains metal ions that are attracted to the image area (the area with the least resistance), and a metallic visible image is formed on the coating of the copy paper. The solution is applied to the surface of the paper as it passes over a moist sponge. Although the paper is thus moistened, it emerges comparatively dry. Electrolytic reproduction is used in some microfilm reader-printers, because the process takes only a few seconds.

electronic engraving *See* ENGRAVING, ELECTRONIC.

electronography Printing process in which the ink (toner) is transferred by electrostatic attraction across a gap between the printing plate and the opposing surface, and the receiving material accepts the deposit of ink. *See also* ELECTROSTATIC STENCIL-SCREEN PRINTING PROCESS.

electrophotographic duplication Process of making duplicate copies by utilizing electrostatic forces. It is unrelated to the electrostatic screen printing process.

electroplate To cover with a coating by electrolytic means. *See* ELECTRO-TYPE PLATE.

electrostatic process Copying or printing process in which an image is deposited on a material by means of electrostatic forces. Several methods of utilizing electrostatic forces have been developed. The methods themselves may be distinguished, and so may the purposes for which the equipment is designed. Is the equipment classified as a copying machine or as a printing press? The application of electrostatic forces is distinctive in each case. In one method, termed "xerography," the image is transferred by contact from a selenium-coated plate or drum to stock. In a second method, a machine transfers the image directly from the original to special paper. The fine powder, or toner, is automatically brushed onto the paper and adheres to the image on the drum or plate by electrostatic attraction. A third method differs from those above only in that the toner is mixed with a liquid and becomes "wet ink." The machines using these methods are called copying machines because the image is made from an original.

A fourth method of applying electrostatic forces is pressureless printing, known technically as the electrostatic stencil-screen printing process. Since this method uses a plate stencil through which toner is attracted to and deposited on almost any receiving surface, it can be classified as printing. The word "pressureless" is descriptive of the process because the printing plate does not touch the receiving substratum, as happens in conventional printing. In the electrostatic stencil-screen printing process, a charge is placed on the printing element and an opposite charge on the plate, thus creating a magnetic field. The receiving substratum or article imposed within that field intercepts the ink particles (toner) as they travel to the opposite charge. In the case of a conductive material, the material itself will take the charge and serve as a pole. Common to all electrostatic methods is the toner that is used to form the image instead of the wet or paste ink used with conventional printing presses.

electrostatic stencil-screen printing process (also known as **pressureless printing**) Printing process developed by the Electrostatic Printing Corporation and therefore known as the "EPC process." A thin flexible printing element, with finely screened openings defining the image to be printed, is used. An electric field is established between the image element and the surface to be printed. Finely divided dry ink particles are metered through the image openings and are attracted to the printing surface where they are firmly held by electrostatic forces until they are fixed by heat or chemical means.

Full color reproduction requires a series of printing elements representing the color separations. The material to be printed passes under a

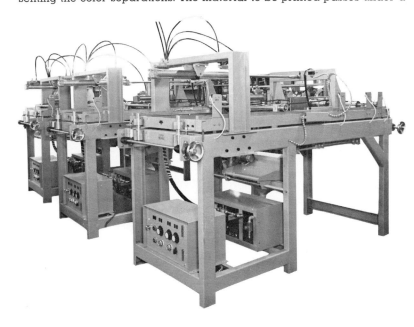

**Fig. E-1   Ceramic tile printer.
(Electrostatic Printing Corporation.)**

Fig. E-2 Pipe printer using the EPC process. (Japan, *Electrostatic Printing Corporation.*)

succession of these elements, and a multicolored powder image is formed, ready for fixing. Dry ink with the proper characteristics for the material to be printed has been formulated. For the most part, these are resin-colorant combinations that are pulverized to a controlled particle-size range. However, they can be made of finely ground glass particles for printing on glass that is subsequently fired at high heat to become an integral part of the glass. Since the image-forming element does not touch the image-receiving surface, quality is not dependent on the finish of the material. Rough textures and irregular surfaces take clear and legible images. In addition, because of the noncontact features, the process has the ability to apply images or markings to glass, ceramics, or metal at a point in the manufacturing process where the article may have a retained heat of 1,000°F or more. There is renewed interest in the potential of this printing process because the solvent-free inks would aid in pollution control, reduce fire hazards, and consume less energy.

The EPC process has enjoyed considerable success in Japan in two noteworthy applications. One application involves the use of some 80 electrostatic printing presses used to decorate ceramic tile where successive deposits of dry glaze has produced unique effects. Figure E-1 shows a ceramic tile printer. Tray-loaded tiles move under a succession of printing units for a multicolor decoration prior to firing. Decoration is applied directly to raw glaze. These tiles enjoy worldwide success. The other Japanese application is a computer-controlled marking method that weighs cast pipe, measures the length of the pipe, and prints information on it. See Figures E-2 and E-3. Eight major steel companies are presently using the equipment. Another application of using the EPC process involves using the Case Marker, a machine manufactured by Jas. H. Matthews & Company that provides an in-line printer capable of printing on a filled corrugated container with a label image that matches the graphics of the preprinted portions. Figure E-4 shows the Case Marker printing the universal product code on packaged equipment. Speed of the printer in this instance is at the rate of 60 feet (18.29 m) per minute. The Case Marker

Fig. E-3 Seamless pipe ready for marking. *(Electrostatic Printing Corporation.)*

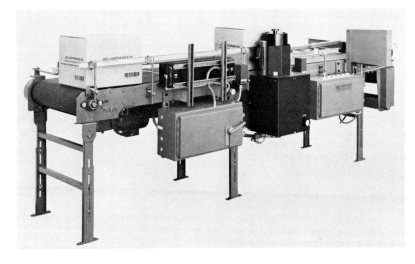

Fig. E-4 Case Marker printing on cartons. (Jas. H. Matthews & Company.)

has proven economically attractive, since it provides quality printing for the specifics of the container and allows for a reduction in inventory.

A promise of the EPC process extends to possible uses in fields currently supplied by screen printing, letterpress, and lithography. A major research effort has been launched with prototype equipment in operation for the application of dry adhesives. While this particular application is used more as an industrial tool, it utilizes a pattern of dry adhesives for bonding in place that can also be used in the manufacture of clothing, box sealing, and the production of numerous fabricated articles.

electrotype plate Duplicate printing plate produced by electrolysis. The image of the original plate is impressed under pressure into a mineral wax, a vinyl compound, sheet lead, or a wax-coated sheet of paper or metal to form the mold. Silver spray or a graphite coating is applied to the mold to make it electrically conductive, and the mold is then suspended from the negative pole of a direct-current circuit in an electrolytic bath. A bar of metal is suspended in the bath from a positive charge. The metal may be copper, nickel, iron, chromium, or a combination of these materials.

When current is applied, the metal decomposes and a thin film of it is deposited on the mold. The shell now contains an exact duplicate of the printing surface of the original plate. When backed with a low-melting alloy for strength, shaved for proper thickness, leveled, and trimmed, it becomes an electrotype printing plate.

Sheets of lead are often used instead of wax for molding halftones because halftones require fine work. When a vinyl compound such as plastic is used as the molding material, the plastic is lifted from the shell, but wax must be melted away. Sheets must be carefully stripped from the mold when lead is used. Chromium and nickel are used as plating materials for long runs because these metals are durable. Electrotype plates may be flat or curved to fit rotary cylinder printing presses.

Electrotypesetter Operating unit for automatic linecasting control, manufactured by the Radio Corporation of America. It is controlled by punched tape. The reader is cable-connected to a slug-casting machine such as a Linotype or an Intertype. The keyboard of the casting machine is removed, and matrices are released by a solenoidal operation.

electrotypy Art or process of producing electrotype plates. *See* ELECTROTYPE PLATE.

element In advertising, any of the parts, such as display type, text copy, and line or continuous-tone art, that compose an advertisement; in book makeup, any of the components of the front matter, body, and back matter of a publication. *See also* BOOK MAKEUP.

elevation drawing: architecture Rendering of design variations of different models of residences or commercial buildings, often used in conjunction with an architectural floor plan. Different models are indicated by "elevation A," "elevation B," etc. Elevation drawings are made in perspective. *See also* ARCHITECTURAL FLOOR PLAN; ARCHITECTURAL RENDERING.

elevation drawing: engineering Drawing that depicts vertical projections of structures, inboard and outboard profiles of aircraft, automotive and marine equipment, or parts of such equipment. An elevation drawing shows the shapes and sizes of walls, bulkheads, openings, projections, or recesses, space allocation, compartments, the location and arrangement of machinery and fixed equipment, and the like. It may also indicate construction materials.

elite Type size for typewriters approximating 10-point (3.51-mm) printing type. Elite type has 12 characters to the linear inch (2.54 cm) of copy and 6 lines to the vertical inch.

ellipse Enclosed plane forming a regular oval. The shortest dimension through the center of an ellipse is called the minor axis; the longest dimension, the major axis. *See also* AXIS.

elliptical-dot screen Contact screen that incorporates an elliptical-dot structure and produces an elliptical dot in the middle tones. This feature eliminates the sudden jump in density usually encountered in vignetted areas of the reproduction where the corners of square dots join at the same place in the tonal scale. Since only the diagonal corners of elliptical dots join at any one place in the tonal scale, a smoother reproduction is obtained and grain characteristics are minimized. The elliptical-dot screen is used for black-and-white reproduction in the same manner as a square-dot contact screen.

em Type measure equal to the square of the type body. The name is derived from early type practices in which the letter M was cast on a square body. One-half of an em is known as an "en." The quadrat, which is used for horizontal spacing, is measured in ems or ens. *See also* QUADRAT.

em dash Dash 1 em in length, as —. This is the regular dash used in punctuation.

embossing Producing a raised design on paper or other material. A brass or bronze die contains the image to be emossed. When set in intaglio, it serves as a plate on the bed of the press. A soft, pliable material like papier-mâché is placed on the cylinder of the press. As the cylinder revolves, it presses the papier-mâché into the intaglio image on the bed. The papier-mâché, with the relief design on it, is then dried, trimmed, and printed. In a second operation, the relief design on the cylinder forces the printed image facedown into the intaglio counterpart in the die on the bed. Thus a raised surface appears on the material.

embossing press Printing press capable of embossing work as well as regular printing. Some platen presses have this advantage. *See* PLATEN PRESS.

emulsion Coating of a photographic material that is sensitive to light. It is usually made of a diazo compound or silver salts suspended in gelatin.

emulsion speed Rate of response of a photographic emulsion to light, determined under standard conditions of exposure and subsequent development.

en *See* EM.

en dash Short dash, such as the dash used in ranges (e.g., 1900–1950) or to join two compound adjectives.

enameled finish *See* COATED FINISH.

encaustic Method of preparing images by means of heat. An encaustic painting is made with wax to which color has been added; it is then fused with a hot iron, which fixes the color.

endleaf (book endpaper; book lining; flyleaf paper) Paper at the beginning or end of a book, half of which is pasted to the cover and half of which forms a flyleaf. It must have sufficient strength to hold the inside of the book and the cover together, and it must accept paste without crinkling.

endpaper Two sheets of folded paper of a stock heavier than the main body of sheets making up a book. One sheet is pasted to the inside front or back cover of the book, and the other half is pasted to the first or last page across the base at the horizontal dimension. It is also called a "flyleaf" or "endleaf." The endpaper often bears printing, such as in dictionaries and text books; but the endpaper should not bear front matter such as book titles, the name of the publisher, or the copyright notice.

engine sizing In paper manufacturing, application of emulsified resin in the beater. Almost all chemical wood papers are sized in this way.

engineering document Any specification, drawing, sketch, list, standard, pamphlet, report, or other written information on the design, procurement, manufacture, test, or inspection of equipment or services.

engineering drawing In standard usage, an orthographic drawing of a piece of equipment or an article or of its detailed parts, containing information and instructions sufficient to manufacture the equipment, article, or parts. Some engineering drawings are not orthographic, but give a perspective or an isometric view of an article. Such drawings, which are made for commercial reasons, are known as "sales drawings." Engineering drawings are made on tracing paper, linen, or film, all of which are translucent for the reproduction of copies, usually by the whiteprint process. Pencil is generally used. The use of perspective and isometric projection on engineering drawings intended for government services is discouraged. *See also* ORTHOGRAPHIC PROJECTION: ENGINEERING DRAWINGS.

english Old type size. The nearest equivalent in the point system is 14 point (4.92 mm).

English finish Paper finish that is smoother than machine finish, but not so smooth as that of supercalendered stock. It is popular for magazines, brochures, and illustrated booklets for which halftone screening is employed and for which paper must be of reasonably good quality. *See also* UNCOATED BOOK PAPER.

engrave To incise designs or images on the surface of a material from which printing impressions can be made. *See* PHOTOENGRAVING.

engraver's proof Proof of a line cut or halftone engraving. The proof is inspected to determine whether the image has acceptable printing characteristics.

engraving, electronic Engraving for the production of printing plates by electronic means. Figure E-5 shows HCM Corporation's Chromagraph DC 300 electronic scanner, designed for the production of corrected continuous-tone and screened color separations for all printing processes. Color transparencies, color negatives, or flexible color-reflection pictures are suitable as scanning copy. A special mask scanning head and a scanning drum for mounting a control mask are provided for combinations of several picture subjects; for the insertion of lettering, live subjects, and picture cutouts; for partial picture corrections; and for colored borders. Enlargements or reductions can be carried out in a wide range between 33⅓ and 1/1685 percent by means of three scanning drums of different sizes combined with digital storage. The maximum size of 16 by 20 inches (40.6 by 50.8 cm) for originals, mask, and separation films permits the production of color separations for full-page illustrations, large picture combinations, and complete magazine and journal pages in one operation. Pre-angled contact screens, which are inserted with the separation film (lithographic film) in daylight cassettes and mounted on the recording drum automatically and without distortion by actuation of a lever, enable

Fig. E-5 HCM Corporation's Chromagraph DC 300 electronic scanner.

the separations for letterpress and lithographic printing to be screened in one operation. The color separations for gravure are recorded on commercial continuous-tone film. Directly screened separations can be prepared in the scanner by exposing lithographic film through a contact lens. Recording resolutions are 350 lines per inch (140 lines/cm), 500 lines per inch (200 lines/cm), 750 lines per inch (300 lines/cm), and 1,500 lines per inch (600 lines/cm). Production time required for continuous-tone color separations varies from 7 seconds for 350 lines per inch (140 lines/cm) to 210 seconds for 500 lines per inch (200 lines/cm). Time required for direct screening varies from 15 seconds for 750 lines per inch (300 lines/cm) to 630 seconds for 1,500 lines per inch (600 lines/cm).

Figure E-6 shows HCM Corporation's Helio-Klischograph Model K200

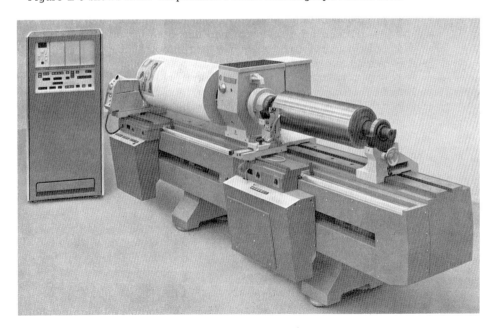

Fig. E-6 HCM Corporation's Helio-Klischograph Model K200 electronic engraving machine.

electronic engraving machine. The machine provides electronic engraving of cylinders for rotogravure printing of magazines, catalogs, and decorative and packaged printing. Continuous-tone or line copy on opaque film of any size up to the size of the printing cylinder is suitable. Both positive and negative copies (separations) may be scanned. Functional features of the machine are (1) multiple engraving in a circumferential direction; (2) seamless engraving in a circumferential direction; (3) subsequent engraving in register; (4) multiple engraving in a lateral direction; (5) mirror effect; (6) shifting; (7) shifting with a staggered base line in a circumferential direction; and (8) size change in a lateral direction. The cylinder circumference range is from $9\frac{8}{10}$ to 55 inches (23.6 to 139.7 cm), and the corresponding diameter is from $3\frac{1}{10}$ to $17\frac{1}{2}$ inches (7.62 to 44.5 cm). The cylinder length, including shafts, is 76 inches (193.04 cm), and engraving width of the cylinder is 48 inches (121.92 cm). By exchanging the engraving heads, available screens are 100, 120, 137, 150, 175, 200, and 250 lines per inch (40, 48, 54, 60, 70, 80, and 100 lines per centimeter), respectively. The engraving output is determined to a certain extent by the cylinder circumference. It is slightly reduced with smaller cylinder circumferences and increased with larger.

Figure E-7 shows the Magnascan 460 electronic color scanner. The scanner produces three or four colors, positive or negative, continuous-tone or screened. The machine is versatile in that it also provides facsimile reproduction or electronic retouching of originals, and separations are in precise register through a register pin system. The 460 provides six color controls for each color channel and four tone controls for highlights, mid-tones, shadows, and catch lights. The black printer is automatically computed and fully adjustable from skeleton to full-range black. Originals are transparencies or reflection copy, and maximum input size is 10 by 12 inches (25.4 by 30.48 cm). Maximum output film sizes is 20 by 24 inches (50.8 by 60.96 cm), and the enlargement or reduction ratios are 0.3X to 16.5X. Output scanning speeds are as follows:

Fig. E-7 Magnascan 460 electronic color scanner. (Rutho-Graphics Division, Sun Chemical Corp.)

	Enlargement ratio	Standard resolution		High resolution	
Continuous-tone	$\times 0.3-\times 1$	—		1 in/min	2.5 cm/min
	$\times 1.0-\times 9.0$	4 in/min	10 cm/min	1 in/min	2.5 cm/min
	$\times 9.0-\times 16.5$	2 in/min	5 cm/min	1 in/min	2.5 cm/min
Screened	$\times 0.3-\times 1.5$	—		1 in/min	2.5 cm/min
	$\times 1.5-\times 9.0$	—		2 in/min	5.0 cm/min
	$\times 9.0-\times 16.5$	—		1 in/min	2.5 cm/min

engraving, mechanical The Hermes Model ITF-K Engravograph (Figure E-8) is a portable engraving machine that enlarges and reduces images, operating on the same principle as the pantograph. The operator composes the inscription by setting individual brass master letters into an adjustable and self-centering slide. The operator then traces the grooved master letters (or any other master template). The movement is transmitted to the engraving cutter, which does the actual engraving. The depth of cut is controlled by an automatic depth regulator. One set of type can create up to 20 different sizes. Engraving cutters are inserted from the top without the use of wrenches, and change of the cutter from bold to fine and back

Fig. E-8 Model ITF-K Engravograph engraving machine. (New Hermes Engraving Machine Corp.)

again can be accomplished. The most popular sizes of type range from $\frac{1}{16}$ to 1-inch (0.158 to 2.54-cm) high letters, but lettering up to 4 inches (10.16 cm) can be engraved as well. The machine has a large variety of uses, producing such items as small name tags, large instrument panels, directional and safety signs, desk plates, badges, awards, and flowcharts on plastic, metal, or wood. The Model ITF-K Engravograph has a capacity of 19 inches (48.26 cm) by any length. The engraving cutter will cut a width up to $\frac{11}{64}$ of an inch (4.366 cm). Ratios are from 21 to 7, and the machine is adjustable to 21 different engraving sizes. Hermes manufactures many different models of their engraver for various applications. A wide assortment of templates (master copy types) are available in various typefaces, sizes, and styles. In addition, templates for foreign languages, engineering symbols, fraternal insignias, and sport templates and templates for engraving jewelry, trophies, and other ornamentals are available.

envelope drawing In engineering drafting, a drawing that shows an item in sufficient detail to identify it for procurement purposes. The drawing gives such information as mounting and mating dimensions, tolerances, weight limitations, finishes, and other physical requirements.

envelopes Figure E-9 shows a number of styles and sizes of envelopes for a variety of purposes. (The names suffixed with an Ⓡ are the United States Envelope Company's registered trade names.) An envelope must be uniform in die cut, size, folding, gumming, quality of paper stock, weight, surface characteristics, and color. Any lack of uniformity could cause delay and expense because of printing difficulties.

EPC Abbreviation for Electrostatic Printing Corporation of America and for the electrostatic screen printing process developed by this firm. *See* ELECTROSTATIC STENCIL-SCREEN PRINTING PROCESS.

epidiascope (optical lantern) Lantern that projects enlarged images on a screen from illustrations, text copy, or photographs imposed on a transparent material. In its simplest form, the epidiascope consists of a lantern body, a light source, and lenses that magnify the object. The light source may be a carbon arc lamp or a strong incandescent lamp. The epidiascope is useful in illustrating lectures.

equivalent weight *See* BASIS WEIGHT.

erasing and eradicating Errors may be removed from copy by applying an abrasive material or a chemical solvent. Successful erasing with rubber erasers and eradication by means of a fluid depend on such factors as the surface finish of the material, the grit content of the eraser, the strength and potency of the eradicating fluid, and the manner in which the erasing or eradicating is done. Proper erasing and eradicating are important to the appearance and reproduction quality of cold-composition copy, engineering drawings, and technical artwork. High-grade tracing papers and linens are manufactured to withstand erasure pressure. Careful erasing on linen or tracing papers with a high rag content therefore presents no

V-FLAP

6¼ – 3½ x 6
6¾ – 3⅝ x 6½
9 – 3⅞ x 8⅞
*10 – 4⅛ x 9½

*Also available in
Postage-Saver style
with Spot of Gum

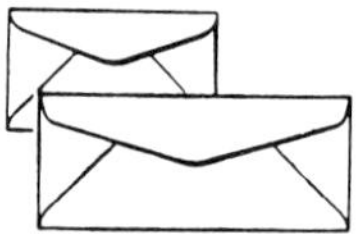

COMMERCIAL AND OFFICIAL

5 – 3-1/16 x 5½
6¼ – 3½ x 6
6¾ – 3⅝ x 6½
7 – 3¾ x 6¾
7¾ – 3⅞ x 7½
Monarch – 3⅞ x 7½
8⅝ – 3⅝ x 8⅝
9 – 3⅞ x 8⅞
10 – 4⅛ x 9½
11 – 4½ x 10⅜
12 – 4¾ x 11
14 – 5 x 11½

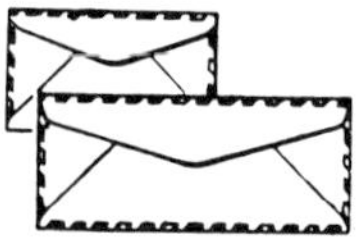

AIRMAIL

6¾ – 3⅝ x 6½
10 – 4⅛ x 9½

OUTLOOK^R AIRMAIL

10 – 4⅛ x 9½

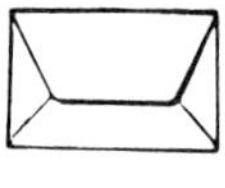

WALLET FLAP

Aylesford – 3⅜ x 5⅜
Lenox – 3½ x 6
Astor – 3-9/16 x 5-9/16
Court – 3⅝ x 6½
Viceroy – 3⅞ x 7½

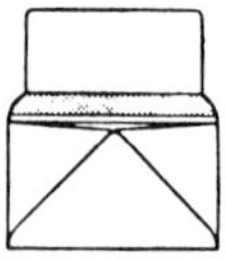

COUPON

6¼ – 3½ x 6
6¾ – 3⅝ x 6½

SOUVENIR

6¼ – 3½ x 6
6¾ – 3⅝ x 6½

POINTED FLAP

Winthrop – 3⅜ x 5⅜
Sultan – 3½ x 6
Gladstone – 3-9/16 x 5-9/16
Sovereign – 3⅝ x 6½
Monarch – 3⅞ x 7½

BARONIAL

4 – 3⅝ x 4-11/16
5 – 4⅛ x 5⅛
5½ – 4⅜ x 5⅝
5¾ – 4⅝ x 5-15/16
6 – 5 x 6
5 Card – 4½ x 5½
5⅛ Card – 4½ x 5¾

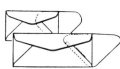

POSTAGE SAVER
Regular and Spot of Gum*

6¼ – 3½ x 6
*6¾ – 3⅝ x 6½
7 – 3¾ x 6¾
7¾ – 3⅞ x 7½
8⅝ – 3⅝ x 8⅝
*9 – 3⅞ x 8⅞
*10 – 4⅛ x 9½
11 – 4½ x 10⅜
12 – 4¾ x 11
14 – 5 x 11½

*Available in both styles.

SELF-SEAL^®
Commercial and Official Sizes

6¾ – 3⅝ x 6½
7¾ – 3⅞ x 7½
10 – 4⅛ x 9½

Social Stationery Sizes

3¾ x 5¾
3⅞ x 7½

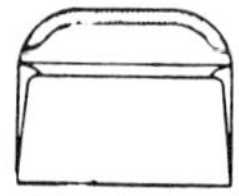

TYPEWRITER

6¾ – 3⅝ x 6½
9 – 3⅞ x 8⅞
10 – 4⅛ x 9½

SQUARE FLAP
Regular and Outlook^®

7¾ – 3⅞ x 7½
9 – 3⅞ x 8⅞
10 – 4⅛ x 9½
10½ – 4½ x 9½
11 – 4½ x 10⅜
12 – 4¾ x 11
14 – 5 x 11½

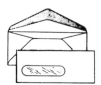

BANKERS FLAP
Regular and Outlook^®

7¾ – 3⅞ x 7½
9 – 3⅞ x 8⅞
10 – 4⅛ x 9½
10½ – 4½ x 9½
11 – 4½ x 10⅜
12 – 4¾ x 11
14 – 5 x 11½
*16 – 6 x 12

*Not in Outlook Style.

COLUMBIAN^® CLASP

0 – 2½ x 4¼
5 – 3⅛ x 5½
10 – 3⅜ x 6
15 – 4 x 6⅜
11 – 4½ x 10⅜
25 – 4⅝ x 6¾
35 – 5 x 7½
14 – 5 x 11½
50 – 5½ x 8¼
55 – 6 x 9
63 – 6½ x 9½
68 – 7 x 10
75 – 7½ x 10½
80 – 8 x 11
83 – 8½ x 11½
87 – 8¾ x 11¼
90 – 9 x 12
93 – 9½ x 12½
94 – 9¼ x 14½
95 – 10 x 12
97 – 10 x 13
98 – 10 x 15
105 – 11½ x 14½
110 – 12 x 15½

Fig. E-9 Envelopes and mailing pieces. (United States Envelope Company.)

problems. In contrast, erasing on bond or paper stock manufactured from wood pulp with little or no rag content is extremely difficult. It is easy to erase on paper stock having a coated or enameled surface because the surface itself is removed in erasing. Only high-quality coated or enameled stock having a glazed finish should be used for reproduction proofs or for camera-ready copy prepared on office composing machines. Supercalendered stock without a coated finish should not be used. Some paper stocks have the appearance of being coated because of their high luster and glossy finish. This appearance is obtained by passing the paper through the calender rolls many times during the manufacturing process. The degree of gloss and smoothness varies with the number of times the paper has been calendered. Such paper stocks should not be used for producing camera-ready cold-composition copy because they are very poorly suited to erasing. The eradicating fluids recommended by the manufacturer of the material should be used for tracing paper, linen, and film.

erection drawing Engineering drawing that shows the procedure and sequence for the erection or assembly of individual items or subassemblies of items.

erratum Error in writing or printing; also, an acknowledgment of such an error. Errata sheets are often sent to recipients of technical books to correct technical, typographical, and other errors.

escapement Mechanism in a linecasting machine that dislodges individual matrices from their respective magazines. The matrices thus dislodged are arranged to form a line from which slugs or lines of type are cast with molten metal. The term "escapement" also applies to a ratchet device on a typewriter. When a typewriter key is struck, the carriage moves, or "escapes," to the left and space is provided for typing the next character.

etch To corrode with an acid or similar material; also, to make a design on a metal plate by employing a corrosive substance. The metal plate is coated with a varnishlike material. The design is made with a sharp instrument, which destroys the material and exposes the metal. Then acid is used to eat out the exposed metal, thus forming an image from which an impression can be made.

etch proof See REPRODUCTION PROOF.

excelsior Old 3-point type size, now seldom used.

Executive Name of a series of proportional-spacing typewriters produced by IBM's Office Products Division. See TYPEWRITER.

expanded type (extended type) Type with a wider face than that of usual type of the same family.

exploded view Line drawing or photograph of a piece of equipment, an article, or a component or part of an article in which the parts are drawn separately in perspective or isometric projection to show their relationship to each other (*See* Figures E-10 and E-11). Each part is identified by a number that is keyed to a parts list or legend. Exploded views are used extensively in technical manuals to assist mechanics in overhauling and maintaining equipment. They are also used in conjunction with text matter for the disassembly, inspection, repair or replacement, and reassembly of parts. The numbers applied to each part must be assigned in the order of proper disassembly.

Several features shown in Figure E-10 are important in the construction of an exploded view: (1) the assembled view, enclosed within a shadow box or a "TV screen," is oriented in the same plane as the exploded parts; (2) use of the shadow box greatly improves the drawing because it separates the assembled view from the exploded parts; (3) all parts are shaded to show that the light source is coming from the upper left corner; (4) part 9, which is a subassembly, has been disassembled into parts 10 through 12 by the use of a brace (this means that parts 10 through 12 can be ordered and replaced as separate parts belonging to assembly parts 9); (5) the part directly above part 5, which has no number, appears in phantom with broken lines (this indicates that it cannot be ordered and replaced as a separate part but is a component of part 2); (6) arrowheads are used with lead lines because there are relatively few parts and they do not clog the

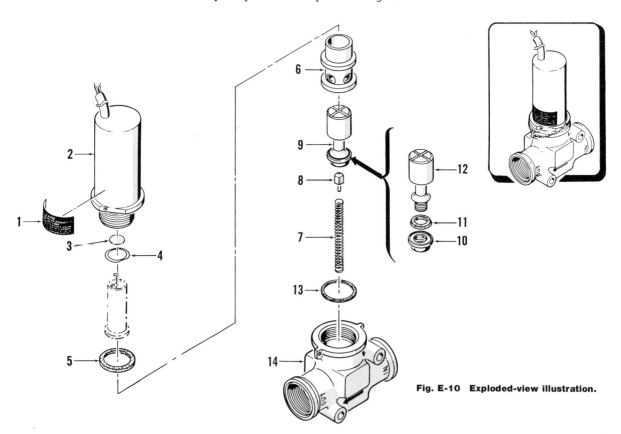

Fig. E-10 Exploded-view illustration.

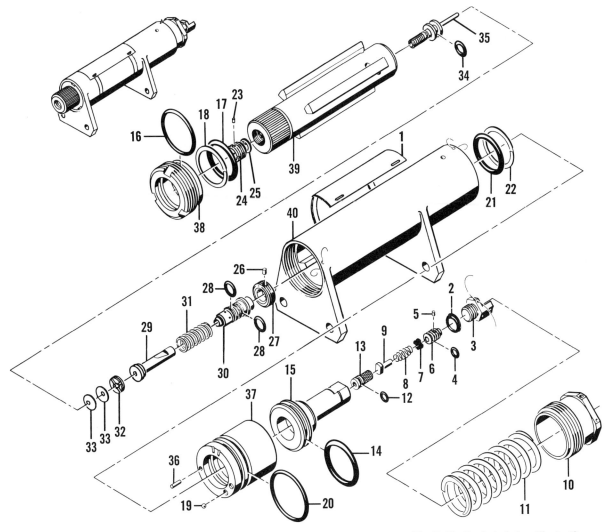

Fig. E-11 Exploded-view illustration.

drawing or detract from its appearance; and (7) gaskets 5, 11, and 13 are shaded to indicate that they are nonmetallic.

The exploded view in Figure E-11 also shows proper shading for the light source, but here the assembled view merges with the exploded parts because it is not enclosed. Both views, however, are oriented in the same plane. Arrowheads are not used because they would congest the drawing. O rings are shown in black with highlighted areas. Springs 8, 11, and 31 and the configuration of such parts as 15, 30, 37, and 39, as well as the threaded parts, add to the cost of the view because drawing these parts is time-consuming.

exposure Quantity of light that is allowed to act on a photographic material. The product of the intensity and the duration of the light acting on the emulsion is the amount of exposure.

exposure index Number assigned to a photographic material and intended for use with an exposure meter to determine the correct aperture and exposure time for best results.

exposure meter Instrument used to determine the intensity of light falling on or reflected by the subject that is being photographed.

extended type See EXPANDED TYPE.

extension line In orthographic engineering and mechanical drawings, a line used to indicate the extent of a dimension. It is designated as a "thin" line. Extension lines should not touch the object to which they refer. See also LINE CONVENTIONS: ENGINEERING DRAWINGS.

external projection Exposure of the sensitized copy paper of a microfilm reader-printer outside the machine with room illumination. Speed and light intensity are important factors in quality reproduction. See also INTERNAL PROJECTION.

extract Material quoted from another work, usually set in smaller type, indented, or otherwise displayed to distinguish it from the text.

eyeball Colloquial term meaning to draw lines and objects without reference to scale.

face Portion of a type piece that receives the ink and comes in direct contact with the printed surface, thus forming the image. The term is used also as an equivalent of typeface. *See* TYPEFACES.

facsimile Exact reproduction of an original.

facsimile transceiver Machine capable of making facsimiles of communications that are transmitted and received via ordinary telephone lines. The machines are plugged into any standard electrical outlets. Facsimile documents can be sent from one facility to another across plant grounds, a city, or a country—in fact, wherever a telephone call can be placed—providing a transceiver is located at the called station. Sending or receiving transmissions can be made without operator attendance during or after working hours. Anything written, printed, or illustrated, such as engineering drawings, change notices, tabulated data, charts, graphs, and photographs, can be transmitted.

Figure F-1 is the Xerox Telecopier 200 transceiver. The machine automatically feeds up to 50 documents and prints incoming messages from a self-feeding paper supply on 20-pound (9.08-kg) bond paper. The machine handles document sizes from 5 by 7 inches (12.7 by 17.7 cm) to 9 inches (22.8 cm) by any length; the 8½ inch by 350-foot (21.6 cm by 106.7-m) roll allows almost unlimited reception. The Telecopier 200 has four transmit speeds that can be selected, using the 8½ by 11-inch (21.6 by 27.9-cm) size for each document: two minutes for high-volume applications, three minutes for greater resolution for difficult to read documents, and four or six minutes for compatibility with other Xerox Telecopier units. A line control permits the operator to bypass the automatic hang-up to reestablish voice control after transmission or to reload documents on manually fed units. Flexibility in line selection permits a line selector to connect the equipment to any two telephone lines. A take-up reel is provided for storage and accessing of multipage messages at high-volume unattended Telecopier 200 stations.

Xerox manufactures and distributes other models of transceivers. Telecopier 410 is a desk-top device that operates automatically when unattended during or after working hours. The transceiver automatically feeds and sends or receives 75 documents from 5 to 11 inches (12.7 to 27.9 cm) in length. Its output is on 8½ by 11-inch (21.6 by 27.9-cm) recording paper. Speeds for 8½ by 11-inch (21.6 by 27.9-cm) documents are four minutes and six minutes for higher resolution. Half-size documents are faster. Black-on-white images are produced from all kinds of originals, and originals may be typewritten or printed in pen or pencil. Photographs also can be reproduced. The Telecopier 410 is compatible with other transceivers manufactured by Xerox. The Xerox Telecopier 400 transceiver is portable (it weighs 18 pounds [8.17 kg]) and practical for offices. An ordinary wall outlet and telephone constitutes the portable Telecopier terminal. The machine sends or receives an 8½ by 11-inch (21.6 by 27.9-cm) page in four minutes and it has a six-minute speed for higher resolution. Output is on 8½ by 11-inch (21.6 by 27.9-cm) recording paper. It can be equipped with a device for unattended document transmission and reception. Telecopiers III and V are similar in design and performance, except that model III is

Fig. F-1 Xerox Telecopier 200 transceiver.

used for facsimile broadcasting and model V for international facsimile communications. Input materials are 8½ by 14 inches (21.6 by 35.5 cm) maximum with no minimum size. Output materials are 8½ inches (21.6 cm) wide by any length, with a minimum of 7½ by 9½ inches (19 by 24 cm). Both models have a speed of four minutes per 8½ by 11-inch (21.6 by 27.9-cm) document, or six minutes for high resolution. Partial-page documents require less time.

fade-out blue Very light sky-blue color that is not reproduced by the camera unless it is filtered. It is used for writing on reproduction line copy. Fade-out blue is used also for printing forms employed in the preparation of photographic copy for reproduction. Guidelines showing margin limitations, marginal-data location, columnar arrangement, page-number location, and the like are drawn in black india ink on the original form, which is printed in fade-out blue.

fadeback (also called **ghosting**) Depiction of the central object of an image with full tonal values and the area around the object in flat or less pronounced tones. The heavier tones emphasize the central object. An example is an advertisement showing an automobile engine with an air filter. The manufacturer of the filter shows his product in full, distinct tones and the engine in lesser tones. Thus the physical relationship of the filter to the engine is recognized, and the filter appears as the main object.

family of type Typefaces of a group, regardless of size, that have similar design features. When mixed, these typefaces show a compatible and balanced relationship.

fan delivery Unit on a printing press that transfers folded signatures from a folding section to a conveyor belt. The fan operates in waterwheel fashion. Blades assist in picking up and dislodging a signature at each revolution.

fan fold Method of folding perforated paper which provides for automatic paper stacking after printing. This method is also referred to as "accordian fold" or "Z-fold." A typical example is the paper used in tabulated computer runs.

fatty Photographic internegative mask which slightly enlarges copy. This technique, performed in a contact printer, makes possible precision butting and kissing of tints, screens, colors, and halftones. Most common use is for accurately overlapping two stripped elements.

feather In a printed or duplicated image, an undesirable bleeding effect in which microscopic featherlike indications surround the characters. The effect may be caused by incorrect pressure between printing plate and printing stock, overexposure, excessive diffusion of chemicals, coarse printing stock, or other factors.

featheredge *See* DECKLE EDGE.

felt finish Finish applied by a special marking felt on a web of paper as it goes through the papermaking machine.

felt pens *See* PENS, TECHNICAL.

felt side Printing side of paper. The felt side is the top side of the paper as it comes off the papermaking machine; it is the opposite of the wire side.

ferrotype Photograph produced on a thin metal plate by a process in which collodion is used as a vehicle for sensitive salts. As a verb, "ferrotype" means to burnish a photograph by squeegeeing it while wet on a lacquered plate.

figure Line illustration or photograph of any kind used in a publication. A figure may be a graph, a chart, an exploded view, a rendering, a halftone, or any other illustration in which artwork or photography is used to produce the image. Figures in a technical publication should be numbered consecutively throughout or double-numbered by chapter or section, and they should appear immediately following their first reference in text. The figure number and title are placed below the figure.

figure number Number assigned to an illustration in a publication. Single or double arabic numbers should be used. The two numbers in a double number are separated by a hyphen or an en dash, the first number indicating the section or chapter and the second the sequential order of the figure within that section or chapter.

figure title Title of an illustration in a publication, usually preceded by a figure number in a technical work. It should be as brief as possible.

file number *See* ART FILE NUMBER.

filler Copy used to fill space in a page or column of a magazine or newspaper. Brief poems, witty sayings, parables, proverbs, and jokes are examples. Cartoons, photographs, and the like may also be used as fillers.

fillet Line impressed on the cover of a book for decorative purposes.

filling in (or **filling up**) Condition when printing halftones where the ink fills areas between the dots and produces a solid rather than a sharp halftone print. The condition also may occur in the printing of type matter.

film Flexible, translucent or transparent plastic or other chemically formed base coated with a photographic emulsion. The term may also be applied to a similar material without the emulsion, such as a "wrapping" film.

film base *See* FILMS AND PLATES.

film color sensitivity *See* FILMS AND PLATES.

film, mechanized processing (MP) Films specifically designed for processing in mechanized film processors. The Kodak MP films consist of six products, briefly described as follows:

Kodak MP Phototypesetting Film 2592 (Estar Base). High-contrast, orthochromatic film on dimensionally stable 4-mil Estar base, designed for use on phototypesetting machines that expose with either tungsten or xenon flash lamps. The film yields sharp, high-density images which provide intermediates for printing directly either on metal plates or on photographic film.

Kodalith MP Ortho Films. Orthochromatic, high-contrast films designed primarily for making line and halftone negatives and positives for photomechanical reproduction. The films are available on three different thicknesses of dimensionally stable Estar base, and on a medium thickness acetate support. Their special antihalation backing permits practical exposure times and excellent results when exposed through the base.

Kodalith MP Contact Films. Available on two thicknesses of dimensionally stable Estar base, these films are blue-sensitive and yield high contrast. They are designed for making contact line or halftone negatives or positives. A special antihalation backing permits practical exposure times and provides excellent results when the films are exposed through the base side (such as when laterally reversed negatives or positives are being made). The emulsion and base sides are sufficiently matte to minimize Newton's rings and drawdown times in vacuum printing frames.

Kodalith MP High Speed Duplicating Films. Moderately high-contrast, contact-speed films intended for making high-quality duplicates with high maximum density from line or halftone negative or positive film originals. Exposures can be made to the emulsion side or through the base. They are available in two thicknesses of dimensionally stable Estar base. Because of their speed, these films can also be exposed on a process camera in special applications such as copy-dot work or making facsimile enlargements or reductions from reflection or transmission copy.

Kodalith MP Line Films. High contrast, camera-speed orthochromatic films designed primarily for making camera line negatives and positives for photomechanical reproduction. Coated on dimensionally stable Estar base, these films have a special antihalation backing which permits practical exposure times and provides excellent results when the films are exposed through the base. These films are designed for processing suitable mechanized film processors.

Kodalith MP Pan Film 2558 (Estar base). High-contrast, fast panchromatic film coated on dimensionally stable 4-mil Estar base and designed for processing in mechanized film processors. It yields halftone, direct color-separation negatives and positives of high quality by either projection or contact-printing methods. It is also suitable for line work. The film produces excellent halftone dots well-suited to dot etching. (Refer to Kodak Publication No. Q-2M for further specifications, detailed description, and handling.)

film negative Photolithographic negative produced by a process camera. The negative has a film base and reflects a translucent (white) image on a black background; it may be a line negative or a halftone negative. While it is called a negative, however, the image is right-reading. The term "negative" is derived from the fact that it is camera-produced. *See also* NEGATIVE, PHOTOLITHOGRAPHIC.

film, photographic (color sensitivity and types of sensitizing) *See* FILMS AND PLATES.

film, photographic (composition and physical properties) *See* FILMS AND PLATES.

film, photographic (photographic properties) *See* FILMS AND PLATES.

film positive Film or material of acetate composition having a black image or definition and a translucent or clear background. It has a right-reading image. Film positives are useful in making additional reference copies on whiteprint machines and as intermediates. The term is also applied to a positive contact print on film-base material that has been produced from a stripped-up negative mask and used for burning in a deep-etch offset plate to expose a silk-screen photostencil. In the case of a continuous-tone print, the film is used for masking an intaglio plate.

film processing *See* MICROFILM PROCESSING; PROCESSING, FILM; PROCESSING, NITROGEN-BURST.

films and plates The following discussion on films and plates has been made possible through the courtesy of the Eastman Kodak Company and extracted from the copyrighted Kodak publication *Kodak Graphic Arts Films and Plates.* Because of space limitations it was necessary to condense the material from this publication.

Composition and physical properties: Generally speaking, photographic films and plates are made up of several layers of extremely thin, carefully coated materials. The most important layers are illustrated in Figure F-2.

Base. Film base or glass is the transparent material that serves as the support for the thin, light-sensitive emulsion. The film base for most Kodak graphic arts films is an improved safety type of great clarity and high dimensional stability. For the utmost in dimensional stability, Kodalith Ortho Type 3 is available on a polystyrene base. Kodak plates are coated on specially selected glass, ranging in thickness with the size of the plate from 0.060 to 0.190 inch (1.524 to 4.826 mm). Other thicknesses can be furnished on special order.

Dimensional stability. The dimensional stability of a photographic film depends on many factors. These include not only the chemical composition of the film and the treatment it receives during manufacture but also the form and conditions under which it is stored before and after exposure. The dimensional changes which occur in any photographic film are of two types: temporary, or reversible, and permanent, or irreversible. Temporary expansion or contraction is due to (1) loss or gain of moisture, which is determined almost solely by the relative humidity of the air in contact with the film; and (2) changes in temperature. This temporary type of dimensional change is important in graphic arts use. Expansion due to moisture

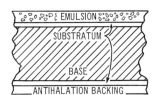

Fig. F-2 Layers of typical photographic materials.

in the air is generally greater than thermal expansion. Since the relative humidity of most shops and laboratories is more apt to vary than the temperature, the problems caused by humidity changes are the main ones. Permanent shrinkage in a photographic film is caused by loss of residual solvents and plasticizer (softening agent) from the base, plastic flow (shrinkage caused by contraction of the emulsion), and release of mechanical strain. Permanent shrinkage during storage prior to exposure is generally very low and is also unimportant because there is no image on the film.

Film swells during processing and contracts again during drying. If it is brought to equilibrium with the same relative humidity after processing as existed before, a small net shrinkage called "process shrinkage" is usually found. Kodak films for the graphic arts are in equilibrium with air at approximately 40 percent relative humidity at the time of shipment. When the utmost in dimensional stability is required, sheets of film should be conditioned to the air of the workroom before exposure by being hung in the dark for approximately one hour. Gentle circulation of air is beneficial.

If the film is reconditioned in the same atmosphere after processing, all dimensional changes caused by humidity are eliminated. All Kodak graphic arts films have high dimensional stability, provided they are not stored after processing at relatively high humidities, that is, over 60 percent. It is desirable for conditions in the workroom to resemble those in the storage room. If the relative humidity of the workroom is either low or high, each sheet of film should be conditioned to room air before exposure. A temperature from 70 to 75°F and a relative humidity between 40 and 50 percent are most satisfactory. Too low a humidity is undesirable because it increases static. If this occurs, dust adheres to unprotected unexposed film and spots appear after the film has been exposed and developed. Light penetrating all the way through an emulsion may reflect from the back of the base and strike the emulsion once more, causing halation. Halation is particularly noticeable in areas of negatives that represent excessively bright areas of the original copy.

In graphic arts films, a light-absorbing material is incorporated in the backing layer, which then serves the double purpose of preventing both halation and curling of the film. The light-absorbing material is always bleached out, but the backing is not removed during processing. In graphic arts plates, the backing is bleached and dissolved during processing. An exception is the Kodak Infrared Sensitive plate from which the black backing must be removed by rubbing lightly with cotton after the plate has been fixed. A weak alkali or developer solution often makes this operation easier.

Photographic properties. The photographic properties of a film or plate determine the type of image that results after exposure and processing. If the type of image needed for a particular purpose is known, the proper film or plate can be selected to do the job. Specifying such properties as speed, contrast, and color sensitivity usually narrows the choice to a few materials. The first consideration in the choice of a photographic film or plate is generally the color sensitivity needed. In most cases, this is primarily a choice between materials for use in black-and-white reproduction, on the one hand, and those for use in color reproduction on the other. The former are sensitive to a few colors of light, while many of the latter are sensitive to all colors.

Color sensitivity and types of sensitizing. All photographic emulsions are sensitive to blue, violet, and the invisible ultraviolet light. For many applications, however, this sensitivity is not enough. The photographic emulsions used in photomechanical color reproduction must be able to record densities for the broader range of colors which the human eye can see, that is, the greens, yellows, oranges, and reds. During manufacture, dyes are added to make the emulsions sensitive to these colors. Blue-sensitive photographic materials record high negative densities for blue areas of the original and, in the final reproduction, render blues very light and reds, yellows, and greens very dark. They are very useful in such specialized work as copying black-and-white photographs.

Orthochromatic films and plates are not sensitive to red light and therefore render reds as very dark in reproduction. These materials are normally faster than blue-sensitive materials because they are sensitive to a wider range of colors. Panchromatic films and plates are sensitive to all visible colors, as well as to ultraviolet, and therefore give excellent mono-chromatic rendering of colored copy. Infrared materials possess a particularly high sensitivity to infrared radiation. Their principal use in photomechanical reproduction is in making black-printer negatives.

Filters. A filter is a device which transmits light of certain colors while it absorbs light of others. The most common types are thin sheets or disks of gelatin or glass that are placed in front of the lens of the camera or in a slot in the lens mounting. By using the proper filters, selected colors of light from a multicolored object are filtered out or reduced. A photograph will then record only the colors transmitted through the filter. Kodak Wratten filters in the form of dyed gelatin sheets are used extensively in graphic arts photography because of their consistently high quality. A filter never changes the color of light. It can only allow a part of some colors to pass through and stop other colors. A "red" filter appears to be red because it transmits red light to the eye and absorbs most other colors. This is shown in Figure F-3. All filters absorb some of the light which strikes them, and under the same conditions of illumination longer exposures are necessary than when no filter is used.

There are two basic applications of filters in photomechanical work. In one, filters are used to emphasize tonal areas in making black-and-white reproductions from colored or soiled copy. In the other, filters are used in

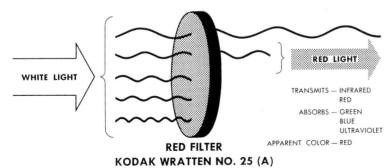

WHITE LIGHT

RED LIGHT

TRANSMITS — INFRARED
RED
ABSORBS — GREEN
BLUE
ULTRAVIOLET
APPARENT COLOR — RED

RED FILTER
KODAK WRATTEN NO. 25 (A)

Fig. F-3 Characteristics of a "red" filter.

making color reproductions from color copy. In the latter case, the original is photographed successively through each of three color-separation filters. The three black-and-white negatives thus obtained are called "color-separation negatives" and are used in making the three printing plates that print the respective colors on the paper. (A fourth plate, the black printer, is usually employed to add density to the dark areas of the picture.) Each of the two applications requires a separate method of calculating the correct exposure. The first is based on filter factors and the second on filter ratios.

The recommended filters for photomechanical work are the Kodak Wratten filters, which are made by carefully mixing prepared dyes in gelatin and forming the resulting mixture into thin sheets. Each filter is standardized by comparison with a permanent standard in specially designed instruments. Selected Wratten gelatin filters are available for critical photomechanical work. These filters, designated as Kodak Wratten Photomechanical filters, are particularly useful when partial exposures are to be made through each of several filters, as in the split-filter method of making a black printer. The Kodak Wratten photomechanical filters are PM8, PM25, PM29, PM33, PM47B, PM58, PM61, PM85B, PM23A, PM47, and PM96 (0.60 and 1.00 densities only).

Materials for general use. The fundamental requirement in a film or plate for photomechanical line work and screened halftone work is high contrast. In negatives of line work, dark lines will then be rendered as clear areas and background areas as extremely dense areas even if the original copy has light or weak lines. In halftone work, the high contrast of the emulsion will produce sharp, crisp halftone dots. A fine-grain emulsion is necessary so that edges of lines and dots will not be ragged. Halftone dots must be of such quality that they can be altered in size by chemical means after development and still retain their opacity. For color copy, it is necessary to use a color-sensitized material that can record colors in their relative black-and-white tone values.

Although emulsions with extreme contrast are slower than continuous-tone materials, high film and plate speed is important in reducing costs by saving time. Kodak graphic arts films and plates combine sufficient speed and sensitivity to provide ease in handling. Of equal importance, films and plates must be physically stable to withstand handling under production conditions. Each of the many photographic materials has characteristics which meet specific needs.

For a more thorough technical discussion of films and plates, it is recommended that the publication *Kodak Graphic Arts Films and Plates,* a copyrighted Kodak publication, be obtained from a Kodak graphic arts dealer.

filmsetter Name given to a machine that sets copy automatically on film or on photographic paper. While this term more appropriately describes such a machine because it does not set metal type, the trade has accepted the name "typesetter" as definitive. However, because a photographic process is used, the machine is more correctly called a photographic typesetter or a photocomposing machine. *See also* TYPESETTERS, PHOTOGRAPHIC.

filmstrip   Strip of rolled film containing still phtographs projected as slides, as opposed to strips of film whose images are projected by motion-picture cameras in rapid succession to simulate motion.

filter   Device, commonly of gelatin or glass, placed between the subject being photographed and the photographic material in order to reduce or eliminate the light of certain colors while allowing that of others to reach the emulsion. *See also* FILMS AND PLATES.

filter factor   Multiplication of exposure time necessary when using a color filter under the same conditions as without the filter.

filter ratio   Number indicating the ratio of exposure when using a given filter such as Kodak Wratten Fiber No. 25. This system of exposure determination is for color-separation work. The ratios allow for the reciprocity effect and are determined for separation negatives developed to the same contrast.

final draft   Text material or copy that is ready in all respects for setting in type.

fine arts   Arts created with concern for aesthetic values rather than for utility. Among them are architecture, sculpture, drawing, painting, and ceramics, insofar as they manifest taste, are responsive to beauty, and are susceptible to aesthetic influences.

finished-sheet size   Overall dimensions of an engineering drawing and of a full-size reproduction made from it.

finisher (inker)   One who applies ink on artwork and generally finishes the work after another has drawn it in pencil.

finishes, paper   *See* PAPER FINISHES.

first generation   Photographically reproduced copy made from an original, either by contact or by photographic reproduction; also, the first impression or copy made from the original.

first parallel fold   Paper fold made in the jaw folder immediately following the former fold. (It is called a "tabloid fold" when the web has been slit in half along the longitudinal dimension.) The result is the printing of eight-page signatures of multiples of the number of webs in the press, the signature size being one-half of the cutoff length by one-half of the web width.

fitting copy   *See* COPYFITTING.

fixative   Any clear solution sprayed or coated on artwork or other material, such as reproduction copy, that "fixes," or stabilizes, the image, rendering it more resistant to wear or smudging. A fixative protects and preserves drawings, photographs, documents, and other papers. An example is a spray coating trade-named Krylon.

flapping *See* MOUNTING AND FLAPPING.

flare Non-image-forming light which reaches the film plane of the process camera; noted in photomechanical reproduction work. Such light may be due to multiple reflections from the lens surfaces, to reflections from the interior of the lens barrel or camera bellows, or to reflections from the front case of the camera. Flare may also be caused by light scatter due to dirt or scratches on the lens or on a filter used in the lens system. Other sources of flare include reflections from the copyboard, reflections from the room walls, and light shining directly into the lens. Excessive flare contributes to tone-scale distortion. When continuous-tone negatives are being made, the net effect of excessive flare is a loss of shadow contrast, which the eye sees as reduced shadow detail. When halftone negatives are being made, flare acts like a flash exposure and its effect is not always apparent. However, a loss of control in the screening process can occur, since the amount of flare varies with the type of original copy and the working conditions. It is better, therefore, to eliminate flare as far as possible and to use controlled flash for shadow exposure.

Flare can be even more undesirable when positives are being made, since it causes loss of highlight contrast and detail. In masking and color-separation work, modern techniques emphasize the importance of standardized curve shapes in the mask and negative to obtain proper tone rendition and color balance in the reproduction. Excessive flare makes it difficult to obtain the right curve shapes and results in poor reproductions. Means of determining the percent of flare present in a particular optical system are discussed in Kodak Pamphlet Nos. Q-107A and Q-107.

flash exposure Second of two process-camera exposures used only in halftone work. The first exposure, the main or detail exposure, is not sufficient to bring out the dot formation required in dark areas of a halftone for proper reproduction in printing. The dots formed during the main exposure will run together, and the halftone will print as solid black in the shadow areas. An additional flash exposure through the contact screen to the negative is required to form halftone dots in the dark areas without affecting the lighter areas.

A flashing lamp is used to make exposures remotely with some cameras. The lamp is located in the darkroom, where it can illuminate the entire film back area evenly. Exposure is controlled manually. During exposure, the vacuum back film holder is lowered and the vacuum retained to keep the film and screen from moving. The exposure must be made on the dots already started on the negative, and any movements of the screen or film would begin new dots, creating a moiré effect.

Flash exposures are also made by retaining the camera setup and flashing through white paper covering the copy on the copyboard. The flashing lamp is gallery-operated, connected to the timer, and mounted on the front-case lens board.

flat In photographic platemaking for offset lithography, the arrangement of assembled pages of copy that are to be printed on one side of the sheet. The sheet, or flat, is loaded into the camera copyholder for photographing. The term also denotes combined page negatives masked and stripped into an orange-colored masking paper, hence the term "goldenrod flat." The flats are inserted in a vacuum frame in contact with a sensitized plate which, after exposure, is developed and becomes the printing plate. Copy pages and page negatives are so arranged on the flat, that when cut, folded, and trimmed, they will be right-reading and fall in numerical sequence. *See also* GOLDENROD FLATS; IMPOSITION.

flat cast In newspaper production, a flat printing plate cast from newspaper matrices.

flat copy In photomechanics, images that lack depth, such as line copy, in contrast to images that have varying depths, such as are encountered when photographing outdoors with an ordinary camera.

flat-size copy Copy made from an original engineering drawing that has a printed format and, because of its relatively small size, can be filed flat.

flat tone (screen tint) In lithography, a tone without gradation that has only one tone value in the dot formation.

flatbed press Printing press having a horizontal bed on which forms are locked for relief (letterpress) printing.

flexographic ink Highly pigmented opaque ink used almost exclusively in flexographic printing. The colors are brilliant and solid.

flexographic printing Printing with rubber plates and with a liquid ink instead of paste ink, such as that used in letterpress printing. The image is set in relief. The flexographic press prints from rolled stock such as foil, cellophane, and enameled or coated paper. Because of the fluidity of the ink used, the dots in halftones may be lost and papers that are manufactured to absorb ink readily may absorb too much ink, but such items as food cartons, candy and gum wrappers, cellophane bags, and waxed papers are ideally suited for this type of printing. The presses operate at 300 feet (91.4 m) to almost 1,000 feet (305 m) per minute, the speed depending on the material to which the image is being transferred. A wide range of opaque colors is available for printing, such as those seen on holiday gift wrappings.

flip chart *See* BRIEFING CHART.

floating Technique of attaching peeled film to another film support base. The peeled emulsion is laid sticky side up on a flat surface, and the other film is dropped carefully on top of it. This eliminates the chance of wrinkles or bubbles forming.

flocking Minute fiberlike particles of wood or cloth in various colors that are blown onto printed matter or painted objects having an adhesive ink. The particles adhere to the ink or paint, producing a decorative effect.

flong Damp mixture of papier-mâché used as a matrix or negative. The image is impressed in the papier-mâché, which dries and serves as the matrix or negative.

flow diagram Schematic diagram indicating the course of a material through an object or article, as in hydraulic and pneumatic systems. It shows the direction of flow through the system and the relationship of the components (*see* Figure F-4). Arrows used to indicate direction of flow may be shaded, dotted, or cross-sectioned to show condition or state. Colors

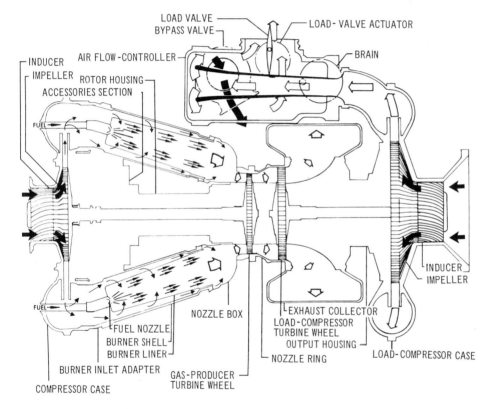

Fig. F-4 Pneumatic flow diagram.

LEGEND	
➡	INLET AIR
→	COMPRESSED AIR
⇉	COMBUSTION
◁	PRODUCTS OF COMBUSTION (EXHAUST)
▭▷	LOAD AIR
➡	BYPASS AIR

may be employed. An accompanying legend, which should be part of the diagram, may show the arrows and key them to the flow system for clarity. If possible, the flow in a system should originate at the left of the diagram so that the direction is from left to right.

flow line Line that indicates the physical relationship of parts of an object when the parts are separated in the drawing. It is broken into alternate short and long lines. *See also* EXPLODED VIEW.

fluid duplicating *See* SPIRIT DUPLICATING.

fluorescent ink Very bright poster and printing ink that contains natural or synthetic phosphorus. It throws off a broad spectrum of visible light while absorbing ultraviolet light. Such inks are effective in briefing charts and advertising displays.

flush Even with a predetermined point, said of lines of text or of line or halftone copy. For example, this line is flush left and right (because it is justified) with the lines above and below it. When lines are not flush, particularly at the right margin, they are said to "run ragged" (and are therefore not justified). *See also* JUSTIFICATION.

flush blocking Trimming so that a plate and a printing surface are even.

flush cover Book cover having the same dimensions as the inserted book.

flyer Broadside, announcement, or circular, usually of inferior quality, printed on one side of the sheet and generally used for advertising purposes.

flying paster Automatic device that splices a new web of paper onto a depleted roll without stopping the press.

flyleaf paper *See* ENDLEAF.

fog Veil of silver of low density on a photographic material. It is most commonly caused by nonimage ink that strikes the material or by incorrect chemical treatment. Correct treatment is of particular importance in maintaining quality in microfilm processing. Fogging is sometimes done intentionally by means of uniform light of low intensity.

foil Very thin sheet or leaf of metal, such as gold foil, silver foil, and the like, that is used to embellish designs and lettering in a stamping process. The term also denotes a transparent, sensitized acetate film that is used chiefly in whiteprint reproduction to produce intermediates and in making projecturals for overhead projection.

foil stamping Method of using gold and silver foil to impress an image on a surface. The foil, or leaf, is stamped and laid on the surface by using heat in the relief matrix.

foldor Printed circular folded and used as a mailing piece.

folding: paper Folding paper into various shapes and sizes is a major field in the graphic arts industry, and complete coverage of the subject is not possible in this work because the subject is too extensive and would require a complete volume of its own. Folds range from a single fold to as much as those required for multipage magazines and newspapers. Equipment manufacturers will gladly furnish folding charts for machines of their manufacture. The following are some of the considerations that must be taken into account where folding paper is a requirement: paper size, weight, finish, ply, and grain; imposition (the arrangement of printed pages on a press form so that pages will be in numerical sequence after being folded); the number of pages in a signature or copies required in relation to the capability of the folding equipment; and paper-feed and paper-delivery capacities, i.e., volume, speed, and flexibility of the equipment. Figure F-5 is A. B. Dick Company's folding machine, designed for offices, schools, churches, and associations having office duplicating equipment. Paper feed is automatic, and adjustable paper-stacking guides ensure continuous delivery of folded paper to top of desk, work table, or removable receiving tray. The folder handles paper sizes from 3 by 5 inches (7.62 by 12.7 cm) to 9 by 15 inches (22.8 by 38.1 cm). Paper weights that can be folded are for single-run folds 16 to 36 pound (7.26 to 16.3 kg) for single-run folds, from 16 to 28 pound (7.26 to 12.7 kg) for double-run folds and french folds, and from 16 to 20-pound (7.26 to 9.08-kg) stock for small envelope folds. Approximately 12,000 sheets 8½ by 11 inches (21.6 by 28 cm) letter-folded can be folded per hour.

Fig. F-5 A. B. Dick Company's Model 52 folding machine.

Fig. F-6 General Binding Corporation's O&M Module 1 folding machine.

Figure F-6 is General Binding Corporation's O&M Module 1 folding machine, which features variable-speed controls on both folder and feeder, rubber fold rollers, self-aligning bearings, a full blanket stacker, hinged deflectors, and perforating, scoring, and slitting capabilities. It accommodates a sheet size of 17½ by 22½ inches (44.4 by 57 cm). An added swinger section, when placed parallel with the folder, provides multiple folds, with plate No. 1 having a roller width of 18 inches (45.7 cm) and a plate depth of 15 inches (38.1 cm), and plate No. 2 having a roller width of 18 inches (45.7 cm) and a plate depth of 12¼ inches (31 cm). When the swinger section is placed at a right angle to the folder, two parallel folds (three additional folds) are provided. For this position of the swinger section, all four plates (Nos. 1 through 4) have a roller width of 18 inches (45.7 cm) and a plate depth of 12¼ inches (31 cm). The pump drive motor has a ¾-horsepower motor and the folder motor a ½-horsepower motor.

Figure F-7 is General Binding Corporation's O&M Pro-Fold heavyweight tabletop folding machine. The machine is designed for use by small, medium, and in-plant printing shops, and can be used as a satellite folder for the large binder. It features a see-through protective shield over all rollers as a safety measure and is available with a right-angle fold attachment. Maximum sheet size is 11.69 by 18 inches (29 by 45.7 cm). Fold roll speed is 4,500 inches per minute (114.25 m per minute). Minimum fold is 1½ inches (3.8 cm). Plate depth for No. 1 and No. 2 plates is 12 inches (30.4 cm). The motor is rated at ⅓-horsepower, and weight of the machine is 107 pounds (48.5 kg).

Fig. F-7 General Binding Corporation's O&M Pro-Fold heavyweight tabletop folding machine.

folding: prints Blueprints, whiteprints, and any prints taken from original engineering, construction, or architectural drawings may be folded to size. A standard method of folding prints ensures visible identifying numbers when the prints are filed or stored. Regardless of the size of flat prints, all are folded to 8½ by 11 inches (21.6 by 27.9 cm) and filed so that the drawing number is visible on the outside in the upper right corner when a print is being selected (the drawing number also appears in the title block in the lower right corner). So-called "accordion-pleated" folding may be used.

Folding requires a folding board of sheet metal, plastic, or wood, measuring 8⅜ by 10⅞ inches (21.2 by 27.6 cm) with rounded corners, and a small block of smooth wood for creasing. The duplicate drawing number must appear in the upper right corner after folding. Fold procedures for various sizes are as follows:

Size, in.	Size, cm	Folding
8½ by 11	21.6 by 28	None required
11 by 17	28 by 43	One fold to 8½ by 11 in. (21.6 by 28 cm)
17 by 22	43 by 55.8	First fold to 17 by 11 in. (43 by 28 cm); second fold to 8½ by 11 in. (21.6 by 28 cm)
22 by 34	55.8 by 86.3	First fold to 34 by 11 in. (86.3 by 28 cm); second fold to 11 by 17 in. (28 by 43 cm); third fold to 8½ by 11 in. (21.6 by 28 cm)

Size, in.	Size, cm	Folding
11 by 34	28 by 86.3	First fold to 11 by 17 (28 cm to 43 cm); second fold to 8½ by 11 in. (21.6 by 28 cm)

For all roll-size and flat prints not listed above, accordion folds are made by using the folding board. In each case, the first fold is an 11-inch (27.9-cm) fold made from the end that carries the drawing number. Each fold thereafter also is 11 inches (27.9 cm) except the last, which may be smaller. After the length of the print has been folded into the required number of 11-inch accordion folds, the width is folded in 8½-inch (21.6-cm) folds.

foldout (gatefold)   Insert wider than the page width of a publication. It may require one or more vertical folds so that it will occupy the same area as the page. Foldouts are used to accommodate large illustrations, charts, and the like.

For technical publications measuring 8½ by 11 inches (21.6 by 28 cm), right-hand page foldouts should have the figure number and title on the right 4½-inch (11.4 cm) dimension of the 8½-inch (21.6 cm) width. When a left-hand foldout backs up a right-hand foldout, figure number and title are centered across the page. If a single foldout is interspersed with text, it should be a right-hand page.

folio   In papermaking, a paper size measuring 17 by 22 inches (43 by 55.8 cm); in printing, a sheet of paper folded once; in a publication, a page number.

follow copy   Direction to compose or type copy exactly like the manuscript copy without making any changes.

font, phototypesetting   Number of typeface designs and typeface sizes in points that can be mixed at any one time in a machine setup. A photomatrix contains the typeface designs, and the lens system has the ability to enlarge or reduce in a given number of sizes measured in points. The number of typeface designs multiplied by the number of sizes determines the number of fonts. For example, a machine setup has a photomatrix drum (or disk) that hold four different type designs and the lens assembly contains eight typeface sizes. The number of fonts in the setup is 32.

font, printing   Complete assortment of characters of one size and style of type, including capitals, small capitals, lowercase, numbers, and punctuation marks. Matching italic and bold characters are often available.

foolscap   Any of various sizes of paper measuring from about 12 by 15 inches (30.5 by 38.1 cm) to about 13½ by 17 inches (34.3 by 43.1 cm).

foot margin   Space between the image area and the bottom of the page.

footnote   Note of comment, explanation, or citation appearing at the bottom of a page or table. It is usually set in smaller type than the text or table on which it comments. If necessary, a long footnote may be carried over to the foot of the succeeding page. Footnotes are usually referred to in text by superior numbers and in tables by reference marks. When superior numbers are used in text, numbering is generally by chapter in nontechnical books and by page in technical works.

In a publication divided into chapters, sections, or articles, each beginning a new page, text footnotes begin with number 1 in each such division. In a publication without such divisional grouping, footnotes are numbered from 1 to 99 and then begin with 1 again. In supplemental sections such as appendixes and bibliographies, which are not part of the publication proper, footnotes begin with number 1. Footnotes are set in paragraphs and are separated from the text by a 50-point (17.56-mm) rule on a 6-point (2.11-mm) body, flush on the left, with 1 lead above and below the rule. For typewritten matter, use a 1-inch (2.54-cm) rule to separate text from the footnote.

When symbols or signs are used for footnote reference marks, their sequence should be as follows: * asterisk, † dagger, ‡ double dagger, § section mark, and ¶ paragraph.

forced aging Subjection of a light-sensitive emulsion or material to increased temperature in order to estimate its shelf life in advance of natural aging.

foreshorten In illustrating, to depict an object or line in less than its true perspective.

foreword Statement forming part of the front matter of a book, frequently written by someone other than the author or editor. The term may be used synonymously with preface. *See also* PREFACE.

form Type and material secured in a chase and ready for printing or electrotyping.

form roller Roller in the ink distribution system of a printing press. The roller comes in direct contact with the printing plate and transfers ink to form the image on a substrate.

format General form of a book, brochure, direct-mail piece, or other printed matter, with particular reference to composition, layout, size, and general appearance.

former Triangular device used on a web-fed printing press to make a longitudinal fold. The paper travels over the former and converges at the apex, or nose, of the triangle to make the fold. A roller keeps the web smooth before forming begins. Small air jets along the edges and nose of the former reduce the heat caused by friction. A double former folder will produce two folds. *See also* DOUBLE FORMER FOLDER.

former fold (newspaper fold) In a web-fed press, a longitudinal fold made by a former as the web travels over it.

foundry proof Last or final proof of type and material locked in a form before electrotyping or stereotyping.

foundry type Type cast in individual pieces.

fountain Ink receptacle attached to a printing press or machine. There is provision for direct application of the ink to distributing plates or rollers.

fountain roller Roller that revolves in the ink fountain. In lithography, it is also the roller that revolves in the dampening solution.

fountain solution (also **dampening solution**) In lithography, generally a mixture of water, acid, buffer, and a gum to prevent the nonprinting areas of the plate from receiving ink. Alcohol is added to some solutions. A proper balance between the solution and the ink is an important factor for quality printing.

Fourdrinier machine Papermaking machine whose name is derived from two brothers, Sealy and Henry Fourdrinier of London, who built a successful machine in Bermondsey, England, in 1803. Their machine was perfected from a crude paper machine invented in France in 1799 by Nicolas Robert.

fourth cover Exposed back cover of a book or magazine.

fpm Abbreviation for feet per minute.

frame Lines drawn or printed around an illustration or other copy in the form of a rectangle. An illustration should never be enclosed in a frame on original artwork; instead, the lines should be ruled on the basic reproduction page of which the illustration becomes a part when copy is prepared for photo-offset reproduction. The term "frame" also denotes an individual picture in a strip of motion-picture film.

free sheet Sheet of paper without wood particles.

French fold Method of folding in which a sheet of stock is printed on one side only and folded twice to form an uncut four-page folder.

friction feed Method of feeding sheet paper into a printing press or other device in which rubber rollers are used to transport the paper in its initial progress through the press. Friction feed may be distinguished from suction and hand feeding.

friction-glazed finish Highly polished finish given to coated papers by using wax and processing the paper through friction rollers.

fringe Soft halo surrounding small black dots on a large, clear field that shows on the original first-generation-halftone. *See also* SOFT DOT.

frisket (or **art knife**) Any small knife with a fine cutting edge used by artists, illustrators, and others for precise cutting of graphic arts materials. Figure F-8 illustrates an art knife (top), a frisket knife, and a scalpel. The art knife incorporates a strong nylon handle which is shaped to prevent rolling on drafting tables, and a machined aluminum locking mechanism. The frisket knife has a No. 11 blade which is permanently molded into the handle. A locking safety cap protects the user and the blade when not in use. The frisket knife is disposable. The scalpel is a straight razor which folds for safe storage. Figure F-9 shows a blade dispenser and two blade configurations used with the knives.

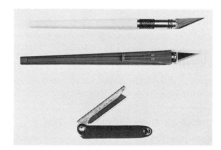

Fig. F-8 Chartpak's graphic arts knives and scalpel.

frisket paper Thin transparent paper used to block out or mask portions of art during retouching or airbrushing. The paper is cut with a sharp knife after the art has been mounted on a mounting board. *See also* AIRBRUSHING.

front cover Face of a book or magazine. The cover may be soft and flexible or hard, as in a case-bound book. *See also* COVER PAPER.

front jacket flap Front, folded-inside portion of a jacket on a case-bound book. It usually contains copy that is continued to the back jacket flap and may include a photograph of the author.

front matter All matter that precedes the text of a publication, which should begin on page 1, a right-hand page. The preceding material is front matter and may include a half title, frontispiece, title page, copyright, foreword, preface, abstract, table of contents, list of illustrations, list of tables, and the like. Front-matter pages are generally numbered with lowercase roman numerals, but printed numbers do not appear until after the copyright page.

frontispiece Formerly, the first page or title page of a book; now a photograph, sketch, drawing, portrait, or other illustration prefacing a book or other publication. In a commercial publication, a frontispiece may consist of one or more line drawings or photographs that serve as a visual introduction to the article under discussion. If such a frontispiece is a line drawing, it should be drawn in perspective as an assembled view and show the best angle of view.

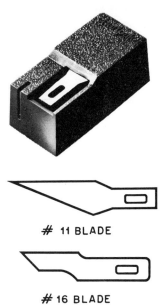

11 BLADE

16 BLADE

Fig. F-9 Chartpak's dispenser and knife blades.

fugitive color Colored ink or other color that is sensitive to light and fades or changes hue with age and exposure.

full binding All-leather binding of a book.

full measure Entire width of a line of type measured in picas. A line of type set full measure is flush with both margins.

full shadow Typographic effect created by outlining an entire letter or line of type.

full space Horizontal space between lines of type or a space between lines of typewritten matter. Quite frequently the term "double space" is used in connection with typewritten matter and can be understood to mean two spaces, whereas to double-space means to strike the carriage return key twice, resulting in leaving only one space between lines. The expression "one full space" or "two full spaces" to indicate space between typewritten lines is preferable.

full-word wrap Method of moving a word intact to the beginning of the next line instead of breaking the word when an entire word does not fit at the end of a line on the video display terminal. This is a function of the phototypesetter.

furniture In hot-metal linecasting work, wood or metal pieces used to fill in the blank areas of typeforms that are locked in a chase.

fuzz Loose or projecting fibers on a paper surface.

gallery In process-camera work, the area in and around the copyboard, camera tracks, exterior control panels, and so on.

galley Long, shallow metal tray used by compositors to hold type after it has been set. Proofs called galley proofs are pulled from the galley. The type in the galley is later divided into pages.

galley proof Proof taken from type while still on the galley, before the material has been divided into pages. It is about 24 inches (61 cm) long. In cold-composition work, the prejustified reproduction copy is sometimes called a galley proof to identify the copy.

gamma In photographic work, the degree of contrast of a photographic image as represented by the slope of the straight-line portion of the characteristic curve. The gamma is numerically equal to the tangent of the angle which the straight-line portion makes with the base line.

gang shooting In photolithographic platemaking, photographing several pages of original copy, such as pages of a book or booklet, at the same time. The pages are arranged on a surface so that after printing, folding, binding, and trimming they will be in numerical sequence. To save the cost of separate negatives, unrelated images may also be grouped for gang shooting if reduction or enlargement is the same for all.

gate page Page having a gatefold.

gatefold *See* FOLDOUT.

GATF Abbreviation for Graphic Arts Technical Foundation, a member-supported, nonprofit, scientific technical and educational organization that serves the graphic communications industries.

gathering Collating signatures in the order in which they are to appear in a book. Machines which automatically gather sheets or signatures in page sequence are used when a great number of copies are required. *See also* COLLATING.

gelatin process Direct-image duplicating process. Writing, typed matter, or drawn images are impressed on a master paper by special carbon ribbon or with a hectograph pencil or ink. The image on the master is pressed into a gelatin mass or pad and then transferred from the gelatin to duplicator paper. The copy is referred to as a gelatin or "jelly" print.

generation Single step in a reproduction process. First-generation halftones are those made with a contact screen. Second-generation halftones are contacts made from first-generation originals.

geometry symbols *See* TABLE 10, *page 446.*

ghost Colloquial term used by drafters and others for a smudge or smear, such as a portion of an image left by poor erasing.

ghosting *See* FADEBACK.

glassine papers Papers produced from highly hydrated paper pulp. It is semi-transparent and resists grease. Glassine paper is used to package food products. Certain special waxes are applied to produce heat-sealable packaging material for foods having moisture. Glassine papers are usually printed by flexography and gravure processes.

glossary List of terms in a particular field with their definitions.

glossy print Photoprint having a glossy finish, as distinguished from one having a matte finish. Such a print is not adaptable for rework, as the glazed surface does not readily absorb ink. If nomenclature is required, an acetate overlay containing the nomenclature should be used. If artwork is not required on the face of a print, a glossy should be used for screening into a fine reproduction halftone. If ink work must be done on a glossy print, the gloss may be erased and the surface will then accept ink.

goldenrod flats Orange-colored masking paper used in layout and makeup work for stripping in line and halftone negatives for lithographic reproduction. It is preprinted and ruled to serve as a guide for the place-ment of the stripped-in negative. The paper is opaque so that light cannot pass through it when the negative is exposed, yet it has sufficient translu-cency so that it may be cut over a light table.

gothic Typeface that is square-cut, sans serif, and without hairlines.

gradation Variation in tonal values from white to black; also, the passing of one tint or shade into another by insensible degrees. The tones between the two extremes are called middle tones.

grain: paper Alignment of paper fibers as a result of the manufacturing process. The grain of paper should be parallel with the binding edge. Grains are classified as long and short. Grain may be determined by tearing the paper; if the paper tears easily with relatively few broken edges, it is torn with the grain. A smooth and even crease results when paper is folded with the grain.

grain: photography Minute variations of density in a developed photo-graphic emulsion. The variations are caused by irregular distribution of the silver crystals.

graining Treating the surface of a lithograph plate to ensure retention of water on the nonimage area to repel ink.

graph Diagrammatic representation of changes in a variable quantity in comparison with those of other variables. The term is used in preference to "chart" in scientific and technical work.

graphic arts Arts represented by drawing or imposing on a flat surface an image that communicates a message; also the methods, processes, and techniques employed in these arts. The three components necessary for any graphic arts function are the products and tools with which the image is made, the kind of image produced, and the material on which the image is applied or formed. These three components are the theme around which the *Encyclopedia* has been written.

graphic scale *See* SCALE: ENGINEERING DRAWINGS.

graphical map Graphic representation of an area that shows various factors in addition to geographical features. A weather map, for example, reflects conditions such as wind movements and velocities, temperatures, pressures, and rainfall. A graphical map may be constructed to show pictorially farm and industrial products in their respective locations.

graphoscope Optical instrument used to magnify engravings, photographs, and the like.

Graphotype Trade name of a machine that embosses characters on a thin metal plate. It is used largely in producing addresses and lists.

gravure printing *See* INTAGLIO PRINTING; PRINTING METHODS.

great primer Old type size. The nearest equivalent in the point system is 18 point.

grid drawing, proportional Method of drawing objects in a larger or smaller size by using a grid with evenly spaced vertical and horizontal lines. A translucent or transparent overlay is placed over the original artwork, and the grid lines are drawn on it. A second grid is then drawn on paper with lines in proportion to the reduction or enlargement desired. A reference point is established at each point where a line of the object crosses a grid line. For fine details, finer evenly spaced grid lines are used in the same proportion. For example, to reduce artwork by one-half, a 1-inch (2.54-cm) grid line is used for the original art and a ½-inch (1.27-cm) grid line for the reduced art. For fine details, ¼, ⅛, or 1/16 -inch (6.350, 3.175, or 1.588-mm) grid lines are used with the ½-inch (1.27-cm) grid scale.

grid, photocomposition Grid photomatrix containing an assortment of typeface designs that is used in photocomposition equipment. Each character bears a transparent image for light emission with an opaque background. The number of typeface designs on the grid multiplied by the number of type sizes employed by the lens system is the mixing capability and is equivalent to the number of fonts available at a one-time machine setup for mixing. Because of the interchangeability of matrices, the number of fonts will vary in proportion to the number of typeface designs on the photomatrix.

grid, preprinted Spaced vertical and horizontal lines imposed by preprinting or by drawing on a plane surface. Grid lines may be imposed by the arithmetic or by the logarithmic scale. Preprinted grid forms are useful for drawing charts, block diagrams, sketches, and graphs. Artwork may be prepared directly on the grid. Brown or black preprinted grid lines are employed if the lines are to be reproduced photographically, but light blue preprinted or drawn lines should be used if the lines are not to be reproduced. *See also* GRID DRAWING, PROPORTIONAL.

gripper edge (gripper margin) Forward, or leading, edge of paper held by grippers of the printing press. In calculating the total paper area, an allowance must be made for gripper edges, especially in printing from forms.

grippers Metal fingers that clamp on paper and control its flow as it passes through the printing press.

groundwood Inexpensive wood pulp, such as that used in the manufacture of newsprint.

groundwood paper Paper used originally for newsprint. It is manufactured from groundwood pulp and bleached or unbleached chemical pulp. With modern papermaking machines and techniques, the utilization of groundwood pulp has been extended to include the manufacture of many varieties and grades of paper for magazines, catalogs, directories, books, and wallpaper, as well as commercial printing paper.

guide roller *See* COCKING ROLLER.

gum Protective substance used to coat offset printing plates when they are not in use.

gumming Method of applying a protective gum film to the surface of a lithographic plate.

gutter Inner margins of two facing pages in a book or other publication; also, the space between two columns.

gutter bleed Unbroken image that extends across the gutter in the double spread of a newspaper, magazine, or other publication.

H and J Abbreviation for hyphenation and justification, a term used in typesetting of any kind.

hairline Finest of an assortment of printing rules. The term also denotes an unfavorable characteristic of the text image mass that shows as impressions around and between printed characters. Found only in hot-metal linecasting work, the hairline condition is caused by the frequent collision of matrices with one another, resulting in a breakdown of their sidewalls. The breakdown leaves a space between adjacent matrices where molten lead escapes and appears on the type slug, thus causing the printed hairline.

halation Blurring of a photographic image, particularly in highlight areas, caused by light reflection from the back surface of the base of the film. *See* ANTIHALATION BACKING; *see also* FILMS AND PLATES.

half title (bastard title) Title of a book appearing in the front matter, usually immediately following the front flyleaf and preceding the full title page, which not only repeats the title but adds other information such as the author's name and the publisher's name and location. In some technical publications, a half title page is one that bears the title on the upper portion of the first page of text. Such a page must conform to specifications. In government parlance, a half title page is a panel title page. It may also be called a short title page.

halftone Tone pattern of shades from white through black of a continuous-tone image, made by photographing the image through a finely ruled glass screen with crossing opaque lines. The screening reduces the tones to a dot formation for reproduction by printing. It is claimed that half of the original image is thus eliminated and half of the full tone remains. *See also* CONTINUOUS-TONE ART; LINE CONVERSION.

halftone blowup Enlargement of a prescreened photolithographic negative to effect a course dot formation.

halftone paper Smooth paper prepared especially for the reproduction of halftones.

halftone percentage Percent of the total area covered by halftone dots.

halftone screen Screen placed in front of the negative material in a process camera to break up a continuous-tone image into a dot formation. There are two types of halftone screens, ruled glass screens and contact screens.

halftone screening Since letterpress or lithographic printing presses cannot lay down varying densities of ink, they cannot differentiate tones. Therefore, to obtain the illusion of tone gradations in printing, continuous-tone images such as photographs must be broken up into tiny dots. When the printing press deposits ink in these dot areas, the eye interprets the mixture of ink dots and unprinted specks of white paper as gray tones. In letterpress printing, metal plates are exposed to halftone negatives. Etching the metal plate creates a relief image. The raised areas in the relief surface pick up ink and are the printing areas. Photolithographic methods are based on the principle that water repels greasy ink. By treating either a smooth or grained plate so that water adheres in areas around the dots, ink is repelled from all but the dot surface. In black-and-white photomechanical printing without the dot pattern, no tones between the solid black of the ink and the white of the paper used would be printed. Dots of different sizes in a uniform grid, therefore, are the means of mechanically reproducing intermediate gray tones.

One method of preparing halftone negatives requires a cross-line screen consisting of two pieces of glass cemented together. Figure H-1A shows an enlarged pattern of a glass halftone screen. Each piece of glass has parallel lines which are etched into the surface and filled with an opaque material. The two sheets of glass are cemented together with the lines at right angles to each other to form a grid. The areas between the lines form transparent squares. In use, the glass screen is mounted in a holder in a process camera and positioned just in front of a sheet of lithographic film. The spacing between the film and the glass screen is adjustable and is determined by the screen ruling and by the lens opening used. Screen distance is critical because it affects the halftone contrast as well as dot shape and dot quality.

Another method of making halftone negatives utilizes a contact screen. A contact screen is composed of vignetted dots on a flexible support. See Figure H-1B, which is an enlarged pattern of a Kodak magenta contact screen. As the name implies, the film is used in contact with a light-sensitive film. Because it is essential that the contact is as close as possible, a vacuum holder and vacuum pump are used to remove the air between the two materials. Kodak has a variety of contact screens available for use in photolithography, photoengraving, and photogravure. Many are offered in either conventional or elliptical-dot patterns.

Halftone screens vary in quality. Screens are defined and classified by the number of dots that appear per linear inch. The most commonly used screens are 55, 65, 85, 100, 120, 133, and 150-line screens. Screens defined as 55, 65, and 85-line screens contain fewer dots and produce coarse halftones as compared with, for example, the 150-line screen. The coarse halftone screens are used for newspaper reproduction and other work not requiring fine quality. The 100, 110, and 120-line screens are used for supercalendered papers, and the 133 and 150-line screens are used for printing halftones on coated papers when a very high quality of reproduction is desired. If one looks at a halftone through an ordinary magnifying glass, the rows of dots are readily recognized.

Fig. H-1A Enlarged patterns of glass halftone screen.

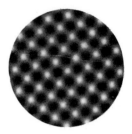

Fig. H-1B Kodak Magenta contact screen.

hand composition Setting type by hand. The type is set on a measured composing stick. When a full measure is being set, quadrats are inserted to make the line flush right with other lines. This is called "justifying" or "justification." *See also* COMPOSING STICK.

hand lettering *See* BRUSHES, ART; PENS, STEEL-BRUSH; SPEEDBALL PENS; STYLUS.

handbill Printed sheet, usually containing advertising, that is circulated by hand.

hanger marks (edge marks) Objectionable marks produced on film by the developing hanger. They are usually due to poor agitation in the first developer.

hardcopy Copy of any kind, except on film, that is produced on paper or any substrate that can be used as an end item for proofing, checking, revising, or redrawing; typed, printed, or copied matter (as opposed to film, cathode-ray tube, and digital displays). Examples are tabulated computer printouts, camera-ready reproducible copy, photographic reproductions, printing and copying of any kind, and outputs from disks, punched paper, and magnetic tape.

hardcover book *See* CASE-BOUND BOOK.

hard dot Expression used to describe second- or third-generation contacted halftones whose dots are crisp and lacking in fringe or veiling.

head rule First or top rule of a boxhead in the layout of tables. It extends the full width of the table.

head-to-foot arrangement Arrangement of copy on both sides of a sheet with the foot of the opposite page aligned with the top of the first page. It is necessary to flip the sheet to view the opposite page for normal reading.

head-to-head arrangement Arrangement of copy so that the top of the page is at the same end on both sides of a sheet.

heading Caption or title of a division of a brochure, book, or other publication. Center headings are centered on a page or column. Sideheads may be flush with one side or indented in alignment with other page elements. Headings are printed in type chosen to set them apart from the text and to make a distinction between main and subsidiary headings.

headless paragraph Paragraph that stands alone without the support of a sidehead.

headline Major caption set above a newspaper or magazine article or advertising text. The size of the type indicates the importance the editor attaches to the topic.

Headliner Trade name of a display typesetter. *See* TYPESETTERS, PHOTO-GRAPHIC.

headpiece Illustrative image used to decorate a chapter or section heading.

headwriter Nonphotographic headline composing machine.

heat-set ink Special ink used for high-speed printing. It dries rapidly when the web (paper roll) is passed through a dryer at approximately 350°F and then chilled by cooling rollers. The setting temperature is approximately 80 to 90°F.

hectograph Device for making duplicate copies from a prepared gelatin surface to which the original image has been transferred.

height Distance between two points along the vertical dimension. It is perpendicular to the width. When measurements are given for line and continuous-tone copy, the width and the height are stated in that order. *See also* VERTICAL DIMENSION.

Helios Line of opaque papers and cloths and transparent papers, cloths, and films manufactured especially for dry diazo reproduction. Helios is a registered trade name of the Keuffel and Esser Company. The opaque materials comprise a series of papers and cloths with black, blue, and maroon lines. The opaque prints, which are produced from right-reading translucent originals, serve as working prints in engineering and production departments and may be used for the reproduction of maps and other types of drawings. They are also used for business forms, duplicate copies, manuals, handbooks, and bulletin-board notices. The blackline papers are obtainable in white, yellow, pink, green, and blue. The several transparent papers are all 100 percent rag papers with sepia lines. The plastic-coated transparent cloths and clear or matte acetate safety films have sepia lines; they are used primarily for making intermediates.

Herculene drafting film Trade name of durable, translucent, and tear-resistant drafting film manufactured by the Keuffel and Esser Company. It has excellent erasing qualities for ink, pencil, or typewritten copy. Herculene film may be obtained in sheet sizes as ordered or in 20-yard (18.3-m) rolls with widths of 30, 36, 42, or 54 inches (76, 91.4, 106.6, or 137 cm). Base thicknesses are 0.003 and 0.002 inch (0.0762 and 0.0508 mm); a matte finish is available on one or both sides of either thickness. The film accepts printer's ink for title blocks, logotypes, or forms. When a material is translucent, excellent copies are obtained by using the whiteprint reproduction process.

hickles Defects in a print appearing as specks surrounded by an unprinted "halo."

hidden line Line used to show a hidden feature of a part or article. As used in orthographic engineering and mechanical drawings, it is designated as a "medium" line and consists of evenly spaced short dashes. Hidden lines should always begin with a dash in contact with the line from which they start unless such a dash would form a continuation of a full line. Dashes should touch at corners, and arcs should start with dashes on the tangent points. *See also* LINE CONVENTIONS: ENGINEERING DRAWINGS.

High Contrast Pan film Du Pont separation negative film on Cronar polyester film base. It is used when high gammas are required in making continuous-tone color-separation negatives from reflection (opaque) copy or from low-contrast color transparencies.

high finish Smooth high-polished paper finish.

highlight Light portion of a photograph. In a negative, highlights are the areas of highest density since these correspond to the lightest areas of the original.

highlight halftone Halftone plate in which the dots usually present in highlights have been etched away. The act of etching out or eliminating halftone dots in negatives is called "dropout." Practically all dropouts are confined to continuous-tone copy other than photographs, such as wash drawings, crayons, and charcoal drawings with large white areas.

hologram Image recorded on a photographic plate produced by coherent light waves which inherently set up interference paths. The hologram is produced by exposing the plate to light reflected from an object and a reference source. A laser beam can furnish light of the required degree of coherence. Three-dimensional objects will produce three-dimensional images of the object by proper illumination; in addition, if color film is used, the color can be reproduced. Because highly coherent light is required to produce the hologram, research in holography was advanced with the advent of the laser.

honing Mechanical method used to remove unwanted image areas from a printing plate.

horizontal bar chart *See* BAR CHART.

horizontal dimension Dimension of a plane that extends parallel to the horizon. It represents the width of an image when the image is viewed from the correct left-to-right position. The horizontal dimension is the major controlling dimension in graphic arts insofar as proportions are concerned. Its correlative is the vertical dimension. When used as the controlling dimension, the horizontal dimension governs the reduction or enlargement of line and halftone art as well as text copy and nomenclature for paste-ups. For oversize line and halftone art, the width of the image to be reproduced, from crop mark to crop mark, is the controlling dimension. For a page of solid text that has been set or typed oversize, the dimension is the width of the text area. When a single strip of nomenclature has been set or typed for paste-up and an enlargement or a reduction of the letters is desired, the horizontal dimension is the distance from the left edge to the right edge of the copy. *See also* SCALING.

horizontal page *See* BROADSIDE PAGE.

hot composition Setting type by machine, as with the Linotype, Intertype, Monotype, and other composing machines, in which characters are cast into slugs of molten metal or as single pieces of type.

house organ   Periodical published by a business organization for its employees or customers.

hydrographic chart   Map that depicts a body of water, sometimes with adjacent land, showing its location, flow, depth, and other significant phenomena.

hydrophilic   Property of a substance that makes it more receptive to water and fountain solutions than to oils and inks; used in lithography.

hydrophobic   Property of a substance that makes it more receptive to oils and inks than to water and fountain solutions; used in lithography.

hygroscope   Instrument for recording changes of atmospheric humidity in paper which result from attracting and absorbing moisture from the air. The hygroscope, having the configuration of a sword, is inserted between paper stock. A sensitive element in the blade of the instrument expands with increasing relative humidity and contracts with decreasing relative humidity. As the element contracts or expands, the movement is mechanically magnified to cause a needle or other indicating device to show a reading on a calibrated scale.

hygroscopic   Property in paper and other substances that makes them absorb moisture.

hyperbolic functions: symbols   *See* TABLE 10, *page 446.*

hypo   Short term for hyposulfite, or sodium thiosulphate, a white translucent, crystalline compound used as a photographic fixing agent and as a bleach.

idler rollers *See* WEB LEAD ROLLERS.

illustration *See* FIGURE.

illustration board (artist's board) Heavy paperboard manufactured especially for artists, for both oil and watercolor application. Standard sizes are 22 by 30, 22 by 28, 28 by 44, 30 by 40, and 40 by 60 inches (55.8 by 76.2, 55.8 by 71.1, 71.1 by 111.7, 76.2 by 101.6, and 101.6 by 152.4 cm); weights vary from thick to heavy. Thick board is about 8-ply (0.762 mm) heavy, 24- to 30-ply (2.134 to 2.742 mm). Colors range from white gray to snow white.

illustration file number *See* ART FILE NUMBER.

illustration request Form that requests that an individual piece of art be executed. It is usually filled in by the writer of the text that the illustration is to accompany.

illustration title *See* FIGURE TITLE.

image Any representation of a concept or an object on a paper sheet, plate, or other material. It may be drawn, typewritten, stamped, printed, marked, cut, carved, engraved, typeset, or photographed and may be applied by any method or process. The image may be a type mass of text, a line drawing, a photograph, a symbol, or a dot, but only if it was made intentionally and communicates a message. An image is not an ink smear, an erasure ghost, or an unintended mark.

image area Square or rectangular area that encompasses a printed, drawn, or photographed image and the white or dark background space around the image. It is enclosed by imaginary perpendicular and horizontal lines. For artwork, the four sides of the area are established by using crop marks that limit the horizontal and vertical dimensions but are not printed. In text matter, the image area is defined by a line measure along the horizontal dimension and a line count along the vertical dimension, both expressed in picas. The image area may also be expressed in inches, particularly when oversize copy is to be reduced.

imposition Arrangement of the pages that are to be printed on one side of a sheet so that, when cut, folded, and trimmed, they will be right-reading and fall in numerical sequence. After margins have been determined for the outside dimensions of the sheet, it is the practice to allow additional margins of ⅛ to ¼ inch (3.175 to 6.350 mm) for trimming. When work is tumbled, that is, when a sheet is first sent through the press in a normal operation and then tumbled forward with the top of the second printing engaging the bottom of the first printing, it is imperative that all sheets have the same dimensions to register properly. Figure I-1 shows how various folders and booklets may be printed for correct imposition. Illustration *A* is the simplest form of imposition, if it can be termed imposition at all. One typing is made on the top half of a direct plate or stencil and run

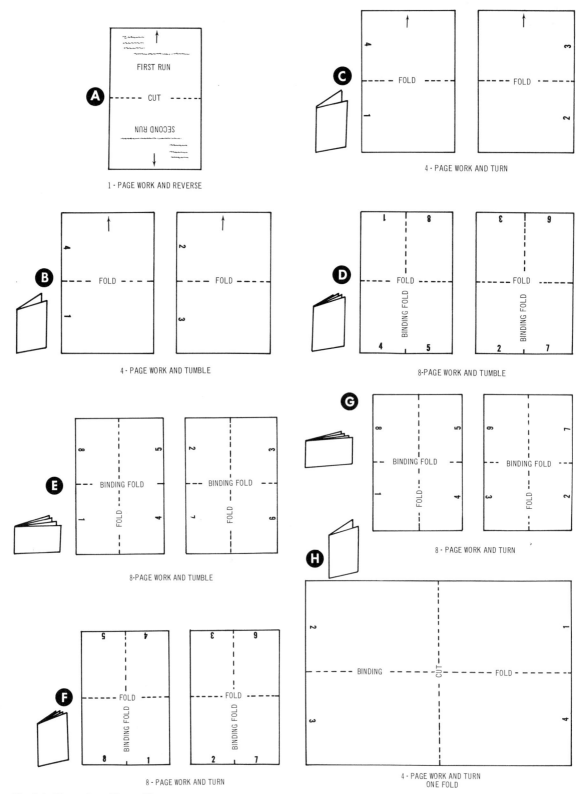

Fig. I-1   Examples of imposition.

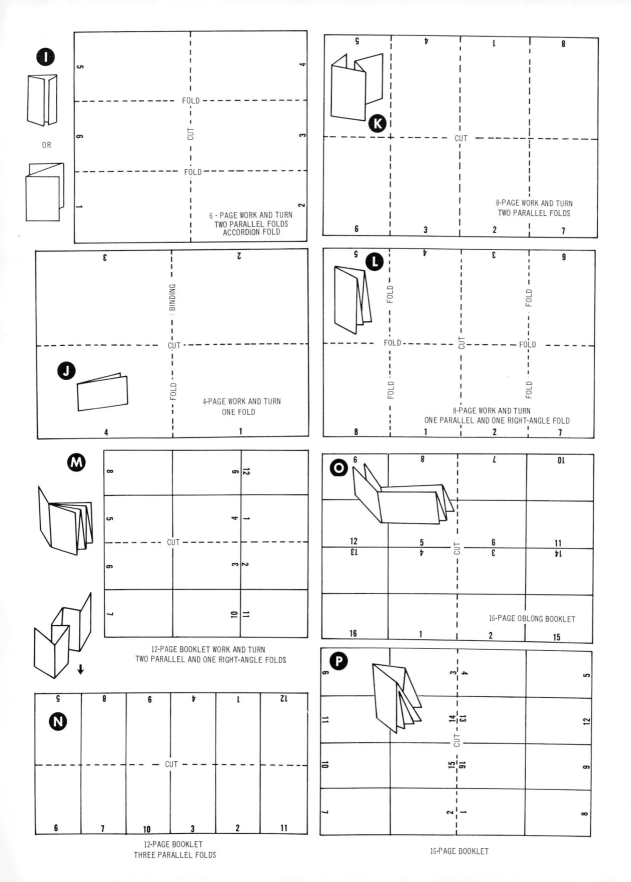

I

OR

5   FOLD   4

6   CUT   3

1   FOLD   2

6 - PAGE WORK AND TURN
TWO PARALLEL FOLDS
ACCORDION FOLD

K

5   4   1   8

CUT

6   3   2   7

8-PAGE WORK AND TURN
TWO PARALLEL FOLDS

J

3   BINDING   2

CUT

4   FOLD   1

4-PAGE WORK AND TURN
ONE FOLD

L

5   4   3   6

FOLD   FOLD

FOLD   CUT   FOLD

FOLD   FOLD

8   1   2   7

8-PAGE WORK AND TURN
ONE PARALLEL AND ONE RIGHT-ANGLE FOLD

M

8   6   12

5   4   1

CUT

6   3   2

7   10   11

12-PAGE BOOKLET WORK AND TURN
TWO PARALLEL AND ONE RIGHT-ANGLE FOLDS

O

9   8   7   10

12   5   6   11
13   4   CUT   3   14

16   1   2   15

16-PAGE OBLONG BOOKLET

N

5   8   9   4   1   12

CUT

6   7   10   3   2   11

12-PAGE BOOKLET
THREE PARALLEL FOLDS

P

6   3   4   5

11   14   13   12

10   15   16   9

CUT

7   2   1   8

16-PAGE BOOKLET

through the machine. The paper is then reversed, run through the machine again, and cut in half. Illustrations *A* through *H* show types of imposition suitable for duplicators, whereas those shown in illustrations *I* through *P* must be done on printing presses.

impression Degree of pressure or force required between the printing plate or form and the printing stock. A "kiss" impression is the ideal contact between plate and stock. An impression is also each individual piece of printed matter made during a pressrun, as well as an image of any kind imposed on a surface, such as the impression that printing type makes on a material when the type is inked or in embossing without ink. The term also denotes a printing, or all the copies made in one pressrun.

impression cylinder In a rotary printing press, the cylinder that impresses the paper against the plate or blanket cylinder containing the image.

impression paper Paper that receives the image in any duplicating or printing operation. It is known in the printing trade as printing stock or as the web (rolled paper) and in the reproduction field as copy paper.

imprint Matter printed on a page or sheet which has already been printed. Imprinting is generally confined to printing a name and address, perhaps with a logotype. The term "imprint" also was applied to the first book face that was designed and used in mechanical linecasting composition (1912). Its success proved that it was possible to draw and cut new type designs pantographically and that mechanically set type could rival in appearance the best examples of hand composition.

imprint unit Device used to print imprints on one side of a web (paper roll), usually from rubber plates. For example, each copy of *This Week Magazine*, a Sunday newspaper supplement, bears the imprint and usually the logotype of one of the newspapers whose publishers subscribe to it.

incunabula Books printed before 1501.

indention Holding of one or more lines of printed or typewritten matter in from the margin. The first word of a paragraph is usually indented. In a hanging indention, the first line is flush left and subsequent lines are indented 1 or more ems from the left.

index, alphabetical Alphabetical list of subjects, place names, and personal names presented as main entries and subentries, giving the page numbers of where they appear in the main body of text. The main purpose of an index is to make the book more useful to the reader. A good index is also influential in promoting sales because it readily identifies a book's contents for prospective purchasers. The index is usually prepared by the author from a duplicate set of page proofs. *See also* AUTHOR'S PROOF.

index guide Printed tab or other device marking a division of a publication, card file, ledger, or filing system for quick reference. Several kinds of index guides are used. One method involves printing divisions (dividers) on sheets of the same size as the publication. The guides are not visible when the book is closed but become apparent when it is fanned to locate the division. This type of index is printed with the book and generally on the same grade of paper. Text matter appears on the same sheet.

A second kind of indexing, called "thumb indexing," is often used in dictionaries. A single letter is printed on a black or colored half-round portion of the margin of a page at the beginning of each alphabetical section (sometimes a half-round printed tab is affixed to the page). Pages appearing before the index guide are die-cut to expose the letter. The guides are visible when the book is closed.

A third type of indexing guide extends beyond the standard sheet or card size and is usually printed separately on heavier stock. Such guides are used extensively in industry. Figure I-2 shows a typical arrangement of index guides for a book. There are six units, each of which contains three divisions. The broken lines represent notches that will be cut out. All the divisions are in the order in which they will appear in the assembled book.

To prepare index guides as shown in Figure I-2, follow this procedure:

1. Mark off three even divisions on the edge of the 11-inch (27.9-cm) dimension of a sheet of quality reproduction paper, using a fade-out blue pencil. Leave ¼-inch (6.35-mm) blank spaces at the right- and left-hand margins.

2. Draw lines for tabs either ⅜ or ½ inch (9.525 or 12.70 mm) wide from the edge of the paper along the 11-inch (27.9-cm) dimension.

3. Apply nomenclature to each position by paste-up, taking care that copy is spaced evenly within each tab. (If this cannot be done, the compositor will make the index tabs from furnished instructions.)

4. Use separate sheets of paper for each three-position unit and complete the paste-up.

The index guides are now ready for the printer, who will print from a plate for each unit. After printing, the sheets are notched with a circular die cut.

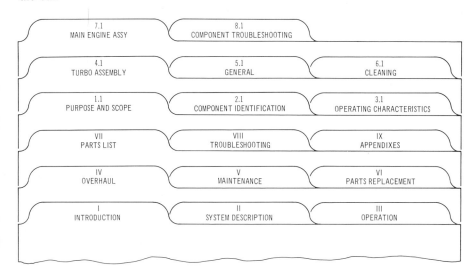

Fig. I-2 Arrangement of index guides for printing.

index letter Letter of the alphabet, usually a capital letter, used to key a part or item depicted in an illustration to a legend or to a discussion in text. Index numbers are used for the same purpose. *See also* KEY NUMBERS.

india ink Pigment made of lampblack and binding material; also this pigment suspended in water as a fluid ink. For good delineation, india ink should be solid black. Some india inks are gray in comparison with others.

india paper *see* BIBLE PAPER.

indirect color separation Color separation in which the various separation exposures are made on a continuous-tone film or plate and halftone screening is accomplished as one of the later steps of the process. Masks for color correction can be applied to the continuous-tone negatives.

infeed rollers *See* METERING UNIT.

inferior Subscript; a letter, numeral, or symbol written below the line and to the right of another character, in contrast to a superscript. It is set in a type size smaller than the text size. *See also* SUPERIOR.

initial First letter of a chapter, section, or article that is set in a type size larger than the text size. When the base of the initial is aligned with the base of the first text line, the initial is said to be a "stickup" initial. When the top of the initial is aligned with the top of the first text line and carry-over lines run around the lower part of the initial, the initial is said to be a "cut-in" initial.

initial caps Abbreviation for initial capital letters. As a direction to the printer, it indicates that the first letter of a word or the first letter of a series of words begins with a capital letter.

ink drier Prepared chemical added to printing inks to improve drying time and to prevent ink smearing. To test drying qualities, rub a finger over the ink rather firmly after ten minutes of drying. A smear largely confined to the area around the smear indicates good drying quality.

inked art Artwork that has been completed in ink after the penciled drawing has been checked for accuracy. When inked art is ready for reproduction, it is called reproduction or camera-ready copy.

inker *See* FINISHER.

inker, printing press System of ink distribution consisting of a series of rubber-to-steel rollers that mesh to transfer ink from the fountain to the plate cylinder. Some rollers vibrate or oscillate laterally (called a "stroke") to give a more even distribution and breakup of ink. The vibrator rollers in some high-speed presses are cooled with circulating water to control the temperature of the ink vibrators, thus keeping the ink from losing its quick-drying characteristics.

inks, printing The extent and impact that printing inks have had on the civilized world is so vast that it is almost difficult to conceive. The spread of knowledge and culture and the ability to pass on to successive generations the experience of the past have all been made possible largely through the application of ink to paper. Printing inks are found in almost every aspect of human activity. We are educated, informed, and entertained by books, newspapers, and magazines and through visual aids. Paintings, photographs, and countless packages and containers of all types are printed or colored with inks, from food packages and beverage cans to postage stamps, billboards, roadway signs, advertising literature, circuit boards, and a host of other uses. The list is endless because new uses are continually being found.

For more than 2,000 years, ink making has been a craft and a historic art. It had its beginnings in two of the oldest civilizations known to man: China and Egypt. Records show that the Chinese were experimenting with different ingredients and formulations as early as 200 B.C., more than 1,600 years before Gutenberg's development of movable type and the advent of the mechanical printing press. There are even mentions of ink in both the Old and New Testaments of the Bible. Even after Johann Gutenberg made his historic breakthrough of movable type in the fifteenth century, printing ink making remained a handicraft consisting of the simple physical mixing of familiar pigments and vehicles. In all those centuries, lampblack (soot) remained the principal pigment and varnish made by boiling linseed oil remained the vehicle of choice. It wasn't until the mid-nineteenth century, when such chemical advances as coal tar dyes and synthetic pigments, new solvents, and better vehicles were discovered, that ink making moved into the modern age.

Ink making today has become a major industry and a science. It requires high technology and the application of a variety of scientific disciplines and technical and management skills. Each advancement in the printing process, every new and complex piece of equipment, and each addition to the ever-growing list of materials which can be printed upon has called for chemical and physical changes in printing inks. Ink making now holds an important place within the chemical industry, converting the basic products of chemical manufacturers into end products for the graphic arts and allied industries. Research, coupled with increased knowledge of organic and colloidal chemistry, has enabled the industry to cope with the problems of producing inks for modern high-speed publication printing, package printing, and printing on a wide variety of surfaces and materials.

Ink is basically a chemical compound, different types of which have specific physical properties. Ink is manufactured from a variety of natural and synthetic materials and is made in modern, efficient plants which rely on the latest in automated and computer-directed machinery as well as the experience of a dozen kinds of skilled artisans.

While several specialty processes are also used, most printing inks may be classified into one of four basic categories according to the type of printing process by which they are applied. These four major printing processes are letterpress, lithography, gravure, and flexographic printing.

Letterpress. Letterpress inks are viscous, tacky systems. The vehicles are oil- or varnish-based and generally contain resins that cure by oxidation. The main exception is news ink, which generally consists solely of pigment dispersed in mineral oil, and drying, such as it is, is accomplished by absorption. While final drying of the ink film is due to oxidation of the resin or drying oil component, initial setting may take place by means of absorption of ink into the substrate or by evaporation by the application of heat-set inks. In some cases, especially where the letterpress image is being transferred to a rigid surface such as plastic or a two-piece metal container, the image is transferred to a blanket and then to the printed surface. This special form of letterpress printing has become known as "letterset" or "dry offset" since an offset blanket is used but no water is present in the printing process as in offset lithography.

Lithographic. Lithographic inks are viscous inks with varnish systems similar to letterpress varnishes. They differ in that the ink films applied are thinner than in letterpress; therefore, pigment contents must be higher. Also they must be formulated to run in the presence of water, since water is used to create the nonimage areas of the plate. In the lithographic process, ink is usually transferred from the plate to a rubber blanket which, in turn, transfers the image to the surface being printed. Since most lithographic printing is done with an offset blanket, the term "offset" has become synonymous with lithography. In certain limited applications, such as business-form printing, ink may be transferred directly from the lithographic plate to the printed surface. In this case the process is known as direct lithography.

Web offset printing, because of its higher running speeds, requires inks with lower viscosities and tack, but high resistance to emulsification with the fountain solution (water). Web offset inks can be separated into two categories: non-heat-set, which air dry, and heat-set, which dry with the assistance of drying ovens. Non-heat-set web offset inks are ink oils which are absorbed into the substrate during the drying process. Heat-set web offset inks, like heat-set letterpress inks, are set by driving off the ink oil in an oven. Most sheet offset inks are used for general commercial printing and are quickset types. Like quickset letterpress, these inks set rapidly as the ink oil component penetrates the substrate and subsequently dry as the vehicle cures by oxidation. High gloss and more abrasion-resistant inks, such as those used in carton printing, are modified with harder resins and often represent a compromise between quicksetting and better abrasion-resistant properties. Sheet offset inks are not dried with heat dryers, though some sheet presses do have low-level heat assist. Metal-decorating inks are lithographic inks which are specially formulated with synthetic resin varnishes to dry on metal surfaces with high-temperature baking. To decorate formed containers, special offset presses are used which may be either wet or dry offset processes. In either case, the ink systems are similar.

Flexographic. Flexographic inks are chemically different from paste inks used for letterpress and lithographic printing. They are low-viscosity (liquid) inks which dry by solvent evaporation, absorption into the substrate, and decomposition. There are two main types of flexographic inks: water and solvent. Water inks are used on absorbent paper stocks such as kraft or lightweight paper. Solvent types are used on films such as cellophane, polyethylene, or polypropylene. They may also be used on some paper substrates.

Gravure.   Gravure inks are low-viscosity (liquid) inks which dry by solvent evaporation. They are very versatile and may be formulated with an exceptionally wide range of resin vehicles. There are four main types of gravure inks. Each has certain specific applications which designate the type of binder and solvent used. Type A is used for publication printing and is the cheaper grade of the gravure inks. Type B is used for publications printed on better-grade stocks than is Type A. Type C is used for various types of packaging. Type T is used for package printing, primarily food cartons. There are also other miscellaneous types of gravure inks for special applications.

Metallic inks.   These inks consist of a suspension of fine metal flakes in vehicles that serve to bind the powders to the surface being printed. The high brilliancy and lustre characterizing these inks are caused by the "leafing" of metal flakes when they float to the ink surface. Metallic powders, such as aluminum, bronze, and copper, consist of metal in the form of flakes, plates, or flat granules. The flake form is most desirable because it covers a maximum surface and shows better leafing properties and lustre. Aluminum powders give better leafing properties than do gold bronzes because of the flakelike form and low specific gravity of the particles. Aluminum powder, because of the tenacious film of oxide which coats each particle, is not as prone to tarnish or darken when mixed with vehicles as is gold bronze. The bronze powder and vehicle for preparing "gold" inks are generally supplied separately, to be mixed in the correct proportion by the printer just before use. This is necessary because most gold inks tarnish rapidly once the powder has been mixed with the vehicle. The tarnishing probably is caused by the acidity of the vehicle.

Watercolor inks.   These inks are generally employed in the printing of wallpaper, greeting cards, and novelties. Watercolor inks are based on a vehicle composed essentially of gum arabic, dextrin, glycerin, and water. Pigments or dyes can be used as the colorant in this type of ink. Special rollers are required; water is used to wash the press.

Cold-set inks.   Inks of this type are solid rather than viscous liquids at room temperature. They consist of pigments dispersed in plasticized waxes having melting points ranging from 150 to 200°F. They are used on presses with fountains which are heated above the melting point of the inks. The inks are melted and maintained in a fluid condition until they are impressed on the relatively cold paper, where they revert almost instantly to their normal solid state. The advantages claimed for these inks are that they do not smudge or "set off," they are almost tack-free when in the fluid state, they neither skin in the cans nor dry on the presses, and they yield sharper printing results because they do not penetrate into the pores of the paper. However, technical and economic considerations involved in providing and maintaining the highly complicated heating and cooling devices on the presses have proved to be a great obstacle, and the process is used only for special applications, such as hot-spot carbon and transfer printing.

Magnetic inks.   Magnetic inks are used where an electronic system for character recognition is used for sorting and calculating as in bank checks, business forms, etc. Magnetic inks are made with pigments which can be magnetized after printing so that the printed characters can later be recognized by the electronic reading equipment. These inks must be formulated to produce exceptionally high-grade printing which will meet the rigid requirements of the reading equipment. Other systems of character recognition are being developed based on the optical characteristics of the printed sheet, using differences in the reflective properties of ink and paper.

General Printing Ink, a division of Sun Chemical Corporation, has developed a systems approach to drying ink called Suncure, a method that utilizes ultraviolet light to instantly change a photosensitive liquid ink to a solid film. The system involves no solvent and is one that improves rub, scratch, and grease. The system is composed of ultraviolet tube units that are mounted on the press and powered from a console interlocked with press controls. The number of units required depends upon the speed of the particular press and whether units are installed between color stations for dry trapping. Each unit is designed to focus light on the fast-moving substrate. Then, upon exposure to the ultraviolet light, the special Suncure inks (that contain photosensitors and monomers) rapidly polymerize and develop their dry film properties, with little external heat involved. As soon as the printed material leaves the press, it is ready for post-press operations such as die-cutting, folding, or the like. Because inks cure instantly, it is possible to dry trap print, or dry after each color station, with a gravure quality impression. (The foregoing discussion was provided through the courtesy of the National Association of Printing Ink Manufacturers, Inc., and Sun Chemical Corporation, General Printing Ink Division.)

insert Page or group of pages added to a publication during binding. The term also denotes, particularly in rough manuscript copy (copy in the process of being reproduced in one form or another), added text that is keyed to fall in its correct place in the copy. If all pages of the manuscript copy are right-hand pages, the insert may be typed on a separate sheet facing the page in which it is to appear. This procedure necessitates binding the insert at the right margin. It is a good plan to type inserts on paper of a different color from that used for the original manuscript copy. This lessens the chance of the insert's being overlooked by the typist preparing the final copy.

For copy that is to be set on a linecasting machine, an insert should be stripped in place by cutting the sheet where it falls. When stripping in an insert will leave a sheet longer than other sheets, the copy should be broken at the bottom of the page and carried over to another sheet. When additional sheets are thus required, letters are added to the page number, as in 236A, 236B, 236C, etc.

inspection drawing *See* DIMENSION DRAWING.

installation control drawing Engineering drawing that sets forth the dimensions of an item in terms of area and space, sway and access clearances, and pipe and cable attachments for installation and functioning with related items.

installation drawing In engineering drafting, an outline drawing that shows the form, location, and position of an item and provides mounting instructions with respect to its fixed points and other parts.

Instant Negative Conversion *See* NEGATIVE CONVERSION.

intaglio printing (gravure printing) Method of printing used in steel and copperplate engraving. An engraved plate is an exact opposite of a relief plate, the image being depressed below the surface of the plate. Ink floods over the plate and into the depressed areas. The top of the plate is then wiped clean with a "doctor blade," leaving ink only in the depressions. When paper is applied to the plate, the ink held in the depressed areas adheres to the paper and the image is printed. Ink used in intaglio printing must be more fluid than letterpress ink to maintain the flow into the engraved areas. *See also* PRINTING METHODS.

intensification Addition of density to negatives or prints, usually made by chemical treatment.

interconnection diagram Connection or wiring drawing that shows the external connections between units. Connections within the units themselves are usually omitted.

interleave *See* SLIP-SHEET.

interlock Effect of joining type characters, produced usually in display type set with a photographic typesetter. An interlock is similar to a ligature. *See* LIGATURE.

intermediate Copy of an original on translucent or transparentized film, paper, or cloth from which subsequent copies are made. An intermediate serves as a master only in the sense that it is used to make additional copies so that the original may be filed and saved from wear and tear. More than one intermediate may be made from the same original, thus saving production time in running off copies. Used largely in the whiteprint process, intermediates are required to intensify weak originals and to permit design and copy changes while leaving the original unaltered.

1. Make intermediate prints of original tracings and drawings. Use the intermediates as working originals and keep the originals in the files, where they will be spared frequent handling.

2. If the original is weak, torn, or faded, make an intermediate print of the original copy on translucent material. Use this translucent print in place of the original to produce subsequent prints in the machine.

3. Make design changes without altering or tracing the original by producing a translucent print of the original. Make the changes on the print with pencil or ink and produce as many prints of the design change as are needed.

4. When two or more drawings are to contain basic elements common to all, intermediates eliminate the need for tracing or redrawing the constant elements each time. Make a drawing containing only the constant elements

and as many copies of the original as there are different drawings required. Complete the individual drawings at the drafting board by adding the respective design variations to the translucent prints.

5. Make composite prints of two or more originals by (*a*) reproducing each original on translucent material, blocking out or later eradicating any unwanted portions of the original design; (*b*) superimposing the prints or placing them next to each other in desired registration; and (*c*) running them through the machine as a single original is run.

6. Make several reproducible prints of the original translucent material. Use these as multiple "duplicate originals" in the machine to speed production.

internal projection   Exposure of the sensitized copy paper of a microfilm reader-printer so that light falls on it within the machine. *See also* EXTERNAL PROJECTION.

introduction   Preliminary explanatory statement in a book or other publication. There are two kinds of introductions. One, which appears as part of the front matter, comments on the scope and content of the book, how it should be used, and the like. This type of introduction may be made by someone other than the author. The second kind of introduction is the opening chapter or section of a book in which the author introduces the reader to the subject matter.

I/O   Designation for input/output.

IPH   Abbreviation for impressions per hour.

isometric projection   *See* AXONOMETRIC PROJECTION.

italic   Slanting type used to emphasize a letter, word, or series of words in text and to print foreign words or phrases. *This sentence is set in italic.* To indicate to the compositor that a word or phrase is to be set in italic, underscore it with a single line; in proof, underscore the word or phrase and write "ital" in the margin.

jacket, book Protective temporary covering for a hardcover (case-bound) book, bearing the book title, the author's and publisher's names, and other information as desired. Its elements consist of the front and back faces, the spine, the folded-inside front jacket flap, and the folded-inside back jacket flap. The jacket is designed to have sales appeal. The spine carries the name of the book, its author, the name or logotype of the publisher, the number of the edition, and the publisher's identification number, as desired. Care should be taken to distinguish between the book jacket and the book cover when these terms are used in the production and manufacturing phases.

jaw fold Fold made by the jaw folder. Also called a "tucker fold" or "parallel fold."

jaw folder Paper folder used with a web-fed printing press. It consists of three cylinders between which the web passes to make one or two parallel folds at right angles to the direction of web travel. First, the leading edge of the web is caught on pins that carry it around the first cylinder. Halfway around, tucker blades on the cylinder force the center of the signature-to-be into folding jaws on the second cylinder. At the same time, a cutoff knife separates the tail of the signature from the web. The signature is then carried around and released by the jaws, and the cycle continues. The signature can be passed to a third cylinder in a similar manner to make a second parallel fold. The folds thus made are called jaw folds or parallel folds.

jelly print *See* GELATIN PROCESS.

jet printing Process wherein charged ink droplets are emitted from a nozzle and deflected vertically and horizontally by electrodes that are charged positively and negatively. The operation is similar to an electron beam tracing as found in cathode-ray (television) tubes. Speeds of over 1,200 words per minute are achieved.

job case *See* CASE.

job press Small printing press into which stock is fed by hand. The platen and bed open and close to receive the stock, which is pressed against the typeform on the bed.

job stick *See* COMPOSING STICK.

jogger Vibrating device used to align the edges of stock before trimming, folding, and binding, or to align and position any material for any purpose during production. The jogger may be a separate unit (*see* Figures J-1 and J-2), or a printing press delivery system may employ vibration to jog printed matter into alignment. Joggers are of many types and may be designed for multiple or specific uses. They are employed at the press or cutter in small printing shops or binderies, in offices and stores, in label factories, and in the gathering machines of newspaper plants. Specific

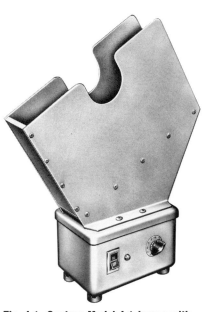

Fig. J-1 Syntron Model J-1 jogger with single-bin rack. *(FMC Corp.)*

uses include settling the contents of envelopes prior to opening them by automatic machine; aligning invoices, tabulating cards, statements, canceled checks, premium notices, and forms; aligning heavy board stock to onionskin; and adjusting addresses in window envelopes.

Figure J-1 shows the Syntron Model J-1 jogger with single-bin rack. This jogger is designed for use with small offset presses, duplicators, or copying machines. It will handle 1½ reams (750 sheets) of tightly packed copy paper. The J-1 is also used for aligning paper stock for sales, service and instruction manuals, invoices and file papers for microfilming, and other paper forms; it handles items from the size of small cards to 8½ by 14-inch (21.6 by 35.5-cm) stock. The jogger is portable and weighs 25 pounds (11.35 kg). Figure J-2 show the Syntron Model J-50 tilted-rack jogger. It is designed for use by printers for cutting and trimming stock and is used prior to collating or folding. The angle of the rack is set at 45°. The jogger is available with either a 14 by 20-inch (35.5 by 50.8-cm) or a 17 by 22-inch (43 by 55.8-cm) hardwood, open rack with 4-inch (10.16-cm) sides.

jump Trade term indicating the continuation of text matter from the initial page to a succeeding page in a magazine, newspaper, or publication.

justification Spacing of lines of type to a predetermined measure so that the margins are aligned. Linecasting machines automatically justify copy, but copy composed on a typewriter and other cold-composition machines must be pretyped (prejustified) to determine the required unit count of each line. Although the VariTyper justifies copy automatically, prejustification is required. Manual justification is accomplished with typewriters that feature proportional spacing such as IBM's Executive series of electric typewriters. *See also* PROPORTIONAL SPACING; TYPEWRITER.

Fig. J-2 Syntron Model J-50 tilted-rack jogger. (FMC Corp.)

kern That part of the face of a type character which projects beyond the body of the character. The term "kerning" is used in phototypesetting to indicate adding space between characters.

key Legend or index identifying components, parts, or other features of an illustration. Keys are used with numerals, letters, or drawn symbols. The term "key" also denotes a code used in an advertiser's address to identify the magazine or newspaper from which an inquiry originates. The advertiser can thus determine the effectiveness of his advertising in a particular medium.

key art *See* BLACK ART.

key letters Identifying letters (or words) used in a layout comprehensive or dummy to indicate that such letters (or words) are to appear as part of the copy at that particular place. The completed text is furnished separately.

key numbers In technical illustrating, index numbers used in sequence with lead lines and arrowheads to key items on an illustration to an identifying legend. When it appears that arrowheads may congest the illustration, only lead lines are used. *See also* CALL OUT.

key plate *See* BLACK PRINTER.

keyboard Typewriter with a standard keyboard arrangement with control keys added to perform additional functions. The term "keyboarding" is a spin-off definition resulting from the advent of word processing and the growing popularity of phototypesetters. Some keyboards are equipped with cathode-ray tubes (CRTs) that are of the same class and type as the ordinary television screen. This visual display, known also as a video display terminal (VDT), which is the preferred term, is viewed by the operator for immediate editing and correcting while the copy is being typed, and before the copy is sent to the phototypesetter for typesetting. While being typed (and changed or corrected), the copy is stored on magnetic tape or on magnetic tape cassettes and, if required for future use, can be retrieved from the typeface library for replay and for further changes or revisions as required. The entire unit, both keyboard and visual display, is also known as an editing, proofing, or correcting terminal.

keyboard equipment, photographic typesetter composition Device with a universal standard keyboard used to provide output data to another device and produce hard copy or "soft" copy such as viewed on a video display screen.

Figure K-1 is Alphatype Corporation's AlphaSette keyboard/editor. The machine is a visual display input/editing system, full function, counting input keyboard. It generates magnetic tape and displays the keyboarded copy and all function codes on a large cathode-ray tube screen. It is also capable of reviewing previously keyboarded copy and performing typesetting corrections, revisions, and styling changes with no extraneous or redundant keyboarding.

Figure K-2 is Alphatype Corporation's AlphaSette system. The basic system consists of a keyboard/recorder and printout unit. The keyboard will accept 20 strokes per second, permitting operator keyboarding at maximum efficiency. Copy and instructional codes typed on the keyboard are stored on magnetic tape on the recorder. The recorder's incremental digital coding system advances the tape with each keystroke. When the Multimix keyboard/recorder is added to a basic system, the operator can switch to as many as 10 different alphabets (one after the other) by pushing buttons on the keyboard. Mixing functions (style width programs and line measures) are preprogrammed on the recorder. As changes in programs and measures are required for particular font styles or sizes, they are automatically set on the recorder as the operator calls for a font change. Some features of the system are automatic justification in unit increment of any line length to over 66 picas (279 mm); a single justification space expansion to as much as 1,000 units (over 50 ems) with a minimum justifying space control to zero ems; automatic controls on the keyboard for quad left, quad right, quad center, leadering, and ruling; 18-unit character width system with automatic 1-unit kern and letterspace control; and operator control to delete an improperly keyboarded line or tab column that simplifies underscoring and double ruling.

Fig. K-1   Alphatype Corporation's AlphaSette keyboard/editor.

The Multimix printout unit is fully automatic and self-monitoring. The printout production rate is 10 characters per second over 30,000 exposures per hour; galley depth is 11½ inches (29.2 cm) with 14½ inches (36.8 cm) available; right- or wrong-reading film or right-reading paper is produced; and the unit has a range exposure control for different photographic emulsions. In addition, primary line feed and/or secondary line feed of up to 39½ points (13.86 mm) per signal in ½-point (0.1756-mm) increments is produced; line and paragraph feed signals can be repeated for unlimited line spacing; the printout line length is over 66 picas (279 mm) with 94 picas (398 mm) available; and the unit has a five-font (10 alphabets) unmonitored mixing capability.

Figure K-3 shows the Mergenthaler MVP Editing System. It incorporates a built-in programmable computer, a display which includes split-screen capabilities, and 15 programmable format keys for single-stroke access to up to fifteen 256-character formats. It is designed to operate in a six, seven, or eight-level tape mode with Mergenthaler phototypesetters or phototypesetters of other manufacturers. The machine is designed to provide text-editing functions for commercial, in-plant, or newspaper work. The split-screen capability and the sort and merge software, plus the option for a second tape reader, make it suitable for such applications as newspaper classified advertising functions, commercial catalogs, directories, and other work that requires updating. It also serves as an input device for typographic functions such as tables, charts, box scores, etc., where the ability to display the formatted copy is an advantage for editing and correcting functions. The 14-inch (35.6-cm) screen is capable of displaying twenty-four 80-character lines (including the control line); twenty-three 80-character, single-column lines; 46 lines of 40 characters each in two columns; or via split-screen, 23 lines of 40 characters for each side. A full 128 uppercase and lowercase character set is programmable by the operator.

Fig. K-2   Alphatype Corporation's AlphaSette system.

Fig. K-3   Mergenthaler MVP Editing System.

The Harris 1100 editing and proofing terminal (Figure K-4) is designed for correcting, editing, and proofreading text prior to typesetting and is used primarily for newspapers having a circulation from 10,000 to 500,000 copies. The machine accepts input from paper tape, from optical scanners, or directly from a computer; it stores input in memory; and it displays the input on an 8⅓ by 11-inch (21 by 28-cm) display screen in green phosphor 14-point (4.916-mm) characters. Input is accepted at a minimum of 120 characters per second. Display capacity is 2,000 characters, and storage

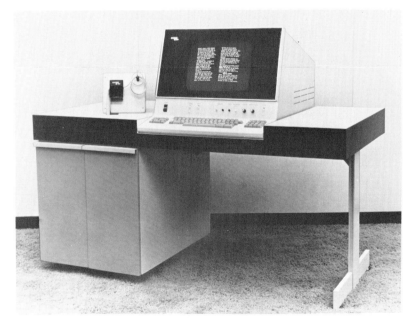

Fig. K-4   Harris 1100 editing and proofing terminal.

capacity is 2,000 characters, expandable to 6,000. The unit is compatible with special-purpose typesetting computers and photo units: PDP-8, RCA Spectra 70, IBM 1130, and IBM 360. TTS standard and ASCII/EBCDIC code are optional. The paper tape punch is handled at 60 characters a second as standard, with an option of 110 characters a second. Six- to eight-level tape is advanced or in-line-fed. The console desk is 30 inches (76.2 cm) deep, 60 inches (152.4 cm) long, and 29 inches (73.6 cm) high. The unit weighs 350 pounds (159 kg).

Figure K-5 shows the Harris 1500 editing and proofing terminal. The machine is equipped for newspaper production, with circulations of from 40,000 to 250,000 copies. The machine displays the writer's copy on a 5 by 10-inch (12.7 by 25.4-cm) cathode-ray tube display as the copy is being written. A scroll-back or recall capability permits the reporter to review and revise any portion of a story before it is sent to the computer memory. Editors may then retrieve the copy for evaluation and final copy-cutting, for updating, or for making additions. The editor presses a button marked "set it," and the copy is dispatched for composition by the phototypesetter. The system also generates an index or "directory" of all local wire service stories available for the day's news columns and lists the length of each. When the editor sees the title of a story that is of interest in the directory, another button is pressed and the complete text appears on the screen of the editing terminal. The 1500 is a self-contained unit with its own buffer memory, refresh and character-generating logic, and editing logic. The screen display consists of 12 lines of up to 80 characters each. Characters are formed by a 7 by 9-dot martix. A total of 112 different symbols may be displayed. The buffer memory contains only one screen with 12 lines worth of information. A host computer supports the terminal by providing scrolling and block-move functions. The 1500 keyboard is interfaced to the host 2500 system by means of a 34,700-baud bit-serial data-transmission line. (See Figure K-6.)

Figure K-7 shows the Edit/Set video display terminal (VDT) that is self-contained and based on the programmable Amtrol mini-computer. The terminal provides editing, correcting, and formatting functions to convert

Fig. K-5 Harris 1500 editing and proofing terminal.

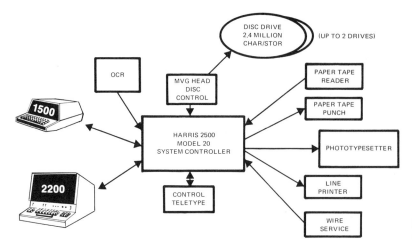

Fig. K-6 Harris editorial input system copy flow.

raw copy as a complement to phototypesetting systems. Copy is read into the Edit/Set terminal from an on-line perforated tape reader at approximately 150 characters per second or from an on-line Scan/Set optical character reader (OCR). The text area of the VDT screen contains up to 18 working lines of copy with characters displayed in 18-point size and constructed in an 8 by 10-inch (20.32 by 25.4-cm) dot matrix. The 15-inch (38.1-cm) screen viewing area is 8½ by 11 inches (21.6 by 27.94 cm) wide. The character set consists of 128 characters and symbols. Four fonts are identified by number and display mode: font 1, normal; font 2, normal with underline; font 3, bold; and font 4, bold with underline. Additional fonts are identified by number and repeat of above sequence of display modes. Screen capacity is 18 working lines with a 2-line insert buffer and 22 lines, including a 2-line function field. The input is 6, 7, and 8-level perforated tape; the photoelectric reader operates at 150 cps. The output consists of 6, 7, and 8-level perforated paper tape (in-line feed) or 6-level perforated paper tape (advance feed); the punch operates at 40 cps.

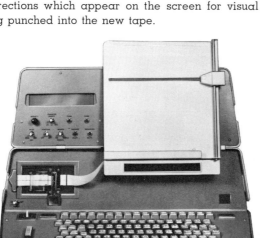

Fig. K-7 Edit/Set video display terminal _(Addressograph-Multigraph Corp., VariTyper Division.)_

The Electro/Set 450 (Figure K-8) is a dual-purpose correcting terminal and input keyboard that introduces error-free tapes for input to phototypesetters and tape-operated linecasters. The Electro/Set 450 is equipped with an easy-to-read visual display, which, at the operator's discretion, displays sixty-four 14-point (4.92-mm) characters, or thirty-two 28-point (9.83-mm) characters. The screen provides a 64-character buffer; copy is committed to tape only as it is "dumped" from the screen. The movable cursor is under keyboard control, and convenient controls reduce correction functions to a single keystroke. The original tape is inserted in the high-speed reader (pictured to the left of the keyboard in the photograph), and the operator keyboards an identifying "tag" for the first correction location. The tape is read at 40 cps, and the copy moves across the screen as new tape is punched. Operation stops automatically at the preselected location with copy displayed on the screen. The operator intervenes to make the required corrections which appear on the screen for visual verification before being punched into the new tape.

Fig. K-8 Electro/Set 450® dual-purpose correcting terminal _(Addressograph-Multigraph Corp., VariTyper Division.)_

With the movable cursor pointing to the erroneous character, the correct character is keyboarded, instantly replacing the incorrect one on the screen. The movable cursor indicates the character, word, sentence, or paragraph to be deleted. The character, word, sentence, or paragraph delete key is pressed, the deletion shows on the screen, and copy to the right of the deletion advances to take its place. With the cursor at the point at which copy is to be inserted, the insert key is pressed and new copy is keyboarded. It enters the screen at the cursor location, "pushing" the preceding copy off the screen and onto the new tape. Copy to the right of the cursor remains in position. Where blocks of copy are to be merged in from existing tape, the reader is switched to merge and the new tape is placed in the reader. With the cursor at the point of the insertion, the new copy is entered automatically from the reader. The 74-key keyboard with solid-state key modules includes 43 alphanumeric and 31 control keys and TTS or secretary shift; functions and keytop designations are as required for the phototypesetter with which unit will be used. Indicators are supplied as required for the phototypesetter to be used. The output is non-justified, 6-level advanced feed on ⅞-inch (22.2-mm) tape or 6, 7, or 8-level in-line feed on ⅞-inch (22.2-mm) or 1-inch (25.4-mm) tape. Code is standard TTS or other as specified.

keyline   Outline drawing indicating exact position and size for halftones and line drawings in artwork.

keyline art   *See* COMPREHENSIVE.

keystoning   Distortion of the screen image in overhead projection. As the height of the image is increased, the image becomes wider at the top than at the bottom. Keystoning is corrected by tilting the top of the screen forward.

kid finish   Paper finish similar to that of unfinished kid leather. It is comparatively smooth.

killed matter   *See* DEAD MATTER.

kiss impression   Near-perfect impression produced by the ideal contact between printing plate and paper. In offset and letterpress work, it may be necessary to build up the plate, form, or blanket with paper to secure a kiss impression.

kit drawing   Engineering drawing that depicts a packaged unit, item, or group of items, instructions, photographs, and drawings, such as are used in modification, installation, or survival but in themselves do not necessarily constitute a complete functioning engineering assembly. A kit drawing usually includes a listing of all item numbers, commercial products, and hardware (as applicable) to complete a modification or installation. Only one drawing is usually prepared for a particular kit modification.

kneaded eraser   Gum eraser of a special type that is kneaded into a desired shape for pencil erasing. When a portion is kneaded to a fine point, this type of eraser is excellent for cleaning excessive toner from open xerographic plates before the image on the plate is fixed by fusing.

Kodagraph Autopositive paper *See* KODAK AUTOPOSITIVE MATERIALS.

Kodak Autopositive materials Photographic films, plates, and paper proprietary with the Eastman Kodak Company. They are divided into four classifications: (1) Kodak Autopositive film (Estar base), a clear-base film that is thin enough for printing through for lateral image reversal; (2) Kodak Autopositive plates, designed for precision color work and applications for which the utmost dimensional stability is required; (3) Kodak Autopositive projection film (Estar base), for use in the process camera or enlarger in making positive transparencies from line originals and coarse-halftone originals; and (4) Kodagraph Autopositive paper "Ultra-thin, A1," which is used for quick proofing from positives, thus eliminating the need for an intermediate negative.

The basic operating principles are the same for all four Kodak Autopositive materials. The individual processing required in each case is described in instruction sheets packed with the material. With these materials, a negative can be made directly from a negative and a positive from a positive. The materials can be used to make outline effects on lettering and line work in a few simple steps. Portions of a single negative can be reversed so that positive and negative combinations and effects can be combined on the same sheet of film without stripping. Such effects as solid, clear, or tint lettering on halftone backgrounds, halftone tint joined to halftone tint with a clean division between the two, and clear or solid areas set in halftone-tint backgrounds are all produced without stripping. Reflex copies can be made of drawings or printed matter without the use of a camera or an intermediate negative. Blue-key positives can be simply produced instead of the usual blue-key negatives. Exposure is made by high-intensity ultraviolet light; the print is developed, stopped, and washed, but fixing is not required. The printout image has a blue or purplish color; hence the term "blue-key." Stripping to positive keys is easier and more accurate than stripping to negative keys.

The reader is referred to Kodak Pamphlet No. Q-23.

Kodak Control Guide C-2 *See* CONTROL GUIDE, CONTACT.

Kodak gray contact screen Photographic screen available in rulings of 65, 85, 100, 110, 120, 133, 150, and 220 lines per inch (2.54 cm). Screens of 110, 120, 133, and 150 lines have elliptical dots only. The gray contact screen is designed for making halftone negatives and direct halftone separations from colored originals. It is recommended for processes that do not require the magenta dye for controlling tone reproduction. The controlled-flash method is recommended for controlling halftone contrast. The Kodak gray contact screen will give adequate highlight contrast for most work. For any application requiring additional highlight contrast, however, a no-screen, or highlighting, exposure should be made. Such an exposure is made before the screen is put in place for the main exposure. The highlighting exposure time is 2 to 15 percent of the main exposure time.

If this time becomes too short for control, a neutral density filter is used. With a filter having a neutral density of 1.00, the same exposure time as is used for the main exposure will yield a 10 percent highlighting exposure.

Kodak gray contact screen (negative) *See* CONTACT SCREEN.

Kodak magenta contact screen Screen developed by the Eastman Kodak Company and used to make halftone negatives for photolithography and photoengraving. It is usable for either the conventional etching or the powderless etch process directly from black-and-white copy, as well as for making lithographic screen positives. The screen is also an improved means of making screened color-separation negatives or positives by the indirect method. One of the advantages of the magenta contact screen is an improvement in sharpness and in reproduction of fine details. Improved tone rendering, especially in the middle tones and highlights, without distortion of dot shapes, simplified contrast control, and elimination of the problems of screen distance ratios are other advantages. The use of multiple lens stops, required with conventional crossline screens, is also eliminated.

Since the lens opening does not affect contrast or dot formation, lens apertures other than $f/16$ can be used. Most process lenses give sharper results in the apertures of $f/16$ and $f/32$. When enlargements or reductions are made, either the aperture or the exposure time can be changed in compensation. An enlargement of the image size necessitates more exposure; a reduction, less. Contrast may be controlled by any of four methods: controlled flash, highlighting exposures with a screen, the use of an appropriate filter, and controlled agitation. Often these methods are used in combination.

Kodak magenta contact screens are supplied in three basic types: (1) Kodak magenta contact screen (negative), for making halftone negatives for photomechanical reproduction; (2) Kodak magenta contact screen (positive), for making halftone positives from continuous-tone negatives; and (3) Kodak magenta contact screen (for photogravure), for making gravure reproductions of high quality. When any positive or negative type of screen is used for its intended purpose, it gives excellent results without complicated exposure techniques. If a positive screen is used in a normal manner for making negatives or if a negative screen is used for making positives, however, the resulting reproduction usually lacks sufficient highlight contrast. Again, although excellent halftone negatives can be made with a positive screen if a no-screen or highlighting exposure is added, there is no way to overcome the loss of highlight contrast when positives are made with a negative screen.

For further information on these screens, the reader is referred to Kodak Pamphlet No. Q-21. Instructions for using Kodak magenta contact screen (for photogravure) are given in Kodak Pamphlet No. Q-22, *How to Use the Kodak Magenta Contact Screen for Photogravure.*

Kodak magenta contact screen (negative) *See* CONTACT SCREEN.

Kodak magenta contact screen (photogravure) *See* CONTACT SCREEN.

Kodak magenta contact screen (positive) *See* CONTACT SCREEN.

Kodak MP films *See* FILM, MECHANIZED PROCESSING.

Kodak MPT gray contact screen *See* CONTACT SCREEN.

Kodak Polymatic Litho Plate LN-L Precoated, presensitized printing plate for use on all conventional lithographic printing presses. It is designed to eliminate the lacquering step and to give predictable performance and high quality for long pressruns. It will produce quality printing from a wide range of line or halftone negatives. There is a uniform light-sensitive coating on one side of the plate. The other side is not sensitized. This plate is made in a variety of sizes and with different end patterns. The exposure and process of the LN-L plate is similar to that of other presensitized, subtractive plates. The plate is coated on grained anodized aluminum and is contact-speed. It is also negative-working, has short exposure and process time, and is subtractive-processed. The sensitized coating is a special colored photopolymer which is made insoluble when it is sufficiently exposed to light. The unexposed areas are softened and removed during development. The exposed (insoluble) photopolymer is formulated to have outstanding ink-carrying and ink-release capabilities. It is designed for processing at room temperature or in a range between 13 and 32°C (55 to 90°F). It is not necessary to process the plate immediately after exposure. A tusche is available for making additions. Deletions are made by honing. For detailed instructions, refer to Kodak Publication No. Q-210.

Kodak preangled gray contact screen (negative). *See* CONTACT SCREEN, PREANGLED.

Kodak preangled magenta contact screen (photogravure) *See* CONTACT SCREEN, PREANGLED.

Kodak preangled magenta contact screen (positive) *See* CONTACT SCREEN, PREANGLED.

Kodalith Autoscreen Ortho film Film produced by the Eastman Kodak Company which is used for making halftone negatives from continuous-tone photographs for use in lithographic or letterpress printing. Halftones can be exposed in either a process camera or a conventional view camera. When the film is exposed to a continuous-tone image, a dot pattern is automatically produced as though a halftone screen had been used in the process camera. The film can be exposed in an ordinary view-camera film holder without a vacuum frame. Because no screen is used, the film is capable of greatly improving detail. All image light reaches the film, and the result is a higher effective speed than is obtained with the conventional screen and film combination. This film has a 133-line-per-inch (2.54 cm) screen built into the film. Each of the minute sensitive areas on the emulsion produces a dot, the size of which is dependent on the amount of exposure received. Unlike most films, this material is not equally sensitive to light throughout its emulsion surface. Instead, the emulsion is composed of

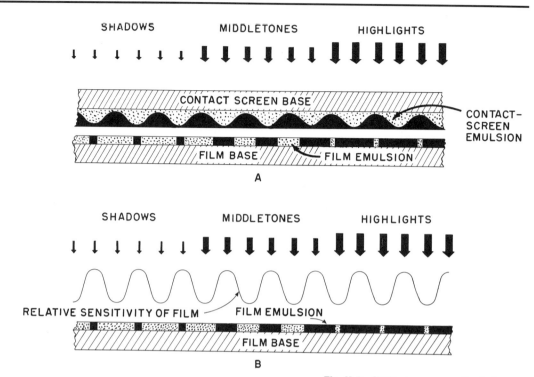

Fig. K-9 Contact screen method of producing halftones (A), and Autoscreen Ortho film method of producing halftones (B).

thousands of light-sensitive areas, each acutely sensitive at the center but gradually decreasing in sensitivity around the center. A weak exposure from the dark areas of the original produces an image only in the most sensitive portions of the emulsion, which are at the centers of the dots. A stronger exposure from the middle tones exposes less sensitive areas also, thus producing larger dots. With a maximum exposure from the highlights, the light is strong enough to form an image in all but small areas. The method of making halftones on conventional film by using the contact-screen method is shown in Figure K-9A. In this method, light striking film through a contact screen must penetrate varying density in the form of a dot pattern on the screen in order to reach and expose the film. Intense light from highlight areas in the original penetrates even dense areas on the screen and exposes a large-dot pattern on the film. The slight amount of light coming from dark areas, on the other hand, yields only small dots. Figure K-9B illustrates that although the same dot pattern is achieved on Autoscreen Ortho film, there is no screen through which the light is filtered. Instead, the film's sensitivity varies across the surface of the emulsion, and the size of the dots is proportional to the amount of light striking the film. For further information, refer to Kodak Pamphlet No. P-21.

Kodalith MP High Speed Duplicating film Highly stable, moderately high contrast, contact-speed film designed for processing in mechanized film processors. Film No. 2565 has an Estar base and No. 4565 has an Estar thick base. The films are designed for making duplicates having high maximum density from line or halftone negative or positive originals on transparent materials. The film, which can be used to duplicate scribed images and ink, pencil, or crayon lines, is of sufficient speed for exposure on a process camera. Duplicate negatives or positives that are to have the same orientation as the original negative or positive should be made with the base side of the positive or negative in contact with the emulsion side of the duplicating film. Equally good results can be obtained if the emulsion side of the original is in contact with the base side of the duplicating film. For laterally reversed duplicates, the emulsion side of the positive or negative should be in contact with the emulsion side of the duplicating film. This film can also be exposed on a process camera in special applications such as copy-dot work or for making facsimile enlargements or reductions from reflection or transmission copy. For example, when making a same-size line duplicate from reflection copy with pulsed-xenon illumination, expose for 30 to 45 seconds at $f/16$. When exposing through the base, increase exposure 2 times. (Refer to Kodak Publications Q-2 and Q-127 for detailed instructions.)

Koh-I-Noor pen *See* PENS, TECHNICAL.

Krylon Registered trade name of Krylon, Inc., for a crystal-clear spray coating used to protect artwork, drawings, photographs, documents, papers, or any other material that is to be preserved. The copy is held at a distance, and Krylon is first sprayed to one side to determine the strength of the spray. The image area is then sprayed lightly, the arm moving back and forth over the copy. Several passes with the spray should be sufficient to coat the material.

lacquering *See* VARNISHING.

laid antique paper Antique paper with a pattern of vertical and horizontal lines produced either by a hand process or by laid wires in the dandy roll of a papermaking machine.

lamination Flattening into a thin plate; in the graphic arts industry, uniting plastic film by heat and pressure to a sheet of paper to protect the paper and improve its appearance. Lamination is used to protect, preserve, and add luster to documents, valuable drawings and papers, covers for books, booklets, proposals, and specifications, and any material that might suffer from heat, aging, chemicals, water, grease, and other stains. Figure L-1 illustrates the laminating process.

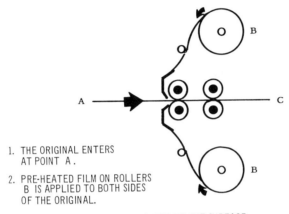

1. THE ORIGINAL ENTERS AT POINT A.
2. PRE-HEATED FILM ON ROLLERS B IS APPLIED TO BOTH SIDES OF THE ORIGINAL.
3. THE FILM IS PERMANENTLY BONDED TO THE SURFACE OF THE ORIGINAL BY PRESSURE AND HEAT.
4. THE ORIGINAL EMERGES AT POINT C LAMINATED.

Fig. L-1 Laminating process illustrated.

landscape page *See* BROADSIDE PAGE.

lantern slide A glass-mounted slide, usually 3¼ by 4 inches (8.25 by 10.16 cm), used in special shade projectors.

laser Device that converts incident electromagnetic radiation of mixed frequencies to one or more discrete frequencies of highly amplified and coherent visible radiations.

lateral reversal Left-to-right, or mirror-image, reversal of an image.

latitude Range of exposures within which a film will produce an acceptable image.

lawn finish Linenlike paper finish.

lay Character of the bed on which paper rests before it enters a flatbed printing press. Register controls, sheet-size alteration, and type of paper grippers are considerations of lay.

layout Arrangement of a book, magazine, or other publication so that text and illustrations follow a desired format. Layout includes directions for marginal data, pagination, marginal allowances, center headings and sideheads, placement and size of display and body type, and placement of illustrations. If time permits, a dummy layout may be made to show how the final layout will appear. Layout may also be defined as "makeup," but this term is usually confined to work handled by compositors, whereas "layout" is used for cold-composition copy.

Figure L-2 illustrates a multiple-page layout form for a soft-cover report consisting of 4 pages of front matter and 19 pages of the body of the report. Such a form is used before or with individual page makeup, primarily as an advance indication of the placement of copy and its relation to right- and left-hand pages. Note that all right-hand pages have odd numbers and left-hand pages even numbers. The cover or title page does not take a

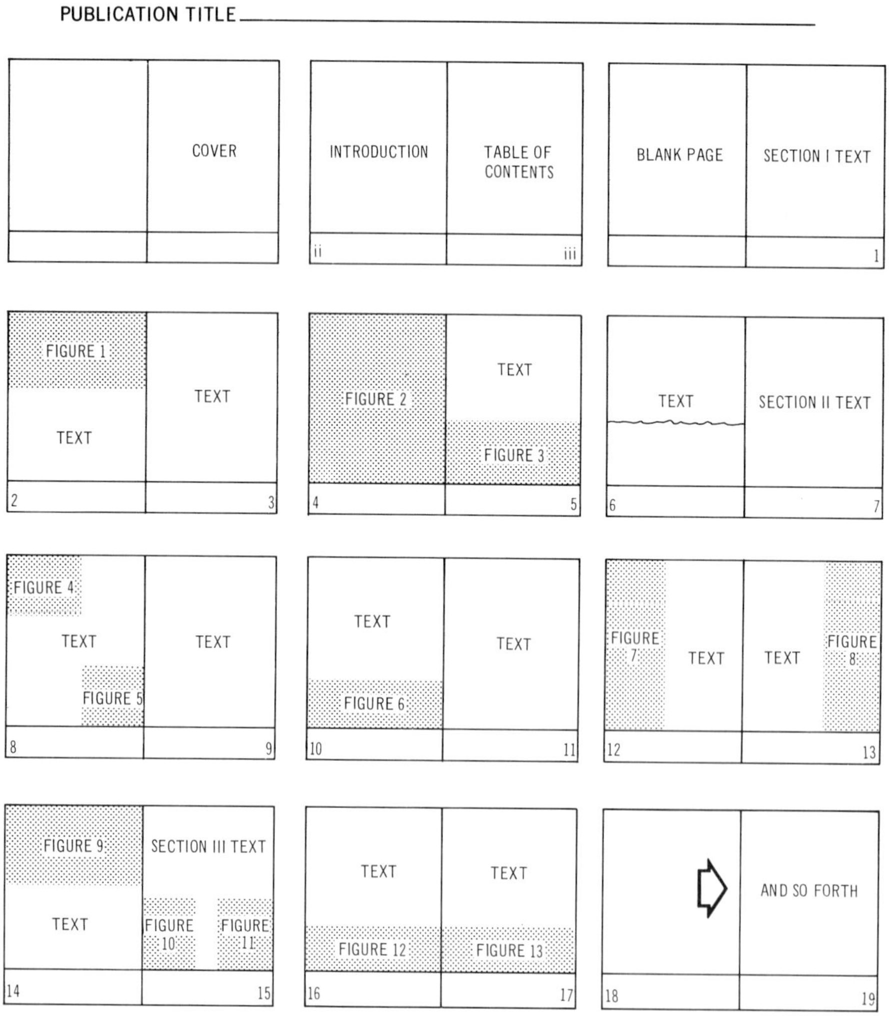

PUBLICATION TITLE _____

Fig. L-2 Advance multiple-page book layout.

A

POOR LAYOUT

B

GOOD LAYOUT

Fig. L-3 Art layout.

page number, but the page is counted (blind-folioed), as is shown by the succeeding page, which is numbered ii. All front-matter pages preceeding page 1 are numbered with lowercase roman numerals. Page ii will back up the title page. Page iv is left blank so that page 1 can be a right-hand page. From the illustration, one can see that each section begins on a right-hand page.

Figures may be designated "F/P" (full-page), "H/P" (half-page), etc. Line art may be identified as "Line," halftones as "H/T," and page foldouts as "F/O." While it is customary for a foldout page to be a right-hand page with the opposite side left blank, an ideal arrangement exists when one page foldout backs up another page foldout. The size of the sheet for the foldouts is determined by the longer illustration of the two. A blank space called an "apron" may be left on either foldout next to the binding margin if one illustration is not of the same length as the other.

Page 19 of the report is backed up with a blank page because it is a right-hand page. The blank page serves as the back cover. When the last page ends as a left-hand page, copy on the page should be protected with a dust cover by adding a blank sheet to the publication.

The term "layout" is also applied to the arrangement of art and of nomenclature used with art. Art should supplement the text and be in proportion to the object depicted, of the right size, and pleasing to the eye. Without benefit of enlargement or reduction, it can be seen that in Figure L-3A the object is drawn in too large a scale because its shape does not lend itself to the size. The layout of Figure L-3B is more in keeping with proper size.

layout typing Typing text for reproduction copy while allowing space for illustrations or other material. Considerable skill and experience are required for this kind of typing because page layout must conform to acceptable standards. Illustration dimensions, particularly height, must be known. A convenient method of layout typing employs layout sheets printed with fade-out blue perimeters that show the space limitations of the page. Each line of text should be numbered, beginning with 1 at the left margin and proceeding in sequence to the last line on the preprinted page. A line count for each line of text is thus established. Allowance for illustration numbers and titles should be made and the number of lines for titles predetermined.

lead line (leader line) Line that leads to and points out an object or a point of interest or reference. Arrowheads may be used with lead lines. When preprinted wax-backed paste-ups are employed, a white lead line (or white arrowhead) should be used when leading into a dark area and a black lead line (or black arrowhead) when leading into a white or highlighted area. A white-and-black lead line should be used to cross both white and dark areas. Figure L-4 illustrates the use of lead lines. *See also* LINE CONVENTIONS: ENGINEERING DRAWINGS.

lead time Time allocated for a specific job or a series of incremental tasks for the job in order to ensure completion and delivery on schedule.

leaders Row of dots, called dot leaders, or dashes used in lists or tabular matter to guide the eye from one item to another. An example follows:
   Introduction 1-1

leading Spacing between lines of type, measured in points. Narrow metal strips less than the overall height of the type are inserted between the lines, or the type is cast on a slug that is wider than the point size of the type. If no leading is used, the type is said to be "set solid." If 8 point (2.81 mm) is cast on a 10-point (3.51-mm) body (called "8 on 10"), the effect is of leading 2 points (0.702-mm).

leading edge Front portion of a moving object that extends beyond, or leads, the remaining portion. An example is the leading edge of a web (paper roll) as it is fed into the printing press or the front edge of an airplane wing. The term is opposed to "trailing edge."

leaf Sheet of paper in a book. Each of its two sides is a page. The term "leaf" also denotes a thin sheet of gold or similar materials used in die stamping or lettering.

leatherette finish Paper finish giving the appearance of leather. It is made by embossing.

ledger paper (record paper) Smooth-finished paper used for business ledgers and other purposes for which strength, absence of glare, and suitability for pen writing are required. It must be readily erasable. In addition, it must meet requirements for printing headings and ruling. Colors include white, blue, pink, and salmon. Basis weights are 24, 28, 32, and 36 pounds (10.9, 12.7, 14.5, and 16.3 kg) for 500 sheets of the basic size of 17 by 22 inches (43.18 by 58.8 cm).

left-hand page *See* PAGE NUMBERING.

legal cap White legal-size writing paper.

legal-size paper Paper measuring 8½ by 13 or 8½ by 14 inches (21.6 by 33 or 21.6 by 35.5 cm). *See also* BOXED PAPER.

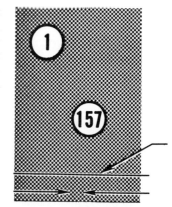
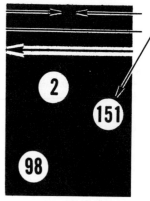

Fig. L-4 Using preprinted lead lines.

legend Key accompanying an illustration; also an illustration title. *See* FIGURE TITLE; KEY.

length Longer of the straight-line dimensions of a plane surface, the shorter dimension being the width. While longer drawings, such as engineering schematics, are described as having length, the term is not used in scaling enlargements or reductions of artwork. For this purpose, the horizontal dimension is the width and the vertical dimension the height.

leroy pens *See* PENS, TECHNICAL.

letter designations: engineering drawings There are ten sizes of engineering drawings, each of which is designated by a letter for flat and roll sizes. For flat sizes, A is 8½ by 11 inches (21.6 by 27.9 cm), used both as a vertical and horizontal sheet; B is 11 by 17 inches (27.9 by 43.1 cm); C is 17 by 22 inches (43.1 by 55.8 cm); D is 22 by 34 inches (55.8 by 86.3 cm); E is 34 by 44 inches (86.3 by 111.7 cm); and F is 28 by 40 inches (71.1 by 101.6 cm). For roll sizes, G is 11 by 42 inches (27.9 by 106.6 cm); H is 28 by 48 inches (71.1 by 121.9 cm); J is 34 by 48 inches (86.3 by 121.9 cm); and K is 40 by 48 inches (101.6 by 121.9 cm). The four roll sizes, G, H, J, and K, may extend from the minimum length shown to a maximum length of 144 inches (365.7 cm).

letter paper Paper, regardless of size, that is manufactured for correspondence.

letter size Boxed-paper size, ordinarily 8½ by 11 inches (21.6 by 27.9 cm).

letterhead Information printed or engraved as a heading on a sheet of stationery; also the printed or engraved sheet itself. The name and address of a person or an organization and sometimes the telephone number, logotype, and other information are included in a letterhead. A properly executed letterhead that reflects the characteristics of the individual or firm it represents is an important factor in graphic communication.

lettering, hand *See* BRUSHES, ART; PENS, STEEL-BRUSH; SPEEDBALL PENS; STYLUS.

lettering: engineering drawings Single-stroke uppercase commercial Gothic lettering is generally used for engineering drawings unless typewritten characters are employed. Letters may be freehand or made by means of a template, typewriter, or lettering machine. To ensure legibility after reproduction, inclined or vertical letters are used. Except for titles, lowercase letters may be used on construction drawings. When office typewriters with standard pica (0.10-inch) letters are used, the typewritten characters are uppercase.

Regardless of the lettering method used, all lines must be sufficiently opaque to be legible, either in full size or after reduction, by any method of reproduction. Underlining may be used for emphasis, but it must be less than 0.03 inch (0.762 mm) below the characters. The division line of a common fraction should be parallel to the direction in which the dimension reads and separated from the characters by a minimum of 0.03 inch (0.762 mm). When a fraction is included in a typewritten note, table, or list, however, an oblique line may be used. The size of lettering and the spacing are determined by the size of the original drawing and the amount of reduction to which it will be subjected. Characters should not touch lines, symbols, figures, or other characters. The minimum space between lines of lettering is 0.03 inch (0.762 mm). The minimum size of lettering should be in accordance with the following table.

Use	Size, in.	Size, mm
Drawing and part number in title block	0.20	5.08
Title	0.12	3.05
Subtitle for special views	0.12	3.05
Letters and numerals for body of drawing	0.12	3.05
Dimensions, fractions, and tolerances	0.12	3.05
Designation of section and detail views		
"Section," "Detail"	0.12	3.05
"A-A," "B"	0.18	4.57

When the need arises, larger characters may be used to provide the required legibility. Lettering and numbering for special notices may be of any suitable size. The spacing between round, full figures such as O, Q, and 6 is smaller than that between straight figures such as I, H, and P. Spacing between words should be not less than the width of one letter O; that between sentences, not less than twice the width of the letter O. Spacing between paragraphs should be at least as wide as a line of lettering. No type smaller than the standard pica (0.10-inch) size should be used. The regular line spacing of typewriters and other lettering machines is acceptable.

lettering guides Transparent green stenciling aids (Figure L-5). The guides are rectangles with tapered openings for forming letters and numbers in various sizes and faces to be used in stenciling and reproduction by the direct-plate (stencil) process employed with duplicators such as the mimeograph. They are used also with mechanical negatives in making presensitized plates for offset duplicating.

lettering or type reduction When lettering or type must be reduced, it must be large enough to be legible after reduction. Furthermore, when a series of drawings (electrical schematics, for example) is to be included under one cover, as in a technical publication, the lettering of all the drawings should be consistent in size. All drawings should have the same image width. When the drawings are reduced, the lettering will be reduced proportionately. If it is not possible to have the same image width on all drawings, the lettering or type applied to them must be proportionately larger or smaller. Lettering or type smaller than 6 point (2.10 mm) is too small for easy reading. Sizes from 6 to 10 point (2.10 to 3.51 mm) are recommended. The 12-point size (4.21 mm) is generally too large for a page size of 8½ by 11 inches (21.6 by 28 cm).

Lettering and type sizes and drawing-image widths should always be planned beforehand. Figure L-6 is a simple explanation of how this can be accomplished when these factors are known: (1) the image width of the

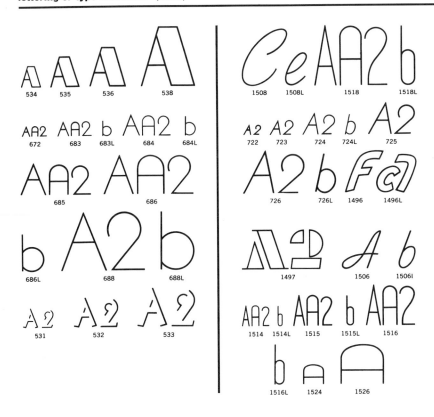

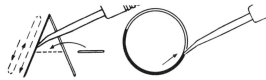

Fig. L-5 Lettering guides used for stencil work. *(Courtesy of A. B. Dick Company.)*

original, (2) the fact that the type size must not be less than 6 point (2.11 mm) or more than 12 point (4.21 mm) and that a range from 8 to 10 point (2.81 to 3.51 mm) is desirable, and (3) the image width of the reduced drawing. The drawing-image width is 30 inches (76.2 cm), and it is to be reduced to 20 inches (50.8 cm). If 30 inches (76.2 cm) is reduced by one-half to 15 inches (38.1 cm) and 12-point (4.21 mm) lettering is applied, the 12 point (4.21 mm) will be reduced proportionately, to 6 point (2.11 mm). Since the required reduction is to be 20 inches (50.8 cm) instead of 15 inches (38.1 cm), however, a size larger than 6 point (2.11 mm) must be used. If 14-point (4.92 mm) lettering is applied to the original copy, the size of the type after reduction can be determined by means of the following formula:

30 in. (76.2 cm) is to 14 pt (4.92 mm) as
20 in. (50.8 cm) is to ?

Algebraically expressed,

$30/14::20/x$

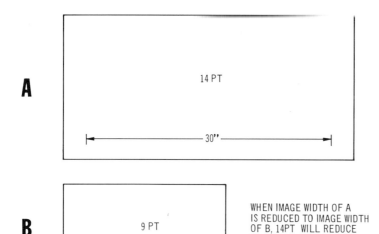

Fig. L-6 Determining type size requirements.

A

14 PT

30"

B

9 PT

20"

WHEN IMAGE WIDTH OF A IS REDUCED TO IMAGE WIDTH OF B, 14PT WILL REDUCE TO 9PT

Multiply crisscross:

$14 \times 20 = 280$

$280 \div 30 = 9$ pt (3.16 mm) approximately

lettering pens *See* PENS, STEEL-BRUSH; SPEEDBALL PENS.

letterpress printing Relief printing method in which raised inked surfaces come in direct contact with the paper and the impression or image is transferred. (For the printing process known as offset letterpress, dry offset, or letterset, *see* LETTERSET PRINTING; *see also* PRINTING METHODS.)

Letterpress is one of the major divisions of printing. It includes both hand-set and machine composition. Foundry type, cast in individual pieces, is used in hand composition. In machine composition, type may be cast in slugs of equal lengths or measures by linecasting machines such as the Linotype and the Intertype. These are hot-metal composition machines.

Many books are printed by having the copy first composed by letterpress and then using it to produce plates by the photolithographic process. The printer furnishes etch or reproduction proofs. Since these proofs are page size, they do not require reduction by the process camera and actual type sizes are used.

letterset printing (also called **dry offset; offset letterpress; offset relief**) Relief offset printing process. The word "letterset" combines the "letter" in "letterpress" and "set" from "offset." The term "dry offset" is used to describe the opposite of the wet process of planographic printing. Letterset printing differs from planographic printing in that the printing plate is in relief. The image is transferred to a rubber blanket and then to the printing surface. Dampening is not required. Any printing process in which an intermediate surface transfers the image from the plate to the stock is an offset process whether the plates are in relief or not. In letterset printing, a thin, flexible, compact relief plate is substituted for the conventional lithographic plate. Ordinary letterpress relief plates and forms must "read wrong" because the impression on stock, which must "read right," comes in direct contact with the plate. In offset printing, however, the plate must read right in order to read right when printed because of the intermediate step of transferring the image from plate to blanket.

letterspacing Placing of additional space between the letters of words to expand the length of a line or to improve and balance typography. Some typewriters letterspace automatically when a control button is pushed. It is difficult to letterspace lowercase letters without deforming the copy, but headings set in capital letters may be letterspaced to improve their appearance.

lift Greatest number of sheets of paper that can be cut at one time with a paper-cutting machine; also the number of sheets that can be handled in an operation of any kind.

ligature Two or more characters cast on the same body of type and partially joined, as æ, ff.

light integrator Electronic device used to monitor and control exposing light output. It gathers information on exposing light output through a meter probe, translates that information into precise exposure needs, and holds the contact light on (or the shutter open) long enough to allow only the amount of light needed. Once calibrated, the light integrator compensates electronically for changes in lamp intensity or voltage output.

light table (stripping table) Table having a transparent glass top through which artificial light is reflected from below. Light tables are used for mortising, opaquing, retouching, alignment, and stripping negatives into masking paper called "goldenrod flats." Adequate light tables are easy to construct and, of course, may be purchased. When a table is being utilized, fluorescent lights should be used instead of incandescent lights to minimize heat and glare.

lightface Typeface composed of fine lines, used for the body of the text, as distinguished from boldface.

line conventions: engineering drawings In engineering drafting there are various standard practices for drawing lines. Ink lines must be opaque and of uniform width. As shown in Figure L-7, three widths of lines, thin, medium, and thick, in the proportions of $1:2:4$, are used. The actual width of each type of line is governed by the size and style of the drawing. The relative widths of the lines are shown in Figure L-8. Pencil lines must be of uniform width and have the same density throughout. Cutting-plane and viewing-plane lines are the thickest lines on a drawing. Outline and other visible lines are drawn prominently. Hidden, sectioning, center, phantom, extension, dimension, and leader lines are not so prominent as outline lines. The minimum space between parallel lines is 0.03 inch (0.762 mm).

NAME	CONVENTION	DESCRIPTION AND APPLICATION	EXAMPLE
VISIBLE LINES		HEAVY UNBROKEN LINES / USED TO INDICATE VISIBLE EDGES OF AN OBJECT	
HIDDEN LINES		MEDIUM LINES WITH SHORT EVENLY SPACED DASHES / USED TO INDICATE CONCEALED EDGES	
CENTER LINES		THIN LINES MADE UP OF LONG AND SHORT DASHES ALTERNATELY SPACED AND CONSISTENT IN LENGTH / USED TO INDICATE SYMMETRY ABOUT AN AXIS AND LOCATION OF CENTERS	
DIMENSION LINES		THIN LINES TERMINATED WITH ARROWHEADS AT EACH END / USED TO INDICATE DISTANCE MEASURED	
EXTENSION LINES		THIN UNBROKEN LINES / USED TO INDICATE EXTENT OF DIMENSIONS	

NAME	CONVENTION	DESCRIPTION AND APPLICATION	EXAMPLE
LEADER		THIN LINE TERMINATED WITH ARROWHEAD OR DOT AT ONE END / USED TO INDICATE A PART, DIMENSION, OR OTHER REFERENCE	$\frac{1}{4}$ X 20 THD
PHANTOM OR DATUM LINE		MEDIUM SERIES OF ONE LONG DASH AND TWO SHORT DASHES EVENLY SPACED ENDING WITH LONG DASH / USED TO INDICATE ALTERNATE POSITION OF PARTS, REPEATED DETAIL, OR TO INDICATE A DATUM PLANE	
STITCH LINE		MEDIUM LINE OF SHORT DASHES EVENLY SPACED AND LABELED / USED TO INDICATE STITCHING OR SEWING	STITCH
BREAK (LONG)	(WOOD)	THIN SOLID RULED LINES WITH FREEHAND ZIGZAGS / USED TO REDUCE SIZE OF DRAWING REQUIRED TO DELINEATE OBJECT AND REDUCE DETAIL	
BREAK (SHORT)		THICK SOLID FREEHAND LINES / USED TO INDICATE A SHORT BREAK	
CUTTING OR VIEWING PLANE; VIEWING PLANE OPTIONAL		THICK SOLID LINES WITH ARROWHEAD TO INDICATE DIRECTION IN WHICH SECTION OR PLANE IS VIEWED OR TAKEN	
CUTTING PLANE FOR COMPLEX OR OFFSET VIEWS		THICK SHORT DASHES / USED TO SHOW OFFSET WITH ARROWHEADS TO SHOW DIRECTION VIEWED	

Fig. L-7 Line conventions for engineering drawings.

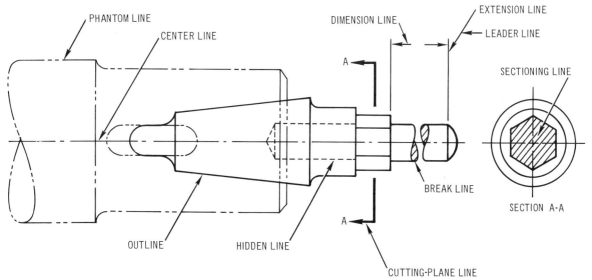

Fig. L-8 Line convention widths.

Center lines are composed of alternate long and short dashes, with a long dash at each end. They must cross without voids (see Figure L-9). Short center lines may be unbroken if they cannot be confused with other lines. Center lines may be used to indicate the travel of a center in an alternate position (see Figure L-10). Dimension lines terminate in arrowheads at each end (see Figure L-8). They are unbroken except where space is required to insert the dimension.

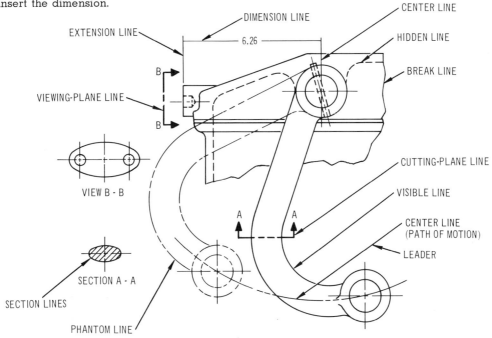

Fig. L-9 Line convention characteristics.

Leaders are used to indicate a part or a portion to which a number, note, or other reference applies; they terminate in an arrowhead or a dot. Arrowheads always terminate at a line; dots should be within the outline of an object, such as an outline indicating a surface. Leaders should terminate at any suitable portion of the note, reference, or dimension (*see* Figure L-9). Short break lines are indicated by solid freehand lines. For long breaks, full ruled lines with freehand zigzags are used. When a portion of the length of a shaft, rod, tube, or the like is broken out, the ends of the break are drawn as illustrated in Figure L-11. Phantom lines, composed of a series of one long and two short dashes evenly spaced with a long dash at each end (*see* Figures L-9 and L-10), are used to indicate the alternate position of parts, repeated detail, or the relative position of an absent part. Sectioning lines are used to indicate the exposed surfaces of an object in a sectional view. The spacing of sectioning lines may vary with the shape and size of the part but should never be narrower than is necessary for clarity. Hidden lines are evenly spaced short dashes used to show the hidden features of a part. They always begin and end with a dash in contact with the lines from which they start and end unless such a dash would continue a full line. Dashes touch at corners; arcs start with dashes at the point of tangency (*see* Figure L-9).

Stitch lines, which are used to indicate stitching or sewing, consist of evenly spaced short dashes. They are labeled (*see* Figure L-7).

Other conventional lines are visible, datum, cutting-plane, and viewing-plane lines. Visible lines, or outlines, are used to represent the visible lines on an object (*see* Figures L-7, L-8, and L-9). Datum lines, which are used to indicate the position of a datum plane, consist of a series of one long dash and two short dashes evenly spaced unless the plane is established by another line, such as an outline or an extension line (*see* Figure L-7). A cutting-plane line is used to indicate a plane or planes in which a section is taken; a viewing-plane line, the plane or planes from which the surface of an object is viewed.

Arrowheads vary with the size of the object depicted, the ratio of length to width being held to approximately 3:1. An arrowhead denotes the termination of a dimension or leader line, and the tip should end on the line to which it is drawn. *See also* LETTERING: ENGINEERING DRAWINGS; ORTHOGRAPHIC PROJECTION: ENGINEERING DRAWINGS; SCALE: ENGINEERING DRAWINGS; SIZES: ENGINEERING DRAWINGS.

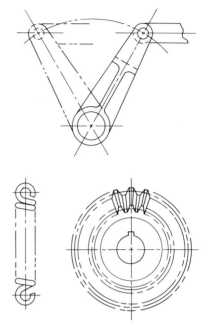

Fig. L-10 Alternate-position and repeated-detail lines.

line conversion Photographic process whereby continuous-tone copy is converted to line work. Emphasis is placed on the most important feature of the subject. The process can be used to make duotones from black-and-white photographs, to eliminate halftone screening for wash drawings, and to give photographs a hand-drawn appearance. It also provides contrast from dropouts to solid black, and it can be used in combination with line and halftone work or with other line-conversion special effects. While the process is adaptable to all forms of reproduction, conversion to line work is especially suitable for letterpress, screen-process, and flexographic printing. Special effects have been particularly successful in advertising copy for magazine, newspaper, brochure, poster, and billboard use.

Figure L-12 was produced from an 8 by 10-inch (20.3 by 25.4-cm) portrait

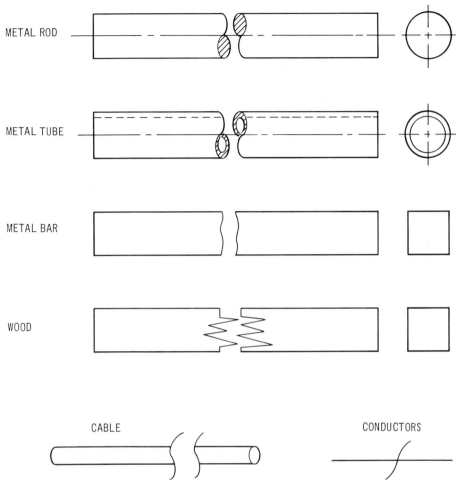

METAL ROD

METAL TUBE

METAL BAR

WOOD

CABLE

CONDUCTORS

Fig. L-11   Line conventions for broken objects.

by using a 133-line standard screen. Because of the fine screen, a magnifying glass must be used to observe the dot formation that was necessary for faithful reproduction. However, visible line formations, as shown in Figure L-13, can be used to advantage. These special effects were produced from the photograph used in Figure L-12 and other subjects.

The straight-line effect gives photographs or drawings a scratchboard or hand-engraved appearance. Lines are parallel; they can be horizontal, vertical, or oblique. The angle of the lines and the coarseness of the screen can be selected to intensify dramatic action or to accentuate a subject's characteristics. The mezzoprint adds a hand-drawn effect to photographs or artwork. Contrast is controllable so that textures and details can be held or white dropped out or lost in black shadows. The texture can be fine or extremely coarse.

The contour-line process gives the subject a rounded texture having the appearance of open weaving. The full range, from dropout whites through wavy lines to contour lines of solid blacks, is controlled to give the effect of

lines forming and modeling the rounded shapes. Tonal separation simplifies the original copy, resolving continuous tones into clearly separated
ones. The process is excellent for multicolor separations from black-and-
white copy. As many tones (or colors) can be separated as the original
copy allows. Separation can be made on film positives for screen-process
printing. The process is effective for billboard and newspaper reproduction, where a posterlike appearance is desired.

The spiral effect of converting continuous-tone copy to line work is
effective in focusing the reader's attention on a predetermined point, as
shown in the spinning top. The method is effective in combination with line
art and continuous-tone copy. The number of lines per inch (2.54 cm) is
controllable to provide spacing as desired. The tone-line effect is distinct
because of the complete separation of continuous tones into definite lines.
The appearance is one of fine pen work, as in a crow-quill drawing in
india ink. Tone-line effects are therefore useful in adding an artistic and
realistic touch to artwork.

**Fig. L-12   Portraiture using 133-line
screen. *(Portraiture by Bernie Alden of
June E. Lindeman, Miss California.)***

line copy   Composition of solid black lines and masses without gradation
of tone. It is one of two kinds of copy, the other being continuous-tone copy.
In text, line copy consists of letters, numerals, punctuation marks, rules,
borders, dots, or any other marks in black and white. Blackline illustrations
prepared on white paper are also line copy. The use of preprinted shading
mediums does not alter black-and-white illustrations from being line copy.
Photoprints made from original line drawings are black and white and
therefore are line copy.

line engraving   Method of cutting line images into a copper or steel plate
or the like, from which an ink print is taken. Line engraving is distinguished
from drypoint, in which ridges of metal are thrown up in relief with a sharp
instrument to form the image. In line engraving the background metal is
cut away, leaving the image in relief. The term also denotes the engraved
plate, or linecut, made by this process and the print made from the plate.

line measure   *See* MEASURE.

line negative   *See* NEGATIVE, PHOTOLITHOGRAPHIC.

line shot   Process camera operator's term for photographing copy without
using a screen. A line negative results.

line-tone process   *See* TONE-LINE PROCESS.

line weight   Thickness of pencil, ink, or other lines in artwork or in ruling.
Line weights should be consistent within a given group of illustrations
regardless of the number of weights used for any one illustration. The
amount of reduction of artwork must be taken into consideration. As a
simple example, if the width of the original oversize image is reduced from
14 to 7 inches (35.5 to 17.7 cm), a line 1/16 inch (1.588 mm) thick will be
reduced to a thickness of 1/32 inch (0.794 mm). For pencil drawings, the pencil
should be sharpened almost constantly to provide a hard, firm line.

STRAIGHT LINE

MEZZOPRINT

CONTOUR LINE

TONAL SEPARATION

SPIRAL

TONE LINE

Fig. L-13 Line-conversion effects.

Present-day process cameras will produce almost as good an image from a good pencil drawing as from ink copy.

linecasting machine (slugcasting machine) Machine that automatically sets slugs of type, such as the Linotype and Intertype machines. Before tape was used in linecasting control, a linecasting machine was run solely by an operator who "keyboarded" the words into the machine as a typist does on a typewriter. With automation it became possible to set type automatically by using punched tape to command the keyboard.

linecut Metal plate of a line illustration used for printing.

lineup table Device designed to facilitate close register work and alignment of materials before and after plate making. It is used for aligning the components of a paste-up, such as finished art and nomenclature, and for laying out and stripping negatives into goldenrod flats, ruling and scribing, checking press proofs for dimensional accuracy, handling imposition, assuring correct register for complementary and multiple flats, and many other applications for which accuracy and precise alignment are desired.

Fig. L-14 nuArc's Model RR41F lineup table.

Figure L-14 is nuArc's Model RR41F lineup table. The table is used for ruling multiple layout sheets, checking positives or proofs, scribing plates for step and repeat register, checking press sheets, ruling bindery sheets, and ruling forms. Some features of this table are precision engraved front and side scales in 32-inch (81.2-cm) increments; a double hairline indicator for straightedge positioning; a straightedge which rides on gears on precision tracks and can then be locked in place; a paper side guide which holds down the work and then locks in place; and fluorescent lighting. Beneath the glass top is a permanent light-diffusion plastic sheet, and a storage shelf and leveling screws are provided. The RR41F table has a glass area of 31 by 41 inches (79 by 105 cm).

Linkrule Device to find proportions for enlargement or reduction by "stretching" it across the copy. Measuring an illustration or photograph with an enlarged or contracted ruler produces the same measurements that would result if the copy itself were reduced or enlarged. No scaling is necessary. A direct reading of the measured copy produces final reproduction sizes. Three graduated color scales are provided to give a wide range of enlargments or reductions. The readings of measurements on the ruler are zigzag as shown in Figure L-15, view *B*, and correspond to a straight ruler as shown in view *A*. It is first extended along the horizontal dimension of the copy to the desired size. Without changing the setting, it is then placed along the vertical dimension and the required dimension is read on the same scale. The Linkrule measures in meters, inches, picas, or any unit of measurement. To measure in the metric system, the dots are counted on the ruler as centimeters instead of picas or inches.

linoleum-block printing *See* BLOCK PRINTING.

Linotype Automatic typecasting machine that casts an entire line of type in a single slug. It employs a hot-composition process of typesetting. *See* LINECASTING MACHINE.

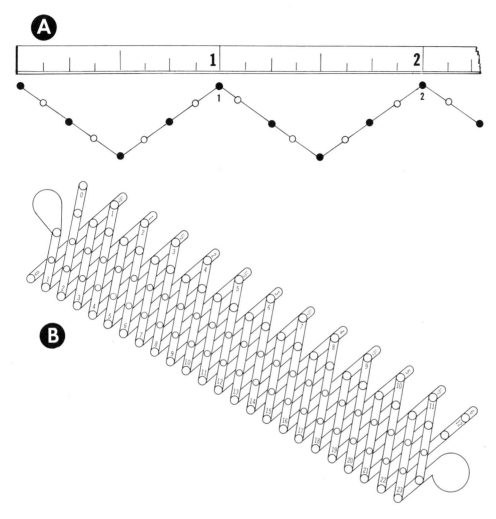

Fig. L-15 Linkrule proportional scale.

liquid toner Carbon particles suspended in a liquid solvent, used to produce an image by electrostatic attraction.

list of illustrations Element of the front matter of a publication. It includes the figure numbers and titles and the page numbers on which the figures appear. The list of illustrations, when used, should immediately follow the table of contents. The titles shown in the list should be identical with those appearing with the illustrations.

list of tables Element of the front matter of a publication. It includes the table numbers and titles and the page numbers on which the tables appear. The list of tables, when used, should immediately follow the list of illustrations.

Litho T photographic paper Transparent flexible Du Pont photographic paper on a waterproof base. It is a low-cost paper that combines fine resolving power with high contrast. The paper is used for line reproductions for lithography, quick paper negatives, map reproduction, and other photographic or photomechanical processes.

Lithofilm Special-purpose sensitized transparent film, used as an intermediate and for the projection of overlays. Lithofilm is a trade name registered to the Ozalid Corporation.

lithograph Print produced by lithography.

lithographer One who specializes in the art and process of lithographic printing.

lithographic printing Printing from a plane surface, as opposed to printing by the relief or intaglio processes. *See* PRINTING METHODS.

live matter Printing forms or copy in current use.

locator *See* SPOT.

lock up In letterpress printing, to secure a form in a chase by means of clamps known as "quoins."

logarithmic scale Proportional scale often used on a chart or graph as a vertical scale with lines varying as to distance; the distances so represented have equal ratios. The horizontal arithmetic scale is often used to represent time; lines are equidistant, representing equal values.

logic mode Automatic operating mode used in keyboard phototypesetting, inserted by the keyboard operator. It can be inhibited by the operator when required, however. For example, a switch on the keyboard sets the logic hyphenation mode desired. The hyphenation logic can then be inhibited if the operator wishes to override the automatic mode at his or her own discretion (discretionary hyphenation).

logotype (abbreviated **logo**) Piece of type bearing the name of a company or any name or trademark used with or without a design as a symbol. Figure L-16 shows three examples of logotypes.

long fold Having the grain running along the long dimension, said of paper. It is the opposite of broad fold.

long ink Property of an ink whereby it can be stretched out into a long thread without breaking. These inks have good flow in the inking fountain.

long page Page having one or two more lines of text than the normal page in a publication. One or two lines may be added to a page in order to avoid a bad break during makeup.

long primer Old type size. The nearest equivalent in the point system is 10 point (3.51 mm).

Fig. L-16 Logotypes.

loose-leaf binding *See* BINDING, MECHANICAL.

Low Contrast Pan film Du Pont separation negative film on a Cronar polyester film base. It is used for making color-separation negatives when low contrast is desired.

low finish Paper finish without gloss or enamel.

Low Gamma Pan film Du Pont separation negative film on a Cronar polyster film base. It is recommended particularly for gravure work because it offers the negative density range and response to high-activity developers that are required for the separation of long-scale transparencies without correction.

lowercase Small letters of the alphabet. The term is also applied to small roman numerals.

machine finish Finish applied to paper as it goes through the paper-making machine. It is smoother than eggshell but not so smooth as English finish.

machine-glazed paper Paper to one side of which a highly polished finish has been applied during manufacture.

machine language Language designed for internal interpretation and use by a specific machine without having to be translated; used in computer work.

magazine Storage unit. In hot-metal linecasting machines, such as the Linotype and the Intertype, a magazine holds the brass matrices that constitute a font of a specific typeface and type size. A machine may have several magazines at a time, making possible a variety of faces and sizes. A single matrix contains the impression for an individual character. When a key is operated on the keyboard, the respective matrix drops into its proper position in an assembler. As each line is completed, molten lead pours into the impressions of the assembled matrices and a single slug of type is produced. The matrices return automatically to their position in the magazine at the top of the machine and are used repeatedly.

magenta Purplish red color, classed as a secondary color in printing inks.

magenta contact screen *See* CONTACT SCREEN.

magnesium plate Printing plate of any kind made of magnesium, a metal noted for its durability, light weight, and adaptability for fast etching.

magnetic ink Special ink containing iron oxide. Its magnetic characteristics permit image code recognition by an electronic reader. The image can thus be sensed for the sorting of bank deposit slips and checks and other applications. Special magnetic inks are required for letterpress and lithographic printing, which vary in the way they deposit ink. A uniform quantity of ink on the receiving substratum is a requirement when images are being sorted by an electronic reader. The silk-screen printing process is used for information recording and storage because a heavier deposit of magnetic ink must be printed in uniform strips for recording.

Magnetic Tape Selectric typewriter *See* COLD COMPOSITION.

mail fold *See* SECOND CHOPPER FOLD.

main exposure First of two process-camera exposures used only in halftone work. The main, or detail, exposure is not sufficient to bring out the dot formation required in dark areas of a halftone for proper reproduction in printing. The dots formed during the main exposure will run together, and the halftone will print as solid black in the shadow areas. An additional flash exposure is therefore required. *See also* FLASH EXPOSURE.

major axis *See* AXIS.

makeready Preparation of a press for printing; specifically, the adjustment of the platen or impression cylinder to compensate for high or low spots in the printing form. The term can also refer to all preparatory operations preceding a pressrun.

makeup Arrangement of text and illustrations on a page, generally in conformity with standard practices of the industry or with particular publication requirements. In cold-composition work, it is known as layout. *See also* LAYOUT.

manifold paper *See* ONIONSKIN.

manuscript copy Text that requires further preparation before it is ready for printing or copying. The term is generally applied to copy in the process of being reproduced. Reproducible manuscript copy is copy that is ready to be converted into reproduction copy.

map *See* GRAPHICAL MAP.

marble finish Paper finish resembling the veins of marble.

marking felt In the manufacture of paper, a felt containing a pattern with which the paper pulp comes in contact. The pattern is thus impressed on the felt side of the web of paper as it is processed, resulting in a felt finish.

mask Photographic image mounted in register with a negative or a positive to modify certain tones or colors.

masking Blocking out a portion of an illustration by pasting paper over it to prevent it from being reproduced. Masking is used on reproducible copy before exposure. Opaque material may similarly be used to protect printing surfaces while plates for offset printing are being made. In addition, masking is used in the whiteprint process for changing copy.

masking, color-separation Any of several methods in which photographic masks are used to obtain better rendition of colors in reproduction. *See* FILMS AND PLATES.

Masking (Blue-sensitive) film Du Pont film on a Cronar polyester film base. It is used in making overlay masks for contrast adjustment and color correction of separation negatives, as well as in black-and-white camera-copy work.

masking paper *See* GOLDENROD FLAT.

masking sheeting Stripping material of paper, plastic, or vinyl sheets of orange, yellow, or green, used for assembling flats for contacting and platemaking. The sheeting holds back light in nonimage areas of the flat;

windows are cut to strike the image areas of the flat. Example: goldenrod flats.

masking and stripping materials Materials and films used in the production of line and halftone work platemaking, visual aids, overhead projection, screen-process printing, and many other applications. Rubylith and Amberlith*, registered trademarks of the Ulano Company, are two popular types of film used extensively in the graphic arts industry to produce effects such as open windows, outlining, dropouts, color separation, masks, color overlays, and the like. Ulano Rubylith is a red, light-safe stripping film coated on a polyester backing sheet. A special adhesive permits stripped portions to be replaced on the polyester for corrections; or if desired, those films with a tacky adhesive can be transferred to film negatives or positives. Rubylith photographs as black or gray, depending on the film and exposure time. When contacting or projecting through an enlarger, Rubylith will print white. Ulano Amberlith is the same as Rubylith except it is amber in color. Amberlith cuts, peels, and performs the same as Rubylith on lithographic plates and it provides better see-through quality. Amberlith photographs as black or gray, depending on the film and exposure time. When contacting or projecting through an enlarger, Amberlith will also print white. Rubylith films RM3, DM3, D3R, 5DR, and 5DM are available in 40 by 150, 40 by 300, 44 by 300, 52 by 300, and 60 by 300-inch rolls (101.6 by 381, 101.6 by 762, 111.7 by 762, 132 by 762, and 152.4 by 762-cm rolls). Rubylith 7DM is available in sheets only. Amberlith A3A, 3Da, and 5DA films are available in 40, 44, 52, and 60-inch (101.6, 111.7, 132.08, and 152.4-cm) widths. Table M-1 shows characteristics of Rubylith and Amberlith films. Rubylith and Amberlith films are used in the following way:

TABLE M-1 Characteristics of Rubylith and Amberlith films

	Color	Base Polyester	Performance
Ulano Rubylith RM3	Red	.003 in. (.0762 mm)	Tacky
Ulano Rubylith DM3	Red	.003 in. (.0762 mm)	Tacky
Ulano Rubylith D3R	Red	.003 in. (.0762 mm)	Quick stripping
Ulano Rubylith 5DR	Red	.005 in. (.1270 mm)	Quick stripping
Ulano Rubylith 5DM	Red	.005 in. (.1270 mm)	Tacky
Ulano Rubylith 7DM	Red	.007 in. (.1778 mm)	Tacky
Ulano Amberlith A3A	Amber	.003 in. (.0762 mm)	Tacky
Ulano Amberlith 3DA	Amber	.003 in. (.0762 mm)	Quick stripping
Ulano Amberlith 5DA	Amber	.005 in. (.1270 mm)	Quick stripping

How to lay in color or tints. (1) Apply register marks to art. Place Amberlith dull side up on illustration. (2) Tape top of Amberlith to art to ensure working registration. (3) With a sharp blade, cut a clean line through the Amberlith emulsion, outlining the area intended for color. Do not cut hard enough to go through the polyester base. (4) Use tip of knife blade (or stripping tweezers) and lift up a corner of the film, separating it from the support base. Peel away the unwanted Amberlith emulsion. Leave overlay cell on top of art. (5) Place a sheet of white paper under the Amberlith. The color-art is now camera-ready. Do not cover register

*Rubylith and Amberlith are registered trademarks of the Ulano Companies.

marks. The amber area will photograph as black and the film negative will develop clear in the panel where Amberlith appears. Tints may be placed in the panel, or a solid color can be printed. (6) If several colors are being used, a different overlay cell should be prepared for each color or color-percentage printed. Tape each overlay cell at a different side of the art and cut successive color cell overlays in position over previously cut masks to ensure proper fit.

How to prepare halftone windows on art. (1) Position line art under sheet of Amberlith with dull side up. With a sharp blade, carefully outline an area slightly larger than the halftone as it will finally print. Peel the Amberlith emulsion and apply it to the camera-ready art. (2) Outline the exact area that is to be the halftone window. (3) Burnish the center area of the Amberlith with a fingertip to ensure adhesion to the art. Lift up the Amberlith emulsion outside the window just cut and peel it away. (4) Expose and develop the line negative. Opaque the negative as required. In some cases it may be necessary to bleach or etch away pinholes in the window caused by dust particles or improper development. (5) Place the halftone negative in the window in the line negative. Mark the negative for trim marks. Do not trim the halftone negative on top of the line negative, because cutting through the halftone would scratch the emulsion of the film underneath. (6) Place the trimmed negative in position on the line negative. Both negatives should be emulsion side up. Thinned rubber cement can be used to adhere the halftone in the window where cropping is tight; if space permits, tape can be used.

How to outline halftone negatives. (1) Place a sheet of Rubylith on a light table with dull side up and on top of the film-support-base side of a dry halftone negative. Use a sharp blade and cut the Rubylith at least 1 inch wider than the area to be outlined. (2) With the tip of the blade, lift up a corner and carefully peel back the Rubylith. Smooth it out, adhesive side up. (3) Holding the halftone negative (emulsion side up) over the Rubylith, let the negative float onto the light table in such a manner that all the areas to be outlined are under the Rubylith. Smooth out and burnish with a stripper's blotter to ensure adhesion of the Rubylith to the negative. (4) Outline the exact area to be included in the halftone. Use care not to cut through the negative. (5) With blade tip or stripping tweezers, lift up a corner of the Rubylith emulsion that has just been cut and peel it away. (6) Insert the negative in position in the plate-exposing flat.

How to fake a wash art effect from simple line art. (1) Scale, expose, develop, dry, and opaque the line negative. If three percentages of black are to be combined with the line negative, place three sheets of Rubylith on top of the negative with dull side up. The negative should be right-reading. Punch-register the Rubylith sheets and negative. Make sure that the Rubylith sheets are at least as large as the negative. (2) Mark each Rubylith sheet with the percentage to be printed. Place a sheet of Rubylith over the negative, on the register pins, and cut a clean line around the area to be screened. (3) Lift up an inside corner of the panel cut, and strip away Rubylith emulsion. Repeat steps 2 and 3 for each percentage on other sheets of punch-registered Rubylith. Check masks with each other for proper fit and overlap. (4) After finishing all Rubylith masks, make an internegative film positive by doing the following: Punch, in matched register, a piece of unexposed film, emulsion side up. Place the line negative on register pins in a darkroom contact printing frame. Expose the original line negative, emulsion to emulsion, to new sheet of film. (5) Expose each of the Rubylith masks, using the pins for perfect register. Insert a tint screen of the value required between the masks and the film. When all exposures have been made on the internegative, develop exposed film in fresh developer for best dot reproduction. (6) The result will be a positive, right-reading, emulsion-side-up image. Check for effect. If desired, the film can be contacted back to a negative. The film is now ready for the flat and for final plate exposing.

How to outline and add extra color to duotones. (1) Expose, develop, and dry two identically sized halftone negatives. It may be desired to expose each negative for different highlight and shadow values. Use the proper screen angles to avoid a moiré effect. Mark each negative as to its proper color. (2) Using a sharp blade, cut a fine line around the area to be printed on the final press sheet. (3) Lift up the inside corner of the Rubylith. (4) Peel away the area that is to print in the halftone, leaving the Rubylith in the area to be masked. (5) Place another sheet of Rubylith on top of the negative. Cut an outline of the area that is to print 100 percent on the final press sheet. Lift up and peel away that area. (6) These elements are now ready for platemaking. One mask is used for exposing both negatives to both plates. The other mask is used to double-burn the color plate only.

How to reduce background density in a photograph. (1) Expose, develop, and dry a normal highlight and shadow halftone to the size required. In a contact printing frame, expose the negative to another piece of film. When this is developed, a screened positive image results. Punch-register the film. (2) Place the film positive on register pins, emulsion side up. Then place on top of that film a sheet of punched Amberlith, dull side up. (3) With a sharp blade, outline the exact area to remain in normal density. Peel away the Amberlith leaving a mask over the area that will remain in normal density. (4) Working on register pins in a contact printing frame, make a regular exposure of the halftone positive only, to a piece of negative-acting film. (5) After the above exposure is completed, open the contact frame and insert the Ulano mask on the register pins. (6) Make a supplemental exposure. Generally, the exposure time should be about 25 percent of the first exposure. Because the Ulano mask is in position, the only area affected by this exposure will be the background area. The longer the exposure, the tighter the background dot will become, thereby reducing ink-lay on the final press sheet.

How to prepare knockouts or island dropouts. (1) Punch-register the halftone negative, a sheet of Rubylith, and an outline of the design to be deleted from the final press sheet. (2) Place the Rubylith over the negative on register pins. Both the Rubylith and the negative must be emulsion side up. Carefully cut the exact outline to be dropped. (3) Peel away the Rubylith emulsion from the outside area. This will leave a light-safe mask in the shape of the design that is not intended to print. (4) Position the mask over the negative in the plate-exposing flat. (5) If the job is to be multicolored, use the mask in position during each plate exposure. (6) If a color or a tint screen effect is desired inside the dropped panel, cut a mask to cover all other areas of the film. Make a double plate burn using this mask with or without a halftone screen.

How to create color art from simple line art. (1) Punch-register four sheets of Rubylith, emulsion side up, and key negative with the design elements outline on it. (2) Mark each Rubylith overlay cell with a crayon indicating the color it is to represent on the final press sheet. (3) Work with one Rubylith cell at a time on register pins over the black key illustration. (4) Cut each color panel. (5) Insert each mask in its respective color flat. Expose the plates. If screens are to be incorporated into panels, place tint screens between mask and plate before exposing. (6) Prepare a second flat for the black printer. Double-burn the black plate, using the black Rubylith mask and the key negative.

How to selectively stage negatives or positives. (1) Working on a light table, place a halftone emulsion side up. Place a sheet of Rubylith 5DM, dull side up, on top of the film. With a sharp blade, cut a section at least 1 inch larger than the area that is to be etched back. (2) Peel the Rubylith emulsion. Smooth it out, adhesive side up. Float the halftone (emulsion side down) in position on the Rubylith. Use a stripper's blotter to adhere the Rubylith to the film. (3) Cut an outline around the area not to be etched back or staged. Do not cut too deep or the film emulsion will be cut. Peel away the Rubylith in the area that is to be staged. (4) Etch or stage the film, using potassium ferricyanide and sodium thiosulphate as recommended by the manufacturer. When properly applied, this solution gives the experienced technician more control in dissolving developed black silver deposits from the film. (5) After inspecting the film to make sure that the proper etch-back has been achieved, peel off the protective Rubylith emulsion. Wash and dry film. (6) When film has dried, inspect it carefully. If there are scratches along the outlined area, use a finger to gently rub the emulsion back in place so the scratch will not print. (Courtesy of the Ulano Companies.)

master Original typed, drawn, typeset, or hand-lettered copy. It may be produced on film, paper, cloth, or almost any other material. Various copy methods and processes are used to produce some form of copy from the master. Additional copies, prints, negatives, or intermediates may be used as masters to produce other copies, but the master itself is the original and first image in the process.

master cylinder Cylinder on a printing press that receives the ink from the ink distribution system. The cylinder comes in contact with the printing plate and transfers ink to make the image on a substrate. Also called a "form roller."

master paper *See* DUPLICATOR PAPER.

master-plan drawing Drawing that is sufficiently detailed to serve as a guide for the long-range development of an area. Such drawings are used in architectural planning and construction.

master plate Paper, plastic, or metal plate installed on a press for offset printing. The image may be applied to the plate directly or indirectly.

mat Abbreviation for matrix.

matched negative Combination of negatives of a piece of work that is too large to be accommodated by the available process camera at one exposure. The image must be photographed more than once and the separate negatives "matched" and spliced by taping or other means. When a drawing such as a large schematic is being separated for matching, vertical breaks should be made where horizontal lines are fewest.

matched-parts drawing (matched-set drawing) Engineering drawing that depicts parts, such as special-application parts, which are machine-matched or otherwise mated and which must be replaced as a matched set or pair.

mathematical symbols *See* TABLE 10, *page 446.*

matrix (abbreviated **mat**) Mold in which the face of type is cast, as by using a "flong," a mixture of moist or wet papier-mâché. The papier-mâché dries and forms a mold into which lead is poured. The matrix is then used in stereotyping. Brass dies employed in hot-metal composition are also called matrices.

matrix paper (dry mat paper) Paper ranging in thickness to 0.036 inch (0.914 mm), used for making flongs. Matrix paper is a papier-mâché material moistened to make the mold. After molding, the paper is heat-dried and hot metal is poured into it to form the mold.

matte finish Dull paper finish without gloss or luster.

matte print Photoprint having a dull finish. When line art must be imposed directly on a photographic print, a matte finish should be requested from the photographer. This finish has ink-absorbing qualities not found in a glossy print with its glazed surface. However, if line art is imposed directly on a photographic print without an acetate overlay, it will be screened when the image is screened for plate making. If it is necessary to rework the surface of a glossy photograph, the glaze can be erased from the portion where ink is to be applied.

maximum density *See* DENSITY, MAXIMUM.

measure Printer's term for the length of a line of type measured in picas (1 pica = 4.23 mm). The ideal length is about 40 characters of any size. Lines of less than 30 or more than 50 characters should generally be avoided. A good rule to follow is to use 1½ alphabets of lowercase letters, or 39 characters, to the line measure. When printing by typesetters is ordered, the line measure should be specified in picas.

mechanical Page or layout prepared as an original for photomechanical reproduction. It may be a single unit with all the elements of the finished page ready for single-shot photography, or it may have hinged overlays that can be swung into position for making successive exposures of various elements on the same negative.

mechanical binding *See* BINDING, MECHANICAL.

mechanical schematic Engineering drawing that illustrates the operational sequence or arrangement of a mechanical device. Dimensions and relative sizes of items may be shown to indicate mechanical relationships.

mechanical spacing *See* OPTICAL SPACING.

media Means of audio and visual communication, such as books, magazines, newspapers, billboards, direct-mail advertising, radio, and television.

medieval laid finish Finish in paper made by chain lines during manufacture. There is an effect of shading adjacent to the vertical chain-line marks.

Medium Contrast Pan film Du Pont film used to make color-separation negatives from normal transparencies or opaque copy and to serve as camera-copy film when a commercial level of contrast is required.

memory Equipment and devices that have the ability to collect and hold information in a control system until such time it is needed by the computer.

metallic finish Paper finish having a metallic luster.

metallic ink Ink composed of aluminum or bronze powders in the vehicle varnish to produce gold or silver color effects.

metering unit Series of three infeed rollers mounted on the roll stand of a web-fed press. The rollers smooth the web and control paper tension and speed as the web feeds from the roll into the first printing unit.

mezzoprint Line print converted from a continuous-tone photograph or tone artwork by a photographic screening process. *See also* LINE CONVERSION.

mezzo-relievo Image sculptured in half relief, between bas-relief and high relief.

mezzotint Method of engraving on copper or steel to produce variations in tone; also the engraving so produced.

MF Abbreviation for machine finish.

mica finish Coated paper finish that contains mica particles. It is some-times used on greeting cards.

microfiche Sheet of film containing the microimages of pages of technical documents and reports, records, correspondence, instruction manuals, catalogs, or other publications. Each page of the microfiche form can be enlarged and the image read on a reader or viewer or on a reader-printer, which combines showing the page on a screen with making an enlarged printout of the desired page or pages. Microfiches may be 3 by 5, 4 by 6, 5 by 8, 6½ by 8½, and 6 by 9 inches (7.62 by 12.7, 10.1 by 15.2, 12.7 by 20.3, 16.5 by 21.6, and 15.2 by 22.8 cm) in size. Capacities range from 30 to 100 pages. A 5 by 8-inch (12.7 by 20.3-cm) microfiche, for example, will hold 84 pages of a standard image on 8½ by 11-inch (21.6 by 28-cm) paper (Figure M-1). It would take only four such microfiche forms to produce a book of 336 pages. Although microfiche sizes vary, United States government agencies now require a standard 4 by 6-inch (10.1 by 15.2-cm) size. Index and filing information are produced in type of normal size to permit reading with the naked eye.

When duplicate copies of microfiches are required, a microfiche copy is used as an intermediate and a contact print made by such methods as the diazo process or heat-developing film sheets. Duplicates can be extended to four generations without losing readability and reproduction quality.

Fig. M-1 Microfiche form (not actual size).

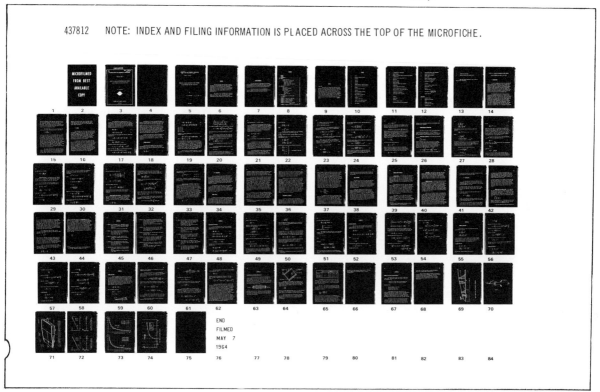

Microfiches may be filed by document number or by cross-indexing the subject matter to the index in a conventional filing cabinet. Filing and selection are generally done by hand, but patented devices are available to speed this work if volume warrants their use. *See also* MICROFILM; MICROFILM EQUIPMENT; MICROFILM PROCESSING; MICROFILM READER; MICROFORM; PRINTER.

microfilm Sensitized film on which microform images are produced. *See also* MICROFICHE; MICROFORM.

microfilm equipment Machine or devices capable of projecting an enlarged microform image on a screen for viewing. Some machines are capable of making duplicate copies as well. Machines may have either a diazo or a thermal method of reproduction. Figure M-2 shows Bruning's OP-49/88 diazo microfiche duplicator. This duplicator system automatically produces cut-to-size, collated microfiche in one operation. The OP-49, with or without its optional OP-88 collator, can be operated in either the automatic or semi-automatic mode.

In the automatic mode, a 105-mm roll of master film is required to have sensing marks identified with each microfiche on the roll. The machine automatically positions each master microfiche into the exposure station and produces the preselected number of copies from each master as required. This cycle of operations repeats automatically until all master images on the roll have been duplicated. If an OP-88 collator is used with the OP-49, finished copies will be either arranged in collated distribution sets or separated into groups in the same sequence as the master roll microfiche.

In the semi-automatic mode, individual microfiche on master rolls, or jackets, or cut film are positioned in the exposure station. The required

Fig. M-2 Bruning's OP-49/88 diazo microfiche duplicator. (Addressograph-Multigraph Corp.)

number of copies is preset, without output automatically collated or separated as required by means of the OP-88 collator.

The master carrier features a built-in viewer for use when the machine is operated in the semi-automatic mode. This permits the operator to read headings or titles easily over a back-lighted screen beneath the film carrier. For ease of master microfiche selection, operator controls permit either variable speeds of master roll transport or automatic incremental transport of sequential microfiche on the master rolls. With cut microfiche and jackets, ready stations permit preloading of microfiche while production is occurring. Production speeds in excess of 750 cut-to-size microfiche per hour are thus obtained. Up to 99 copies of any master can be produced in one continuous cycle.

Master microfiche made for duplication to COSATI, NMA, ISO, and other standards can be used to produce 105 by 148-mm copies that meet accepted standards. The system is compatible with COM and other configurations. It uses a direct process, producing negative copies from negatives, or positive copies from positives. The OP-49 duplicator uses 105-mm diazo microfilm in rolls up to 1,000 feet (305 m) in length. Exposure, development, and cutting to size are performed automatically without operator involvement. The anhydrous ammonia developer system is sealed and can be used in any office environment. Bruning provides other duplicator models which use the diazo and thermal methods, with or without automatic master roll feed and with automatic collators as optional.

Figure M-3 is Bruning's self-contained tabletop diazo microfiche duplicator Model OP-10. The machine produces 150 microfiche copies per hour. The original and diazo film is placed in the exposure area, and the diazo film is inserted in the developer slot. It is 17 inches (43.18 cm) in length, 17½ inches (44.4 cm) in depth, and 9¾ inches (24.77 cm) high, and it weighs 44 pounds (19.98 kg).

Figure M-4 shows Dukane Corporation's Model 27A25B microfilm reader with roll film attachment that accommodates 16 and 35-millimeter film. In addition, the reader can be adapted to 3 by 5-inch (7.62 by 12.7-cm) and 4 by 6-inch (10.16 by 15.24-cm) microfiche jacketed film and aperture cards. The screen is 14 by 14 inches (35.56 by 35.56 cm) and is composed of nonglare, coated plexiglass. Magnification is changed by inserting one of four different lenses: 15X, 18X, 24X, or 27X. The intensity of a 1,000-hour 7724 quartz-halogen, fan-cooled lamp can be varied to compensate for light conditions and various densities of microfilm material with three positions of 102, medium, and high. Size of the reader is 26 by 15 by 18 inches (66.04 by 38.1 by 45.72 cm).

Figure M-5 shows the Dukane Model 576-90, used for reading 35-millimeter microfilm mounted in aperture cards. It is designed for desktop use and is equipped with spring-loaded glass flats for easy loading. A three-position card feed accommodates vertical and horizontal aperture cards as large as military D drawings (22 by 34 inches) 55.8 by 86.3 cm and can be removed for cleaning of the aperture glass. Screen size is 12 by 10½ inches (30.4 by 26.6 cm) and magnification is 15X.

Figure M-6 is 3M's 3400 microfilm cartridge camera, which can record up to 2,400 letter-size documents on one 100-foot (30.48-m), 16-mm microfilm cartridge. A film odometer indicates paper documents filmed, which

Fig. M-3 Bruning's tabletop diazo microfiche duplicator. Model OP-10 (Addressograph-Multigraph Corp.)

Fig. M-4 Dukane's Model 27A25B microform reader.

Fig. M-5 Dukane's Model 576-90 aperture card reader.

provides retrieval with corresponding odometers on 3M microfilm readers or other reader-printers. The odometer also allows removal of the cartridge for later filming. The unexposed cartridge is snapped in position, the film-load button is pushed, and the film automatically self-threads. For exposed film protection, an interlock prevents removal of threaded cartridges. A warning light indicates when the full 100 feet (30.48 m) of film has been exposed. Microfilming speed is up to 60 documents per minute. Maximum document size is up to 12 inches (30.4 cm) wide. The reduction ratio is 24X.

Figure M-7 is 3M's 500CT microfilm reader-printer. The 500CT produces dry copies utilizing 3M's dry silver-print process. The print time is ten seconds, and 6 prints of the same document can be produced in one minute. A motorized film drive features a variable-speed control which allows film to be scanned as slowly as 10 inches (25.4 cm) per minute, or the entire 100-foot (30.48-m) cartridge roll can be scanned in fifteen seconds. A film odometer ensures retrieval from zero setting to scan the document location as noted on the cartridge during microfilming. Film threading is automatic. The dry silver-print paper is provided in 500-foot (152.4-m) rolls. The screen image is 11½ by 16 inches (29.3 cm by 40.6 cm), and print size is 8½ by 12½ to 12¾ inches (21.6 by 31.7 to 32.3 cm) nominal. Microform acceptance is 16-millimeter, 100-foot (30.48-m) cartridges. Available lenses are 14.88X, 15.7X, 18.25X, 20.78X, 23X, 25X, and 29X.

Bruning's Model 96 automated microfiche retrieval display printer is shown in Figure M-8. The machine provides access to page information on any of 30 microfiche housed in specially designed cartridge frames. Frames on the same microfiche are displayed in less than one second; frames on different microfiche are displayed in less than three seconds, including the refilling of the previous microfiche. Image positioning and focus are achieved by controls. By pushing a "print" button, an 8½ by 11-inch (21.6 by 28-cm) copy is produced. The display screen is 12 by 11½ inches (30.5 by 29 cm). Print cycle time is ten seconds, and the imaging system produces electrostatic prints, negative or positive, with no warm-up time. Magnifications are 20X and 48X. The machine is 29 inches (73.66 cm) high, 17 inches (43.18 cm) wide, and 34 inches (86.36 cm) deep. Weight is 130 pounds (59 kg).

Figure M-9 is Bruning's Model OP-60 tabletop semi-automatic aperture card duplicator. The machine automatically feeds copy cards which are stored in the unit's hopper. Once exposed and developed, diazo copy cards are then stacked in the output hopper. Duplicate copies are produced at the rate of approximately one every five seconds. Master aperture cards, either negative or positive, are fed into the machine, and the duplicating cycle is started by activating a button or optional foot switch. Diazo copy cards are fed automatically. It accepts Bruning's copy cards or any other MIL D specification diazo copy card. An add-on module (OP-61) allows the operator to automatically reproduce up to 99 copies of any master card without using the foot switch or panel button for each copy. The module is a plug-in accessory requiring no technical installation. A running counter records the number of copies made from each master. If one or more copies are needed on a rush basis, a "hold" button allows the operator to interrupt a long run without affecting the running counter. The machine is

Fig. M-6 3M's 3400 microfilm cartridge camera.

Fig. M-7 3M's 500CT microfilm reader-printer.

Fig. M-8 Bruning's Model 96 automated microfiche retrieval display printer. (Addressograph-Multigraph Corp.)

10⅞ inches (27.6 cm) in height, 21⅝ inches (54.9 cm) in length, and 23⅛ inches (58.7 cm) in depth. Weight of the machine is 103 pounds (46.7 kg).

Figure M-10 is Bruning's Model 5500 microfiche reader-printer. It is operated by inserting a microfiche into the carrier, selecting the desired frame (or page) by moving the pointer of the carrier to the corresponding grid position, setting the desired copy length and contrast, and pushing the print button. Dry electrostatic prints are delivered at the rate of eight per minute. Print paper is available in 460-foot (140-m) rolls. One 11-inch (28-cm) roll provides approximately 650 8½ by 11-inch (21.6 by 28-cm) copies. Viewing screen size is 11 by 11 inches (27.9 by 27.9 cm). Magnifications are 18X, 24X, 32X, and 40X with additional special magnifications available. Height of the machine is 23 inches (58.4 cm), width is 15 inches (38.1 cm), and depth is 28 inches (71.1 cm). Weight of the machine is 70 pounds (31.8 kg).

Fig. M-9 Bruning's Model OP-60 tabletop aperture card duplicator. (Addressograph-Multigraph Corp.)

microfilm processing Development of exposed microfilm to bring out the latent image. Microfilm containing silver halides as the light-sensitive emulsion requires chemical development and washing. This process may be handled by a machine such as the Recordak Prostar. Any length from 2 to 100 feet (0.61 to 30.5m) of 16 or 35-millimeter film can be processed automatically in less than two minutes. The processor is 28½ inches (72.3 cm) high, 25 inches (63.5 cm) wide, and 12½ inches (31.7 cm) deep and weighs approximately 90 pounds (40.8 kg).

microfilm reader Device capable of projecting an enlarged microform image on a screen for viewing.

microform (also called **microtransparency**) Any microimage imposed on film, whether as a microfilm sheet, microfiche, rolled film, individual film, or filmstrip. It may be cut as a unit and mounted in an aperture card. Microforms replace bulk storage of newspapers, books, technical reports, documents, or any other printed or drawn images. They not only save space but facilitate the rapid acquisition and transmission of data. The data thus stored may be retrieved for reading in enlarged form on a viewing screen, or an enlarged printout may be obtained by using a printer or a reader-printer.

Microforms may be positive, negative, or microopaque. A positive microform reflects a black image on a white background on a printout, whereas a negative microform reflects a white image on a black background. (The terms "black" and "white" as used here denote variations of black and white that depend on exposure time and the degree of magnification and development.) A microopaque image is a positive printed on white paper. The paper, of course, reflects light in and around the image area, and the image is produced by reflection and magnification. With negative and positive transparencies, the light passes through translucent areas on the film and reading and printing are also aided by magnification.

Regardless of the type of microform used, original copy must be reduced by photography for storage. In order to be viewed again with the naked

Fig. M-10 Bruning's Model 5500 microfiche reader-printer. (Addressograph-Multigraph Corp.)

eye, the copy must be enlarged to normal or greater size and "read" on a viewing screen. The equipment used to enlarge and read microforms is called a microfilm reader. When a copy of the image is required, a printout of the image is obtained on a microfilm printer. When the image can be viewed and a printout made on the same machine, the equipment is referred to as a reader-printer. If a duplicate copy of a microform is required, it is produced by an exposure unit, a reproducer, or a microfilm duplicator by the processing steps of exposure and development.

Microforms are produced in rolled films of 16, 35, 70, and 105 millimeters. In addition, individual frames may be cut from rolled microfilm and mounted in aperture cards to be used with electrical accounting machines, or the original image can be photographed directly on sensitized film already mounted in an aperture card. Methods of reproduction vary with different manufacturers. Xerography, electrolytic and stabilization processes, diffusion transfer, and conventional photography may all be used in making printouts from microforms.

microimage Image produced on microfilm; a microform. *See* MICROFORM.

microopaque *See* MICROFORM.

microphotography Art or practice of producing microscopic photographs. A microphotograph is the photograph so produced.

microtransparency *See* MICROFORM.

middle tones Intermediate tones between black and white that compose continuous-tone copy and halftone printed copy.

milestone chart Chart that lists such information as the elements required to produce an item. By using bars and data points that show scheduled dates in terms of days, weeks, months, or years, production goals can be set and measured. Stages such as prototype manufacture, assembly, first test runs, final delivery, and other aspects are listed on the left side of the chart, and horizontal bars are drawn from them to denote time. When data-point symbols are used, a key should be added to clarify the meaning of each point. Figure M-11 shows symbols used on milestone charts.

Milestone charts are also useful for controlling the production of technical and other publications. Such steps as the starting date, first-draft completion, first-draft review, rewrite or rework, final-draft completion, editing, final-draft review, rewrite or rework as the result of final-draft review, quality control, collating or book makeup, printing, and delivery are milestones that can help control documents as work progresses.

milline rate Advertising rate based on the cost of one agate line per 1 million copies of a publication's circulation. Milline rates of various publications may be compared for evaluation. The rate is determined by multiplying the line rate by 1 million and dividing by the circulation number.

MILESTONE SYMBOLS

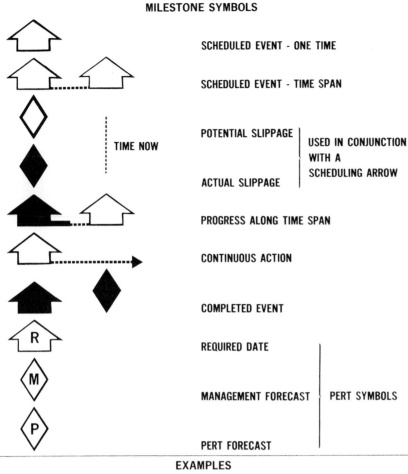

SCHEDULED EVENT - ONE TIME

SCHEDULED EVENT - TIME SPAN

TIME NOW

POTENTIAL SLIPPAGE

ACTUAL SLIPPAGE

USED IN CONJUNCTION WITH A SCHEDULING ARROW

PROGRESS ALONG TIME SPAN

CONTINUOUS ACTION

COMPLETED EVENT

REQUIRED DATE

MANAGEMENT FORECAST

PERT FORECAST

PERT SYMBOLS

EXAMPLES

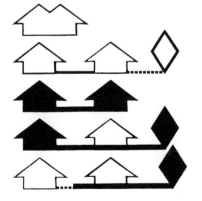

SHORT TIME SPAN

EVENT NOT STARTED - POTENTIAL SLIPPAGE

COMPLETED EVENT (NO SLIPPAGE)

COMPLETED EVENT - ACTUAL SLIPPAGE

COMPLETED EVENT - STARTED LATE

Fig. M-11   Milestone chart symbols.

mimeograph Duplicating machine that employs a direct-plate stencil process. It is a product of the A. B. Dick Company. Figure M-12 shows the principles of operation of this method of duplication, which has four elements: the stencil, ink, paper, and the mimeograph itself. The stencil, which may be typed, handwritten, or drawn, is placed on the outside cylinder of the mimeograph. As the paper passes through the mimeograph (Figure M-13), the impression roller rises automatically and presses it against the stencil on the cylinder. At the same time, ink flow from the cylinder through the ink pad and the stencil openings make a copy of the image on paper. The Model 565 mimeograph stencil printer produces copies at variable speeds from 115 to 200 copies per minute with fluid, and 65 to 130 copies per minute with paste. It counts copies to 2,000, and when the run is completed, a bell rings and the counter shuts off the feed. The three-way jogging tray is adjustable for sizes from 3 by 5 inches to 9 by 15 inches (7.6 by 12.7 cm to 22.8 by 38 cm). It handles paper sizes of these same dimensions. The machine accommodates paper weights from 16 to 100-pound (7.26 to 45.4-kg) index. Maximum duplicating area is 7½ by 14 inches (19 by 35.5 cm). The duplicator weighs 115 pounds (52.2 kg). Various colored inks are available. Paper colors include blue, pink, green, canary, buff, goldenrod, granite, tan, terra-cotta, yellow, india, and gray. The A. B. Dick Company publishes a booklet, *Techniques of Mimeographing*, that includes instructions for the operator, typist, and artist and information on such subjects as using colored inks, inking, filing stencils for reruns, ink and pad blockouts, and copy blowouts. In addition to regular typing or drawing stencils, die-impressed and photographically or electronically prepared stencils are available.

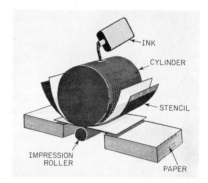

Fig. M-12 Mimeograph principles of operation.

mimeograph paper Paper with good ink-absorbing qualities, available in a laid or a wove finish. Considered a boxed paper, it is cut to the letter size of 8½ by 11 inches (21.6 by 28 cm) and the legal size of 8½ by 14 inches (21.6 by 35.6 cm). Basis weights are 16, 20, and 24 pounds (7.3, 9.08, and 10.9 kg) for 500 sheets of the basic size of 17 by 22 inches (43.1 by 55.8 cm).

mimeoscope Illuminated drawing board or light table (Figure M-14) used in drawing, tracing, or otherwise preparing stencils for mimeographing. Mimeoscope is a registered trademark of the A. B. Dick Company. Sliding straightedges are used for ruling and measuring. The height and slant of the board are adjustable. *See also* MIMEOGRAPH; STYLUS.

minimum density *See* DENSITY, MINIMUM.

minion Old type size. The nearest equivalent in the point system is 7 point (2.46 mm).

minor axis *See* AXIS.

mixing Total number of typeface styles, designs, and sizes that can be combined for producing copy during a one-time machine setup without changing photomatrices.

Fig. M-13 A. B. Dick Company's Model 565 mimeograph stencil printer.

mock-up Preliminary visualization, especially of a package or other printed piece, to show size, color, type positioning, folds, and the like.

moiré Undesirable wavelike or checkered effect that results when a halftone is photographed through a screen. This effect, which is caused by parallel mesh dots, can be avoided by turning the second screen 15° away from that of the halftone.

mold Wax or other form in which an electrotype is shaped.

monochromatic Having a single color.

monochrome Continuous-tone painting or drawing or a printed halftone painting or drawing having a single color or hue. The continuous tone does not become a halftone until it has been screened.

monodetail drawing In engineering drafting, a separate drawing for a single part.

monofilament Type of fabric used in screen printing.

monogram Combination of two or more interwoven or overlapping letters to represent a name.

monograph Written account of a particular subject; a learned treatise on a single topic.

montage Combination of drawings or photographs usually related to one subject and consisting of distinct as well as indistinct images that blend into each other. When only photographs are used, the term "photomontage" is more common.

mortise (mortice) To secure copy in position on the basic reproduction page; also to cut a hole in two layers of material and replace the undesired cutout piece with the desired cutout piece. The piece to be replaced may consist of one character, a line, a solid block of text, or a complete illustration. To mortise a correction for a word, for example, the word is first retyped on a separate piece of paper of the same kind as the reproduction paper. Ample space is left around the retyped word. The reproduction-copy page is then placed on a light table and the retyped word positioned over the word to be replaced. A sharp knife is used to cut out both layers of paper. The cutout retyped word is set aside. The reproduction-copy page is turned over and a strip of pressure-sensitive mortising tape affixed over the cutout. The paper should not be pulled or wrinkled. The reproduction-copy page is turned over again. The retyped word is picked up with the point of the knife and placed in the cutout space. The adhesive tape will serve as a base for holding the new word in position. When the page has been turned over once more and pressed lightly but firmly, the correction is complete.

Practically anything can be mortised into position. Printing cuts, for

Fig. M-14 A. B. Dick Company's Mimeoscope.

example, may be mortised to hold type. While the word "stripping" may be used to define mortising, the former is derived from lithography. Lithographers strip negatives into goldenrod flats before exposing the flats for platemaking.

mother-of-pearl finish   Paper finish having the effect of a lustrous change of colors.

mottle   Objectionable cloudy pattern appearing in film because of insufficient agitation in the first developer. Mottle appears especially in color-transparency films exposed to low densities. The same effect is produced in black-and-white film at about 1.0 density unit.

mottled finish   Paper finish showing diversified spots or blotches.

mounting, dry   *See* DRY MOUNTING.

mounting and flapping   Proper protection of line and photographic art requires mounting and flapping. This procedure also makes space available for identifying the art and facilitates filing. Figure M-15 shows a suitable method. The mounting board should be of proper dimensional stability so that it will not warp or bend. A minimum of ¾ inch (19.05 mm) should be provided between the paper edge of the art and the mounting board on all four sides. The tissue overlay, cut to the same size as the board, should be free from wax or grease. It is taped across the top and in

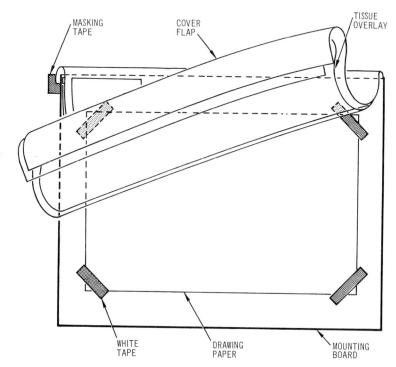

Fig. M-15 Mounting and flapping art.

two places on the face of the board. The overlay protects the art and may be used for notes and correction marks. It should not be removed until the art has been given a final check. If necessary, a second tissue overlay may be added, but the first one should not be removed. When the art has been completed, a clean tissue overlay is used to replace marked overlays.

Kraft paper is an excellent covering material. It is cut to the width of the mounting board and at least 1 inch longer to permit it to be folded over the top of the board. The corners of the folded edge are tapered, and the flap is affixed with rubber cement. Line art should be fastened in four places with white tape approximately 1¾ to 2 inches (4.45 to 5.08 cm) long and ½ inch (1.27 cm) wide. Pasting is not recommended because line art must be easily removed from the board for any necessary reworking. Continuous-tone art, however, should be pasted or dry-mounted.

mounting board Heavy paperboard in standard sizes of 20 by 20, 22 by 28, 28 by 44, and 30 by 40 inches (50.8 by 50.8, 55.8 by 71, 71 by 111.7, and 76.2 by 101.6 cm). The most popular thicknesses are 14, 24, and 30-ply (1.22, 2.13, and 2.74-mm). Mounting boards are used for mounting photographs, renderings, and other artwork. They have a smooth finish and vary in color from a slate gray to snow white. The 24- and 30-ply (2.13 and 2.74-mm) boards are suitable for mounting large illustrations and are sufficiently stable to withstand handling.

mouse See PICKUP.

movable type Type consisting of single pieces, as opposed to slugs of type which make up complete lines which are then cast as one piece. Johann Gutenberg is credited with inventing printing from movable type in the fifteenth century.

MT/ST Abbreviation for the Magnetic Tape Selectric typewriter. See COLD COMPOSITION.

muller tester Instrument, usually made of glass, used for grinding pigments in varnish for test purposes. Power-driven automatic mullers have two circular glass grinding surfaces.

multidetail drawing Engineering drawing that depicts more than one item.

multifilament Type of fabric used in screen printing.

Multilith See OFFSET DUPLICATOR.

Multilith Duplimat masters Paper and metal plates used for Multilith duplicators. To meet varying requirements, the plates are available in four styles. The style used depends on the type of master-cylinder clamp on the duplicator and the requirements of the particular application. Guidelines may or may not be furnished on masters.

The Duplimat masters are classified in numbered series. Series 2000, consisting of direct-image masters, is designed to produce comparatively few permanent high-quality copies. It is well suited to systems duplicating that requires the making of a master from a master to preserve the original format. Information may be added or deleted for each generation. Series 3000 direct-image masters are intended for short and medium runs. Information can be added for reruns. Series 3001 masters combine the surface characteristics of Series 2000 and the body strength of Series 3000. They are suitable for systems duplicating that requires the making of a master from a master, and they can be filed for reruns. Series 4000 direct-image masters produce a greater number of clean, sharp copies than the Series 2000 or 3000 masters; they are used for systems and general office duplicating. Series 5000 direct-image masters are suited for long-run requirements when a fabric ribbon is used; Series 5001, when a paper ribbon is used.

Systemat direct-image masters may be preprinted with business forms, letterheads, or any desired layout in reproducing or nonreproducing ink. Other direct-image masters are available in plain flat packs of various sizes as well as in printed continuous forms with carbon-interleaved work copies. Teletype rolls 8½ inches (21.6 cm) wide and 333 feet (101.2 m) long are also available.

Series 3000 and Series 4000 transfer-image masters are used in the xerographic transfer method. The image may be enlarged or reduced when the xerographic equipment contains a lens. Series 9000 Premier paper masters are presensitized for fine photographic reproduction. They may be exposed to arc lamps, exposure frames, or diazotype machines. Series 9001 presensitized economy master plates are also designed for photographic reproduction. Both types of masters can produce as many as 10,000 copies with a shelf life of one year.

Series 6000 aluminum masters are presensitized for photographic reproduction. The material is resistant to scratches and has a grained surface that simplifies the balancing of ink and moisture. The Pacemaster is a photographic acetate master that is interchangeable with a direct-image master without machine adjustment. It has a short exposure time and is easy to process. The Enco aluminum master is presensitized and exposes any positive image on translucent paper that is applied directly to it.

multiple flats   Separate printing flats, the details of which must match for a particular job, such as successive pages of multiple forms to be printed from separate plates. Multiple flats thus differ from complementary flats, in which several flats are used for the same plate.

multiple-frame microfilm   Arrangement in which two or more frames of microfilm are used to depict a single sheet of an engineering document.

multiple shadows   Series of shadows used to create a typographic effect on letters or lines of type.

multisheet drawing   Drawing in which two or more sheets are required to cover one item. Each sheet is identified with the same drawing number and numbered as sheet 1 of 5, sheet 2 of 5, etc.

Mylar Tough, highly stable polyester film used as a base for films for engineering drawings, photographic materials, and other applications. Mylar is a registered trade name of Du Pont. When sensitized, Mylar makes an excellent intermediate for the whiteprint process. The clear film may be used for laminating.

negative, photolithographic Film negative having a translucent image and a black background, produced by a process camera and used primarily to make printing plates. An enlargement or a reduction is made from original photographed material. After being developed, the negative is stripped into masking paper called a goldenrod flat, which is placed in a vacuum frame next to a sensitized printing plate. The image is then "burned" through the negative to the plate by exposure to strong light. The light penetrates the translucent image but is blocked by the opaque background of the negative and the masking paper.

There are two kinds of photolithographic negatives: line copy and continuous-tone copy. Line copy is black and white without intermediate tones. The reproduced image will appear as type matter, lines, dots, or other image-forming deposits. Continuous-tone copy has gradations of tone from white to black; when screened, it is a halftone. The printing press cannot reproduce the tone gradations by laying varying amounts of ink on the paper. Instead, it prints various sizes of ink dots. Small dots are printed for light tones and large dots more closely together for dark tones.

The process camera introduces this halftone pattern into the negative by means of a contact halftone screen between the film and the camera lens. Magenta and gray contact screens are widely employed. They are made on a flexible film base that can be used over the film on the vacuum back of the camera. Screens are provided in various rulings and are designated by the number of lines per inch, ranging from a coarse screen of 65 lines per inch (2.54 cm), suitable for reproduction on newsprint, to 133-line or finer screens used for quality reproduction of halftones on offset and enamel paper.

Because line copy does not require screening and continuous-tone work does, certain techniques must be introduced when both line and continuous-tone copy are to appear on the same printed page. One method is to take a line exposure of the line work and then, in a second operation, a screened halftone exposure of the continuous-tone copy. The halftone negative is stripped into the line negative, and the result is a combination negative from which a combination printing plate can be made. A second method leading to a combination printing plate is to use masking and stripping film such as Rubylith or Amberlith. Two overlays are required. The first mask covers all the line portions of the image that fall outside the tone area, and a second mask covers the tone values. With the first mask in position covering the line copy and the tone areas exposed, a halftone contact screen is placed over the film and the halftone main and flash exposures are made. With the first mask removed, the second mask is positioned over the copy with the tone areas covered and the line work exposed. A line exposure is made, thus completing the double-exposed film and producing a line and halftone combination negative. This method has many advantages over that of stripping the halftone negative into the line negative.

If art must be reworked, a strip of masking tape may be placed along the bottom of the corresponding negative extending to the width of the crop marks but outside them. Vertical lines are drawn on the tape to show the horizontal limitations of the image. Size instructions are noted on the tape, and the printer will accordingly enlarge or reduce the image to provide a photoprint for reworking.

Photolithographic negatives are excellent for producing reference copies by the whiteprint process. In this process, everything that is white stays white and everything that is black stays black on the copy paper. As the photolithographic negative has a translucent image and a black background, the image on the copy paper will have a white image and a black background. If an 8- by 10-inch (20.3 by 25.4 cm) negative is positioned to register evenly in the upper right corner of 8½ by 11-inch (21.6 by 28-cm) copy paper, white space is left for a binding margin and for the figure number and title at the bottom.

negative conversion System of converting metal typeforms to lithographic negatives, developed by the Printing Arts Research Laboratories and designated as the "Instant Negative Conversion" process.

Use of a darkroom and camera is not required. To produce a negative, a reproduction proof is made on paper. The proof is then covered with a sheet of instant negative film and heated briefly in a vacuum platen. The film is developed by being wiped.

A special low-tack ink is used in the proof press. The image is transferred immediately after proofing. Vacuum contact and heat between 135 and 145°F transfer the image to the film in about thirty seconds. The latent image is completed when the film is swabbed with a clearing solution. The film is then ready for making an offset printing plate.

negative-reading *See* REVERSE-READING.

neutral density filter Filter that reduces all colors of light uniformly.

newspaper fold *See* FORMER FOLD.

newsprint Low-grade printing paper having loose fibers and high ink-absorbency characteristics, designed especially for printing newspapers. The ink permeates the paper and leaves carbon-black pigment on the surface. While letterpress is used to print many newspapers, a strong trend toward using web-offset presses was first begun by weekly newspapers and is expanding rapidly to large dailies.

newsprint inks Carbon-black or colored pigments with mineral oil as a vehicle, manufactured especially for printing on newsprint. These inks dry by absorption. Emulsion, oxidation, and heat-set systems are recent developments for fast drying. A recent development by Sun Chemical Corporation, General Printing Ink Division, is their Suncure solventless, pollution-free ink and drying system that has been designed especially to meet OSHA requirements and other contingencies involving the printing ink industry. *See also* SUNCURE SYSTEM and INKS, PRINTING.

Newton's rings Light-interference patterns created where a plane surface and a convex lens (or two lenses with different curvatures) meet, found in photomechanical work during exposure.

nick Notch found in the body of a piece of type. In hand composition nicks are aligned by the compositor so that type will print properly. *See also* TYPE DESCRIPTION.

nickeltype (also called **"steelfaced" plate**) Copper electrotype plate having a first coating of nickel, used for long pressruns.

Nitex Trademark for a monofilament fabric used in screen printing.

nitrogen-burst process *See* PROCESSING, NITROGEN-BURST.

nomenclature In artwork, words or symbols used to identify and call out an object (*see* Figure N-1). Nomenclature can be applied in several ways. If it is applied by using wax-backed preprints or transfer sheets, it may be on either transparent or opaque paper and be pasted, mortised, or burnished into place. If the background is white, either opaque or transparent preprints or transfers may be used. If the background is gray to black, the nomenclature should have an opaque backing, but preprints should be true rectangles because their background will be defined on the art. If wire numbers are desired for a wiring diagram in which each wire has a number or color designation, the lines should be drawn without breaks. When preprints that have an opaque background are placed over a line, they will then "break" it.

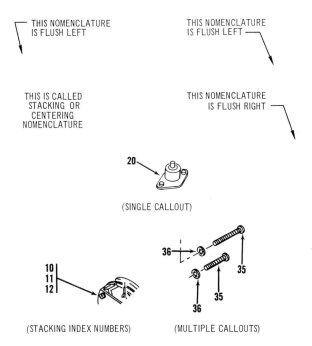

Fig. N-1 Using nomenclature with art.

nomograph (nomogram) Graph or chart that enables one to find the value of a dependent variable by aligning a straightedge with the given independent variable; also a graphic representation of the relation of numerical values.

nonimpact printing Printing whereby the printed image is produced without an impression cylinder or other image-bearing plate or screen coming in contact with the paper or other substrate. Examples are the use of writing heads as used in computer-adapted output units. Electrostatic screen printing (also referred to as pressureless printing) can be classified as nonimpact printing because the image-bearing plate does not come in contact with the surface upon which the image is imposed.

nonpareil Old type size. The nearest equivalent in the point system is 6 point (2.11 mm).

Occupational Safety and Health Act (OSHA) Act passed in the United States in 1970 which permits inspectors to examine and inspect any company for violation of occupational safety and health standards established by the act.

off-line Functional setup of equipment in which related operating units do not interface directly with other units during operation; for example, a folding machine, collator, or plate maker operating independently of the printing press. In computer graphics, a system configuration in which the operation of peripheral equipment is not under direct control of the central processor.

office-composition copy Reproduction copy composed on office or similar cold-composition machines. *See* COLD COMPOSITION.

offset Unwanted image transferred to the back of a printed sheet by the sheet beneath it as the sheets are stacked after printing. When heavy ink is used on a nonporous stock, a slip sheet must be placed between each two printed sheets. The offset effect is also found on the back of a printed page when the image has been unintentionally imposed on the impression roller because paper and printing plate have not been synchronized. In printing, the term "offset" also refers to the transfer of the image from the plate to a rubber blanket to stock as in photo-offset lithography and letterset printing.

offset duplicator Small offset printing machine that uses the planographic method, or printing from a plane surface by the application of lithography. The image may be applied to the printing plate directly or indirectly. In direct platemaking, preprinted matter, an ink pen, graphite or grease pencil, ball-point pen, rubber stamp, brush, crayon, or other means is used to compose the image on the plate without intermediate steps. Indirect platemaking is accomplished by photomechanical means.

The offset method of printing is based on the fact that grease and water do not mix. The master plate is placed on the master cylinder. An aqueous solution applied to the plate is repelled by the grease-receptive image on the master but is accepted by the nonimage area. The ink adheres only to the image and is repelled from the wet nonimage area. As the master cylinder revolves, the various rollers continue to supply the solution and ink to the plate. The image is transferred from the master plate to a cylinder on which a rubber blanket has been mounted. An impression cylinder then brings the paper stock in contact with the blanket cylinder, thus transferring the image from the blanket to paper. (*See also* DIRECT PLATEMAKING; PRINTING METHODS.)

Figure O-1 is A.B. Dick Company's tabletop offset duplicator Model 326. The feed table accommodates 500 sheets of 20-pound (9.08-kg) paper or the equivalent. The table automatically elevates to maintain proper feeding level. The paper feed with twin feed rollers is automatic, and the receiving tray is adjustable for various paper sizes. Paper sizes are 3 by 5 to 11 by 14 inches (7.62 by 12.7 to 27.9 by 35.5 cm) for automatic feed and 3 by 5 to 11½ by 16 inches (7.62 by 12.7 to 29.2 by 40.6 cm) for single-sheet feed. Paper weights are 13-pound (5.9-kg) bond to postcard stock (94 pound; 42.6 kg). The maximum copy area is 9½ by 13 inches (24 by 33 cm). The reset counter counts copies up to 9,999. Speed of the machine is variable from 4,500 to 7,500 impressions per hour. Weight of the unit is 222 pounds (101 kg).

Figure O-2 is A.B. Dick Company's Model 369 offset duplicator. The programmer includes drive and pump switches for manual, automatic, and off control. Other main features are a preset counter to 100 copies that automatically resets, a counter on-off switch, a blanket-cleaning cycle selector for 3 to 15 revolutions, and a shut-off for feed at the desired point that actuates the master ejector and engages and disengages the blanket washer. The water and ink rolling system consists of three oscillating rollers, two ductor rollers, five distribution rollers, and two form rollers. The loading table for masters accommodates dry masters from 1 to 100 of any size from 4½ by 6 inches (11.4 by 15.2 cm) to 11 by 18½ inches (27.9 by 47 cm). The feed table accommodates a 20½-inch (51.3-cm) stack of paper.

Figure O-3 shows American Type Founders' offset copy duplicator system with the duplicator, master maker, and processor designed as their 1014 copy duplicating system. The master maker produces up to 11-inch masters in variable lengths of 8 to 17 inches (20.3 to 43 cm) from a 300-foot (91.4-m) roll of paper stock, although manually fed masters cut to size may be made and used. The processor produces ready-to-mount masters in several seconds. The 1014 duplicator produces copies at the rate of 8,500 impressions per hour with a three-step operation; the master is inserted into an automatic clamping device, the desired number of copies is punched into the control panel, and a single control lever is moved through the water, ink, and run cycles. Blanket wash and ink-system cleaning are automatic. Solid-state electronics are used.

Figure O-4 is A.B. Dick Company's Model 1500 copy system. The master-making station automatically images, converts, dries, and delivers electrostatic masters to the offset duplicator for printing of copies. The master-making station copies colors of printing, writing, or drawings from all types of originals including transparencies. Copies are made from single-sheet originals or from bound materials. A two-level counter programs the number of copies needed from the master at the duplicating station, and masters immediately follow. The control panel contains the following: power button; automatic start button for the duplication station; pre-etch switch to prime the duplicating station if the machine has been idle; print button to start production of the master; sort button that controls on-line sorter if used; emergency stop button; and a reset button. A button on the control panel lights when dispersant is to be added. A load light is provided to signal when a new original may be loaded. The offset duplicator may be used independently of the master-making station. The duplicator feed table accommodates 5,000 sheets of 20-pound (9.08-kg) stock. The master loading table holds up to 20 masters in continuous operating using the master transport and 50 masters when placed manually on the loading table. Paper sizes for the duplicator are 3 by 5 to 11 by 17 inches (7.62 by 12.7 to 27.9 by 43 cm). Paper weights range from 12 pound to 110 pound (5.4 to 50 kg) index. The offset duplicator operates at speeds from 5,000 to 9,000 copies per hour, and speeds from exposure to the first copy at the master-making station is approximately thirty seconds

Fig. O-1 A. B. Dick Company's tabletop offset duplicator Model 326.

Fig. O-2 A. B. Dick Company's Model 369 offset duplicator.

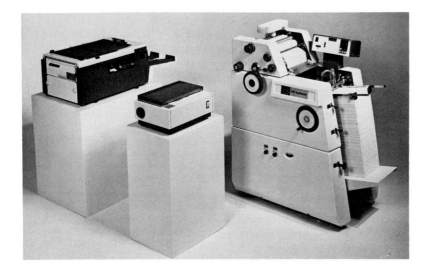

Fig. O-3 American Type Found[...] 1014 copy duplicating system.

Fig. O-4 A. B. Dick Company's 1500 copy system.

from exposure of the first copy; operation is continuous thereafter. A reset counter counts to 99,999.

offset letterpress *See* LETTERSET PRINTING.

offset lithography Lithographic printing by the method of transferring the image to paper from a rubber blanket. The inked plate prints on the blanket, which then offsets the image to paper stock. *See also* PRINTING METHODS.

offset paper Type of book paper. Since the lithographic offset process of printing is based on the fact that grease (ink) and water do not mix, offset paper must be acid-free. Offset book papers are divided into uncoated and

)ups may be obtained in basis weights of 50, 60, 70,
inds (22.7, 27.2, 31.7, 36.3, 45.4, 53.4, and 68 kg) for
ize of 25 by 38 inches (63.5 by 96.5 cm). Uncoated
for magazines, advertising pieces, house organs,
igle-color and multicolor work. Woven and other
.... Special sizing techniques during manufacture
....ie or minimize fuzz. Coated offset paper is manufactured especially
to eliminate fuzz and picking, and sizing processes are included to repel
water. This type of paper will reproduce better halftones and colors than
uncoated offset paper.

offset plate Paper or metal plate having a right-reading image that is
affixed to an offset press for printing. A single plate carries all copy and
artwork to complete one impression. The metal plate, which may be made
of aluminum, magnesium, stainless steel, or other material, curves around
the cylinder of the press. One side of the plate is grained to hold moisture
and coated with a solution that is sensitive to light. The coated plate is
placed in a vacuum frame with the assembled negative containing the
image in front, and the combination is then exposed to arc lights that
penetrate the translucent image of the negative. The latent image on the
plate is developed by being washed with developer and water. The
emulsion on the part of the plate that receives the image hardens and
resists the action of the developer, and thus the image is disclosed on the
plate.

offset printing press Rotary press using the offset method of lithographic
printing. Offset printing presses are available in a wide variety of designs,
sizes, and modes of operation to meet requirements ranging from those of
the small job shop to those of medium and large printing establishments
and newspaper publishers. Common to all the presses are the rotary
cylinders. These in the main are the master cylinder that holds the plate,
the blanket cylinder to which the image is transferred from the master
cylinder, and the impression cylinder, which serves as a cushion in
conjunction with the blanket cylinder so that the image can be impressed
on stock. The stock may be sheet-fed or fed from a roll called a web.
Printing-press designers continue to automate offset presses insofar as
practicable, arranging for most aspects of operation to be handled at a
single control station and incorporating automatic devices to ensure safety
and to detect malfunctions.

Figure O-5 shows HCM Corporation's Champion four-color sheet-fed
offset press. The main operator's station, at the delivery, contains push-
button controls for starting, sheet flow, ink and dampening, pressure
adjustment, tachometer reading, sheet counting, and the like. Colored
lamps signal the degree to which the press is switched on and the tripping
of the control and safety devices. The press can handle a sheet size of 28⅜
by 42½ inches (72 by 108 cm) and it has a printing area of 27⅗₁₆ by 41¾
inches (70 by 106 cm). Maximum speed is 7,200 sheets per hour.

American Type Founders' Profiteer 25-1 (Figure O-6) is a sheet-fed offset
printing press designed to print a variety of jobs on different paper sizes,
thicknesses, and stock. Paper sizes range from 8 by 10 inches (20.3 by

Fig. O-5   HCM Corporation's Champion four-color sheet-fed offset press.

25.4 cm) to 19 by 25¼ inches (48.2 by 6.41 cm). Thicknesses of stock from 9-pound (4.08-kg) onionskin to 6-ply (0.610 mm) card stock can be used. The Profiteer 25-1 handles stock such as bond, ledger, offset book, eggshell, handfinish, tag, and blotter in four colors when desired. The printing area is 18½ by 25 inches (47 by 63.5 cm), and plate size is 21 by 25⅜ by 0.016 inches (53.5 by 64.4 cm by 0.406 mm) thick (with packing). There are 20 inking rollers, 3 ink form rollers, and 5 dampening rollers. Feeder pile height is 33¾ inches (85.7 cm), and delivery pile height is 16⅛ inches (41 cm). Maximum printing speed is 8,500 impressions per hour.

The Chief 15-inch (38.1-cm) offset press (Figure O-7) is designed to augment the work of larger presses when makeready time and operating costs are significant. It handles sheets from 3 by 5 inches (7.62 by 12.7 cm) to 11 by 15 inches (27.9 by 38.1 cm) and paper weights from 11-pound (5-kg) manifold to 2-ply card stock (0.010 inch; 0.025 mm). The maximum printing area is 9¾ by 13¼ inches (24.7 by 34.3 cm). Speed varies from 7,200 to 9,000 impressions per hour. The inking unit contains 10 rollers, and the damping unit contains 4 rollers. The gripper margin can be adjusted from 3/16 to 5/16 inch (4.76 to 7.94 mm).

Figure O-8 shows the Schriber Model H 500 press, designed to produce short to medium pressruns of business forms. Forty-inch (101.6 cm) unwind rolls can be run at speeds up to 800 feet (244 m) per minute and web widths to 17½ inches (44.4 cm). (An optional speed of 600 feet [183 m] per minute is available.) It is available with standard 14, 17, 22, and 24-inch (35.6, 43.1, 55.8, and 61-cm) cylinder circumferences and one through four printing towers for color flexibility. A power roll lift, air-expandable mill roll shaft, and electric-eye press stop, and a manual side adjustment of roll position are provided. A cylinder and modified drum infeed, for the first offset only, provides the printing register control. Once the register control is set, it is not necessary to compensate for different press speeds under normal operating conditions. Printing towers feature controls for the ink fountain roller, ink ductor, plate cylinder side adjustment, and impression cylinder. The Micro-Flo dampening system features the Schriber follower-circuit which automatically controls the ink and water balance throughout the speed range of the press. The H 500 also features a redesigned horizontal configuration of the processing unit, a 24-inch (61-cm) diameter rewind that is equipped with an air-controlled rewind dancer, an eccentric web-separating idler, and a cantilevered air-expandable shaft for fast roll

Fig. O-6   American Type Founders' Profiteer 25-1 sheet-fed offset printing press.

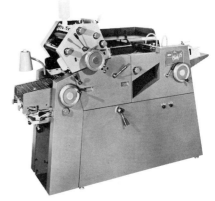

Fig. O-7   American Type Founders' Chief 15-inch offset press.

Fig. O-8 Schriber Model H 500 press.

changes. Each press is provided with a double numbering unit with a common impression cylinder and ink fountain. Optional accessories are a press rapid folder, double numbering tower, sheeter, and a carbon paper attaching unit.

Figure O-9 shows the Miehle 36 two-color offset press, having a minimum sheet size of 11 by 16 inches (27.9 by 40.6 cm), a maximum sheet size of 25 by 36 inches (63.5 by 91.4 cm), and plate size of 29½ by 36⁷⁄₁₆ inches (75 by 92.5 cm). Blanket size is 32¾ by 36⁷⁄₁₆ inches (83 by 92.5 cm). The press has a high starting torque and wide range of speed control with speeds up to 10,000 impressions per hour. Feeder capacity is 47 inches (119.3 cm) to the floor and delivery capacity is 49 inches (124.4 cm) to the floor. Dimensions are 16 feet 10 inches (4.87 m 25.4 cm) in length, 9 feet 7 inches (2.74 m 17.8 cm) wide, and 6 feet 6 inches (1.82 m 15.2 cm) in height. Additional allowance for the length must be made for operation of the nonstop feeder and sheet catcher for continuous delivery. Models of this press also are available for single- and four-color work.

The Miehle Super 60 offset press is shown in Figure O-10. This model has a capability of from one to six colors. Minimum sheet size is 22 by 34 inches (55.8 by 86.3 cm), maximum sheet size 43 by 60 inches (109 by 152.4 cm), plate size is 47¼ by 60½ inches (120 by 154 cm), and blanket size 48 by 61¼ inches (122 by 156 cm). Press speeds are up to 8,000 impressions per hour. The feeder has an all-electric nonstop operation and feeds a range of stock

Fig. O-9 Miehle 36 two-color sheet-fed offset press. (*MGD Graphics Division, North American Rockwell.*)

Fig. O-10   Miehle Super 60 six-color offset press. (*MGD Graphics Division, North American Rockwell.*)

from thin paper to heavy caliper board. The pile mechanism is designed to handle commercial mill skids. A four-way register control, which is part of the off-press operating console, permits an overall adjustment of the front guide system while the press is operating. Guides can be raised, lowered, or moved forward or back to change gripper margins or to cock the sheet as a unit or individually. A remote ink fountain color control console, which can be had at option, reduces makeready time up to 50 percent. Ink fountain individual blades can be adjusted in increments of 0.000125 inch (0.00318 mm) through a digital readout counter. The automatic dampening system is independent of the inker system. It supplies a dampening solution to the plate on a continuous and precisely controlled basis. A refrigerated and filtered circulating system reduces evaporation of the fountain solution, maintains a uniform level of the solution, and filters out solid contaminants. Automatic push-button delivery controls are operated from a console. The Miehle Super 60 press has an overall length of 52 feet (15.8 m), width is 16 feet 1½ inches (4.9 m) including the drive side ink mixing slab, and height is 7 feet 11 inches (2.4 m). In addition, the Super 60 models are available for single-, two- and four-color work.

Designed for printing continuous stock tabulating forms, the Schriber High-Speed press (Figure O-11) is a long-run, single-color offset press producing forms up to 1,500 feet (457 m) per minute roll to roll, or 1,200 feet (367 m) per minute roll to fold. The press is available in 22 or 24-inch (55.8 or 61-cm) cylinder circumferences and will accept 50-inch (127-cm) rolls up to 32½ inches (83 cm) wide. It will handle 10-pound (4.54 kg) bond up to 24-pound (10.9-kg) ledger stock. The press consists of an unwind unit, dry offset printing tower, modified drum feed, processing unit, 1,200 feet (367 m) per minute cylinder folder, and 40-inch (101.6-cm) rewinder. Additional standard features include a plate-bending fixture, a predetermining press-stop counter, tachometer, web-break detectors, and an automatic lubrication system. The processing unit consists of marginal punch, cross-perforating, and vertical slitting/perforation units and provision for one file punch position. The printing tower is dry offset with an option for conversion to wet offset by adding a dampening system. The 22-inch

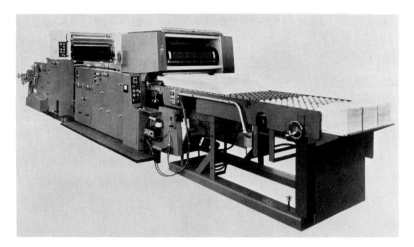

Fig. O-11   Schriber High-Speed stock forms press.

(55.8-cm) cylinder circumference press handles a web length of 32½ inches (82.5 cm), maximum printing length is 21⅝ inches (55 cm), form size folding is 11 inches (27.9 cm), and folding speed is up to 1,200 feet (366 m) per minute based on 15-pound (6.81-kg) stock. Rewinding speed is up to 1,500 feet (457 m) per minute. The 24-inch (61-cm) cylinder circumference press handles a web length of 32½ inches (82.5 cm), maximum printing length is 23⅝ inches (60 cm), form size folding is from 8 or 12 inches (20 or 30.4 cm), and folding speed is up to 1,200 feet (366 m) per minute for the 12-inch (30.4-cm) fold and up to 875 feet (267 m) per minute for the 8-inch (20.3-cm) fold.

Figure O-12 shows the Harris Model 1000 web offset press. This model, available in two standard usage sizes (22¾ or 23½ by 38 inches; 57.7 or 59.6 by 96.6 m) is designed for the production of catalogues, tabloids, newspapers, and magazines. Two different folders are offered in both sizes as standard; a combination folder (former-jaw-chopper) or a two-former, four-delivery folder. The press accommodates web supply devices such as reels, pasters, or unwind stands for feeding from a roll of paper. Roll stands may be specified in tandem or as dual units and may be located in-line or on the drive side of the press or both. Controlled metering is handled by a preset web-tension automatic infeed unit. A speed determinator roll produces the desired tension and can be preset by a control, which combined with an indicator, gives a readout of the total web tension. Each perfecting unit simultaneously prints one color on each side of the web as it travels through the press horizontally at speeds up to 32,000

**Fig. O-12
Harris Model 1000
web offset press.**

impressions per hour. Cylinder circumference (cutoff) is 23¾ or 23½ inches
(60.3 or 59.6 cm). Maximum transfer size is 22⅜ or 23⅛ by 37½ inches (56.7
or 58.7 by 95.2 cm). Maximum web width for a full roll is 38 inches (96.5 cm),
and minimum web width for a full roll is 26 inches (66 cm). Maximum web
width for a half roll is 19 inches (48.3 cm), and minimum web width for a
half roll is 13 inches (33 cm). Plate and blanket sizes for the two usage sizes
are as follows:

Plate size: 22¾ press 24⅝ by 38 inches (57.7 press 62.4 by 96.6 cm)
23½ press 25⅜ by 38 inches (59.6 press 64.4 by 96.6 cm)
Blanket size: 22¾ press 52¼ by 38⅜ inches (57.7 press 132.7 by 97.4 cm)
23½ press 53½ by 38⅜ inches (59.6 press 135.8 by 97.4 cm)

offset relief *See* LETTERSET PRINTING.

offset spray Device that applies a fine mist of powder between two sheets
during the pressrun to prevent the moist ink of one sheet from printing on
the back of the succeeding sheet.

offset toning Method of applying liquid toner in which the toner is sprayed
onto a roller traveling in contact with the paper. The toner is applied at a
rate directly proportional to the speed of the paper. This method is used in
computer graphics.

oiled paper Paper treated with oil to give it sealing characteristics, often
used as a wrapping paper.

on-line Functional system of related operating units which are attached to
or placed in a position where all units operate simultaneously to achieve
two or more functions. For example, original copy is exposed to make the
printing plates, the plates are delivered to the master cylinder of the press,
and printed pages are collated in an automatic continuous operation. In
computer graphics, a system configuration in which the operation of
peripheral equipment is under direct control of the central processing unit
(CPU).

once and a half up In drawing, to a size 1½ times that of artwork as it will
appear on the printed page. If a printed page is to have an image width of
7 inches (17.8 cm), the art is drawn to that width plus one-half, or 10½
inches (26.7 cm), without allowance for boxing. Height must be increased in
proportion.

one-scale chart Bar chart that shows only one quantity by using one
scale. The bars, drawn horizontally on the chart from left to right, represent
quantity. Such a chart may serve as the basis for constructing other charts
in which more than one value can be expressed. A "pie chart" is another
example of a one-scale chart. *See also* BAR CHART; COLUMN CHART; CURVE
CHART; PIE CHART; SURFACE CHART.

one-view drawing *See* ORTHOGRAPHIC PROJECTION: ENGINEERING DRAWINGS.

onionskin (manifold paper) Thin, translucent paper used to make a typewriter carbon copy or to serve as a tissue overlay for work requiring correction or protection. The rag content may be 25 to 100 percent, and the finish may be dull or glazed. Basis weights are 7 and 9 pounds (3.17 and 4.08 kg) for 500 sheets of the basic size of 17 by 22 inches (43 by 55.8 cm). Onionskin is available in the letter size of 8½ by 11 inches (21.6 by 28 cm) and in the legal sizes of 8½ by 13 and 8½ by 14 inches (21.6 by 33 and 21.6 by 35.6 cm). It comes packaged in boxes of 100 or 500 sheets.

Onyx Line of opaque papers and cloth and transparent paper, cloth, and film manufactured for moist diazo reproduction. Onyx is a registered trade name of the Keuffel and Esser Company. Opaque blackline and blueline paper and cloth are produced from right-reading translucent originals. The transparent Onyx paper, cloth, and film produce sepia-line intermediates.

opaque Impermeable to light; not transparent or translucent. As a verb, opaque means to paint over unwanted areas of a negative with an opaque solution before the negative is exposed for plate making. The painted areas are made impervious to light.

opaque circular Bond and offset book paper manufactured to provide great opacity. It is used for direct-mail advertising, booklets, house organs, leaf inserts, technical data sheets, and illustrated leaflets.

operating unit *See* READER.

optical center Point slightly above the geometric center of a rectangular plane. Objects placed at the optical center appear to be at the geometric center.

optical character recognition (OCR) System of employing an optical device which scans an image and "reads" the characters for phototypesetting.

optical lantern *See* EPIDIASCOPE.

optical printing Any printing method in which a process camera is employed as one step in producing the end item. Reductions, enlargements, or same-size negatives may be produced. If a camera lens is used in the copying process, various sizes may be obtained from the original copy; if a camera is not used, only contact, or same-size, reproduction copies may be had.

optical spacing Arrangement of spacing between letters for legibility and appearance, as opposed to mechanical spacing, in which the same space is used between all characters. The spacing varies with the shape of the letters to achieve optical equalization.

orange backing Orange-colored carbon paper used for typing on vellum or other translucent material. The carbon paper is reversed and impresses an image on the back of the original. Orange backing is used to create a dense image and accomplish better reproduction during exposure in the whiteprint machine. Corrections can only be made by erasing, although erasing is difficult because of the carbon characteristics of the orange backing.

order In styling a manuscript, the ranking of the various headings according to their importance. The major subdivisions of a chapter or section carry first-order headings, their chief subdivisions second-order headings, and so on. The compositor is given detailed instructions on the desired typeface, point size and leading, indention, and the like for each heading. Compositor's language—picas as a measurement instead of inches, leading, points, and ems—should be used. If key numbers are used to designate the headings, detailed type marking of the manuscript is unnecessary. A similar system may be used in preparing a manuscript for the reproduction typist.

organization chart Block chart or diagram showing the names, titles, departments, and responsibilities of personnel in an organization (*see* Figure O-13). Such a chart serves to outline responsibilities and to show the chain of command. When the information given in each block is not extensive, it should be stacked; that is, each line of type should be centered beneath the preceding line. When a breakdown of the duties of a person or a department or other extended information is given, however, each line should be flush left. The primary title of each block should be set or typed

Fig. O-13 Simple organization chart.

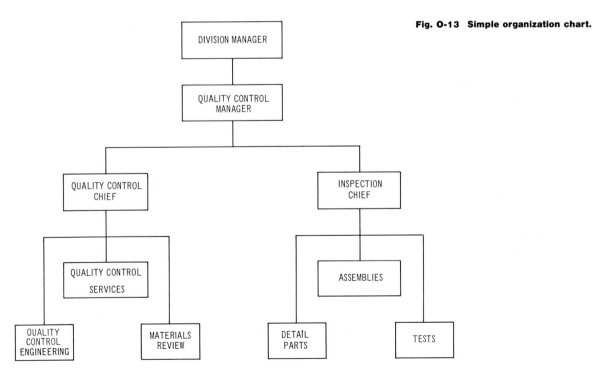

in capital letters and subordinate information in capitals and lowercase. For example, if the subject of a chart is departments or divisions, the department or division name should be in capital letters and other copy in the block in capitals and lowercase. If the subject is the personnel of an organization, then the names of the persons should be in capitals and the other copy in capitals and lowercase.

original *See* MASTER.

orphan In copy layout and page makeup, a colloquial term for a word or syllable that stands alone at the top of a column or page. An orphan is an indication of poor layout and should be avoided. *See also* WIDOW.

Ortho A film Du Pont lithographic film on a Cronar polyester film base. Ortho A is designed for halftone and line negatives or positives employed in lithography, photoengraving, gravure, and screen-process printing, and it can also be used to make highlight and color-correction masks. In addition, it finds favor in contact operations because of its ability to perform well in universal developers.

Ortho D film Du Pont lithographic film on a Cronar polyester film base. Ortho D is designed to produce high-quality line and halftone negatives for Dycril printing plates. Because it has a low-level nonhalation backing, it can also be used on deep-etch positives and photoengraving negatives with laterally reversed images for exposure through the back of the film.

Ortho M film Du Pont lithographic film on a Cronar polyester film base. Ortho M has special surfaces to minimize Newton's rings and characteristics that facilitate contact printing and platemaking. It is designed for both camera and contact negatives or positives for the major printing processes, and it can be used for either halftone or line work.

Ortho S film Du Pont lithographic film on a Cronar polyester film base. Ortho S is used in making halftone and line negatives or positives for lithography, photoengraving, gravure, and screen printing. The film is recommended for applications where maximum dimensional stability and high-quality camera halftone work are required.

orthochromatic Designating photographic materials that are sensitive to green as well as blue and ultraviolet light. *See* FILMS AND PLATES.

orthographic projection: engineering drawings Orthographic projection, a method of third-angle projection, is graphically illustrated in Figure O-14*A*, *B*, and *C*. There are six principal views of an object as represented in Figure O-14*C*. Figure O-14*B* shows an object placed in a transparent box, and *C* shows the box unfolded. The projection in Figure O-14*C* shows the object seen by looking straight through each side of the box. When the box shown in O-14*B* is opened and laid flat, the result is a six-view third-angle orthographic-projection drawing. It is seldom necessary to draw all six views to portray an object clearly for fabrication purposes.

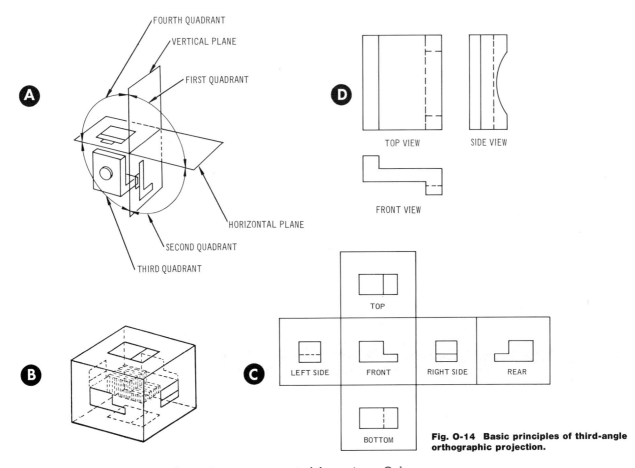

Fig. O-14 Basic principles of third-angle orthographic projection.

Figure O-14D illustrates an alternative arrangement of three views. Only the views that are necessary to illustrate the required characteristics of an object should be drawn. Almost all engineering drawings used in fabrication are in orthographic projection.

One-view drawings are drawings of objects that are cylindrical, spherical, hexagonal, square, rectangular, or the like or of objects that can be completely defined by one view and by a note of such features as thickness or length (see Figure O-15A, B). Figure O-15A shows a cylindrical object, while Figure O-15B is a plate.

Partial views of symmetrical objects may be represented by half views, as shown in Figure O-15C and D. Half views extend slightly beyond the center line of symmetry and terminate in a break line. If the adjacent view is nonstructural, the near half of the symmetrical view is drawn as in Figure O-15C; if the adjacent view is a full or half section, the far half of the symmetrical view is drawn as in Figure O-15D.

Three-view drawings may be arranged with any three adjacent views in the relation shown in Figure O-14C. When space is limited or the part can thus be more clearly indicated, the side view may be placed near the top view, as shown in Figure O-14D. When two side views are required to

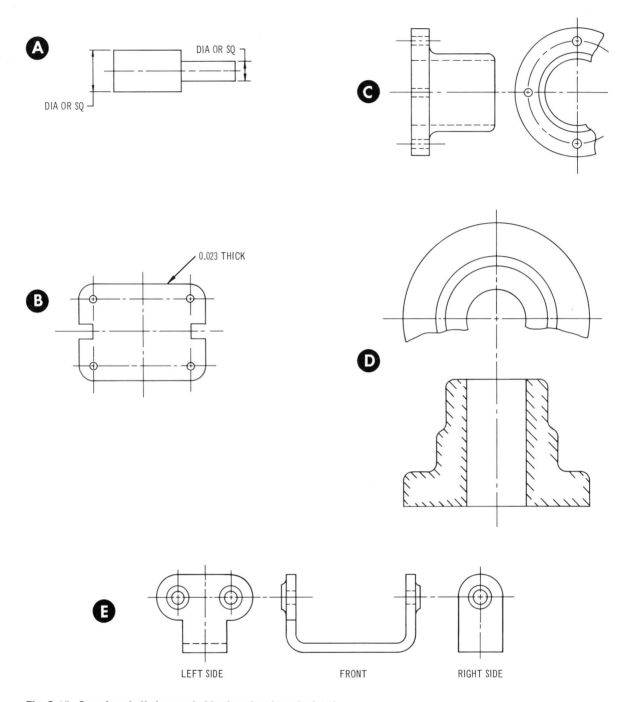

Fig. O-15 One-view, half-view, and side-view drawings depicted in orthographic projection.

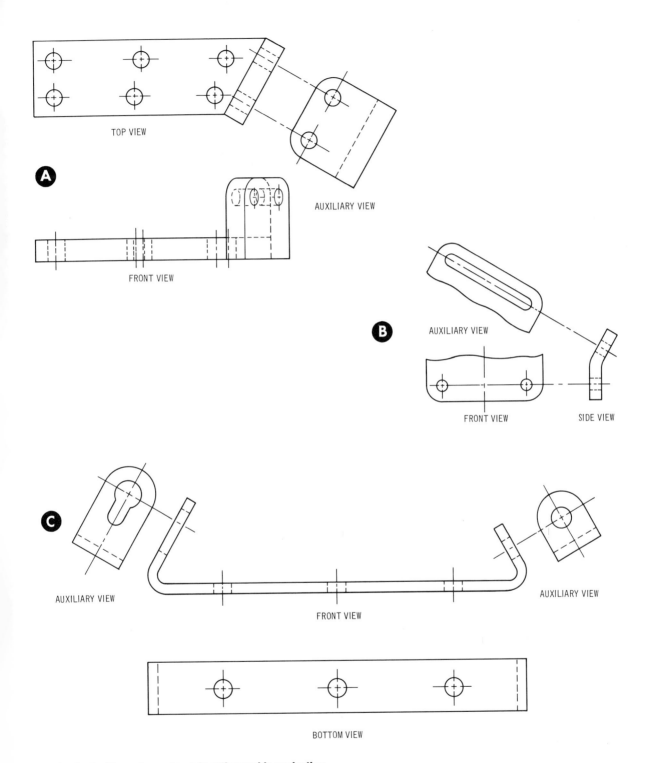

Fig. O-16 Auxiliary views shown in orthographic projection.

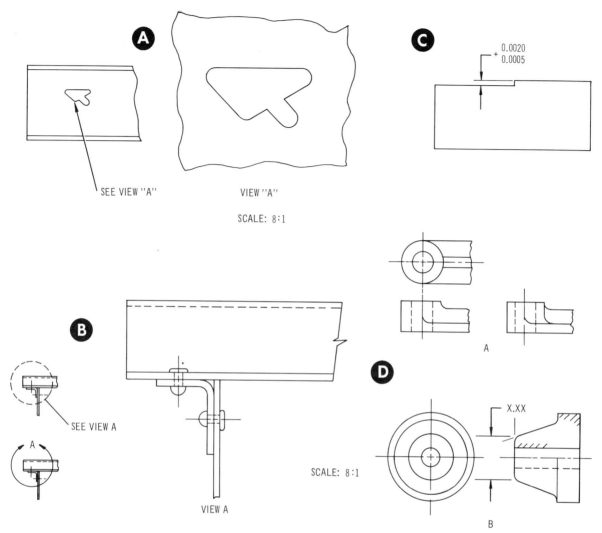

SEE VIEW "A"

VIEW "A"

SCALE: 8:1

SEE VIEW A

A

VIEW A

SCALE: 8:1

0.0020
+ 0.0005

A

X.XX

B

Fig. O-17   Detail views, exaggerated view, and contour lines in orthographic projection.

illustrate an object, they may be complete views if together they depict the shape of the object, as in Figure O-15E.

Objects having inclined faces or other features not parallel to any of the three principal planes of projection require auxiliary views to show the true shape of these features. Partial auxiliary views showing only the pertinent features are employed to illustrate features not clearly shown by the principal views (see Figure O-16A, B, C).

Auxiliary sectional views may also be employed to advantage to illustrate features not clearly shown by principal views. Views not directly projected must be clearly marked to indicate the location and the direction from which the object is viewed.

A detail shows part of the drawing in the same plane and in the same arrangement but in greater detail and, if necessary, to a larger scale than the principal view. The part of the drawing to be detailed must be suitably identified (*see* Figure O-17*A, B*). When a feature is too small to be drawn to scale, it may be exaggerated, as shown in Figure O-17*C*. Variations from true projection may be drawn for clarity. For example, the rounded or filleted intersection of two surfaces theoretically shows no line in projection but may be indicated by a conventional line. Contour should be drawn as shown in Figure O-17*D*.

outline   *See* VISIBLE LINE.

outline drawing   In engineering drafting, a drawing that shows the contour of an object, which is usually projected with three views.

overexposure   In platemaking, overexposure results when the light source is too close to the vacuum frame that holds the negative and plate. Underexposure results when the light source is too distant from the vacuum frame.

overhang cover   Cover larger than the page size of a book. It is the opposite of a flush cover.

overhead projection   System of projecting images over the shoulder of a lecturer, who sits and faces the audience while controlling the projector, which projects the image on a tilted screen. This technique is a flexible method of visual communication and has many advantages over the system in which the lecturer addresses the audience while the projector is operated by a second person. Transparencies, also called "projecturals," visuals, slides, or vu-graphs, are projected from the front of the room with the aid of the projector. By facing the audience at all times, the lecturer not only is in a position to set the pace of the discussion but can observe audience reaction, alter the sequence of projecturals, and operate the projector without interrupting his or her talk to give an operator instructions.

Figure O-18 illustrates a typical overhead-projection setup, including the communicator and the tilted screen. The projection stage of the projector (flat surface on which the projectural is placed) permits the communicator to use the screen as a blackboard. Without turning away from the audience, the lecturer can write or draw at will with a grease pencil on projecturals or sheets of transparent plastic. A pointer or a pencil may also be used to emphasize important details that are reflected on the screen.

Several sheets of transparent film may be superimposed on the stage and various colors used to identify the elements of the projected image. The communicator can unmask transparent projecturals during progressive disclosure of information, or several components can be built into a composite image. For instance, it is possible to project the framework of a house in black and, after discussion, to add the electrical system in blue, the plumbing in red, and so forth. Projection is accomplished under normal room lighting conditions.

Standard image-projection sizes are 10 by 10, 8 by 10, 7½ by 10, 7 by 7, and 5 by 5 inches (25.4 by 25.4, 20.3 by 25.4, 19 by 25.4, 17.8 by 17.8, and 12.7 by 12.7 cm). The larger sizes simplify preparation of artwork and eliminate

Fig. O-18 Typical small conference room for viewing overhead projection. (*Scott Graphics, Inc.*)

the need for reduction in most cases. The size of the projection screen is determined by the maximum viewing distance. The width should be not less than one-sixth of the distance from the screen to the last row of viewers. The projector should be adjusted to fill the screen with the projected image. The projector-to-screen location is determined by the size of the screen image desired. The image grows larger as the projector is moved farther from the screen. For example, at a distance of 6 feet (1.83 m) from the screen, a 7½ by 10-inch (19 by 25.4-cm) projector produces a 34.4 by 46-inch (86.3 by 117 cm) image; at 8 feet (2.44 m), the projected image is 46.4 by 62 inches (117 by 157.4 cm). Another rule to follow for screen projector and audience relationship for proper viewing is known as the "2 by 6 rule." The distance from the screen to the first row of seats should be twice the width of the screen, and the distance from the screen to the last row of seats should be 6 times the width of the screen. This rule holds true of any screen size. For example, if an overhead projection screen is 8 feet (2.44 m) wide, the first row of seats should be 16 feet (4.87 m) from the screen and the last row of seats should be 48 feet (14.6 m) from the screen. It is therefore possible to lay out the seating arrangement and determine how many people can be seated for adequate viewing.

Figure O-19 shows the Proto-Printer (left) and the "pickle jar" developer (right). The Proto-Printer, designed especially for printing transparencies, is a compact, portable, diazo printer that produces prints in registration. The light source is a No. 4 photo-flood lamp, controlled by an exposure timer and cooled by a centrifugal blower. The light source is readily replaceable. The contact printing assembly consists of a pin board which holds the master and film in registration, a compression tray and pad, and two tempered printing glasses, one of which is a spare. The jar is composed of a widemouthed glass jar equipped with an evaporator sponge and a neoprene screen. It is fitted with a hinged, spring-mounted lid for fume-free insertion and removal of materials. The sponge is charged with ammonia by inserting the spout of a polyethylene feed-bottle in an opening in the lid. Aqua-ammonia is poured from the bottle through a stainless steel tube built into the jar, to the sponge in the bottom. The jar is 16 inches (40.6 cm) high. The image must first be exposed for several minutes in a printer (Proto-Printer) in contact with the diazo-treated material. The copy material containing the latent image is then rolled and inserted in the jar.

Fig. O-19 Pro-Printer and "pickle jar" developer. (*Scott Graphics, Inc.*)

The latent image can be seen coming to life through the sides of the jar. The completed print is removed in a dry condition.

overhead transparency Chartpak offers a line of materials and accessories for making overhead transparencies, consisting of color and matte acetate tapes, transfer lettering, color film, and accessories such as mounting frames, frisket knives and blades, tracing papers, layout guides, and the like. *See* Figure O-20. Figure O-21 shows a shading film being added to a major part of a 35-millimeter camera that is the subject. First, a sheet of shading film is placed over the transparency and a section of the film is scored slightly larger than the area to be covered. Then cut through the film but not through the backing sheet. To position the film, hold one edge of the film above the transparency, and gently place the other edge on the overhead. Smooth gently with fingers, dropping the remaining film with care. When applying film, do not rub with fingers, but gently place the film on the transparency and let the adhesive seek its own level. This procedure will reduce the number of air bubbles. Trim off any excess film with a frisket knife. If the film is not positioned correctly, lift it off the transparency and reapply. Chartpak pressure-sensitive materials can be removed and repositioned without leaving any marks or residue on the transparency.

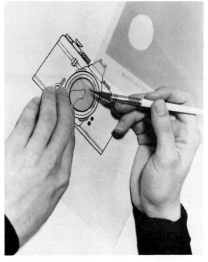

Fig. O-21 Chartpak shading film being applied to artwork.

The next step is to apply pressure-sensitive tapes. (*See* Figure O-22.) These tapes have four basic functions: (1) title positioning lines, (2) label identification lines, (3) definition lines which serve to outline an entire figure or diagram, and (4) information lines, such as a line on a graph. To apply, place the end of the tape at the desired starting point on the transparency and unroll it until it is approximately one inch beyond the cutoff point. To cut the tape, place the knife at the desired cutting point. Holding the tape with thumb and forefinger, pull the tape up against the edge of the knife with a diagonal movement while applying slight downward pressure with the knife. As with color and shading films, the tape is lifted and repositioned in making revisions and corrections.

The final step in the completion of the transparency is to rub on transfer lettering and symbols. (*See* Figure O-23.) Position letters directly on the transparency by lining up the bottoms of the letters with lines of the grid

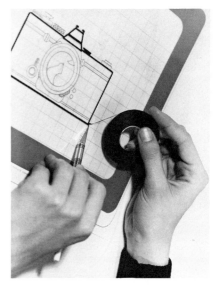

Fig. O-22 Chartpak tape being applied to artwork.

master. The letter is transferred to the film by rubbing it lightly with a burnishing tool, ball-point pen, or other hard object. Be sure that all edges are burnished, and then pull away the letter sheet and a letter appears on the transparency. After lettering is applied, the transparency is completed. (*See* Figure O-24.)

overlay *See* ACETATE OVERLAY; CORRECTION OVERLAY; TISSUE OVERLAY.

overleaf The leaf of a right-hand page referred to as being on the opposite side of the sheet.

overprinting Printing of an image over another impression. Overprinting is used particularly in color work. If a tint or a pattern is desired, a secondary color is printed over a primary color.

overrun Printed or duplicated copies of sheets or pages in excess of the specified number.

oversize Designating copy produced in a size larger than the size it will be after it has been reduced for reproduction. The copy may consist of text or line and halftone illustrations. A good deal of copy for reproduction is produced oversize. Technical illustrations, for example, are seldom drawn less than 1½ times the final reduced size, and many are drawn twice up.

The reasons for drawing oversize copy are simple. Critical areas and lines may thus be drawn easily and rapidly with good delineation, and reduction eliminates such small imperfections as fuzziness, smudges, and erasure ghosts. In addition, open spaces are closed up for better appearance.

When nomenclature applied to art is too large, it dominates the object depicted, whereas the object itself should be the dominant factor. If nomenclature is smaller than 6 point (2.11 mm), the illustration loses its ability to convey a message. The accompanying table shows the size to which nomenclature will be reduced when the reduced image width is held to 7 inches (17.8 cm). *See also* LETTERING OR TYPE REDUCTION.

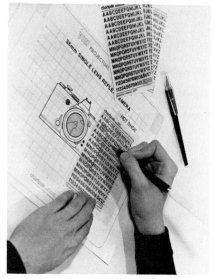

Fig. O-23 Chartpak lettering and symbols being applied to artwork.

Fig. O-24 Completed overhead transparency mounted in frame.

Width of oversize art	Oversize nomenclature, pt.	Reduced nomenclature, pt.
10½ in (26.7 cm)	12	8.0
14 in (35.6 cm)	14	7.0
17½ in (44.4 cm)	24	9.5

packing Paper sheets placed under a printing plate or the rubber blanket of an offset press to raise contact surfaces and so improve their printing qualities.

padding Binding printed or blank sheets in units for scratch pads. Base stock is used to separate the units. The pads are secured as a batch, and cement is applied to one side. The units are then separated to form individual tablets.

page One side of a sheet of paper. It should not be called a page until it contains copy or is identified in some manner to show its sequential arrangement.

page-content heading Heading that appears at the top of a page to identify its contents. The headings in dictionaries and encyclopedias that give the first and last entries on a page are examples of page-content headings. In some publications, such as those issued by United States government services, headings showing the section number and paragraph numbers contained on each page are required. The page-content heading is flush right for right-hand pages and flush left for left-hand pages.

page frame Page prepared for insertion of a photograph or line illustration that will subsequently be morticed, pasted in place, or otherwise inserted on the page. The page frame includes information such as the figure number and title of the insert, page number, running head or foot, or other information that is marginal to the insert. Also known as a "skeleton page."

page layout *See* LAYOUT.

page makeup *See* MAKEUP.

page numbering For most publications pages are numbered with lowercase roman and arabic numerals. Roman numerals are used for pages preceding the first chapter, part, or section of the text. These pages are termed "front matter." The first page of the first chapter, part, or section is then numbered with the arabic numeral 1, and subsequent pages are numbered in sequence. Right-hand pages should always be odd-numbered and left-hand pages even-numbered.

Numbers may appear in the lower right corner of each page for right-hand pages and in the lower left corner for left-hand pages, centered at the bottom of each page, or in the upper right or left corners. Pages are sometimes numbered within each chapter, part, or section. In such a case, the first page of section I is numbered 1-1, the second page 1-2, etc. The fourth page of section III is numbered 3-4. (The roman numeral for the section number is converted to an arabic numeral.) This method of pagination is useful when a contract proposal or other document is being prepared by several departments in an organization. Each department assigns its own page numbers to its sections without waiting until all the material has been collated. Individual sections of the publication can thus be printed before the complete work. If back matter, such as appendixes and indexes, is required, pages are numbered consecutively beginning in most instances with the numeral 1. Exhibits should be identified with capital letters in sequence, such as A-1 or C-5.

page plate Paper or metal printing plate used to print a single page. The term is generally used with reference to offset duplicators. With large offset printing presses that can accommodate 4, 16, 32, 64, or more pages, the plate is referred to as a "flat." *See also* FLAT.

page proof Proof taken from each page and proofread as a final check. The galley corrections have been made, and illustrations and footnotes have been arranged in their proper places.

paginate To number pages.

pamphlet Publication consisting of several sheets of unbound printed matter, either stitched or stapled, or folded only, and having a soft cover or self-cover. It is smaller than a booklet. The term also denotes a treatise published in this format, usually on a controversial topic of interest. *See also* BOOKLET.

Pan Litho film Du Pont lithographic film on a Cronar polyester film base, used for filtered highlight masks. It can also be used in three- and four-color separation systems in which halftone separation negatives are made directly in the camera or enlarger.

Pan Masking film Du Pont film on a Cronar polyester film base, used as a negative masking material in the contrast adjustment and color correction of color copy. A 0.007-inch (0.178-mm) version of this film, without anti-halation backing, was developed for camera-back masking techniques and for preparing unsharp premasks for transparencies. For multiple overlays and additional image sharpness, the 0.004-inch (0.102-mm) version of the film is recommended.

panchromatic Designating photographic materials that are sensitive to light of all colors. Their color-sensitivity range approximates that of the human eye.

panel drawing In engineering drafting and technical illustrating, a drawing that depicts operating controls and indicators for an item such as a hydraulic or electrical panel. It is used for operating instructions. Relationships and locations appear on the drawing as they do on the item. It is essential that nomenclature appears on the drawing exactly as it does on the equipment and in the same relative location.

panel title page *See* HALF TITLE.

pantograph Instrument for enlarging or reducing maps or drawings. It features a hinged parallelogram with a pole, a tracer point, and a pencil point set in the line of the parallelogram's diagonal. If the pole is at one corner and the tracer point at the opposite corner, the pencil will produce a reduction. If the tracer point and pencil are reversed, an enlargement is made.

Pantone matching system (trademark of Panton, Inc.) Coordinated system for matching printing inks and coordinating color reproduction and color reproduction materials.

paper, origin of Three thousand years before Christ, the Egyptians used a material called papyrus to write on. The papyrus plant was the most important source of writing material before the invention of paper. The Chinese, in about 150 B.C., are credited with making the first pulp from which paper was manufactured. Bamboo shoots were soaked in lime and water, and the fibers were first separated and then pressed together by striking them with stones against a flat surface. The material was dried in the sun. The secret of papermaking reached medieval Europe through the Arabs, who made paper in Spain in the eleventh century. It spread to Italy, France, and Germany between 1190 and 1390, then through the Netherlands to England sometime before 1495.

The first paper mill in America was built on the Delaware River in Germantown, Pennsylvania, in 1690; it was operated by William Rittenhouse. The first paper machine was invented in 1799 by Nicolas Robert, a Frenchman. This machine was later perfected by John Gamble and Bryan Donkin. Henry and Sealy Fourdrinier of London purchased the patent rights and built their first machine in 1803 in Bermondsey, England. The Fourdrinier machine has since become synonymous with paper manufacturing.

paper, reproduction *See* REPRODUCTION MASTER.

paper-base film Sensitized photographic film having paper as a base. It is used in making plates for photo-offset printing.

paper-cutting charts *See* TABLES 3, 4, and 5 (*pages 442–443*).

paper finishes For discussions of particular paper finishes, *see* ANTIQUE FINISH; ANTIQUE WOVE PAPER; CALENDERED FINISH; COATED FINISH; COCKLE FINISH; CRASH FINISH; DOUBLE-COATED PAPER; DRY FINISH; DULL COATED PAPER; DULL FINISH; EGGSHELL FINISH; ENGLISH FINISH; FELT FINISH; FRICTION-GLAZED FINISH; HIGH FINISH; KID FINISH; LAID ANTIQUE PAPER; LAWN FINISH; LOW FINISH; MACHINE FINISH; MACHINE-GLAZED PAPER; MARBLE FINISH; MARKING FELT; MATTE FINISH; MEDIEVAL LAID FINISH; METALLIC FINISH; MICA FINISH; MOTHER-OF-PEARL FINISH; MOTTLED FINISH; OILED PAPER; PARCHMENT FINISH; PLATER FINISH; PYROXYLIN-COATED PAPER; REP FINISH; RIPPLE FINISH; SATIN FINISH; SINGLE-COATED PAPER; SUPERCALENDERED FINISH; SUPERFINE; TEXT FINISH; UNGLAZED FINISH; VELLUM FINISH; WATER FINISH; WOVE FINISH; ZINC FINISH.

paper manufacturing Paper may be manufactured from wood, rags, straw, rope, jute butts, esparto grass, or other materials. Such woods as hemlock, poplar, birch, gum, spruce, and fir are commonly used for paper pulp. Wood may be transformed to pulp by mechanical or chemical means. Mechanical pulp is manufactured by grinding the wood into a fibrous condition. Newsprint, some wrapping papers, and paper bags are made from mechanical pulp. Sulfite, soda, and kraft processes are chemical methods of making pulp from wood. The wood is reduced to fine chips, which are conveyed to a huge digester. There they are pressure-cooked with chemicals until the material has been reduced to a fibrous mass called cellulose, the chemicals having removed such unwanted elements as resin, sap, and lignin. The cooking mixture is drained from the cellulose by continued washing and separation. The pulp is then bleached, washed, drained, and sent to a beating machine. Here begins the actual process of papermaking, in which such additives as clay, rags, various stocks, coloring, and sizing are put in the pulp to give it its special quality and character. At this stage the pulp has the appearance and consistency of milk.

In the sulfite process, the chips are cooked under pressure in a solution of calcium bisulfite. This method produces high-quality fibers for fine book papers. When wood such as gum, birch, or poplar is cooked under pressure with a caustic soda solution, the fibers are soft and short and form a more compact surface than sulfite fibers. Soda fibers are desirable for book papers. The sulfate and kraft processes are used, for the most part, in making wrapping papers and papers for bags.

When the pulp has been reduced to a fine milklike substance, it is piped to the Fourdrinier papermaking machine. The pulp is conveyed along a traveling belt of fine cloth meshed with wire on the underside. The weight of stock to be produced determines the speed of the belt: a speed of 1 inch (2.54 cm) per second ultimately produces heavier stock than a speed of 10 feet (3.05 m) or more per second. The belt vibrates as it moves to set the fibers. At the same time, the liquid content of the pulp either passes through the bottom of the mesh or is sucked off.

After the paper has been dried by heated iron rollers, it is passed through additional rollers, or calenders, where it is finished to the desired quality. Rag pulp is treated in much the same manner as wood pulp. Although the processes of cleaning, sorting, thrashing, bleaching, and digesting differ, the end result is the same when the pulp is ready for the beating process. Rag pulp may be added in various quantities to wood pulp during beating, or paper called "100 percent rag" may be manufactured from rag alone. Rag content, of course, lends a highly desirable quality to paper.

paper master *See* PAPER PLATE.

paper negative Inexpensive negative used for producing printing plates when quality is not of prime importance.

paper plate (paper master) Printing plate used in the direct plate method of reproduction. Typewritten copy, hand-drawn characters, drawings, or any other image may be applied directly to the plate. As no photography is involved, all reproductions are of the same size as the original. If art requires reduction or enlargement, the image may be applied to a paper plate indirectly by means of xerographic equipment or other photographic and exposure units. *See also* COPYING MACHINES; DIRECT PLATE MAKING.

paper qualities It is impossible to become an expert on paper without devoting many hours of study to its manufacture and to its use in printing, duplicating, and copying. Whenever an image is created with ink, crayon, camera, airbrush, or pencil, it is paper or a paper-base material that usually receives the image, either poorly or to good advantage. Paper is designed for a particular application, and it can be judged only by how well it fulfills the purpose for which it was manufactured.

Paper should first be judged by the degree of uniformity on both sides of the sheet. Uniformity in a paper surface can be appraised by close inspection under a good light. When paper fibers are compact and uniform, the type impression has less chance of falling on a nonprinting area. Paper may be judged as to whiteness, if this quality is desired, by comparing several samples against a dark background.

There are several tests to determine grain in paper. The most common is to fold the paper in both directions. A fold with the grain is smoother than a fold against the grain. If the paper is fingered delicately, less resistance to coarse friction is experienced when the paper is creased with the grain. Grain may also be determined by tearing a sample of paper slowly in both directions into strips no more than 1 inch (2.54 cm) wide. In tearing with the grain, the paper has a tendency to tear from edge to edge, whereas in tearing against the grain greater resistance is encountered and a complete tear from edge to edge is seldom achieved.

Durability and tearing resistance are significant primarily in binding and handling. If, for example, paper is to be used in a loose-leaf or other binder and must therefore be perforated or serrated, ability to withstand handling and avoid tearing is most important.

Good folding qualities are considered of prime importance by paper manufacturers and merchants. To test folding characteristics, one can compare a paper of known folding ability with a sample. One can fold and refold the two papers the same number of times, applying equal pressure to both creases across each fold. When the folds have broken the resistance of the paper, each sample should be torn slowly and the difference in resistance noted. This test cannot be applied to 100 percent rag-content paper, which can be folded 500 to 1,000 times before showing any evidence of breakdown.

Good erasure qualities are desirable in certain papers. Paper with rag content and gelatin sizing is better than sulfite-treated paper. To test for erasure qualities, the surface of the paper should be scraped. If the residue is fine and powdery, the paper has good erasing qualities; if it is coarse and fibrous, wood sulfite and starch sizing are evident and erasing qualities are inferior. When good erasure characteristics are desired, papers with gelatin surface sizing are preferable to those with starch surface sizing.

The undesirable surface characteristic called "picking" may be eliminated or minimized by sizing. To test for picking, one can moisten a finger and press it firmly against the paper. When the finger is pulled away quickly, it can be examined for flecks of paper. *See also* PICKING.

Another important consideration in determining suitable paper for printing is "show-through" when the copy is printed on both sides of the sheet. If show-through is present, either another grade of paper should be considered or a heavier stock of the same grade selected. *See also* SHOW-THROUGH.

The weight of paper is an important factor in book and magazine publishing since postal rates are based on weight. While coated-two-sides book paper will reproduce fine-screen halftones and have remarkable printing qualities, volume mailing costs are considerably higher than if uncoated stock is used. Obviously, additives in paper make it much heavier.

paperboard Stock used primarily for boxes that require folding such as boxboard, paper signs, and the like. Major categories are boxboard, fiberboard, and corrugated (kraft) container board. Boxboards fall into several classes: patent-coated, clay-coated, manila, and bleached manila. Board stock must resist handling, and inks used on it are long, soft, and have little tack. All major printing methods are used in printing boxboard. To avoid crushing of corrugated boxboard during printing, they are printed from rubber plates by either letterpress or flexography. Finish and density in different paperboards are relative to changes in weight. The National Paperboard Association has adopted four standard finishes: No. 1, low density and generally having a rough surface; No. 2, greater density and smoother finish than No. 1 and satisfactory for ordinary printing; No. 3, greater density and smoother surface than No. 2 and intended for high-quality printing; and No. 4, very dense board with extreme smoothness.

papier-mâché Mixture of paper pulp, clay, chalk, sand, and materials such as glue, resin, and lead acetate. It is molded into shape while moist and then dried until it is firm. Molten metal is poured into a papier-mâché mold for making stereotype printing plates.

papyrus Most important writing material used before the discovery of paper by the Chinese in about 150 B.C. It was made from thin strips of pith from the papyrus plant, which were pressed while wet, covered with a paste, dried, cut to size, and polished with a smooth stone or shell. Papyrus was used by the Egyptians to make writing material 3,000 years before Christ.

parallel fold *See* FIRST PARALLEL FOLD; SECOND PARALLEL FOLD.

parallel lines *See* LINE CONVENTIONS: ENGINEERING DRAWINGS.

parchment finish Finish that makes paper resemble parchment.

partial view *See* ORTHOGRAPHIC PROJECTION: ENGINEERING DRAWINGS.

pasted blanks Stock pasted together to form a thicker ply. Only 12, 14, and 16-ply (1.067, 1.220, and 1.422-mm) blanks are pasted. *See also* PLY.

pastel Coloring matter mixed with gum to form crayons. The word "pastel" also denotes both such a crayon and a picture produced with the crayon. Pastels are used widely by commercial artists for comprehensives, expecially in the range of grays that correspond to the range of tones desired. Pastel colors are those having soft or pale hues.

paster In a web-fed press, a device that applies a fine line of paste to one or both sides of the paper roll to produce finished booklets.

paste-up Process of pasting an image or part of an image on a repro-duction page or sheet that is to be photographed for plate making and printing. It includes pasting blocks of text, art, preprints, or any other image in position. Before copy is pasted, the paste-up areas should be outlined with a fade-out–blue pencil. Rubber cement is an excellent adhesive for paste-up work. Some types of rubber cement need be used on only one pasting surface, but if a worker is not sure of the cement, it should be applied to both surfaces. All excess cement must be removed. If particles of cement are permitted to adhere to the paper, dust and dirt are attracted and the reflection will show on the negative. A small "pickup" should be used to remove the surplus cement. If the copy is to be stored, it should be covered with a tissue overlay.

patch Piece of metal with a correction that is affixed to a printing plate, usually by soldering.

patent base Metal base used for the lockup of irregularly shaped types and designs. It has proved quite successful in the accurate registration of long printing runs.

patent drawing Precise, carefully executed drawing that depicts all the operational and functional characteristics of an invention, discovery, or design. It should show as many views as patent reviewers may require to understand the invention. Shading mediums, cross-hatching of sectional views, line drawing to portray shapes, and index numbers keyed to explanatory text may all be used. Drawings must be executed in india ink. It is suggested that a patent drafter or attorney be consulted before making patent drawings if their preparation and handling are not thoroughly understood.

pearl Old type size. The nearest equivalent in the point system is 5 point (1.76 mm).

pebble board Board stock having a very coarse surface. When it is drawn upon with charcoal or stick pastels, dots are produced, the size of the dots depending on the pressure applied. The work gives a continuous-tone effect but is reproduced as line work.

pencil art Drawing made with an ordinary graphite or other pencil. It may include lines or renderings (shaded areas) as desired. When pencil drawings or renderings with hard, definite lines are reproduced by the photolithographic process, it is difficult to determine whether pencil or ink has been used. Modern cameras provide quality reproduction of good pencil art.

pencil artist Technical illustrator who draws in pencil work to be completed in ink by others. Such illustrators are employed in large art departments where volume production is the rule. They are accomplished in art layout and drawing and must be able to convert parts and objects depicted on orthographic engineering drawings into perspective or isometric illustrations. Their work is completed in ink by finishers, or inkers.

The system of employing pencil artists and finishers has both advantages and disadvantages. Good technical illustrators are at a premium, and their knowledge should be employed where the need is most critical. Large art groups are placed at a disadvantage because of volume output and are therefore forced to distinguish between illustrators and finishers. While the distinction discourages initiative, it is followed of necessity. A disadvantage is that the pencil artist, knowing that his or her responsibility ends when the pencil art is completed, may get out of touch with inking and finishing problems and may not remain so close to the art as if he or she were to complete the job. The finisher, too, works under a handicap in attempting to interpret what the pencil artist has done. Moreover, the pencil artist may not be given an opportunity to do creative work or to work with engineering drawings and thus advance to higher illustration techniques.

pens, Speedball lettering *See* PENS, STEEL-BRUSH; SPEEDBALL PENS.

pens, steel-brush Flexible pens manufactured by the Hunt Manufacturing Company. They are designed especially for large poster lettering. The pens may also be used as auxiliary brushes for watercolor and oil painting, particularly to fill in large areas of black-ink and color work. The pens work with any india ink or color diluted to a usable consistency. Lettering instruction charts are available on request.

pens, technical Pens suitable for technical illustrating. Some of the requirements of good technical pens used with regular drawing and writing inks are (1) freedom from clogging, (2) consistency in line weights, (3) ease of filling and cleaning, (4) cleanliness during use, (5) interchangeability of writing points, and (6) adhesion to the material drawn upon.

Figure P-1 is the Koh-I-Noor Rapidograph technical fountain pen Model 3060. The pen, used with regular drawing and writing inks, is used especially for drawing, drafting lettering, technical illustrating, and for various commercial and fine art techniques. It is also used for inking in pencil tracings, freehand and guide lettering, and template work. It is available in 18 Kolor-Koded pen weight widths (Figure P-2) for quick identification. Stainless steel points are used in drafting on paper and

cloth. A jewel point was developed for drafting on coated polyester drafting films, and an abrasion-resistant tungsten carbide point was developed for use on automated drafting machines. Figure P-3 shows the Rapidograph Model 300 lettering scriber, and Figure P-4 is the scriber engaged with a scriber lettering template. The drawing point section is threaded into the scriber's bushing such that the point-to-point paper contact is balanced with the movement of the scriber. Templates contain 12 sizes of uppercase and lowercase Gothic type (from 0.060 to 0.500-inch [1.52 to 12.7-mm] high) numbers and punctuation marks. Guides are available in sets. Another Koh-I-Noor Rapidometric template has a cut-through, double-row design feature. The cut-through principle permits the pen point to extend through the template, permitting removal of the template without danger of smudging. Figure P-5 is the Rapidograph 3065 HRS12 humidified revolving selector set. A humidified interior prevents ink from drying in points when drawing sections are stored uncapped and point down in sleeves during work intervals.

Figure P-6 is the Pelikan Graphos (Koh-I-Noor) drawing ink fountain pen, primarily used in technical drawing applications and freehand drawing and lettering work. The flow of drawing ink may be varied by changing the feed. Figure P-7 shows the Graphos pen and nib assortment. Figure P-8 illustrates seven types of nibs used with the pen, the range of widths supplied (in millimeters), and the style of work that can be accomplished with each type of pen. Figure P-9 is an example of design work produced by using the Type O style nib. The range of art work that can be accomplished for each type of nib is as follows:

A   Fine nibs for ruling and for freehand and technical drawings

T   Broad nibs for ruling, poster work, and technical drawings

S   Nibs for fine freehand drawing, sketching, cartography, touching up, and Spencerian script

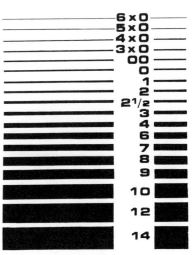

Fig. P-2   Koh-I-Noor Rapidograph pen line weights (actual size.)

Fig. P-3   Koh-I-Noor Rapidograph lettering scriber with drawing point section.

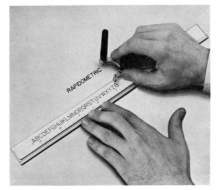

Fig. P-4   Koh-I-Noor Rapidograph scriber engaged with a lettering template.

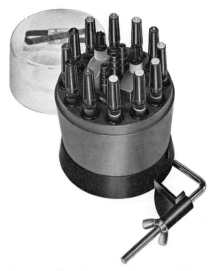

Fig. P-5 Koh-I-Noor Rapidograph 3065 HRS12 humidified revolving selector set.

Fig. P-6 Pelikan Graphos (*Koh-I-Noor*) drawing ink fountain pen.

Fig. P-7 Pelikan Graphos pen and nib assortment.

R   Tubular nibs for stencilling with lettering guides and for drawing contour lines

O   Round nibs (14) for freehand lettering and sketching. (*see* Figure P-8)

N   Right-hand slant nibs for oblique lines

Z   Left-hand slant nibs for oblique lines

Figure P-10 shows the configuration of the Leroy reservoir technical pen, holders, technical pencil, ink cartridge, and the Leroy waterproof black lettering ink pen. Figure P-11 shows the range of line weights from 0000 to 14. Figure P-12 shows the Leroy scriber with a mounted reservoir pen and lettering template. Figure P-13 shows a reservoir pen set that contains seven pens (line-weight sizes 00, 0, 1, 2, 3, 4, and 5) with holder, ink filler bottle, and bottle of pen cleaner; the set is packed in a revolving caddy that will hold up to a dozen pens and three holders. The base of the caddy holds a sponge for humidifying, so that when uncapped pens are stored with point down, the pens will not dry out and are ready for immediate use.

Reservoir pens are threaded to accept the pen holder for use as a freehand drawing and ruling pen. Pen sizes 0000 to 5 have a thicker tip and a "step" in the diameter, which permits a free ink flow. To use the lettering pen, proceed as follows: (1) a template is chosen in the size and style desired (there are many sizes and styles of alphabets, numerals, and symbols, including Greek letters) and then placed along a straightedge; (2) the tailpin of the scriber is set in the straight guide groove of the template; (3) the recessed letters on the template are traced with the tracer pin on the scriber, and the pen reproduces the character in full view above the template. One model of the scriber permits the height and slant of characters to be varied. Other templates produce line weights up to ¼-inch (6.35 mm) wide with characters 2 inches (5.08 cm) high. A letter-size

ITEM NUMBER	NIB	TYPE	WIDTHS SUPPLIED (in mm)	KIND
9010-A	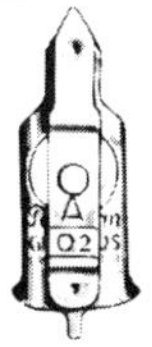	A	0,1 0,13 0,18 0,2 0,25 0,3 0,35 0,4 0,5 0,6 0,7	RULING NIBS *FOR* FINE LINES
9010-T	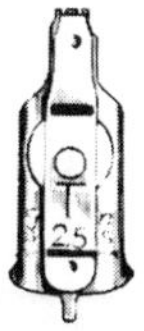	T	0,8 1,0 1,25 1,6 2,5 4,0 6,4 10,0	**RULING NIBS** for broad lines and for **poster work**
9010-S	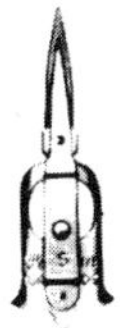	S	B = SOFT HB = MEDIUM HARD H = HARD K = EXTRA HARD	*Drawing Nibs* *for fine freehand drawing sketching, cartography and touch-up work*
9010-R		R	0,3 0,4 0,5 0,6 0,7 0,8 1,0 1,25 1,5 1,75 2,0 2,5 3,0	**TUBULAR NIBS** **FOR STENCILLING WITH LETTERING GUIDES AND FOR CONTOUR LINES**
9010-O		O	0,2 0,3 0,4 0,5 0,6 0,7 0,8 1,0 1,25 1,6 2,0 2,5 3,2 5,0	*ROUND NIBS for freehand lettering and sketching*
9010-N		N	0,8 1,25 2,0 2,5 3,2 4,0	*Right hand slant nibs for oblique lines*
9010-Z	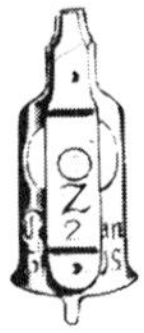	Z	0,8 1,25 2,0 3,2	*Left hand slant nibs for oblique lines*

Fig. P-8 Pelikan Graphos nib types, widths (in millimeters), and drawing styles.

Fig. P-9   Example of line widths made with Graphos type O nib.

Fig. P-10   Leroy reservoir technical pen, holders, pencil, and ink cartridge. (*Keuffel & Esser Company.*)

Fig. P-11   Leroy pen and line-weight sizes (actual size). (*Keuffel & Esser Company.*)

0000	000	00	0	1	2	3	4	5	6	7	8	9	10	12	14
.008	.010	.013	.017	.021	.026	.035	.043	.055	.067	.083	.098	.125	.150	.200	.250

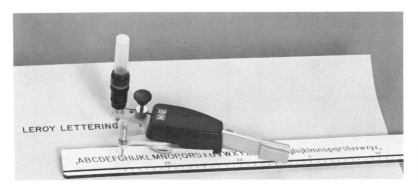

Fig. P-12 Leroy scriber with reservoir pen and lettering template. (*Keuffel & Esser Company.*)

Fig. P-13 Leroy pen set with revolving caddy. (*Keuffel & Esser Company.*)

Fig. P-14 Three views of the Mars-700 technical pen. (*J. S. Staedtler, Inc.*)

adapter, used with certain scribers, extends and condenses letters by increasing or decreasing heights by as much as one-third. The Leroy reservoir pens are color-coded and numbered for identification of point size to prevent mismatching them while cleaning.

Figure P-14 shows three views of the Mars-700 technical pen. The pen consists of a point section, holder, and cap with clip. The point, holder, and

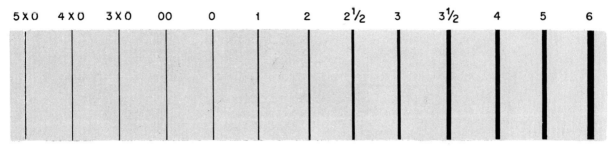

| 5X0 | 4X0 | 3X0 | 00 | 0 | 1 | 2 | 2½ | 3 | 3½ | 4 | 5 | 6 |

Fig. P-15 Line widths of the Mars-700 technical pen. (J. S. Staedtler, Inc.)

cap are color-coded so that line widths (Figure P-15) are readily identified when the pen is either open or closed. A radiused tube tip provides a constant contact between point and drawing surface even when the pen is not held vertically, and line widths can be maintained at a drawing angle of 80°. The point tube is shouldered at the tip to prevent smudging when straight edges, templates, or letter guides are used. The tube is press-fitted into a molded chromium-plated metal cylinder. This reinforcement eliminates any danger of bending or flexing caused by hand pressure. A one-valve capillary action allows an even airflow through the air vent and breather hole into the ink cartridge. A drop of water into the hygro-cell will maintain humidity around the point, thus ensuring instant starting. Figure P-16 shows the Mars scriber used with a lettering template. An additional lettering joint that screws into the barrel provides a grip and angle of adjustment for comfortable handling and lettering. By using a compass attachment, the front section of the Mars pen affords an adjustable pivot bearing that permits the pen to be angled in any plane for drawing small circles.

Fig. P-16 The Mars scriber with point section. (J. S. Staedtler, Inc.)

Fig. P-17 Davidson offset perfecting press with roll converter.

perfecting press (perfector press) Printing press of any kind that prints simultaneously on both sides of a sheet in one operation for each unit. The Davidson offset perfecting press, with roll converter installed but having a sheet capability as well (Figure P-17), is designed for printing invoices, brochures, direct-mail pieces, and other light-to-medium forms. Paper sizes that can be used are from 4 by 6 inches to 15 by 18 inches (10.1 by 15.2 cm to 38.1 by 45.7 cm). The maximum printing area is 13 by 17 inches (33 by 43.1 cm). Feeder capacity for sheets is 6,000 of 20-pound (9.08-kg) stock. Speeds are variable from 4,000 to 8,000 sheets per hour. One individual can install a 600-pound roll of 38,000 sheets in several minutes with the roll converter. Using the roll converter permits running the press 6 times longer without reloading.

perforate To cut minute holes in stock in order to facilitate separation of individual units, as in sheets of postage stamps. Perforation may be performed on machines designed for the purpose. It may also be accomplished during or after the printing run by inserting cutting dies. Perforation differs from scoring in that it is used to separate units, whereas scoring breaks the molecular structure of the stock to permit easy folding.

perforating, schoolbook Perforation of sheets during the printing cycle, made parallel to the binding edge of jaw-folded signatures. This type of perforation is used extensively in school examination books from which students tear answer sheets, leaving the question portions of pages bound in the books. A similar perforation is used for checkbooks, from which checks are detached, leaving the stubs bound.

perforator *See* TAPE PERFORATOR.

perspective drawing View of an object as it appears to the naked eye. A perspective drawing shows a solid object on a flat surface so that the position, distance, and magnitude of the object appear as seen with the eye. A camera photographs pictures in perspective. *See* Figure P-18.

PERT chart Flow-chart network that shows the relationship between events and activities in a program. PERT (program-evaluation and review technique), which was first developed by a project team in the Navy Special Projects Office, was used successfully in the Polaris weapons system and became popular in military and industrial applications. The PERT display of information may be adapted to many phases of programming projects. The basic concept is to control the completion time of a project by showing the events that must take place, the activities required to accomplish them, and the relationship and interdependency of the events. During the course of a program, the chart will reveal remedies that must be adopted to control the program with respect to time. Figure P-19 illustrates a simple PERT chart without identifying events.

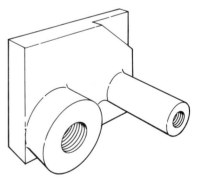

Fig. P-18 Simple line drawing in perspective.

pH Symbol used to express hydrogen-ion concentration and thus acidity and alkalinity. The relative acidity or alkalinity of the solution used in offset press work has a tendency to change, primarily because of exposure

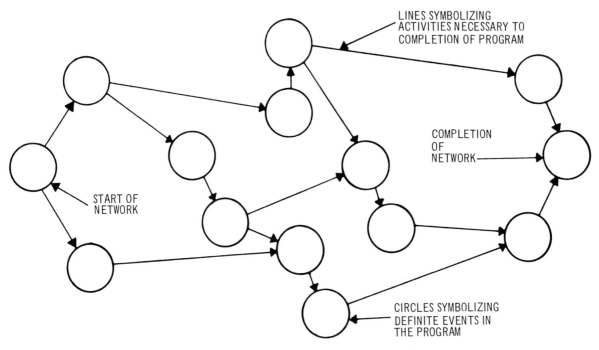

LINES SYMBOLIZING
ACTIVITIES NECESSARY TO
COMPLETION OF PROGRAM

COMPLETION
OF
NETWORK

START OF
NETWORK

CIRCLES SYMBOLIZING
DEFINITE EVENTS IN
THE PROGRAM

Fig. P-19 Simple PERT chart without identifying events.

to the atmosphere. Small kits with litmus paper and a color chart are provided to test this condition. The paper is dipped in the solution fountain, and the color it assumes is compared with the colors on the chart. Corrective action is taken if the solution is unbalanced.

phantom lines (alternate-position lines) Lines used in orthographic projection on engineering and mechanical drawings, consisting of one long and two short dashes, evenly spaced, with a long line at the end. Designated as "thin" lines, they indicate the alternate position of parts of the object delineated, repeated detail, or the relative position of an absent part. *See also* LINE CONVENTIONS: ENGINEERING DRAWINGS.

photoarc process Conventional method of preparing a printing plate by photographing the original with a process camera and then using an arc light to "burn" the image from the negative onto the plate. *See* ARC LAMP.

photocomposition System of producing copy by photographic means. A camera photographs each letter of a desired font as the operator operates a keyboard in much the same manner as an automatic typesetting machine. Justified copy is produced on film or paper. Different sizes of a font are produced by enlargement or reduction. *See also* TYPESETTERS, PHOTOGRAPHIC.

photocontact paper negative Contact negative made from an opaque or a translucent material. The scale maintained is good, and the material is permanent. Such a negative has a reverse reading from which positive prints may be made by the reflection process. Any part of the image not wanted in the positive print can be opaqued.

photodrafting Drafting by revision or tracing onto a print, such as a "printout" or a "blowback," of an engineering or design drawing. The printouts may be made in any manner; the blowbacks are derived from microfilm images. Photodrafting is useful for revising similar drawing configurations or for tracing the desired portion of an image.

photoengraving Making a relief printing plate by utilizing photographic means to obtain a chemically resistant image on a metal surface. The unprotected metal is etched away, leaving the protected areas in relief. The term also denotes the plate made by this process. *See also* CUT.

photogelatin process (collotype process) Planographic, screenless printing process similar to lithography. It is based on the fact that oil (ink) and water do not mix. The image area on the gelatin plate is made water-repellent, whereas the nonimage area is receptive to water.

A bichromated gelatin solution is floated onto a thick sheet of glass, which becomes the plate. When dry, the sensitized gelatin coating is exposed through a continuous-tone negative. The plate is developed by a wetting process. The tones from white to black reject or accept the water in the proportion to which they have been exposed to light. With the introduction of reticulation, the entire surface of the plate is divided into minute and mutually independent areas that repel or accept water and ink in direct proportion to tone values. The printing stock is brought in contact with the gelatin plate.

Copy prepared for the photogelatin process may be a paste-up or any other form suitable for photo-offset printing. The process is effective for short runs of fine color work. *See also* PRINTING METHODS; RETICULATION.

photogrammetry System of making maps from photographs, especially aerial photographs.

photograph Picture of an object formed on sensitized paper, film, or other material by the action of light.

photographic properties *See* FILMS AND PLATES.

photographic typesetters *See* TYPESETTERS, PHOTOGRAPHIC.

photogravure Intaglio printing in which photographic methods are used in the production of the printing plate. *See also* PRINTING METHODS.

photolithographic camera *See* CAMERA, PROCESS.

photolithographic negative *See* NEGATIVE, PHOTOLITHOGRAPHIC.

photolithography (photo-offset) Photographic method of planographic printing, based on the fact that grease (ink) and water do not mix. Photolithography encompasses all the steps necessary to arrive at the end item: photographing the copy, developing the negative, making the printing plate, and printing the image on stock from the plate. *See also* PRINTING METHODS.

photomap Map constructed from a series of photographs taken from an airplane. The photographs are matched to compose the photomap. Photomapping is also used extensively in space technology to photograph planets through satellite control from the earth. *See also* PHOTOGRAMMETRY.

photomatrix Grid, disk, or drum used in phototypesetting having an assortment of type characters of various type designs and sizes. The number of typeface designs multiplied by the number of type sizes in the lens system indicates machine mixing capability and equals the number of fonts in the one-time machine setup. For example, one disk contains an assortment of four different type designs, and the phototypesetter has a lens system capability to enlarge or reduce in eight different point sizes. The phototypesetter will therefore have a 32-font capability. The number of fonts will vary in proportion to the number of type designs on the photomatrix because of interchangeability.

photomechanical Pertaining to any process of printing or duplicating images by mechanical means from a photographically prepared printing plate.

photomechanical transfer *See* DIFFUSION-TRANSFER PROCESS.

photomicrography Art or practice of producing photographs of minute objects such as organisms by using a camera and a microscope. A photomicrograph is the photograph so produced.

photomicroscope Combination camera-microscope for taking photographs of microscopic objects.

photomontage *See* MONTAGE.

photomural Photograph enlarged many times to serve as a decorative piece, especially for wall display.

photo-offset *See* PHOTOLITHOGRAPHY.

photosensitive material Any material coated with a light-sensitive emulsion; any material which responds chemically to light.

Photostat Registered trademark of the Photostat Corporation for a photographic copying machine. The Photostat machine has a prism attached to the front of the lens that turns the image to read from left to right instead of in reverse. Thus a right-reading image is made directly. A particular feature of the many Photostat models is the ability to produce copies continuously while developing, fixing, washing, and drying are handled successively in various contained units without attention from the operator. Depending on the model, copies of original material may be made at the same time with a 50 percent reduction and a 200 percent enlargement, as desired. Copies may also be made in sizes between these extremes. Special models used in advertising work enlarge by as much as 350 percent. Sensitized paper for the photoprints is furnished on rolls and housed in the unit. Some Photostat models have a cycle control that permits continuous operation for producing as many as 23 (or 399) prints without the operator's attention. Some of the models may be adapted to make paper prints from 16, 35, and 70-millimeter film.

phototypesetting Cold-composition method of producing text matter by successively projecting the images of evenly spaced characters on light-sensitive film or on photographic paper. The images may be developed automatically within the machine as the images are set, or the latent images may be developed in a remote darkroom. The term "phototype-setting" is a misnomer because actual type is not used, but it is accepted in the printing trade as the photographic equivalent of setting type. See also TYPESETTERS, PHOTOGRAPHIC.

pi Spilled type. When the type in a galley has been pied, it often must be completely reset.

pica Unit of measurement used in printing. The pica is equal to 12 points; for practical purposes, 6 picas are equal to 1 inch ($2.54 \text{ cm} = 25.40 \text{ mm} = 1$ pica). The pica is used to measure the width and length of pages, columns, slugs, and so on. The term "pica" also denotes a size of typewriter type measuring 6 lines to the vertical inch (2.54 cm) and 10 characters to the horizontal inch (2.54 cm).

picking Lifting of particles of paper from stock during printing. The ink may be sticky or the paper inadequate. In addition, a rubber blanket on an offset press may tend to pick up particles because of suction created by the blanket.

pickle jar Tubular glass jar with a sponge in the bottom that absorbs pure ammonia. A lid prevents the escape of ammonia fumes. The jar is used to develop latent images exposed on diazo-treated foil (film), paper, and cloth. The image must first be exposed for several minutes in a printer in contact with the diazo-treated material. The copy material containing the latent image is then rolled and inserted in the jar. The latent image can be seen coming to life through the sides of the jar. The completed print is removed in a dry state.

This method of exposing and developing images is a whiteprint process of reproduction, for which whiteprint machines may also be used. This process is well suited to the making of projecturals for overhead projection, when the image must be on transparent film. See also WHITEPRINT PROCESS.

pickup Small rubberlike pad or sponge used to pick up excess rubber cement from a paste-up. A pickup is sometimes called a "mouse" by those

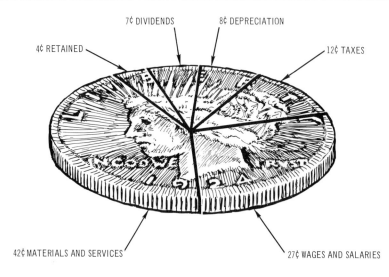

7¢ DIVIDENDS   8¢ DEPRECIATION

4¢ RETAINED

12¢ TAXES

42¢ MATERIALS AND SERVICES   27¢ WAGES AND SALARIES   **Fig. P-20   Pie chart.**

working in the trade. As a verb, "pick up" means to reuse an illustration or text for a new publication.

pictorial drawing Any drawing that depicts an object with such clarity that it can be recognized. This type of drawing is used with electrical, pneumatic, and hydraulic schematics to show the relationship of a system's components. Pictorial drawings are also used to advantage in overhead projection if the projectural is not cluttered with copy.

picture Photograph, halftone, illustration, or artwork. The term "picture" is rarely used in the graphic arts professions and should be avoided because it has a nonprofessional connotation.

pie chart Circular chart divided into wedges resembling the cuts of a pie (Figure P-20). Each wedge represents a percentage of the whole "pie." This type of chart is easy to understand, but its use is limited because only one quantity can be compared with the whole. *See also* BAR CHART; COLUMN CHART; CURVE CHART; SURFACE CHART.

pigment Fine solid particles used to give color to printing inks. They are substantially insoluble in the vehicle and in water. *See also* INKS, PRINTING.

pile height Height of a pile of sheets of stock that equals the normal maximum capacity of the feeder and delivery mechanisms of a printing press. The term is also used to indicate the maximum pile height of other types of machines, such as paper joggers and cutters.

piling Undesirable accumulation of residue on inking rollers, rubber blankets, and printing plates.

pin register Method of holding elements in place in overlay work such as registering negatives and positives, platemaking, and in overhead-projection work.

pinhole Very small light spot that appears on a developed photographic negative. Pinholes result from photographing particles of dust and lint deposited on the unexposed negative, camera lens, vacuum-board glass, or other parts of a camera. The negative may be placed over a light table and the pinholes blotted out with a small brush and opaque solution.

piping diagram Line drawing of a fluid system or of part of such a system. It shows the routing of components, their physical location and arrangement, and such other characteristics as differences in levels, pipe diameters, materials, types and sizes of fittings, flow, pressure, and volume. Information may be listed in tabular form on the engineering drawing.

pitch The number of characters of a given typeface that are counted to a measure of one inch (2.54 cm) along the typed line. The measure holds true only of such typewriters that do not have proportional spacing.

placard drawing Drawing that shows instructions for the maintenance and operation of an article. It can be reproduced in a reduced size and mounted on the article itself. It may be affixed to the underside of the cover of the article or printed on its surface.

plan drawing Drawing that depicts plans for the foundation, framing, floor or deck, or roof of a structure. It may indicate the shapes, sizes, and materials of foundations, their relation to the superstructure, and their elevation with reference to a fixed datum plane; the location of walls, partitions, bulkheads, stanchions, companionways, openings, columns, and stairs; and the shapes and sizes of roofs, parapet walls, skylights, stacks, and ventilators. The drawing shows materials for construction, arrangement of structural framing, and location of equipment or furniture as appropriate. A plan drawing for services may depict individual layouts for heating, plumbing, air-conditioning, electrical, and other utility systems.

planimeter Precision instrument for measuring any plane area. A tracing point or lens is moved around the perimeter of the plane, and the area is read from a measuring wheel and indicator dial.

planographic printing Printing from a flat surface. See PRINTING METHODS.

planography Art or practice of planographic printing.

plastic binding See COMB BINDING; see also BINDING, MECHANICAL.

plastic film Films such as cellophane, polyethylene and polypropylene. These films are manufactured in various grades of thicknesses and stability characteristics. They are used for many applications, such as laminating, point of sale advertising of merchandise, and decorative packaging when visibility of the article is required. Flexographic solvent-type inks are excellent when printing on these films because the inks are of low viscosity, dry by solvent evaporation and absorption into the substrate, and by decomposition. The Suncure method of drying ink, developed by Sun

Chemical Corporation, rapidly polymerizes and develops drying properties with little external heat involved. When in doubt as to what ink to use for these films, the ink manufacturer should be given a sample of the stock to be printed on, its manufacturer's code designation, the type and speed of the press used, and the end use of the product. *See also* SUNCURE.

plastic plate   Direct printing plate made on a plastic base. *See* DIRECT PLATE MAKING.

plat drawing   Engineering drawing of an area in which structures are shown together with detailed information on their relation to other structures, to existing and proposed utilities, and to the terrain, roads, boundary lines, walks, fences, and the like.

plate, photographic   Rigid glass base coated with a photographic emulsion.

plate, printing   Any printing surface except a form. A form, which is the surface used in letterpress printing, is known as such in the trade. The plate may be an offset plate, a gravure plate, or a photogelatin plate. *See also* PRINTING METHODS.

Fig. P-21   nuArc's Model FT40UP Ultra-Plus Flip-Top platemaker.

plate cylinder   Printing-press cylinder to which the printing plate is attached. In letterpress printing, the opposing cylinder is the impression cylinder, which cushions the stock as it is fed between them. In photo-offset or letterset printing, the opposing cylinder is the blanket cylinder and, in turn, the impression cylinder.

plate finish   *See* PLATER FINISH.

platemaking equipment   Photo-offset printing plates are made in exposure units. Some units are complex self-contained devices, such as the Itek Platemaster, which produces duplicate plates from original copy. Other units use photolithographic negatives through which the image is "burned" onto presensitized paper or metal plates. A platemaking troubleshooting chart is shown in Table P-1.

Figure P-21 is nuArc's Model FT40UP Ultra-Plus Flip-Top platemaker shown in the loading position. The platemaker is operated in three steps: loading, flipping, and exposing. The unit was developed for the graphic arts industries for plate coatings, proofing materials, resists, and for other coatings including daylight contact film. A new lamp design, having a metal halide tube light source, covers the 3,500 to 4,500-angstrom range for exposing both photopolymer and diazo-coated materials. The control panel is operated for warmup by pushing the ON button; when warmed up, it reduces to a standby idle intensity. The FT40UP has a blanket size of 30 by 40 inches (77 by 102 cm). The platemaker is also available in "Non-Stop" models with vacuum frame on both sides for greater productivity.

Figure P-22 shows 3M's Dual platemaker. The machine uses the 3M brand "ESP" paper plate for runs under 1,000 and the 3M brand "XL" polyester plate for runs up to 10,000 impressions. In addition to plates, the

Fig. P-22   3M's Dual platemaker.

TABLE P-1   Platemaking Troubleshooting Information.

Problem	Appearance	Solution
Blinding	Image may look strong on the plate, but the plate prints very weakly or not at all.	1. Excess gum on the plate may be covering the image so that it will not accept ink. Use correct chemicals as directed for final gumming. Have press operator rub the plate down with fountain solution to remove excess gum. Certain plates require going over with developer. Follow the manufacturer's directions. 2. Plate will not accept ink because ink rollers are glazed. Fountain solution may be too strong and may have worked into the ink, causing the ink to emulsify.
Scumming	Plate picks up ink in the clear areas and transfers it to nonimage areas of the press sheet.	1. Nonimage areas of the plate may not be desensitized properly to resist ink. Re-etch the plate or make a new plate. Always work the entire plate, including nonimage as well as image areas, with gum and developer. 2. Scumming may be a press problem because of dirty damping rollers, skidding from the roller, a loose blanket, or an improper fountain-solution mixture. Check press conditions.
Halation	This condition appears as dot spreading, copy enlarged at the edges, and shadows of type.	1. Overexposure may accent poorly stripped areas. Use nuArc Sensitivity Guide to check exposure and replace the guide periodically. A yellowed guide can cause overexposure. 2. There is poor contact during exposure. Check flat for improper stripping, such as "fat" stripped areas, thick tape, or overlapped film. Check vacuum gauge and also check contact visually when making the exposure. 3. Use a strong point-light source for exposing plates to avoid long exposure and undercutting.
Broken images	Image is missing in certain areas; fingerprints develop on the plate.	1. Examine stripped flat. Tape or opaquing solution may be covering the portion of the image that is broken. 2. Check vacuum-frame glass. Wet opaquing solution or tape adhesive may come off on the underside. Always make sure the glass is clean. 3. The plate may be underexposed. It may appear to develop properly, but the image "walks off" after a few impressions. Check exposure with nuArc Sensitivity Guide. *(Continued next page)*

TABLE P-1 *(Continued)*

Problem	Appearance	Solution
		4. Irregular areas of broken image may be due to moisture on the plate prior to exposure. Handle plates by the edges only and avoid fingerprinting. Store plates in lighttight containers away from moisture.
Plugging	Press sheet looks dirty, dots have been filled in, or "plugged," and the image is spotty.	1. Old, dried developer in the plate sponge or pad may be dissolving in the fresh developer, causing plugging. Always use a clean sponge and pad. 2. Dried gum and developer on the plate working surface or table may work into the plate when it is wet with new solution. Keep the developing table clean. Always use a flat surface so that low areas on the table will not cause incomplete development. Apply additional developer on a clean surface and redevelop according to the manufacturer's instructions to correct plugging.

platemaker produces instant positive polyester stats as well as halftones, line negatives, and transparencies. The machine therefore combines as an electrostatic platemaker, a photo direct platemaker, and a stat maker. Both rolls of plate material, the ESP and the XL, are contained within the platemaker magazine, and selection is made from one brand to the other by operating a switch. Copyboard sheet size is 30 by 40 inches (76.2 by 102 cm), and the maximum image that can be reproduced is 24 by 36 inches (61 by 91.4 cm). The range of focus for reduction is 45 percent and enlargement 150 percent. The first XL plate is produced in 1½ minutes and then up to 240 plates per hour. An ESP plate is produced in less than 20 seconds. Chemical capacity is 4 gallons (15.14 liters) each for both the developer and activator, and toner capacity is ½ pound (0.227 kg). Controls are at eye level and plumbing is not required.

Itek Graphic Products features a series of Platemaster paper and metal platemakers (two of which are discussed in this section) that serve a variety of purposes. Figure P-23 shows their Model 175VFE variable focus electrostatic platemaker. This machine is designed for use by commercial printers; fast duplicating shops; in-plant reproduction departments; federal, state, and local government agencies; and schools and colleges. The focal range extends from 45 to 150 percent.

Figure P-24 is Itek's 20/24 Platemaster. The platemaker can duplicate 8½ by 11-inch (26 by 28-cm) pages four-up and full page newspaper advertising proofs. Size E engineering drawings (34 by 44 inches; 86.3 by 111.8 cm) can be reduced for easier handling, and size C engineering drawings (17 by 22 inches; 43.18 by 56 cm) are reproduced at the same size.

plate type edges Edges of paper and metal plates that fit particular clamping devices of presses and duplicators.

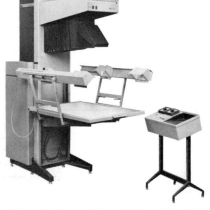

Fig. P-23 Itek's Model 175VFE variable focus electrostatic platemaker.

Fig. P-24 Itek's Model 20/24 Platemaster.

platen In a job press, the flat surface that holds the paper as it is pressed against the printing form. In a cold-composition machine such as a typewriter, the platen is the round rubber cylinder that supports the paper and receives the impact when the keys are operated.

platen press Printing press in which an impression is taken by bringing together two flat surfaces, one holding the stock and the other the printing surface. In some presses, the form moves up against the platen; in the universal type, the platen is first placed in a position parallel to the bed and then pressed against the bed. Platen presses are used for simple-one-color work and for high-quality color work in which fine register is required. Large platen presses are used for stamping, die cutting, creasing, and embossing.

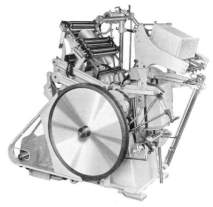

Fig. P-25 D Series Kluge automatic platen press.

Figure P-25 shows a D series Kluge automatic platen press. The D series includes models with sheet sizes of 11 by 17 inches (27.9 by 43.1 cm), 13 by 19 inches (33 by 48.3 cm), and 14 by 22 inches (35.6 by 55.8 cm). While designed primarily for printing, the presses are also used for die-cutting, embossing, and foil-stamping work. If a steel die-cutting plate is added, the press is converted into an automatic die-cutting press. If a die-heating plate is added, hot embossing work is produced. The presses will accommodate thicknesses from onionskin to wallboard (to 0.200 inch; 0.508 cm). They will die cut shapes varying from circles to quadrilaterals and will print on materials ranging from tags to wooden rulers and snap-out forms.

The minimum sheet sizes for these presses is 1⅞ by 3 inches (4.8 by 7.62 cm) for models 11 by 17 and 13 by 19 (28 by 43.1 cm and 33 by 48.2 cm), and 3 by 3 inches (7.62 by 7.62 cm) for model 14 by 22 (36 by 56 cm). Feed- and delivery-pile heights are 14 inches (36 cm) for all three models. Speeds are 4,000 impressions per hour for model 11 by 17 (28 by 43.1 cm), 3,500 for model 13 by 19 (33 by 48.2 cm), and 3,300 for model 14 by 22 (36 by 56 cm). The roll-leaf feeder is available as an optional feature. The feeder operates mechanically from the action of the press. Accurate foil advancements are from 0 to the height of the platen. Foil brackets offer capacities to 1,000-foot (305-m) rolls, and foil-rewind units dispose of used foil. Three different foils of various widths and lengths can be used.

Kluge platen presses are designed for delayed dwell, which is the time delay necessary in quality foil-stamping and embossing work. A combination of heat, impressional strength, and dwell-on impression is required. The heat is necessary to soften the binders and coatings in paper, board stock, and other materials. Once softened, the fibers in the stock can be realigned and reshaped to permit a sharp embossment. Heat is also required for foil stamping, and the increased dwell allows time for the heat to penetrate from the embossing or stamping die to the foil and then to the stock. Otherwise the foil would not adhere properly to the stock.

The Kluge EHD-Series automatic die-cutting, foil-stamping, and embossing press is shown in Figure P-26. Two models are available: the 13 by 19-inch (33 by 49-cm) model and the 14 by 22-inch (36 by 56-cm) model. The presses die cut special configurations, or produce die cutting, foil applications, and embossing work in combination. Foil may be stamped flat or embossed in a single pressrun. A roll-leaf feeder transport, equipped with ball bearings, operates mechanically with the operation of the press and

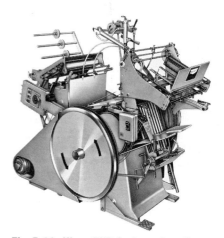

Fig. P-26 Kluge EHD-Series automatic die cutting, foil stamping and embossing press.

advances foil from 0 to the height of the platen. A full foil width may be used and with the three-draw model transport, three parallel colors of three different widths and lengths may be used in one pressrun. The foil rewind permits disposal of used roll leaf. The foil is fed from the top of the press, and foil brackets offer a capacity of 1,000-foot (305-m) foil rolls.

The model 13 by 12-inch (33 by 30.4-cm) press has a maximum sheet size (commercial register) of 14 by 20 inches (36 by 51 cm) and a maximum sheet size (hairline register) of 13 by 19 inches (33 by 49 cm). The model has a minimum sheet size of 2 by 3 inches (5.08 by 7.62 cm), a magazine and delivery capacity of 14 inches (36 cm), and a maximum speed of 3,500 impressions per hour. The 14 by 22-inch (36 by 56-cm) model press has a maximum sheet size for both commercial and hairline register of 14 by 22 inches (36 by 56 cm) and a minimum sheet size of 3 by 3 inches (7.62 by 7.62 cm). Magazine and delivery capacities are both 14 inches (36 cm). Maximum speed of this press is 3,300 impressions per hour.

plater finish (plate finish) Glazed paper finish achieved by introducing sheets of paper between platers, or plate calenders.

plot To establish reference points on a grid. The points so plotted are connected by lines.

plugging In photomechanical platemaking, an unfavorable condition of printed copy in which the copy looks dirty, dot areas have been filled in, or "plugged," and the image is spotty. Deposits of dried developer on the sponge or pad may have dissolved in the fresh developer, causing plugging. A clean sponge and pad should always be used. In addition, dried gum and developer on the plate working surface or table may penetrate the plate when it is wet with new solution. A flat surface should always be used and the table kept clean. The condition is corrected by applying additional developer on a clean surface and redeveloping according to the manufacturer's directions.

ply Thickness of blanks and heavy paper stock expressed in the number of layers of which they are composed. The following table gives the equivalent of ply ratings in fractions of an inch.

ply	in.	mm
2	0.012	0.305
3	0.015	0.381
4	0.018	0.456
5	0.021	0.533
6	0.024	0.610
8	0.030	0.762
10	0.036	0.914
12	0.042*	1.067
14	0.048*	1.220
16	0.056*	1.422

*Double-pasted sheets.

point body Portion of type whose sides are measured from end to end on the same plane and direction as the top and bottom of the face. This measurement indicates the size of the type in points. *See* Figure T-8.

point-of-sale (point-of-purchase) In advertising, designating a device or display of any kind installed near merchandise to aid sales. Display racks, animated and action pieces, and banners are point-of-sale devices.

point: paper Thickness equivalent to 0.001 inch (0.0254 mm).

point system Method of measuring type sizes. The point system is based on the pica, which is equivalent to 12 points. Each point measures 0.013837 inch (0.3514 mm), or almost $\frac{1}{72}$ inch. One pica is equivalent to 4.233 mm. When 12-point (4.21-mm) type is set solid, without leading, 6 vertical lines of type measure 72 points, or almost 1 inch (2.54 cm). The point size of type is determined by dividing 72 by the number of lines per column-inch when the type is set solid. Thus, 12 lines of type to the column-inch divided into 72 is 6 point (2.11 mm), 8 lines is 9 point (3.16 mm), and 6 lines is 12 point (4.21 mm).

Polaroid MP-4 Multipurpose Land camera Camera designed primarily for use in science and industry. It delivers photographs on the site in the same manner as the regular Polaroid camera popular in family picture taking but has greater capabilities. The MP-4 system permits rapid interchange of both film format and camera function. It is used for copying simple charts and graphs, producing 35-millimeter transparencies for projection, photomacrography, photomicrography, and off-stand studio or laboratory photography. There are three cameras in the modular MP-4 system: the Standard, the XL, and the XLR. All feature reflex viewing and ground-glass focusing, full-adjustable lighting, precision alignment, interchangeable lenses, and a removable camera head which can be mounted on a tripod. A condenser-enlarger head converts the MP-4 to a professional-quality enlarger. All models feature a rotating camera head with a scale for reading the exact number of degrees off vertical when copying wall-mounted charts or making mural-size enlargements. The column on the XLR model rotates 360° for recording large subjects on the floor, or in combination with the rotating camera head, to make perspective photographs. The MP-4 Land photographic system (Figure P-27A) offers modular options including (clockwise from lower left): tripod mount for off-stand use, universal camera mount, negative carriers and condenser-enlarger head, choice of lenses or lensless microscope adapter, rigid macro extensions, accessory filter kit, choice of ground glasses including folding viewing hood, and choice of Polaroid Land film holders.

The MP-4 camera has a flexible 10-inch (25.4 cm) bellows mounted on twin focusing rails with a built-in metric scale for easy measurement of bellows extension. There are two camera heads for making photographs with the MP-4: a sliding head and a fixed head. Both heads accept Polaroid 4 by 5-inch (10.16 by 12.7-cm) Land film holders, a specially designed Polaroid Land pack-film holder which slips under the spring-loaded ground glass, and a Polaroid Land roll-film holder, as well as most wet-process 4 by 5-inch (10.16 by 12.7-cm) film holders.

A laterally sliding camera head features a movable carriage that holds the ground glass and reflex viewer on one side and film holder on the other. One motion changes the head from the viewing position to the

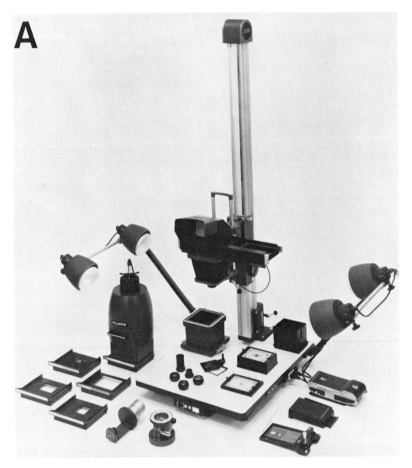

Fig. P-27 Polaroid's Multipurpose Land camera showing: (*A*) the photographic system's modular options; (*B*) the unit used as a tripod-mounted studio or clinical camera; (*C*) the unit used as a view camera; and (*D*) the condenser enlarger.

photographing position without adjusting the dark slide on the film holder. The fixed camera head holds the ground glass, reflex viewer, and film holder. With the fixed head, the film holder must be completely removed from the camera for focusing.

A condenser-enlarger head, which attaches onto the basic camera, doubles the capability of the MP-4 camera system. A supplemental condenser and heat-shield glass allow higher magnification enlargements. Glassless negative carriers for the MP-4 enlarger are available in 35-millimeter, 2¼ by 2¼-inch, 2¼ by 3¼-inch, and 4 by 5-inch formats (5.7 by 5.7-cm, 5.7 by 8.3-cm, and 10.1 by 12.7-cm formats). The MP-4 camera head can be removed from the column and mounted on a tripod by means of a special adapter for in-plant, studio, and clinical photography. Once the camera head has been taken off the column, a universal camera mount will accept most still, motion-picture, or video cameras for copy work, slide duplication, or animation. The Polaroid SX-70 Land camera may be mated with the MP-4 system by means of its standard tripod mount.

Four light sockets with reflectors accept 150-watt reflector flood lamps for even illumination over the entire baseboard. The lights, fully adjustable along the length of their cross-bars, may be removed for creating special lighting effects. Cross-bars are secured by arms attached to the rear of the baseboard, allowing the largest copy to be moved about freely under the camera lens and removing front-light arms as an operator obstacle. A locking lever on each mount provides positive positioning of the arms in any attitude—from fully vertical to below the plane of the baseboard for a wide variety of flat, direct, or oblique lighting effects. Guides built into both the cross-bars and light-arm mounts make it simple to return lights to the optimum copy position. The column and baseboard of each Polaroid MP-4 Land camera are calibrated at the point of manufacture for precise alignment. The camera carriage is counterbalanced by a spring mounted on the top of the column and operated by means of a crank which activates a smooth friction drive. Fixed to the column is a metric scale for repositioning of the camera for repetition of photographic results.

Increased magnification is obtained by inserting rigid macro-extensions into the camera system. Special quick-release clips make it possible to place one or two macro-extensions between the camera back and the bellows to obtain higher magnification. With the line of MP-4 lenses and two bellows extensions, the camera will cover a total macro-range from 1:1 up to 14.8X.

Figure P-27B shows the camera off its stand and set up as a tripod-mounted studio or clinical camera through use of an accessory adapter; it is designated as a copy camera in this setup. Figure P-27C shows the MP-4 set up as a view camera. Small-parts photography for research reports and quality-control applications are typical uses for the MP-4. An accessory filter holder, shown in place, offers choice of filters most commonly used with Polacolor Land film emulsions. The folding hood permits viewing the image on the ground glass when the camera is in the horizontal position and the tripod adapter enables the camera to be used with any tripod. Producing images on all Polaroid materials is possible and with 4 by 5-inch (10.16 by 12.7-cm) roll-film holders. Figure P-27D shows the MP-4 condenser-enlarger. The enlarger converts the MP-4 into a 4 by 5-inch

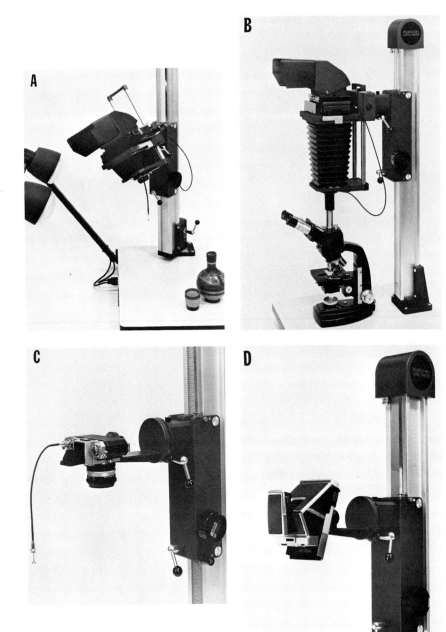

Fig. P-28   Polaroid's MP-4 XLR Land camera with rotating camera head: (*A*) alone; (*B*) using lensless baffle tube for photomicrography; (*C*) using universal camera mount for various formats and functions; and (*D*) mated with the MP-4 camera mount.

(10.16 by 12.7-cm) enlarger. The enlarger is of conventional condenser design and has negative carriers available in 4 by 5, 3¼ by 4¼, 2¼ by 3¼ inches (10.16 by 12.7, 8.3 by 10.8, 5.7 by 8.3 cm) and 35-millimeter formats. The enlarger used the 135-millimeter and 105-millimeter lenses and the

75-millimeter lens with an auxiliary condenser unit. The lamp housing provides adjustments for positioning the light source for even illumination on the baseboard. There is a filter drawer above the condensers that permanently holds a glass heat shield and accepts a 4 by 5-inch (10.16 by 12.7-cm) acetate filter, or if preferred, a 3-inch (7.62-cm) or 2-inch (5.08-cm) gelatin filter can be used below the lens.

Figure P-28A shows the fully rotating column on the MP-4 XLR Land camera that combines with a rotating camera head to allow the user to make a wide variety of perspective photographs not possible with most vertical camera systems. The rotating feature also allows copying of floor- and wall-mounted originals, as well as production of mural-size enlargements with the MP-4 enlarger head. Figure P-28B shows the lensless baffle tube for photomicrography. The produced quality of the photograph is in proportion to that viewed in the user's microscope. Rotating the camera head permits the unit to be used upright with trinocular microscopes, as shown, or at any angle for photographing through the microscope eyepiece. Figure P-28C illustrates how the universal camera mount that is available for the MP-4 Land camera allows the use of any standard-thread camera—still, motion-picture, or video, with a large or small format, and with the MP-4's stand and adjustable lighting system. Figure P-28D shows how the Polaroid SX-70 Land camera, a fully automatic single-lens reflex camera, which ejects a hard, dry, full-color print in 1.2 seconds after the shutter button is pushed, can be mated with the MP-4 by means of a universal camera mount.

polyester film base *See* CRONAR.

porosity Quality or state of being porous, or permeable to liquids; used to describe papers.

portraiture Process or art of depicting an individual by drawing, painting, or photographing from life, particularly an individual's face; also, the depiction so produced. *See also* LINE CONVERSION.

positive Photographic image usually made from a negative, in which tones are not reversed as in a negative. A positive on paper is called a "print"; one on a transparent base such as film, a "positive transparency." *See also* FILM POSITIVE.

positive-reading *See* RIGHT-READING.

poster Large cardboard or thick-paper display sign. It is known as a poster chart when it is used as a visual aid in a presentation.

posterization Graphic arts or photographic technique for adding posterlike qualities to a photograph or art illustration by separating the normal tones of a subject into distinctly separated strong tones.

pounce Powderlike material distributed by the Keuffel and Esser Company for improving the ink-absorbing qualities of reproduction tracing cloths and papers. The powder is sprinkled on the surface, and the excess is removed by brushing with a felt pad or brush.

powder ink: toner   *See* DRY INK.

PP   Abbreviation for pages.

preface   Statement forming part of the front matter of a book in which the author or editor states the purpose of the work and expectations for it and sometimes expresses appreciation for assistance.

prejustification   *See* JUSTIFICATION; *see also* COLD COMPOSITION.

preprint   Any letter, number, symbol, design, logotype, shading, or line that is printed beforehand and subsequently pasted or mortised in place on a material or a mechanical for reproduction. Preprints are used in visual aids, television and screen titles, display advertising, commercial art, technical illustrations, and other applications. Almost any design, letterhead, trademark, or logotype may be had on order. Preprints may be typed or drawn on adhesive-backed transparent sheets, or the sheets or images may be opaque. Special preprints may be ordered from the typesetter for paste-up or mortising. In addition, preprints may be typed on coated stock and pasted as desired. The underside of the image should be covered with rubber cement and, when dry, placed lightly on a piece of waxed paper with the adhesive side down. Only sufficient pressure should be applied to make the preprint adhere to the paper. Burnishing is not necessary. The surface of the drawing or other material is then painted with a light coat of rubber cement, and the preprint is ready to be pasted in place by pressing it lightly. Excess rubber cement is removed with a pickup. The tissue overlay should be burnished lightly and care used in handling so that the work is not smeared.

presensitized plate   Aluminum printing plate or a paper plate used in offset printing that has been coated with a sensitive emulsion for image reception.

press proof   Proof removed from the press to inspect line and color values, registration, quality, and so forth. It is the last proof taken before the complete run.

press-wire tape converter   *See* TAPE CONVERTER.

pressrun (run)   Total number of copies of a publication printed during one printing.

pressure diazo copying process   Whiteprint copying process that offers a dry, odorless operation; because heaters or ammonia fumes are not required for development, venting is not required for this process. Mixing of chemicals is not required. The development system is replenished with a cartridge of activator. In this process, the exposed copy material travels through the developer section where a thin film of activator is metered under pressure for development of the diazo material. Metering and pressure blades withdraw automatically from contact with the applicator rollers when the machine is turned off. When the machine is turned on for operation, the blades return to position for development. *See also* WHITE-PRINT PROCESS.

pressure frame Frame for holding copy while the copy is being photographed; also, a frame for holding plate and negative during exposure. Such a frame holds the elements by pressure alone, without the use of a vacuum. *See also* COPYBOARD.

pressure-sensitive material Any material, such as adhesive- and wax-backed tapes, that will stick to another material when lightly pressed on that material. (For pressure-sensitive tapes and sheets, *see* CHARTPAK; *see also* ARTIST AID; AVERY; CRAFTINT.)

pressureless printing *See* ELECTROSTATIC STENCIL-SCREEN PRINTING PROCESS; *see also* PRINTING METHODS.

primary colors In printing inks, yellow, red, and blue. Orange, green, and magenta are secondary, or derivative, colors. The primary colors are used with black. Tints and patterns in color may be overprinted with a combination of primary and secondary colors.

print and tumble *See* WORK AND TUMBLE.

print and turn *See* WORK AND TURN.

printed circuit Electrical or electronic circuit reproduced by a printing process.

printer Machine other than a printing press that prints out a previously made original, operating either from opaque, translucent, or transparent copy or from a microfilm image. It has a lens for reduction or enlargement of the original. Printers thus differ from copying machines, which produce an exact facsimile of the original. Photocomposing machines, too, are in a class of their own. They are neither printers nor copying machines because their primary purpose is to compose cold-composition copy. With the advent of xerography, electrostatic screen printing, stabilization and electrolytic reproduction, and other processes, the classification of equipment has become complex. A printing press imposes an image by depositing ink on a surface, whereas electrostatic copying and printing utilize a very fine powder called "toner" that ultimately forms the image. Not only are the steps required to place an image on a surface entirely different, but magnification, mirror projection, and image sources vary.

printing density Measure of the opacity of an image to the exposing radiation. In the whiteprint process, a mercury arc is the usual light source, and the 3660, 4046, and 4358 A lines of mercury are the exposing radiation.

printing down   Making a photographic print by placing the original film image between a light-sensitive coated material and a source of light. The material may be intended for letterpress, gravure, or photo-offset. The film image and the sensitive material should be kept in close contact by using a vacuum frame during exposure. The term "printing down" is also used in making a printing plate from a photolithographic negative.

printing frame   Graphic arts device used to hold a negative or positive in tight contact with printing plates or other material for exposure. Also termed a "vacuum printing frame" when a vacuum is employed.

printing inks   *See* INKS, PRINTING.

printing methods   Printing is the art of causing a plate image to be transferred to a surface regardless of the method used. Conceptions of the major divisions and the various subdivisions of printing differ. With the many advances and the introduction of new technology in printing methods, the identity of the major divisions and subdivisions is open to discussion. Probably no industry has been hindered so much by differences in terminology as the graphic arts. The graphic arts industry has elected to call the function of printing on small offset presses "duplicating," whereas in fact it is printing. The size of the press has nothing to do with the method. The industry has also elected to call certain machines "printers." These machines are copiers because they do not themselves make originals; they merely copy from originals made by another method.

It is important to understand the various methods of printing and the selection of the best one for the particular application. These methods may be classified into major divisions by several criteria: the type of printing plate or material containing the image to be printed, the method of forming the image on the plate or material, and the way in which the image is transferred to a surface. These divisions are relief, planographic, intaglio, letterset, and stencil printing (*See* Figure P-29).

Relief Printing

Letterpress.   The printing plate is in relief, and the image is transferred directly from plate to stock. The image on the plate always reads wrong because the printed image must read right. Most letterpress printing is set with hot-metal linecasting or Monotype machines, although type is also set by hand. Whether set by machine or by hand, the copy is said to be "typeset."

Multigraphing.   Type is set on a composing stick and transferred to a drum incised with slots for receiving lines of type. A large inked fabric ribbon covers the type mass on the drum, which is rotated to impress the image on paper. Paste ink may also be used in Multigraph work.

Flexography.   Rubber plates having a relief image are used in flexographic printing. The flexographic press prints from rolled stock such as foil, enameled or coated paper, and cellophane. Food cartons, candy and gum wrappers, waxed bags, and similar items are ideally suited for this type of printing. The flexographic method is excellent for printing solid opaque colors such as are found in Christmas wrappings. A fluid ink is used.

Fig. P-29 Methods of printing.

RELIEF
(LETTERPRESS, MULTIGRAPHING, FLEXOGRAPHY, RUBBER STAMPS)

INTAGLIO (GRAVURE)

PLANOGRAPHIC
(LITHOGRAPHY, SPIRIT DUPLICATING, PHOTOGELATIN, HECTOGRAPHIC)

LETTERSET

STENCIL
(PAPER STENCIL, SCREEN PROCESS, ELECTROSTATIC SCREEN)

Planographic Printing

There are more variations of planographic printing, or printing from a flat surface, than there are of any other major division.

Lithography. The most popular method of planographic printing, lithography is based on the fact that grease (ink) and water (aqueous solution) do not mix. It begins with a process camera that photographs original copy to produce a photolithographic negative. The translucent image on the negative is transferred to a sensitized flexible metal printing plate by light exposure. The exposed and unexposed image areas on the plate vary in molecular structure because of the breakdown of image-area emulsions during exposure, and a latent image is formed on the plate in the areas that have been penetrated by light.

In contrast to letterpress printing, in which the image is transferred directly from plate to stock, an additional cylinder containing a rubber blanket is used in lithography. When the plate cylinder is rotated, the aqueous solution and ink are transferred to the flat image. The inked image repels the solution and therefore accepts ink, whereas the nonimage area accepts water, which repels the ink. The operating sequence is plate to blanket to stock.

The lithographic method is also called "photo-offset" because photography is used and the image is offset from the rubber blanket cylinder to stock. In addition, it is known as "offset lithography."

Spirit duplicating.   The image is typed, drawn, or written on a paper master that is backed with a separate sheet coated with aniline dye. The dye is transferred to the back of the master and reflects a wrong-reading image. The master is then attached to the cylinder of the spirit duplicator with the dye side up. With the rotation of the cylinder, spirit vapors activate the dye image, transferring the image to stock.

Photogelatin process.   This process, which is similar to lithography, is also based on the fact that grease and water do not mix. The image area on a gelatin plate accepts ink but repels water, and the nonimage area accepts water, which repels ink. A bichromated gelatin solution is floated onto a sheet of glass, which becomes the plate. When dry, the coating is exposed through a continuous-tone negative. The amount of light passing through the negative hardens the gelatin in proportion to the light and dark areas. Thus the tones reject water and accept ink through the range of tonal values. The photogelatin process is effective for short runs of fine color work. High-fidelity reproductions of posters, murals, calendars, and oil and water paintings may be made by this process.

Hectographic printing.   An aniline dye is deposited on a master by typing, drawing, or writing with a special hectograph ribbon, ink, or pencil. The master is then placed facedown on a moistened gelatin plate, to which the image is transferred. Copies are made by pressing paper lightly against the plate.

Intaglio Printing

This method of printing is used in steel and copperplate engraving. The intaglio plate is the exact opposite of a relief plate, the image being formed by incised cuts. As the plate cylinder rotates, fluid ink floods over the plate and into the recesses of the image. The top of the plate is then wiped clean with a doctor blade, and the ink that remains in the recesses is transferred to stock to form the image. Intaglio printing is also known as "gravure printing," as "photogravure" when photography is used, and as "roto-gravure" when rotary cylinders are employed.

Letterset Printing

In this method of printing, a relief image is produced and is then transferred to a rubber blanket, from which it is offset to stock. The process is also referred to as "offset letterpress," as "offset relief," and as "dry offset" because an aqueous solution is not required. Letterset forms a division of its own because it is neither letterpress (the relief image is not transferred directly to stock) nor lithography (a damping solution is not required). A thin, flexible, compact relief plate taken from the relief image is substituted for the conventional lithographic plate. The image is transferred from the relief plate to the rubber blanket and then to stock.

Stencil Printing

A printing stencil is a paper or metal sheet in which an image is perforated. The perforated image permits ink or other substances to pass through the openings onto stock or other material. A paper stencil is typed, written, or drawn and is then placed on the cylinder of a mimeograph, or duplicator. As the paper passes through the duplicator, the impression roller rises automatically and presses it against the stencil. Ink flows from inside the stencil cylinder through the ink pad on the cylinder and the stencil openings and prints the image on paper.

Screen-process printing. This method of printing utilizes a silk, nylon, or metal screen containing the image. A squeegee forces the ink through the screen to form an image on paper or other material. Early screens were made by painting the image on silk with a fluid, resistant to ink. Masking materials blocked out unwanted printing areas. Now hand-cut stencils or photomechanical means are used in screen-process work. One technique involves coating the material with a light-sensitive emulsion and placing a photographic film positive in contact with it. Exposure hardens the surface of the screen in proportion to the penetration of light; hardened areas are then made insoluble to water, while the image area is made soluble to water.

Thick deposits of ink compounds and paint make a wide variety of printing possible. Fabrics, plastics, metal, heavy card stock, and paper are a few of the materials that are receptive to screen-process printing.

Electrostatic screen printing. In this process, electrostatic forces cause the image to be formed on the receiving surface. Electrostatic screen printing is known also as "electronography" and as "pressureless printing" because the plate containing the image does not come in contact with the material to be printed. A thin, flexible printing element (stencil), with finely screened openings defining the image to be printed, is used. Electroscopic dry-ink particles, known originally as toner, are metered through the stencil and attracted to the printing surface, where they are held by electrostatic attraction until they have been fixed by heat or chemical means to make the image permanent.

printout Enlarged copy made from an original microform, particularly by a microform reader-printer or printer. Printouts are used for reference or for correction and revision of engineering drawings or other images. They are sometimes called "blowbacks."

process camera *See* CAMERA, PROCESS.

process lens Lens for use with a process camera. It is designed to give best results with flat copy of about the same size as the original rather than with subjects of varying depth, such as are photographed with a snapshot camera. *See also* CAMERA, PROCESS.

process plates Two or more color plates used together to reproduce artwork or other copy. The primary colors for printing inks, yellow, red, and blue, are used with black; tints and patterns may be produced by overprinting with a combination of primary and secondary colors.

processing, film or paper Development and treatment of film or sensitized paper by chemical means or washing after exposure. Eastman Kodak Company's Ektamatic 214K processor is shown in Figure P-30. The processor is designed for use by newspaper printers, commercial typographers, in-plant printers, business-forms printers, and other users of stabilization processing. It processes Kodak Ektamatic SC photomechanical papers, Grades S and T, and Kodak Ektamatic SC paper. The processor

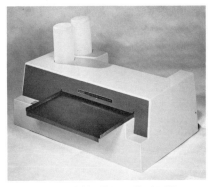

Fig. P-30 Kodak's Ektamatic 214K stabilization processor.

accepts paper up to 14 inches (35.6 cm) wide in continuous lengths up to 3 feet (0.914 m). Transport speed is 5.9 feet (1.80 m) per minute. Premixed chemicals are used at normal room temperatures. Processing time is fifteen seconds or less.

Figure P-31 shows Kodak's Readymatic Processor, Model 420A. The processor provides processing of certain Kodak photographic materials, or equivalent, in widths of 20 inches (50.8 cm) and in lengths from 10 inches to 18 feet (25.4 cm to 5.49 m). If lengths of roll film or paper are longer than 8 feet (2.43 m), the capacity of the receiving bin can be exceeded while they are being processed. When processing roll film or paper in lengths between 8 and 18 feet (2.44 and 5.49 m), care should be taken so that the processed material does not slip to the floor. Materials fed into the processor are developed, fixed, washed, and dried. Chemicals consist of a developer, stop bath, and fixer. The operator feeds exposed material into the first two rollers, and the material is transported into the developer tray where it is developed. As the film or paper passes between the developer-fixer rollers, the stop-bath solution is applied to the emulsion of the material by the lower roller. The material is then transported through two fixer trays and then into a spray wash. Excess water is squeegeed from the material as it passes into the dryer. In the dryer, warm air is blown against both sides of the material via the upper and lower dryer plenums. From the dryer, the photographic material is transported into the film-receiving bin and is ready for use or storage. Processing time is less than two minutes at 3 feet (0.914 m) per minute. Transport speed is from 2 to 4 feet (0.61 to 1.22 m) per minute.

Fig. P-31 Kodak's Readymatic Processor Model 420A.

Figure P-32 is LogEtronics' LogEflo PC-18 photocomposition film and paper processor. This machine processes photocomposition film or resin-coated paper in cassettes up to 24 inches (61 cm) wide from any photocomposition system and at the rate of up to 15 feet (4.57 m) per minute. A darkroom is not required because the processor operates in daylight. Developing time is infinitely variable from 20 to 120 seconds. Changes for film and chemicals are adjusted on the control panel, and indicators display when material has entered the developer and when the feed tray is clear. Replenishment of developer is automatic or dial-operated and takes place as long as material is passing over the feed microswitch. The rate of flow of the fixer is controlled by a flowmeter, and fixer replenishment is automatic as the developer is replenished. The drying temperature is adjustable from ambient to 145°F with automatic cutoff. Film or paper size (without leaders) is 4 to 18 inches (10.16 to 45.7 cm) and length is 10 inches (25.4 cm) and up. Short film or paper requires that leaders be attached for feeding.

Figure P-33 shows LogEtronics' LogEflo RAP 20 processor. The machine develops, fixes, washes, and dries graphic arts film and waterproof paper. It can be installed in a darkroom (through-the-wall) or used in daylight with optional cassette cover for cassette-fed applications. The RAP 20 is designed for use by newspaper publishers, printers, photo platemakers, and phototypesetters. Materials are film and RC type papers for high-temperature, rapid-access processing. Film or paper sizes (without leaders) are from 4 to 20 inches (10.1 to 50.8 cm) wide and 10 inches to 20 feet (25.4 cm to 6.1 m) long. Developing time is 90 seconds or less, dry to dry.

Fig. P-32 LogEtronics' PC-18 photocomposition film paper processor.

processing, nitrogen-burst   System of using inert nitrogen gas to agitate sensitized materials during the film-developing process. The advantage of the nitrogen-burst process is that each set of developed films exhibits the same density, contrast, and evenness regardless of the operator or the time of day.

A basic processing machine contains four lighttight nitrogen-burst tanks and one quick-dump washing tank. Separation negatives usually require a developer tank, a second tank for diluted masking developer, a short-stop (stop bath), and a fixer. For screened material, the masking tank developer is replaced by a high-contrast replenishing developer. The setup also requires the connection of a ½-inch (1.27-cm) hot- and cold-water line, a 1½-inch (3.81-cm) drain manifold in the bottom of the unit, and a flexible nitrogen pressure hose from a nitrogen bottle.

The film is loaded in a film sheath similar to that of the conventional film hanger, which supports it on all four sides. The sheath is dimpled and allows the solution to flow freely on both front and back of the film. After loading, the sheath is placed in a channel hanger rack. Film guides facilitate darkroom loading. The nitrogen burst is timed automatically. The operator first turns on the nitrogen-burst system and inserts the rack in the lighttight developing tank. (White light may therefore be turned on during the developing cycle.) An even layer of gas is injected through a distributor into the tank, where it immediately displaces the entire solution, moving it upward and thus agitating the material. The vigorous boil produced as the gas moves upward mixes the development byproducts and moves fresh chemical to all parts of the sensitized material. The washing tanks also receive a nitrogen burst. When the process has been completed, the film is squeegeed and dried in the conventional manner.

Fig. P-33   LogEtronics' LogEflo RAP 20 processor.

processing, stabilization   Developing process that makes use of light-sensitive material incorporated into the emulsion of photostabilization papers. Stabilization is a method of processing black-and-white prints more quickly than is possible by the customary develop-stop-fix-wash method. Stabilized prints are not permanent because the chemical reactions within the emulsion have been stopped only temporarily. However, such prints last long enough to serve a number of practical purposes. In fact, stabilized prints often remain unchanged for many months if they are not exposed to strong light, high temperatures, or excessive humidity.

The main difference between stabilization processing and ordinary print processing are in the speed of activation or development and in the method of treating the unexposed light-sensitive silver halide left in the emulsion after development. Stabilization processing is a machine operation. The prints are processed in about fifteen seconds, and they are slightly damp when they leave the machine. They dry completely in a few minutes and are then ready for use. In conventional processing, the unused silver halide is dissolved by the fixer (hypo) and any traces of silver left after fixing are removed by subsequent washing. Thus, conventionally processed prints are stable for long periods. In stabilization processing, however, the silver halide is converted to only temporarily stable compounds; therefore, the prints have a limited keeping time. Stabilized prints can be made permanent by fixing and washing after their initial purpose has been served.

Common stabilization processes can be divided into two groups according to the number of chemical solutions involved:

1. Two or more solutions (an activator and one or more stabilizers). The two-solution process is most often used for good quality continuous-tone prints.

2. The monobath, or one-solution process. This is generally more suitable for drawings and other line work. Development and stabilization are simultaneous.

In many stabilization processes, developing agents are incorporated in the paper emulsion. Development is achieved by applying an alkaline activator to the emulsion surface. The stabilizer is then applied to neutralize the activator and to convert any remaining silver halide to relatively stable, colorless compounds.

Ordinary printing papers cannot be developed by this type of stabilization process because there is no developing agent present in either the emulsion or the activator. However, a stabilization paper with developing agents in the emulsion can be processed in ordinary print-processing chemicals if desired.

The use of stabilization processing has increased greatly in the last few years, and it continues to grow as photographers, and others who use photography as a tool, realize its value. In stabilization processing, a measure of print stability is exchanged for the following advantages:

1. Stabilization processing is fast; prints are ready for use in a matter of seconds.

2. Speed and simplicity make the process adaptable to uncomplicated systems of mechanization. Photography, then, is a more easily used tool for those who are not experts in photographic processing.

3. Darkroom space and plumbing are greatly reduced. In fact, some applications of the process do not require a darkroom.

4. Stabilized prints do not need washing. This is a significant advantage since water conservation is important in many areas.

5. Mechanically processed prints have greater uniformity in density than those processed manually.

6. Most stabilized prints can be fixed and washed to make them permanent. Thus, the speed of stabilization processing is combined with having a permanent print if desirable.

7. Kodak Ektamatic SC papers are used in stabilization processing. These are variable-contrast stabilization materials that can also be processed with conventional chemicals.

Some modern applications for stabilized prints are proofing; quality deadline work; industrial and commercial applications where speed of production is essential; phototypesetting and photocomposing; medical, military, and police photography; newspaper work; immediate enlargements of microfilmed documents; and instrumentation or recording photography.

There are important points to remember in stabilization processing:

1. Correct exposure is essential because the development time is constant.

2. The processor must be kept clean. The manufacturer's recommendations for cleaning and maintaining the processor should be followed.

3. Chemical solutions should not be overworked. Observe the manufacturer's recommendations about the capacity and renewal of solutions.

4. Make sure that the processing trays in the machine are dry before loading them with the chemicals, because some stabilization solutions are not compatible with water.

5. Avoid contamination of the activator with stabilizer. This results in chemical fog on the prints.

6. Avoid handling unprocessed paper after handling stabilized prints. Such prints are impregnated with chemicals that easily mark or stain unprocessed material.

7. Stabilized prints must not be washed unless they have been fixed in an ordinary fixing bath. Washing without fixing renders the print sensitive to light.

8. Stabilized prints must not be heat-dried. The combination of heat and moisture stains the prints an overall yellowish brown.

9. Because stabilized prints are impregnated with chemicals, do not use the same racks or blotters for drying conventionally processed prints. For the same reason, do not file stabilized prints in contact with negatives or any other valuable printing materials.

This discussion of stabilization processing was made possible through the courtesy of Eastman Kodak Company, extracts of which were taken from their Kodak Pamphlet No. G-25. *Refer also to* PROCESSING, FILM OR PAPER.

profile grid *See* RECTANGULAR GRID.

progressive proofs *See* PROOFS, PROGRESSIVE.

projection Act or art of projecting lines and planes in isometric, dimetric, trimetric, perspective, and orthographic drawings. In mapmaking, projection is the representation of a plane on the earth's surface; in visual communications, it is the causing of an image to fall on a surface.

projection, overhead *See* OVERHEAD PROJECTION.

projection machine Any mechanical device that throws an image on a surface from transparent or opaque material by utilizing light and lenses.

projection print Print made from a photolithographic negative by projecting the image. An enlarged or reduced matte or glossy print is obtained. The desired size is indicated by (1) placing a strip of masking tape along the controlling dimension of the copy, (2) drawing a line on the tape with arrowheads to show the image width, and (3) noting the size in inches of the reduction or enlargement. A matte or glossy print having the same dimensions as the negative is called a "contact print."

projectural (also called **visual; vu-graph**) Transparent or opaque material from which an image is projected on a screen; also, the image so projected. *See also* OVERHEAD PROJECTION; OVERHEAD TRANSPARENCY.

proof: photography Sample test print made from a negative.

proof press Hand-operated press for running off proofs; also, any press used to produce reproduction proofs.

proof: printing Impression of the type image taken for examination.

proofreader's marks Standard marks that indicate corrections to be made in typeset copy (*see* Figure P-34). They are placed in the margin that is nearer to the word being corrected.

proofreading Reading copy to detect typographical or other errors. Proofreading should be performed by two persons and from the original copy rather than from an intermediate draft copy, such as that used in prejustifying cold-composition copy. If the material to be proofread is manuscript or other typed copy, a typist should not hold and read his or her own typing while proofreading. When two persons proofread copy, one is called the "copyholder" and the other the "proofreader," who uses proofreader's marks to correct any errors. Exceptional alertness is required for good proofreading. The copyholder should speak distinctly and fairly quickly. Slow reading places a burden on the proofreader, whose eyes can follow copy much more quickly than the copy can be read. Reading speed is increased when such abbreviated forms as "semi" for "semicolon" and "super" for "superscript" are used. Words difficult to spell or pronounce should be spelled out.

proofs, progressive Set of proofs of all color plates used separately for one operation and of the plates in combination. Progressive proofs give an indication of color quality and serve as a check against requirements. Registration, tonal values, impression characteristics, and the like are determined before the pressrun.

proportional grid drawing *See* GRID DRAWING, PROPORTIONAL.

proportional spacing (differential letterspacing) Spacing of characters in proportion to size by means of the typewriters and office composing machines used in the preparation of cold-composition copy. The keyboard characters have different values that are measured in units. The letter M, for example, has a unit count of 5 and the letter i a count of 2. Thus, characters are well balanced and spaced in proportion to their respective sizes.

With the attachment of a mechanical device, typewriters equipped with proportional spacing may be used to justify copy. Justifying may also be accomplished manually by subtracting units between words on lines that exceed the line measure and adding units between words on lines that are shorter than the line measure. The variTyper is a proportional-spacing machine that justifies copy automatically after the first typing to establish the line count. The IBM Executive series of typewriters are also proportional-spacing machines. *See also* TYPEWRITER.

	Marginal Marks	Example
Delete; take out	*ℓ*	Draw a diagonal line thus; show/ the symbol in margin.
Left out; insert	*ar*	Use a caret and write in mgin. ∧
Insert a question mark	?	Use a caret. What∧
Insert a colon	⊙:	Use a caret and circle. As follows∧
Insert an exclamation mark	!	Use a caret in text. Write in margin. No∧
Insert an apostrophe	∨	Proofreaders marks. Insert it in margin. ∧
Insert a semicolon	;/	Use a caret in text∧write in margin.
Insert a hyphen	=/	Checkout. Show two parallel lines in mar∧gin.
Delete and close up	*ℓ*	Counter/ clockwise.
Insert en dash	$\frac{1}{n}$	Counterclockwise∧
Insert em dash	$\frac{1}{m}$	Counterclockwise∧
Insert a comma	∧	Use a caret in text∧write in margin.
Insert a period	⊙	Use a caret in text∧ Draw circle around it in margin.
Insert quotation marks	∨⟨⟨ ∨⟩⟩	He said, ∧I will not.∧
Insert brackets	[/]	The result: ∧H2O∧
Insert parentheses	(/)	The result: ∧H2O∧
Stet; let it stand	*stet*	Do not ~~make~~ correction. Place dots under crossed-out word.
Insert space	#	For better∧reading.
Equalize spacing between words	*eq* #	Too ✓many ✓spaces are not good.
Spell out	(*sp*)	The (U. S.) government.
Transpose	*tr*	Writt∧e for a purpose. Or, in order reverse.
Align text or columnar matter	‖	‖43879 76120 34827 63001

Fig. P-34 Proofreader's marks.

	Marginal Marks	Example
Change capital letters to lowercase	*lc*	Do not use C̶A̶P̶S̶.
Change lowercase to capitals	*caps*	Williston, North Dakota
Change to small capital letters	*sc*	Small capital letters.
Use boldface	*bf*	Draw a wavy line under the word. Write in margin.
Use roman letters	*rom*	Use (roman) letters.
Use italic	*ital*	Use italic.
Raise copy; move up	⊓	Use caution in drawing angles.
Lower copy; move down	⊔	Use caution in drawing angles.
Move copy to left	⊏	The word "the" will be moved left to the vertical line.
Move copy to right	⊐	The word "the" will be moved right to the vertical line.
Make a new paragraph	¶	Use the symbol with a caret.⋀This sentence will then begin a new paragraph.
No paragraph	*run in*	Use a line. Connect the sentences.
Insert a superscript	⌄∘	32⋀F.
Insert a subscript	⌃₂	H⋀O
Bad letter; change	X	Circle letter.
Letter is inverted	⊚	Underline and use symbol in mar∂in.
Straighten jumbled type	=	The letters are uneven.
Push space down	⊥	Draw a diagonal/through it; mark in margin.
Indentions	⊡⊡⊡	◻◻◻ This indicates an indention of three ems.
Wrong font; change	*wf*	The letter is not of the same face or size.

proportional wheel Circular scale used to determine proportional reductions and enlargements of copy. It may be made of card stock, plastic, or metal. Linear scales may be used for the same purpose.

Prostar Trade name of the Recordak microfilm processor. *See* MICROFILM PROCESSING.

protective margin *See* APRON.

protractor, orthographic Instrument used to determine the degrees of an isometric ellipse, angle, or plane. The protractor transposes the angle of an orthographic drawing to a like angle on an isometric projection.

pseudoperspective Any deviation from drawing a true isometric image in order to portray the image in perspective to avoid distortion. For example, lines of an assembled view of an engineering item may be foreshortened to produce a lifelike appearance rather than a distorted one as in an isometric projection.

PSM Abbreviation for proportional spacing machine.

public domain Property rights belonging to the public at large because of the loss or lack of patent or copyright protection.

publisher Individual or firm that reproduces for sale to the public books, periodicals, pamphlets, sheet music, maps, and the like. The publisher prints or, more generally, causes to be printed the copies of the work to be sold.

pulsed-xenon arc (film exposure) Specifications for pulsed-xenon arcs, a light source for film exposure work, except in the ultraviolet and blue regions, roughly approximate those for white-flame arcs in color quality. Therefore, the exposure indexes for ortho- and pan-sensitized film will be the same for the two illuminants. The manufacturers of this type of equipment claim that the xenon arc is color-balanced for both color and black-and-white work, maintains constant intensity for the life of the tube, and requires no warm-up period. It has been determined that conventional barrier-layer photoelectric exposure meters do not respond properly to pulsed-xenon illumination. For this reason, the exposure indexes for this illuminant were calculated on the basis of measurements made with a light integrator of a type normally used in the graphic arts industries. On this basis, these values indicate relative speeds only.

punch register Method of punching holes to accomplish close register work. Copy, film, masks, internegatives, and plates are all punched identically, when the elements are used to compose a single job, such that they can be placed on register pins to achieve fast and close register. Any punching device, such as a two-hole or three-hole punch, will serve the purpose.

pyroxylin-coated paper Paper treated with pyroxylin lacquer to make it water-repellent.

QA Abbreviation for "query author," used as a marginal notation to question an author regarding the meaning or accuracy of copy. It is the author's responsibility to check and revise the copy accordingly.

quadrat (usually abbreviated **quad**) Piece of type metal of less than the height of the typeface, used to insert spacing in lines of printed matter. It is measured in ems and ens of the point size of type used. As illustrated in Figure Q-1, an en quad (nut quad) is one-half of the em-quad width, a 3-em space one-third of the width, a 4-em space one-fourth of the width, and so forth.

quarto Book size in which sheets of paper are folded twice to form eight pages.

quartz-iodine lamp (film exposure) Incandescent light of photographic quality with construction consisting of a tungsten filament surrounded by quartz, rather than by a glass envelope. Unlike a conventional incandescent bulb, the envelope contains iodine, which vaporizes as the filament is heated. The principal shortcoming of the old-style tungsten lamp is that it darkens with age. This darkening changes both the color temperature and the intensity of the lamp. In a quartz-iodine tube, however, the tungsten vapor which normally deposits on the glass combines with the iodine and is redeposited on the filament in a continuing cycle when the lamp cools. This action eliminates the troublesome tube blackening and provides a more constant light output.

quire Twenty-four or twenty-five sheets of paper (one-twentieth of a ream) of the same size and quality.

quoin Expandable device used to secure forms in a chase.

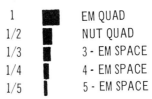

Fig. Q-1 12-point em quad and spaces.

raised printing Printing in which a raised design is produced. *See* EMBOSSING; THERMOGRAPHY.

rapidograph pen *See* PENS, TECHNICAL.

ratchet Toothed wheel installed on the end of a typewriter platen to control vertical spacing. As the carriage return key is operated, a prong engages a tooth on the ratchet, thus moving the platen and paper to the next line of typing. Ratchets may be changed to produce desired spacing between lines. While this is a simple procedure, a repairperson must make the final adjustment because a change of parts is necessary.

rate card Card issued by a publisher showing the insertion rates of display and classified advertising and other pertinent information. It is usually assigned a number, such as Rate Card No. 5, which indicates that four previous rate cards have been superseded. Rate cards may include information on mechanical requirements, contract and copy regulations, finished artwork, bleed pages, inserts, mailing instructions, closing dates, special position of advertisements and cover rates, commissions and discounts, production charges, additional charges, subscription rates, and circulation.

reader (also called **tape interpreter**) Device that operates a linecasting machine such as the Linotype or the Intertype. As the tape runs through the reader, the device senses the code (punched holes in the tape) and automatically translates, or reads, it into mechanical movements. Thus the reader performs the same function as a manually operated keyboard on a linecasting machine.

reader screen Viewing screen for reading enlarged microimages from microforms and microfiches. *See also* MICROFILM READER; READER-PRINTER.

reader-printer Machine that magnifies a microform for reading on a viewing screen and, if necessary, produces an enlarged printout of the image. Light must fall on the microimage or pass through it and be reflected by magnification for the image to become large enough to be read on a viewing screen with the naked eye. A second requirement is that the enlarged image be exposed to a light-sensitive material. The latent image must then be developed by some means, usually a chemical process.

A reader-printer is a form of information storage and retrieval. Using microforms to replace bulky material reduces storage and filing space and facilitates the acquisition and distribution of material needed in research. A reader-printer must (1) produce a readable printout under ordinary room lighting conditions without the necessity for a darkroom, (2) produce a dry or almost dry print instantaneously without recourse to conventional film processing, (3) reflect a readable image on the viewing screen, and (4) be so simple that the operator need have only minimal skill and knowledge. Electrolytic processing, stabilization processing, diffusion transfer, and xerography are several methods used to reproduce the enlarged printout.

reading head Columnar heading in a table under which reading matter appears, as opposed to numbers and dates.

reading type *See* BODY TYPE.

ream Unit of quantity consisting of 500 sheets of fine writing or printing paper or 480 sheets of wrapping or tissue paper.

remainders Books that have been published for which there is no longer a demand and therefore additional printings are not warranted. The book may be "out-of-print" or the publisher may wish to sell the overstock. The books are sold at reduced prices.

reciprocity-law failure Apparent mathematical exception in photography. Whereas 6 times 4 is the same as 12 times 2, photographic materials do not attain the same density from an exposure by a high-intensity light source acting for a short time as from an exposure by a low-intensity light source acting for a longer time even though the product of time and intensity is the same in both cases. For example, when the intensity of the light is doubled, halving the exposure times does not result in exactly the same density. Reciprocity-law failure occurs to some degree in all photographic materials.

record paper *See* LEDGER PAPER.

rectangular grid (profile grid) Grid of lines that are closer together in one direction than in the other. Rectangular grids are used in sketching vertical sections (profiles) for railroads, roads, embankments, subsurface formations, reservoirs, and so forth. Contractors use profile grids to determine grades for sewers, inlets, flumes, aqueducts, and the like.

recto Odd-numbered, right-hand page. The even-numbered, left-hand page is the "verso."

red streak Streak of red ink appearing along the right margin of the front page of some newspapers to indicate a specific edition, such as the final edition, when more than one daily edition is published. Ink is applied with a cylinder wheel mounted on the press. The device has its own ink supply.

reducer Chemical that decreases the density of a photographic image by removing silver halides.

reference marks Symbols used to key text or tabular matter to footnotes. They are *, †, ‡, §, ¶, used in that order.

references Books, articles, or papers cited by the author of a published work. The name of the author of the cited work, the title of the work, the publisher, the place and date of publication, the volume and page or pages from which the material is cited, and any other pertinent information should be given for each reference. References may be listed in the back matter or included in footnotes appearing at the bottom of the pages in which the works are cited. *See also* FOOTNOTE.

reflected light Light that is reflected on an image and is then directed back through the camera lens.

reflection copy Original copy for reproduction that is viewed and must be photographed by light reflected from its surface. Examples are photographs, paintings, dye-transfer prints, and Ektacolor and Kodacolor prints.

reflex copy Copy made by placing a special photosensitive material, emulsion side down, on an original and exposing the original through the back of the material. More light is reflected from the light areas of the original than from the dark areas. *See also* REFLEX EXPOSURE.

reflex exposure Method of making copies from originals by light reflection during exposure. As shown in Figure R-1, the original A is placed facedown on the emulsion side of the sensitized material B. Light rays pass through the underside of the sensitized paper and are reflected by the bright areas (nonimage area) indicated by the letters D and are absorbed by the dark areas (image area) indicated by the letters C. The areas of the sensitized material under the light-absorbing image area remain white during development. When a very thin original is copied by the reflex method, a sheet of white paper should be placed on top of it. This paper will have a tendency to reflect the light where further light is absorbed around the dark areas.

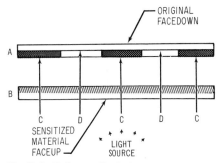

Fig. R-1 Reflex method of exposure.

reflex print Print made by the reflex method during exposure.

register In printing, to align a type page so that it exactly backs the type page on the reverse side of the sheet; to match the position of successive color impressions; also, the alignment of any corresponding elements of an image or impression.

register marks *See* ACETATE OVERLAY.

register motor Optional attachment to a printing press that permits circumferential and lateral register adjustments to be monitored by remote control.

register pins Small pins used to align elements of a single job for close registration such as that for copy, film, masks, plates, and the like. Size of pins should correspond to punched holes for close register.

regular number Number of sheets of 1,000 square inches (6,451 square centimeters) each of a paperboard stock required to make a bundle of 50 pounds (22.7 kg).

relief Raised printing surface such as that used in letterpress or flexographic printing. *See* PRINTING METHODS.

relief printing *See* PRINTING METHODS.

rendering Drawing in which tonal values vary from white through black or from light to dark shades. It may be executed in watercolors, oils, pencil, pen and ink, charcoal, chalk, or airbrush, singly or in combination. A typical rendering is a wash drawing of a house, such as those displayed by real estate firms. For fine reproduction, any drawing with a gradation of tones must be screened for printing as a halftone. *See also* ARCHITECTURAL RENDERING; WASH DRAWING.

rep finish Ribbed paper finish produced during the manufacturing process.

reprint Reprinted version of a publication or book that has already been published. A reprinting differs from a revision in that the revision requires a new copyright notice to protect rights to the added material, whereas a reprinted book does not include new material, and does not call for a new copyright. However, some publishers take the opportunity, before issuing a reprint. to make minor corrections of printer's errors, inaccurate dates, misspellings, and so on. Some publishers use a system of placing numerals on the copyright notice page to identify the number of reprints issued. The numerals are placed in sequence on a line. For the first original printing, the numeral 1 appears. For the next reprinting, the 1 is deleted and the 2 remains, thus indicating the second printing, and so forth through each reprinting. *See also* REVISION.

reproduce To make a copy from an original. When a camera is employed in the copying process, the image may be reduced or enlarged or be produced in the same size as the original.

reproducibility Ability of line or halftone copy to be reproduced as acceptable and legible copy. Firm definitions of black and white produce good copy, but grays and broken lines do not photograph well. Gray, weak, soiled, or broken copy will photograph as seen by the camera and will be reproduced slightly better than as seen by the eye. Modern cameras are of such good quality that a fine, hard pencil line will reproduce almost as well as an inked line. For reproducing text material, a good grade of coated paper with a basis weight of 60 to 80 pounds (27.24 to 36.32 kg) should be used. The paper should be sufficiently translucent so that corrections can be made by mortising over a light table. Reproduction proofs of typeset copy are produced on much lighter stock.

reproducible area Image area on reproducible copy or on a typeset reproduction proof that will appear in final form. Crop and register marks, title blocks, and file numbers are excluded.

reproducible art Second generation of art made from the original art and mortised into or pasted on the basic reproduction page. Original art is generally drawn oversize. Reproducible art consists of a matte or glossy print made from the art negative of the original art and reduced to the size of the area it will occupy on the basic reproduction page. It should remain free from revisions; only the original art should be altered. The term "reproducible art" may also denote art from which a quality image can be obtained. *See also* BOARD ART.

reproduction copy (also called **camera-ready copy**) Typeset copy or copy composed on an office machine, together with line drawings and continuous-tone copy, that is ready in all respects for photomechanical reproduction. When copy is typeset, the printer refers to it as "etch proofs" or "reproduction proofs." Reproduction copy may also be called "black and white" when continuous-tone copy is not included.

A page of copy is called a "basic reproduction page." Each such page is photographed by the process camera, and a right-reading photolithographic negative is produced. The image is translucent, but the rest of the negative is black and therefore opaque. For printing, the negative is stripped in position on ruled orange-colored masking paper called a "goldenrod flat." The flat is then placed in a vacuum frame in front of a sensitized plate and the image "burned" into the plate with a strong arc light. After processing, the plate is attached to the press for printing. Reproduction copy may be oversize or of actual page size. Figure R-2 shows an assembly of reproduction copy ready for the camera. Note that the small line art has been mortised or pasted in position on the basic reproduction page. It will be photographed with the text material on the

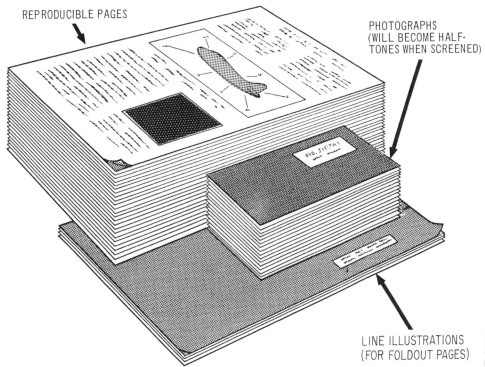

REPRODUCIBLE PAGES

PHOTOGRAPHS
(WILL BECOME HALF-
TONES WHEN SCREENED)

LINE ILLUSTRATIONS
(FOR FOLDOUT PAGES)

**Fig. R-2
Reproduction copy
assembled as a
publication.**

page because the text also is line copy. Note also the black patch on the page. The area that the black patch occupies will be occupied on the page negative by one of the photographs keyed to it after the photograph has been screened and stripped into the negative. The large line illustrations, of course, are too large to be mortised into the basic reproduction page. They will become separate pages with their own page numbers.

The reproducible pages shown may be of the same size as those produced by letterpress printing, or they may be oversize when composed on a cold-composition machine. In the latter case, each page will be reduced to page size; for an 8½ by 11-inch (21.6 by 28-cm) publication, the image width will be reduced to 7 inches (17.8 cm). The letterpress copy requires no reduction, as the copy is set in actual type size. The photograph will be screened for halftone reproduction and reduced to the exact proportions of the area covered by the black patch. The halftone negative is then stripped into position in the negative on the basic reproduction page.

Nomenclature should be of relatively the same size on all art in a given publication. It must be large enough so that when it has been reduced, it will be legible, comparable in size to the nomenclature of other art in the publication, and of good appearance. Reductions of the art for normal reproduction pages and of the large line art are not the same. Therefore, care must be taken that marginal data such as the page-content heading, page number, and illustrations title for large line art are consistent in size with marginal data in other pages of the publication. The practice is to type or typeset all such data on a separate sheet of paper of the same quality and texture as that of the other pages. Following instructions, the photographer will reduce the marginal data to the same size as that on other pages. From this negative, the data will be stripped into the negative of the large line illustration.

reproduction flow   Processes and steps taken in producing and reproducing an image on a material. Various methods are used depending upon what is expected of the end item. The following fundamental points and characteristics should be taken into consideration:

1. An enlargement or a reduction can be made only when a camera lens is used.

2. When light is employed to penetrate sensitized copy paper during exposure, the original must be on a translucent or transparent material for whiteprinting.

3. A camera lens can photograph any object seen by the eye.

4. An intermediate is a copy on paper, cloth, or film of the original from which additional copies are made.

5. A negative may be right-reading or wrong-reading.

6. There are only two kinds of copy, line and continuous-tone.

7. In direct, or contact, printing the original is in direct contact with the copy paper, cloth, or film during exposure. Therefore the copy will be of the same size as the original.

8. Continuous-tone copy requires screening, whereas line copy does not.

9. The image can be on translucent, transparent, or opaque material.

10. The image is either right-reading or wrong-reading.

reproduction master Any master used to make copies by the whiteprint or other copy processes. The typesetter refers to the set copy as "reproduction proofs," "etch proofs," or "black and whites." All three terms denote copy that is to be printed by some method. The term "reproduction proofs" is the most common. Copies (usually two or three are furnished) are run off on a proof press. The typesetter has the copy set on a linecasting or Monotype machine (some large type may be set by hand) on a good-quality coated stock, which may be coated on one side only. Paper weights vary from 45 to 70 pounds (20.4 to 31.8 kg), the lighter papers being more popular. A hard coated stock gives high-fidelity reproduction because the typeface makes a solid impression with good serif definition.

Reproduction paper for cold-composition copy, which is prepared by office composing machines, should be chosen not only for its image-accepting characteristics but for its erasing and mortising qualities. This stock should be coated and have a glossy finish. It should be surface-sized, that is, coated with a gelatin (animal) or starch (mineral) sizing. Gelatin sizing is desirable when erasing qualities are being considered. It is obvious that when a sized surface receives a typed image, the image is produced on the sizing because the paper is serving merely as a base. When the sizing is removed by erasing, the image is also removed. A surface-sized paper can be detected by scraping it with a knife. If the residue is fine and powdery, the paper will have good erasing qualities. If the residue is coarse and fibrous, wood sulfite and starch are evident and the paper will erase poorly.

A paper should not be used for reproduction typing unless it has been surface-sized. Some papers with a high gloss or a semigloss give the illusion of good reproduction tendencies. These papers, however, possess a glossy finish merely because they have been supercalendered by being passed many times through the calender rolls of the papermaking machine.

reproduction photostat (abbreviated **reprostat**) High-quality glossy Photostat used for reproduction.

reproduction proof (etch proof; black and white) Letterpress copy, composed either by machine or by hand, that is subsequently photographed for platemaking and printing by the photo-offset or gravure processes. It is not a proof in the sense that an advance copy is printed for inspection and approval before the pressrun. Copy composed on an office composing machine is not a reproduction proof but is termed "reproduction copy."

reproduction typing Production by a typist of composition copy that is ultimately printed. Technical reports, proposals, manuals, brochures, and house organs are among the kinds of publications that the reproduction typist may be called upon to type. The degree of skill required varies from simple typing to complete production, including typing prejustified and justified copy, proofreading, sizing and proportioning art and nomenclature, window masking for halftones, mortising, stripping, ruling, and page layout. Very few reproduction typists can accomplish all these tasks. These are, however, occupational skills for which a strong demand exists and which must be acquired on the job.

reprographics Branch of the graphic arts that is concerned with the reproduction of images and especially with copying machines and their methods and processes.

reprostat Abbreviation for reproduction Photostat.

resist Enameled or bichromated coating that remains on a relief or offset plate after "burning" in and development and protects the printing area from the acid etch.

resolution In computer graphics, the fineness of detail in a reproduced spatial pattern, expressed in points per inch or points per millimeter.

resolving power Ability of a photographic emulsion or lens to record fine detail, usually expressed in lines per millimeter.

retarder Mechanical device attached to a sheet-fed printing press to stop a sheet of paper and knock it down so that the next sheet falls into place in the stack.

reticulation Molecular conversion of a gelatin emulsion into a fine pattern of lines caused by changes in temperature between solutions. *See also* PHOTOGELATIN PROCESS.

retouch To delete unwanted printing or marks on reproducible copy, masters, negatives, or the like by painting out with an opaque solution of any kind. Also, to repair or emphasize certain details of a photograph or other piece of artwork.

reversal generation Reproduction in which the original image has been reversed by a negative-working process.

reverse blueline (also called **white on black; whiteline print**) Copy made from a photolithographic negative by running the negative through the whiteprint machine. During exposure, light penetrates the translucent image of the negative but cannot penetrate the opaque background. A white image is therefore produced on a black or dark blue background. Reverse bluelines of illustrations are excellent for check-out and approval before printing, and they are also useful as reference copies. An 8 by 10-inch (20.3 by 25.4-cm) negative should be specified for an illustration. The negative is placed over the copy paper so as to preserve white space for binding and identification.

reverse plate Plate on which line copy is reversed, the image being white and the background black. Reverse plates are common with logotypes and imprints.

reverse-reading (negative-reading; wrong-reading) Designating text material or copy that reads backward. It is the opposite of "right-reading."

reverse-reading intermediate Image imposed on a translucent material that offers greater contrast on the opposite side of the sheet when the sheet is held for right reading. When extra-thin and thin paper or film intermediates are used, a more clearly defined image is obtained by reversing the master so that the dense side of the image on the master is in direct contact with the copy paper or film. Figure R-3*A* is grossly exaggerated to show the master placed on the paper or film faceup. View *B* shows the master in reverse with the image facedown. The better contact thus produced between image and copy paper or film results in high-fidelity reproduction. Prints made from reverse-reading intermediates are, of course, right-reading. Pencil or ink revisions are made easily on these intermediates.

revision New edition of a publication or published work containing revisions. Textbooks, handbooks, and reference, professional, and technical books are of the type that require revision. Before a publication is revised, however, the publisher must decide (1) whether the book is successful enough to warrant a revision, and (2) what is to be the extent of the revision. The typical revision cycle for a textbook is every five years, but this is not always a hard-and-fast rule. Some books may be revised in their second or third year of publication, depending on market conditions, competition, and changes in fact, philosophy, or technology that call for new content. Other successful books may not require revision until they have been on the market six, or even seven, years. Generally the publisher's editor will know within two years after publication whether the book warrants a revision. The extent of a revision will vary greatly from one book to another. For some books the subject matter will change very little from year to year and revision is minimal. Other books will require a very heavy revision because of advances in the subject area or its technology or changes in teaching methods. The publication of competitive texts may even force an author to completely rewrite a book. *See also* REPRINT.

rewinder Device on a web-fed printing press that rewinds the printed web when sheeting and folding are not required.

ribbon copy Copy made with a typewriter or other machine in which keys are struck against a ribbon to form the impression. The ribbon may be of paper or of fabric.

ribbons, typewriter There are two kinds of typewriter ribbons, fabric and paper ribbons. The fabric ribbons, which are those commonly used in ordinary typewriters, may be made of cotton, silk, or nylon. All are preinked and are used repeatedly until the ink wears off. The highly absorbent cotton fabric ribbon retains a good ink content. The silk ribbon, which has excellent tensile strength and resists blows, produces the sharpest image of the fabric ribbons. The nylon ribbon produces a sharp, strong image and resists abrasion. Paper ribbons resemble carbon paper;

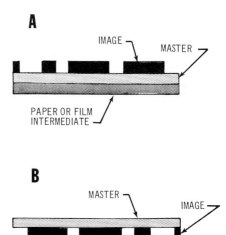

Fig. R-3 Exposure method of making reverse-reading intermediates.

they are used once and then discarded. The acetate paper ribbon, which has a high-quality coat of carbon, produces an exceptionally sharp black image and is used for reproduction copy. Some carbon paper ribbons are manufactured especially for typing on vellum. While the image is not so sharply defined as that on coated stock, the carbon produces a dense image for whiteprint production.

rider Provision added to and made part of a document such as an insurance policy.

rider roller Cylinder, such as an inking roller in a printing press, that rotates by friction with another roller instead of meshing gears directly with a driving force. In a web printing press, the rider roller is referred to as a "dancer roll." It rides on the paper roll between the latter and the metering unit to take up slack and to keep the paper under a uniform tension. The rider roller is interlocked with a brake to control paper unwinding.

right-angle fold *See* CHOPPER FOLD.

right-hand page *See* PAGE NUMBERING.

right-reading (positive-reading) Designating text material or copy that reads in normal fashion. It is the opposite of reverse-reading.

ripple finish Paper finish with a wavy appearance. It is produced by embossing or by using a plater, a calender in the papermaking machine.

river Effect of open space or a stream of "air" running through a type mass, caused by excessive spacing between words. A river may be detected by scanning the length of a page with the eyes slightly squinted.

roll-size drawings Large engineering drawings that, because of their length, are filed in rolls and do not usually have a printed format.

roll stand In a web-fed printing press, the frame that supports the web (paper roll) as the web unwinds and feeds into the press. *See also* AUXIL-IARY ROLL STAND.

roll-up Used in press work, this term refers to the preparatory checks taken of first impressions while inking the plate on the press. Checks should be made independent of the previous pressrun. Considerations such as proper register, solution balance, ink density, image distortion, oper-ating pressures, and paper or stock receptivity are taken into account.

rolled art Artwork that can be rolled, but particularly large technical or engineering drawings such as electrical, piping, wiring, hydraulic, and pneumatic schematics. When nomenclature is applied to art that will be rolled or a configuration is to be altered on the art by paste-up, an opaque thick substance (sticky back) should never be used to apply nomenclature or changes. The affixed copy will not adhere to the surface of the stock completely when the artwork is rolled and it will require constant patching. Further, when copies are produced such as with a whiteprint machine, the copy has a tendency to come off because of heat exposure during development. In addition, if the art is on a translucent or transparent material, exposure is inhibited. Instead, use a thin, transparent material manufactured especially for this purpose.

roman numerals Numerals i, ii, iii, iv, or I, II, III, IV, etc., as distinguished from arabic numerals. Lowercase roman numerals are used to number front-matter pages. Uppercase roman numerals may be used for numbering chapters, parts, and sections.

ROP Abbreviation for run-of-press, a term used to describe the colored inks available as "standard" for a newspaper publisher.

rotary press Printing press in which the printing material is locked on a rotating cylinder. The material must therefore be on a curved plate, either an electrotype or a stereotype. Presses of this type produce either one-color or multicolored work with fine register and speed. In a sheet-fed rotary press, the paper is fed from a pile, printed, and delivered in a pile. In contrast, a web perfecting rotary press prints from a continuous roll of paper called a web, which is printed and folded as a unit. A newspaper is an example of work produced on this type of rotary press. Units may be added to some rotary presses to increase their capacity. Single presses combined with additional units are called "quadruple," "sextuple," etc., an octuple press being composed of four units. *See also* WEB OFFSET PRINTING.

rotogravure Print made by intaglio printing on a rotary press; also, the intaglio rotary printing process. *See also* PRINTING METHODS.

rotogravure paper Book paper manufactured especially for intaglio (gravure) printing. It has an English finish and is supercalendered to produce a smooth, even surface on both sides of the sheet. Rotogravure paper is used for magazines, catalogs, advertising pieces, labels, etc. Basis weights are 35, 40, and 45 pounds (15.9, 18.1, and 20.4 kg) for 500 sheets of the basic size of 25 by 38 inches (63.5 by 96.6 cm).

rough (or visual) Page sketch of actual page size that accurately portrays space allocated for copy, line art, photographs, headings, text copy, and the like with the elements featured; used primarily in advertising.

rough draft Text material that requires editing and possibly reworking before it becomes a final draft.

routing Cutting away nonprinting surfaces of a plate with a machine; also, removing unwanted background in a metal form or wooden block by drilling or gouging.

royal Paper size measuring 19 by 24 inches (48.2 by 61 cm).

royalty Compensation paid for the use of property; hence, in publishing, an author's share of the profits from the sale of copies of his or her work.

rub-ons Transfer sheets of clear acetate paper containing reprinted characters, symbols, numerals, and the like, that are applied by a dry-transfer method of burnishing. The character or symbol is placed over the desired position on the drawing surface and is transferred by burnishing. This dry-transfer method differs from applying wax-backed characters or symbols in that it is not necessary to cut and paste the characters in place. An excellent application for this method is preparing copy in which equations and Greek letters predominate. Another example is using transfer lettering in preparing overhead transparencies for overhead projection. The method is fast, economical, and accurate. *See also* TRANSFER SHEET.

rubbing Impression taken from a stone inscription. While inscriptions cut in stone cannot be considered printing, reproductions from such inscriptions are deemed to have led directly to making books by means of inked impressions from wood and, from that method, to printing from movable type. The earliest-known dated rubbing is from the T'ang dynasty of China. Found at Tunhuang by Paul Pelliot, it bears a date equivalent to 653–654.

The rubbing process is as follows: A piece of felt is laid on the stone inscription, and a thin, tough, moistened sheet of paper is applied to the felt. The paper, with the felt behind it, is then hammered with a mallet and rubbed with a brush until it fits every depression and crevice of the stone. As soon as the paper is dry, a stuffed pad of silk or cotton is dipped in sized ink and passed lightly and evenly over it. When the paper is finally peeled off, it bears a durable impression of the inscription, which appears in white on a black background.

rubometer (or **rub tester**) Instrument used for the measurement of rub or scuff resistance of a printed surface.

Rubylith (Ulano) Red light-safe masking and stripping film coated on a polyester backing sheet. *See* MASKING AND STRIPPING MATERIALS.

rule In letterpress printing, a strip of metal that prints a line. Rules are measured in points. *See* Figure R-4.

run *See* PRESSRUN.

run in Notation to set copy in the same paragraph although a break is shown. A line is drawn from the last word of the sentence before the break to the first word of the following sentence.

run-in heading Heading appearing on the same line with the text that follows it.

run-of-press Designating color work offered by a publisher, such as one who publishes a trade journal. The color work is regularly offered and

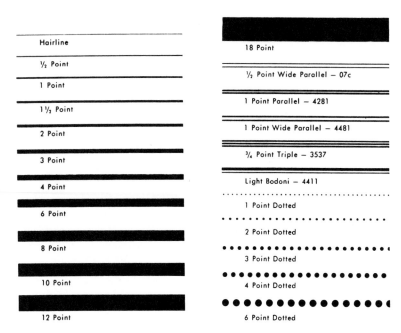

Hairline

½ Point

1 Point

1½ Point

2 Point

3 Point

4 Point

6 Point

8 Point

10 Point

12 Point

18 Point

½ Point Wide Parallel — 07c

1 Point Parallel — 4281

1 Point Wide Parallel — 4481

¾ Point Triple — 3537

Light Bodoni — 4411

1 Point Dotted

2 Point Dotted

3 Point Dotted

4 Point Dotted

6 Point Dotted

printed as stock-in-trade. The term is also applied to multicolored printing in newspapers during high-speed pressruns.

run ragged To be uneven, or unjustified. The right margin in typewritten text is not justified.

runaround Arrangement of text copy around an illustration of less than column or page width. A right runaround places the text copy to the right of the illustration; a left runaround, to the left. The use of runarounds often involves resetting text to a shorter measure after the position of a publication. Examples are a security classification and a company logotype or address.

running head Heading that runs across the top of a page, giving the title of the publication or the chapter title. *See also* PAGE-CONTENT HEADING.

running register Device which enables circumferential or side register adjustments of the printing plate from a remote control console while the press is operating.

running text *See* STRAIGHT MATTER.

saddle stitching (sometimes called **saddle-wire stitching**) Method of mechanical binding that permits a book or magazine to be opened to its full extent. The book or magazine is opened to the center spread and wire-stapled or cord-stitched through the saddle in two or three places. *Newsweek* and *Business Week*, for example, are both saddle-wired. *See also* BINDING, MECHANICAL.

safelight In photomechanics, a filtered darkroom lamp that will not affect photographic material in a reasonable length of time. Different photographic materials require different safelight filters.

safety paper Sensitized paper on which it is impossible to erase or make changes without detection.

sans serif Without serifs, said of a letter that does not have a finishing stroke or line projecting from the end of the main stroke. Modern gothic faces are typical of typefaces without serifs. Figure S-1 compares gothic sans-serif type and a face with serifs.

satin finish Smooth paper finish that resembles satin.

satin white Coating mixture for quality coated and enameled papers, consisting of calcium sulfate and aluminum hydroxide.

scale drawing Drawing such as a map, profile, or plan that shows relative sizes and proportions.

scale: engineering drawings When practicable, engineering drawings should show an object or an assembly in full size. If a full-size view is not practicable, drawings may be made to reduced or enlarged scales. An enlarged scale is used when an object is so small that full-size representation will not clearly show its features. A reduced scale is employed to facilitate presentation of an object or an arrangement of such size that it exceeds the drawing space available, but such a scale should be used only if clarity can be maintained. In the selection of a reduced scale it may also be necessary to consider the degree of reduction contemplated in making a reproduction. Wherever practicable, detail drawings should be prepared to the same scale as the pertinent subassembly and assembly drawings, but this is not mandatory.

Three methods may be used in preparing drawings to scale: the fractional method (engineering), the equation method (engineering and architectural), and the graphic method. The first expresses, in the form of a common fraction, the ratio of the size of the object drawn to its true scale. This method is used on drawings for which the equation method is not appropriate. The scales commonly used are full size ($\frac{1}{1}$), enlarged ($\frac{10}{1}$, $\frac{4}{1}$, $\frac{2}{1}$), and reduced ($\frac{1}{2}$, $\frac{1}{4}$, $\frac{1}{10}$, $\frac{1}{20}$, $\frac{1}{30}$, $\frac{1}{40}$, $\frac{1}{50}$, $\frac{1}{60}$, $\frac{1}{100}$).

The equation method expresses, in the form of an equation, the relationship of the size of the object drawn to its true dimensions. This method is

Gothics

SANS SERIF

Modern

WITH SERIFS

Fig. S-1 Sans-serif typeface and typeface with serifs.

generally used on drawings where dimensions are expressed in feet and inches. The scales most commonly used are as follows:

Full size	Reduced	Enlarged
12 in. = 1 ft 0 in.	⅛ in. = 1 ft 0 in.	24 in. = 1 ft 0 in.
(30.4 cm–30.5 cm 0 cm)	(0.317 cm–30.5 cm 0 cm)	(61 cm–30.5 cm 0 cm)
	¼ in. = 1 ft 0 in.	48 in. = 1 ft 0 in
	(0.634 cm–30.5 cm 0 cm)	(122 cm–30.5 cm 0 cm)
	⅜ in. = 1 ft 0 in.	
	(0.951 cm–30.5 cm 0 cm)	
	½ in. = 1 ft 0 in.	
	(1.27 cm–30.5 cm 0 cm)	
	¾ in. = 1 ft 0 in.	
	(1.902 cm–30.5 cm 0 cm)	
	1 in. = 1 ft 0 in.	
	(2.54 cm–30.5 cm 0 cm)	
	1½ in. = 1 ft 0 in.	
	(3.81 cm–30.5 cm 0 cm)	
	3 in. = 1 ft 0 in.	
	(7.62 cm–30.5 cm 0 cm)	
	6 in. = 1 ft 0 in.	
	(15.2 cm–30.5 cm 0 cm)	
	1 in. = 10 ft 0 in.	
	(2.54 cm–3.05 m 0 cm)	
	1 in. = 20 ft 0 in.	
	(2.54 cm–61 m 0 cm)	
	1 in. = 30 ft 0 in.	
	(2.54 cm–9 m 0 cm)	

In the graphic method, an actual measuring scale is shown on the drawing. This scale permits the approximate dimensions of the object in an enlarged or reduced reproduction to be determined.

scaling (dimensioning; sizing) Determining the proper dimensions for an image that is to be reduced or enlarged to occupy a given area when printed. In order to delineate fine details, most art is drawn in a size larger than the final reproduction or page size. Oversize art may be drawn once and a half up, twice up, or larger. The oversize measurements are determined from the final page size. If the final page size is 42 picas, or 7 inches (17.7 cm), wide and the art is to be drawn once and a half up, the width of the oversize art is 10½ inches (26.7 cm). Twice-up art would have a width of 14 inches (35.5 cm). If the art is to be boxed, a small area around the image is defined by crop marks for this purpose. The lines of the box are drawn on the basic reproduction page after the art has been pasted or mortised in position rather than on the art itself.

Only two dimensions are considered in art: the width, or horizontal dimension, and the height, or vertical dimension. The width should always be stated first. The controlling dimension for scaling art may be either the width or the height, but in most cases it is the width. When a rectangle must be enlarged or reduced to fit a given area, the width and height must be enlarged or reduced in proportion to that area. If the oversize height of the art comes within the limits of the required size, the width is the controlling dimension. If the oversize height of the art is out of proportion to the area the width must occupy, then the height is the controlling dimension.

Several systems are used to determine the proportions to which a rectangle can be reduced or enlarged. Proportional wheels and slide rules are commonly employed. A simple formula may also be used. For example, if a piece of art 14 inches (35.5 cm) wide and 20 inches (50.8 cm) high must be reduced to a page width of 7 inches (17.7 cm), three dimensions are known and the fourth, the height of the reduced art, must be found. Since 14 inches (35.6 cm) is to 20 inches (50.8 cm) as 7 inches (17.7 cm) is to X, $14X = 140$, or $X = 10$; ($35.6X = 355.6$, or $X = 25.4$ cm).

Figure S-2 illustrates another method of scaling art.

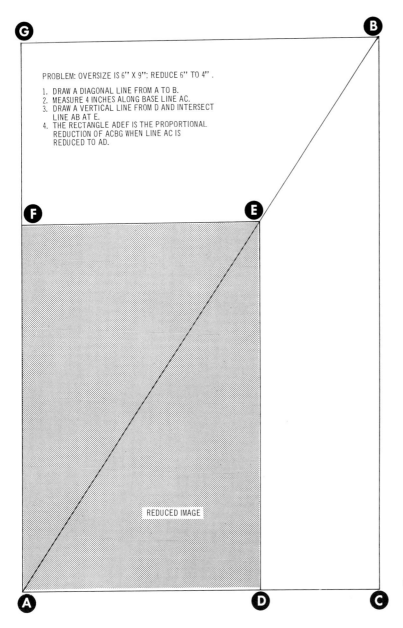

PROBLEM: OVERSIZE IS 6" X 9"; REDUCE 6" TO 4".

1. DRAW A DIAGONAL LINE FROM A TO B.
2. MEASURE 4 INCHES ALONG BASE LINE AC.
3. DRAW A VERTICAL LINE FROM D AND INTERSECT LINE AB AT E.
4. THE RECTANGLE ADEF IS THE PROPORTIONAL REDUCTION OF ACBG WHEN LINE AC IS REDUCED TO AD.

REDUCED IMAGE

Fig. S-2 Scaling art.

In technical illustrating, scaling is drawing an object in proportion to the area it will occupy without either congestion or excessive open space. Figure S-3 is out of proportion for the object illustrated. The object should be larger, and there should be less emphasis on the hand that is holding it. Only a sufficient portion of the hand to identify it as such is necessary. The object should always predominate.

scanning engraver Automatic mechanical photoengraver that scans continuous-tone and line art, both horizontally and vertically, while activating a stylus that engraves halftone dots and lines on a plate. See also ENGRAVING, ELECTRONIC.

schematic Drawing that shows the layout of a system. It may be a pneumatic or hydraulic flow diagram that shows the relationship and flow between components in the system. Schematics are classed as electrical, pneumatic, plumbing, hydraulic, and the like. See also FLOW DIAGRAM.

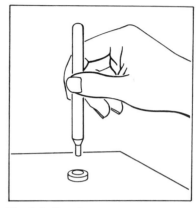

Fig. S-3 Drawing an object to scale.

schoolbook perforating See PERFORATING, SCHOOLBOOK.

scissors editing Cutting out unwanted copy. Scissors editing is particularly adaptable to the whiteprint process, in which light penetrates a translucent or transparent master, leaving a white background. Light will penetrate the cutout portion of the master as well as any translucent or transparent area. The cutout portion should terminate with the apex or a V pointing toward the edge of the master that enters the whiteprint machine first. This precaution avoids fouling the master and copy paper between the rollers in the machine. Cutting across lines that have already been cut should be avoided, as should ragged edges. Depending on the size of the master and the capacity of the machine, it is sometimes possible to run the original through the machine so as to accommodate large cutouts.

scoring Making a partial cut in stock to facilitate folding. Cartons and boxes for display are scored.

scotch print Dimensionally stable proofing material used frequently to convert letterpress forms to film.

scratchboard Type of illustration drawing board that has a chalky surface over which ink is spread as required and then scratched off to show detail and highlight effects of the object. The technique presents an attractive, meticulously detailed, black-and-white drawing. The board is relatively nonabsorbent, smooth, hard, and somewhat brittle. The board is first brush-painted with ink, and the object is traced on the dried-ink surface. Scratching tools such as multiple-point scoring tools, pointed knives, and styli are used to form the image. Brushes and pens are used extensively. The scratchboard technique is excellent for pictorials in which eye appeal and sharp emphasis are desired.

Screen-process film Du Pont camera-speed stencil film. It has an orthochromatic emulsion on a stable supporting base. After the processed emulsion has adhered firmly to the silk screen, the base is stripped away, leaving the emulsion on the silk as the actual stencil for screen printing.

screen-process printing Form of stencil printing that utilizes a silk, nylon, or metal screen containing the image. A squeegee implement forces the ink through the screen to form the image on paper or other material. Early screens were made by painting the image on silk with a fluid resistant to ink. Masking materials were used to block out unwanted printing areas. Hand-cut stencils and photomechanical means may both be used in screen-process work. One technique involves coating the material with a light-sensitive emulsion. Exposure is made through a photographic film positive placed in contact with the screen. The surface of the screen is hardened in proportion to the degree of penetration of light; the hardened areas are then made insoluble to water, but the image is made soluble.

Thick deposits of ink compounds and paint make a wide variety of printing possible. Fabrics, plastics, metal, heavy card stock, and paper are only a few of the materials that are receptive to the screen process.

It is difficult to ascribe the birth of the screen printing process to any one individual. There is evidence, however, that crude stencil processes were used both in the United States and England during the first decade of this century. Reports also indicate that stencils were used in ancient China as well as by the early Egyptians. The ancient Japanese, however, were the first to combine a stencil with a screen that was the beginning of the "silk" screen process, now known in the industry as screen printing or screen-process printing because screens are now composed of materials other than silk. The Japanese used two pieces of paper which served as the combined stencil, cutting the image through on both pieces of paper. Strands of silk or hair were sandwiched in both directions between the papers to form the screen.

Because of the great versatility of this process and because of the demand from new markets producing such products as plastic containers and sheets, outdoor advertising, textiles, wallpapers, nameplates, glass, printed circuits, many different kinds of signs, and materials not conducive to other printing methods, screen printing technology has advanced to where it has had an annual growth rate of approximately 17 percent. No other branch of the printing industry offers such a wide variety of skills as does screen printing; there are close to 40 administrative and production jobs found in the various plants that can be culled from the many specialized and varied functions.

Figure S-4 shows the Aladdin cylinder screen printing press designed for printing on all weights of paper, decals, foil, vinyls, display and corrugated board, hardboard, light-gage metals, and the like. The press prints with all types of inks, lacquers, enamels, and adhesives that can be screened, with speeds of the press up to 2,000 impressions per hour. The squeegee prints over the cylinder for fine-line contact printing, and squeegee pressure is adjustable while the press is operating. The screen area is accessible from top or bottom for touch-up or wipe-up. Four clamps hold the screen firmly in place against register stops. The press can be adjusted for off-contact printing, and it uses an ordinary or adjustable screen chase as desired. Optional features include a standard take-off

Fig. S-4 Aladdin cylinder screen printing press. (*Lawson Printing and Drying Machine Company.*)

conveyor, electric brake for accurate stopping, both a plastic and neo-prene squeegee, a split-fountain ink device, and an adjustable stroke for preset screen travel. Other optional extra features include a vacuum cylinder for light stock, electrostatic eliminators, a setup board for pre-register, a jack shaft take-off for wicket drive, and a vacuum-type (tapes) delivery conveyor. While the printing area size of the Aladdin shown in the illustration is 35 by 46 inches (90 by 117 cm), other Aladdin presses are available that have printing area sizes of 24 by 34, 30 by 45, 38 by 50, and 45 by 65 inches (61 by 86.3, 76.2 by 114.3, 97 by 127, and 114.3 by 165.1 cm). In addition, an Aladdin Jr. is available in printing area sizes of 13 by 20, 14 by 24, and 16 by 24 inches (33 by 50.8, 36 by 61, and 40.6 by 61 cm).

The Genie Mark VI, shown in Figure S-5, is a mobile, floor-model flatbed printing press that prints on all screenable materials from 0.001 inch

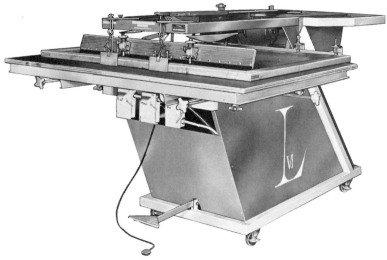

Fig. S-5 Genie Mark VI flatbed screen printing press. (*Lawson Printing and Drying Machine Company.*)

(0.025 mm) to 1 inch (2.54 cm) thick. (The average thickness accepted is ¾ inch [1.902 cm]). The press can print one image at a time or adjust to variable speeds up to 1,000 impressions per hour. The press has an average ratio of 4 times open to 1 of print time with accurate registration of maximum speeds. Because the press is open on three sides, printing can be accomplished with rolled stock or feed-through of such items as jar caps and game boards (wood or plastic); jigs are available for printing small objects such as ash trays, lids, circuit boards, and the like. Two motors operate the press. One motor raises and lowers the screen, and the other motor operates the squeegee. Each motor can be adjusted individually for speed, allowing for a variety of adjustments for open time and squeegee travel. The Genie Mark VI press is available in as many as nine sizes having printing areas from 16 by 22 inches (40.6 by 56 cm) to 52 by 80 inches (132 by 203 cm) in sizes.

Figure S-6 shows the Lawson Mini portable/bench screen printing press; it weighs 40 pounds (18.16 kg) and is 36 inches (91.4 cm) in length. The press prints most screenable materials and prints up to a 2-inch (5.08-cm)

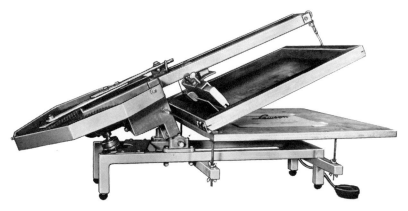

Fig. S-6 Lawson Mini portable/bench screen printing press. (*Lawson Printing and Drying Machine Company*.)

thickness that is adjustable by using wing nuts. The print size is 8 by 10 inches (20.3 by 25.4 cm). The squeegee adjusts for angle, pressure, length of stroke and position, and the assembly includes a precoating (doctor) blade and a ³⁄₁₆ by ¾-inch (0.477 by 1.902-cm) polyurethane blade. The bed adjusts to a height of 2 inches (5.08 cm), enabling wide acceptance of various materials.

The Imp flatbed screen printing press (Figure S-7) has the capability of printing on all screenable materials from thicknesses of 0.001 inch (0.025 mm) up to 4 inches (10.6 cm). The press prints with all proper paints, inks, resists, adhesives, and the like and is designed for adaptation to conveyorized or turntable operation. Speeds are adjustable up to 1,450 impressions per hour. Print sizes for the Imp press are 8½ by 11, 11 by 14, 13 by 20, and 15 by 15 inches (21.6 by 28, 28 by 36, 33 by 50.8 and 38.1 by 38.1 cm). The squeegee is adjustable for angle, pressure, length of stroke, and position. The following optional equipment is available: a vacuum table with high-volume pump, a table that is adjustable to micrometers, a bed-high adjustment from 0 to 4 inches (10.16 cm), a delay time dweller, a print counter, a bottle printer attachment, frame, and the like.

Fig. S-7 Lawson Imp flatbed screen printing press. (*Lawson Printing and Drying Machine Company.*)

The Argon Speed-O-Mat automatic screen printing press is shown in Figure S-8. The press is capable of printing on both rigid and flexible sheets of most thicknesses, regardless of weight, with variable speed control from 500 impressions per hour to a maximum press output of up to 2,000 sheets. Four models of the press are available, designated according to the maximum printing area of each as 20 by 30, 30 by 40, 40 by 55, and 47¼ by 64 inches (50.8 by 76.2, 76.2 by 101.6, 101,6 by 140, and 121 by 163 cm). Some features of the Speed-O-Mat include micro-adjustment of off contact, multiple micro squeegee pressure adjustment knobs, squeegee angle adjustment, fast removal of squeegee and flood bar assembly, accessibility of bottom of screen by means of a finger control for lifting of

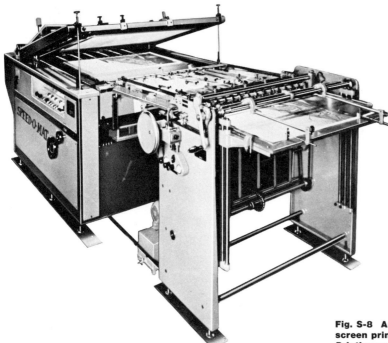

Fig. S-8 Argon Speed-O-Mat automatic screen printing press. (*Cincinnati Printing and Drying Systems, Inc.*)

screen and frame assembly, an adjustable device that peels the mesh with selected mechanical precision during each printing stroke, automatic low-torque acceleration start-up speed control, a no-sheet detector that prevents the squeegee from printing if there is no sheet on the printing bed, and fittings for the addition of antistatic bar (optional) directly to the squeegee carriage. An important feature of the press is that all operations of the press, including the gripper travel, are controlled by one cam shaft driven by a gear motor which is coupled to the shaft. This ensures positive synchronization between the grippers, the screen, and other moving parts of the machine. The danger of phase difference exists in screen printing machines when the grippers, which move at high speed under the screen, are operated by a driving gear different from that which controls the raising and lowering of the screen and other movements of the press. A control center contains the start-and-stop control of the progressive vacuum printing bed, the feeder, squeegee and flood bar, lift control for screen cleaning, manual operation of a handwheel (used for setup), speed adjustment control, and an impressions per hour indicator and resetable sheet counter.

Figure S-9 shows the Argon Compact semi-automatic screen printing press. The press is available in six models, Models 0, 1, 2, 35, 3, and 4, with maximum printing areas, respectively, of 15⅜ by 20, 20 by 30, 30 by 40, 35 by 45, 41 by 61, and 49½ by 65 inches (39 by 50.8, 50.8 by 76.2, 76.2 by 101.6, 89 by 114.3, 104.3 by 155, and 126 by 165 cm). Printing impressions per hour vary from 600 to 1,200 depending upon the model; maximum stock thickness is 1 inch (2.54 cm) for all models. The Compact series are semi-automatic, electro-pneumatically powered, and designed to print on flat rigid or flexible materials. The presses feature a suction blower system that employs a foot-operated prevacuum control to hold sheets in position prior to printing, and a postvacuum control for holding sheets after printing is mounted on a control panel. This control is useful when printing items such as pressure-sensitive plastic sheeting and rigid plastics that tend to warp or adhere to the bottom of the screen because of excessive static. Speed of the squeegee, from minimum to maximum, is easily adjusted according to the requirement of the type of prints such as halftone or fine-line reverses. The squeegee is driven by a square shaft dual-chain system that gives a uniform running speed, even at very low print stroke speed. Squeegee angle is adjustable from 62° to 80° for additional control of print quality. The return, or flood-stroke speed, is also adjustable, allowing a uniform and variable coating on the return or flood coat. Squeegee and flood bar carriage are easily removable for fast washing of the entire system. A special screen-cleaning control switch is also supplied which makes sure that the squeegee stops in the forward position, after the last print, leaving the screen free of ink and easily accessible for cleanup.

Fig. S-9 Argon Compact semi-automatic screen printing press. (*Cincinnati Printing and Drying Systems, Inc.*)

All operating adjustments are made from the control panel, and each knob is legibly marked. All presses operate on either a single or automatic cycle. Single-print cycling is controlled by the operator using a foot switch. When put on automatic cycling, a built-in nonelectric dwell-timer operates which delays the lowering of the screen for a dwell period of zero to ten seconds. It is also possible to delay the raising of the frame at the end of the print stroke by means of a similar device; this delay is particularly useful when printing large areas with high-viscosity inks. By enabling the fabric to release completely from the substrate, it eliminates the possibility of halos or smears caused when the screen is released too quickly. Registration is accomplished by moving the printing base in all directions under the screen with micrometer screws. Movement of the printing base is adjustable in a longitudinal transversal as well as rotary direction. Each is dependent on the other and thus undesired movements during the registration operation are avoided. Locking devices are supplied for locking registration, thereby preventing any table movement during a print cycle.

Figure S-10 shows the Super-Jet III automatic conveyorized dryer used for drying printed materials and substrates. The machine employs more air

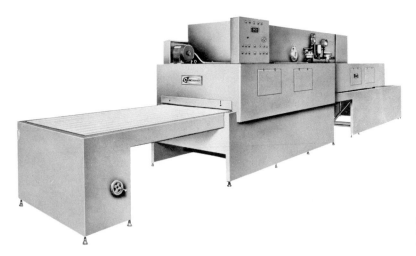

Fig. S-10 Super-Jet III automatic conveyorized dryer. (*Cincinnati Printing and Drying Systems, Inc.*)

and less temperature for high-efficiency drying. Fresh, warm air, driven through specially designed orifices at optimum velocity, scrubs solvents from screen prints on the moving conveyor. Captured solvents are emitted from the shop through an exhaust system. Proper air balance in the drying chamber and the dryer's suction belt conveyor holds the lightest of materials flat and flutter-free. Twin-wall construction of the dryer packed with high-density insulation eliminates heat or temperature radiation, and efficiency of combustion holds fuel consumption to the minimum. Heating or air conditioning balance is not disturbed in the shop. Some features of the Super-Jet III are a modulated gas and automatic safety shutdown valve, a high and low gas pressure control, variable-speed conveyor control, a variety of available conveyor belts, a simplified design of the control panel equipped with GO–NO GO circuit lights that identify each control circuit, and a modulated temperature control for contrast temperature levels. In addition, the dryer has an automatic sequence control and a self-powered, automatic, fail-safe safety valve.

Figure S-11 is the Electro-Jet modular drying system. The machine is an electric jet dryer capable of supplying heated air of up to 200°F for drying poster inks, lacquers, vinyls, and most evaporative-type inks. A variable-speed conveyor drive system provides up to thirty-two seconds of drying time. Standard belt width of the conveyor is 48 inches (122 cm) for Model

Fig. S-11 Electro-Jet modular drying system. (*Cincinnati Printing and Drying Systems, Inc.*)

E-48-8/6M and 66 inches (168 cm) for Model E66-12/8M. The Model E-48-8/6M dryer is 23 feet (7 m) long, 57 inches (145 cm) wide, and 44 inches (111.7 cm) high. The Model E66-12/8M dryer is 29 feet (8.84 m) long, 57 inches (145 cm) wide, and 44 inches (111.7 cm) high. Because of its modular construction, additional jet sections can be added to meet increased drying requirements. Controls are mounted on a safety interlocked electric panel for safe operation.

Figure S-12 shows the Arrow-Matic automatic screen printing press. The operator and presswork are handled simultaneously; the stock is prefed by the operator to registration guides outside the printing head at the same time the sheet is being printed. Following printing, an automatic take-off removes the printed sheet while the prefed sheet is transferred into registration on the printing bed. Print sizes for the Arrow-Matic are 24 by 30, 25 by 38, and 35 by 45 inches (61 by 76.2, 63.5 by 97, and 89 by 114.3 cm). The following are some additional features of the press: automatic feeding of the stock from the feed table to the print position; a mechanical gripper infeed which holds the sheet in exact registration during the print cycle; and a head-lift mechanism which raises the screen for easy cleanup and

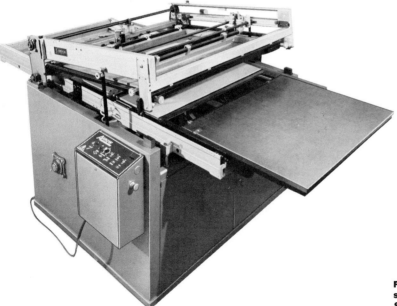

Fig. S-12 Arrow-Matic automatic screen printing press. (*American Screen Printing Equipment Company.*)

inspection. The screen of the press is accessible from four sides, and all controls are solid-state. In addition, the squeegee and flood bar speeds are independently controlled. The press also features a three-way, micro-adjustable feed table; a solid-state time control with dwell adjustable to from one to fifteen seconds; micrometer pressure adjustments on the squeegee and floor bar; and an adjustable squeegee printing angle.

Figure S-13 shows the Cameo Multi-Printer textile printer. The press is of rotary index design and is available in six- and eight-station models. The rotary indexer is automatically registered to the printing station for printing T-shirts, finished garments, fabric cut pieces, and plastic items with up to seven colors simultaneously in a controlled automatic sequence. Six models, three having six stations and three models having eight stations, accommodate print sizes of 12 by 12, 14 by 14, and 22 by 22 inches (30.4 by 30.4, 35.6 by 35.6, and 56 by 56 cm), respectively. The six-station indexer prints five positions for combinations of print, dry, load and unload, and one to four colors (textile) at a production rate up to 70 dozen per hour with two operators, which is a fast rate of production. It will also print five colors at a good production rate with one operator, print two- and three-color jobs at the same time with two operators, and print up to three colors and dry in between with one operator. The eight-station indexer prints seven positions for combinations of print, dry, load and unload, and one to six colors (textile) at the fastest production rate of 70 dozen per hour with two operators. It will also print seven colors at a good production rate with one operator, print two- and three-color jobs at the same time with two operators, and print up to four colors and dry in between with one operator.

Standard features of the Multi-Printer are an individual stop-start control on each printing head, mechanical action (air is not required), a three-way micro-registration rear-screen holder, and nonwarping aluminum pallets on the press. In addition, a three-way adjustability for individual pallets, a three-point leveling system for each printing bed, an easily removable squeegee and flood bar, a solid-state one- to fifteen-second low time controller, a micro-adjustable pressure setting on the squeegee and flood bar, a variable stroke length control, and a five-digit resettable counter are featured.

Fig. S-13 Cameo Multi-Printer textile printer. (*American Screen Printing Equipment Company*.)

The Masterprint Glider screen printing press is shown in Figure S-14. The press is available in three models according to model print sizes of 38 by 55, 44 by 64, and 54 by 80 inches (97 by 139.7, 111.7 by 163, and 137 by 203 cm). Largest sheet sizes for the three models are listed, respectively, as

Fig. S-14   Masterprint Glider screen printing press. (*American Screen Printing Equipment Company.*)

follows: 48 by 65, 54 by 86, and 64 by 103 inches (122 by 165, 137 by 218.44, and 163 by 262 cm). An optional Masterprint takeoff is available that features positive pickup and delivery of stock to the conveyor belt either across the belt or down its length. The takeoff employs a unique drop-edge design and permits printing as close as ¼ inch (6.350 cm) from the edge of all printed stock. Speed ranges vary for the three models from 450 to 1,000 impressions per hour. The Glider's detachable Masterframe and removable squeegee and flood bar allow fast screen changes and washups without affecting micro-adjustments or copy positioning.

The Glider, which is all-mechanical, features the following: an automatically controlled off-contact peel, a three-way micro-adjustable vacuum bed, an automatic blow-back, high-volume turbo-vacuum system, a wrap-around safety bar and dynamic braking system, and a micro-adjustable squeegee and flood bar. In addition, the press has a single adjustment stroke control and a cycle foot switch.

The Vecto-Jet dryer is shown in Figure S-15. Standard widths denote four models, i.e., 48, 60, 72, and 80 inches (122, 152.4, 183, and 203.2 cm), respectively. Three length sizes of master heating units are available as standard for the four models: 10, 15, and 20 feet (3.048, 4.572 and 6.096 m). Similarly, three length sizes of cooling units are available as standard: 10, 12, and 15 feet (3.048, 3.668 and 4.57 m). The Vecto-Jet uses large volumes of fresh air that have been forced through a direct-fired burner (on a gas unit) for maximum heat-transfer efficiency. The heated air is then impinged in continuous streams by air knives across the printed sheet, releasing and absorbing volatiles. The saturated air is then exhausted through a Resomite belt in the base cabinet. The solvent-laden, saturated air is never reused. The high-volume base cabinet exhausts at a greater extent than that of the intake blower. This creates a partial vacuum or negative

pressure condition that causes the stock to be held onto the vacuum belt. The cooling unit uses unrefrigerated air from either an outside or a room air-intake, and forces it through the main blower. No exhaust is necessary. The Resomite belt is a special solvent-resistant durable woven-mesh belting with unique construction features that form the heart of the vacuum belt. Some standard features of the Vecto-Jet are the following: the press is available for use with a gas, electric, oil, or steam heat source; it uses the lowest temperature necessary for drying with the air-knife principle; it dries a wide range of evaporative and oxidizing inks and coatings; a panel is provided for safety and ultimate temperature control; and stock can be stacked immediately after drying without slip-sheeting.

screen ruling Number of lines per inch on a contact screen or ruled glass halftone screen.

screen tint *See* FLAT TONE.

screened paper print Halftone illustration made on photographic paper. It can be mounted with line copy on a page layout so that the entire page can be photographed at the same time as line copy for reproduction.

screened print Print made from continuous-tone copy and screened during photographic exposure. A Velox is a screened print. It is not necessary to screen the print again for reproduction printing; only a line shot is used. *See also* VELOX.

screening *See* HALFTONE SCREENING.

scriber (colloquial name **bug**) Device used in conjunction with a template to form characters, symbols, and the like. *See also* PENS, TECHNICAL.

scribing Scratching clear lines on the emulsion of blackened film or on metal to produce, change, or complete an image.

script Type characters that resemble handwritten copy.

scufftester *See* RUBOMETER.

scumming In photomechanical plate making, an unfavorable condition in which the printing plate picks up ink in the clear areas and transfers it to nonimage areas of the sheet. The nonimage areas of the plate may not be desensitized properly to resist ink. Either the plate should be reetched or a new plate made. The entire plate, including nonimage as well as image areas, should always be worked with gum and developer. Scumming may also be caused by soiled damping rollers or other press problems, such as skidding from the roller, a loose blanket, or by an improperly balanced fountain solution.

second chopper fold (mail fold) Fold made in a web-fed printing press in the same manner as the first chopper fold. It immediately follows the first chopper fold and is parallel to it. Long narrow signatures that are 32-page multiples of the number of webs in the press are produced. The signature size is one-half of the web width by one-fourth of the cutoff length. *See also* CHOPPER FOLD.

second cover Inside surface of the front cover of a publication, usually identified as such for advertising purposes. The third cover is the inside surface of the back cover.

second parallel fold In a web-fed press, a paper fold made in the jaw folder immediately after the first parallel fold and parallel to it. The second parallel fold results in 16-page signatures of multiples of the number of webs used during the printing operation. The signature size is one-half of the width of the web by one-fourth of the cutoff length.

secondary colors In printing, orange, green, and magenta. They are obtained by overprinting on primary colors. The primary colors for printing inks are yellow, red, and blue.

section Usually, part of a chapter of a publication. Sometimes, however, sections may replace chapters as the highest divisions of a publication.

sectional view View obtained by cutting away part of an object in an illustration or engineering drawing in order to show the shape and construction of the interior. *See* SECTIONS: ENGINEERING DRAWINGS.

sectionalizing Arranging a technical publication in sections. Each section begins with a right-hand page, and paragraphs, pages, illustrations, and tables may be double-numbered within the section. The first number of the paragraph, page, illustration, or table represents the section. If the section number is in roman capital numerals, the number here should be converted to arabic. The second number represents the paragraph, page, illustration, or table within the particular section. For example, the third page of section IV is numbered 4-3, the fifth illustration of section VI is numbered 6-5, etc. Small publications should not be sectionalized. *See also* PAGE NUMBERING.

sectioning lines In engineering and mechanical drawings, lines used in orthographic projection to indicate exposed surfaces of an object in a sectional view. They are generally thin, full lines but may vary with the material shown in the section. Sectioning lines are uniformly spaced lines drawn at an angle of 45° to the base line of a section. On adjacent parts, the 45° angles are drawn in opposite directions. On a third part adjacent to two other parts, the sectioning lines may be drawn at an angle of 30° to 60°. When the 45° sectioning lines are parallel or nearly parallel to the outline of an object, another angle should be selected. *See also* LINE CONVENTIONS: ENGINEERING DRAWINGS; SECTIONS: ENGINEERING DRAWINGS.

sections; engineering drawings A section, or sectional view, is obtained by cutting away part of an object to show the shape and construction at the cutting plane. Such a view is used when the interior construction or hidden features of an object cannot be shown clearly by an outside view. Hidden lines and details beyond the cutting plane may be omitted unless they are

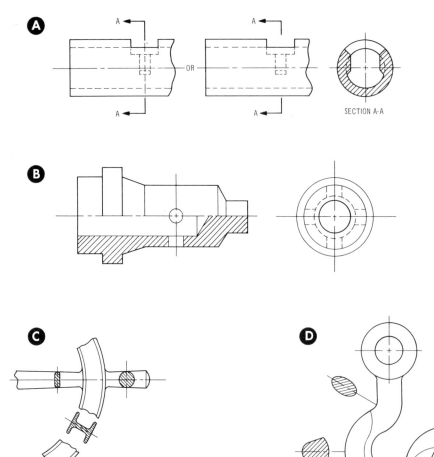

Fig. S-16 Sections and sectioning used on engineering drawings.

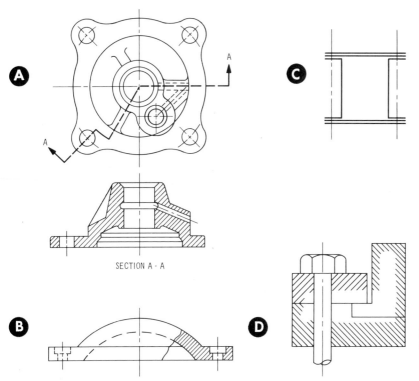

SECTION A - A

Fig. S-17 Sections and sectioning used on engineering drawings.

necessary to portray the object adequately. A sectional view is made through an outside view and not through another sectional view unless such a procedure would clarify a drawing. A view may be rotated if an explanatory note, such as "Section A-A rotated 45° clockwise," is shown next to it.

The cutting-plane lines described in LINE CONVENTIONS: ENGINEERING DRAWINGS, together with arrows and letters, make up the cutting-plane indication. The arrows at the ends of the lines show the direction in which the sections are viewed. The cutting plane may be a single continuous plane, or it may be offset if details can thus be shown to better advantage. In simple views, the cutting plane is indicated as in Figure S-16. In complex views or views in which the cutting plane is offset, the cutting plane is shown as in Figure S-17.

Viewing planes are indicated in a similar manner, except that they are placed outside the object to indicate the surfaces shown in the auxiliary views. All cutting-plane indications are identified by reference letters placed near the ends of the arrowheads. When a change in the direction of the cutting plane is not clear, reference letters may be placed at each change of direction. If more than one sectional view appears on a drawing, the cutting-plane indications are identified in alphabetical series. The letters identifying the cutting plane appear as part of the title under the sectional view, as in "Section A-A," "Section B-B." When the alphabet is exhausted, double letters may be used, as in "Section AA-AA," "Section BB-BB."

If possible, sectional views should appear on the same sheet as the subassembly, assembly, or detail drawings from which they have been taken. When sectional views must be drawn on a separate sheet, they are arranged from left to right in alphabetical order or with suitable cross-references by zone designations. If a sectional view appears on a sheet separated from the sheet containing the cutting-plane indication, the number of the latter is entered with the section title thus: "Section *B-B*, Sheet No. 3."

A full section is a view obtained when the cutting plane extends entirely across an object, as in Figure S-16*A*. For sections taken on the center line of a symmetrical view, the cutting-plane indications and the section title may be omitted if the section view is in correct orthographic projection. In all other cases, the section title and projection cutting-plane indications are shown.

A half section of a symmetrical object shows internal and external features by passing two cutting planes at right angles to each other along the center lines or symmetrical axes. One-quarter of the object is considered to have been removed and the interior exposed to view. Cutting-plane indications and section titles are omitted (*see* Figure S-16*B*).

A revolved section drawn directly on an exterior view shows the shape of the cross section of a part, such as the spoke of a wheel. The cutting plane is passed perpendicular to the center line or axis of the part to be sectioned, and the resulting section is rotated into place. Cutting-plane indications are omitted (*see* Figure S-16*C*).

Removed sections may be used to illustrate particular features of an object; they are drawn in the same manner as revolved sections. They are placed to one side and are often drawn to a larger scale to bring out details (*see* Figure S-16*D*). If the cutting plane is not continuous, the resulting section is an offset section (*see* Figure S-17*A*). When a sectional view of only part of an object is needed, broken-out sections may be used. The break-line convention is employed to separate the sectional view, as in Figure S-17*B*.

When the true projection of a piece may be misleading, parts such as ribs or spokes are drawn as if they were rotated into or out of the cutting plane. The method of representing the lower spoke shown in Figure S-18*A* is preferred to the true projection. When the cutting plane passes through the rib, web, or similar element, sectioning lines may be omitted from these parts (see Figure S-17*A*).

Structural shapes, sheet metal, packing, gaskets, and the like that are too thin for section lining may be shown solid. If solid lines are used and two or more thicknesses are shown, a space as narrow as possible is left between them (*see* Figure S-17*A*). Shafts, bolts, nuts, rods, rivets, keys, pins, and similar parts whose axes lie in the cutting plane are not sectioned (*see* Figure S-17*D*). When the cutting plane passes at right angles to the axis of such parts, however, they are sectioned.

It is preferable to draw sectional views to the same scale as the outside views from which they were taken. When a different scale is used, the procedure is as outlined in SCALE: ENGINEERING DRAWINGS. In addition to showing shape and construction, sectional views may be used to distinguish individual components of an assembly or subassembly (*see* Figure

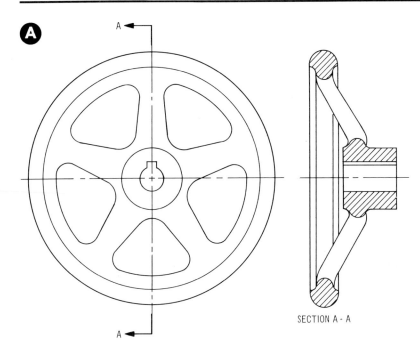

SECTION A - A

METALS

GLASS, CERAMICS AND PLASTICS

GENERAL

* SHOW TYPE OF MATERIAL ABBREVIATION

Fig. S-18 Sections and sectioning used on engineering drawings.

S-17D). This is done by arranging these lines in section conventions on the exposed surfaces of the sectional view. Section conventions (*see* Figure S-18B) must not cross dimensions or obscure other conventions. When clarity is not thereby sacrificed, section conventions may be shown along the borders of a part. In section views, the metals symbol (Figure S-18B) is used to indicate other materials. Section lining is composed of uniformly spaced lines at an angle of 45° to the base line of the section. On adjacent parts, the 45° angles are drawn in opposite directions. On a third part adjacent to two other parts, the section lining is drawn at an angle of 30° to 60° (*see* Figure S-17D). When a 45° section lining is parallel or nearly parallel to the outline of an object, another angle is chosen.

see-through *See* SHOW-THROUGH.

self-cover Cover of the same stock as the inside pages of a publication. The self-cover is printed at the same time as the inside pages.

self-mailer Folder, broadside, or other mailing piece on which the address is printed directly, without use of an envelope.

self-quadder Automatic quadder mechanism in Linotype machines. It consists of space matrices used in conjunction with spacebands. The quadder mechanism in Intertypes is called an "autospacer."

semilogarithmic grid Grid composed of equal abscissa (horizontal) and ordinate (vertical) divisions laid out in a logarithmic ratio. A graph drawn on such a grid shows rate of change and changes in ratios or percentages.

sensitive material Any material—diazo paper, plastic plate, photographic film—which is coated with diazo salts, bichromate solutions, or other chemicals that render its surface sensitive to light.

sensitivity, color *See* FILMS AND PLATES.

sensitometry Science of measuring the sensitivity and other photographic characteristics of photographic materials.

sepia Dark yellowish-brown color of low brilliance.

sepia intermediate Intermediate used in making duplicate transparencies by the whiteprint process. The original may be filed and the sepia intermediate revised and used to produce copies. When sepia intermediates are made, exposure should be approximately one-third slower than for ordinary blueline or blackline papers. Normally, they should be made in reverse. Rather than placing the master over the treated paper with image side up, the master is placed facedown with the image in direct contact with the copy paper. *See also* REVERSE-READING INTERMEDIATE.

serif Finishing stroke or line projecting from the end of the main stroke of many letters in some typefaces. Letters that do not have such terminal strokes are said to be sans serif. Text typefaces have serifs, while gothic and similar faces are sans serif. The latter are generally used for forms, tabulated text matter, directories, headings, and display advertising. *See also* SANS SERIF.

serigraph Color print made by the silk-screen process and executed by the artist himself. The production of serigraphs by either amateurs or accomplished artists can be a stimulating hobby or a profitable undertaking.

set off Undesirable transfer of ink from the printed sheet to the back of the sheet that immediately follows during a pressrun.

set solid To set type without additional leading. *See* LEADING.

sextodecimo Book having a page size of 4½ by 6½ inches (11.43 by 17 cm) and consisting of 32 pages. Sixteen pages are printed on both sides. Also called a "sixteenmo."

shading: drawings Shading may be added to drawings with ink or pencil or by affixing preprints and hand-cut screening materials of various patterns. In an exploded view, shading effects on the various parts should indicate that the light is coming from the same source. If, for example, the light is coming from the upper corner of the drawing, the shading should be applied to the opposite side of the parts. An area should not be shaded when it appears that the source light will strike the part. In Figure S-19A, light is coming from the upper right corner; in Figure S-19B, from the upper left corner. View A is an example of excessive shading. Shading in both cases was applied with preprinted patterns having an adhesive back, cut to the appropriate size, and burnished down. *See also* SHADING MEDIUMS.

Figure S-20 is an exploded view showing proper use of shading. The light source is coming from the upper left corner. Note the shading in the interior of housing 44. Note also that parts 4, 15, 22, 27, and 28 are filled in solidly except for highlights, which indicates that these parts are nonmetallic. Heavier lines are used to delineate the larger parts.

shading mediums Sheets of preprinted tones and patterns with adhesive or developing characteristics that are used to improve the appearance of copy, especially artwork. The Craftint Manufacturing Company's Craf-Tone sheets are available in approximately 300 shadings and tones with

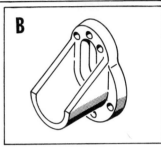

Fig. S-19   Shading on drawings.

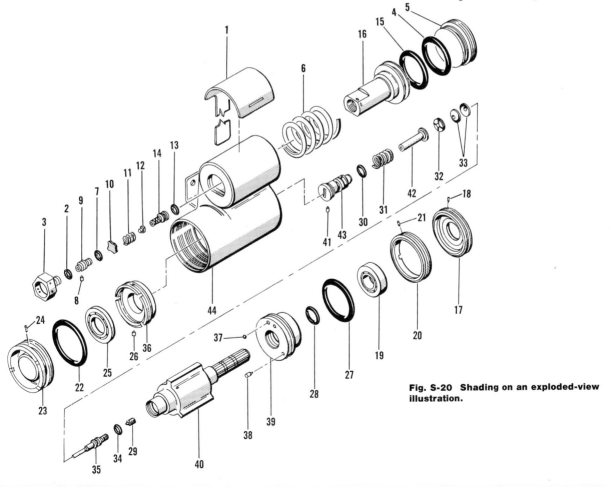

Fig. S-20   Shading on an exploded-view illustration.

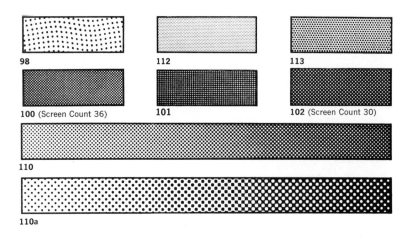

98   112   113

100 (Screen Count 36)   101   102 (Screen Count 30)

110

110a

Fig. S-21   Craf-Tone shading-medium patterns.

patterns on thin adhesive-backed matte acetate. Some of the patterns are shown in Figure S-21. These shading mediums are used for borders, unusual lettering effects, maps, graphs, catalogs, yearbooks, posters, brochures, letterheads, technical illustrations, and other printed matter.

In applying Craf-Tone, remove sufficient shading from the sheet to cover the area to be shaded. Place the shading over the copy and flatten it by using mild pressure. It is better to start at the bottom and rub from left to right, working upward as the pattern adheres to the copy. Remove excess or unwanted shading by cutting it with a sharp frisket knife, but be careful to cut only the shading. After the excess shading has been removed, place a sheet of tissue over the area and burnish the shading through the overlay.

Craftint has developed a process in which shadings of various styles and tones are applied by the artist directly on the drawing. Doubletone drawing paper, which resembles ordinary high-grade bristol board, has two hidden patterns. The Doubletone sheet is processed with two invisible shading screens, one having a light tone and the other a dark tone. By the application of two different developers, either the light or the dark tone is caused to appear on the drawing. Singletone drawing paper has one latent screen. The drawing is first outlined in pencil on the Singletone sheet. Ink is then used to make permanent lines. Developer is applied with pen or brush to the areas where the tone is desired and blotted immediately (see Figure S-22). Both Doubletone and Singletone sheets are available in various patterns.

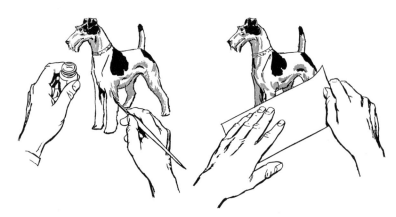

Fig. S-22   Using Singletone shading.

Craftint also produces engraver's top-sheet shading film with opaque patterns. The top sheet is placed over artwork or negatives to break up black solids. A white top-sheet dot can be made black by applying a developer. The white sheet breaks up solid black, whereas a black top sheet shades black on white.

shading: stenciling Producing a shading effect on a stencil by means of a transparent plastic plate with a raised pattern and a stylus. Shading is transferred to the stencil by placing it between the screen plate and a screen-plate stylus (see Figure S-23). With the stencil mounted on the duplicating machine (mimeograph), ink passes through openings in the stencil, thus transferring the image to paper. See also MIMEOGRAPH; MIMEOSCOPE; STYLUS.

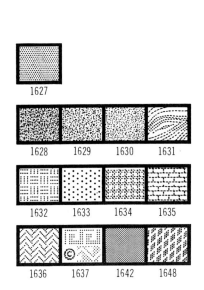

Fig. S-23 Stencil shading plates and styli.

shadow Darkest portion of a picture or image. In a negative, the low-density areas are called the shadow areas because they correspond to the high-density (dark) portions of the original copy.

shadow box Frame drawn around copy to give the illusion of a shadow. The lines of the box may be straight or wavy or be drawn heavier on one side (see Figure S-24).

sharpness In photographic material, the ability to reproduce the sharp edge of a line.

sheet Piece of paper with or without copy. A page is one side of a sheet.

sheet-fed Designating a printing press to which paper is fed in sheets rather than in rolls, or webs.

Fig. S-24 Shadow boxes.

sheeter Rotary device employed at the end of the last printing unit of a web-fed printing press which produces cutoff flat sheets in specific sizes for further folding, to be cut and folded, or to be finished in the bindery as booklets, broadsides, or flat-printed pieces. The web passes over the sheeter, which cuts individual sheets for stacking in a delivery pile. A former folder also may be used for the cutoff.

shelf life Length of time before sensitized materials such as diazo copy paper, film, and chemicals deteriorate with age. These materials have a limited use because their chemical properties are gradually lost.

shelf talker Any printed sales message used to attract attention and describe merchandise on display. The material, which is pressure-sensitive, is affixed above or below the shelf on which the merchandise rests.

shelfback *See* BACKBONE.

shop print Engineering, construction, or architectural blueprint used in the shop or field. Shop prints are produced from original drawings made on vellum, tracing paper, cloth, or film. Blueprints, which have a white image on a black or dark blue background, can withstand hard usage and are impervious to grease and dirt. Even though they are exposed to sunlight, they will not fade for a reasonable length of time. *See also* BLUEPRINT.

short ink Printing ink characterized by its lack of flow; the opposite of long ink.

short page Page having fewer lines of text than are normally allocated to the pages of a publication. One or two lines may sometimes be omitted from a page to improve page makeup.

short title page *See* HALF TITLE.

shoulder In photomechanics, the portion of a characteristic curve above the straight-line section; in printing type, the portion of the surface on which the typeface rests.

show-through (see-through) Visibility of printed matter on the opposite side of a sheet. The effect is due largely to a poor choice of paper, but it may also be caused by excessive ink penetration of the paper or too heavy an impression between the printing plate and the impression cylinder.

side roll stand Roll stand for holding a web (paper roll) that is located to the side rather than in a direct line with the press. This arrangement is used when space is not available in line. The paper is turned and guided into line with angle bars.

sidehead Caption or title that appears at the side (generally the left side) of a page or column. It may be flush or indented.

sidestitching (side-wire stitching) Method of mechanical binding in which a booklet or a signature is stitched at the sides. "At the sides" means that the booklet or signature is stitched in the closed position. The pages therefore cannot be opened to their full width. *See also* BINDING, MECHANICAL.

sign paper Paper used for indoor and outdoor advertising signs and posters. The back of the paper readily accepts paste for mounting, and the face is receptive to printer's ink. Sign paper comes in various colors and in sheets as well as in rolls as long as 1,000 feet (305 m).

signature Sheet of paper printed on both sides and folded to make up part of a publication. For example, a sheet of paper with 2 printed pages on each side is folded once to form a 4-page signature. One with 4 pages on each side is folded twice to form an 8-page signature, and so on up to a 64-page signature with 32 pages on each side of the sheet. A 16-page signature is ideally suited to bookbinding machines. The proper arrangement of pages in signatures is called "imposition." *See also* IMPOSITION.

silhouette Outline of an object, especially a portrait profile, filled in with black or another solid color. Silhouettes are often cut from black or colored construction paper and mounted on a white background. *See* Figure S-25.

silhouetted halftone Halftone from which the background has been deleted entirely or in part so that the image is silhouetted.

silk-screen printing process *See* SCREEN-PROCESS PRINTING.

silver-generated Designating a reproduction made from a silver image.

silver halide A halide is a binary chemical compound formed by the direct union of a halogen, such as chlorine, iodine, or bromine, with another element or radical. Silver nitrate, one of the silver salts, is obtained by treating silver with nitric acid. It appears as colorless crystals on white fused or molded masses. A silver halide results from the union of silver salts with, usually, the halogen bromine. A remarkable susceptibility to light makes silver halides useful in photography and in graphic arts reproduction and photomechanical work.

Fig. S-25 Silhouette.

silver print *See* BROMIDE PRINT; BROWNLINE PRINT.

silver salts *See* SILVER HALIDE.

single-coated paper Coated or enameled paper to which only one coat has been applied.

single-color press Printing press that is capable of printing only one color at a time. To produce multicolor work, various color plates are used and the sheet is run through the press for each color.

single printing Printing first on one side of a sheet and then on the reverse side by either the work-and-turn or the work-and-tumble method. The process is the opposite of perfector printing, in which both sides of a sheet are printed in one run through the press. *See also* PERFECTING PRESS.

Singletone Sheet of high-grade board stock processed with an invisible shading screen. The artist applies a developer to bring out the tone desired on the drawing. *See also* SHADING MEDIUMS.

sinkage Distance below the top margin of a page at which chapter openings and similar material are set.

size (also called **sizing**) Any of various gelatinous materials made from starch, clay, glue, casein, and the like and used for glazing or coating papers and cloths during the manufacturing process. Size is also used in the tempera process of painting. *See* TEMPERA.

In printing, a clear size may be laid on stock by preprinting to seal the surface against ink penetration. Sizing is used especially in color work for better definition of the image when a porous stock is desired.

sizes: engineering drawings The sizes of engineering drawings as set forth in military specifications are accepted as standard by almost all the concerns that make or reproduce such drawings. Flat-size drawings, which are relatively small, usually have a printed format and may be filed flat. Roll-size drawings, because of their length, are filed in rolls and usually do not have a printed format. The finished-sheet size of drawings refers to overall dimensions of drawing forms and of full-size reproductions made from them. As shown in the table below, sizes are designated by letters. To provide protection for roll-size drawings, a 4-inch (10.16-cm) margin should be added to the right end of the minimum lengths specified. When practicable, the maximum length of roll drawings should be 144 inches (365.7 cm). The table shows finished-sheet sizes of the various drawings.

Size	Flat sizes in.	cm	Size	Roll sizes in.	cm
A	8½ by 11 (22 by 28 cm)		G	11 by 42 (28 by 107 cm)	
B	11 by 17 (28 by 43 cm)		H	28 by 48 (71 by 1.22 cm)	
C	17 by 22 (43 by 56 cm)		J	34 by 48 (86.3 by 122 cm)	
D	22 by 34 (56 by 86.3 cm)		K	40 by 48 (101.6 by 122 cm)	
E	34 by 44 (86.3 by 111.7 cm)				
F	28 by 40 (71 by 101.6 cm)				

sizing *See* SCALING; SIZE.

skeleton page *See* PAGE FRAME.

skid Platform for stacking paper temporarily.

slip-sheet (interleave) To insert paper or other material between printed sheets in order to avoid offsetting an image on one sheet onto the back of the next sheet. In the preparation of copy, the term "slip-sheet" means to insert pages in proper sequence to designate the placement of illustrations that are still being prepared. Each such page identifies its particular illustration with a notation as to whether the illustration is line or halftone, foldout or horizontal, as well as the size, the negative or art file number, the figure number and title, and any other information that serves to key the illustration to its proper page for printing or collating.

slip-tracing Tracing an object by shifting its position under a translucent paper on which the tracing is made. A different configuration can thus be drawn or the layout improved over the original.

slug (slugline) Line of type cast by a linecasting machine; also, a metal strip wider than leading used for spacing between lines.

slugcasting machine *See* LINECASTING MACHINE.

slugline *See* SLUG.

small capital letters (abbreviated **small caps**) Capital letters set in a size smaller than regular capitals of the same font. A double underline is used to direct the printer to set words in small capital letters.

small pica Old type size. The nearest equivalent in the point system is 11 point (3.86 mm).

snake slip Abrasive stick for removing dirt or unwanted printing from an offset plate.

soft copy Text copy typed on vellum or other paper, as opposed to camera-ready copy. It is provided for check-out and approval of the style and accuracy of the text. Soft copy is not final copy.

softcover Any book cover other than a hardcover or a self-cover. It may consist of any type of stock as long as the stock is not the same as that on which the pages are printed. *See also* SELF-COVER.

soft dot Expression used to describe first-generation halftones where dots are characterized by fringe or veiling. All original halftone negatives and positives made with a contact screen are "soft," the amount of softness depending on the choice of film, developer activity level, proper contact of the contact halftone screen, and other factors. *See also* VEILING; FRINGE.

soft-roll To roll a typewriter platen by hand above or below the normal line of typing in order to type superscripts or subscripts. If the typewriter is already equipped with a half-ratchet spacer, there is no need to soft-roll. To avoid soft-rolling, which requires estimating the space needed, ratchets can be installed to accommodate half spacing. Superscripts and subscripts can thus be accurately aligned.

solid copy *See* STRAIGHT MATTER.

solid step In offset platemaking and photolithographic negative work, the critical step number on the sensitivity guide recommended by the manufacturer of the printing plate as the proper density to achieve. *See also* SENSITIVITY GUIDE.

sorts Symbols, designs, braces, stars, and the like that are not included in a regular font of type characters. (*See* Figure S-26 for an example of miscellaneous sorts.)

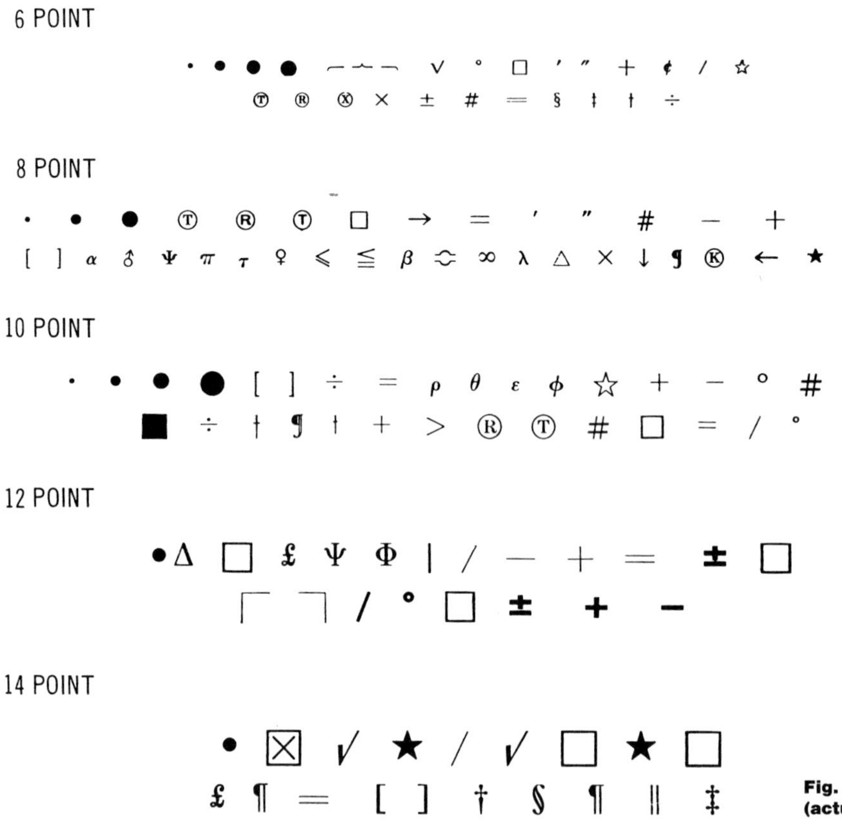

6 POINT

8 POINT

10 POINT

12 POINT

14 POINT

Fig. S-26 Miscellaneous sorts (actual size).

source-control drawing Engineering drawing that specifies the source that exclusively provides the performance, installation, and interchangeability characteristics of an item selected and tested for specific application by a design activity. The drawing is identified by the contractor design group's name and number and shows the vendor's name, address, and part number. When the source-control drawing number is used as the identifying number on an assembly drawing or list, however, a note such as the following is placed on the drawing or list: "For procurement or part number, see source-control drawing."

A source-control drawing is identified by the words "Source-control drawing" adjacent to the title block. It also contains the following notice: "Only the item listed on this drawing and identified by vendor's name, address, and part number has been tested and approved by [name of the equipment design activity] for use in [name of item]. A substitute item must not be used without prior testing and approval by [name of equipment design activity]."

spanner heading Primary heading in the boxhead of a table that covers two or more columnar headings.

specification-control drawing Engineering drawing that discloses the configuration, design, and test requirements for the items (other than military standard items) designed and manufactured by vendors. Vendors' part numbers and names and addresses are included in the drawing. A specification-control drawing number is not considered a part number. When the number is used as the identifying number on an assembly drawing or list, however, a note such as the following is placed on the drawing or list: "For procurement or part number, *see* specification-control drawing." A specification-control drawing must be identified by the words "Specification-control drawing" adjacent to the title block.

specification tree *See* CHECK-OUT CHART.

spectral sensitivity Response of a photographic emulsion to certain wavelengths of light. The spectral sensitivity of an orthochromatic film is low or nonexistent in the red region of the spectrum and very high in the green and blue regions.

spectrogram Diagram showing the relative sensitivity of a photographic material to different colors of light.

Speedball pens Lettering and drawing pens manufactured by the Hunt Manufacturing Company, of which Speedball is a registered trademark. Five styles of Speedball pens, together with samples of lettering, are illustrated in Figures S-27 and S-28. The flicker lettering pens break open for easy cleaning and maintenance.

SPH Abbreviation for sheets per hour.

spine *See* BACKBONE.

spiral binding *See* BINDING, MECHANICAL.

spirit duplicating (fluid duplicating) Direct-image duplicating process in which the image is typed, written, or drawn on a master that is backed by an aniline-dye carbon sheet. A deposit of dye is transferred to the back of the master, where it forms the image in reverse reading. When placed on the spirit duplicator, the copy paper comes in direct contact with the master. As the paper goes through the machine, it is moistened with the vapor of a duplicating fluid and a small amount of carbon dissolves to produce the image. The carbon paper is obtainable in purple, red, and green. Paper or card stock from a minimum size of 3 by 5 inches (7.62 by

Style A square pens.

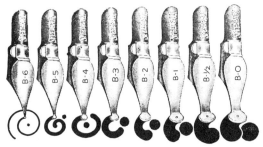

Style B round pens.

Style C flat pens.

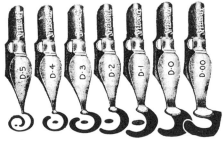

Style D oval pens.

Lettering with C-1 pen.

Lettering with Style D pen.

Fig. S-27 Speedball pens and samples of lettering.

12.7 cm) can be handled by various models of spirit duplicators. Masters are provided in grades designed for maximum performance and long runs as well as in economy grades for low cost and short runs.

The A.B. Dick Company's Model 217 tabletop spirit duplicator (Figure S-29) handles masters in sizes as large as 9 by 14 inches (22.8 by 35.6 cm) and paper ranging from 3 by 5 (7.62 by 12.7 cm) to 9 by 14 inches (22.8 by 36 cm), fed automatically or by hand from 16-pound to 100-pound (7.26-kg to 45.4-kg) card stock. Speed of the machine is 120 copies per minute.

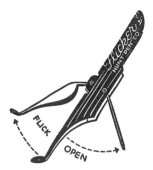

Fig. S-28 Speedball flicker pen.

spot (locator) In technical illustrating, an object that forms part of an assembly and is drawn in solid black in a small drawing adjacent to the drawing of the complete assembly. The spot indicates origin only and is used as a reference point. The part or section indicated by the spot constitutes the main illustration. The spot in the aircraft in Figure S-30 shows a portion of the inboard nacelle.

spotting Painting out small defects on a negative or other material by using opaquing fluid or white paint.

spread In advertising, two facing pages in a publication, with or without a gutter. *See also* CENTER SPREAD.

spreads (spreading) Contact process by which letters, solids, or other shapes are made "fatter" without altering their shape or relative position. The amount of spread is controlled by exposure.

sprocketed film Roll film with sprocket holes that engage sprocket wheels so that the film may be guided and controlled as it passes between reels.

square grid (cross-section grid) Grid ruled in squares and designated by the number of lines per inch (2.54 cm). A 4-by-4 grid, for example, has four lines per inch in both directions, usually with every fourth line heavier than the others; a 5-by-5 grid has five lines per inch in both directions, with every fifth line heavier; and so forth. The basic unit is not always an inch, however, and a 10-by-10 grid may have a 2½-inch (6.35-cm) grid. Because the square-ruled sheet can represent any assigned dimension or value, a square grid is frequently used for engineering sketches, block diagrams, and plant or office layouts.

squeegee Implement used on screen-process printing presses that forces ink and ink compounds through the screen stencil onto a printing surface to form the image. Squeegee open and travel time are set to correspond with press speed. As a verb, "squeegee" means to remove excess or unwanted chemical or water from the surface of a sheet of film or an offset printing plate.

SS or **ss.** Abbreviation for same size, indicating that the copy is not to be enlarged or reduced.

stabilene film Tear-resistant film made by the Keuffel and Esser Company in thicknesses of 0.003, 0.005, and 0.0075 inch (0.0762, 0.127, and 0.905 mm). It is available in various coatings, surfaces, and colors and may be opaque or translucent. Stabilene films are manufactured for mapmaking, drafting, illustrating, and the drawing of printed circuits as well as for certain mechanical applications.

stabilization reproduction *See* PROCESSING, STABILIZATION.

stacker Device attached to a delivery conveyor that collects, compresses, and bundles signatures.

stacking In technical illustrating, placing nomenclature on an illustration so that a vertical line drawn through it shows balanced copy. Lines are neither flush right nor flush left but are centered on the first line of copy.

stand-alone system Photocomposition system that performs the end-line function of producing typeset copy on paper or film, such as a photo-typesetter with an on-line keyboard; it may be driven by other means as with paper tape through its tape reader or by magnetic tape through a cassette reader.

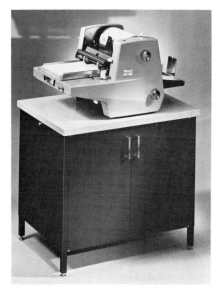

Fig. S-29 A. B. Dick Company's Model 217 spirit duplicator.

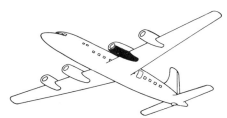

Fig. S-30 Using a spot in technical illustrating.

standing form Printing form that will be used repeatedly and therefore will not be disassembled or melted down.

stat *See* PHOTOSTAT.

static neutralizer Device that neutralizes electrostatic charges that interfere with paper during transportation in a printing press or other machines that move paper or other substrate.

status lines First line or lines initiated on a display console that are keyboarded to show characters identifying a specific job. The lines show parameters such as type point size, line spacing, typeface, line length in picas and points, depth of copy in picas and points, rejustify, insert, search, and the like. When all parameters have been entered, the machine is in the entry mode and is ready for input.

steelfaced plate *See* NICKELTYPE.

stencil sheet Sheet of fine paper backed with heavier material on which an impression can be cut by typewriter percussion or by a stylus. When the stencil is mounted on the duplicator cylinder, fast-drying ink penetrates the cut impression. The ink is thus transferred to paper to form the image. This type of stencil is used in mimeographing.

Figure S-31 shows A. B. Dick Company's stencil maker for mimeographing. This machine images stencils automatically from typed material, halftones, drawings, paste-up copy, newspaper and magazine clippings, solids, and continuous-tone photographs. The original is placed under an acetate sheet and both are positioned on the drum, which moves laterally past the imaging system to make the stencil. Warm-up of machine is not required because of its solid-state circuitry. Line density is infinitely adjustable from 125 to 750 lines per inch (per 2.54 cm). The maximum original size of the printed material is 8⅝ by 13⅜ inches (22 by 34 cm). Size of the image area is up to 8½ by 12⅝ inches (21.6 by 32 cm). Stencil imaging time is variable from 2½ minutes to 16 minutes. When the stencil is imaged, the drum automatically stops. A safety interlock stops the imaging process and drum movement when the lid is raised. The exhaust is filtered to eliminate odor and stencil particles.

Fig. S-31   A. B. Dick Company's stencil maker.

step-and-repeat machine Machine that repeats a series of operations to produce multiple images from negatives or positives in register on photosensitive materials. The materials include metal plates and photographic glass or film for photo-offset, photogravure, silk-screen printing, printed-circuit production, and other industrial applications. The carriages of the machines may operate vertically or horizontally.

stereotype mat Matrix into which molten metal is poured to produce a stereotype plate. *See* MATRIX.

stereotype plate Duplicate printing plate made from a type image. The face of the type or engraving is pressed into pulp material by a molding press. The stereotype matrix is then filled with molten metal and becomes a new printing surface that can be mounted on wood to the conventional height of type. Less expensive than electrotypes, stereotypes are popular in newspaper printing. They are curved and mounted on the plate cylinder of the newspaper press.

stet Latin word meaning "let it stand," used to indicate that a change is not to be made and that copy should remain as it was originally written. A row of dots placed beneath the copy is the proofreader's instruction not to make the change. The word "stet" is written in the margin.

stickup initial *See* INITIAL.

sticky back *See* AVERY.

stippling Drawing, engraving, or painting by means of dots or small, short touches that together produce a softly graded tone, instead of using continuous lines and solid areas.

stitch line In orthographic engineering and mechanical drawings, a line used to indicate sewing. Designated as a "medium" line, it consists of a series of evenly spaced short dashes. *See also* LINE CONVENTIONS: ENGINEERING DRAWINGS.

stock Paper, paperboard, or other paper product on which an image is printed, copied, or duplicated.

stomp Soft pencil made of paper or other soft material. Artists use stomp for blending chalks, pastels, or pencil graphite to produce shading and graded tones on drawings.

stop out Liquid chemical used to delete film edges and other unwanted copy on positive plates.

storyboard Panel presentation of rough sketches of a proposed series of views such as may be used on film slides or transparencies for overhead projection. Storyboards are also used in cartoon animation.

straight-line portion In photomechanics, the section of a characteristic curve that is essentially a straight line. It represents the range of exposure in which an increase in density is proportional to an increase in the logarithm of the exposure.

straight matter (running text; solid copy) Text that is not interrupted by headings, tables, illustrations, or displayed equations.

straightedge Instrument with one or more straight long edges, particularly a ruler having measured increments, used in artwork. The C-Thru ruler is a transparent straightedge that is popular with technical illustrators, layout personnel, and artists. It is inscribed with grid divisions for alignment of copy and has a beveled edge that prevents ink from smearing.

strike-on composition Method of composing text copy by using a typewriter or other percussion keyboard whereby the impact of keys forms the image. Also, any impact of keys directly on a substrate, particularly for producing copy for printing.

stripper's blotter Pliable material such as cardboard or bristol board used as a burnisher to rub out air bubbles or to apply adhesive-backed film to another support base. The term originates from photoengravers using cuts to squeeze moisture from under stripping film as it is applied to glass plate.

stripping Cutting out and placing in position, particularly with reference to arranging a photolithographic negative in masking paper for a plate. Stripping also means removing all or part of text copy or an illustration by mortising and replacing the material with something else, particularly with reference to reproduction copy. A screened halftone negative stripped in a line negative is a "strip-in"; the combination is called a "composite."

stripping film Film having a light-sensitive emulsion laid on a membrane 0.0005 inch (0.0127 mm) thick. The membrane is bonded to a thicker base material. After the film has been developed, the base can be stripped away, leaving the membrane to hold the photographic image. With stripping film, wrong- or right-reading copy can be produced by placing the image between a light-sensitive coated material and a source of light. Close contact is achieved by using a vacuum frame. A disadvantage of stripping film is that the membrane is usually unstable because of shrinkage and stretching. These characteristics must be calculated and allowed for in planning.

stripping and masking film See MASKING AND STRIPPING MATERIALS.

stripping table See LIGHT TABLE.

stripping tweezers Sharp, thin tweezers used to separate any two unlike materials such as masking films and other adhesive-backed materials.

stubhead Heading that appears in the left-hand column of a boxhead in tables. The stub column is the column which is the listing under the stubhead.

studio finish In photographic work, the finished surface of the photograph which is a matte or unglazed finish as opposed to a glossy finish.

stuffer Printed circular enclosed in an envelope with regularly mailed material, such as an invoice.

style Uniform spelling, punctuation, abbreviation, capitalization, ruling, headings, typography, and the like used throughout a publication.

stylus Precision-made penlike instrument used for drawing, tracing, lettering, shading, ruling, and writing on stencil sheets for mimeographing; also, such an instrument used for engraving or etching. Also, in computer graphics, the conducting point which places the electrolitic charge on the printing medium.

subhead Heading or subdivision of text copy; a subordinate heading or title.

subscript *See* INFERIOR.

subsidy publisher Publisher who publishes books initially at the expense of the author but who may, under certain conditions, aid in financing.

subspanner head Heading in the boxhead of tables that is subordinate to a spanner head and which is the heading for two or more columnar headings.

substance Descriptive of the basis weight of paper expressed in pounds.

substrate Base material that is coated, or any substance that receives an impression on its printing surface.

suction feed Method of employing air suction to pick up paper and start to feed it through a printing press or similar machine. An automatic device introduces the air suction to pick up the paper and then cuts off the air at the proper instant to release the paper, which is caught between feed rollers. Suction feed may be distinguished from friction feed.

sulphate pulp *See* PAPER MANUFACTURING.

sulphite pulp *See* PAPER MANUFACTURING.

summary Supplement to the abstract of a publication, usually consisting of technical data. It precedes the body of the text. A summary is included only when a publication is lengthy or complicated. It should state concisely the reason for the publication, the matter covered, results and how they were obtained, and conclusions. The reader should be able to determine from it whether or not the subject matter is of interest. A summary is written last, after the author has a complete grasp of the subject.

Suncure system System developed by General Printing Ink, Division of Sun Chemical Corporation, that uses a systems approach to drying ink. The system uses ultraviolet light to instantly change a photosensitive liquid ink to a solid film. The system involves no solvent and improves on rub, scratch, and grease. The basic system comprises ultraviolet tube units mounted on the press and powered from a console interlocked with press controls. The number of units required depends on the speed of the particular press and whether units are installed between color stations for dry trapping. Each unit is designed to focus light on the fast-moving substrate. Upon exposure to the ultraviolet light, the Suncure inks that contain photosensitors and monomers polymerize and develop their dry-film properties, with little external heat involved. When the printed material leaves the press, it is ready for postpress operations.

supercalendered finish Glossy finish applied to paper by passing it repeatedly through the calender rolls of a papermaking machine.

superfine Designating high-grade writing paper.

superior Superscript or exponent; a letter, numeral, or symbol written above and to the right of another character, in contrast to an inferior, or subscript. It is set in a type size smaller than the text size. *See also* INFERIOR.

supplement Addition to a book or a newspaper or other periodical, intended to supply deficiencies or add special interest to a subject. It can be a separate publication printed to augment or change an original publication. A good example of a supplement is *Parade*, which is added to many large Sunday newspapers and bears the imprint (the name and sometimes the logotype) of the newspaper subscribing to it.

surface chart Graphical representation with plotted points moving across it from left to right in a logical sequence. The pattern thus reflected is extended to the base of the chart by shading or crosshatching. The shaded area is the predominant feature of the chart. The vertical scale may indicate quantities, while the base may reflect periods of time, expressed in hours, days, weeks, months, or years. An example of a surface chart is shown in Figure S-32. *See also* BAR CHART; COLUMN CHART; CURVE CHART; PIE CHART.

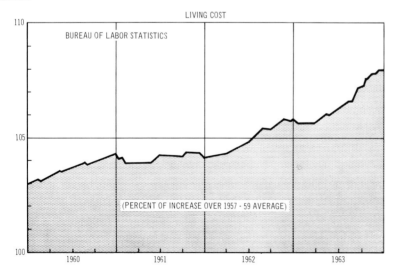

Fig. S-32 Surface chart.

surface sizing Sizing applied to paper by spraying it on both sides before it has run over the last series of dryer rolls in the papermaking machine. A sealed surface, such as that found on rag-content bond papers, is provided for ruling, typing, and printing.

surprinting Imposing unscreened line art on a plate on which halftone art has already been printed. In this procedure, the continuous-tone art has become a halftone by prior screening, but the line art remains unscreened and therefore presents a better definition without a dot formation. The term "surprinting" may also mean printing over copy that has already been printed.

swatch In printing, a color sample. When a printing color that may prove difficult to reproduce is desired, a swatch should be given to the printer. The printer will furnish a color proof if so requested.

symbol Any character, letter, or drawn configuration that is identified with or serves to explain the meaning of something. Unless a symbol is universally understood, a key or legend should be furnished to explain its intent.

symmetrical Designating an object whose parts are in balanced proportions on either side of a dividing line. Examples are cylinders, butterfly or airplane wings, and revolving doors.

tab *See* INDEX GUIDE.

table of contents *See* CONTENTS.

tabloid Newspaper about half the size of a regular newspaper. Text matter is compressed, and emphasis is placed on photographs.

tabloid fold *See* FIRST PARALLEL FOLD.

tabulated drawing Engineering drawing that depicts fixed characteristics only once but shows all differences in characteristics, dimensions, materials, finishes, or other requirements. Another drawing number or a double number is used to identify the difference. Since such a drawing may show many deviations from the basic characteristics of an item, it is unnecessary to make an individual drawing for each difference.

tack As used in printing inks, the stickiness or adhesive condition of the ink. If too adhesive, the ink can be conditioned by using a reducing compound. Tack is a quality of stickiness and is not to be confused with the viscosity of ink. If an ink is too thick, it can be thinned out by using a thinning additive.

tailpiece Decorative design employed at the end of a chapter or section to mark the conclusion of the chapter or section.

tandem roll stand Dual or single roll stand located at the front of a web-fed press that permits multiple webs (rolled stock) to be fed to the press at the same time.

tape converter Device that converts press-wire tape for photomechanical typesetting.

tape interpreter *See* READER.

tape perforator Machine designed to punch holes in coded tape for subsequent translation. It is used in conjunction with linecasting-control typesetters such as the Linotype and the Intertype to compose news text, editorial and market matter, box scores, and classified ads. Tape perforators have a standard keyboard arrangement, which is supplemented by additional keys and controls. An operator types the information in much the same manner as he or she would operate a typewriter. As a character or functional key is struck, not only is a visual copy produced but the coded character or function is simultaneously punched in the tape. The tape then contains information in the form of text matter. When it is fed into another machine, such as an interpreter, or reader, the device senses the code, automatically translates, or "reads," the coded characters and functions, and thus actuates the movements of the linecasting machine. *See also* READER.

tape, pressure-sensitive Tape having an adhesive back, available in many sizes, colors, and finishes and used in a variety of applications in the graphic arts. Very common uses are direct and indirect visual presentations such as flip charts, graphs, posters, signs, maps, diagrams, slides, overhead transparencies, overlays, training aids, flow plans, displays, office and plant layouts, and the like. Chartpak offers a large assortment of tapes in addition to transfer lettering, graphic films, symbols, and accessories. Tape sizes range in width increments of $\frac{1}{32}$ inch (0.794 mm) up to 2 inches (5.08 cm) wide and are available in all colors and shades. Tapes with a glossy surface are recommended for use in direct visual presentations because of their vivid color properties. Tapes having a matte finish are used for photographic reproduction because of their solid, nonreflective colors. They are also used for direct presentation before large groups where glare and lighting could make viewing difficult. Transparent and projectable color tapes are available for use in preparing slides, transparencies, projecturals, overlays, and all color compositions. Other tapes are color tapes or crepe paper that are flexible and curve with little or no distortion and are suitable for close-tolerance work. Pattern tapes in either a glossy or matte finish, with spacing between pattern lines and bars, are used for making charts, graphs, newspaper borders, training aids, technical illustrations, displays, exhibits, and the like. Fluorescent tapes, statistical and symbol tapes, plant and office layout tapes, decorative-border tapes, and mechanical production and custom-printed tapes are also available.

To apply the tape, place the end of the tape at the desired starting point on the drawing surface and unroll it until it is approximately 1 inch (2.54 cm) beyond the cutoff point. To cut the tape, place the frisket knife at the desired cutting point. Holding the tape with thumb and forefinger, pull the tape up against the edge of the knife with a diagonal movement while applying slight downward pressure with the knife. If tape is mispositioned or if revisions or corrections are required, the tape is easily lifted and repositioned. Chartpak provides a precision tape pen for applying tapes. The pen contains the roll of tape and can be used with drafting guides such as rules and French curves or can be used independently for freehand applications. Figure T-1 shows application of pressure-sensitive tape to a column chart.

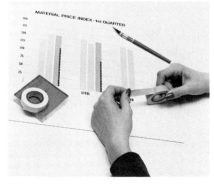

Fig. T-1 Applying pressure-sensitive tape to a column chart. (*Courtesy of Chartpak.*)

target date Date set for completing a task that presumably will allow ample time for quality control before the deadline.

teacher's manual (teacher's key) Guide for use by teachers in classroom instruction. Such a manual supplements a specific textbook but is printed and bound separately. Suggested elements for inclusion in a manual are instructions in how to use it, instructions in how to use the textbook to which it pertains, recommended questions and answers, methods of reviewing the subject matter, student problem areas, practice sheets, examination questions or suggestions, time schedules for assignments, study periods, and recommendations that will enable the teacher to conduct the course in accordance with good teaching practices.

tear sheet Sheet extracted from a publication that contains an advertisement or other matter. Tear sheets may be distributed to a select group or to an interested individual. A tearsheet containing an advertisement is usually furnished free to the advertiser on request.

technical illustration Graphic arts profession that embraces the art of making drawings for technical reports, proposals, manuals, and catalogs, as well as visual aids such as briefing charts, projecturals, slides, posters, and the like. Technical illustrations include wiring diagrams, cutaways, electrical schematics, pneumatic and hydraulic schematics, organization charts, graphs, pictorial and functional flow diagrams, and assembled and exploded views. Crayon, pastel, airbrush, pen and ink, pencil, oils, watercolors, and other equipment are utilized to produce images. A good knowledge of paper, types, paste-up, and reproduction equipment is required.

Technical illustrating did not come into its own as a professional field until World War II, when United States government agencies began to require instruction, maintenance, service, operation, flight, and other handbooks and manuals for use in maintaining and operating the equipment which they requisitioned. The field may now be divided into two main divisions: military illustrating for government agencies and commercial illustrating for private industry. On the military side, the art is created solely to serve as guidance, instruction, and planning material. Government standards and specifications must be followed. Sources of information for technical illustrators include engineering drawings whose orthographic projections must be converted to isometrics or perspectives, photographs, catalogs showing components and parts, observation of the equipment itself if it has been manufactured, and discussion of the equipment with engineers and others.

Not until the latter part of 1939 and the early part of 1940 were the first exploded views of an object photographed. The parts of the article were disassembled and placed in sequence on a flat surface, small parts being held in position with putty. An alternative method involved hanging the parts with string or wire against a bulkhead. These methods proved expensive and inadequate because airbrushing was required to remove the marks of the putty and strings. Moreover, it was practically impossible to obtain good perspective because flow lines were not exact. The next step was to trace the photograph of an exploded view in ink in order to improve its perspective and layout, but this method was time-consuming and expensive. The obvious answer to the problem was to draw exploded views directly from available information. Orthographic, isometric, perspective, and trimetric methods of projection are now used for exploded views. Figure T-2 illustrates the flow of art in a technical art department.

telephotography Method of photographing objects at a distance by using a telephoto lens or telescope with a camera; also, the technique of transmitting photographic or pictorial images over a distance. An example is Telstar, a privately financed communications satellite used to transmit television pictures and telephone messages.

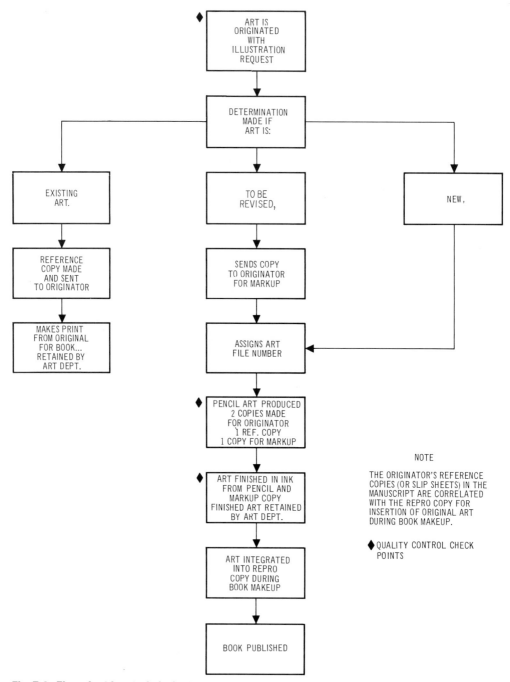

Fig. T-2 Flow of art in a technical art department.

technical pens *See* PENS, TECHNICAL.

Teletypesetter Tape-controlled operating unit for automatic linecasting control. Teletypesetter is a trademark of the Fairchild Graphic Equipment Corporation. The device is used extensively in newspaper work and in industry generally. The reader is attached to a slugcasting machine, such as the Linotype or the Intertype, to control keyboard operation. The name has come into general usage to refer to the coding system of this machine.

tempera Painting process in which the color is bound either with a size such as starch, glue, or casein or, especially, with egg instead of oil. The yolk or white of egg may be employed in combination or separately. Tempera was the most widespread method of painting among the early Egyptians, Babylonians, and Italians, who used such ingredients as fish oil, milk, and honey for painting on mummy cases, the walls of tombs, papyrus, parchment rolls, and panels. In modern usage, tempera is known as "distemper."

template Guide made of highly polished transparent or translucent plastic material, containing patterns for use in pencil and ink work. Edges and shapes are designed to suit requirements. The use of color makes templates easy to identify as work progresses and also prevents glare. Templates increase drawing and drafting output because shapes may thus be drawn quickly and accurately.

tension control Device used in web presses to control delivery of the web as it is fed through the press.

test setup Type of technical illustration used in a manual. It may be an orthographic drawing, as in Figure T-3, or a drawing showing components in either isometric or perspective projection. The isometric and perspective

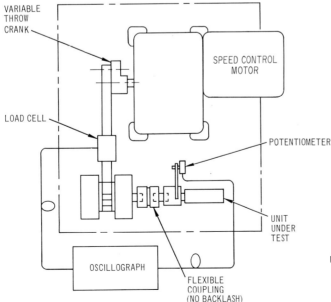

Fig. T-3 Test setup.

drawings present a true likeness of the components, whereas the ortho
graphic presentation is symbolic. Illustrations of test setups are supported
in the text of the manual with instructions on conducting the test.

text Typewritten or printed matter forming the main body of a work, as
opposed to front and back matter, illustrative material, tables, extracts,
and so on.

text finish Paper finish that is smoother than antique finish but not so
smooth as machine finish.

text paper High-quality uncoated paper of good appearance used for
books, booklets, brochures, programs, and the like. It may be obtained in
various colors. The basis weight is 60 pounds (27.2 kg) for 500 sheets of the
basic size of 25 by 38 inches (63.5 by 96.5 cm).

text type *See* BODY TYPE.

textured screen Sheet of material, usually film, used to add a textured
appearance to art subjects.

thermographic copying Dry heat-transfer process of producing copies
from an original. The image is heated with infrared radiation and transferred to copy paper that is sensitive to light.

thermography Inexpensive method of imitating engraved printing by the
use of heat. While the printing ink is still moist, the sheets are conveyed to
a machine that dusts the image with a powdered compound. Surplus
powder is vacuumed off, and the sheets are conveyed through an oven to
fix the powder. When the sheets are cooled, the result is raised lettering.
Colors include copper, gold, silver, and white. The finish may be dull or
glossy.

thin space Thin piece of type metal used to insert space between characters.

third-angle projection *See* ORTHOGRAPHIC PROJECTION: ENGINEERING DRAW-
INGS.

third cover *See* SECOND COVER.

third-dimension printing System of producing the illusion of depth in an
image by adding a third dimension to width and height. One method
involves coating a printed surface with plastic. Three-dimensional printing
promises to be a factor in display work, packaging, and point-of-sale
advertising.

three-view drawing *See* ORTHOGRAPHIC PROJECTION: ENGINEERING DRAWINGS.

throughput Operational unit of elapsed time; the interval of time from the
start of any task or job until the task or job is completed. The initial effort of

a task is the input, and the end product is the output. For example, a word-processing system will start with keyboarding a page of text; then the text is edited, corrected, and sent to a computer. A phototypesetter produces justified copy on paper or film as commanded by the computer. The paper or film so produced is the end product (output). Another example of an operational unit that illustrates throughput is one of production: a page is photographed with a process camera that produces a negative; the image on the negative is burned onto a sensitized printing plate; the plate is developed and attached to a printing press; and copies are printed, resulting in the end product.

thumb indexing *See* INDEX GUIDE.

thumbnail sketch Page layout, often used in advertising agencies, showing the allocation of space for headings, photographs or line artwork, and text copy. These sketches are the simplest form of layout used to present an idea. Following thumbnail sketches, more advanced layouts are known as the "rough" (or visual) and the comprehensive.

tick marks Short, fine lines imposed on a chart or graph to represent evenly spaced points on a scale between the vertical or horizontal division lines.

time card, illustration Card used in an illustration department for the record control of a piece of art. Figure T-4 shows a typical card. In a

ART WORK TIME CARD

ART SIZE _____   JOB NO. _____

REDUCTION _____   CODE NO. _____

OVER SIZE _____   PUB. NO. _____

REPRO SIZE _____   FIG. NO. _____

NOMENCLATURE _____   DATE OF ISSUE _____

ISSUED BY _____

ENGINEERING & PENCIL LAYOUT			INKING			OPAQUING			RETOUCHING			NOMENCLATURE		
DATE	TIME	INIT.	DATE	TIME	INIT.	DATE	TIME	INIT.	DATE	TIME	INIT.	DATE	TIME	INIT.
EST.			EST.			EST.			EST.			EST.		

NOTES: _____

_____

_____

_____

_____

Fig. T-4 Typical illustration time card.

technical publications department, the technical writer requests the illustration, but time estimates are entered by the art director or art supervisor because time and costs are the responsibility of the art department. The director or supervisor assigns the job and enters pertinent instructions for the illustrator on the card. The card is retained by the illustrator until the assignment has been completed. It is then returned to the director or supervisor with the completed art.

time-gamma curve In photography, a curve that indicates the development times necessary at various temperatures to produce approximately the same degree of contrast as is given by the recommended times at 68°F. The chart on which the curve is shown is called a time-temperature chart.

time-temperature chart Chart that indicates the development times necessary at various development temperatures to produce approximately the same degree of contrast as given by the recommended times at 68°F (20°C).

tint Light shade made by adding a small amount of color to an extender.

tint block Cut processed to print a panel of color. One or more tint blocks may be printed on a sheet. For example, if a color is to be printed at the top and bottom of a leaflet, tint blocks are used to print the colors and the colors are then overprinted with text or other line copy. Tint blocks are also often used behind halftones to produce an economical pseudoduotone effect.

tint plate Printing plate with an image bearing a tint block.

tinting In lithography, the uniform discoloring of a background caused by the bleeding or washing of the pigment in the fountain solution.

tip-in Separate page or other printed matter, such as postage-paid inquiry card, pasted in a publication. *See also* INSERT.

tip-on Object or material glued, stapled, or otherwise fastened to an advertising display or other printed matter. Tip-ons are used extensively in greeting cards.

tissue overlay Thin, translucent paper placed over artwork for protection and correction. Register marks are used on the overlay to ensure proper register for corrections. Overlays may also be placed over reproduction copy to mark corrections and to protect the copy while paste-ups are being burnished. Any light, inexpensive onionskin that does not have oily characteristics may serve as an overlay. Overlays should be retained on artwork or copy until all indicated corrections have been made. *See also* MOUNTING AND FLAPPING.

tissue proof Additional proof printed on tissue by some typesetters and furnished to a customer as an act of courtesy with a regular order for reproduction proofs. It can be used as a file copy.

title page Page of a book or other publication containing the full title and other information deemed necessary by the publisher, such as a brief synopsis, the author's name, the edition number, the name of the publisher, and the publisher's address. A half title precedes the full title page and is generally the first printed page of the book. Various United States government agencies issue specifications that set forth requirements for full- and half-title pages. Type sizes and faces, spacing, and the inclusion of information on contents are specified. These pages are typeset as reproduction proofs and are usually printed by photo-offset. *See also* HALF TITLE.

title slide Photographic slide used to show the title or titles for a slide presentation.

toe In photomechanics, the portion of the characteristic curve below the straight-line section. It represents the area of minimum useful exposure.

tone art Abbreviation for halftone art.

tone-line process Method of converting continuous-tone art to line art. A continuous-tone negative and a film positive are made of the subject in equal tone values. The two are then placed in precise register. They cancel each other out except at the edges of contrasting tones, where sufficient light penetrates to form a line rendering during exposure for platemaking.

toner Carbon particles that may be used dry or as a liquid when suspended in a liquid solvent, used to produce an image in electrostatic duplicating and copying machines.

tooth Ability of paper to take printing ink, drawing ink, pencil, and the like. If paper readily accepts these materials, it is said to have "tooth."

tracing cloth Duplicate drawing with a black image made on blue or white waterproof cloth. It is probably the longest-lasting type of duplicate. The tracing cloth may be produced from any negative and in widths as large as 54 inches (137 cm) by any length. Pencil or ink corrections are easily made, since the image may be removed with a dampened eraser tip. Rather than make an ink drawing, which requires expensive drawing time, it is advisable to make a good pencil drawing and have a duplicate tracing cloth made. The scale is fair to good.

tracing paper *See* DRAFTING AND TRACING MATERIALS.

trade book Books published for sale to the general public, including fiction, biographies, children's books, cookbooks, and the like, sold through bookstores, mail-order houses, and newsstands. Contrary to general thinking, it does not mean books written especially for the various trades.

trailing edge Last portion of a moving object that follows the remaining portion. An example is the trailing edge of a web (paper roll). The term is opposed to "leading edge."

transfer Sheet or gelatinlike film containing the image that is to be transferred to a metal printing surface.

Transfer-Key Proprietary name of 3M Company for a method of prepress proofing color separations. The process involves the following steps: (1) a cyan Transfer-Key is laminated to base stock; (2) the clear plastic liner is removed from the Transfer-Key and only the cyan color coating remains on base stock; (3) the cyan negative is positioned for exposure to ultraviolet light; (4) after exposure, the negative Color-Key developer is applied; (5) Transfer-Key processes the same as Color-Key and the unexposed pigment is removed; (6) the same procedure is followed for other colors (for example, yellow is developed over the cyan); (7) next, magenta is applied, exposed, and developed over yellow and cyan; and (8) the addition of black Transfer-Key produces full color on a single proof sheet. *See also* CONTACT IMAGING MATERIALS.

Fig. T-5 Applying letters from a Chartpak transfer sheet using a burnisher.

transfer sheet Sheet of clear acetate paper containing preprinted characters and symbols, used in preparing cold-composition, camera-ready reproduction copy. The character or symbol is placed over the desired position on the reproduction copy and is transferred in place by burnishing. The method differs from applying a wax-backed character or symbol in that it is not necessary to cut, paste, and burnish the character or symbol in place. An excellent application for this transfer method is copy in which equations and Greek letters predominate. The method is fast, economical, and accurate. *See* Figure T-5.

translucent Designating a material that permits the passage of light. Such a material is not transparent because the image is indistinct when viewed through it. Translucent materials such as cloths, films, drawing and tracing papers, and vellums are used as originals from which copies are made by whiteprint, blueprint, and other processes in which light penetration is required during exposure.

transmitted light Light that passes through a material.

transmitted-light exposure Method of making copies from originals during exposure by transmitted light, as opposed to exposure by reflex method. As indicated in Figure T-6, the original *B* is placed with the copy faceup. The emulsion side of the sensitized material *A* is placed facedown over the original. Light rays pass through the original *B* at points indicated by the letters *d* and reach the emulsion side of the sensitized material *A*, but they are intercepted by the image area (dark areas) indicated by the letters *c*. Therefore, the parts of the sensitized material above the dark areas are not exposed to light and do not form the image (or blacken) during development.

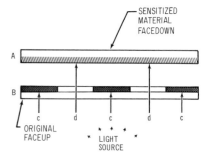

Fig. T-6 Method of exposure by transmitted light.

transparency Any transparent material that bears an image.

transparency, overhead *See* OVERHEAD TRANSPARENCY.

transparent Designating a material such as clear glass or clear acetate that permits the passage of light so that objects behind it are completely visible. Materials such as drawing and tracing papers, cloths, films, and vellums are not transparent; they are translucent. A distinct image must be seen through a material before it can be correctly termed "transparent."

transparent inks Inks that permit the passage of light, thus allowing previous printing or substrates to show through.

transparentizer Chemical available in spray cans, used to increase the reproduction quality of opaque originals.

transversing carriage Component of some phototypesetters. The carriage moves along the line being composed and reflects the image of the character onto a photographic paper or film.

triangular grid Grid used for plotting the curves of three variables with a constant sum. Problems involving three elements that are expressed in percentages can thus be graphically portrayed for comparison.

trigonometry symbols *See* TABLE 10, *page 446.*

trim marks Marks used on printed sheets or other substrate to indicate where the stock is to be cut or trimmed on both the horizontal and vertical dimensions. They perform the same purpose as crop marks, that is, they define the limits of the reproduction area of artwork or other defined areas.

trimetric projection *See* AXONOMETRIC PROJECTION.

trimmed size Size of a publication or a page after it has been trimmed to its final dimensions. Books are trimmed during the binding process.

tub sizing In the manufacture of paper, immersing the paper in a solution of glue. Better grades of rag-content bond paper are tub-sized.

tucker blade Reciprocating knifelike blade used in a web-fed printing press to form signatures into jaws when making a jaw fold or between rollers when making a chopper fold.

tucker fold Fold made by a jaw folder.

tumble *See* WORK AND TUMBLE.

turnaround Time from the acceptance or beginning of a job until the completed job is delivered.

turning bar *See* ANGLE BAR.

tusche Substance used for drawing in lithography and as a resist in etching and screen-process printing work.

TV screen Shadow box used to frame an illustration, as in Figure T-7. A TV screen sets off an assembled view from the main illustration and, depending on company practice, may be inserted with the exploded view in the upper left or right corner of the main illustration. It should be a true rectangle or square with heavier lines opposite the assumed source of light. The lines must not be so heavy as to detract from the view they enclose. Note that in the illustration the base line is broken at one point.

twice up In drawing, to a width twice that of artwork as it will appear on the printed page. If the illustration is to have a printed-page width of 7 inches (17.8 cm), it is drawn to a width of 14 inches (35.6 cm). The height must be increased proportionately.

two-scale chart Column chart in which two values are compared. The vertical columns usually represent quantity, and the horizontal dimension represents time. Comparisons of salaries, employment, sales, progress rates, distances, growth, and the like may be charted. Such charts may be expanded to show many factors. *See also* BAR CHART; COLUMN CHART; CURVE CHART; PIE CHART; SURFACE CHART.

tympan Hard-surfaced material used to cover the impression cylinder of a printing press. It serves as a cushion behind the paper receiving the impression.

type description Typography is an extensive field. Knowledge of common typefaces, relative sizes, measurements, leading and spacing, and the elements that compose type is a basic requirement for graphic arts students. The size of the typeface does not indicate or determine the size of the type in points, which is the standard system used to measure type. Note in Figure T-8 that the point measurement is the depth of the point body, which includes the shoulder, and that it is greater than the depth of the typeface. The body must be large enough to accommodate the ascenders and descenders of the particular typeface. Type set without other spacing between lines than that furnished by the shoulders is said to be "set solid." Additional spacing is provided by leading. *See also* LEADING; TYPE SPECIMENS; TYPEFACES.

type-high Designating the measurement from the base of the type to the top of the typeface. This dimension, which measures 0.918 inch (23.32 mm), was established as the standard by the Association of Type Founders of the United States.

type page Part of the page on which type is printed; the image area inside all margins.

type-size range Range in typeface sizes from the smallest to the largest size as measured in points.

type specimens Samples of type showing the various names, sizes, faces, and other information, offered for sale or available to the customer as a

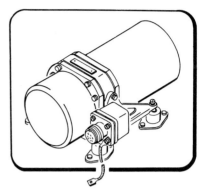

Fig. T-7 TV screen.

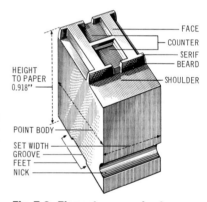

Fig. T-8 Elements composing type. (*Courtesy of American Type Founders.*)

Bodoni

Series Number 22

Characters in complete font

A B C D E F G H I J K L M N
O P Q R S T U V W X Y Z &
$ 1 2 3 4 5 6 7 8 9 0
a b c d e f g h i j k l m n o p q
r s t u v w x y z . , - : ; ! ? ' ' " "
fi ff fl ffi ffl

( ) [ ] Included in 6 to 18 pt.

Bodoni Italic

Series Number 23

Characters in complete font

*A B C D E F G H I J K L M N
O P Q R S T U V W X Y Z &
$ 1 2 3 4 5 6 7 8 9 0
a b c d e f g h i j k l m n o p q
r s t u v w x y z . , - : ; ! ? ' ' " "
fi ff fl ffi ffl*

Bulmer Roman

Series Number 497

Characters in complete font

A B C D E F G H I J K L M N
O P Q R S T U V W X Y Z &
$ 1 2 3 4 5 6 7 8 9 0
a b c d e f g h i j k l m n o p q
r s t u v w x y z . , - : ; ! ? ' '
fi ff fl ffi ffl

Caslon Oldstyle No. 471

Series Number 50

Characters in complete font

A B C D E F G H I J K L M N
O P Q R S T U V W X Y Z &
$ 1 2 3 4 5 6 7 8 9 0
a b c d e f g h i j k l m n o p q
r s t u v w x y z . , - : ; ! ? ')]
fi ff fl ffi ffl ct
Qu QU 6 to 18 pt. only

Caslon No. 540

Series Number 233

Characters in complete font

A B C D E F G H I J K L M N
O P Q R S T U V W X Y Z &
$ 1 2 3 4 5 6 7 8 9 0
a b c d e f g h i j k l m n o p q
r s t u v w x y z . , - : ; ! ? ' ( ) [ ]
fi ff fl ffi ffl ct

Caslon Bold

Series Number 817

Characters in complete font

A B C D E F G H I J K L M N
O P Q R S T U V W X Y Z &
$ 1 2 3 4 5 6 7 8 9 0
a b c d e f g h i j k l m n o p q
r s t u v w x y z . , - : ; ! ? ' ct st

Fig. T-9 Type specimens. (*Courtesy of American Type Founders.*)

Century Expanded
Series No. 59
Characters in complete font

A B C D E F G H I J K L M N
O P Q R S T U V W X Y Z &
$1234567890

abcdefghijklmnopqrst
uvwxyz.,-:;!?')[fiffflffiffl

Characters) are furnished only with sizes 4 to 36 point
Characters [are furnished only with sizes 4 to 18 point

Small Caps, 6 to 12 point

A B C D E F G H I J K L M
N O P Q R S T U V W X Y Z &

Century Schoolbook
Series Number 454
Characters in complete font

A B C D E F G H I J K L M N
O P Q R S T U V W X Y Z &
$ 1 2 3 4 5 6 7 8 9 0

a b c d e f g h i j k l m n o p q
r s t u v w x y z . , - : ; ! ? ' '
fi ff fl ffi ffl

Cheltenham Bold
Series Number 67
Characters in complete font

A B C D E F G H I J K L M N
O P Q R S T U V W X Y Z &
$ 1 2 3 4 5 6 7 8 9 0

a b c d e f g h i j k l m n o p q
r s t u v w x y z . , - : ; ! ? '

Cheltenham Bold Extra Condensed
Series Number 70
Characters in complete font

A B C D E F G H I J K L M N
O P Q R S T U V W X Y Z &
$ 1 2 3 4 5 6 7 8 9 0

a b c d e f g h i j k l m n o p q
r r s t u v w x y z . , - : ; ! ? '
fi ff fl ffi ffl

Garamond
Series Number 459
Characters in complete font

A B C D E F G H I J K L M N
O P Q R S T U V W X Y Z &
$ 1 2 3 4 5 6 7 8 9 0
a b c d e f g h i j k l m n o p q
r s t u v w x y z . , - : ; ! ? ' '
fi ff fl ffi ffl ct st

Garamond Bold
Series Number 474
Characters in complete font

A B C D E F G H I J K L M N
O P Q R S T U V W X Y Z &
$ 1 2 3 4 5 6 7 8 9 0
a b c d e f g h i j k l m n o p q
r s t u v w x y z . , - : ; ! ? ' '
fi ff fl ffi ffl

Goudy Bold

Series Number 446

Characters in complete font

A B C D E F G H I J K L M N
O P Q R S T U V W X Y Z &
$ 1 2 3 4 5 6 7 8 9 0
a b c d e f g h i j k l m n o p q
r s t u v w x y z . , - : ; ! ? ' '
fi ff fl ffi ffl

Goudy Bold Italic

Series Number 464

Characters in complete font

A B C D E F G H I J K L M N
O P Q R S T U V W X Y Z &
$ 1 2 3 4 5 6 7 8 9 0
a b c d e f g h i j k l m n o p q
r s t u v w x y z . , - : ; ! ? ' '
fi ff fl ffi ffl ct

Spartan Book

Series No. 707

Characters in complete font

A B C D E F G H I J K L M N
O P Q R S T U V W X Y Z &
$ 1 2 3 4 5 6 7 8 9 0 * ¢ %
a b c d e f g h i j k l m n o p q
r s t u v w x y z . , - : ; ! ? ' ' " " ( )

Ligatures are included in fonts of 6 to 18 point
sizes, and are obtainable in 24 to 36 point sizes
in foundry lines.

ff fi fl ffi ffl

Spartan Medium

Series Number 680

Characters in complete font

A B C D E F G H I J K L M N
O P Q R S T U V W X Y Z &
$ 1 2 3 4 5 6 7 8 9 0 * ¢ %
a b c d e f g h i j k l m n o p q
r s t u v w x y z . , - : ; ! ? ' ' " " ( )

Ligatures are included in fonts of 6 to 18 point
sizes, and are obtainable in 24 to 120 point
sizes in foundry lines.

fi ff fl ffi ffl

Spartan Black

Series Number 683

Characters in complete font

A B C D E F G H I J K L M N
O P Q R S T U V W X Y Z &
$ 1 2 3 4 5 6 7 8 9 0 ¢ %
a b c d e f g h i j k l m n o p q
r s t u v w x y z . , - : ; ! ? ' ' " " ( )

Ligatures are included in fonts of 6 to 18 point
sizes, and are obtainable in 24 to 120 point
sizes in foundry lines.

fi ff fl ffi ffl

Spartan Black Condensed

Series Number 687

Characters in complete font

A B C D E F G H I J K L M N
O P Q R S T U V W X Y Z &
$ 1 2 3 4 5 6 7 8 9 0 ¢ %
a b c d e f g h i j k l m n o p q
r s t u v w x y z . , - : ; ! ? ' ' " " ( )

Ligatures are included in fonts of 10 to 18 point
sizes, and are obtainable in 24 to 120 point
sizes in foundry lines.

fi ff fl ffi ffl

Stymie Light

Series Number 553

Characters in complete font

A B C D E F G H I J K L M N
O P Q R S T U V W X Y Z &
$ 1 2 3 4 5 6 7 8 9 0
a b c d e f g h i j k l m n o p q
r s t u v w x y z . , - : ; ! ? ' ' « » ( ) § *

Superior $ furnished only with sizes 24 to 48 pt.

Stymie Medium

Series Number 552

Characters in complete font

A B C D E F G H I J K L M N
O P Q R S T U V W X Y Z &
$ 1 2 3 4 5 6 7 8 9 0
a b c d e f g h i j k l m n o p q
r s t u v w x y z . , - : ; ! ? ' ' ( )

Superior $ furnished with sizes 24 to 72/60 pt.

Franklin Gothic

Series Number 162

Characters in complete font

A B C D E F G H I J K L M N
O P Q R S T U V W X Y Z &
$ 1 2 3 4 5 6 7 8 9 0
a b c d e f g h i j k l m n o p q
r s t u v w x y z . , - : ; ! ? '

Franklin Gothic Wide

Series Number 701

Characters in complete font

A B C D E F G H I J K L M N
O P Q R S T U V W X Y Z &
$ 1 2 3 4 5 6 7 8 9 0
a b c d e f g h i j k l m n o p q
r s t u v w x y z . , - : ; ! ? ' ' " "

News Gothic

Series Number 338

Characters in complete font

A B C D E F G H I J K L M N
O P Q R S T U V W X Y Z &
$ 1 2 3 4 5 6 7 8 9 0
a b c d e f g h i j k l m n o p q
r s t u v w x y z . , - : ; ! ? '

News Gothic Extra Condensed

Series Number 340

Characters in complete font

A B C D E F G H I J K L M N
O P Q R S T U V W X Y Z &
$ 1 2 3 4 5 6 7 8 9 0
a b c d e f g h i j k l m n o p q
r s t u v w x y z . , - : ; ! ? '

Murray Hill Bold

24 pt. 5A 19a 8-1   L. c. alphabet 200 pts.   Char. per pica 1.7

Brazil and Colombia exported to Europe
pottery impregnated with delicate perfumes.
It shows civilizations at a time so remote

Bernhard Gothic Medium
Italic

24 pt. 6A 13a 5-1   Lower case alphabet 260 pts.   Characters per pica 1.3

BRAZIL AND THE OTHERS
*It shows that civilization at a time
so remote could establish at that*

Caslon 641

24 pt. 6A 12a 8-1   Lower case alphabet 323 pts.   Characters per pica 1.0

Rail and road transportation
close at hand plus a network

Cooper Black

24 pt. 5A 10a 6-1   Lower case alphabet 376 pts.   Characters per pica .91

TO THE BUSY EXEC IN
the hustle and bustle of

Craw Clarendon Condensed

24 pt. 9A 13a 7-1   L. c. alphabet 277 pts.   Char. per pica 1.2

GRAPHIC DESIGNER, RESPONSIVE
to all the needs and requirements

24 pt. 5A 7a 4-1   L. c. alphabet 535 pts.   Char. per pica .64

LETTER FORMS
is truly excellent

Dom Bold

24 pt. 10A 18a 8-1   Lower case alphabet 202 pts.   Characters per pica 1.7

BRAZIL AND OTHER COUNTRIES ARE
It shows civilization at a time so remote

Franklin Gothic

24 pt. 6A 11a 5-1   Lower case alphabet 349 pts.   Characters per pica .98

Brazil and Peru export to

HEADLINE GOTHIC

48 pt. 4A 3-1

ZERO IS A MARK

Lydian Italic

30 pt. 7A 12a 5-1   Lower case alphabet 314 pts.   Characters per pica 1.1

JADE VARIES IN COLOR
It is used for jewelry or carve

New Caslon

24 pt.   5A 12a 7-1   Lower case alphabet 328 pts.   Characters per pica 1.0

BRAZIL AND OTHER
Shows civilization at a time
so remote that it is doubtful

UNIVERS 46

24-L pt. 6A 11a 6-1   Lower case alphabet 327 pts.   Characters per pica 1.0

| ABCDEFGHIJKLMNOPQR
| abcdefghijklmnopqrstuvw.

News Gothic

30 pt. 6A 11a 5-1   Lower case alphabet 343 pts.   Characters per pica 1.0

JADE VARIES IN COLOR
It is used for jewelry and

UNIVERS 65

24-L pt. 5A 10a 5-1   Lower case alphabet 352 pts.   Characters per pica .97

| ABCDEFGHIJKLMNOP
| abcdefghijklmnopqrstuv

printing service. Figure T-9 shows examples of type specimens. Compositors stock a variety of sizes and faces, and most have type books that show specimens available to users. Unless the customer is familiar with the type a printer stocks, he or she should order the desired face and size with the notation "or equivalent." This leaves the compositor free to recommend and select an equivalent face and size carried in stock.

Type may be divided into two main divisions: text type, which is suited to solid blocks of text; and display type, which is used for display advertising, headings, and nomenclature applied to artwork and visual aids when large sizes are required.

Text type generally ranges from 8 to 10 points (2.8 to 3.51 mm), although 12-point (4.21-mm) and even 14-point (4.9-mm) and larger type may be used for children's reading books and textbooks in the lower grades. An 8-point (2.8-mm) size is quite small, but dictionaries and similar publications may have text as small as 6 points (2.11 mm). The ideal size for newspaper text is 9 points (3.16 mm); 10-point (3.51-mm) type is popular for magazines, trade journals, typewritten matter, books, proposals, technical manuals, reports, and numerous other applications. Although 12-point (4.21-mm) type is too large for large blocks of text in conventional adult books, it is ideally suited for small blocks of text for mechanicals and for descriptive text in fine proposal work when used as a cutline with illustrative material. In general, there is a tendency to select type that is too small as text type.

Display typefaces are large faces that draw attention. A text type in 10 points can become a display type in 36 or 72 points (12.6 or 25.3 mm). Typefaces have distinctive design characteristics that make them suitable for particular tasks. Type creates an illusion. Its appearance can suggest a thought, an idea, a statement, or a fact that it represents in copy. Type also conveys a mood or a condition, such as humor, happiness, gaiety, frivolity, anxiety, stateliness, solidarity, even sadness. Or, it can be feminine or masculine, soft or hard. It can whisper or shout and be bold or delicate. These illusions are the result of thick and thin lines, curves, boldfaces and heavy lines, solid masses of black and color, the presence or absence of serifs, and embellishments.

typefaces The face of the type is the printing surface. A typeface may be judged by its design, printability, wearability, and position on the body. Past and present masters of the art of letter design and typographic layout have contributed much to the creation of artistic and practical type. Printability depends on deeply engraved matrices in hard nickel brass, from which the type is cast, on matrices made to provide crisp, clean edges on the finished product, on finishing tools that produce sharp edges and well-incised crotches, and on matrices chromium-plated to impart a mirror-smooth printing surface to the type cast from them. Wearability depends on the use of high-quality metal cast at a high temperature under extreme pressure in a water-cooled mold. Type so made is tightly compressed and uniform in grain. It will print sharp images and last for a long time. The position of the face on the body is important for proper alignment and spacing. A strong and durable type results from the liberal use of tin, antimony, and copper, as well as from casting under rigidly controlled conditions.

Many faces and sizes of type have been manufactured since the first black-letter design, now sometimes used for German. This was the only design until roman and italic faces made their appearance. In the early eighteenth century, William Caslon of England designed the classic roman face. Later in the century, Giambattista Bodoni of Italy designed the first modern letter.

There are four basic forms of typefaces: text, roman, italic, and script (*see* Figure T-10). The roman faces, in one variation or another, make up the modern faces known today. All present-day type is based on these designs; it may be divided into two groups of faces, Old Style and modern. Figure T-11 shows the names used to describe the various lines of typefaces.

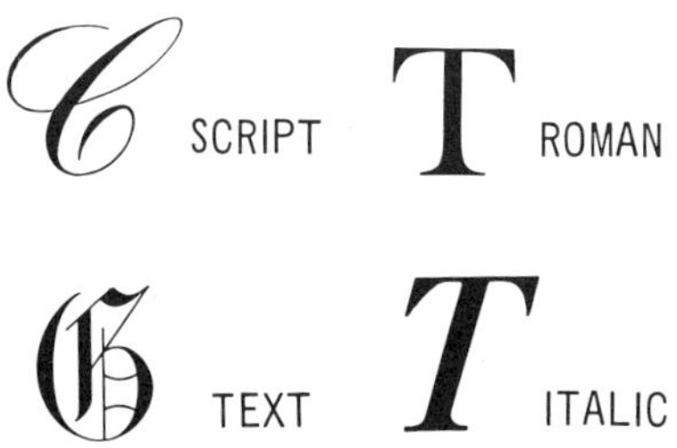

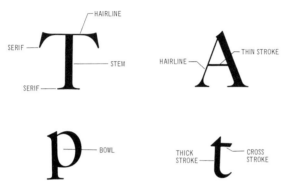

Fig. T-10 Basic letter forms of typefaces.

Fig. T-11 Typeface composition.

typescript Typewritten text copy.

typeset matter, ordering of Typesetting costs can be reduced and better quality assured when the compositor is intelligently informed of all requirements. The compositor's task is to follow copy, that is, to set exactly as it was submitted. Before ordering typeset matter, copy should be proofread for errors in spelling, punctuation, capitalization, and the like and checked for paragraph numbering (if any), indention, page numbering, and general format. Changes made to the typescript should be neat and legible and written in lowercase and capital letters as they are to be set. Copy should be double-spaced, typed on one side of a sheet, and paginated in sequence, preferably in the upper right corner of each page. Long tables should be typed on separate pages.

The following suggestions for ordering typeset matter should be considered:

1. Specify the typefaces for text and headings and make certain that the printer has the available faces and sizes. If this is not certain, the notation "or equivalent" should be included on the purchase order.

2. Specify the type size in points or request the compositor to recommend a size.

3. For text copy, keep the line measure to approximately 39 characters (1½ alphabets is considered an ideal measure).

4. Give the line measure in picas, not in inches.

5. Specify copy that is to run ragged. Otherwise, the compositor will justify the lines.

6. Designate the leading desired (*see* LEADING).

7. If other than normal reproduction proofs are desired, specify "Avery" for adhesive-backed paper, "dull seal" for transparent stock with an adhesive back, and "cell" for transparent stock without an adhesive back; or specify the particular paper desired.

typesetters, photographic The advent of computerized photographic typesetting, coupled with composition systems such as the keyboarded text editing and correction video-display terminals, has been one of the greatest steps forward in the printing industry since Mergenthaler patented his Linotype in 1885. The experimental stage for the development of automated composition and related peripherals ended in 1972; 1973 began a period of great technical advances. The abundance of technology was enormous, and manufacturers placed emphasis on equipment capability and cost effectiveness to catch up with technology. The following methods and materials have been developed: Typemasters (or disks), magnetic cards, paper tape and cassette tapes, automatic hyphenation and justification, type capacity sizes and styles, video display terminals, correcting and editing terminals, optical character recognition, exposure methods, format, line-composition speeds, computer technology, and keyboarding. Emphasis was placed on the total systems approach by most manufacturers and on software and hardware from input to output.

Large and small in-house production centers, the job printer, magazine and book publishers, and newspaper publishers are converting at a rapid rate to computerized photographic typesetting. The steady growth rate and popularity of lithographic printing continues to rise and fits hand-in-glove with computerized text processing. Phototypesetting machines are versatile in supplying a variety of type designs and sizes with great flexibility. In addition, the price of machines has gone down and the quality of output, ease of operation, ease of equipment maintenance, and personnel training have progressed.

Fig. T-12 VariTyper's Headliner Model 820 photolettering display typewriter.

VariTyper's Headliner Model 820 (Figure T-12) composes one or more lines of type at the rate of 30 or more characters per minute. A wide assortment of type and other characters from 10 to 84 points (3.51 to 29.5 mm) may be selected. Each character is automatically letterspaced on transparent film or plastic-coated opaque paper, 35-millimeter sprocketed, plain or with an adhesive back, and packed in disposable daylight-loading cartridges. The film may be used as a transparency for projection. Type is selected by placing the desired font, a plastic disk called a "Typemaster," in operating position on the machine. A print key is pressed for each character in the copy. The Headliner automatically develops, fixes, and washes the type proof and delivers it ready for use in about ninety seconds. Up to five lines may be produced on the strip when using multiple-line Typemaster discs. Line selection is made by dialing for proper lighthouse mask aperture.

Figure T-13 shows Alphatype Corporation's Signal-Set desk-top phototypesetting headliner. An incremental spacing control is set that automat-

Fig. T-13 Alphatype Corporation's Signal-Set desk-top phototypesetting headliner.

ically spaces the headline to suit the allotted space. A variable incremental spacing control justifies lines in the desired typeface. Each reel (font) can hold 10 to 12 alphabets, and over 2,800 fonts are available from 12 to 144 point (4.21 to 50.6 mm). Special symbols, logotypes, reverse lettering (white letters on a black background), borders, shadow lettering, and other effects are produced. A foot pedal is pressed to expose the letter. Printing is on paper or film.

Figure T-14 is the Comp/Set 500 direct-entry phototypesetter. The typesetter is designed for use by the newspaper printer, the sophisticated printing establishment, the small job shop compositor, and the in-house printing plant. There are about 70 type sizes on-line ranging from 5½ to 74 points (1.93 to 26 mm). Four type styles are on-line and are unrestricted as to size and font mixing. Alphanumerics are virtually identical with the universal keyboard except that color-separated designations indicate locations of nontypewriter characters such as fractions and symbols. Command and format keys are separately color-identified and are grouped adjacent to the alphanumeric keys for ready access. Keytop designations are designed to be easily understood by both the novice and experienced operator. The machine's video screen displays 14-point green characters on an 8 by 11-inch (20.3 by 27.9-cm) background. The main body of the screen contains the equivalent of two full lines of type, i.e., the line being keyboarded and the line being set by the phototypesetter. Each of these can contain up to 256 characters, the maximum content of a 45-pica (190-mm) line in 5½ point (1.93 mm) type of average width. Typographical characteristics of the Comp/Set 500 are four fonts on-line, 112 characters per font, 33 sizes on-line from 5½ to 36 point (1.93 to 12.6 mm), instant font and size selection from the keyboard, 45-pica (190-mm) line length capa-

Fig. T-14 Comp/Set 500 direct-entry phototypesetter. (*Addressograph-Multigraph Corp.*)

bility in all sizes, all type base-aligned, and font and size mixing. Typeface selection consists of over one hundred faces.

The Comp/Set Series 4500 phototypesetters (Figure T-15) includes six models: three models for English language composition and three for foreign composition. The phototypesetter is equipped with a multidisk turret (see insert) that permits the unit to operate with 16 fonts of 112 characters each on-line. However, a dual floppy disk model is available. The 4500 Series is capable of setting type in sizes ranging from 5½ to 74 points (1.93 to 26 mm) in 70 different-size graduations. The series accommodates logic hyphenation with operator-programmable exception dictionary. The type library consists of over 200 type styles. The phototypesetters operate at 50 lines per minute (speed is based on 9 point [3.16 mm] type, 11-pica [47-mm] lines) with proofed-copy output at 70 lines per minute. When equipped with an optional 503 or 504 record/playback module, the 4500 handles input from multiple off-line sources.

The keyboard is color-coded for simplicity of operation, alphanumerics are identical with those of the standard keyboard typewriter, and command and format keys are grouped for ready access. There are no off-keyboard dials or switches to distract the operator. The video display consists of an 11 by 8-inch (28 by 20.3-cm) screen with 14-point (4.91-mm) characters displayed on a black background, two typeset lines of up to 256 characters each, and a two-line function field. Mixing is unlimited of all on-line sizes and styles, and line length is a maximum of 45 picas (190 mm) in all sizes. Leading is primary, secondary, and add-lead, each from 0 to 99½ points (34.8 mm) in ½-point (0.1756-mm) graduations.

Fig. T-15 Comp/Set Series 4500 phototypesetter. (*Addressograph-Multigraph Corp., VariTyper Division.*)

Compugraphic's UniSetter typesetter (*see* Figure T-16) can be utilized as a stand-alone or on-line system component such as a direct-entry keyboard. The UniSetter provides 96 different fonts (6 to 72 point) (2.11 to 25.2 mm) and positions copy anywhere on a line measure up to 45 picas (190 mm). It allows mixing on all type styles within the same line and has a dual output speed of 50 and 80 lines per minute. Over 600 text and display typefaces are available. In addition, copy can be aligned with the right margin, the left margin, or both margins, with or without hyphenation, and centered within line measures by command. Input to the typesetter is 6-level justified or unjustified TTS-coded paper tape, on-line to terminal or computer. Up to eight different typefaces of 118 characters each on two interchangeable filmstrips serve as the typeface capacity, and there are 12 base-aligning type sizes in high and low range from 6 to 72 points. Photographic paper in 3, 6, or 8-inch (7.62, 15.2, or 20.3-cm) widths is used.

Compugraphic Corporation provides a series of direct-input photo-typesetters: the CompuWriter IV, CompuWriter 88, and CompuWriter 48. Figure T-17 shows the CompuWriter 88. The only difference between the three designs is in the number of type styles and sizes offered to meet specific requirements. All other features are identical. Typeface capacity of the series ranges from four through eight typefaces of 118 characters each on two interchangeable filmstrips. There are eight or twelve base-aligning type sizes that range from 6 through 72 point (2.11 through 25.2 mm), depending upon the design. Font mixing is unrestricted of all styles and sizes within a line, and any line measure up to 45 picas (190 mm) can be programmed. Reverse leading can be had from 1 to 72 points (0.351 to 25.2 mm) in 1-point increments. Switch or keystroke control of leading from 0 to 127½ points (0 to 44.8 mm) in ½-point (0.175-mm) increments is provided. Character compensation, letterspacing, kerning, typographic formats, and displays are designed into the series. Photographic paper is in 3, 6, or 8-inch (7.62, 15.2, or 20.3-cm) widths.

Compugraphic's EditWriter 7500 typesetter is shown in Figure T-18. This is a stand-alone system with a composition management keyboard, video display terminal, computer-managed storage and retrieval, and outputting photograph paper widths of 2, 3, 4, 6, and 9 inches (5.08, 7.62, 10.16, 15.2, and 20.3 cm). The video display terminal has a 15-inch (38.1-cm) (diagonal) cathode-ray tube utilizing 12 inches (30.4 cm) for distortion-free display. Character size on the screen is approximately 18 point (6.32 mm), with formatting instructions shown at half intensity of easy identification. Character complement is 256 uppercase and lowercase alphanumerics and function symbols, and the screen has a capacity of 15 lines: one "message line," one "status line," and 13 copy lines out of a scrolling memory of up to 200 lines (6,000 characters). Storage is the random-access floppy-disk type, with 128 variable-length files per disk and 300,000 characters. More than 100 formats can be stored. There are 12 type sizes on-line, with the high range from 6 through 72 point (2.11 through 25.2 mm) and the low range from 6 through 36 point (2.11 through 12.6 mm). Font capacity is 96 points (33.7 mm) on-line, with two film masters of four faces each in 12 sizes. There are 118 characters per font and a total character capacity of 11,328 characters on-line. Line measurement is up to 45 picas (190 mm) in all sizes. Justification, hyphenation, and quadding are auto-

Fig. T-16 Compugraphic's UniSetter photographic typesetter.

Fig. T-17 Compugraphic's CompuWriter 88.

Fig. T-18 Compugraphic's EditWriter 7500 photographic typesetter.

matic or manual with logic and discretionary characteristics as required.

Figure T-19 is Compugraphic's CompuWriter II photographic typesetter. Some of the features of this machine are a 32-character correctable display; a display of the line length remaining after keyboarding, which enables the operator to achieve the best possible line ending; a front indicator that shows possible selection of four type styles with indicator light showing what style the machine is setting; automatic line ending; discretionary hyphenation; line length selection up to 45 picas (190 mm); and line spacing from 0 to 31½ points (0 to 11 mm). Two different line lengths, leading values, and type sizes can be programmed and then selectively accessed for cut-runarounds, tabular work, and other jobs requiring frequent changes in typographic format and type size. Space between characters and lines can be added, characters may be kerned, and reverse leading in 1-point (0.175-mm) increments to 24 points (8.42 mm) can be achieved. Input is direct-entry, font capacity is four 96-character fonts, type sizes are same size or double size at a keystroke, type size range is 6 through 24 point (2.11 through 8.43 mm), and photographic paper is in 3, 6, or 8-inch (7.62, 15.24, or 20.3 cm) sizes.

Figure T-20 is Compugraphic's Display Composition System (DCS). The system is a computer-assisted area composition setup for handling text, classified and display advertisements, charts and forms, and periodical, catalog, and book pages. Its components include the Unified Composer, PreView, a hard-copy printer, and the VideoSetter Universal. The combination provides for input, markup, hyphenation and justification, storage and retrieval, proofing, and setting of complex matter. Copy may be introduced as input from a variety of sources and then formatted at the Unified Composer. In addition to its editing capabilities, the Unified Composer is a copy management system. The system's computer-con-

Fig. T-19 Compugraphic's CompuWriter II photographic typesetter.

Fig. T-20 Compugraphic's Display Composition System.

trolled floppy-disk storage system provides recall for proofing, editing, and incorporation of changes in copy. The system allows definition of file names, which are automatically indexed and stored on the floppy disk. The storage and retrieval system increases productivity by automatic management of composition.

The Unified Composer serves as the graphics center of the DCS to receive, code, store, and retrieve copy for all copy changes. It allows storage and retrieval of composition, and operators can see all line-ending decisions. Other features include complete editing operations at the terminal; the ability to correct, delete, and insert characters and words and full copy blocks; 14 viewable lines of copy with message line; scrolling capacity up to 128 lines; search capability of stored files; index display and 300,000 characters stored per disk; and automatic sorting and merging by keyboard coding and discretionary hyphenation and justification. Also, copy can be sent on-line from the Unified Composer screen or disk to the PreView for display or to the VideoSetter Universal for typesetting.

The PreView utilizes the VideoSetter Universal to display a "soft proof" copy on the 19-inch (48.2-cm) viewing screen. Once input is completed and set to the VideoSetter Universal, the PreView becomes a window to the typesetter and the type is displayed in the same point size, typeface, and position specified. The position of each copy block, rule, and box is displayed as it will appear in the typeset copy, size for size. Thus, the operator sees the job as it will be in the finished galley or page form.

An option to the system is a hard-copy printer which produces a direct, full-size proof print of the image seen on the PreView screen. This process allows the operator to receive an immediate proof of the material without going through a typesetting pass.

The VideoSetter Universal has options for reverse leading and ruling and reverse type. Output is approximately 400 lines per minute. Seventy-six type sizes and 96 styles are produced from eight machine-resident and interchangeable glass grids of 106 characters each. Character compensation is automatic with full kerning, offering character fit on display ads. Hyphenation is automatic and discretionary. Justified, ragged-left, and ragged-right composition is also automatic by input command. Two methods of tabbing, automatic and sequential, may be intermixed to produce an unlimited number of columns across a full line length of up to 45 picas (190 mm). Optional reverse leading, up to 24 inches (61 cm), minimizes paste-ups and makes possible setting pages up to 10 full columns in position at high speed. Ruling (optional) and reverse-leading features combine to electronically produce boxes of any size. Rules are set to any depth up to 24 inches (61 cm) in up to 73 weights. The machine also features direct production of reverse type, from 5 to 60 points, within one job. Reverse leading, electronic ruling, and direct production of reverse type are available under keyboard command for easy control and increased productivity.

Figure T-21 is the VariTyper AM 748 photographic typesetter. The typesetter is designed to meet requirements of the newspaper plant, the printer, and in-house industrial capabilities. Input consists of 6, 7, or 8-channel perforated tape and in-line or advanced feed. All types may be used interchangeably. There are eight type sizes ranging from 5 to 72 point (1.76 mm to 25.3 mm), including any four text sizes with any four display sizes. Text sizes are 5, 5½, 6, 7, 8, 9, 10, 11, and 12 point (1.76, 1.9, 2.11, 2.5, 2.8, 3.2, 3.5, 3.9, and 4.2 mm). Display sizes are 14, 18, 24, 30, 36, 48, 60, and 72 point (4.9, 6.3, 8.4, 11.0, 12.6, 16.9, 21.0, and 25.3 mm). The type disc contains 112 character fonts. Font selection is by tape command and disk change time is less than one minute. Type design is based on 18 units to the em, base-aligned. Line length is up to 45 picas as follows: type sizes are 5, 5½, 6, 7, 8, 9, and 10 point (1.76, 1.93, 2.11, 2.5, 2.8, 3.2, and 3.6 mm) and larger; maximum picas are 20½, 24, 28½, 39, 42, and 45 (87, 102, 121, 165, 178, and 190 mm). Primary and secondary leading can be selected singly or in combination for one or more feeds. Values are entered on control panel dials to a maximum of 49½ points (17.3 mm) for type up to 30 point (11 mm) and a maximum of 99 points (34.8 mm) for type larger than 36 point (12.6 mm). Additional leading values can be entered in any amount up to 99½ points (35 mm) on a line-by-line basis from tape command. Speed is 50 lines per minute, based on 9 point (3.16 mm) type with an 11-pica (47 mm) line. Xenon flash is the light source. Output is phototypesetting paper or film up to 8 inches wide. Imaging material is removed from the phototypesetter in lighttight cassettes for processing. The AM 748 typesetter has a height of 57 inches (145 cm), a width of 23 inches (58 cm), and a depth of 45 inches (114 cm).

Figure T-22 shows Mergenthaler's Linocomp 2 phototypesetter. This is a direct-entry phototypesetter having the keyboard and typesetting component combined as a single unit. It serves as a stand-alone production backup device for Mergenthaler's line of second-generation cathode-ray tube (CRT) typesetters. (The CRT is the character exposure method used.) Capabilities include the full range of Mergenthaler and ITC typefaces; complete inter- and intraline mixing of four typefaces; 14 type sizes ranging from 6 to 36 points (2.11 to 12.6 mm); optional tape reader and punch; and a 32-character uppercase and lowercase message display.

Fig. T-21 VariTyper AM 748 phototypesetter. (Addressograph-Multigraph Corp.)

Fig. T-22 Mergenthaler's Linocomp 2 phototypesetter.

Other features include microprocessor control, fully automatic aesthetic kerning in ⅑ relative units, expanded automatic tab capabilities, access from memory of up to 20 variable-width table columns with full control over typefaces, sizes, quadding, and line lengths, in addition to 19 gutters with the ability to specify any size gutter. Line-length capability is 45 picas (190 mm) maximum, and paper sizes are variable with 3, 4, 6¾, and 9-inch (7.62, 10.16, 17.14, and 23-cm) widths.

Figure T-23 is Mergenthaler's Linotron 606 typesetter designed for large-volume typesetting, including newspapers, books, directories, timetables, and statistics. The machine consists of a single, compact cabinet that contains a high-speed magnetic disk, a minicomputer, interface and electronic control circuits, a microspot cathode-ray tube system, and a film magazine. Text for typesetting can be input to the Linotron 606 by means of paper tape, magnetic tape (7- to 9-level), or direct connection to a computer. The paper tape reader accepts either 6-level tape with advanced feed hole or 8-level tape with in-line feed hole. The reading speed is approximately 700 characters per second. The number of characters in a typical font is between 100 and 130, depending on the type style, but the disk storage space occupied by a single font varies according to the point size range. For example, there is room on the disk for approximately 2,000 fonts in sizes up to 12 points (4.21 mm), 700 fonts in sizes up to 24 points (8.43 mm), 250 fonts in sizes up to 48 points (16.9 mm), and 125 fonts in sizes up to 96 points (34 mm). The machine produces right-reading or wrong-reading outputs on film or paper. The photographic material may be in any width from 8 to 17 inches (20.3 to 43 cm), and the exposed text lines can be in any measure up to 100 picas (423 mm), variable in 1-point steps.

Fig. T-23 Mergenthaler's Linotron 606 typesetter.

The film magazine contains a feed cassette that holds up to 400 feet (122 m) of film or paper and an output cassette that holds up to 150 feet (46 m) of exposed material. To load a tape, the operator inserts the output cassette into the front of the machine and presses a button. The machine threads itself automatically and stops at a point where type can be correctly exposed. On completion of the typesetting run, the exposed film or paper is advanced into the output cassette and cut off by an automatic knife.

Mergenthaler has developed four modularly designed, interactive computer systems based around its variable-input phototypesetters (VIP) as production systems for commercial, book, in-plant, and other typographic needs. Designated VIP Systems 10, 20, 30, and 40 are designed around the concept that while the VIP user has a wide range of typographic functions under the control of the computer built into the phototypesetter, there are situations where more data storage and retrieval and formatting capabilities are required. The systems interface to the VIP phototypesetters with a 32K computer, a 12.5 megabyte disk, a line printer, and up to six Linoscreen 300 video display terminals (VDTs), with optical scanning and paper tape punch optionally offered. The system is on-line except for input, which is tape-oriented. System 10 (Figure T-24) is the basic system that interfaces with one VIP typesetter, a line printer, up to three VDTs, and the computer. System 20 involves two VIP phototypesetters, one of which may operate off-line when required. System 30 involves two duplexed computers and simultaneous operation of up to six

Fig. T-24 Mergenthaler's VIP Basic System 10.

VDTs. This configuration provides expanded production capabilities and is partially redundant. System 40 provides complete redundancy, because in addition to the duplexed computer, the 12.5 megabyte disks are also duplicated.

The Harris Fototronic 7400 system-oriented CRT phototypesetter (Figure T-25) combines typesetting speeds with mixing speed. For straight text, it sets type at 500 lines per minute with the standard paper tape reader. With optional on-line interface to an information handling system, such as the Harris 2500 system, it can set up to 1,000 lines of text per minute. The 7400 also accepts 6-level TTS justified stock market input to typeset multicolumn stock listings. The typesetter is designed with a 68 pica (288 mm) line length; however, the length can be expanded to 100 picas (423 mm) if required. The 5 through 96 point (1.76 through 34 mm) size range is sizable in 1-point (0.3514 mm) increments. The basic 7400 system includes digital storage for 20 on-line typefaces, with up to 128 characters in each font in the full 5 through 96 point (1.76 through 34 mm) size range. Expanded digital storage of up to 80 typefaces is optional. Reverse leading up to 30 inches (76.2 mm) in increments of 1 point (0.3514 mm) is standard. Horizontal and vertical rules are also standard. Input modes are 6 or 8-level paper tape, on-line interface, and other input auxiliary modes. Photographic material is stabilization paper, RC paper, or film up to 475 feet (145 mm). The system accepts film or paper for line lengths of 18, 30, 42, 45, 51, 54, 60, and 68 picas (76, 127, 178, 190, 216, 229, 254, and 288 mm).

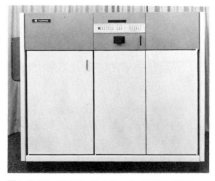

Fig. T-25 Harris Fototronic 7400 CRT phototypesetter.

Figure T-26 is the Harris Fototronic TxT system. Specifications for this machine are 150 lines per minute using the TxT disk and 90 lines per minute using the 120-character 10-point (3.51-mm) font type disk. Operating modes are 6-level TTS-format-justified or unjustified paper tape (system justifies and will hyphenate), 6-level TTS-format-justified paper tape (system will rejustify and hyphenate in any different measure and point size configuration than that called for in the input tape), 8-level Fototronic 1200 format justified paper tape, and 9-channel magnetic tape (optional feature). Character capacity is up to 1,200 different characters on-line. Type size range is 5 through 72 point (1.76 through 25.3 mm), and sizes on the machine are up to 12 sizes on-line at one time, chosen from different standard lenses. Standard point size lenses currently available are 5, 5½, 6, 7, 8, 9, 10, 11, 12, 14, 16, 18, 20, 24, 30, 36, 42, 48, 60, and 72 (1.76, 1.93, 2.11, 2.46, 2.8, 3.16, 3.51, 3.87, 4.21, 4.91, 5.6, 6.3, 7.02, 8.43, 11, 12.6, 14.8, 16.9, 21, and 25.3 mm). Line length is 42 picas (178 mm). The Fototronic TxT system accepts film and paper in widths of 18, 30, and 42 picas (76, 127, and 178 mm). Photo material capacity is 475 feet (145 m) of paper and 200 feet (61 m) of film.

Fig. T-26 Harris Fototronic TxT system.

The typesetters shown in Figure T-27 are Dymo's Pacesetters Mark 4 and 5. The Pacesetters may be configured in a number of speed, typeface, point size, and core (intelligence) configurations. Users may add capabilities as required. Both models of the Pacesetter provide the ability to control negative and positive intercharacter spacing and image density for particular typeface and point size settings. User-modifiable logic hyphenation rules and an optional exception dictionary allows consistent word spacing at preset values. The Dymo library includes more than 1,000 typeface masters and thousands of typeface related pi-characters, logotypes, and symbols. In addition to hundreds of designs based on Roman letterforms, there are such alphabet designs as Cyrillic, Greek, Hebrew, Arabic, and Thai. Classic and modern letterforms for text and display as well as engraver typefaces, including connecting scripts, are available.

Typographic functions for the Pacesetters are 19 point sizes ranging from 5 to 72 points (1.76 to 25.3 mm), and point sizes can be set on maximum line measure equivalents of 25, 30, 35, 40, 45, and 54 picas (106, 127, 148, 169, 190, and 229 mm) wide. Point sizes of 5, 6, 7, and 8 point (1.76, 2.11, 2.46, and 2.8 mm) can additionally set on a 45-pica (190-mm) line measure when using special half-size typeface master disks. The reverse leading feature allows setting of up to nine columns side by side, up to 22 inches (55.8 cm) long, as well as automatic gutter space and column depth, the latter in half-point increments. Standard typeface matrix disks contain 16 different standard point sizes in the 5 to 72-point (1.76 to 25.3-mm) range, and it is possible to mix any combination of 256 fonts on a common base line. Pacesetter segmented disk assemblies have eight segments, each segment containing a different typeface of 108 characters. For language applications, over 150 character combinations can be achieved by the assignment of floating accents as part of the pi-character selection. The typesetters are capable of setting 4 to 16 sizes from 5 to 72 points (1.76 to 25.3 mm) at speeds to 150 lines per minute.

Fig. T-27 Pacesetters Mark 4 and 5. (Dymo Graphic Systems, Inc.)

Input of the typesetters can be any of the following: paper tape of 6, 7, or 8-level standard and computer-generated wire service; magnetic tape cassette options from Redactron or Sperry Remington word-processing units; from IBM/MT/ST, MC/ST, Wang, Xerox, and others with interface; and magnetic tape computer generator, industry-compatible with appropriate interface. For the Mark 4 only, on-line keyboard option selectable justifying or nonjustifying operating modes and on-line to computer can be interfaced to most composition systems. The Pacesetters accept stabilization and resin-coated papers and photocomposition films. Material widths accommodated are 2, 3, 4, 6, 8 and 10-inch (5.08, 7.62, 10.16, 15.24, 20.32, and 25.4-cm) widths, nonsprocketed.

The phototypesetter shown in Figure T-28 is Dymo's Model DLC-1000 laser composer. This machine is equally applicable to newspaper, commercial, and data composition requirements. The DLC-1000 will expose plate-ready negatives with text, line art, and halftones in position on fully composed 100-pica (423-mm) width pages and is capable of operating in a stand-alone mode and as one element of a copy-processing system. All type images are generated on the output media by a high-precision laser at a resolution of 650 lines per inch (2.54 cm). Fonts are coded digitally and stored on a magnetic disk. A complete font library can be stored on file at one time, without the concern of grids, filmstrips, or type disks. This character-generation method permits the composer to access sizes and faces in milliseconds in a complete size range from 5 to 72 points (1.76 to 25.3 mm). Other intermediate type sizes, including those over 72 points (25.3 mm) in size, are optionally available.

Fig. T-28 Dymo's Model DLC-1000 laser composer. (Dymo Graphic Systems, Inc.)

Line-length speed of the DLC-1000 is 1,000 lines per minute of 9-point (3.16-mm) and smaller type sizes and 600 lines per minute at 10-point through 72-point (3.51 through 25.3-mm) type sizes. Input media can be magnetic tape, paper tape, or a host computer; output media may consist of all traditional typesetting films and paper, dry silver, and direct-negative film. Font capacity is approximately 300 fonts of up to 128 characters per disk and up to four disks per unit.

Under control of a central processing unit (CPU) and its resident program, the DLC-1000 responds to input data from several sources as

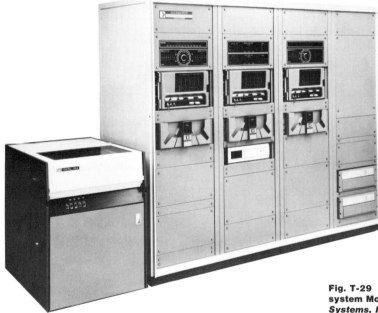

Fig. T-29 Dymo's copy processing system Model CPS-730. (Dymo Graphic Systems, Inc.)

indicated above, as well as parameters that may set on the operator's console. The minimum memory capability associated with the CPU includes the input data buffer, housekeeping program, and font memory organization tables. In the case of a stand-alone version, this CPU memory would also contain character-width tables, as well as the formatting and line-ending decision programs similar to that found in second- and third-generation phototypesetter, such as the Pacesetter models. In the case of the stand-alone configuration of the DLC-1000 as opposed to a slave unit, it would be typical to find added memory for these functions, as well as a more complex operator's console which would enable manual control over key typesetting parameters such as line length, type style, point size, and leading.

The customized central control unit for Dymo's Model CPS-730 copy-processing system is shown in Figure T-29. The CPS-720 is a companion to the 700 series. Three computers, three paper tape readers, two half-million-character-fixed head disks, and one of two (the unit on left) 50-megabyte moving head disks are shown. The software package is designed to expedite newspaper operations, including editorial, classified advertising, and display advertising. Editorial personnel have direct access to video display terminals (VDTs) (the CPS-730 will accommodate as many as 24 VDTs) and therefore complete control of copy at all times. High-speed wire or locally written copy is transmitted into memory, or disk storage, and is automatically segregated into appropriate directories. An editor or writer can call up his or her directory on the VDT by means of a single-stroke command and get a synopsis in one of two forms: the first line of a paragraph or the first 256 characters. While a story is stored in only one directory, it can be called out simultaneously by reporters and editors in other departments. The new software permits the routing of stories from temporary to permanent storage areas on the same disk for archival purposes.

typesetting Composing and setting type by hand, with hot-metal type-casting machines, or with photographic typesetters.

typewriter The history of the typewriter is one of slow progress to which many inventors have contributed. The original concept envisaged a device that would form a readable image faster than a person could write with a pen. However, the need for some means of enabling the blind to read by touch also played a large part in the development of the typewriter. Unlike a great number of inventions, the typewriter cannot be attributed to a single individual, although no doubt some inventors contributed more than others. The accounts are replete with crude, slow devices that were unsuccessful, with trial and error, and with improvement from one device to the next.

The earliest recorded attempt to create a mechanical writing device was made in England in 1714. No drawings of this device are in existence. Seventy years later, in France, a device was constructed to emboss characters that could be translated by the blind. In 1829, the first United States patent was granted for a machine having type mounted on a disk. The disk was rotated to the desired character and a lever operated to impress the character on a surface. It was not until 1868 that a typewriter that could produce letters faster than a person could write was developed. Meanwhile, the platen had come into being as a means of holding paper.

The year 1873 is recognized as the beginning of the period when features were introduced to make the typewriter a workable machine. New developments were added to older models. The platen, the carriage return, typebars, and the advancing inked ribbon were either introduced or assembled as units. An escapement mechanism was devised that permitted the carriage to move to the next space. By providing corresponding capital and lowercase letters on a single typebar, the use of two keyboards, one for capital letters and one for lowercase, was eliminated. Mark Twain was the first author to use a typewriter for a book manuscript.

Development of a standard keyboard placed the most frequently used characters in positions where keys could be manipulated with the least effort and at the greatest speed. Thus, touch typing was introduced and schools were formed to give instruction in this new profession. Once having learned the technique of touch typing, operators were in demand and the profession was regarded as one of great skill. Operators were called typewriters because they wrote with type.

Manual percussion was used to force the relief image on the typebar against the ribbon and so to paper. It was not until 1920 that George Smathers produced a working model of an electric typewriter. A continuously revolving rubber power roller provides the force that propels the typebar of the electric typewriter against the ribbon. When a key is struck, a leg of the typebar is forced momentarily against the roller, which kicks it, thus forcing the typebar to strike the ribbon and form the impression. A subsequent advance in typing technology is represented by the IBM Selectric typewriter. A small interchangeable printing element containing characters in relief is used to form the typed image. During operation, the element moves across the paper typing the line of text. This principle has eliminated typebars and the moving paper carriage. Another advance in typing technology is the Xerox interchangeable typing wheel used with the Xerox 800 electronic typing system. Typing from magnetic tape cassettes or magnetic cards, the wheel enables a typing speed of up to 350 words per minute (see Figures C-11 and C-12).

It became apparent that typewriters could be used effectively to produce reproduction copy for offset printing. The VariTyper and the IBM Executive series are equipped for proportional spacing. Figure T-30 shows an Executive typewriter. All typewriters of the Executive series have various individual typefaces. Unlike the characters on standard typewriters, the characters on these typewriters have assigned unit values. It is this feature which makes them proportional-spacing machines and therefore highly suitable for preparing reproduction copy for offset printing.

Proportional spacing means that each typed character occupies a space equivalent to its width. Small letters such as i, l, j, and f have fewer units than such letters as m, w, and r. The smallest letter has 2 units; the largest, 5. Ordinary typewriters type all letters in the same amount of space (Figure T-31*A*), whereas with proportional spacing each letter is given its required space (Figure T-31*B*).

Fig. T-30   IBM's Executive typewriter.

iiiiiiiiiiiiii

lllllllllllll

A mmmmmmmmmmmmm   (All characters occupy
                       equivalent spaces)

wwwwwwwwwwwwww

MMMMMMMMMMMMMM

LLLLLLLLLLLLLL

- -

iiiiiiiiiiiiiii   (2 units each character)

lllllllllllllll   (2 units each character)

B mmmmmmmmmmmmmm   (5 units each character)

WWWWWWWWWWWWWW   (5 units each character)

MMMMMMMMMMMMMM   (5 units each character)

LLLLLLLLLLLLLL   (4 units each character)

Fig. T-31 Ordinary and proportional spacing of letters.

Justification is made possible because spacing between words is also measured in units. Normal spacing between words has a value of 2 units, which is obtained by striking the 2-unit space bar once. It is thus possible not only to subtract 1 unit between words for long lines but to add 1 or more units for short lines. It is necessary to type the copy twice. The first typing, called "prejustifying," determines the line count, that is, the number of units to be added to or subtracted from each line. Actual justifying is accomplished in the second typing. It is possible to justify copy to any line measure. First, a series of M's is typed to the length of the desired measure. When the operator strikes the last M, without striking the space bar again, the position of the pointer is noted on the right front paper scale. This is the reference point to which lines must be typed by adding or subtracting units. A tab is set to the right of the line for typing the number of units to be added or subtracted for each line.

For prejustifying copy, the operator types the text in normal fashion. When the end of the line approaches the reference point indicated by the pointer on the paper scale, the operator determines whether the line is long or short. If the pointer indicates that the line has been typed beyond the reference point, the backspace key, which has a value of 1 unit, is used to back up to the reference point. The number of units required to reach the reference point is typed at the tab and prefixed by a minus sign. If the typed line falls short of the reference point, the number of units to be added is found by striking the 2-unit space bar until the pointer rests on the reference point. The number of units is then typed at the tab. When a period or a comma comes at the end of a line, it is necessary to backspace once and then count units to be added or subtracted. If a typed line ends exactly on the reference point, justification is not required and a zero is typed at the tab.

Once the unit count has been made for all lines of text, plus or minus marks are inserted between words as shown by the tab numbers. Each mark represents 1 unit. A red pencil is used to denote minus marks and a black pencil plus marks. After all plus and minus marks have been inserted and the copy proofread, it is ready for typing (justification) on reproducible paper. The text is typed exactly as in the first typing except where plus and minus marks have been inserted. The backspace key is used to delete units between words. The 3-unit space bar is used to add 1 unit between words, and the 2-unit space bar is used to add units as desired.

typewriter paper *See* BOND TYPEWRITER PAPER; BOXED PAPER.

typographer One skilled in typography as a designer or as a printer.

typography Art and process of letterpress or similar printing, with reference to the style, format, and general appearance of the printed page.

ultraviolet curing (or **UV curing**) Conversion of a wet coating or printing ink film to a solid film by using ultraviolet radiation. *See* SUNCURE SYSTEM.

ultraviolet light Actinic (shorter wavelength) or useable part of light spectrum needed to react or harden light-sensitive coatings.

uncoated book paper Paper used for the letterpress printing of catalogs, books, direct-mail pieces, folders, etc. It is manufactured in four finishes: machine, antique, English, and supercalendered. The antique finish, which is somewhat rough and reflects light, is used for catalogs, books, folders, and brochures for which bulk is not important. Because of its rough surface, antique finish is not recommended for halftones with screens of more than 85 lines. Standard weights are 30, 35, 40, 45, 50, 60, 70, 80, and 100 pounds (13.6, 16, 18.1, 20.4, 22.7, 27.2, 31.8, 36.3, and 45.4 kg) for 500 sheets of the basic size of 25 by 38 inches (63.5 by 97 cm). Standard basis weights and sizes are the same for all uncoated book papers.

The machine-finished uncoated book paper has a medium-smooth surface and is used for books, catalogs, direct-mail pieces, and broadsides in which line art is important. While the finish is smoother than antique, only halftones with 100-line or coarser screens are recommended.

The supercalendered finish is the smoothest finish of uncoated book paper. Catalogs, books, pamphlets, and magazines are examples of its use. Halftones of 100- to 120-line screens may be employed, the best results being obtained from the 100-line screen. This finish is applied by the same process as the machine and English finishes for uncoated book paper, additional smoothness being obtained by further calendering.

undercut (undercutting) In photoengraving, the effect produced by allowing acid to etch under the printing area and undermine it; during exposure, light creeping under the edges of an image altering the image. When undercutting causes an image to become smaller, the image is said to be "sharpened." When it causes an image to enlarge, the image is said to have "gained." In technical illustrating, it is a break in the outline of an object at the point where the flow line intersects the object.

underlay Subject matter placed under a piece of artwork or photograph to add color or tone or to create a special art effect.

underrule Line drawn beneath text in preparing cold-composition copy.

underrun Printed or duplicated copies of sheets or pages less than the specified number.

underscore Line placed beneath word or text.

undimensioned drawing Engineering drawing that does not show actual dimensions but depicts to scale the loft-line, template, pattern, and printed-circuit information necessary to produce such parts within the allowable manufacturing limits shown on other engineering drawings. Undimensioned drawings are shop accessory drawings used in conjunction with other drawings; as such, they do not show part requirements. They permit quality control of complex contours of templates or patterns that would be difficult to measure in any other way.

unglazed finish Paper finish without luster.

unit: cold-composition copy Measurement of width used in typing with proportional-spacing machines, particularly IBM Executive typewriters. *See* PROPORTIONAL SPACING; TYPEWRITER.

unit perfecting press *See* BLANKET-TO-BLANKET PRESS.

unit: printing Individual printing unit added to a web-fed press to increase its capacity. Each unit has its own inking and roller system and is installed in line with one or more other units. *See also* OFFSET PRESS; WEB OFFSET PRINTING.

unitized film Filmstrip of individual microforms, each containing a related image or unit, as opposed to a roll of microfilm.

Universal Product Code (UPC) Method by which retail outlets use an automated product coding system in checkout operations. A 10-digit number is used to code and identify each product, and a linear-bar symbol is employed to further identify transaction data. *See* Figure U-1. In operation, the code number and symbol for each product is exposed to an optical scanner located in the counter. The scanner "reads" the symbols, translates it into a code number, and sends the number to a local computer for processing. The information is sent back to the checkout counter where a data printout receipt on tape is provided for the customer. In addition, transaction information is flashed on a small display screen for the benefit of the customer and the checkout clerk.

It is the printer's responsibility to reproduce the symbol within tolerances so it can be scanned electronically without causing errors in the readout. At nominal size, the symbol is 1.498 inch (38.0492 mm) across, and the tolerance for the bars is approximately ±0.004 inch (±0.1016 mm). The tolerance for the UPC film master is ±0.0002 inch (±0.00508 mm). While the manufacturer is responsible for providing the proper code, it is the printer who must reproduce the symbol such that it is machine-readable. The size and placement of the bars are the concern of the manufacture as a general rule. It is the ratio between the bars and spaces that is critical and not the actual width of the bars. The tolerance of bars is checked with a UPC press operator's gage. Resolution and density for various substrates is determined by using a UPC printability gage. The gage can also be used as a quality control device during the pressrun. More detailed information concerning the UPC can be obtained from Distribution Codes, Inc., 401 Wythe Street, Alexandria, Virginia 22314.

unretouched photograph Photograph that has not been altered or improved by airbrushing, hand, or other means. It is therefore an exact facsimile of the original view.

Fig. U-1 Universal Product Code with example of grocery checklist.

```
CONTINENTAL MARKETS-M.V.

     GROCERY        .75
     GROCERY        .79
     GROCERY       1.19
     CHICKEN THGH  1.00
     GROCERY        .89
     GROCERY        .29
     LOW FAT MILK   .68
     SAFFOLA MARG   .65
     GROCERY       2.39
     CUBED STEAK   1.35
     CHUCK ROAST   3.18
     MEAT          3.49
 .90# TOMATO@  .49  .44
     TAX DUE        .00
     TOTAL        17.09

     CSH TEND     20.00
     CHG DUE       2.91


 4/24/76 12:55  102/ 5
 SAVE $-SHOP CONTINENTAL
```

unsharp premask Photographic material exposed and printed from the original color transparency before color-separation negatives are made. It gives better registration with less probability of showing defects between the two films.

vacuum frame *See* COPYBOARD.

value Relative lightness and darkness of different areas of a picture as represented in tones, shading, line balance, layout, and the like. *See also* DENSITY.

vandyke Term often used to designate a brownprint negative and sometimes a brownline positive. *See* BROWNLINE PRINT; BROWNPRINT.

vanishing point Point at which parallel lines, receding from the observer, appear to come together in a perspective drawing or photograph.

Varigraph Cold-type nonphotographic headline composing machine. *See* COLD COMPOSITION.

Vario-Klishograph Trademark of an automatic electric scanner. *See* ENGRAVING, ELECTRONIC.

VariTyper Cold-composition machine manufactured by the VariTyper Corporation. *See* COLD COMPOSITION.

varnishing (lacquering) Applying fixative to reproduction copy or to a completed printed sheet for protection or appearance.

vector-analysis symbols *See* TABLE 10.

vehicle In printing inks, the fluid element that acts as the carrier for pigment in printing inks.

veiling Soft, fuzzy density that fills the small clear area between large dots on an original first-generation halftone. *See also* SOFT DOT.

vellum Kind of fine paper resembling parchment that is used for duplicating copies made with a whiteprint machine. Vellum is translucent and consequently permits the passage of light during exposure in the whiteprint process. For typing, vellum is sometimes backed with orange carbon paper to make the image more pronounced when it is reproduced. The finish of the paper is of high quality, and the content is 100 percent rag.

vellum finish Paper finish similar to text finish. It is smooth and dull.

vellum master Original produced on vellum paper.

vellum transfer Master copy on vellum, taken from the original and used to make additional copies by the whiteprint process. It is actually an intermediate because it is made from an original to produce copies.

Velox Print of a photograph or other continuous-tone copy which has been prescreened before paste-up or platemaking with line copy and which

may be screened in any manner with or without a darkroom. The necessity of making a composite negative (halftone art stripped into line art) is eliminated because only a line shot is required.

verso *See* RECTO.

vertical column chart *See* COLUMN CHART.

vertical dimension Distance between the top and bottom of an image when the image is held in an upright, or reading, position. It is perpendicular to the horizontal dimension. The vertical dimension is also known as the height, regardless of its length with respect to the horizontal.

When oversize copy is prepared, both dimensions must be in proportion to the reduced image area. If the copy is not in proportion, either the width or the height must be used as the controlling dimension so that the reduced copy will fit the prescribed area.

vertical page Page that contains right-reading copy when it is held in a normal reading position. It is contrasted with a broadside page, which must be turned 90° clockwise to be read.

vertical press Printing press with a flatbed that is held in a vertical position with the pinting forms locked in place. A rotating cylinder draws the paper around itself as it revolves and moves from the top to the bottom of the printing form, thus causing the impression to be made on the paper.

vicinity plan drawing Drawing or map used with construction drawings to show the relationship of a site to features of the surrounding area, such as towns, bodies of water, railroads, and highways.

video display terminal (VDT) A visual display, such as that seen on the ordinary television screen, used in photocomposition work in conjunction with a keyboard. During typing operations, the visual display is viewed by the operator for immediate editing and correcting as the copy is typed and before it is sent to the computer for phototypesetting. The VDT may also be known as an editing, proofing, or correcting terminal.

viewer, microfilm *See* MICROFILM READER.

viewing-plane line *See* LINE CONVENTIONS: ENGINEERING DRAWINGS.

vignette Halftone copy in which the background fades from heavier to lighter tones until it is completely absorbed by the color of the paper. The dots should be graduated beginning ½ inch (1.27 cm) from the edge of the vignette until they seem to disappear.

vignetter Device for printing photographic vignettes; also, one who produces vignettes.

visible line In orthographic mechanical and engineering drawings, the outline line. An unbroken line, it is used for all the visible lines of an object. *See also* LINE CONVENTIONS: ENGINEERING DRAWINGS.

visual: art Preliminary rough layout of artwork, usually produced by a visualizer to exploit the best layout and composition possibilities of the article to be illustrated. A visual is desirable when an article has a complicated or technical design or the layout of the illustration is difficult.

visual: overhead projection *See* OVERHEAD PROJECTION; PROJECTURAL.

vu-graph Projectural consisting of carbon-backed film, used in overhead projection. The communicator writes or draws with a pencil or stylus, producing a white image on a black background. The term "vu-graph" is often used erroneously for a transparent projectural, which produces a black or colored image on a white background. *See also* OVERHEAD PROJECTION; OVERHEAD TRANSPARENCY.

walk-off Loss of the image on a printing plate during the pressrun.

wash drawing Watercolor painting in which the color is applied mainly by washes. A complete drawing should be made before the washes are applied. A first wash of clear water is spread over the drawing. The following washes, from the lightest to the heaviest tones, are applied successively over one another. In the process, white or light areas are passed over. Final touches are added for emphasis.

washed-out drawing (wiped-out drawing) Watercolor in which a portion of the image is washed out with a damp brush while the painting is damp. The technique is used to add soft color on a canvas-grained paper. Dramatic sky effects may be produced. Indelible inks may be used for tinting. When glycerin is mixed with the painting solution, the wash has a tendency to "float" on the surface rather than to penetrate the paper immediately, thus allowing time to apply the washing technique.

washout Washing, drying, and cleaning of negatives, plates, and the like during the developing and processing stage.

washup Process of cleaning the rollers of a printing press, particularly to prepare them for a different color run.

water finish High-quality glossy paper finish, obtained by applying water to one or more calender rolls in the papermaking process.

watercolor printing Printing process in which special watercolor inks and soft, porous stock are used. Unlike oil or varnish inks used in ordinary printing, which are laid for the most part on the surface of the stock, watercolor inks are immediately absorbed by the paper. The process therefore permits colors to overlap and hues to be blended. For certain types of posters for which brilliant contrasting colors are desired, the effect is excellent.

watermark Design, trademark, name, logotype, or the like impressed on paper by the dandy roll or other rollers during the paper-manufacturing process.

wax engraving Method of reproducing forms such as graphs, maps, and charts by cutting lines in wax that is backed with a thin copper sheet. The impression is used as a mold for an electroplate.

web Roll of printing paper formed in the manufacturing process. To the printer, the web is the continuous roll of paper as it is fed through the press. The web or webs are attached to roll stands, which may be installed in line with the printing press or on the side when space is limited. They are diverted to the printing unit by angle bars. A web has a center shaft, or core, around which the paper is wound. The core may be made of metal and intended to be reused or of paper and so be expendable.

web aligner Device used to control the position of the running edge of the web, or the center line of the web. It can be used at both the feeding and folder positions of the press.

web cleaner Vacuum cleaner installed before the first printing unit of a web-fed press to remove foreign particles from stock.

web flow Continuous feeding of a web (paper roll) through a printing press, as opposed to feeding single sheets to the press. The printing of continuous forms is an example.

web lead Amount of paper that remains in the press when the press has been threaded.

web lead rollers (idler rollers) Set of rollers located between printing units of a blanket-to-blanket press in line with the lower blanket cylinder. The rollers support the stock and prevent it from wrinkling between the units and also control the stock as it unrolls from the web.

web offset printing Lithographic printing from rolled stock. The paper manufacturer refers to the roll as a web. The printer uses the term "web" not only for the roll but for the paper itself as it feeds through the press. The web is a continuous roll of paper formed during manufacture and used extensively in printing newspapers. In some offset presses the web is fed between the blanket cylinder and an impression cylinder. Other presses are manufactured with a blanket-to-blanket arrangement, the web being fed between two blanket cylinders, each of which serves as an impression cylinder for the other. A great advantage of blanket-to-blanket web presses is their speed and resulting high productivity. Speeds may be twice those of some other presses because both sides of the web are printed at the same time. They may attain 800 feet (244 m) per minute, or approximately 25,000 impressions per hour. This rate of speed will account for more than nine miles of paper per hour. Most web offset presses have widths of 36 to 38 inches (91.4 to 97 cm).

Web offset presses can be divided into two broad classifications: those that are designed for great productivity but without flexibility for long printing runs; and multipurpose flexible presses for handling many varied sizes of printed matter. They may be subdivided into categories by such design characteristics as cylinder-to-cylinder relationships and features peculiar to individual manufacturers.

web perfecting press Press that performs on the rotary principle with curved plates locked on a plate cylinder. The paper is fed from a web. Units containing inking rollers, an impression cylinder, a plate cylinder, and cylinders for transferring paper, as well as separate ink fountains for various colors, may be added as required. The press will print one color on both sides of the sheet in one operation with one or more printing units.

web tension Tension of the web as the continuous roll of paper or other substrate is transported through the press. A tension control device is used to maintain incoming and ongoing web tension at the proper tension.

weight (paper) *See* BASIS WEIGHT.

wet stripping Removal of the stripping layer from a film after the film has been processed but while it is wet.

wet wash To wash down a lithographic printing plate before dropping the ink from rollers to roll up the plate. The method is excellent for removing storage gum from the plate.

white-flame arc Arc light that uses carbon with a core of chemicals that burn to produce an intense white light.

white on black *See* REVERSE BLUELINE.

whiteline print *See* REVERSE BLUELINE.

whiteprint process Reproduction process based upon the use of light-sensitive dyes. Several features are peculiar to the process: (1) masters must be of translucent or transparent material, (2) all copies are of the same size as the original, (3) all copies are facsimiles of the original, and (4) white on the original stays white and black on the original stays black on the copies. Whiteprint machines range from small models accommodating 8½ by 11-inch (21.6 by 28-cm) paper to large commercial machines that can handle copy paper up to 54 inches (137 cm) wide and of any length.

The whiteprint process is comparatively simple. An original is placed over the sensitized copy faceup, and the two sheets are fed in contact into the machine by the operator. The sheets are conveyed around a high-pressure mercury lamp where ultraviolet light inactivates the dye in the copy paper that is not protected by the opaque image of the original. The original is returned automatically to the operator. Meanwhile, the copy paper, carrying the latent image, is conveyed across ammonia vapors (dry process) or through developer rolls (moist process) that develop the image. The copy emerges as a facsimile of the original. The image is permanent, and the copy is dry. *See also* ANHYDROUS AMMONIA SYSTEM; AQUEOUS AMMONIA SYSTEM; COPYING MACHINES; DRY DIAZO PROCESS.

Depending on the type of copy paper used, the image may have blue, black, red, or sepia lines when it has been developed. Copies may be made on several grades or weights of white paper, on blue, pink, yellow, green, or other colored paper, or on film, cloth, or plastic-coated paper. The image may also be produced on paper or thin flexible plates which are developed by applying a solution and made ready for offset printing.

Photolithographic negatives or any negatives having a translucent image are adaptable to the whiteprint process for obtaining check-out and proof copies. The black background remains black or dark blue, and the image remains white. This type of copy, which has been given the name "reverse blueline," has many advantages, since it withstands smudging and grease marks in the shop or field, may be used for editing and checking, and can serve as a reference copy in a special file. *See also* REVERSE BLUELINE.

In addition to translucent bond and writing paper, vegetable parchment, greaseproof paper, rag tracing paper, and onionskin may be used as masters. While vegetable parchment and greaseproof paper have a high reprint speed, they do not function as well as printing and writing paper because of instability and distortion due to changes in atmospheric conditions. Rag tracing papers, such as those commonly used for engineering drawing work, are satisfactory as whiteprint reproduction masters with pencil and ink work. Such papers that have been transparentized by the addition of resin during manufacture make excellent masters. Films and cloths also make excellent masters, as they are sturdy, handle well, and are easily filed.

In preparing masters, several factors are essential for good reproduction. A master must have a solid definition of the image, composed of hard, even lines. For typewritten material, small drawings, or hand-ruled forms, the master may be backed with orange carbon paper to obtain greater opacity. *See also* ORANGE BACKING.

The machine illustrated in Figure W-1 is Bruning's PD 33 tabletop whiteprint copying machine. The machine features the odorless, dry, patented pressure diazo process. Some whiteprint machines use ammonia vapor as the development agent. The machine is used primarily as a backup or satellite in large whiteprint reproduction departments. Maximum printing width is 18 inches (45.72 cm) by any reasonable length. Exposure source is two high-output intensity fluorescent lamps. Speed is up to 30 feet (9.144 m). Length of the machine is 31½ inches (80 cm), depth is 17 inches (43.18 cm), and height is 12 inches (30.48 cm).

Fig. W-1   Bruning's PD 33 tabletop whiteprint copying machine. (Addressograph-Multigraph Corp.)

Figure W-2 shows Bruning's Revolute 860 dry diazo copier. It is a medium-volume whiteprint machine that automatically separates copy from the original and delivers dry, collated copies of drawings up to 42 inches (107 cm) wide. With most of the 860's copying operations, originals and prints return automatically on extendable front delivery trays. However, when an extra-long original is being copied, the returning print can, if long enough, be rolled out on top of the original tracing. To avoid such interference, an adjustable-read delivery tray has been added to the 860. An adjustment of the space and tray-heater dials controls a close tolerance of the degree of heat and percentage of humidity inside the developing tank. In regular operation, the Revolute 860 delivers prints in the stacked order of the originals. Single prints from a series of tracings emerge in correct sequence when the machine is set for front delivery and when each faceup drawing and its matching copy sheet (sensitized side up) is fed in the normal manner, that is, top sheet first and bottom sheet last. Originals return stacked and collated. The feed board is over 5½ feet (1.68 cm) long and almost 1½ feet (0.456 m) deep. Speed of the machine is 2 feet to 45 feet (0.61 to 13.72 m) per minute. Rated printing width is 42 inches (107 m) by any reasonable length, and maximum printing width is 45 inches (114.3 cm).

Figure W-3 is the Bruning pressure diazo copying machine Model PD 80. This whiteprint process offers a dry, odorless operation, and heaters or ammonia fumes are not required for development; therefore venting or mixing of chemicals is not required. The development system is replenished with a cartridge of activator. In this process, the exposed copy material

Fig. W-2   Bruning's Revolute 860 dry diazo whiteprint copier. (Addressograph-Multigraph Corp.)

Fig. W-3 Bruning's pressure diazo copying machine Model PD 80. (*Addressograph-Multigraph Corp.*)

travels through the developer section where a thin film of activator is metered under pressure for development of the diazo material. Metering and pressure blades withdraw automatically from contact with the applicator rollers when the machine is turned off. When the machine is turned on for operation, the blades return to position for development. The PD 80 model contains one instant-on high-intensity fluorescent exposure lamp. It has a rated printing width of 42 inches (107 cm), and a maximum printing speed of 15 feet (4.572 m) per minute, and front delivery. Originals are

Fig. W-4 Bruning's Revolute 875 whiteprint copying machine. (*Addressograph-Multigraph Corp.*)

separated manually. The machine is 13½ inches (34.29 cm) high, 64 inches (163 cm) wide, and 16 inches (41 cm) in depth and weighs approximately 220 pounds (100 kg). An optional cabinet stand is available.

Figure W-4 shows Bruning's Revolute 875 whiteprint copying machine. The machine produces copies at 80 feet (24.3 m) per minute running speed from originals 42 inches (107 cm) in width by any reasonable length. Delivery of prints can be to the front or rear, and both cut sheets and roll stock can be run with provisions for two 200-yard (183-m) rolls of sensitized paper. A number of dependability features include an automatic drive chain lubrication fixture, an electronic motion-sensing device for shutdown in case a mishap should occur, and torque-tube construction to ensure stability and measurably increased machine life.

widow Short last line of a paragraph that is carried over to the top of the next column or page, where it stands alone. Widows should be avoided during layout or makeup of copy. *See also* ORPHAN.

width In the graphic arts, the distance between two points along the horizontal dimension. With height it is one of the two dimensions that measure a plane. When measurements are given for line and continuous-tone copy, the width and the height should be stated in that order. *See also* HORIZONTAL DIMENSION.

wild copy Text copy that has been typed or printed to be cut and pasted as callouts for illustrations or for use in the composition of graphs, charts, or mechanicals.

window Die-cut opening on the front cover of a publication that reveals the title or other information printed on the title page; also, any such opening that reveals an image of any kind imposed on the succeeding page. The term "window" may also be used as an equivalent of black patch. Also, a clear rectangle, square, or other shaped panel in a lithographic negative in which corresponding halftone negatives are stripped with either tape or cement for platemaking.

wipe-on-plate Offset printing plate that requires the application of a light-sensitive coating before exposure. When the plate is exposed to light through the coating, the exposed areas of the coating harden. Wipe-on plates are chemically or mechanically grained to make them receptive to water.

wiped-out drawing *See* WASHED-OUT DRAWING.

wire side In the manufacture of paper, the side of the paper next to the wire (the underside) as it is conveyed along a belt. It is the opposite of the felt side.

wiring diagram Diagram of an electrical or electronic system in which wire numbers, colors, and sizes are shown together with an orthographic pictorial drawing representing the parts of the system. The parts may also be shown by a listing. A wiring diagram is often used to give instructions or information on wiring functions for assembly, disassembly, repair or replacement, and connections of an electrical system. It may cover internal or external connections, or both, and usually shows the details needed to trace and make connections.

with the grain Folding or using paper with the grain, as opposed to folding against the grain. Grain in paper results from the alignment of fibers during vibration of the pulp along the traveling belt in the manufacturing process. *See also* PAPER MANUFACTURING.

woodcut Engraving cut in a block of wood; also, the impression made from the engraving. The woodcut was an early form of block printing. The image is drawn or written on the block and the background removed with fine cutting tools. A raised surface, representing the image, thus becomes the printing surface, which is used to make a black or white impression. When lines are incised in solid black areas, a range of middle tones is introduced, and the resulting impression is a white-on-black representation. Because there is no perceptible gradation of tone, woodcuts are classified as line art. Fine lines may be so well defined that some objects are better illustrated by woodcuts than by halftones.

wood-pulp bond *See* BOND PAPER.

word processing Transformation of a concept or idea into a printed communication media by using mechanical or automated systems, methods, or processes.

word spacing Adjustment of spacing between words, particularly to shorten or extend a line in order to achieve justification.

work and tumble (print and tumble) To print one side of a sheet of paper and then turn the sheet over from gripper to back while using the same side guide.

work and turn (print and turn) To print one side of a sheet of paper and then turn the sheet over from left to right and print on the opposite side. The same gripper edge is used for both sides of the sheet.

work-up Defect appearing on a printed impression because of leading, furniture, or a slug that has worked up to the surface of a printing form.

wove finish Paper finish that has no visible laid lines. Antique wove is an example of such a finish.

wraparound Cylindrical printing plate that wraps around a plate cylinder. It is used on a rotary printing press.

wraparound cover Soft cover used to bind or hold a booklet, brochure, etc. It consists of one sheet of stock that forms both front and back covers. Any type of mechanical binding may be used.

Wrico pens *See* PENS, TECHNICAL.

writing head In computer graphics, a linear array of styli which comes in contact with the paper during the electrostatic writing process.

writing paper Paper suitable for writing with pen and ink.

wrong-reading *See* REVERSE-READING.

X Twenty-fourth letter of the alphabet, used in the graphic arts to denote magnification of an image such as that of a microfilm. For example, 14X means that an enlargement is 14 times the size of the image on the microfilm.

xenon, xenon flash lamp In phototypesetting, one of the methods used to expose characters during the optical character recognition and typesetting function. Xenon is a gas which, when contained in an arc lamp and subjected to a high voltage, produces an intense peak of radiant energy. Other methods in use are the flash lamp, laser, and cathode-ray tube.

xerography Copying process that utilizes electrostatic forces to form an image. The word is taken from the Greek *xeros*, meaning "dry," and *graphos*, meaning "writing." Xerography is a clean, fast, dry direct-positive process. Two methods may be used to produce the image. In the first, which is based on the drum principle, the image is transferred from a selenium-coated drum to paper. In the second, the image is transferred from a flat photoconductive plate to paper. In the drum operation, the original is placed facedown on a scanning glass and a scanning light passed under the glass. The image is projected onto the selenium-coated photoconductive drum, where a pattern of electrically charged and discharged areas corresponding to the image and nonimage areas of the original is formed. The surface of the drum is positively charged as the drum rotates. The latent electrostatic image is developed by a cascade of powder over the drum, and the powdered image is transferred electrostatically from drum to stock. The image is fused by heat for permanence. *See also* COPYING MACHINES.

The plate method uses a thin selenium-coated photoconductive plate as a substitute for camera film. The camera enlarges or reduces originals and then makes copies. In operation, the photoconductive selenium-coated plate is electrically charged in the charging chamber of a processor. After being charged, the plate is placed in the camera, and the material to be copied is exposed directly to the charged plate. The plate is then placed in a tray assembly of the processor, and the latent image is developed. After development, the image is transferred electrostatically from the plate to ordinary paper, vellum, or a paper or metal offset duplicating plate. The paper, vellum, or offset plate is then placed in a heat fuser and "baked," or fused, to make the image permanent.

Z When used in handwritten copy, the letter Z is often crossed with a small line through the center (Z̵) to indicate that it is a Z and not a 2.

zinc etching Zinc plate on which a photoengraved line image has been etched.

zinc finish Paper finish obtained by using sheets of zinc in the manufacturing process.

zinc halftone Zinc plate on which a halftone has been etched.

General

Anatomy of the nuArc Camera, nuArc Company, Inc., Chicago, 1969.

The ATF Web Story, American Type Founders, Whitinsville, Mass.

Basic Tools and Their Applications, nuArc Company, Inc., Chicago, Ill., 1967.

The Book of American Types, American Type Founders Co., Inc., Elizabeth, N.J.

Carter, John, *ABC for Book-collectors*, 3d ed, rev., Alfred A. Knopf, Inc., New York, 1963.

Catalog of Brushes, Colors, Artists' Materials, M. Grumbacher, Inc., New York, 1963.

Contacting Procedures for the Graphic Arts, Eastman Kodak Company, Rochester, N.Y., 1974.

Continuous-Tone Processor Control for the Graphic Arts, Publication No. Q-37, Eastman Kodak Company, Rochester, N.Y.

Contrast Index—Guide to Proper Development, Pamphlet No. Q-120, Eastman Kodak Company, Rochester, N.Y.

Craftint Quik-Graphics Catalog, No. 5, Craftint Manufacturing Co., Cleveland.

Dentsman, Harold, and J. Morton Schultz, *Photographic Reproduction*, McGraw-Hill Book Company, New York, 1963.

Diazo Microfilm for Miniaturization Systems, 10th Annual Conference, National Microfilm Association, Chicago, April 4–6, 1961.

Diazchrome Projecturals for Instructional Purposes, Scott Graphics, Inc., Holyoke, Mass.

Diazchrome Projecturals for Visual Communication, Scott Graphics, Inc., Holyoke, Mass.

Engineering Reproduction Handbook, E.I. du Pont de Nemours & Co., Wilmington, Del.

Equipment for Graphic Data Reduction, Film Reduction, and Plotting, Gerber Scientific Instrument Co., Hartford, Conn., 1963.

Frankenfield, H., *Block Printing with Linoleum*, 5th ed., Hunt Manufacturing Co., Philadelphia, 1956.

————, *Printmaking*, 6th ed., Hunt Manufacturing Co., Philadelphia, 1964.

Fundamentals of Layout in the Graphic Arts, nuArc Company, Inc., Chicago, Ill., 1967.

George, Ross F., *Speedball Textbook for Pen and Brush Drawings*, 18th ed., Hunt Manufacturing Co., Philadelphia, 1960.

Graphic Arts Background Memorandum, E.I. du Pont de Nemours & Co., Wilmington, Del.

Graphic Arts Handbook, E.I. du Pont de Nemours & Co., Wilmington, Del.

Handy One-line ATF Type Style Selector, American Type Founders Co., Inc., Elizabeth, N.J.

How to Use the Kodak Autopositive Materials, Pamphlet No. Q-23, Eastman Kodak Company, Rochester, N.Y.

How to Use the Kodak Graphic Arts Exposure Computer, Pamphlet No. Q-12A, Eastman Kodak Company, Rochester, N.Y.

How to Use the Kodak Magenta Contact Screen for Photogravure, Pamphlet No. Q-22, Eastman Kodak Company, Rochester, N.Y.

IBM Electric Typewriter, International Business Machines Corp., Office Products Division, New York.

Introduction to Mechanized Processing, Publication Q-91D, Eastman Kodak Company, Rochester, N.Y.

Instructions for the Kodak Graphic Arts Color-Separation Calculator, Pamphlet No. Q-11D, Eastman Kodak Company, Rochester, N.Y.

Instructions for Using the Kodak Copy Alignment Kit, Publication No. Q-206A, Eastman Kodak Company, Rochester, N.Y.

Kodak Angle Indicator, Publication No. Q-31A, Eastman Kodak Company, Rochester, N.Y.

Kodak Contact Control Guide C-2, Publications No. Q-94, Eastman Kodak Company, Rochester, N.Y.

Kodak Contact Direct-Screen Color-Separation Method, Pamphlet No. Q-121, Eastman Kodak Company, Rochester, N.Y.

Kodak Contact Screens, Types and Applications, Pamphlet No. Q-21, Eastman Kodak Company, Rochester, N.Y.

Kodak Direct-Screen Color-Separation Method, Pamphlet No. Q-114, Eastman Kodak Company, Rochester, N.Y.

Kodak MP Films for the Graphic Arts, Publication No. Q-2M, Eastman Kodak Company, Rochester, N.Y.

Kodak Photographic Materials for the Graphic Arts, Publication No. Q-2, Eastman Kodak Company, Rochester, N.Y.

Kodak PMP Materials for Paste-Up, Color Separation, Pamphlet No. Q-201, Eastman Kodak Company, Rochester, N.Y.

Kodak PMT Metal Litho Plate, Publication No. Q-202, Eastman Kodak Company, Rochester, N.Y.

Kodak Polymatic Litho Plate LN-L, Publication No. Q-120, Eastman Kodak Company, Rochester, N.Y.

Melcher, Daniel, and Nancy Larrick, *Printing and Promotion Handbook*, 3d ed., McGraw-Hill Book Company, New York, 1966.

Moore, N. O., *The History of Printing*, Polytechnic High School and Junior College, Riverside, Calif.

Offset Platemaking with the nuArc Flip-Top Platemaker, nuArc Company, Inc., Chicago, 1968.

Plate Maker's Guide for 3M Brand Lithographic Plates, Minnesota Mining and Manufacturing Company, Saint Paul, Minn.

Pressman's Guide for 3M Brand Lithographic Plates, Minnesota Mining and Manufacturing Company, Saint Paul, Minn.

Printing Ink Handbook, National Association of Printing Ink Manufacturers, Inc., Harrison, N.Y., 1976.

Processing Techniques, Chemicals, and Formulas for the Graphic Arts, Publication No. Q-9, Eastman Kodak Company, Rochester, N.Y.

Processor Control for Kodak MP Films, Publication No. Q-38, Eastman Kodak Company, Rochester, N.Y.

Stabilization With Kodak Ektamatic Products, Pamphlet No. G-25, Eastman Kodak Company, Rochester, N.Y.

Techniques of Mimeographing, A.B. Dick Company, Chicago, 1963.

Type Catalog and Production Handbook, Varigraph, Inc., Madison, Wis., 1963.

Visualization Made Easier with Chart-Pak, Chart-Pak, Inc., Leeds, Mass., 1958.

Visucom Equipment and Materials Catalog, Scott Graphics, Inc., Holyoke, Mass.

Military Standards

MIL-STD-1, *General Drawing Practice.*

MIL-STD-2, *Drawing Sizes.*

MIL-STD-3, *Format for Production Drawings.*

MIL-STD-4, *Format for Construction Drawings.*

MIL-STD-7, *Types and Definitions of Engineering Drawings.*

MIL-STD-8, *Dimensioning and Tolerancing.*

MIL-STD-24, *Revision of Drawings.*

Military Specifications

MIL-D-5480, *Data, Engineering and Technical (Reproduction Thereof).*

MIL-D-8510, *Drawing Negative, Reproducible Photographic, Preparation of.*

Classification	Product	See	Manufacturer
Adhesive materials	Avery	AVERY	Avery Label Company
	Paste-ups and transfers	ARTIST AID	Jay G. Lissner
		CHARTPAK	Chartpak
	Craftint	CRAFTINT	The Craftint Manufacturing Co.
Art brushes	Art brushes	BRUSHES, ART	M. Grumbacher, Inc.
Binding, mechanical	Autobinder II Model 346 BN	BINDING, MECHANICAL	General Binding Corporation
	Automatic punch	BINDING, MECHANICAL	General Binding Corporation
	Model 123 desk-top binder	BINDING, MECHANICAL	Velo-Bind, Inc.
Block printing	Block-printing instruments	BLOCK PRINTING	Hunt Manufacturing Co.
Bookbinding equipment	High-speed heavy-duty hinge clamp binder	BOOKBINDING	The Sheridan Company
	Hinge-clamp binder	BOOKBINDING	The Sheridan Company
	Straight-line trimmer	BOOKBINDING	The Sheridan Company
	XG standard rotary gatherer	BOOKBINDING	The Sheridan Company
Camera, microfilm	Microfiche camera processor Model 750	CAMERA, MICROFILM	Addressograph-Multigraph Corp., Bruning Division
Camera, Polaroid	Polaroid MP-4	POLAROID MP-4 MULTI-PURPOSE LAND CAMERA	Polaroid Corporation
Camera, process	Model SST-1418 process camera	CAMERA, PROCESS	nuArc Company, Inc.
	Model 2024V Rocket vertical process camera	CAMERA, PROCESS	nuArc Company, Inc.
	Model VV1418 vertical camera	CAMERA, PROCESS	nuArc Company, Inc.
	Robertson 500 graphic arts process overhead camera	CAMERA, PROCESS	LogEtronics, Inc.
	432 Mark II vertical process camera	CAMERA, PROCESS	LogEtronics, Inc.
	480 camera processor	CAMERA, PROCESS	Itek Graphic Products
Cold composition machines	Magnetic Tape Selectric composer	COLD COMPOSITION	IBM, Office Products Division
	Magnetic Tape Selectric typewriter	COLD COMPOSITION	IBM, Office Products Division
	800 electronic typing system	COLD COMPOSITION	Xerox Corporation
Collators	Business forms collator Model 750A	COLLATING	Harris Corporation, Schriber Division
	Model 720 copy sorter	COLLATING	A.B. Dick Company
	Model 7124(S) collator	COLLATING	A.B. Dick Company
	20-Station Rollomatic collator	COLLATING	General Binding Corporation
Composing machines, headline	Leteron automatic lettering system	COLD COMPOSITION	Reynolds/Leteron Company
	Varigraph headline composing machine	COLD COMPOSITION	Varigraph, Inc.
	Varityper Headliner Model 820	TYPESETTERS, PHOTO-GRAPHIC	Addressograph-Multigraph Corp., VariTyper Division
Contact imaging materials	Color-Key	CONTACT IMAGING MATERIALS	Minnesota Mining and Mfg. Company
	Kodak magenta contact screen (negative)	CONTACT SCREEN	Eastman Kodak Company
	Kodak magenta contact screen (positive)	CONTACT SCREEN	Eastman Kodak Company
	Kodak magenta contact screen (photogravure)	CONTACT SCREEN	Eastman Kodak Company
	Kodak gray contact screen (negative)	CONTACT SCREEN	Eastman Kodak Company
	Kodak PMT gray contact screen	CONTACT SCREEN	Eastman Kodak Company
	Transfer-Key	TRANSFER-KEY	Minnesota Mining and Mfg. Company

[1]For complete address of manufacturer or distributor, see MANUFACTURERS' INDEX.

Classification	Product	See	Manufacturer
Copying machines	A.D.S. automatic duplicating system	COPYING MACHINES	Itek Graphic Products
	Both Sides copymaker	COPYING MACHINES	Addressograph-Multigraph Corp., Multigraphics Division
	Copier II	COPYING MACHINES	IBM, Office Products Division
	Electrostatic copier AM 5000	COPYING MACHINES	Addressograph-Multigraph Corp., Multigraphics Division
	IBM Copier	COPYING MACHINES	IBM, Office Products Division
	Model 675 electrostatic copier	COPYING MACHINES	A.B. Dick Company
	Pressure diazo copying machine Model PD 80	COPYING MACHINES	Addressograph-Multigraph Corp., Multigraphics Division
	Total Copy system	COPYING MACHINES	Addressograph-Multigraph Corp., Multigraphics Division
	4500 copier	COPYING MACHINES	Xerox Corporation
	6500 color copier	COPYING MACHINES	Xerox Corporation
	9200 duplication system	COPYING MACHINES	Xerox Corporation
Correction aids	Ko-Rec-Copy	CORRECTION SHEET	Eaton Allen Corporation
	Ko-Rec-Type	CORRECTION SHEET	Eaton Allen Corporation
Drafting, automated	Automatic artwork generator PC-740-E system	DRAFTING, AUTOMATED	Gerber Scientific Instrument Co.
	Interactive Design System	DRAFTING, AUTOMATED	Gerber Scientific Instrument Co.
	Laser-controlled photoplotting system, Model 1434	DRAFTING, AUTOMATED	Gerber Scientific Instrument Co.
Drafting equipment	Paragon drafting machine	DRAFTING MACHINE	Keuffel & Esser Company
Drafting materials	Helios drafting papers and cloths	HELIOS	Keuffel & Esser Company
	Herculene drafting film	HERCULENE DRAFTING FILM	Keuffel & Esser Company
	Onyx papers and cloths	ONYX	Keuffel & Esser Company
Dryers, screen-process printing	Electro-Jet modular drying system	SCREEN-PROCESS PRINTING	Cincinnati Printing and Drying Systems, Inc.
	Super-Jet III automatic conveyorized dryer	SCREEN-PROCESS PRINTING	Cincinnati Printing and Drying Systems, Inc.
	Vecto-Jet dryer	SCREEN-PROCESS PRINTING	American Screen Printing Equipment Company
Duplicators, offset	ATF 1014 copy duplicating system	OFFSET DUPLICATOR	American Type Founders Co., Inc.
	Model 326 tabletop offset duplicator	OFFSET DUPLICATOR	A.B. Dick Company
	Model 369 offset duplicator	OFFSET DUPLICATOR	A.B. Dick Company
	1500 copy system	OFFSET DUPLICATOR	A.B. Dick Company
Duplicators, plate	Multilith Duplimat masters	MULTILITH DUPLIMAT MASTERS	Addressograph-Multigraph Corp., Multigraphics Division
Duplicators, spirit	Model 217 spirit duplicator	SPIRIT DUPLICATING	A.B. Dick Company
Duplicators, stencil	Model 565 mimeograph stencil printer	MIMEOGRAPH	A.B. Dick Company
Engraving, electronic	Chromagraph DC 300 electronic scanner	ENGRAVING, ELECTRONIC	HCM Corporation
	Helio-Klischograph Model K200 electronic engraving machine	ENGRAVING, ELECTRONIC	HCM Corporation
	Magnascan 460 electronic color scanner	ENGRAVING, ELECTRONIC	Sun Chemical Corporation
Engraving, mechanical	Model ITF-K Engravograph engraving machine	ENGRAVING, MECHANICAL	New Hermes Engraving Machine Corporation

Classification	Product	See	Manufacturer
Envelopes	Envelopes	ENVELOPES	United States Envelope Co.
Facsimile transceivers	Telecopiers III and V	FACSIMILE TRANSCEIVER	Xerox Corporation
	Telecopier 200	FACSIMILE TRANSCEIVER	Xerox Corporation
	Telecopier 400	FACSIMILE TRANSCEIVER	Xerox Corporation
	Telecopier 410	FACSIMILE TRANSCEIVER	Xerox Corporation
Film, lithographic and process	Acetate Ortho Litho film	ACETATE ORTHO LITHO FILM	E.I. du Pont de Nemours & Co.
	Clearback Ortho Litho film	CLEARBACK ORTHO LITHO FILM	E.I. du Pont de Nemours & Co.
	Clearbase film	CLEARBASE FILM	E.I. du Pont de Nemours & Co.
	Commercial S film	COMMERCIAL S FILM	E.I. du Pont de Nemours & Co.
	High Contrast Pan film	HIGH CONTRAST PAN FILM	E.I. du Pont de Nemours & Co.
	Kodagraph Autopositive paper	KODAK AUTOPOSITIVE MATERIALS	Eastman Kodak Company
	Kodak Autopositive materials	KODAK AUTOPOSITIVE MATERIALS	Eastman Kodak Company
	Kodak gray contact screen	KODAK GRAY CONTACT SCREEN	Eastman Kodak Company
	Kodak magenta contact screen	KODAK MAGENTA CONTACT SCREEN	Eastman Kodak Company
	Kodalith Autoscreen Ortho screen	KODALITH AUTOSCREEN ORTHO FILM	Eastman Kodak Company
	Lithofilm	LITHOFILM	Ozalid Reproduction Products
	Low Contrast Pan film	LOW CONTRAST PAN FILM	E.I. du Pont de Nemours & Co.
	Low Gamma Pan film	LOW GAMMA PAN FILM	E.I. du Pont de Nemours & Co.
	Masking (Blue-sensitive) film	MASKING (BLUE-SENSITIVE) FILM	E.I. du Pont de Nemours & Co.
	Ortho A film; Ortho D film; Ortho M film; Ortho S film	ORTHO A FILM; ORTHO D FILM; ORTHO M FILM; ORTHO S FILM	E.I. du Pont de Nemours & Co.
	Pan Litho film	PAN LITHO FILM	E.I. du Pont de Nemours & Co.
	Pan Masking film	PAN MASKING FILM	E.I. du Pont de Nemours & Co.
Film bases	Cronar	CRONAR	E.I. du Pont de Nemours & Co.
	Mylar	MYLAR	E.I. du Pont de Nemours & Co.
Film, mechanized processing	Kodak MP phototypesetting film 2592 (Estar Base)	FILM, MECHANIZED PROCESSING	Eastman Kodak Company
	Kodalith MP contact film	FILM, MECHANIZED PROCESSING	Eastman Kodak Company
	Kodalith MP High Speed Duplicating film	FILM, MECHANIZED PROCESSING	Eastman Kodak Company
	Kodalith MP line film	FILM, MECHANIZED PROCESSING	Eastman Kodak Company
	Kodalith MP Ortho film	FILM, MECHANIZED PROCESSING	Eastman Kodak Company
	Kodalith MP pan film 2558 (Estar base)	FILM, MECHANIZED PROCESSING	Eastman Kodak Company
Fixatives	Krylon	KRYLON	Krylon, Inc.
Folding: paper	Model 52 folding machine	FOLDING: PAPER	A.B. Dick Company
	Module 1 folding machine	FOLDING: PAPER	General Binding Corporation
	O&M Pro-Fold folding machine	FOLDING: PAPER	General Binding Corporation
Guide, contact control	Contact control guide and scale	CONTROL GUIDE CONTACT	Eastman Kodak Company
Inks, printing	Inks, printing	INKS, PRINTING	Sun Chemical Corporation
Jogging equipment	Model J-1 jogger	JOGGER	FMC Corporation
	Model J-50 jogger	JOGGER	FMC Corporation

Classification	Product	See	Manufacturer
Keyboard equipment, photographic typesetter composition	AlphaSette keyboard/editor	KEYBOARD EQUIPMENT, PHOTOGRAPHIC TYPESETTER COMPOSITION	Alphatype Corporation
	AlphaSette system	KEYBOARD EQUIPMENT, PHOTOGRAPHIC TYPESETTING COMPOSITION	Alphatype Corporation
	Comp/Set Series 4500 phototypesetter	TYPESETTER, PHOTOGRAPHIC	Addressograph-Multigraph Corp., VariTyper Division
	Comp/Set 500 direct-entry phototypesetter	TYPESETTER, PHOTOGRAPHIC	Addressograph-Multigraph Corp., VariTyper Division
	Edit/Set video display terminal	KEYBOARD EQUIPMENT, PHOTOGRAPHIC TYPESETTER COMPOSITION	Addressograph-Multigraph Corp., VariTyper Division
	Electro/Set 450 dual-purpose correcting terminal	KEYBOARD EQUIPMENT, PHOTOGRAPHIC TYPESETTER COMPOSITION	Addressograph-Multigraph Corp., VariTyper Division
	Harris editorial input system copy flow	KEYBOARD EQUIPMENT, PHOTOGRAPHIC TYPESETTER COMPOSITION	Harris Corporation
	Model 1100 editing and proofing terminal	KEYBOARD EQUIPMENT, PHOTOGRAPHIC TYPESETTER COMPOSITION	Harris Corporation
	Model 1500 editing and proofing terminal	KEYBOARD EQUIPMENT, PHOTOGRAPHIC TYPESETTER COMPOSITION	Harris Corporation
	MVP Editing system	KEYBOARD EQUIPMENT, PHOTOGRAPHIC TYPESETTER COMPOSITION	Mergenthaler Linotype Company
Knives, art	Art knives and scalpel	FRISKET	Chartpak
	Knife blades and dispenser	FRISKET	Chartpak
Layout aids	Copy Block	COPY BLOCK	The Craftint Manufacturing Co.
Lettering guides	Lettering guides	LETTERING GUIDES	A.B. Dick Company
Lineup tables	Model RR41F lineup table	LINEUP TABLE	nuArc Company, Inc.
Masking and stripping materials	Amberlith	MASKING AND STRIPPING MATERIALS	Ulano
	Rubylith	MASKING AND STRIPPING MATERIALS	Ulano
Microfilm equipment	Aperture card reader Model 576-90	MICROFILM EQUIPMENT	Dukane Corporation
	Automated microfiche retrieval display printer Model 96	MICROFILM EQUIPMENT	Addressograph-Multigraph Corp., Bruning Division
	Diazo microfiche duplicator OP-49/88	MICROFILM EQUIPMENT	Addressograph-Multigraph Corp., Bruning Division
	Microfiche reader-printer Model 5500	MICROFILM EQUIPMENT	Addressograph-Multigraph Corp., Bruning Division
	Tabletop aperture card duplicator Model OP-60	MICROFILM EQUIPMENT	Addressograph-Multigraph Corp., Bruning Division
	Tabletop diazo microfiche duplicator Model OP-10	MICROFILM EQUIPMENT	Addressograph-Multigraph Corp., Bruning Division
	500CT microfilm reader-printer	MICROFILM EQUIPMENT	Minnesota Mining and Mfg. Company
	3400 microfilm cartridge camera	MICROFILM EQUIPMENT	Minnesota Mining and Mfg. Company
Mimeoscope	Mimeoscope	MIMEOSCOPE	A.B. Dick Company
Overhead projection	Diazochrome projecturals	DIAZOCHROME PROJECTURALS	Scott Graphics, Inc.
	Kit used in making overhead transparencies	OVERHEAD TRANSPARENCY	Chartpak
	Lettering and symbols	OVERHEAD TRANSPARENCY	Chartpak

Classification	Product	See	Manufacturer
	Mounted overhead transparency	OVERHEAD TRANSPARENCY	Chartpak
	Pickle jar	PICKLE JAR	Scott Graphics, Inc.
	Proto-Printer	OVERHEAD PROJECTION	Scott Graphics, Inc.
	Shading film	OVERHEAD TRANSPARENCY	Chartpak
	Tape applied to artwork	OVERHEAD TRANSPARENCY	Chartpak
Pens, steel-brush	Speedball steel-brush pens	PENS, STEEL-BRUSH	Hunt Manufacturing Co.
	Pens, Speedball	SPEEDBALL PENS	Hunt Manufacturing Co.
	Flicker pen	SPEEDBALL PENS	Hunt Manufacturing Co.
Pens, technical	Koh-I-Noor Rapidograph pens	PENS, TECHNICAL	Koh-I-Noor, Inc.
	Leroy pen sets and scribers	PENS, TECHNICAL	Keuffel & Esser Company
	Mars technical pen	PENS, TECHNICAL	J.S. Staedtler, Inc.
Platemaking equipment	Dual platemaker	PLATEMAKING EQUIPMENT	Minnesota Mining and Mfg. Company
	Model FT40UP Flip-Top platemaker	PLATEMAKING EQUIPMENT	nuArc Company, Inc.
	Model 175VFE electrostatic platemaker	PLATEMAKING EQUIPMENT	Itek Graphic Products
	Model 20/24 Platemaster	PLATEMAKING EQUIPMENT	Itek Graphic Products
	Stencil maker for mimeographing	STENCIL SHEET	A.B. Dick Company
Presses, electrostatic stencil-screen printing	Case Marker electrostatic screen printer	ELECTROSTATIC STENCIL-SCREEN PRINTING PROCESS	Jas. H. Matthews & Company
	Ceramic electrostatic tile printer	ELECTROSTATIC STENCIL-SCREEN PRINTING PROCESS	Electrostatic Printing Corp. of America
	Pipe printer using electrostatic printing process	ELECTROSTATIC STENCIL-SCREEN PRINTING PROCESS	Electrostatic Printing Corp. of America
Presses, offset: sheet-fed	Champion four-color sheet-fed offset press	OFFSET PRINTING PRESS	HCM Corporation
	Chief 15-inch offset press	OFFSET PRINTING PRESS	American Type Founders Co., Inc.
	Miehle 36 two-color sheet-fed offset press	OFFSET PRINTING PRESS	MGD Graphic Systems, North American Rockwell
	Miehle Super 60 offset press	OFFSET PRINTING PRESS	MGD Graphic Systems, North American Rockwell
	Model 1000 web offset press	OFFSET PRINTING PRESS	Harris Corporation, Harris Web Press Division
	Profiteer 25-1 sheet-fed offset printing press	OFFSET PRINTING PRESS	American Type Founders Co., Inc.
	Schriber Model H 500 press	OFFSET PRINTING PRESS	Harris Corporation, Schriber Division
	Schriber High-Speed stock forms press	OFFSET PRINTING PRESS	Harris Corporation, Schriber Division
Presses, perfecting	Davidson offset perfecting press with roll converter	PERFECTING PRESS	American Type Founders Co., Inc.
Presses, platen	D Series Kluge automatic platen press	PLATEN PRESS	Brandtjen & Kluge, Inc.
	EHD Series Kluge automatic die cutting, foil stamping, and embossing press	PLATEN PRESS	Brandtjen & Kluge, Inc.
Presses, screen-process printing	Aladdin cylinder screen printing press	SCREEN-PROCESS PRINTING	Lawson Screen Printing and Drying Machine Company
	Argon Compact semi-automatic screen printing press	SCREEN-PROCESS PRINTING	Cincinnati Printing and Drying Systems, Inc.

Classification	Product	See	Manufacturer
	Pacesetters Mark 4 and 5	TYPESETTERS, PHOTO-GRAPHIC	Dymo Graphic Systems
	Unisetter	TYPESETTERS, PHOTOGRAPHIC	Compugraphic Corporation
	VariTyper AM 748	TYPESETTERS, PHOTO-GRAPHIC	Addressograph-Multigraph Corp., VariTyper Division
	VIP Basic System 10	TYPESETTERS, PHOTO-GRAPHIC	Mergenthaler Linotype Company
Typewriters	IBM Executive	TYPEWRITER	IBM, Office Products Division
Whiteprint process	Diazo copying machine Model PD 80	WHITEPRINT PROCESS	Addressograph-Multigraph Corp., Bruning Division
	Dry diazo whiteprint copier Revolute 860	WHITEPRINT PROCESS	Addressograph-Multigraph Corp., Bruning Division
	Revolute 875 whiteprint copying machine	WHITEPRINT PROCESS	Addressograph-Multigraph Corp., Bruning Division
	Tabletop copying machine	WHITEPRINT PROCESS	Addressograph-Multigraph Corp., Bruning Division

Manufacturer	Product	See
Addressograph-Multigraph Corp. Bruning Division 1834 Walden Office Square Schaumburg, IL 60196	Automated microfiche retrieval display printer Model 96	MICROFILM EQUIPMENT
	Diazo copying machine Model PD 80	WHITEPRINT PROCESS
	Diazo microfiche duplicator OP-49/88	MICROFILM EQUIPMENT
	Dry diazo whiteprint copier Revolute 860	WHITEPRINT PROCESS
	Microfiche camera processor Model 750	CAMERA, MICROFILM
	Microfiche reader-printer Model 5500	MICROFILM EQUIPMENT
	Pressure diazo copying machine Model PD 80	COPYING MACHINES
	Revolute 875 whiteprint copying machine	WHITEPRINT PROCESS
	Tabletop aperture card duplicator Model OP-60	MICROFILM EQUIPMENT
	Tabletop copying machine Model PD 33	WHITEPRINT PROCESS
	Tabletop diazo microfiche duplicator Model OP-10	MICROFILM EQUIPMENT
Addressograph-Multigraph Corp. Multigraphics Division 1800 West Central Road Mount Prospect, IL 60056	Both Sides copymaker	COPYING MACHINES
	Electrostatic copier AM 5000	COPYING MACHINES
	Multilith Duplimat masters	MULTILITH DUPLIMAT MASTERS
	Total Copy system	COPYING MACHINES
Addressograph-Multigraph Corp. VariTyper Division 11 Mt. Pleasant Avenue East Hanover, NJ 07936	Comp/Set 500 direct-entry phototypesetter	TYPESETTERS, PHOTOGRAPHIC
	Comp/Set Series 4500 Phototypesetter	TYPESETTERS, PHOTOGRAPHIC
	Edit/Set video display terminal	KEYBOARD EQUIPMENT, PHOTOGRAPHIC TYPESETTER COMPOSITION
	Electro/Set 450 dual-purpose correcting terminal	KEYBOARD EQUIPMENT, PHOTOGRAPHIC TYPESETTER COMPOSITION
	VariTyper AM 748 phototypesetter	TYPESETTERS, PHOTOGRAPHIC
Alphatype Corporation 7500 McCormick Boulevard Skokie, IL 60076	AlphaSette keyboard/editor	KEYBOARD EQUIPMENT, PHOTOGRAPHIC TYPESETTER COMPOSITION
	AlphaSette system	KEYBOARD EQUIPMENT, PHOTOGRAPHIC TYPESETTER COMPOSITION
American Screen Printing Equipment Company, 505 N. Noble Street, Chicago, IL 60622	Arrow-Matic automatic screen printing press	SCREEN-PROCESS PRINTING
	Cameo Multi-Printer textile printer	SCREEN-PROCESS PRINTING
	Masterprint Glide screen printing press	SCREEN-PROCESS PRINTING
	Vecto-Jet dryer	SCREEN-PROCESS PRINTING
American Type Founders Co., Inc. Whitinsville, MA 01588	ATF 1014 copy duplicating system	OFFSET DUPLICATORS
	Chief 15-inch offset press	OFFSET PRINTING PRESS
	Davidson offset perfecting press with roll converter	PERFECTING PRESS
	Profiteer 25-1 sheet-fed offset printing press	OFFSET PRINTING PRESS
Avery Label Company 1616 South California Avenue Monrovia, CA 91016	Adhesive materials	AVERY
Brandtjen & Kluge, Inc. 653 Galtier Street St. Paul, MN 55103	D Series Kluge automatic platen press	PLATEN PRESS
	EHD-Series Kluge automatic die cutting, foil stamping, and embossing press	PLATEN PRESS
	Kluge web-flow continuous-forms press	CONTINUOUS-FORM PRESS
Cincinnati Printing and Drying Systems, Inc. 1111 Meta Drive, Cincinnati, OH 45237	Argon Speed-O-Mat automatic screen printing press	SCREEN-PROCESS PRINTING
	Argon Compact semi-automatic screen printing press	SCREEN-PROCESS PRINTING
	Super-Jet III automatic conveyorized dryer	SCREEN-PROCESS PRINTING
	Electro-Jet modular drying system	SCREEN-PROCESS PRINTING

Manufacturer	Product	See
Chartpak One River Road Leeds, MA 01053	Adhesive materials	CHARTPAK
	Art knives and scalpel	FRISKET
	Kit used in making overhead transparencies	OVERHEAD TRANSPARENCY
	Knife blades and dispenser	FRISKET
	Lettering and symbols	OVERHEAD TRANSPARENCY
	Mounted overhead transparency	OVERHEAD TRANSPARENCY
	Tape applied to artwork	OVERHEAD TRANSPARENCY
	Tape, pressure-sensitive	OVERHEAD TRANSPARENCY
	Shading film	OVERHEAD TRANSPARENCY
Compugraphic Corporation Industrial Way Wilmington, MA 01887	CompuWriter II	TYPESETTERS, PHOTOGRAPHIC
	CompuWriter 88	TYPESETTERS, PHOTOGRAPHIC
	Display Composition System	TYPESETTERS, PHOTOGRAPHIC
	EditWriter 7500	TYPESETTERS, PHOTOGRAPHIC
	Unisetter	TYPESETTERS, PHOTOGRAPHIC
Craftint Manufacturing Co., The 18501 Euclid Avenue Cleveland, OH 44112	Copy Block	COPY BLOCK
	Doubletone shading	SHADING MEDIUMS
	Craf-Tech	CRAF-TECH
	Craf-Tone shading mediums	SHADING MEDIUMS
	Craf-Type	CRAF-TYPE
	Craft-Color	CRAFT-COLOR
	Craft-Symbols	CRAFT-SYMBOLS
	Paste-ups and transfers	CRAFTINT
	Singletone shading	SHADING MEDIUMS
Dick, A.B., Company 5700 West Touhy Avenue Chicago, IL 60648	Model 52 folding machine	FOLDING: PAPER
	Model 217 spirit duplicator	SPIRIT DUPLICATING
	Model 326 tabletop offset duplicator	OFFSET DUPLICATOR
	Model 369 offset duplicator	OFFSET DUPLICATOR
	Model 565 mimeograph stencil printer	MIMEOGRAPH
	Model 675 electrostatic copier	COPYING MACHINES
	Model 720 copy sorter	COLLATING
	Model 7124(S) collator	COLLATING
	Lettering guides	LETTERING GUIDES
	Mimeoscope	MIMEOSCOPE
	Stencil maker for mimeographing	STENCIL SHEET
	1500 copy system	OFFSET DUPLICATOR
Distribution Codes, Inc. 401 Wythe Street Alexandria, VA 22314	Product code	UNIVERSAL PRODUCT CODE (UPC)
Dukane Corporation Special Products Division St. Charles, IL 60174	Model 576-90 aperture card reader	MICROFILM EQUIPMENT
Du Pont de Nemours, E.I., & Co. Wilmington, DE 19898	Acetate Ortho Litho film	ACETATE ORTHO LITHO FILM
	Clearback Ortho Litho film	CLEARBACK ORTHO LITHO FILM
	Clearbase film	CLEARBASE FILM
	Commercial S film	COMMERCIAL S FILM
	Cronar	CRONAR
	High Contrast Pan film	HIGH CONTRAST PAN FILM
	Low Contrast Pan film	LOW CONTRAST PAN FILM
	Low Gamma Pan film	LOW GAMMA PAN FILM
	Litho T photographic paper	LITHO T PHOTOGRAPHIC PAPER
	Masking (Blue-sensitive) film	MASKING (BLUE-SENSITIVE) FILM
	Mylar	MYLAR
	Ortho A film	ORTHO A FILM
	Ortho D film	ORTHO D FILM
	Ortho M film	ORTHO M FILM
	Ortho S film	ORTHO S FILM
	Pan Litho film	PAN LITHO FILM
	Pan Masking film	PAN MASKING FILM
Dymo Graphic Systems 355 Middlesex Avenue Wilmington, MA 01887	Copy processing system Model CPS-730	TYPESETTERS, PHOTOGRAPHIC
	Model DLC-1000 laser composer	TYPESETTERS, PHOTOGRAPHIC
	Pacesetters Mark 4 and 5	TYPESETTERS, PHOTOGRAPHIC

Manufacturer	Product	See
Eastman Kodak Company 343 State Street Rochester, NY 14650	Contact control guide and scale Ektamatic 214K stabilization processor Kodagraph Autopositive paper Kodak Autopositive materials Kodak gray contact screen Kodak gray contact screen (negative) Kodak magenta contact screen Kodak magenta contact screen (negative) Kodak magenta contact screen (positive) Kodak magenta contact screen (photogravure) Kodak MP Phototypesetting Film 2592 (Estar base) Kodak PMT gray contact screen Kodak Polymatic Litho Plate LN-L Kodalith Autoscreen Ortho film Kodalith MP contact film Kodalith MP High Speed Duplicating film Kodalith MP line film Kodalith MP Ortho film Kodalith MP pan film 2558 (Estar base) Readymatic processor Model 420A	CONTROL GUIDE, CONTACT PROCESSING, FILM OR PAPER KODAK AUTOPOSITIVE MATERIALS KODAK AUTOPOSITIVE MATERIALS KODAK GRAY CONTACT SCREEN CONTACT SCREEN KODAK MAGENTA CONTACT SCREEN CONTACT SCREEN CONTACT SCREEN CONTACT SCREEN FILM, MECHANIZED PROCESSING CONTACT SCREEN KODAK POLYMATIC LITHO PLATE LN-L KODALITH AUTOSCREEN ORTHO FILM FILM, MECHANIZED PROCESSING FILM, MECHANIZED PROCESSING FILM, MECHANIZED PROCESSING FILM, MECHANIZED PROCESSING FILM, MECHANIZED PROCESSING PROCESSING, FILM OR PAPER
Eaton Allen Corporation 67 Kent Avenue Brooklyn, NY 11211	Ko-Rec-Type Ko-Rec-Copy	CORRECTION SHEET CORRECTION SHEET
FMC Corporation Material Handling Equipment Division Homer City, PA 15748	Model J-1 with single bin rack Model J-50 with tilted rack	JOGGER JOGGER
General Binding Corporation 1101 Skokie Boulevard Northbrook, IL 60062	Autobinder II Model 346 BN Automatic punch Module 1 folding machine O&M Pro-Fold folding machine 20-Station Rollomatic collator	BINDING, MECHANICAL BINDING, MECHANICAL FOLDING: PAPER FOLDING: PAPER COLLATING
Gerber Scientific Instrument Co. P.O. Box 305 Hartford, CT 06101	Automatic artwork generator Model PC-740-E system Interactive Design System (IDS) Laser-controlled photoplotting system, Model 1434	DRAFTING, AUTOMATED DRAFTING, AUTOMATED DRAFTING, AUTOMATED
Grumbacher, M., Inc. 460 W. 34th Street New York, NY 10001	Art brushes	BRUSHES, ART
Harris Corporation Harris Composition Systems P.O. Box 2080 Melbourne, FL 32901	Fototronic TxT system Fototronic 7400 CRT Harris editorial input system copy flow Model 1100 editing and proofing terminal Model 1500 editing and proofing terminal	TYPESETTERS, PHOTOGRAPHIC TYPESETTERS, PHOTOGRAPHIC KEYBOARD EQUIPMENT, PHOTOGRAPHIC TYPESETTER COMPOSITION KEYBOARD EQUIPMENT, PHOTOGRAPHIC TYPESETTER COMPOSITION KEYBOARD EQUIPMENT, PHOTOGRAPHIC TYPESETTER COMPOSITION
Harris-Intertype Corporation Harris Web Press Division 55 Public Square Cleveland, OH 44113	Model 1000 web offset press	OFFSET PRINTING PRESS
Harris-Intertype Corporation Schriber Division 4900 Webster Street Dayton, OH 45414	Business forms calculator Model 750A Schriber High-Speed stock forms press Schriber Model H 500 press	COLLATING OFFSET PRINTING PRESS OFFSET PRINTING PRESS

Manufacturer	Product	See
HCM Corporation 115 Cuttermill Road Great Neck, NY 11021	Champion four-color sheet-fed offset press Chromograph DC 300 electronic scanner Helio-Klischograph Model K200 electronic engraving machine	OFFSET PRINTING PRESS ENGRAVING, ELECTRONIC ENGRAVING, ELECTRONIC
Hunt Manufacturing Co. 1405 Locust Street Philadelphia, PA 19102	Block-printing instruments Flicker pen Speedball pens Speedball steel-brush pens	BLOCK PRINTING SPEEDBALL PENS SPEEDBALL PENS PENS, STEEL-BRUSH; SPEEDBALL PENS
International Business Machines Corp. Office Products Division Parson's Pond Drive Franklin Lakes, NJ 07417	Copier II Executive typewriter IBM Copier Magnetic Tape Selectric composer Magnetic Tape Selectric typewriter	COPYING MACHINES TYPEWRITER COPYING MACHINES COLD COMPOSITION COLD COMPOSITION
Itek Graphic Products Division of Itek Corporation 1001 Jefferson Road Rochester, NY 14603	A.D.S. automatic duplicating system Model 20/24 Platemaster Model 175 VFE variable focus electrostatic platemaker 480 camera processor	COPYING MACHINES PLATEMAKING, EQUIPMENT PLATEMAKING EQUIPMENT CAMERA, PROCESS
Keuffel & Esser Company 20 Whippany Road Morristown, NJ 07960	Helios drafting papers and cloths Herculene drafting film Leroy pen sets and scribers Onyx papers and cloths Paragon drafting machine	HELIOS HERCULENE DRAFTING FILM PENS, TECHNICAL ONYX DRAFTING MACHINE
Koh-I-Noor, Inc. 100 North Street Bloomsbury, NJ 08804	Koh-I-Noor Rapidograph pens Pelikan Graphos pens	PENS, TECHNICAL PENS, TECHNICAL
Krylon, Inc. Norristown, PA 19134	Krylon	KRYLON
Lawson Screen Printing and Drying Machine Company 4434 Olive Street St. Louis, MO 63108	Aladdin cylinder screen printing press Genie Mark VI flatbed screen printing press Lawson Imp flatbed printing press Lawson Mini portable/bench screen printing press	SCREEN-PROCESS PRINTING SCREEN-PROCESS PRINTING SCREEN-PROCESS PRINTING SCREEN-PROCESS PRINTING
Linkrule Company P.O. Box 34669 Los Angeles, CA 90034	Proportional scale	LINKRULE
Lissner, Jay G. 3417 West First Street Los Angeles, CA 90004	Adhesive materials	ARTIST
LogEtronics, Inc. 7001 Loisdale Road Springfield, VA 22150	PC-18 processor RAP 20 processor Robertson 500 graphic arts process overhead camera 432 Mark II vertical process camera	PROCESSING, FILM OR PAPER PROCESSING, FILM OR PAPER CAMERA, PROCESS CAMERA, PROCESS
Jas. H. Matthews & Company 6515 Penn Avenue Pittsburgh, PA 15206	Case Marker electrostatic printer	ELECTROSTATIC STENCIL-SCREEN PRINTING PROCESS
Mergenthaler Linotype Company Mergenthaler Drive Plainview, NY 11803	Linocomp 2 Linotron 606 typesetter MVP Editing system VIP Basic System 10	TYPESETTERS, PHOTOGRAPHIC TYPESETTERS, PHOTOGRAPHIC KEYBOARD EQUIPMENT, PHOTOGRAPHIC TYPESETTER COMPOSITION TYPESETTERS, PHOTOGRAPHIC
MGD Graphic Systems North American Rockwell 2011 West Hastings Street Chicago, IL 60608	Miehle Super 60 offset press Miehle 36 two-color sheet-fed offset press	OFFSET PRINTING PRESS OFFSET PRINTING PRESS

Manufacturer	Product	See
Minnesota Mining and Mfg. Company Industrial Graphics Division 3M Center Saint Paul, MN 55101	Color-Key Dual plate maker Transfer-key	CONTACT IMAGING MATERIAL PLATEMAKING EQUIPMENT TRANSFER-KEY
Minnesota Mining and Mfg. Company Microfilm Products Division 3M Center Saint Paul, MN 55101	500CT microfilm reader-printer 3400 microfilm cartridge camera	MICROFILM EQUIPMENT MICROFILM EQUIPMENT
New Hermes Engraving Machine Corporation 20 Cooper Square—Third Avenue & Third Street New York, NY 10003	Model ITF-K Engravograph	ENGRAVING, MECHANICAL

nuArc Company, Inc.
4110 West Grand Avenue
Chicago, IL 60651
	Model FT40UP Flip-Top platemaker
	Model P2500 diffusion-transfer
	   process
	Model RR41F lineup table
	Model SST-1418 process camera
	Model VV1418 vertical camera
	Model 2024V Rocket vertical process
	   camera
		PLATEMAKING EQUIPMENT
		DIFFUSION-TRANSFER PROCESS
		
		LINEUP TABLE
		CAMERA, PROCESS
		CAMERA, PROCESS
		CAMERA, PROCESS

Ozalid Reproduction Products Division of General Aniline and Film Corporation 25 Ozalid Road Binghamton, NY 13903	Lithofilm	LITHOFILM
Polaroid Corporation 549 Technology Square Cambridge, MA 02139	Polaroid MP-4	POLAROID MP-4 MULTIPURPOSE LAND CAMERA
Reynolds/Leteron Company 9830 San Fernando Road Pacoima, CA 91331	Leteron automatic lettering system	COLD COMPOSITION
Scott Graphics, Inc. 195 Appleton Street Holyoke, MA 01040	Diazochrome projecturals Pickle jar Proto-Printer	DIAZOCHROME PROJECTURALS PICKLE JAR OVERHEAD PROJECTION

Sheridan Company, The
Division of Harris-Intertype Corpora-
   tion
P.O. Box 283
Easton, PA 18042
	High-speed heavy-duty hinge-clamp
	   binder
	Hinge-clamp binder
	Straight-line trimmer
	XG standard rotary gatherer
		BOOKBINDING
		
		BOOKBINDING
		BOOKBINDING
		BOOKBINDING

Staedtler, J. S., Inc. P.O. Box 68 One Marks Court Montville, NJ 07045	Mars technical pen	PENS, TECHNICAL
Sun Chemical Corporation 200 Park Avenue New York, NY 10017	Magnascan 460 electronic color scanner Suncure	ENGRAVING, ELECTRONIC INKS, PRINTING
Ulano 610 Dean Street Brooklyn, NY 11238	Amberlith Rubylith	MASKING AND STRIPPING MATERIALS MASKING AND STRIPPING MATERIALS
United States Envelope Co. 21 Cypress Street Springfield, MA 01104	Envelopes	ENVELOPES
Varigraph, Inc. Madison, WI 53701	Varigraph headline composing ma- chine	COLD COMPOSITION
Velo-Bind, Inc. 771 Vaqueros Street Sunnyvale, CA 94086	Model 123 desk-top binder Model 201 Mark IV binder	BINDING, MECHANICAL BINDING, MECHANICAL

Manufacturer	Product	See
Xerox Corporation	800 electronic typing system	COLD COMPOSITION
Xerox Square	4500 copier	COPYING MACHINES
Rochester, NY 14644	6500 color copier	COPYING MACHINES
	9200 duplicating system	COPYING MACHINES
Xerox Corporation	Telecopiers III and V	FACSIMILE TRANSCEIVER
1341 West Mockingbird Lane	Telecopier 200	FACSIMILE TRANSCEIVER
Dallas, TX 75247	Telecopier 400	FACSIMILE TRANSCEIVER
	Telecopier 410	FACSIMILE TRANSCEIVER

Tables

TABLE 1   **Metric Conversion Table**

INCHES/CENTIMETERS						FEET/METERS					
1 to 50			51 to 100			1 to 50			51 to 100		
Inches		Centimeters	Inches		Centimeters	Feet		Meters	Feet		Meters
0.3937	1	2.54	20.079	51	129.54	3.281	1	0.3048	167.3	51	15.54
0.7874	2	5.08	20.472	52	132.08	6.562	2	0.6096	170.6	52	15.85
1.1811	3	7.62	20.866	53	134.62	9.843	3	0.9144	173.9	53	16.15
1.5748	4	10.16	21.26	54	137.16	13.12	4	1.219	177.2	54	16.46
1.9685	5	12.7	21.654	55	139.7	16.4	5	1.524	180.4	55	16.76
2.3622	6	15.24	22.047	56	142.24	19.69	6	1.829	183.7	56	17.07
2.7559	7	17.78	22.441	57	144.78	22.97	7	2.134	187	57	17.37
3.1496	8	20.32	22.835	58	147.32	26.25	8	2.438	190.3	58	17.68
3.5433	9	22.86	23.228	59	149.86	29.53	9	2.743	193.6	59	17.98
3.937	10	25.4	23.622	60	152.4	32.81	10	3.048	196.9	60	18.29
4.3307	11	27.94	24.016	61	154.94	36.09	11	3.353	200.1	61	18.59
4.7244	12	30.48	24.409	62	157.48	39.37	12	3.658	203.4	62	18.9
5.1181	13	33.02	24.803	63	160.02	42.65	13	3.962	206.7	63	19.2
5.5118	14	35.56	25.197	64	162.56	45.93	14	4.267	210	64	19.51
5.9055	15	38.1	25.591	65	165.1	49.21	15	4.572	213.3	65	19.81
6.2992	16	40.64	25.984	66	167.64	52.49	16	4.877	216.5	66	20.12
6.6929	17	43.18	26.378	67	170.18	55.77	17	5.182	219.8	67	20.42
7.0866	18	45.72	26.772	68	172.72	59.06	18	5.486	223.1	68	20.73
7.4803	19	48.26	27.165	69	175.26	62.34	19	5.791	226.4	69	21.03
7.874	20	50.8	27.559	70	177.8	65.62	20	6.096	229.7	70	21.34
8.2677	21	53.34	27.953	71	180.34	68.9	21	6.401	232.9	71	21.64
8.6614	22	55.88	28.346	72	182.88	72.18	22	6.706	236.2	72	21.95
9.0551	23	58.42	28.74	73	185.42	75.46	23	7.01	239.5	73	22.25
9.4488	24	60.96	29.134	74	187.96	78.74	24	7.315	242.8	74	22.56
9.8425	25	63.5	29.528	75	190.5	82.02	25	7.62	246.1	75	22.86
10.236	26	66.04	29.921	76	193.04	85.3	26	7.925	249.3	76	23.16
10.63	27	68.58	30.315	77	195.58	88.58	27	8.23	252.6	77	23.47
11.024	28	71.12	30.709	78	198.12	91.86	28	8.534	255.9	78	23.77
11.417	29	73.66	31.102	79	200.66	95.14	29	8.839	259.2	79	24.08
11.811	30	76.2	31.496	80	203.2	98.43	30	9.144	262.5	80	24.38
12.205	31	78.74	31.89	81	205.74	101.7	31	9.449	265.7	81	24.69
12.598	32	81.28	32.283	82	208.28	105	32	9.754	269	82	24.99
12.992	33	83.82	32.677	83	210.82	108.3	33	10.06	272.3	83	25.3
13.386	34	86.36	33.071	84	213.36	111.5	34	10.36	275.6	84	25.6
13.78	35	88.9	33.465	85	215.9	114.8	35	10.67	278.9	85	25.91
14.173	36	91.44	33.858	86	218.44	118.1	36	10.97	282.2	86	26.21
14.567	37	93.98	34.252	87	220.98	121.4	37	11.28	285.4	87	26.52
14.961	38	96.52	34.646	88	223.52	124.7	38	11.58	288.7	88	26.82
15.354	39	99.06	35.039	89	226.06	128	39	11.89	292	89	27.13
15.748	40	101.6	35.433	90	228.6	131.2	40	12.19	295.3	90	27.43
16.142	41	104.14	35.827	91	231.14	134.5	41	12.5	298.6	91	27.74
16.535	42	106.68	36.22	92	233.68	137.8	42	12.8	301.8	92	28.04
16.929	43	109.22	36.614	93	236.22	141.1	43	13.11	305.1	93	28.35
17.323	44	111.76	37.008	94	238.76	144.4	44	13.41	308.4	94	28.65
17.717	45	114.3	37.402	95	241.3	147.6	45	13.72	311.7	95	28.96
18.11	46	116.84	37.795	96	243.84	150.9	46	14.02	315	96	29.26
18.504	47	119.38	38.189	97	246.38	154.2	47	14.33	318.2	97	29.57
18.898	48	121.92	38.583	98	248.92	157.5	48	14.63	321.5	98	29.87
19.291	49	124.46	38.976	99	251.46	160.8	49	14.94	324.8	99	30.18
19.685	50	127	39.37	100	254	164	50	15.24	328.1	100	30.48

Numbers in boldface type are the number of units, either linear or metric. When converting the linear system to the metric system, the centimeter or meter equivalent is found in the right column. When converting from the metric system to inches or feet, the linear equivalent is found in the left column.

TABLE 1 Metric Conversion Table (*Continued*)

POUNDS/KILOGRAMS 1 to 50			POUNDS/KILOGRAMS 51 to 100		
Pounds		Kilograms	Pounds		Kilograms
2.203	**1**	0.454	112.3	**51**	23.15
4.405	**2**	0.908	114.5	**52**	23.61
6.608	**3**	1.362	116.7	**53**	24.06
8.811	**4**	1.816	118.9	**54**	24.52
11.01	**5**	2.27	121.1	**55**	24.97
13.22	**6**	2.724	123.3	**56**	25.42
15.42	**7**	3.178	125.6	**57**	25.88
17.62	**8**	3.632	127.8	**58**	26.33
19.82	**9**	4.086	130	**59**	26.79
22.03	**10**	4.54	132.2	**60**	27.24
24.23	**11**	4.994	134.4	**61**	27.69
26.43	**12**	5.448	136.6	**62**	28.15
28.63	**13**	5.902	138.8	**63**	28.6
30.84	**14**	6.356	141	**64**	29.06
33.04	**15**	6.81	143.2	**65**	29.51
35.24	**16**	7.264	145.4	**66**	29.96
37.44	**17**	7.718	147.6	**67**	30.42
39.65	**18**	8.172	149.8	**68**	30.87
41.85	**19**	8.626	152	**69**	31.33
44.05	**20**	9.08	154.2	**70**	31.78
46.26	**21**	9.534	156.4	**71**	32.23
48.46	**22**	9.988	158.6	**72**	32.69
50.66	**23**	10.44	160.8	**73**	33.14
52.86	**24**	10.9	163	**74**	33.6
55.07	**25**	11.35	165.2	**75**	34.05
57.27	**26**	11.8	167.4	**76**	34.5
59.47	**27**	12.26	169.6	**77**	34.96
61.67	**28**	12.71	171.8	**78**	35.41
63.88	**29**	13.17	174	**79**	35.87
66.08	**30**	13.62	176.2	**80**	36.32
68.28	**31**	14.07	178.4	**81**	36.77
70.48	**32**	14.53	180.6	**82**	37.23
72.69	**33**	14.98	182.8	**83**	37.68
74.89	**34**	15.44	185	**84**	38.14
77.09	**35**	15.89	187.2	**85**	38.59
79.3	**36**	16.34	189.4	**86**	39.04
81.5	**37**	16.8	191.6	**87**	39.5
83.7	**38**	17.25	193.8	**88**	39.95
85.9	**39**	17.71	196	**89**	40.41
88.11	**40**	18.16	198.2	**90**	40.86
90.31	**41**	18.61	200.4	**91**	41.31
92.51	**42**	19.07	202.6	**92**	41.77
94.71	**43**	19.52	204.8	**93**	42.22
96.92	**44**	19.98	207	**94**	42.68
99.12	**45**	20.43	209.3	**95**	43.13
101.3	**46**	20.88	211.5	**96**	43.58
103.5	**47**	21.34	213.7	**97**	44.04
105.7	**48**	21.79	215.9	**98**	44.49
107.9	**49**	22.25	218.1	**99**	44.95
110.1	**50**	22.7	220.3	**100**	45.4

Numbers in boldface type are the number of units. When converting pounds to kilograms, the kilogram equivalent is found in the right column. When converting kilograms to pounds, the pound equivalent is found in the left column.

TABLE 2 Paper Sizes

Type of paper	Standard size*		Standard weights	
	Inches	Centimeters	Pounds	Kilograms
Bible	25 by 38	63.50 by 96.52	20	9.08
	28 by 42	71.12 by 106.68	24	10.90
	28 by 42	71.12 by 106.68	30	13.62
	32 by 44	81.28 by 111.76	35	15.89
	35 by 45	88.90 by 114.30	...	...
	38 by 50	96.52 by 127.00	...	...
Bond	17 by 22	43.18 by 55.88	9	4.08
	17 by 28	43.18 by 71.12	13	5.90
	19 by 24	48.26 by 60.96	16	7.26
	22 by 24	55.88 by 60.96	...	...
	24 by 38	60.96 by 96.52	20	9.08
	28 by 34	71.12 by 86.36	24	10.90
	34 by 44	86.36 by 111.76	...	...
Book (antique,	22½ by 35	57.15 by 88.90	30	13.62
eggshell, machine	24 by 36	60.96 by 91.44	35	15.89
finish, English finish,	25 by 38	63.50 by 96.52	40	18.16
supercalendered)	28 by 42	71.12 by 106.68	45	20.43
	28 by 44	71.12 by 111.76	50	22.70
	32 by 44	81.28 by 111.76	60	27.24
	35 by 45	88.90 by 114.30	70	31.78
	36 by 48	91.44 by 121.92	80	36.32
	38 by 50	96.52 by 127.00	80	36.32
Book (coated-	22½ by 35	57.15 by 88.90	50	22.70
two-sides,	24 by 36	60.96 by 91.44	60	27.24
glossy or	25 by 38	63.50 by 96.52	70	31.78
matte finish)	26 by 40	66.04 by 101.60	80	36.32
	28 by 42	71.12 by 106.68	90	40.86
	28 by 44	71.12 by 111.76	100	45.40
	32 by 44	81.28 by 111.76	120	54.48
	35 by 45	88.90 by 114.30	...	...
	36 by 48	91.44 by 121.92	...	...
	38 by 50	96.52 by 127.00	...	...
Book (coated-	20 by 26	50.80 by 66.04	50	22.70
one-side,	25 by 38	63.50 by 96.52	60	27.24
glossy finish)	26 by 48	66.04 by 121.92	70	31.78
	28 by 42	71.12 by 106.68	80	36.32
	28 by 44	71.12 by 111.76	...	...
	32 by 44	81.28 by 111.76	...	...
	35 by 45	88.90 by 114.30	...	...
	36 by 48	91.44 by 121.92	...	...
	38 by 50	96.52 by 127.00	...	...
	41 by 54	104.14 by 137.16	...	...
Book (process-	24 by 36	60.96 by 91.44	45	20.43
coated)	25 by 38	63.50 by 96.52	50	22.70
	28 by 42	71.12 by 106.68	60	27.24
	32 by 44	81.28 by 111.76	70	31.78
	35 by 45	88.90 by 114.30	...	...
	38 by 50	96.52 by 127.00	...	...
Cover (uncoated)	20 by 26	50.80 by 66.04	40	18.16
	23 by 35	58.42 by 88.90	50	22.70
	26 by 40	66.04 by 101.60	65	29.51
	35 by 46	88.90 by 116.84	80	36.32
	...	...	90	40.86
	...	...	100	45.40
	...	...	130	59.02
Cover (coated)†	20 by 26	50.80 by 66.04	50	22.70
	23 by 35	58.42 by 88.90	60	27.24
	26 by 40	66.04 by 101.60	65	29.51
	35 by 46	88.90 by 116.84	80	36.32
Gravure	25 by 38†	63.50 by 96.52	35	15.89
	28 by 42	71.12 by 106.68	4	18.16
	28 by 44	71.12 by 111.76	45	20.43
	32 by 44	81.28 by 111.76	50	22.71
	35 by 45	88.90 by 114.30	...	...
	38 by 50	96.52 by 127.00	...	...

TABLE 2 Paper Sizes (*Continued*)

Type of paper	Standard size*		Standard weights	
	Inches	Centimeters	Pounds	Kilograms
Ledger (regular and loose-leaf)	16 by 21	40.62 by 53.34	24	10.90
	17 by 22	43.18 by 55.88	28	12.71
	17 by 28	43.18 by 71.12	32	14.53
	19 by 24	48.26 by 60.96	36	16.34
	22 by 34	55.88 by 86.36	...	...
	24 by 38	60.96 by 96.52	...	...
	28 by 34	71.12 by 86.36	...	...
Newsprint	21 by 32	53.34 by 81.28	28	12.71
	22 by 34	55.88 by 86.36		
	24 by 36	60.96 by 91.44	to	to
	25 by 38	63.50 by 96.52		
	28 by 34	71.12 by 86.36	35	15.89
	28 by 42	71.12 by 106.68	28	12.71
	34 by 44	86.36 by 111.76	to	to
	36 by 48	91.44 by 121.92		
	38 by 50	96.52 by 127.00	35	15.89
Offset (uncoated and coated)	22½ by 35	57.15 by 88.90	50	22.70
	25 by 38	63.50 by 96.52	60	27.24
	28 by 42	71.12 by 106.68	70	31.78
	28 by 44	71.12 by 111.76	80	36.32
	32 by 44	81.28 by 111.76	100	45.40
	35 by 45	88.90 by 114.30	120	54.48
	36 by 48	91.44 by 121.92	150	68.10
	38 by 50	96.52 by 127.00	...	...
	38 by 52	96.52 by 132.08	...	...
	41 by 54	104.14 by 137.16	...	...
	44 by 64	111.76 by 162.56	...	...
Onionskin and manifold	17 by 22	47.18 by 55.88		
	19 by 24	48.26 by 60.96		
	17 by 28	43.18 by 71.12	7	3.17
	21 by 32	53.34 by 81.28		
	22 by 34	55.88 by 86.36	to	to
	24 by 38	60.96 by 96.52		
	26 by 34	66.04 by 86.36	10	4.54
	28 by 34	71.12 by 86.36		
Opaque circular	17 by 22	43.18 by 55.88	16	7.26
	17 by 28	43.18 by 71.12	20	9.08
	22 by 34	55.88 by 86.36	24	10.90
	25 by 38	63.50 by 96.52	28	12.71
	28 by 34	71.12 by 86.36	...	...
	35 by 45	88.90 by 114.30	...	...
	38 by 50	96.52 by 127.00	...	...
Papeterie	17 by 22	43.18 by 55.88	16 to	7.26 to
	22 by 34	55.88 by 86.36	32	14.53
Text	25 by 38	63.50 by 96.52	60	27.24
	26 by 40	66.04 by 101.60	70	31.78
	35 by 45	88.90 by 114.30	...	...
	38 by 50	96.52 by 127.00	...	...
Wedding	17 by 22	43.18 by 55.88	28	12.71
	22 by 34	55.88 by 86.36	32	14.53
	35 by 45	88.90 by 114.30	36	16.34
			40	18.16
Writing	17 by 22	43.18 by 55.88	13	5.90
	17 by 28	43.18 by 71.12	16	7.26
	19 by 24	48.26 by 60.96	20	9.08
	22 by 34	55.88 by 86.36	24	10.90
	24 by 38	60.96 by 96.52	...	...
	28 by 34	71.12 by 86.36	...	...

*Underscored size denotes basis weight size.
†Supercalendered in this size only; weights 30, 35, and 40 lb.

TABLE 3 Paper-Cutting Chart for Booklets

Trimmed page size, inches	Trimmed page size, centimeters	Number printed pages	Number from sheet	Standard paper size, inches	Standard paper size, centimeters	Kinds of paper
3⅛ by 6¼	7.93 by 15.88	4 6 8 12 16 24 48	24 16 12 8 6 4 2	28 by 42	71.12 by 106.68	Bible; book; newsprint; offset; gravure
3⅜ by 6¼	8.57 by 15.30	4 4 6 8 12 16 24 48	24 24 16 12 8 6 4 2	28 by 42	71.12 by 106.68	Bible; book; newsprint; offset; gravure
3¾ by 5⅛	9.52 by 13.00	4 8 16 32 64	32 16 8 4 2	32 by 44	81.28 by 111.76	Bible; book; offset; gravure; text
4¼ by 5⅜	10.80 by 13.65	4 8 16 32 64	32 16 8 4 2	35 by 45	88.90 by 114.30	Bible; book; offset
4½ by 6	11.43 by 15.24	4 8 16 32	32 8 4 2	25 by 38	63.50 by 96.52	Opaque circular; gravure; text
4 by 9⅛	10.16 by 23.17	4 6 12	12 8 4	25 by 38	63.50 by 96.52	Opaque circular; gravure; text
4 by 9⅛	10.16 by 23.17	8 16 48	12 6 2	38 by 50	96.52 by 127.00	Bible; book; newsprint; offset; opaque circular; gravure; text
5¼ by 7⅝	13.33 by 19.36	4 8 16 32	16 8 4 2	32 by 44	81.28 by 111.76	Bible; book; offset; gravure; text
5½ by 8½	13.97 by 21.59	4 8 16 32	16 8 4 2	35 by 45	88.90 by 114.30	Bible; book; offset; opaque circular; gravure; text wedding
6 by 9⅛	15.24 by 23.17	4 8 16	8 4 2	25 by 38	63.50 by 96.52	Opaque circular; gravure; text
7¾ by 10⅝	19.68 by 27.00	4 8 16	8 4 2	32 by 44	81.28 by 111.76	Bible; book; offset; gravure; text
8½ by 11	21.59 by 27.94	4 8 16	8 4 2	35 by 45	88.90 by 114.30	Bible; book; offset; gravure; text
9½ by 12⅛	24.13 by 30.79	4 8 16	8 4 2	38 by 50	96.52 by 127.00	Bible; book; newsprint; offset; opaque circular; gravure; text

TABLE 4 Cover-Paper Cutting Chart for Booklets

Trimmed size of book, inches	Trimmed size of book, centimeters	Cover-paper size without trim, inches	Cover-paper size without trim, centimeters	Number from sheet	Cover-paper size with trim, inches	Cover-paper size with trim, centimeters	Number from sheet
3⅛ by 6¼	7.93 by 15.88	20 by 26	50.80 by 66.04	12*	23 by 35	58.42 by 88.90	15
3⅜ by 6¼	8.57 by 15.88	....		.....	23 by 35	58.42 by 88.90	15
3¾ by 5⅛	9.52 by 13.00	....		.....	23 by 35	58.42 by 88.90	16
4¼ by 5⅜	10.80 by 13.65	23 by 35	58.42 by 88.90	16	20 by 26	50.80 by 66.04	8
4½ by 6	11.43 by 15.24	....		.....	20 by 26	50.80 by 66.04	8
4 by 9⅛	10.16 by 23.17	....		.....	20 by 26	50.80 by 66.04	6
5¼ by 7⅝	13.33 by 19.36	....		.....	23 by 35	58.42 by 88.90	8
5½ by 8½	13.97 by 21.59	....		.....	23 by 35	58.42 by 88.90	8
6 by 9⅛	15.24 by 23.17	....		.....	20 by 26	50.80 by 66.04	4
7¾ by 10⅝	19.68 by 27.00	....		.....	23 by 35	58.42 by 88.90	4
8½ by 11	21.59 by 27.94	23 by 35	58.42 by 88.90	4*	20 by 26	50.80 by 66.04	2
9¼ by 12⅛	23.50 by 30.79				20 by 26	50.80 by 66.04	2

NOTE: Cover paper may also be obtained in other sizes.
* Close trim.

TABLE 5 Blotter-Cutting Chart

Standard type	Cut size, inches	Cut size, centimeters	Number from sheet	Standard sheet size, inches	Standard sheet size, centimeters
No. 6	3 by 6	7.62 by 15.24	24	19 by 24	48.26 by 60.96
No. 9	3⅝ by 8⅝	9.20 by 21.90	12	19 by 24	48.26 by 60.96
No. 10	3⅝ by 8⅝	9.20 by 21.90	12	19 by 24	48.26 by 60.96
Checkerbook	2 × 6	5.08 by 15.24	36	19 by 24	48.26 by 60.96

TABLE 6 Greek Alphabet

Name of letter	English equivalent	Greek letters Capital	Greek letters Small
alpha	α	A	α, a
beta	b	B	β, б
gamma	g	Γ	γ
delta	d	Δ	δ, ∂
epsilon	e	E	ε
zeta	z	Z	ζ
eta	ē	H	η
theta	th	Θ	θ, ϑ
iota	i	I	ι
kappa	k	K	κ, ϰ
lambda	l	Λ	λ
mu	m	M	μ
nu	n	N	ν
xi	x	Ξ	ξ
omicron	o	O	ο
pi	p	Π	π
rho	r	P	ρ
sigma	s	Σ	σ, ς
tau	t	T	τ
upsilon	y, u	Υ	υ
phi	ph	Φ	φ, φ
chi	ch	X	χ
psi	ps	Ψ	ψ
omega	ō	Ω	ω

TABLE 7 Useful Mathematical Rules

To find circumference:
Multiply diameter by 3.1416
Or divide diameter by... 0.3183
To find diameter:
Multiply circumference by... 0.3183
Or divide circumference by 3.1416
To find radius:
Multiply circumference by...0.15915
Or divide circumference by 6.28318
To find side of an inscribed square:
Multiply diameter by 0.7071
Or multiply circumference by 0.2251
Or divide circumference by 4.4428
To find side of an equal square:
Multiply diameter by 0.8862
Or divide diameter by..1.1284
Or multiply circumference by 3.5450

TABLE 8 Constants and Conversion Factors

$$1 \text{ angstrom} = 10^{-8} \text{ centimeter}$$
$$1 \text{ micron} = 0.001 \text{ millimeter}$$
$$1 \text{ centimeter} = 0.39370 \text{ inch}$$
$$1 \text{ inch} = 2.5400 \text{ centimeters}$$
$$1 \text{ foot} = 30.480 \text{ centimeters}$$
$$1 \text{ rad} = 57.2958 \text{ degrees}$$
$$1 \text{ gram} = 15.432 \text{ grains}$$
$$1 \text{ ounce} = 28.350 \text{ grams}$$
$$1 \text{ pound} = 445,000 \text{ dynes}$$
$$1 \text{ atmosphere} = 14.697 \text{ pounds per square inch}$$
$$1 \text{ joule} = 10 \text{ million ergs}$$
$$1 \text{ calorie} = 4.186 \text{ joules}$$
$$1 \text{ coulomb} = 3 \text{ by } 10^{9} \text{ electrostatic units of charge}$$
$$1 \text{ volt} = \tfrac{1}{300} \text{ ergs per electrostatic unit of charge}$$
$$1 \text{ farad} = 9 \text{ by } 10^{11} \text{ electrostatic units of capacitance}$$
$$1 \text{ square inch} = 6.4516 \text{ square centimeters}$$
$$1 \text{ square foot} = 929.03 \text{ square centimeters}$$
$$1 \text{ cubic inch} = 16.387 \text{ cubic centimeters}$$
$$1 \text{ liter} = 1,000 \text{ cubic centimeters}$$
$$1 \text{ gallon} = 231 \text{ cubic inches}$$
$$1 \text{ pound} = 453.59 \text{ grams}$$
$$1 \text{ kilogram} = 2.2046 \text{ pounds}$$
$$1 \text{ foot-pound} = 1.3549 \text{ joules}$$
$$1 \text{ British thermal unit} = 252.00 \text{ calories}$$
$$1 \text{ British thermal unit} = 778 \text{ foot-pounds}$$
$$1 \text{ horsepower} = 746 \text{ watts}$$
$$1 \text{ abampere} = 10 \text{ amperes}$$
$$1 \text{ abvolt} = 10^{-8} \text{ volt}$$
$$1 \text{ faraday} = 96,500 \text{ coulombs}$$

$$\pi = 3.1416 \qquad \varepsilon = 2.17183 \qquad \log 10 = 2.3026$$

$$\text{Charge of electron} = 4.80 \times 10^{-10} \text{ electrostatic unit}$$
$$\text{Mass of electron (at rest)} = 9.11 \times 10^{-28} \text{ gram}$$
$$\text{Avogadro's number} = 6.02 \times 10^{23}$$
$$\text{Planck's constant} = 6.63 \times 10^{-27} \text{ erg-second}$$
$$\text{Mass of hydrogen atom} = 1.661 \times 10^{-24} \text{ gram}$$
$$\text{Velocity of light in vacuum} = 299,776 \text{ kilometers per second}$$

TABLE 9   Numerals

Arabic	Greek	Roman
0		
1	α	I
2	β	II
3	γ	III
4	δ	IV
5	ϵ	V
6	$\digamma$	VI
7	ζ	VII
8	η	VIII
9	ϑ	IX
10	ι	X
11	$\iota\alpha$	XI
12	$\iota\beta$	XII
13	$\iota\gamma$	XIII
14	$\iota\delta$	XIV
15	$\iota\epsilon$	XV
16	$\iota\digamma$	XVI
17	$\iota\zeta$	XVII
18	$\iota\eta$	XVIII
19	$\iota\theta$	XIX
20	κ	XX
30	λ	XXX
40	μ	XL
50	ν	L
60	ξ	LX
70	o	LXX
80	π	LXXX
90	$\varkoppa$	XC
100	ρ	C
200	σ	CC
300	τ	CCC
400	υ	CD or CCCC
500	ϕ	D
600	χ	DC
700	ψ	DCC
800	ω	DCCC
900		CM
1,000		M
2,000		MM

TABLE 10   Mathematical Symbols

	Arithmetic and algebra
$+$	Addition; positive value; underestimation; approach through positive values.
$-$	Subtraction; negative value; overestimation; approach through negative values.
$\pm$	Add or subtract; plus-or-minus value.
$\mp$	Used where $\pm$ has appeared previously, as in $(a \pm b)$ $(a^2 \mp ab \pm b^2) = a^3 \pm b^3$; upper or lower signs are to be taken throughout.
$\cdot$	Multiplication (dot centered; $\times$ used in arithmetic).
$(\ )$	Parentheses; for grouping.
$[\ ]$	Brackets, for grouping.
$\{\ \}$	Braces; for grouping.
$^{-}$(superscript)	Vinculum; for grouping.
%	Percent.
/	Solidus, indicating division.
—	Horizontal rule, indicating division; fraction line.
$\div$	Division sign, used chiefly in arithmetic.
:	Ratio (in proportion).
::	Equals (in proportion).
$=$	Equivalent sign; is equal to.
$\neq$	[Is] not equal [to].
$\approx$	[Is] approximately equal [to].
$\equiv$	[Is] identical with; [is] identically equal [to].
$\equiv_x$	Indicates identity with all values of x for which both terms are defined.
$<$	[Is] less than.
$<<$	[Is] much less than.
$\leqq$ or $\leq$ or $\not>$	Equal to or less than; not greater than.
$>$	[Is] greater than.
$>>$	[Is] much greater than.
$\geqq$ or $\geq$	Greater than or equal to; not less than.
$\propto$	Varies directly as.
$N!$	Factorial; continued product of all integral numbers from 1 to N, where N is an integral number.
^{n} (superscript numbers of letters)	Exponent; raised to the power of degree n (exponent indicates number of iterations.)
$\sqrt[n]{\ }$	Radical sign; superscript n indicates index of degree of root; index omitted in case of square root.
$^{m/n}$ (superscript)	Fractional index; . . . raised to power of degree m/n.
$^{-n}$ (superscript)	Negative exponent; changes the term to its reciprocal.
$\exp f(x, y, \ldots)$	Functional symbol; exponential function.
$\exp u$	Functional symbol; exponential u.
i or j	Imaginary unit; j operator. $\sqrt{-1}$
$a \cdot 10^n$	Scientific notation; notation by powers of 10.
$\cdot$	Decimal point (placed on line); separates whole numbers from numerators of decimal fractions or is placed to the left of the numerator of a decimal fraction.
∞	Infinity symbol; algebraic number positively or negatively larger than any other number.
$\rightarrow$	Arrow; approaches as a limit.
$'$ (superscript)	Prime; notational method of distinguishing between differing variables and constants.
$''$ (superscript)	Double prime; notational method of distinguishing between differing variables and constants.
$'''$ (superscript)	Triple prime; notational method of distinguishing between differing variables and constants.
. . .	Three dots; dots of omission, meaning "and so forth."
$\log_a X$	Logarithm of X to base a.
$\log X$	Logarithm of X to base 10 (common system of logarithms).
$\ln X$	Logarithm of X to base e (Napierian system, or natural logarithms).
e	Base of Napierian (natural) logarithms (2.7182–).
$P(n, r)$	Permutations of n things taken r at a time.
$C(n, r)$	Combinations of n things taken r at a time.
$\|\ \|$	Vertical bars; indicates absolute value of the quantity inside the bars; vector magnitude; determinant.
$\|\ \|\ \|\ \|$	Double vertical bars; indicates a matrix; set of quantities written in specific order of rows and columns.

TABLE 10 Mathematical Symbols (*Continued*)

a_{ij}	Element in row i, column j, of determinant or matrix.
$\det (a_{ij})$	Determinant with elements a_{ij} [or determinant of matrix (a_{ij})].
space or half space	Used instead of commas to separate convenient groups of digits.
subscript number or letter	Notational method of indicating differing values in a set or series.

Elementary geometry

$\angle$, $\angle_s$	Angle(s).
$\perp$, $\perp_s$	Perpendicular(s); perpendicular to.
$\parallel$, $\parallel_s$	Parallel(s), parallel to.
$\triangle$, $\triangle_s$	Triangle(s).
$\bigcirc$, $\bigcirc_s$	Circle(s).
$\square$, $\square_s$	Parallelogram(s).
$\square$, $\square_s$	Square(s). (Do not use symbols for any other types of polygon.)
$\square$, $\square_s$	Trapezoid(s).
$\cong$	[Is] congruent [to].
$\sim$	[Is] similar [to].
$\overline{\wedge}$	[Is] equangular.
$\therefore$	Three dots; hence; therefore.
$\overline{AB}$	Vinculum; chord AB of a circle; length of line segment between A and B.
$\overleftarrow{AB}$	Directed segment B to A.
$\overgroup{AB}$	Arc AB of a circle.
π	Pi; constant ratio of circumference of a circle to its diameter.

Analytic geometry

x, y, z	Rectangular (Cartesian) coordinates of a point in space.
x, y	Rectangular coordinates of a point in a plane.
α	Alpha; indicates direction angle with x axis.
l	Indicates directional cosine (with x axis).
β	Beta; indicates direction angle with y axis.
m	Indicates directional cosine (with y axis).
γ	Gamma; indicates direction angle with z axis.
n	Indicates directional cosine (with z axis).
r, θ, ϕ	Spherical coordinates of a point in space.
r, θ	Polar coordinates of a point in a plane.
ψ	Psi; indicates angle from radius vector to tangent of plane curve.
r, θ, z	Cylindrical coordinates of a point in space.
p, s	Indicates intrinsic coordinates.
e	Eccentricity of a conic.
p	Semilatus rectum.
m	Slope of a curve or line.
C	Circumference of a circle.
r	Radius of a circle.
D	Diameter of a circle.
ρ	Radius of a curvature.
d	Perpendicular distance from a point to a line (length of normal).

Trigonometry

° (superscript)	Indicates degree(s).
θ	Angle measured in rads.
′ (superscript)	Prime; indicates minutes.
″ (superscript)	Double prime; indicates seconds.
sin	Sine of angle.
cos	Cosine of angle.
tan	Tangent of angle.
cot	Cotangent of angle.
sec	Secant of angle.
csc	Cosecant of angle.
vers	Versed sine of angle; $1 - \cos \theta$.
covers	Coversed sine of angle.
hav	Haversine of angle; $\frac{1}{2}(1 - \cos \theta)$.
cis θ	$\cos \theta + 1 \sin \theta$.
arc sin or $\sin^{-1}$	Inverse sine [of]; angle whose sine is.
arc cos or $\cos^{-1}$	Inverse cosine [of]; angle whose cosine is.
$[\sin f(x)]^n$	The nth power [of].

TABLE 10 Mathematical Symbols *(Continued)*

Hyperbolic functions	
sinh	Hyperbolic sine.
cosh	Hyperbolic cosine, etc.
arc sinh or $\sinh^{-1}$	Inverse hyperbolic function [of]; angle whose hyperbolic sine is.
arc cosh or $\cosh^{-1}$	Inverse hyperbolic function [of]; angle whose hyperbolic cosine is, etc.
$[\sinh f(x)]^n$	nth power [of].
$[\cosh f(x)]^n$	nth power [of], etc.

Calculus	
d	Differential operator.
d^n	Differential operator of nth order.
$\dfrac{d}{dx}$	Derivative operator of first order.
$\dfrac{d^n}{dx}$	Derivative operator of nth order.
∂	Curly d; indicates partial differentiation.
D	Differential operator.
D^n	Differential operator of nth order.
$\dot{x}, \ddot{x}$	Indicates first and second derivatives with respect to time (Newton's notation).
$d^n y/dx^n$	Derivative of nth order.
$''$ (superscript)	Double prime; order of differentiation.
$'''$ (superscript)	Triple prime; order of differentiation.
$\int, \iint, \iiint$	Integral signs.
$\int_i^m, \int_a^b, \int_{a'}^b, \int_c^d$	Integral signs, indicating index and limits.
$\oint$	Integral around a closed path.
Δ	Delta; indicates increment.
$\sum\limits_i$	Sigma; indicates summation; sum of terms of index i.

Special functions	
$J_0(x), J_1(x), J_n(x).$	Bessel functions. The notation recommended is in G. N. Watson's *Treatise* (1922), as endorsed by E. P. Adams in the *Smithsonian Tables* (1922).
$B_1, B_3, B_5, \ldots$ $B_1, B_2, B_3, \ldots$	Bernoulli numbers and polynomials.
γ	Gamma; Eulerian (Mascheronis) constant (0.5772−).
$\Gamma(x) = {}_0\!\int^\infty x^{-1} e^{-x}\, dx$	Gamm function of the positive number n; also called the factorial function.
$B(m, n) = {}_0\!\int^r x^{m-1} (1-x)^{n-1}\, dx$	Beta function of any two positive numbers m and n.
$\Gamma x^{(n-1)} = {}_0\!\int_x^r x^n e^{-x}\, dx$	Incomplete gamma function.
$B_x(m, n) = {}_0\!\int^x x^{m-1} (1-x)^{n-1}\, dx$	Incomplete beta function.

TABLE 11 Decimal Equivalents

Fractions, in.	Decimals, in.	mm.	Fractions, in.	Decimals, in.	mm.
1/64	0.01562	0.397	33/64	0.51562	13.097
1/32	0.03125	0.794	17/32	0.53125	13.494
3/64	0.04687	1.191	35/64	0.54687	13.891
1/16	0.0625	1.588	9/16	0.5625	14.288
5/64	0.07812	1.984	37/64	0.57812	14.684
3/32	0.09375	2.381	19/32	0.59375	15.081
7/64	0.10937	2.778	39/64	0.60937	15.478
1/8	0.1250	3.175	5/8	0.625	15.875
9/64	0.14062	3.572	41/64	0.64062	16.272
5/32	0.15625	3.969	21/32	0.65625	16.669
11/64	0.17187	4.366	43/64	0.67187	17.066
3/16	0.1875	4.763	11/16	0.6875	17.463
13/64	0.20312	5.159	45/64	0.70312	17.859
7/32	0.21875	5.556	23/32	0.71875	18.256
15/64	0.23437	5.953	47/64	0.73437	18.653
1/4	0.2500	6.350	3/4	0.750	19.050
17/64	0.26562	6.747	49/64	0.76562	19.447
9/32	0.28125	7.144	25/32	0.78125	19.844
19/64	0.29687	7.541	51/64	0.79687	20.241
5/16	0.3125	7.938	13/16	0.8125	20.638
21/64	0.32812	8.334	53/64	0.82812	21.034
11/32	0.34375	8.731	27/32	0.84375	21.431
23/64	0.35937	9.128	55/64	0.85937	21.828
3/8	0.3750	9.525	7/8	0.875	22.225
25/64	0.39062	9.922	57/64	0.89062	22.622
13/32	0.40625	10.319	29/32	0.90625	23.019
27/64	0.42187	10.716	59/64	0.92187	23.416
7/16	0.4375	11.113	15/16	0.9375	23.813
29/64	0.45312	11.509	61/64	0.95312	24.209
15/32	0.46875	11.906	31/32	0.96875	24.606
31/64	0.48437	12.303	63/64	0.98437	25.003
1/2	0.5	12.700		1.000	25.400

SOURCE: National Bureau of Standards.

TABLE 12 Elements and Symbols

Name	Symbol	Name	Symbol
Actinium	Ac	Mendelevium	Md
Aluminum	Al	Mercury	Hg
Americium	Am	Molybdenum	Mo
Antimony	Sb	Neodymium	Nd
Argon	Ar	Neon	Ne
Arsenic	As	Neptunium	Np
Astatine	At	Nickel	Ni
Barium	Ba	Niobium	Nb
Berkelium	Bk	Nitrogen	N
Beryllium	Be	Nobelium	No
Bismuth	Bi	Osmium	Os
Boron	B	Oxygen	O
Bromine	Br	Palladium	Pd
Cadmium	Cd	Phosphorus	P
Calcium	Ca	Platinum	Pt
Californium	Cf	Plutonium	Pu
Carbon	C	Polonium	Po
Cerium	Ce	Potassium	K
Cesium	Cs	Praseodymium	Pr
Chlorine	Cl	Promethium	Pm
Chromium	Cr	Protactinium	Pa
Cobalt	Co	Radium	Ra
Columbium (niobium)	Cb	Radon	Rn
Copper	Cu	Rhenium	Re
Curium	Cm	Rhodium	Rh
Dysprosium	Dy	Rubidium	Rb
Einsteinium	Es	Ruthenium	Ru
Erbium	Er	Samarium	Sm
Europium	Eu	Scandium	Sc
Fermium	Fm	Selenium	Se
Fluorine	F	Silicon	Si
Francium	Fr	Silver	Ag
Gadolinium	Gd	Sodium	Na
Gallium	Ga	Strontium	Sr
Germanium	Ge	Sulfur	S
Gold	Au	Tantalum	Ta
Hafnium	Hf	Technetium	Tc
Helium	He	Tellurium	Te
Holmium	Ho	Terbium	Tb
Hydrogen	H	Thallium	Tl
Indium	In	Thorium	Th
Iodine	I	Thulium	Tm
Iridium	Ir	Tin	Sn
Iron	Fe	Titanium	Ti
Krypton	Kr	Tungsten (Wolfram)	W
Lanthanum	La	Uranium	U
Lawrencium	Lw	Vanadium	V
Lead	Pb	Wolfram	W
Lithium	Li	Xenon	Xe
Lutetium	Lu	Ytterbium	Tb
Magnesium	Mg	Yttrium	Y
Manganese	Mn	Zinc	An
		Zirconium	Zr

TABLE 13 Temperature Conversion Table

C°	F°	C°	F°	C°	F°	C°	F°
−75	−103	40	104	155	311	537.8	1000
−73.3	−100	43.3	100	160	320	550	1022
−70	−94	45	113	165	329	593.3	1100
−67.8	−90	48.9	120	165.6	330	600	1112
−65	−85	50	122	170	338	648.9	1200
−62.2	−80	54.4	130	171.1	340	650	1202
−60	−76	55	131	175	347	700	1292
−56.7	−70	60	140	176.7	350	704.4	1300
−55	−67	65	149	180	356	750	1382
−51.1	−60	65.6	150	182.2	360	760	1400
−50	−58	70	158	185	365	800	1472
−45.6	−50	71.1	160	187.8	370	815.6	1500
−45	−49	75	167	190	374	850	1562
−40	−40	76.7	170	193.3	380	871.1	1600
−35	−31	80	176	195	383	900	1652
−34.4	−30	82.2	180	198.9	390	926.7	1700
−30	−22	85	185	200	392	950	1742
−28.9	−20	87.8	190	204.4	400	982.2	1800
−25	−13	90	194	225	437	1000	1832
−23.3	−10	93.3	200	232.2	450	1037.8	1900
−20	−4	95	203	250	482	1050	1922
−17.8	0	98.9	210	260	500	1093.3	2000
−15	5	100	212	275	527	1100	2012
−12.2	10	104.4	220	287.8	550	1148.9	2100
−10	14	105	221	300	572	1150	2102
−6.7	20	110	230	315.6	600	1200	2192
−5	23	115	239	325	617	1204.4	2200
−1.1	30	115.6	240	343.3	650	1250	2282
0	32	120	248	350	662	1260	2300
4.4	40	121.1	250	371.1	700	1300	2372
5	41	125	257	375	707	1315.6	2400
10	50	126.7	260	398.9	750	1350	2462
15	59	130	266	400	752	1371.1	2500
15.6	60	132.2	270	425	797	1400	2552
20	68	135	275	426.7	800	1426.7	2600
21.1	70	137.8	280	450	842	1500	2732
25	77	140	284	454.4	850	1537.8	2800
26.7	80	143.3	290	475	887	1550	2822
30	86	145	293	482.2	900	1593.3	2900
32.2	90	148.9	300	500	932	1600	2912
35	95	150	302	510	950	1648.9	3000
37.8	100	154.4	310	525	977	1650	3002

NOTE: $F° = (C° \times \frac{9}{5}) + 32$; $C° = (F° − 32) \times \frac{5}{9}$.